MASTER VISUALLY®

by Joe Kraynak

Optimizing PC Performance

Wiley Publishing, Inc.

Master VISUALLY® Optimizing PC Performance

Published by
Wiley Publishing, Inc.
111 River Street
Hoboken, NJ 07030-5774

Published simultaneously in Canada

Library of Congress Control Number: 2004116568

ISBN: 0-7645-7787-5

Manufactured in the United States of America

10 9 8 7 6 5 4 3 2 1

1V/RU/QR/QV/IN

Trademark Acknowledgments

Contact Us

For general information on our other products and services please contact our Customer Care Department within the U.S. at 800-762-2974, outside the U.S. at 317-572-3993 or fax 317-572-4002.

For technical support please visit www.wiley.com/techsupport.

U.S. Sales

Contact Wiley at (800) 762-2974 or fax (317) 572-4002.

Praise for Visual Books...

"If you have to see it to believe it, this is the book for you!"

—PC World

"A master tutorial/reference — from the leaders in visual learning!"

—Infoworld

"A publishing concept whose time has come!"

—The Globe and Mail

"Just wanted to say THANK YOU to your company for providing books which make learning fast, easy, and exciting! I learn visually so your books have helped me greatly – from Windows instruction to Web development. Best wishes for continued success."

—Angela J. Barker (Springfield, MO)

"I have over the last 10-15 years purchased thousands of dollars worth of computer books but find your books the most easily read, best set out, and most helpful and easily understood books on software and computers I have ever read. Please keep up the good work."

—John Gatt (Adamstown Heights, Australia)

"You're marvelous! I am greatly in your debt."

—Patrick Baird (Lacey, WA)

"I am an avid fan of your Visual books. If I need to learn anything, I just buy one of your books and learn the topic it in no time. Wonders! I have even trained my friends to give me Visual books as gifts."

—Illona Bergstrom (Aventura, FL)

"I have quite a few of your Visual books and have been very pleased with all of them. I love the way the lessons are presented!"

—Mary Jane Newman (Yorba Linda, CA)

"Like a lot of other people, I understand things best when I see them visually. Your books really make learning easy and life more fun."

—John T. Frey (Cadillac, MI)

"Your Visual books have been a great help to me. I now have a number of your books and they are all great. My friends always ask to borrow my Visual books - trouble is, I always have to ask for them back!"

—John Robson
(Brampton, Ontario, Canada)

"I write to extend my thanks and appreciation for your books. They are clear, easy to follow, and straight to the point. Keep up the good work! I bought several of your books and they are just right! No regrets! I will always buy your books because they are the best."

—Seward Kollie (Dakar, Senegal)

"What fantastic teaching books you have produced! Congratulations to you and your staff."

—Bruno Tonon (Melbourne, Australia)

"Thank you for the wonderful books you produce. It wasn't until I was an adult that I discovered how I learn—visually. Although a few publishers claim to present the materially visually, nothing compares to Visual books. I love the simple layout. Everything is easy to follow. I can just grab a book and use it at my computer, lesson by lesson. And I understand the material! You really know the way I think and learn. Thanks so much!"

—Stacey Han (Avondale, AZ)

"The Greatest. This whole series is the best computer-learning tool of any kind I've ever seen."

—Joe Orr (Brooklyn, NY)

Credits

Project Editor
Maureen Spears

Acquisitions Editor
Jody Lefevere

Product Development Manager
Lindsay Sandman

Copy Editor
Kim Heusel

Technical Editor
Dennis R. Cohen

Editorial Manager
Robyn Siesky

Manufacturing
Allan Conley
Linda Cook
Paul Gilchrist
Jennifer Guynn

Screen Artists
Jill A. Proll
Elizabeth Cardenas-Nelson

Illustrator
Ronda David-Burroughs

Book Design
Kathie S. Rickard

Project Coordinator
Maridee Ennis

Layout
Amanda Carter
Jennifer Heleine
Heather Pope

Proofreaders
Laura L. Bowman

Quality Control
Brian H. Walls

Indexer
Richard T. Evans

Vice President and Executive Group Publisher
Richard Swadley

Vice President and Publisher
Barry Pruett

Composition Director
Debbie Stailey

About the Author

Joe Kraynak has been writing and editing training manuals and computer books for over fifteen years. His long list of computer books includes *Internet: Top 100 Simplified Tips & Tricks, Google: Top 100 Simplified Tips & Tricks, Master Visually: Creating Web Pages*, and *The Complete Idiot's Guide to Computer Basics*. Joe has a Bachelor's degree in Philosophy and Creative Writing and a Master's degree in English Literature from Purdue University.

Author's Acknowledgments

Thanks to all of the dedicated editors, artists, and page layout people who fine-tuned the manuscript and transformed a loose collection of electronic files and hand-drawn sketches into such an attractive, bound book. Special thanks to Barry Pruett and Jody Lefevere for choosing me to author this book, to Maureen Spears for guiding the content, to Dennis Cohen for ensuring the technical accuracy of my statements and steps, and to Kim Heusel for pruning my prose and tuning the text.

PART I — Taking Inventory of Your PC

1) Test PC Performance
2) Check Available PC Resources
3) Check Internet Connection Speed and Security
4) Safely Back Up and Optimize Your PC

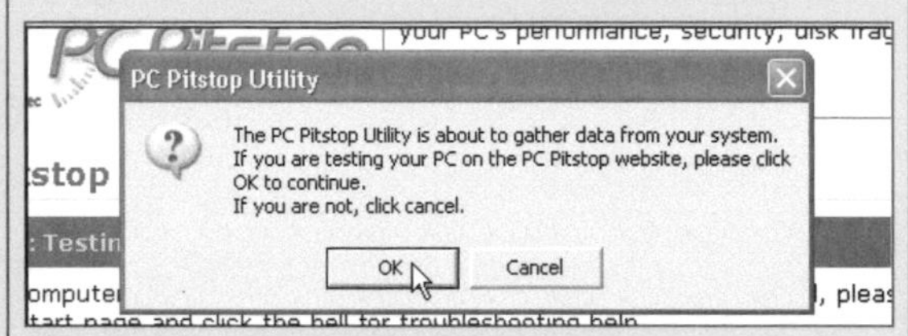

PART II — Reclaiming Disk Drive Space

5) Automate File Removal with Disk Cleanup
6) Unistall Programs You Never Use
7) Find and Delete Other Useless Files
8) Clear Old E-mail Messages from Your System

Select Drive

Select the drive you want to clean up.

Drives:

DISK1PART01 (C:)

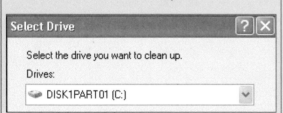

PART III — Optimizing Hard Drive Performance and Memory

9) Convert the Disk Format
10) Optimize a Disk Drive
11) Optimize Processor and Memory Usage

General | Tools | Hardware | Sharing

DISK1PART01

Type: Local Disk

File system: FAT32

Used space: 16,112,058,368 bytes 15.0 GB

Free space: 13,886,799,872 bytes 12.9 GB

PART IV — Making Your PC Start Faster

12) Adjust the BIOS Startup Settings
13) Streamline the Windows Startup

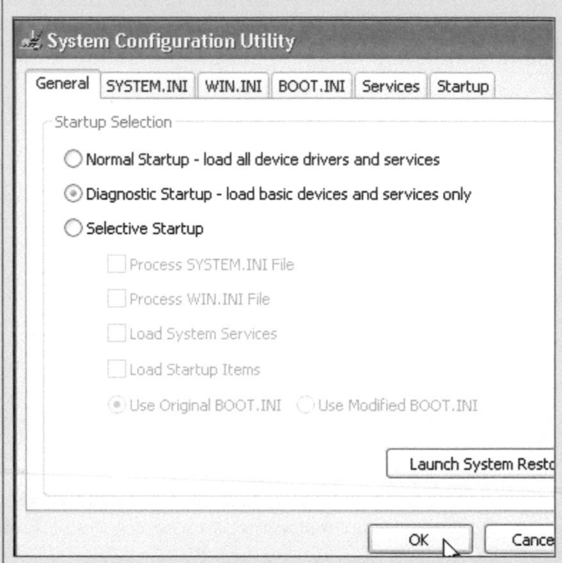

PART V — Improving Internet Performance

14) Eliminate Spyware and Adware
15) Block Pop-up Ads
16) Prevent Spam
17) Optimize Internet Connection Speed
18) Optimize your Web Browser

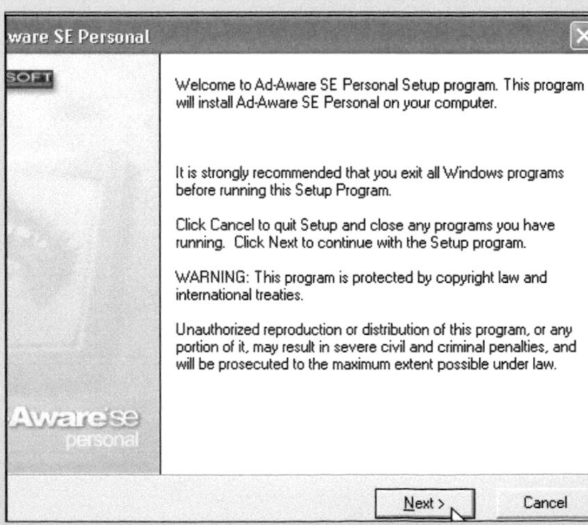

Welcome to Ad-Aware SE Personal Setup program. This program will install Ad-Aware SE Personal on your computer.
It is strongly recommended that you exit all Windows programs before running this Setup Program.
Click Cancel to quit Setup and close any programs you have running. Click Next to continue with the Setup program.
WARNING: This program is protected by copyright law and international treaties.
Unauthorized reproduction or distribution of this program, or any portion of it, may result in severe civil and criminal penalties, and will be prosecuted to the maximum extent possible under law.
Next >
Cancel

WHAT'S INSIDE

PART VI Optimizing the Windows Registry

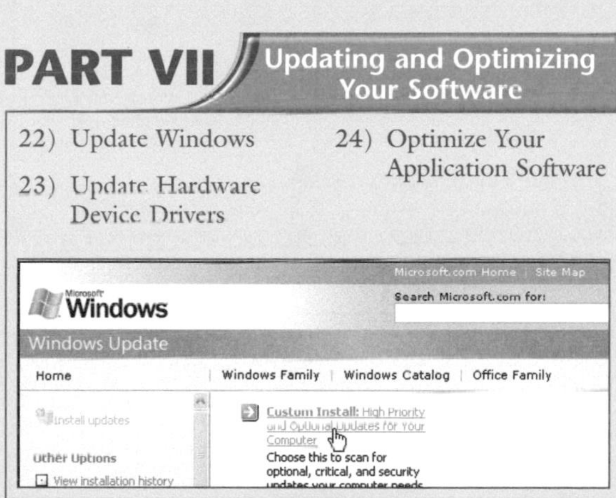

PART VII Updating and Optimizing Your Software

PART VIII Optimizing Your PC's Display

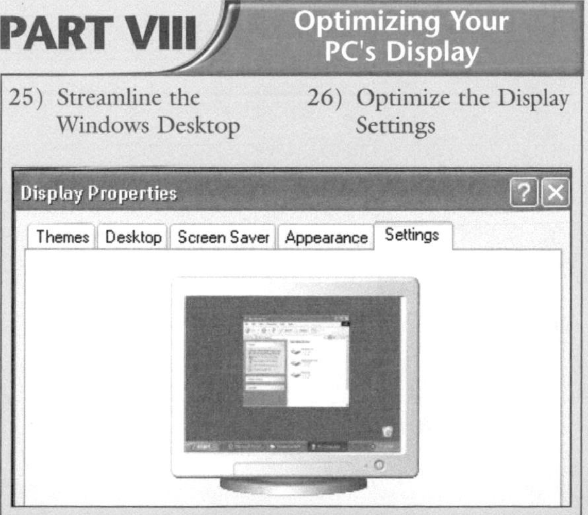

PART IX Protecting Your PC from Viruses and Crackers

PART X Returning Your PC to Pristine Condition

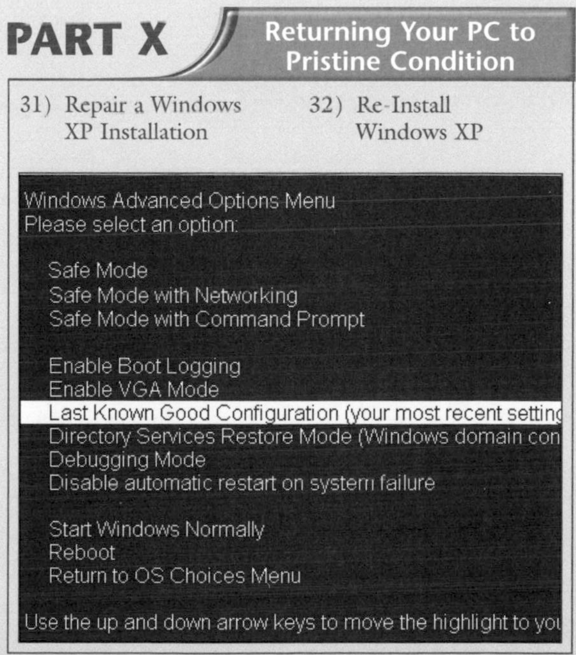

PART I Taking Inventory of Your PC

1 Test PC Performance

PC Pitstop Tests: Analyze Performance
Status: Testing processor...

2 Check Available PC Resources

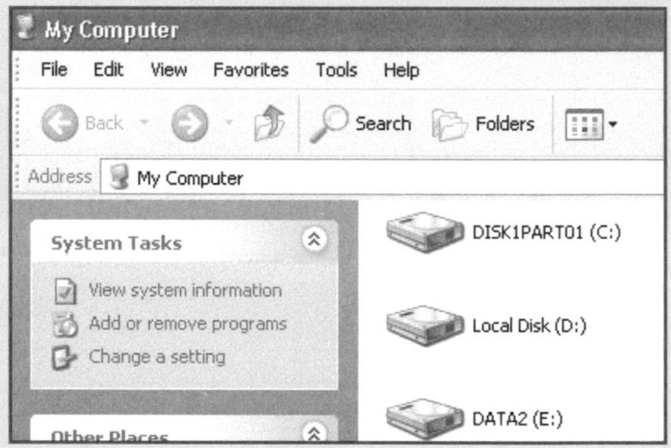

3 Check Internet Connection Speed and Security

4 Safely Back Up and Optimize Your PC

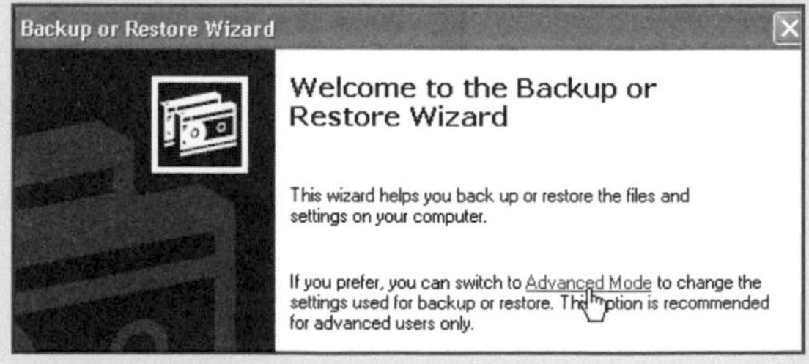

TABLE OF CONTENTS

PART II Reclaiming Disk Drive Space

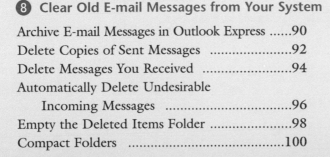

5 Automate File Removal with Disk Cleanup

6 Uninstall Programs You Never Use

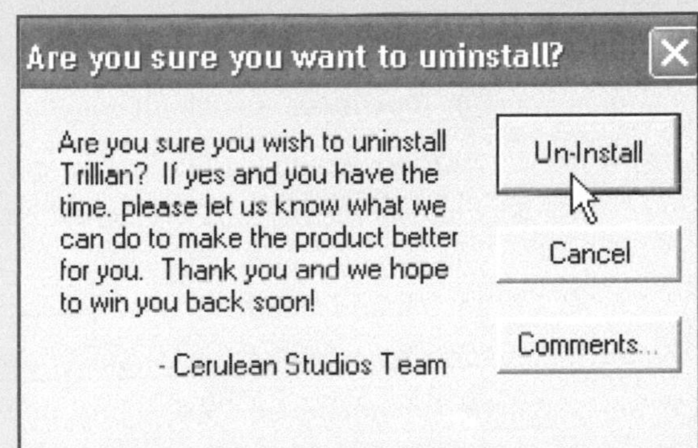

7 Find and Delete Other Useless Files

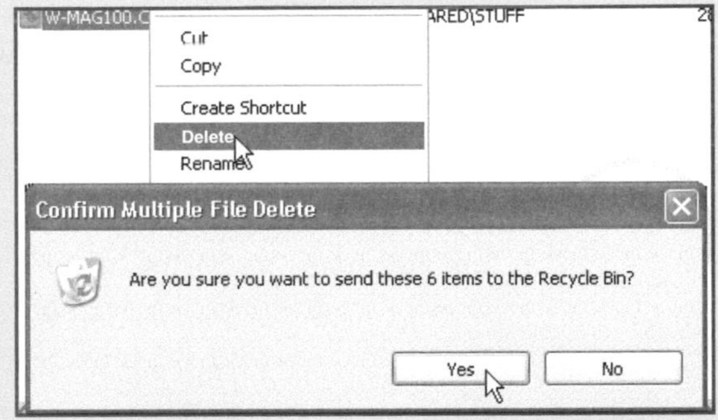

8 Clear Old E-mail Messages from Your System

PART III Optimizing Hard Drive Performance and Memory

9 Convert the Disk Format

10 Optimize a Disk Drive

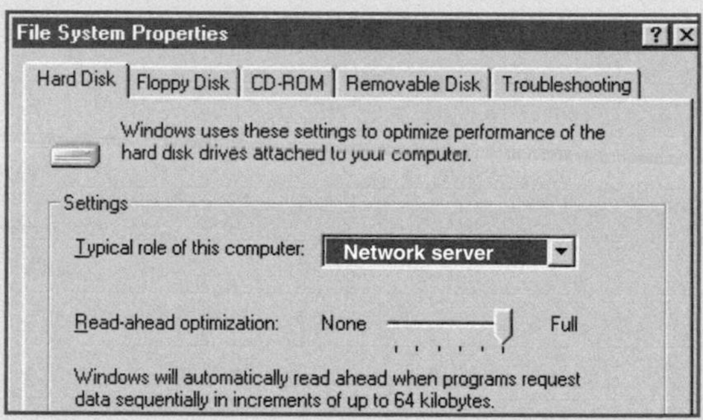

11 Optimize Processor and Memory Usage

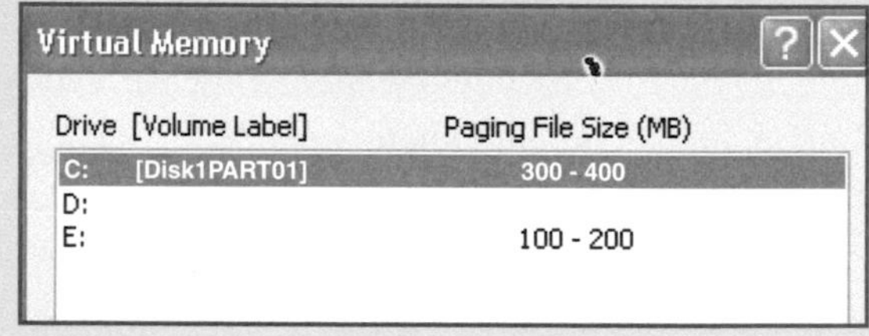

PART IV Making Your PC Start Faster

12 Adjust the BIOS Startup Settings

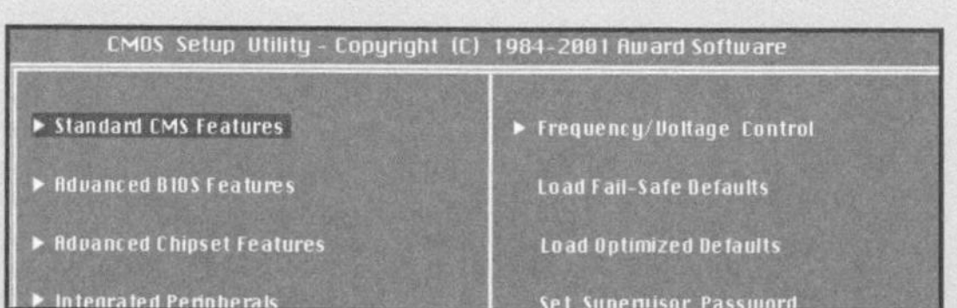

TABLE OF CONTENTS

13 Streamline the Windows Startup

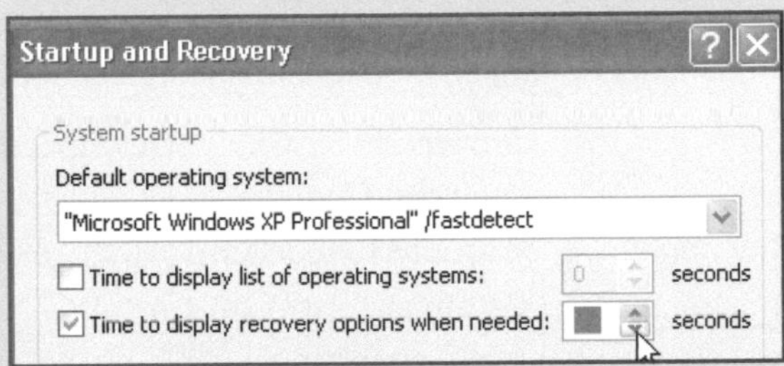

PART V Improving Internet Performance

14 Eliminate Spyware and Adware

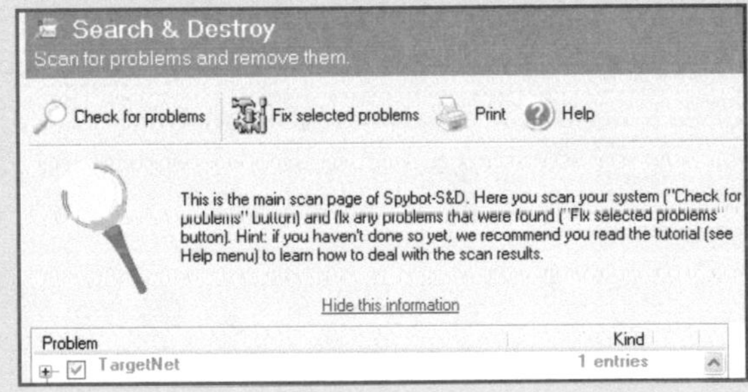

15 Block Pop-up Ads

16 Prevent Spam

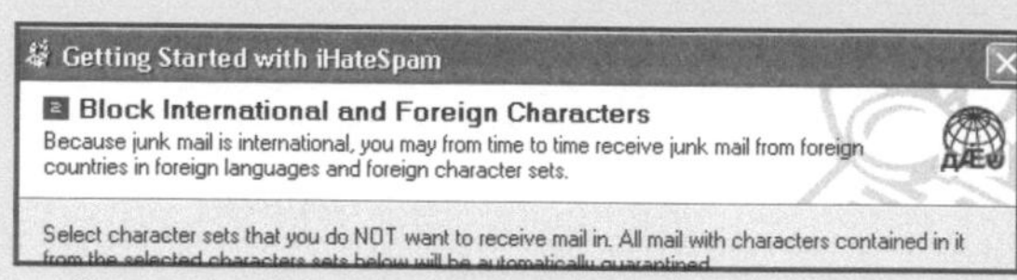

⑰ Optimize Internet Connection Speed

SpeedGuide Programs

TCP Optimizer
Descrip on: The TCP Optimizer is a free Windows program designed to help optimize your Internet connection. Just download and run, no installaion required. The program makes it easy to find the best MaxMTU value, test latency and tweak all the important broadband related registry parameters. The Optimizer can be helpful with tuning any Internet connection type, from dialup to Gigabit+ :) If you need help with the program, read our broadband tweaking articles, the Optimizer FAQ, and/or visit our Forums. As an alternative, you can try one of our generic Registry patches instead.

⑱ Optimize Your Web Browser

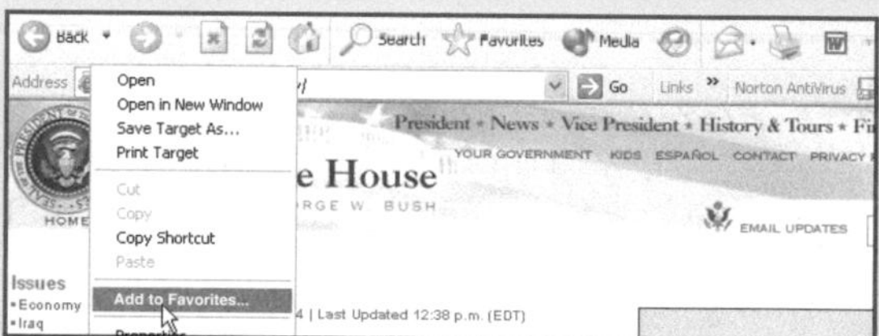

PART VI Optimizing the Windows Registry

⑲ Back Up and Restore the Windows Registry

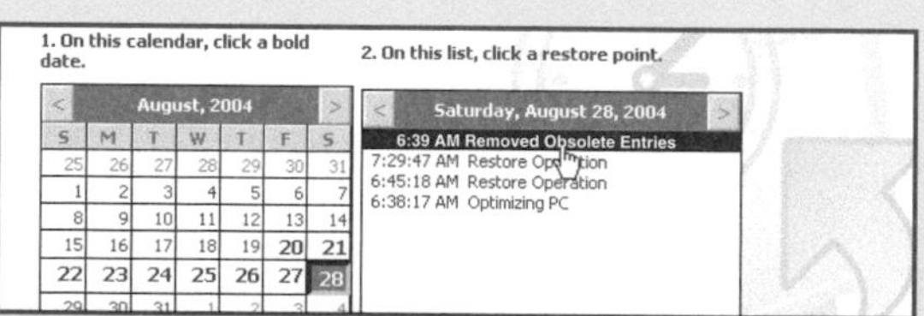

⑳ Remove Unnecessary Registry Entries

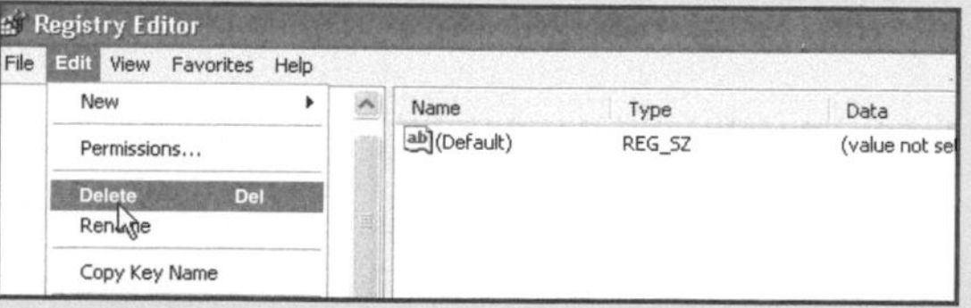

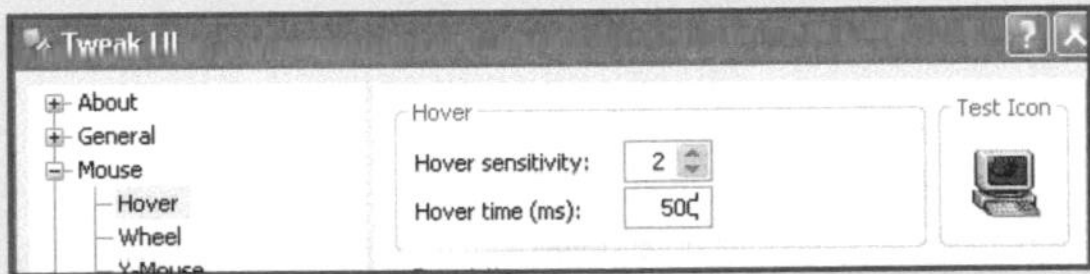

Tweak UI
About
General
Mouse
Hover
Wheel
Hover
Hover sensitivity:
Hover time (ms):
Test Icon

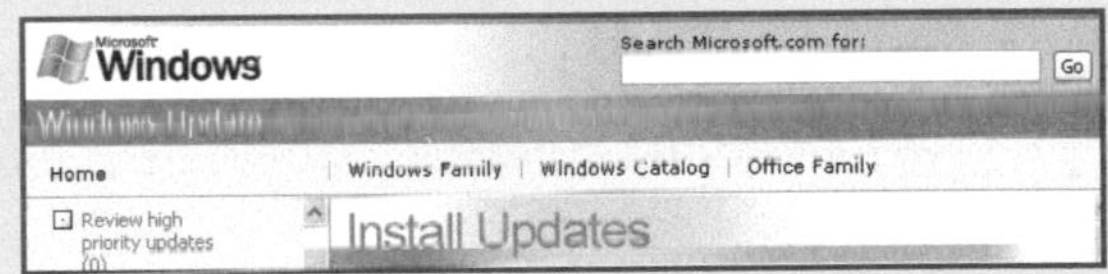

Windows
Search Microsoft.com for:
Go
Home
Windows Family
Windows Catalog
Office Family
Install Updates

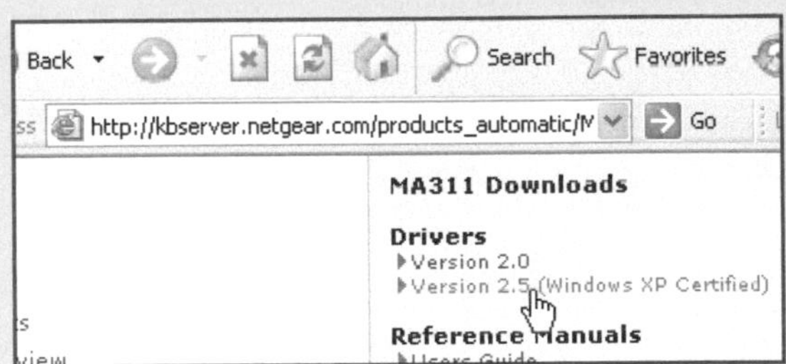

Back
Search
Favorites
http://kbserver.netgear.com/products_automatic/M
Go
MA311 Downloads
Drivers
Version 2.0
Version 2.5 (Windows XP Certified)

PART VIII Optimizing Your PC's Display

25 Streamline the Windows Desktop

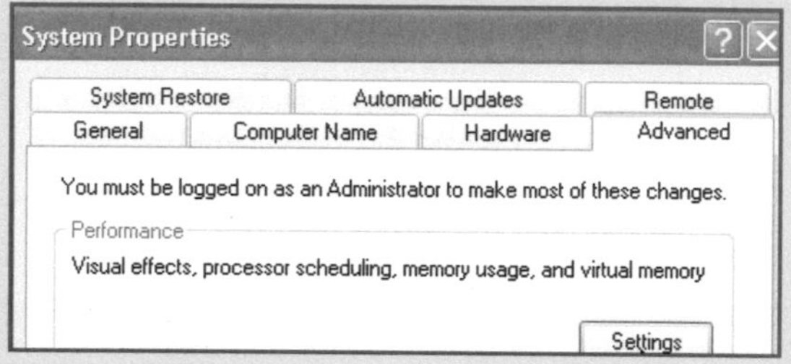

26 Optimize the Display Settings

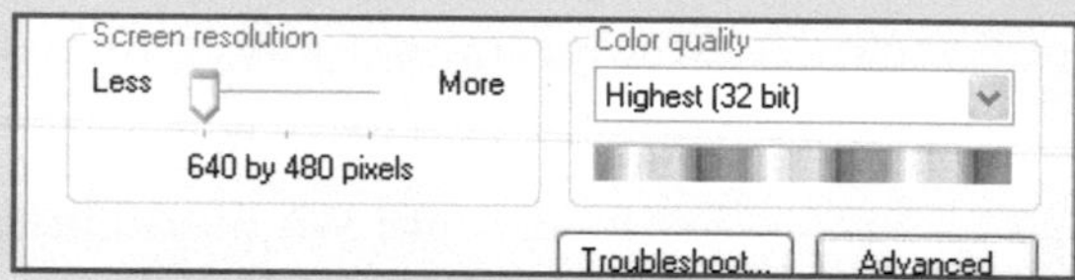

PART IX Protecting Your PC from Viruses and Crackers

27 Install and Configure an AntiVirus Program

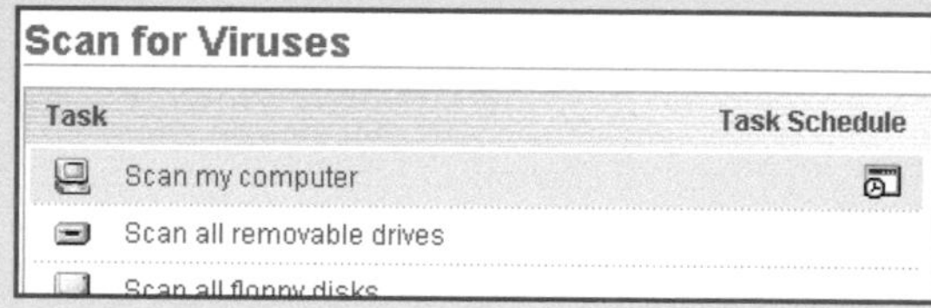

28 Prevent Unauthorized Access to Your PC

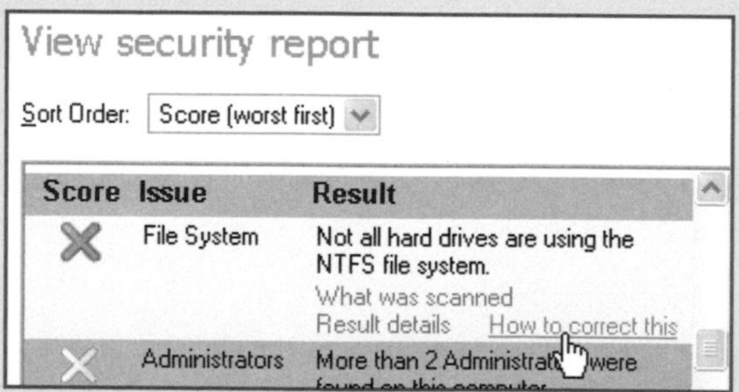

TABLE OF CONTENTS

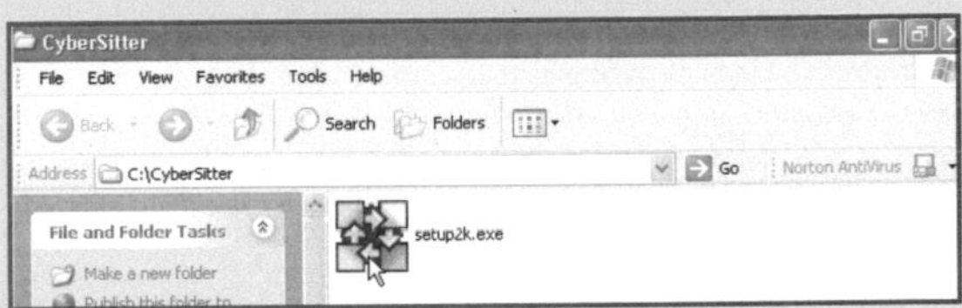

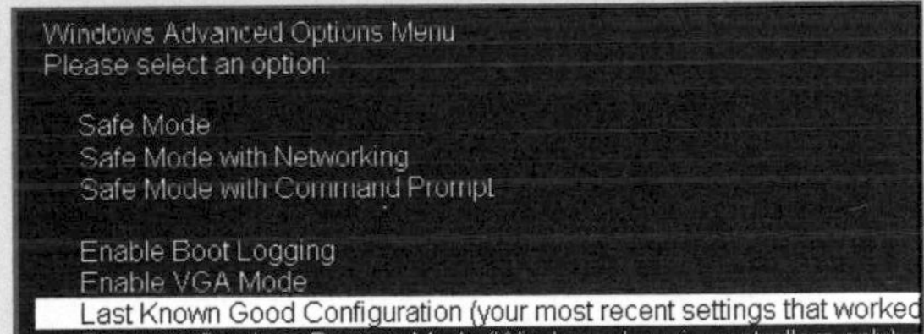

Welcome to Setup.

This portion of the Setup program prepares Microsoft(R) Windows(R) XP to run on your computer.

- To set up Windows XP now, press ENTER.
- To repair a Windows XP installation using Recovery Console, press R.
- To quit Setup without installing Windows XP, press F3.

How to Use this Master VISUALLY Book

Do you look at the pictures in a book or newspaper before anything else on a page? Would you rather see an image than read how to do something? Search no further. This book is for you. Opening *Master VISUALLY Optimizing PC Performance* allows you to read less and learn more about clearing the clutter from your PC's hard drive and enhancing your PC's speed and performance.

Who Needs This Book

This book is for a reader unfamiliar with the various Windows utilities and third-party software designed to protect PCs and enhance their performance. It is also for more computer literate individuals who want to expand their knowledge of different performance features available on their PCs, in Windows, and on the Internet.

Book Organization

Master VISUALLY Optimizing PC Performance has 32 chapters and is divided into 10 parts.

Taking Inventory of Your PC, Part I, shows you how to identify your PC's components, determine total and available disk space, find out which programs are consuming memory, and identify prime areas for performance improvements.

Reclaiming Disk Drive Space, Part II, provides the strategies and steps you need to take to clear useless files from your PC's hard drive and uninstall programs you never use.

Optimizing Hard Drive Performance and Memory, Part III, shows you how to rearrange the files on your PC's hard drive to give your PC quick access to those files. You also learn how to re-allocate system resources to make your PC's processor and memory more responsive.

Making Your PC Start Faster, Part IV, give you complete control over your PC's startup to prevent it from wasting valuable time and resources when you turn it on.

Improving Internet Performance, Part V, helps you rid your PC of malicious software, including adware and spyware, which can significantly slow down your Internet connection speed, optimize your connection, enhance the performance of your Web browser, and reduce the amount of spam you receive via e-mail.

Optimizing the Windows Registry, Part VI, takes you behind the scenes with Windows registry — the file that contains all of the settings that control the way Windows operates and interacts with your other software. Here, you learn how to back up and restore the registry, clear useless setting from the registry, and tweak it to customize Windows.

Updating and Optimizing Your Software, Part VII, shows you how to keep Windows and your other software up-to-date, so your PC runs as efficiently and securely as possible. Here you learn how to download and install Windows updates and schedule updates to install automatically when you are using your PC.

Optimizing Your PC's Display, Part VIII, explores tips and techniques to improve the quality and performance of your PC's display adapter and monitor. Here, you learn everything from changing the screen resolution and color depth to streamlining the Windows desktop.

Protecting Your PC from Viruses and Crackers, Part IX, focuses on securing your PC to prevent it from becoming infected with a virus or other malicious software and to block unauthorized access over the Internet.

Returning Your PC to Pristine Condition, Part X, shows you how to repair to re-install Windows to make your PC run like new. Here, you learn the most important files, settings, and data to back up before re-installing Windows and how to get your PC up and running after a complete re-installation.

Chapter Organization

This book consists of sections, all listed in the book's table of contents. A *section* is a set of steps that show you how to complete a specific computer task.

Each section, usually contained on two facing pages, has an introduction to the task at hand, a set of full-color screen shots and steps that walk you through the task, and a set of tips. This format allows you to quickly look at a topic of interest and learn it instantly.

Chapters group together three or more sections with a common theme. A chapter may also contain pages that give you the background information needed to understand the sections in a chapter.

HOW TO USE THIS BOOK

What You Need to Use This Book

To use this book, you must have a PC running one of the following versions of the Windows operating system: Windows 98, Windows Me, Windows NT, Windows 2000, or Windows XP. Many of the steps also require that you have an Internet connection.

Using the Mouse

This book uses the following conventions to describe the actions you perform when using the mouse:

Click

Press your left mouse button once. You generally click your mouse on something to select something on the screen.

Double-click

Press your left mouse button twice. Double-clicking something on the computer screen generally opens whatever item you have double-clicked.

Right-click

Press your right mouse button. When you right-click anything on the computer screen, the program displays a shortcut menu containing commands specific to the selected item.

Click and Drag, and Release the Mouse

Move your mouse pointer and hover it over an item on the screen. Press and hold down the left mouse button. Now, move the mouse to where you want to place the item and then release the button. You use this method to move an item from one area of the computer screen to another.

The Conventions in This Book

A number of typographic and layout styles have been used throughout *Master VISUALLY Optimizing PC Performance* to distinguish different types of information.

Bold

Bold type represents the names of commands and options that you interact with. Bold type also indicates text and numbers that you must type into a dialog box or window.

Italics

Italic words introduce a new term and are followed by a definition.

Numbered Steps

You must perform the instructions in numbered steps in order to successfully complete a section and achieve the final results.

Bulleted Steps

These steps point out various optional features. You do not have to perform these steps; they simply give additional information about a feature.

Indented Text

Indented text tells you what the program does in response to you following a numbered step. For example, if you click a certain menu command, a dialog box may appear, or a window may open. Indented text may also tell you what the final result is when you follow a set of numbered steps.

Notes

Notes give additional information. They may describe special conditions that may occur during an operation. They may warn you of a situation that you want to avoid, for example, the loss of data. A note may also cross reference a related area of the book. A cross reference may guide you to another chapter, or another section within the current chapter.

Icons and Buttons

Icons and buttons are graphical representations within the text. They show you exactly what you need to click to perform a step.

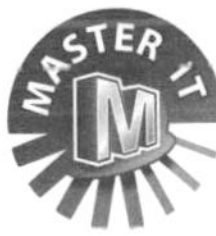

You can easily identify the tips in any section by looking for the Master It icon. Master It offer additional information, including tips, hints, and tricks. You can use the Master It information to go beyond what you have learn learned in the steps.

Operating System Difference

Although most examples in this book illustrate how to perform tasks in Windows XP, the steps cover most versions of Windows starting with Windows 98, including Windows Me and Windows 2000. Steps may differ slightly depending on the PC you own and the way the manufacturer or you configured the appearance and performance of the operating system.

1 Test PC Performance

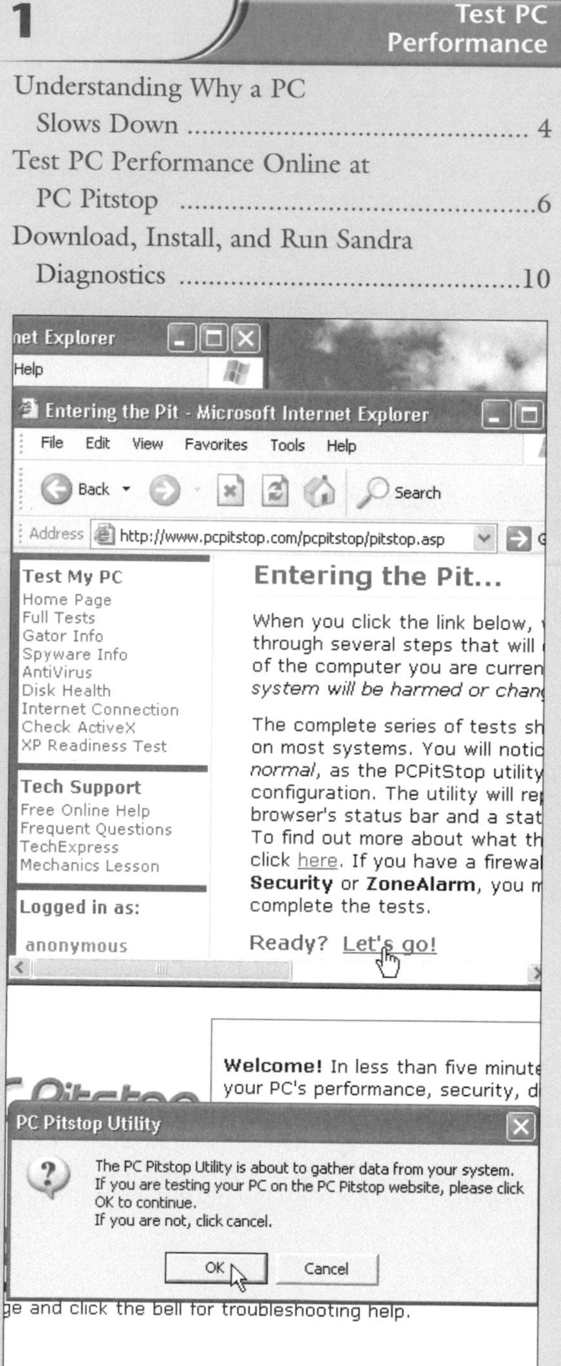

2 Check Available PC Resources

PART I — TAKING INVENTORY OF YOUR PC

3 Check Internet Connection Speed and Security

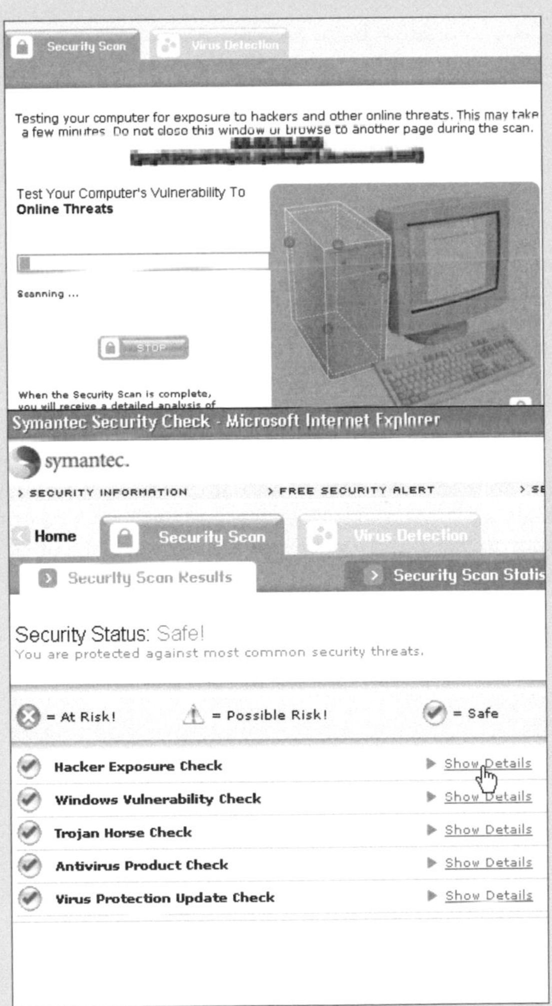

4 Safely Back Up and Optimize Your PC

Understanding Why a PC Slows Down

When you begin using a brand-new computer, Web pages pop up on the screen, documents open in a snap, games respond to every twitch of your finger, and every command you enter executes immediately. Over the course of several months of moderate use, however, the computer begins to slow down.

Most people do not notice a gradual decrease in performance, but one day, while browsing the Web, you begin to realize just how slow your computer has become; it seems tired and unmotivated. Your Windows desktop takes more time to appear when you first turn on your PC. Web pages that used to appear immediately now take several seconds. When you open a document, you have to wait before you can begin working on it. You purchased the best PC you could afford, so what happened?

What happened is that your high-performance computer has finally accumulated enough digital junk to make it run like an old jalopy.

Disk Drive Clutter

On most PCs, the hard drive acts like a digital landfill. It stores important program files and your valuable documents, but it also stores copies of Web pages you recently visited and may never visit again, old e-mails you will probably never read, temporary files that your PC software never bothered to delete, backup copies of files you deleted, and other files you never knew you had.

Disk clutter affects PC performance in two ways. First, it adds to the time it takes a program to load a file. As your disk fills up, free space is harder to come by, so when you save a file, the PC stores parts of the file in any available areas it can find. The file becomes *fragmented* and the drive takes more time to load the scattered parts. Just think how much extra time you spend looking for information if you scatter papers around your office instead of filing them in folders.

Second, a cluttered disk is much less efficient at providing your PC with the *virtual memory* it needs. Your computer uses the hard drive as virtual memory when it runs out of *physical memory* — the electronic form of memory provided by memory chips. When you run a program or open a file, your PC stores the data in physical memory, so it can process it more quickly. If your computer needs more memory than is currently available, it uses an open area of the hard drive to swap data in and out of its physical memory. If your computer does not have a large area of free space to use as virtual memory, it may have trouble running a program or running multiple programs.

Memory Overload

Five primary factors contribute to determining the overall performance of your PC: the *processor* type and speed, the *cache* size and speed, the *bus* type and speed, the size and speed of the *hard drive*, and the amount and speed of the *memory*. These components comprise the engine that drives your PC. Unless you perform hardware upgrades to install a faster processor, motherboard, or hard drive, you can do little to increase the potential top speed of your PC.

However, you can do a great deal to reclaim and optimize your computer's memory without installing an expensive upgrade. This alone can increase the speed of your PC, bringing it into a range that is acceptable to you.

As soon as you start your computer, its memory becomes cluttered with unnecessary data — startup information and programs that you may not even use. Each program you run, every document you open, every task you perform packs more into your computer's memory until it has to begin using the hard drive for additional storage. Even if you close a program to free up some memory, the program may not remove itself entirely.

Chapters 11 and 13 show you how to check available memory, reclaim memory, and optimize its use.

Unsolicited Advertising

Most PCs connected to the Internet act like magnets for unsolicited advertising. E-mail accounts attract junk mail, commonly referred to as *spam*. Web sites use *pop-up ads* to turn your PC's monitor into a miniature billboard. And Web sites and shareware commonly install advertising software, called *adware*, and monitoring software, called *spyware*, right on your computer. All of these unsolicited items consume system resources that your PC could use to run your programs and manage your files. They also reduce your personal productivity by making you delete extra e-mail and close windows that pop up uninvited on your screen.

You may not completely purge your system of these annoyances, but you can significantly reduce them, as explained in Part V.

Windows Registry Bloat

The Windows registry keeps track of Windows and application settings, hardware configurations, and everything else that enables Windows to run and to communicate with the programs and hardware that comprise your system.

The Windows registry quickly becomes bloated, because Windows does a poor job of keeping it trim. When you remove a program from your system, for example, the utility in charge of removing the program is supposed to remove all registry entries that refer to it. In practice, this rarely happens. Over time, the registry collects numerous entries that point to programs, files, and resources that no longer exist. Yet Windows continues to load the entire registry whenever you start your computer.

Fortunately, utilities are available that can safely remove unused entries and streamline the registry, as explained in Part VI.

Test PC Performance Online at PC Pitstop

Before you begin optimizing your PC, you can test its performance and identify any problems online at PC Pitstop for free. PC Pitstop features automated utilities that perform a battery of tests to analyze your PC's processor, memory, hard drives, video, and Internet connection speed. The tests do not change any settings; they simply run on your PC to identify any problems or performance issues. As PC Pitstop performs the tests, you can expect to hear your PC's hard drive run and see the monitor flash various colors and patterns. This is all part of the process.

When you connect to PC Pitstop, you can run the tests anonymously or you can provide your name and e-mail address to have PC Pitstop store the results of your tests for future reference. In either case, PC Pitstop promises to keep any information it obtains about your system confidential. None of the tests accesses documents or other data files on your PC.

PC Pitstop's tests were designed to run exclusively through Internet Explorer. If you are using a Web browser other than Internet Explorer, when you click the link for performing the tests, instructions appear on how to proceed.

Test PC Performance Online at PC Pitstop

1. Close any programs that are currently running.
2. Launch your Web browser.

Note: This example uses Internet Explorer.

3. In the address bar type **www.pcpitstop.com** and press Enter.

   PC Pitstop's home page appears.

4. Click the Click here to test your PC link.

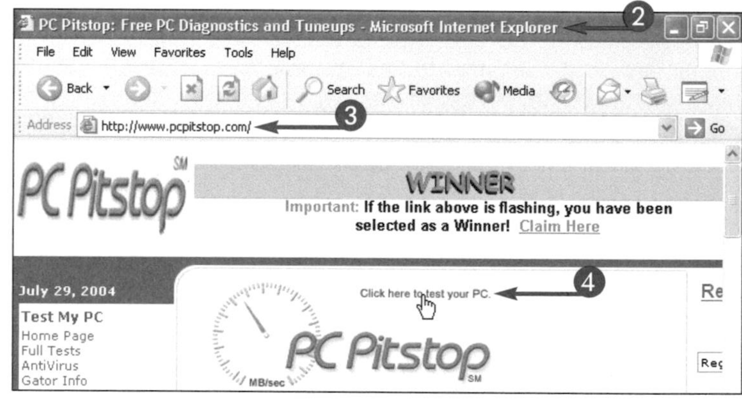

   PC Pitstop's test page appears.

5. Click the link for running the tests.

   The Security Warning dialog box appears, indicating that the authenticity of the PC Pitstop utility has been verified.

6. Click Yes.

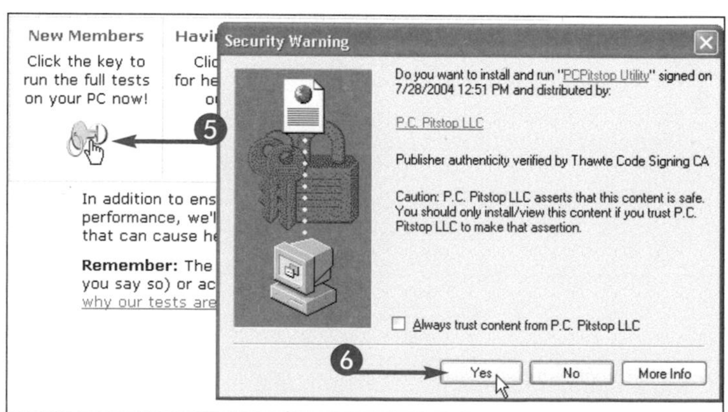

A screen appears prompting you to create an account.

- You can click here and type your name and e-mail address to have PC Pitstop store the test results.

7 Click Test Anonymously.

A screen appears indicating that the tests are ready to begin.

8 Click the link for starting the tests.

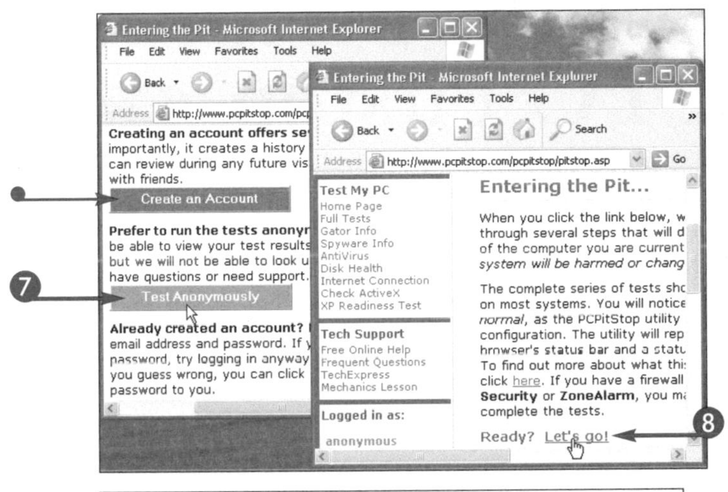

The PC Pitstop Utility dialog box appears prompting you to confirm that you are using the PC Pitstop Web site.

9 Click OK.

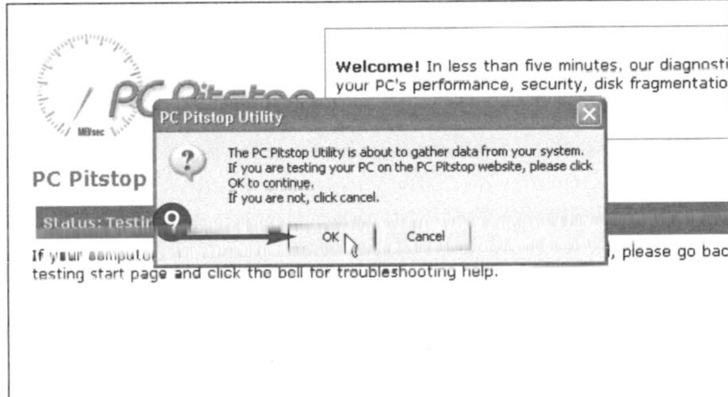

What are the benefits of creating an account at PC Pitstop?

▼ When you create an account, PC Pitstop can identify your computer the next time you connect. If PC Pitstop has any information from manufacturers about possible problems with your PC or any of its devices, it can notify you via e-mail. In addition, if PC Pitstop installs new features to test and improve your PC's performance, it can notify you of these updates. You can perform the tests anonymously and then create an account after you see the results. The screen that displays the results includes a link you can click to type your name and e-mail address and a password for accessing the service.

How can PC Pitstop remain a free service? What's the catch?

▼ PC Pitstop can remain free to users, because it licenses its technology to other companies, including computer manufacturers, technical support services, and Web sites. It also earns money by referring users to software companies that develop PC troubleshooting, maintenance, and security software. You may notice that PC Pitstop's opening page features recommended products. If you click a link and purchase one of these products, PC Pitstop receives a small commission. You can click the Support PC Pitstop link at the bottom of the home page to learn other ways to support PC Pitstop.

continued

Test PC Performance Online at PC Pitstop *(Continued)*

When the tests are complete, PC Pitstop issues a grade card that rates your computer's performance, provides suggestions, and sometimes even supplies a utility that you can download and run to repair a specific problem.

At the top of the results page, PC Pitstop displays an overall description of your PC's performance to indicate whether it is operating on par with other systems of its kind. Below the description is a list of Customized Tune-up Tips, which are links to specific suggestions for optimizing the overall system performance.

Following the Customized Tune-up Tips is a Configuration Summary that highlights the performance of each component. To stay true to its car analogy, PC Pitstop uses auto racing flags and color codes to indicate performance levels. A checkered flag indicates that a component has passed all tests and is running at peak performance. A yellow flag highlights possible problems or performance issues that you have the option of correcting. A red flag indicates a serious problem or security issue that you must address immediately. In addition, PC Pitstop displays a blue dot to indicate any additional suggestions for optimizing performance.

Test PC Performance Online at PC Pitstop *(continued)*

- PC Pitstop starts checking your system and displays messages about the tests it is currently performing.

When testing your monitor and video card, PC Pitstop flashes colors, patterns, and jumbled text on the monitor.

PC Pitstop displays a screen, prompting you to enter information about your system and Internet connection.

10. Type or select the requested information.
11. Click GO.

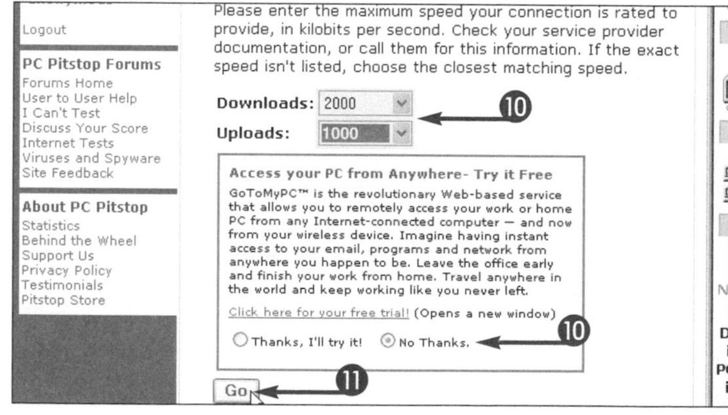

PC Pitstop displays a summary of the test results.

⑫ Scroll down the page to the list of components tested.

⑬ Click a component's link for more information about how to correct a problem or optimize performance.

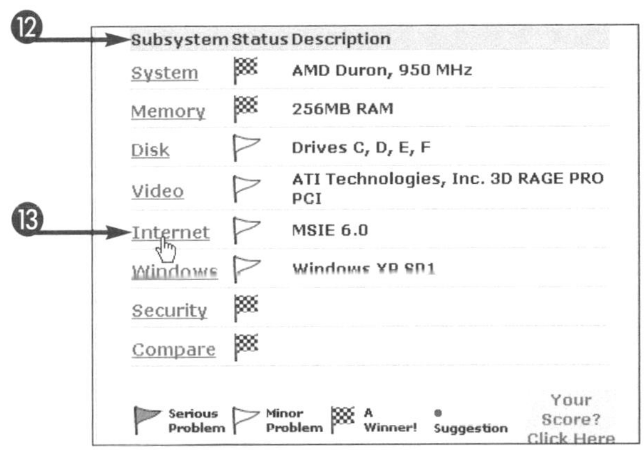

PC Pitstop's recommendations appear.

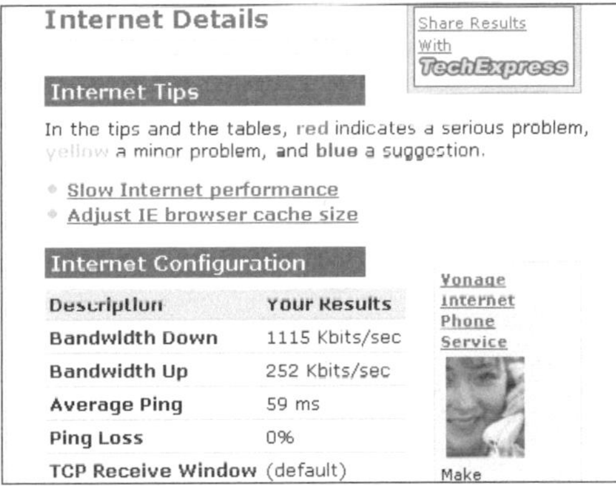

Do these performance tests look for viruses, spyware, and other problems?

▼ No. PC Pitstop's tests focus on your PC's hardware and how it performs. However, PC Pitstop does feature other tests that check your system for viruses and spyware, analyze the health of your hard drive, test your PC's Internet connection speed more thoroughly, and provide additional information on how to optimize your PC. To access these tests and additional information, go to PC Pitstop's home page at www.pcpitstop.com, and click the link for the test or information you want under Test My PC. Many of the links lead to a page that describes a problem and provides a link to a utility that can correct the problem.

PC Pitstop identified some problems, but I still do not know what to do. Can I obtain some additional help?

▼ Yes. This book provides detailed, illustrated instructions to help you identify and correct many of the problems that negatively affect PC performance. If PC Pitstop identifies Windows registry errors, for example, you can skip ahead to Part VI of this book for more on backing up and cleaning the registry safely. PC Pitstop also hosts several technical support forums where you can go for more about PC performance issues, PC Pitstop test results, and ways to configure and customize your PC for optimum performance. Check out the links under PC Pitstop Forums on PC Pitstop's home page.

Download, Install, and Run Sandra Diagnostics

Before you optimize your PC, you should test its components to determine if they are operating correctly. A malfunction on a disk drive or in a memory chip can cause a PC to slow down and crash intermittently or lose important data. More serious problems may indicate that a particular component is bad and in need of replacement. A performance test of your computer may not reveal these problems, but by running a diagnostic utility you can often identify them.

Many PCs come with a CD that includes diagnostic utilities for testing the memory, disk drives, video card, monitor, motherboard, processor, and other key components. If your PC includes such a CD, you can insert it and run the diagnostics from the CD as explained in the manufacturer's instructions. These diagnostic utilities are generally preferred because the manufacturer customizes them for the system you have.

If you do not have a diagnostic utility developed for your system, you can download, install, and run an excellent utility from SiSoftware called Sandra (System ANalyzer, Diagnostic and Reporting Assistant). You can use the utility for free for 30 days, but must pay $34.95 after that time. Although this section shows how to download, install, and run Sandra Diagnostics, you can use the basic steps to run other diagnostic utilities.

Download, Install, and Run Sandra Diagnostics

Download and Install Sandra Diagnostics

1. Launch your Web browser.
2. In the address bar, type **www.sisoftware.net** and press Enter.
3. Click Download.

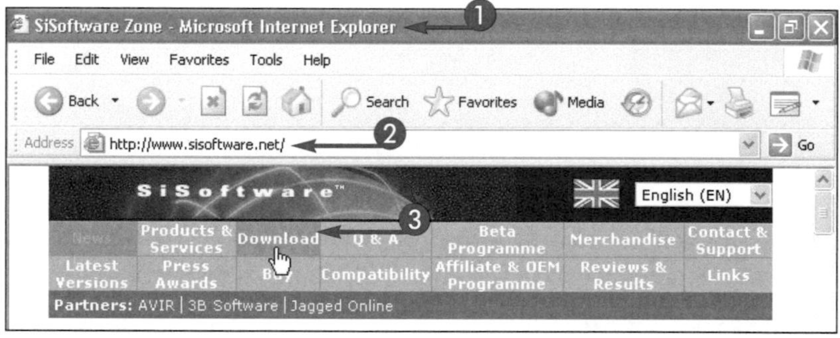

The download page appears.

4. Scroll down to the Affiliate Review/Download Sites list.
5. Click one of the links for downloading the Sandra software.

Note: *Although this example shows the Sandra software being downloaded from Download.com, you can download other diagnostic utilities.*

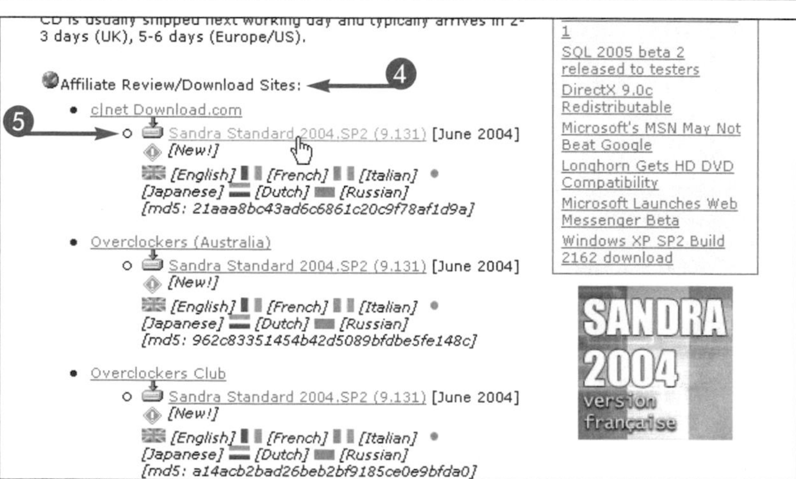

6 Follow the on-screen instructions.

Note: The steps vary depending on the site from which you are downloading the file.

7 When the download is complete, click Open Folder to open the file you just downloaded.

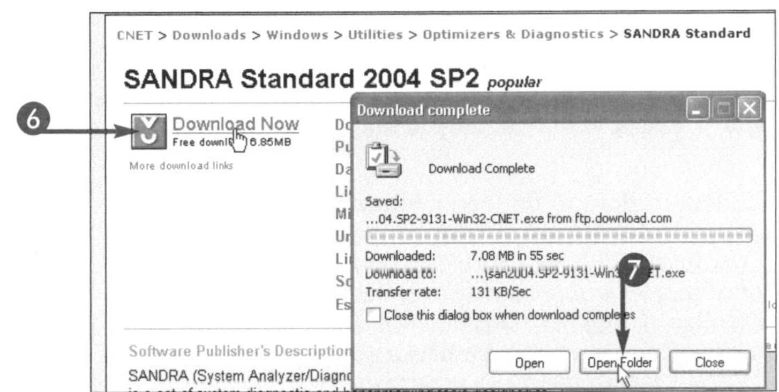

8 Double-click the Sandra installation file.

The installation routine starts.

9 Follow the on-screen instructions to complete the installation.

The installation routine installs Sandra on your PC and displays an icon to run it on the desktop and on the Start ⇨ All Programs menu.

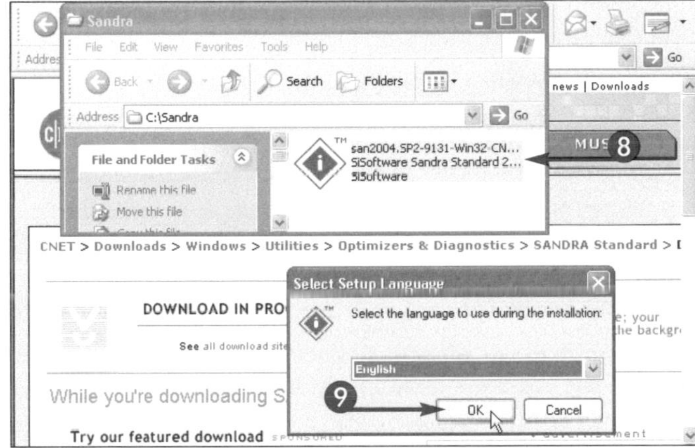

Can I purchase the product now so I do not need to worry about it later?

▼ Yes. On SiSoftware's home page, click the Buy link. A page appears that enables you to purchase a copy of the Sandra software for one or more PCs; you can purchase a copy with multiple licenses at a discount. You can also purchase a copy on CD, so you can reinstall the software if your computer's hard drive fails. If you do not want to order the CD, you can make your own backup CD, as shown in Chapter 4. If you choose to order the CD, you can still download the shareware version and use it until your CD arrives.

Are any other PC diagnostics tools available?

▼ In addition to Sandra and the diagnostic utilities that come bundled with many PCs, there are serveral excellent diagnostic utilities. American MegaTrends at www.amidiag.com features a collection of diagnostic utilities called AMIDiag Suite that you can run in Windows or DOS. It does a thorough system check of all components and provides detailed reports on any errors or problem areas it identifies. AMIDiag Suite is fairly expensive at $250, but you can download a demo version of it to try it for free. BCM Diagnostics, which you can check out at www.bcmdiagnostics.com, is another fine product that retails for less than $30. You can find links to additional diagnostic utilities at dmoz.org/Computers/Software/Diagnostics/.

continued

Download, Install, and Run Sandra Diagnostics *(Continued)*

Sandra functions as both an information tool and a diagnostic utility. As an information tool, it can reveal specifications about your PC that you may not know, such as the processor type and speed, the amount of memory installed, and the hard drive speed. As a diagnostic utility, it can inform you of any malfunctions and potential performance issues so you can repair or replace malfunctioning components or identify settings that you need to change.

Unlike some diagnostic utilities that manufacturers bundle with their PCs, you do not need to boot your computer using a special CD or run Sandra from the DOS prompt, which is very inconvenient. You can run Sandra just as you run your other Windows programs — by selecting it from the Start, All Programs, SiSoftware Utilities menu or by double-clicking its icon on the Windows desktop.

When you launch Sandra, it displays icons for its many tests, grouped by module: Wizard Modules, Information Modules, Benchmarking Modules, Testing Modules, and Listing Modules. When you run a module, a window appears displaying messages that indicate what the module is currently doing. When the module has completed its work, the window displays the results.

Download, Install, and Run Sandra Diagnostics *(continued)*

Run Sandra Diagnostics

1. Double-click the SiSoftware Sandra Standard icon on the Windows desktop.

   The Tip of the Day dialog box appears.

2. Read the tip.

   - You can click Next to display another tip.

3. Click OK.

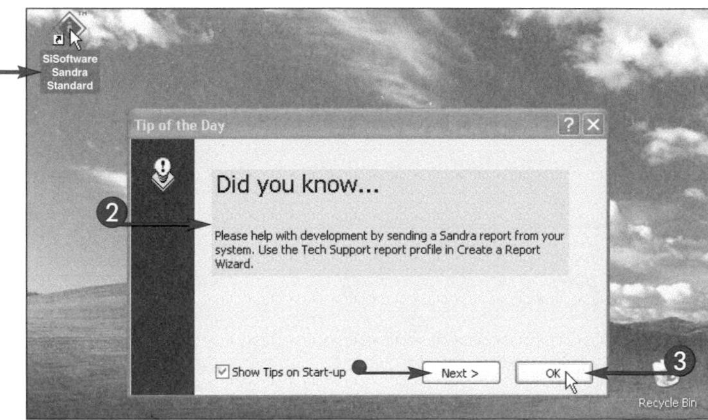

The SiSoftware Standard window appears, displaying icons for its many modules.

4. Double-click the module you want to run.

   This example shows the Windows Memory module.

   If you choose a Wizard Module, follow the on-screen instructions that the Wizard provides.

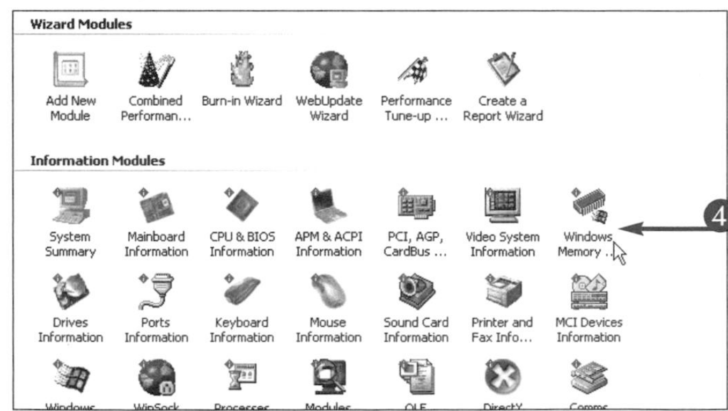

A window appears displaying information about a component or the results of a test or comparison.

5 Click the Next button (⊙) to view information reported by the next Module.

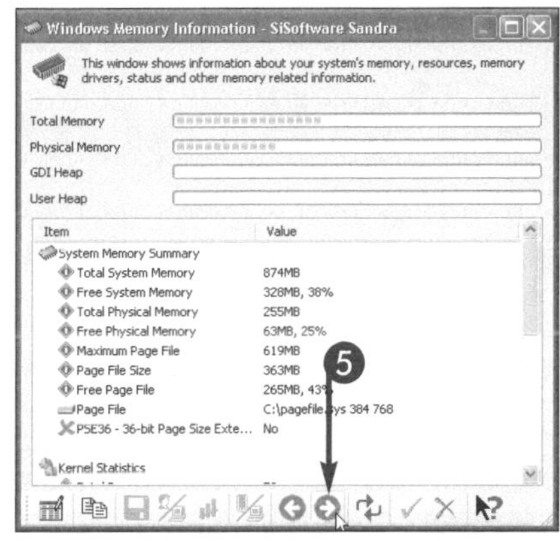

- The Module displays information about the next component, in this example, the hard drives.

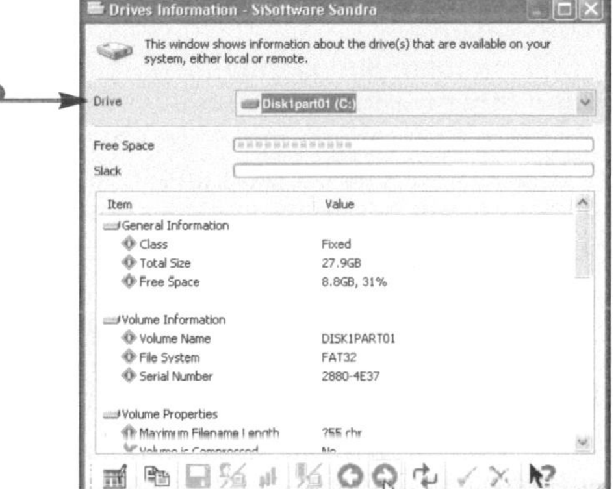

Sandra reports a great deal of information. Do I need to know all of this?

▼ No. Sandra is designed for a wide range of users, from beginners to computer technicians. Each module displays very specific information about your system and its components that you may or may not need right now. For the purposes of tuning the performance of your PC, focus on the Performance Tune-up Wizard, the System Summary Information Module, the Windows Memory Information Module, and the Drives Information Module. These modules provide important information about your PC's system resources that can help you optimize its performance. Feel free to explore other modules.

Some of the information that Sandra reports about my system is incorrect. Is this normal?

▼ Yes. Sandra runs on many different PCs configured in many different ways. Most PCs have software that contains bugs and often does not provide the information that Sandra needs or presents it in a way that Sandra misinterprets. Sandra may, for example, fail to identify a hard drive that you know is installed on your PC. You can ignore the information or obtain additional information to clear up the discrepancy. For general information, click the What's This button (?) and click the item about which you want to know more. For detailed information, go to www.sisoftware.net and click Q&A.

Understanding Your PC's Resources

You can develop a more effective strategy for optimizing your PC by understanding the resources it needs to operate at peak performance. Because the components that comprise a PC work so closely together, when one component runs low on resources, it can slow down the overall operation of the PC. For example, when your system's random access memory (RAM) is full, the PC must use the hard drive, which is much slower, for virtual memory. If the central processing unit (CPU) is constantly busy, data may need to wait in RAM before it processes.

Your computer's system unit — the box into which your monitor, printer, and other devices plug — contains most of the components that store and process instructions and data. These components include the motherboard, CPU, RAM, hard drive, and display adapter.

Motherboard

Your PC's motherboard is the main circuit board to which all of the other components connect. The motherboard has one or more CPU sockets that house the processor; one or more memory sockets for plugging in RAM chips; drive connectors for plugging in disk drives; and expansion slots that can hold circuit boards, such as a display adapter, network card, and an internal modem. The motherboard provides your PC with the communications infrastructure that all other components need to communicate with one another.

The motherboard contains a set of essential instructions, collectively called the Basic Input/Output System (BIOS), which governs the startup operations and provides a common language that the PC's components can use to communicate. As you optimize your PC, you do very little to configure the motherboard settings, but you can tweak the BIOS settings to make your PC start up a little faster. Refer to Chapter 12 for more information.

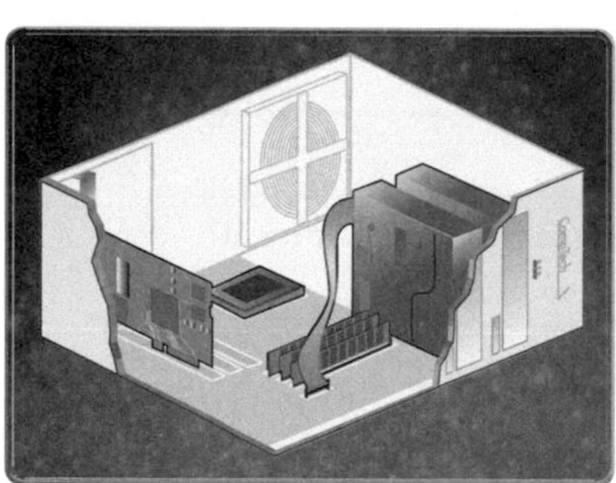

Central Processing Unit

The CPU, commonly called a *microprocessor* on a PC, is often considered the PC's brain, because it processes data and carries out program instructions. Although many people consider this the key component in a PC, a PC that contains a powerful CPU plugged into a slow motherboard with insufficient RAM is often slower than a PC with a less powerful CPU that has a capable motherboard and sufficient RAM.

When optimizing your PC, you do very little to configure the CPU. Some power users perform a technique called *overclocking* to increase the CPU's performance. Overclocking forces the CPU to perform more calculations with each tick of its internal clock. Overclocking can lead to problems, and may even damage the CPU if done incorrectly for an extended period of time, so this book does not recommend overclocking your PC.

Random Access Memory

When you run a program or open a document, your PC reads it from a disk and stores it in RAM. RAM stores data electronically, making it much easier for the PC to access. However, data and instructions remain in RAM only as long as RAM has a steady flow of electricity. When you turn off your PC, any instructions or data stored in RAM are lost. This is why you must save files to a disk before turning off your PC.

Most new PCs are equipped with 256MB of RAM or more, which should be sufficient to run Microsoft Windows and keep a few basic applications running at the same time. However, many programs set themselves up to run in the background, and they can consume a great deal of RAM. In addition, when you exit programs, they may not completely remove themselves from RAM. Eventually, your computer's RAM fills up with programs you do not know are running, or that you do not want to run. This chapter shows you how to check your PC's total memory, find out how much of it is available, and identify the programs that are using it.

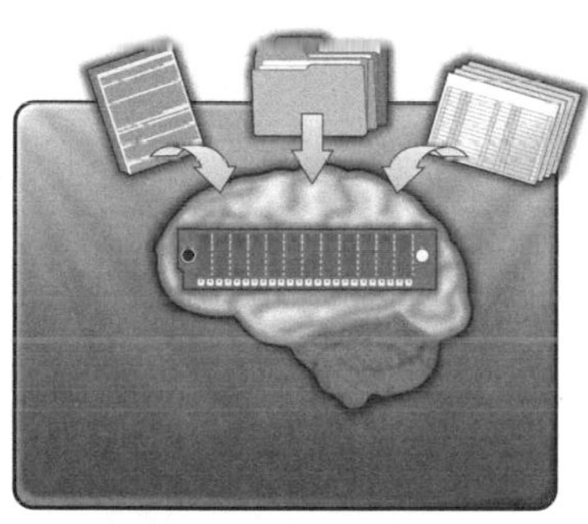

Hard Drive

Unlike RAM, which stores data only as long as the power remains on, your PC's hard drive stores it even after your PC is shut down, using magnetic storage technology that is similar to that for recording cassettes or VHS tapes. When you turn off your PC, the data stored on the disk remains on the disk.

The speed of your PC's hard drive can affect the overall speed of your PC, especially on startup and when you choose to run programs or open documents. You can make your drive work more efficiently by ensuring that it has sufficient free space. This chapter shows you how to identify your PC's disk drives and check the amount of available free space.

Display Adapter

Your PC's display adapter is the circuit board that connects the monitor to the motherboard. Most display adapters include their own RAM, called *video RAM* or *VRAM*, to improve the performance of the adapter and avoid using other valuable PC resources. You can adjust some display settings to improve the video performance, but if your display adapter is slowing down the rest of your PC, sometimes the best option is to replace the adapter. This is a device that PC manufacturers commonly skimp on to lower the cost of the PC.

System Resources

If your PC is running Windows Me or Windows 98, you should be aware of the limitations of Windows System Resources. Windows Me and Windows 98 allocate 64 kilobytes (KB) to user resources and 64KB to graphical device interface (GDI) resources. These limits are set in place to enable older DOS and Windows programs to run in Windows. However, programs can consume all system resources even when your computer has plenty of free memory and disk space, and this can sometimes cause problems. If your PC is running one of these versions of Windows, refer to the section "Check Percentage of Available System Resources," for more information.

Identify Available Disk Drives

You can identify your PC's disk drives to determine the number of drives available and to find out if your PC has more than one hard drive. If your PC has more than one hard drive, you can move files from the drive where Windows resides to another drive to provide Windows with more free space to use as virtual memory.

Most new computers include at least one hard drive and a CD or DVD drive. They may also have a floppy disk drive, which you typically use to transfer files between computers or install small programs.

A PC assigns each drive a letter to identify it. Floppy drives are typically labeled A and B. The hard drive is usually C. The CD drive is usually D. Some PCs have more than one hard drive. The primary hard drive is typically labeled C; additional hard drives are assigned letters such as E, F, and G. You can partition a *physical* hard drive into two or more *logical* hard drives, each of which has its own letter designation. You can identify the available hard drives by opening My Computer.

Identify Available Disk Drives

1. Click Start.
2. Click My Computer.

My Computer appears, displaying an icon for each of your disk drives, including the following:

- Floppy drive
- Hard drive
- CD drive

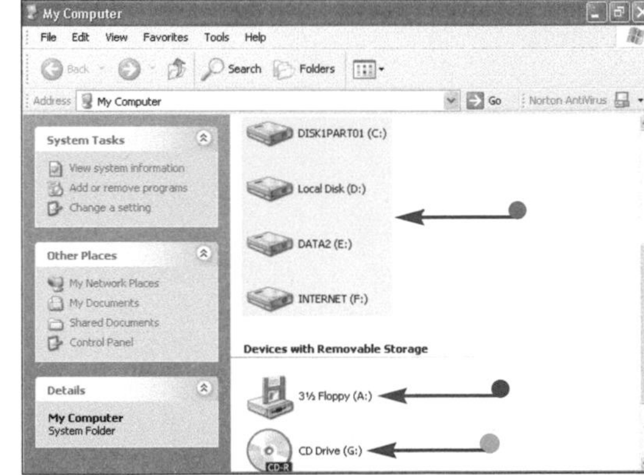

Check Available Disk Storage Space

You can check the amount of storage space that remains on your PC's hard drive to determine if you need to remove files from the drive. As a disk drive fills up, your PC takes more time to find and load files. In addition, if this is the disk drive that Windows uses for virtual memory, the PC may require more time to transfer data between physical RAM and virtual memory. Files on a crowded disk are also more likely to become corrupted.

When you check a drive's properties, Windows displays the size of the drive, the amount of used space, and the amount of free space. You should check your hard drives regularly to determine how much free space is available.

If 10 percent or less of the disk is free, you should back up your files and then remove unused programs and documents from the disk, as explained in Part II.

Can I rank my disk drives according to free space remaining?

▼ Yes. In My Computer, click View, click Arrange Icons By, and then click Free Space. Windows rearranges the disk icons, placing the icon for the disk with the most space at the top.

Check Available Disk Storage Space

1. Click My Computer.

Note: *See the section "Identify Available Disk Drives," for instructions.*

2. Right-click the icon for the drive whose available storage space you want to check.
3. In the menu that appears, click Properties.

The Properties dialog box for the selected disk drive appears, including the following:

- Capacity
- Used space
- Free space

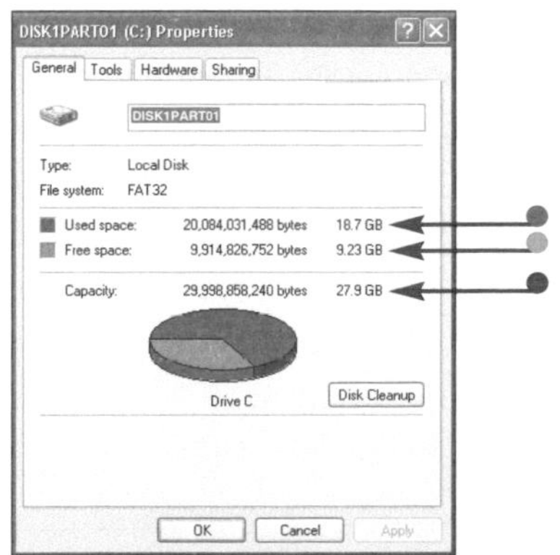

Determine Processor Type and Speed

By identifying the make, model, and speed of the CPU installed in your PC, you can develop realistic expectations concerning performance. If your PC has a 466 megahertz (MHz) Celeron processor, rather than a 2.4 gigahertz (GHz) Pentium 4 processor, for example, you can expect your PC to run a lot slower than most newer PCs. This can help you decide whether you need to optimize the performance of the equipment you already have, upgrade the processor and perhaps other components, or purchase a brand-new PC.

The processor type and speed can also help you determine if a software fix can help improve system performance. For example, if you purchased a top-of-the-line PC several years ago that is still running Windows 98 or Me, you may want to upgrade to Windows XP to equip your computer with a more stable operating system. However, Windows XP requires a 233 MHz processor in the Intel Pentium/Celeron family or the AMD K6/Athlon/Duron family. Unless you know the processor type and speed, you cannot make an informed decision.

The System Properties dialog box can display the processor type and speed.

Determine Processor Type and Speed

1. Click Start.
2. Right-click My Computer.
3. Click Properties.

The System Properties dialog box appears and displays the following:

- Processor manufacturer and model
- Processor speed

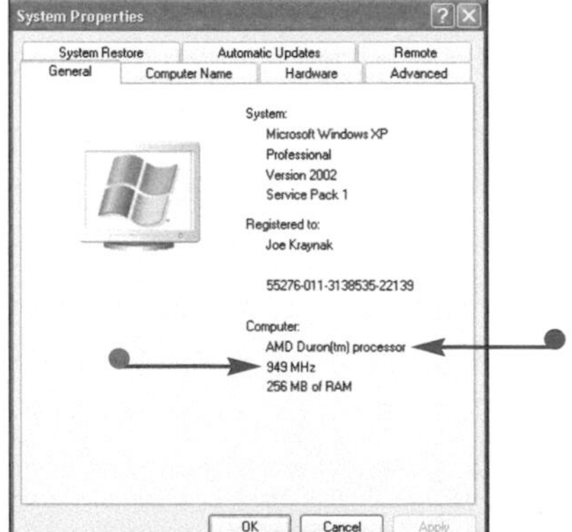

Check Processor Usage

You can check your processor to determine how busy it is processing data, carrying out instructions, and performing calculations. If you check your processor usage and it is consistently showing a high level of usage, even when you are not performing any intensive tasks, such as running programs or opening documents, the usage may indicate that you have programs running in the background that are using the processor.

You can check your processor usage in Windows by displaying the Windows Task Manager. The Windows Task Manager displays the names of all programs currently running along with the percentage of CPU processing power each program is using. By analyzing the list of programs, you can often identify the program that is causing the problem.

MASTER IT

I have something called System Idle Process that accounts for more than 90 percent of the CPU usage. What is it?

▼ System Idle Process indicates the CPU's downtime, its percentage of idle time. A high percentage indicates that the CPU is not working hard at all.

Check Processor Usage

1. Right-click a blank area of the Windows taskbar.
2. In the menu that appears, click Task Manager.

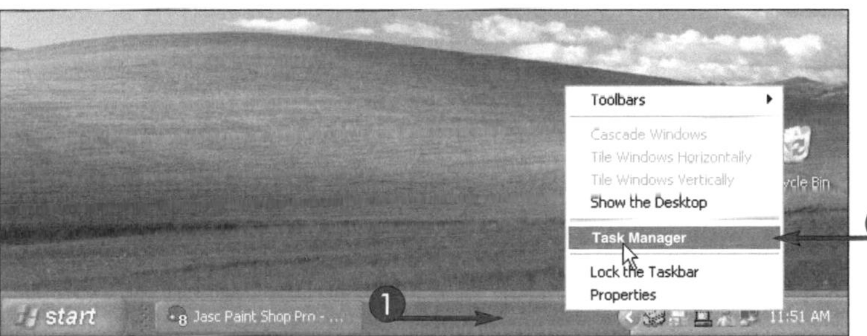

Task Manager appears.

3. Click the Processes tab.

Task Manager displays the currently running processes along with the percentage of CPU usage for each.

- CPU percentages appear in this column.

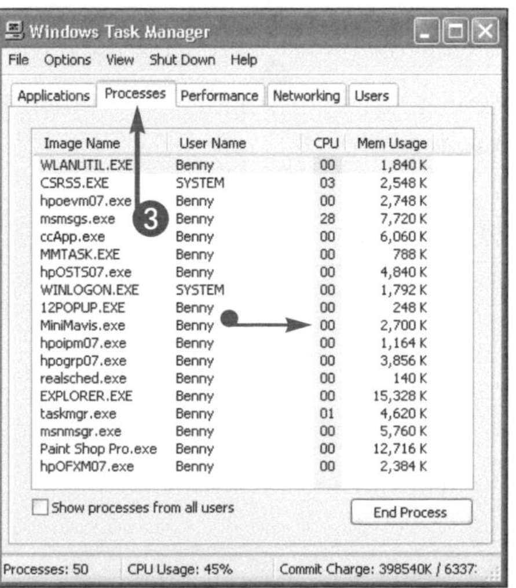

Determine Total Random Access Memory (RAM)

You can check the amount of RAM installed on your PC and the amount of RAM that is available for use to determine if your PC has enough RAM to run Windows and your applications. For your PC to run Windows XP it must have at least 64MB of RAM. However, 64MB is not enough for optimum performance and may not be enough to run many Windows applications. Microsoft recommends 128MB of RAM or more, especially if you plan on running graphics-intensive programs, such as Photoshop. If your PC is running an older version of Windows — Windows 98 or Windows Me — 128MB of RAM is sufficient for most uses.

Your PC's total memory consists of physical memory, RAM, and virtual memory. *Virtual memory* is disk space that Windows uses to supplement RAM. However, virtual memory is a poor substitute for RAM, because RAM is significantly faster and it feeds data directly to the CPU.

In Windows, you can use various techniques to display the total amount of RAM. A quick way is to display the Properties dialog box for My Computer, as shown in the section "Determine Processor Type and Speed." Another way, shown here, is to use the Windows System Information Utility.

Determine Total Random Access Memory (RAM)

1. Click Start.
2. Click All Programs.
3. Click Accessories.
4. Click System Tools.
5. Click System Information.

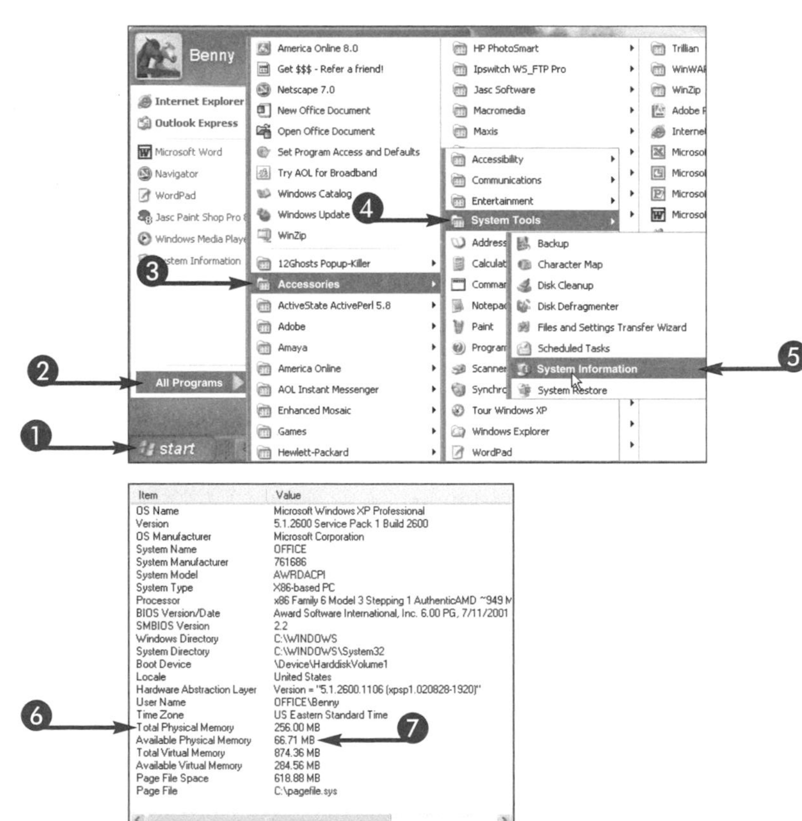

The System Information window appears displaying the System Summary.

6. Note the Total Physical Memory.
7. Note the Available Physical Memory.

8. Note the Total Virtual Memory.
9. Note the Available Virtual Memory.

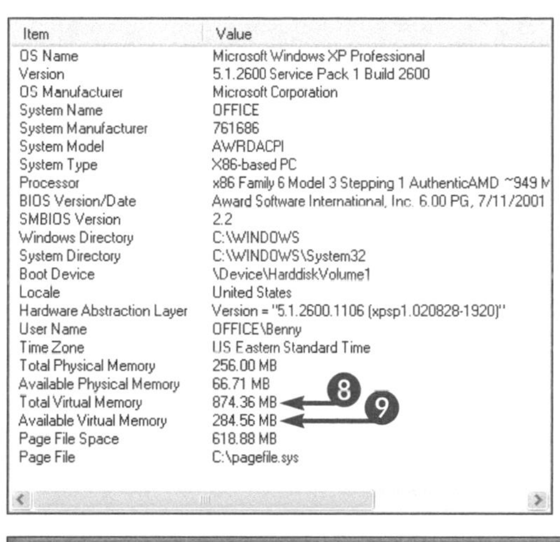

The System Information Window displays other important information about your PC, including:

- The operating system name and version.
- The system type.
- The processor family.
- The BIOS version and date.

10. Click the Close button (☒).

The System Information window closes.

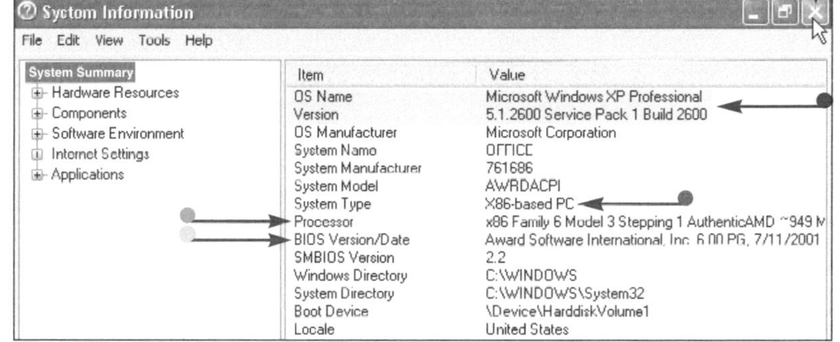

I have only three programs running, but System Information shows that I am using 250MB of RAM. What is using so much?

▼ This is a difficult question to answer. Try closing all programs that you know are running, and then check how much RAM is free. If closing some programs reclaims only a small portion of RAM, you may have a poorly written program that does not return memory on exit. Refer to Chapter 11 for suggestions. Restart Windows and check RAM again. If the RAM usage is still high, you may have too many programs running on startup. See the section "Identify Currently Running Programs," for more information.

How much RAM should my PC have?

▼ The amount of RAM your PC requires depends on the operating system it runs and the types of applications you plan on running. If you are running Windows 98 or Me, your PC should have between 128MB and 256MB of RAM. Any less than 128MB causes Windows performance to suffer, especially if you run several applications or any large applications. Installing more than 256MB of RAM can actually cause problems in Windows 98 or Me due to other Windows limitations. Windows XP runs fairly well with 256MB of RAM, but it runs better with 512MB or more. Windows XP does a better job of managing large amounts of RAM. Check the minimum memory requirements for the software you want to run.

Check Percentage of Available System Resources

If your PC is running Windows 98 or Windows Me, you can monitor your system resources to prevent system crashes and avoid performance problems. When considering system resources, most users think of memory and disk space. In Windows 98 and Windows Me, system resources are 64KB areas of memory that Windows reserves for the user input manager (user.exe) and the graphics display interface manager (gdi.exe). Your PC may have 512MB of RAM, but if either of these system resources dips below 15 percent, Windows may be unable to run additional programs or may crash. A crash makes a program or Windows unresponsive and may display an error message or a blue screen.

Windows 98 and Windows Me include a system resource monitor that displays the percentage of remaining system resources. You can turn on the monitor and keep it running as you perform other tasks in Windows. If the system resources dip below 15 percent, you can shut down programs to reclaim system resources. Sometimes shutting down programs is not enough, because some programs do not free up the system resources they were using. You may need to restart Windows to reclaim additional system resources.

Check Percentage of Available System Resources

1. Click Start.
2. Click Programs.
3. Click Accessories.
4. Click System Tools.
5. Click Resource Meter.

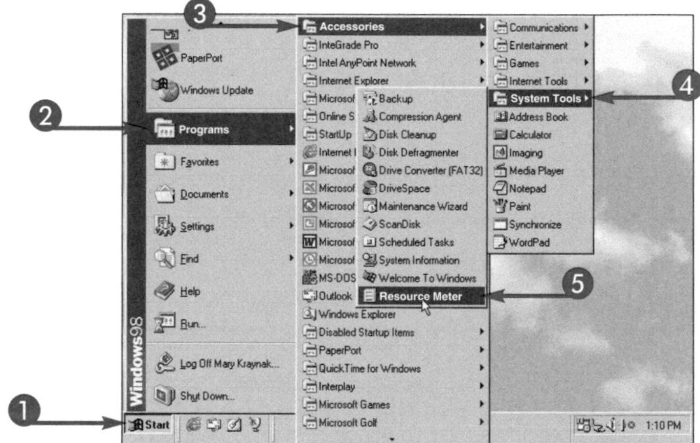

The Resource Meter dialog box appears, indicating that the Resource Meter also uses resources.

6. Click OK.

The Windows Resource Meter appears in the system tray.

7. Position the mouse pointer over the Windows Resource Meter.

- A screen tip appears, displaying the percentage of each system resource remaining.

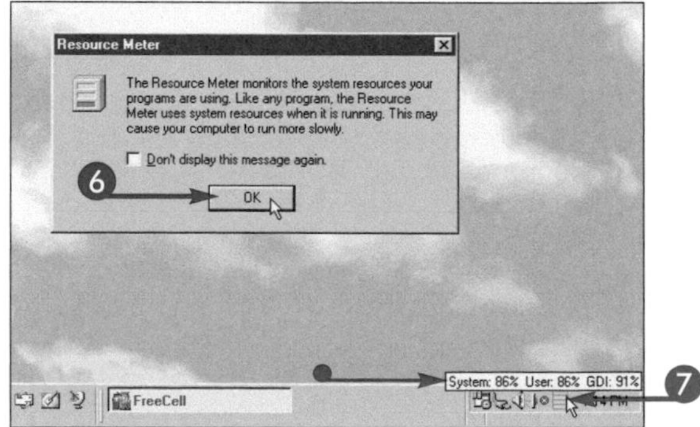

8 Double-click the Windows Resource Meter.

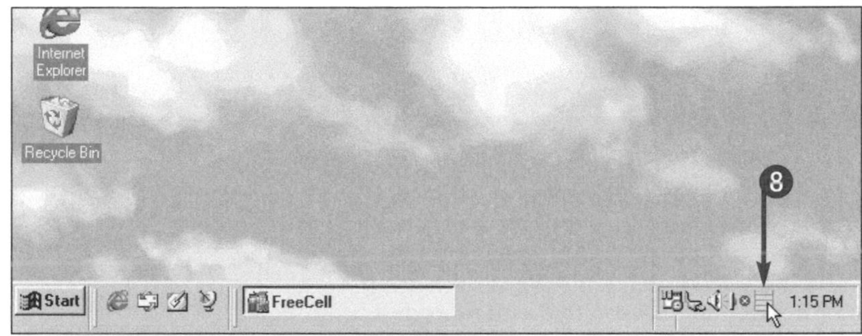

The Resource Meter window appears, displaying the percentage of each system resource remaining.

- In this example, all system resources exceed the lower limit of 15 percent, so no action is required.

9 Click OK.

The Resource Meter window closes, but the icon remains in the system tray.

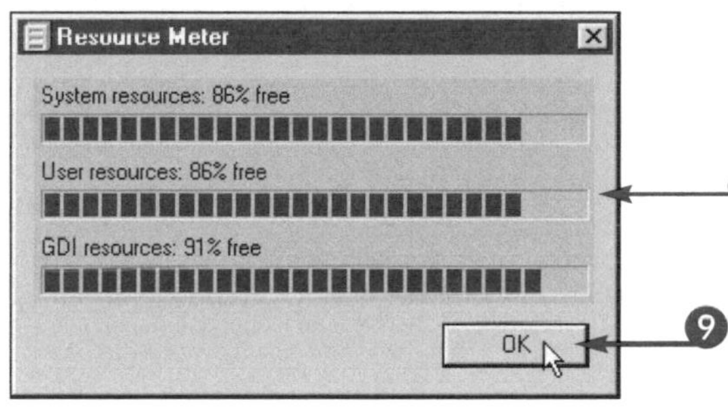

Does Windows 2000 or XP have a feature that is similar to the Windows Resource Meter?

▼ No, but you can use the Windows Task Manager to monitor your PC's CPU usage, memory, and other resources. Right-click a blank area of the Windows taskbar and click Task Manager. When the Task Manager appears, click the Performance tab.

Why is the Resource Meter missing from my System Tools menu?

▼ You may not have the Resource Meter installed on your PC. You can install it from the Windows installation CD by using the Add/Remove Programs utility in the Windows Control Panel to selectively install additional Windows components.

My System Resources commonly run below 50 percent. Is this a problem?

▼ No. System resources can run very low before they become a problem. Be concerned only if they dip below 15 percent. If your PC commonly crashes even when system resources are above 15 percent, the problem is probably due to some other cause — perhaps a bug in a particular program you are using, a corrupt file, or a defective memory module. You can run a diagnostic utility on your computer, as explained in Chapter 1, to check for hardware issues. If the problem is related to a particular program, you may need to install an update, as discussed in Chapter 24, or reinstall the program.

Identify Currently Running Programs

You can identify the programs that are using your PC's memory to determine if you need to have them running. Whenever you run a program, the Windows taskbar displays an icon for the program, so you know the programs you launched. The system tray, on the right end of the taskbar, displays icons for many programs that run automatically when Windows starts. However, you may have other programs running in the background without displaying any indication that they are running.

Windows Task Manager can display a complete list of applications and processes that are currently running. An application is a program that enables you to perform tasks. A process is any executable program, such as Windows Explorer, or a service, such as WINLOGON.EXE. People commonly use Task Manager to force unresponsive programs to close. You can also use it to shut down programs or services that you have no other way of shutting down. However, you must be careful when shutting down services, because Windows may require some services to run. Most services that Windows does not require to function display an icon in the system tray, which you can use to shut down the service.

Identify Currently Running Programs

1. Examine the taskbar for any applications that are currently running.
2. Click the Show hidden icons button ( ).

   The system tray expands to display icons for programs that are running in the background.

   - You can right-click an icon to view a menu of options for the program it represents.
3. Right-click a blank area of the Windows taskbar.
4. Click Task Manager.

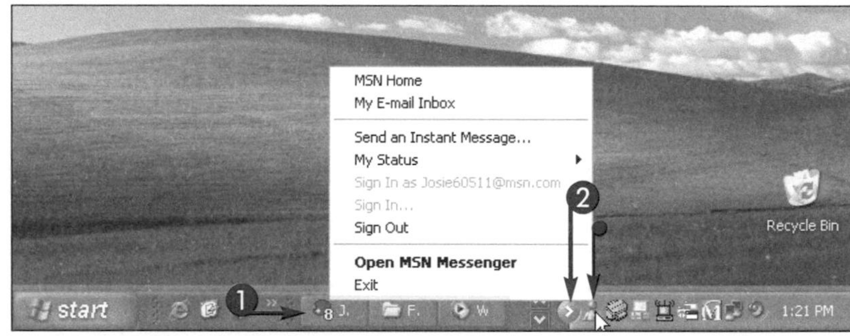

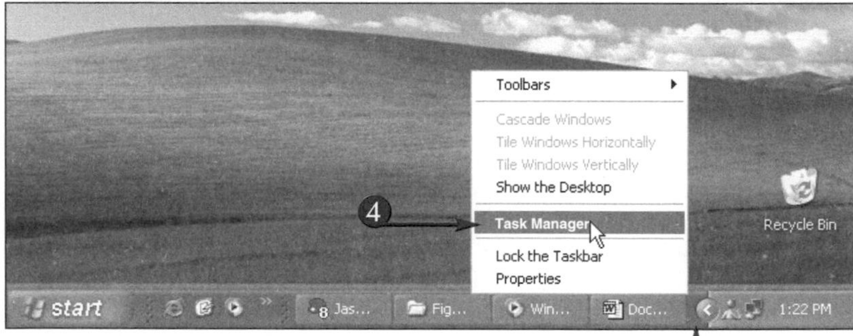

Windows Task Manager appears with the Processes tab in front.

- The Processes list displays the names of all executable program files that are currently running.
- You can end a process by clicking its name and clicking End Process.

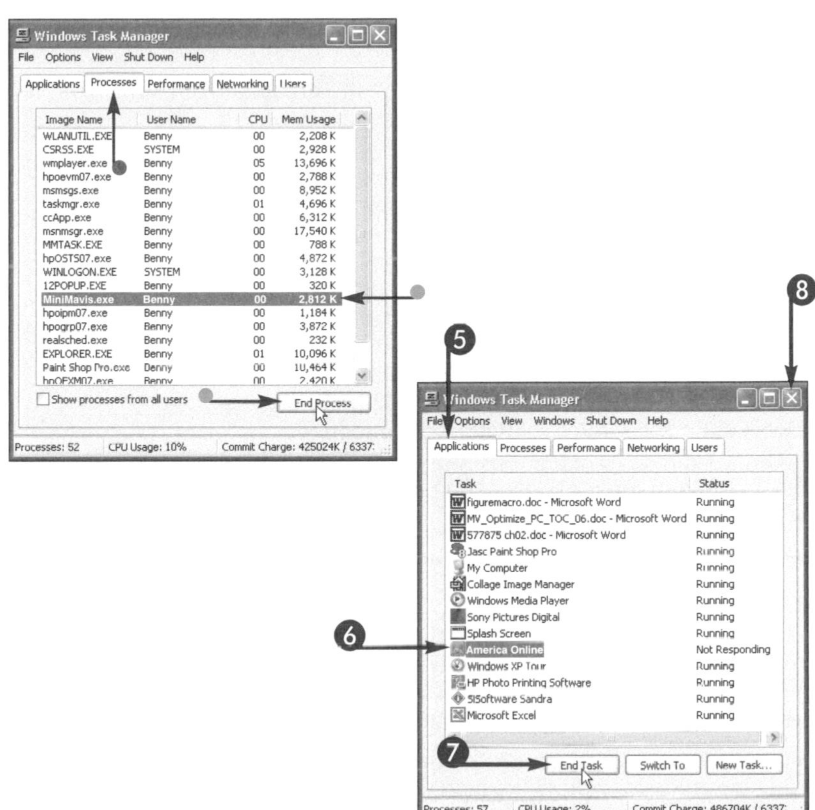

5 Click the Applications tab.

6 If an application is not responding, click its name.

7 Click End Task and respond to any messages that appear.

The program shuts down.

8 Click the Close (☒) button.

Task Manager closes.

If my computer crashes and Windows is not responding, how do I run Task Manager?

▼ If an application locks up, wait one or two minutes before shutting it down. If you shut down an application without saving your work, you may lose valuable data. If the application is still locked up, you can press Ctrl+Alt+Del to display Task Manager. In most cases, Task Manager can restore control of your mouse so you can click the name of the application or process that is not responding and then click End Task or End Process to shut it down. If Task Manager is not responding, press Ctrl+Alt+Del again to restart Windows. In some cases, you may need to press your PC's reset button or power button to shut down.

When I end an application or process in Task Manager, does the process run the next time I start my PC?

▼ Yes. Many programs set themselves up to run automatically whenever you start your PC. To prevent the application from running, you must remove it from the Windows Startup Menu or use the System Information Utility to prevent the program from running. Chapter 13 shows you how to streamline the Windows startup without accidentally preventing essential Windows processes from running on startup. This not only helps keep your PC's memory uncluttered but can also make Windows start faster.

Understanding Internet Connection Types

By understanding the different Internet connection types, you can choose an Internet service provider (ISP) that provides the fastest service possible for your budget. If you use the Internet to browse the Web, send and receive e-mail, chat with friends and relatives, and perform other tasks, the speed of your Internet connection can significantly influence your PC's performance. Downloading audio clips over a standard phone line connection, for example, can take 50 to 100 times as long as downloading the same files using a cable modem connection. You can have the most powerful PC on the market, but if your Internet connection is slow, all of your activity on the Internet drags.

Many factors affect the speed of your Internet connection, including the number of pop-up ads that your computer downloads and displays. The chapters in Part V show you how to optimize your Internet connection. However, the connection itself limits the top speed you can experience. A dial-up modem can establish a connection over a standard phone line, but its top speed is only about 53 kilobits per second (Kbps). The top speed for a cable modem connection is about 4 megabits per second (Mbps).

When you are looking to optimize your Internet connection speed, upgrading your service is the most effective strategy. But you need to know your options.

Dial-Up Modem

With a dial-up modem, you can connect to the Internet over a standard phone line. The fastest dial-up modem you can use is 56 Kbps, but due to phone line restrictions, modems transfer data at a slower rate — typically 53 Kbps or less.

Dial-up modem service is popular for two reasons: It is relatively inexpensive, typically costing $20 or less per month, and you can usually obtain service anywhere, as long as you have a phone line. If you use your Internet connection to correspond with others via e-mail and for some light Web browsing, a dial-up modem may be fast enough to meet your needs.

Cable Modem

If you have cable television service in your area, the cable provider may also offer cable Internet service. Cable Internet service typically costs about $30 to $50 per month. With cable service and a cable modem, you can usually connect to the Internet at speeds of 3 to 4 Mbps. A file that takes two minutes to download over a 56 Kbps connection may take less than three seconds over a cable connection. Upload speeds are typically much slower — 256 Kbps to 512 Kbps.

One drawback to cable Internet service is that the bandwidth — the capacity of data that the cable lines can carry — is shared among a community of users. If the cable service allocates a limited amount of bandwidth to a community where many people use the service, your connection speeds may dip during periods of high use. However, most users who upgrade from dial-up to cable Internet service are more than satisfied with the improvement.

DSL Modem

Many phone companies now offer *digital subscriber line* (DSL) service, which is much faster than a dial-up modem connection but usually not quite as fast as a cable modem connection. With a DSL modem and DSL service, you can achieve data transfer rates of up to 9 Mbps, theoretically. In practice, transfer rates are much slower and typically average about 1.5 Mbps, about half the speed of cable Internet service. The major drawback of DSL is that speed drops the farther you are from the station that services your line. You can expect to pay about $30 per month for the service.

DSL comes in two forms: asymmetric DSL (ADSL) and symmetric DSL (SDSL). ADSL supports downstream data rates of 1.5 to 9 Mbps and upstream data rates of 16 to 640 Kbps. The downstream rate is much faster because most people use the Internet primarily to receive data such as Web pages and e-mail messages. However, when sending e-mail messages that contain large file attachments or when uploading files on the Internet, the low upstream data rate can significantly slow down the operation. SDSL lines provide upstream and downstream data rates that are nearly equivalent.

T1 and T3 Lines

Many businesses connect to the Internet using T1 lines, which are digital phone lines that can carry both voice and data signals. A T1 connection typically carries data at about the same speed as a DSL line, about 1.5 Mbps. ISPs primarily use T3 lines, which form the backbone of the Internet, transferring data at speeds exceeding 43 Mbps. You might hear of a T2 line, which consists of four T1 lines, but most companies skip the T2 designation.

Satellite Service

People in rural areas where cable and DSL service is unavailable commonly use satellite technology to connect to the Internet. In the past, satellite service provided only one-way communication, for receiving data. You needed a separate dial-up modem connection to carry communication and data from your computer to the Internet. Now, satellite services feature two-way communications.

Satellite service is typically more expensive than DSL or cable. You can expect to pay $100 per month or more for satellite service. Internet connection speed is comparable to that of DSL service — about 1.5 Mbps. Satellite service requires the installation of a satellite dish, and service can be interrupted by inclement whether, but if you need broadband service, and DSL or cable service is unavailable in your area, satellite service is a viable option.

Other Options on the Horizon

Other broadband connection technologies are being developed and are already available in some areas, including Wi-Fi (wireless fidelity) and connections through electrical wires. Wi-Fi is especially attractive to users who travel and need a consistent service provider as they move locations.

Understanding Internet Connection Speed Bumps

Your PC may have a broadband connection that is capable of transferring data at 3 Mbps, but many factors can affect speed, including the quality of your phone lines or cables, the number of people using the service, the number of people using the Internet, the reliability of your ISP, the speed of the site you are accessing, and the number of ads that pop up on your computer screen.

By understanding and identifying the Internet connection speed bumps, you can begin to remove them in order to increase the effective speed of your Internet connection. In the next section, "Test Internet Connection Speed," you can check the actual speed at which you can send and receive data. In this section, you discover several factors that can negatively affect your connection speed and reliability.

Physical Limitations

A 56 Kbps modem does not transfer data at 56 Kbps. A cable modem, which theoretically can transfer data at 10 Mbps, is lucky to achieve transfer rates of 2 or 3 Mbps. Physical limitations often prevent a connection from achieving top speeds. For example, an old phone line or a loose connection can cause intermittent connection problems or significantly reduce data transfer rates. Likewise, a cheap cable can prevent a cable modem from transferring data at optimal speeds to a PC. A poorly positioned satellite dish can negatively affect transfer rates over a satellite connection.

Internet Traffic Jams

The Internet is a fairly reliable information superhighway, but with so many people using it, the Internet often experiences backups and traffic jams. At peak usage periods, the entire Internet can slow down, and everybody experiences it. In some cases, a site is so busy that you cannot connect to it. You may think that something is wrong with your system, when the real problem is with the Internet in general or with a specific site.

Web sites are also susceptible to attacks from vandals who try to shut down the sites or overwhelm them with data or requests, simply to have a little fun. The two most popular search sites on the Internet, Yahoo! and Google, have experienced such attacks, making the services unavailable to some users for a period of time.

Internet Service Provider

To connect to the Internet, you connect to a server that your ISP maintains. Your connection is only as reliable and as fast as your ISP makes it. If the provider oversells the service and fails to increase capacity, you may experience times when you cannot establish a connection or your connection slows down considerably.

Cable service providers intentionally limit connection speeds to distribute bandwidth more equitably. Some users employ an illegal hack called *uncapping*, to work around the limitations, which this book does not recommend.

PC Speed

When examining the connection between your PC and the Internet, you can easily overlook the fact that the speed of your PC also has an effect on how you experience the Internet. When you open a Web page, your computer must process the data it receives and display the page. If you choose to download and play audio or video clips, it must process that data, as well. If your PC is not operating at peak performance, it can make your Internet connection seem slow even if your connection is capable of transferring data at high rates of speed.

Pop-Up Advertisements

Some Web sites are set up to display advertisements on-screen, each appearing in a separate browser window. These advertisements, commonly known as *pop-ups*, can slow down your computer in several ways. First, every pop-up consists of data that your computer must download from the Web, which adds to the time it takes to load each page. Second, your computer must expend valuable resources to create a new window and display the advertisement. And finally, the pop-up creates another window that you must take some time to close.

Fortunately, several companies offer free software that can help block most pop-ups, so you and your computer do not need to deal with them. You can find out more about pop-up blockers in Chapter 15.

Spyware and Adware

Some Web sites, shareware programs, and games install software on your computer that can track your browsing habits and display pop-ups on your screen. This software, commonly known as *spyware* or *adware*, provides another source of pop-ups. These pop-ups can appear on-screen even if you have a pop-up blocker installed because adware generates the pop-ups not from the Web but from your PC.

You may find spyware and adware very difficult to remove, because the people who create these programs design it to remain hidden on your system and to avoid any attempts at uninstalling it. Chapter 14 describes programs and techniques to rid your PC of this annoying software.

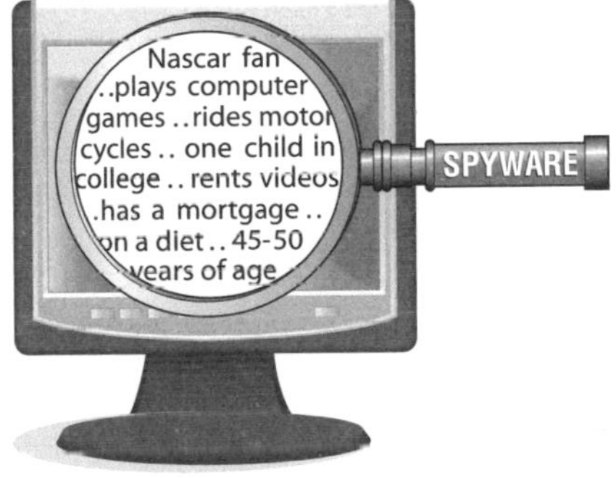

Spam

Like pop-ups, spyware, and adware, *spam* is unsolicited advertising that is distributed over the Internet. In the case of spam, the advertising is sent via e-mail. Chapter 16 shows several techniques for avoiding spam and for preventing it from reaching your inbox.

Test Internet Connection Speed

ISPs often advertise the top speed of their service, claiming that users can connect at 56 Kbps (kilobits per second) or 2 Mbps or "up to 50 times faster than a standard dial-up connection." But what speed are you really experiencing and how does it compare to the advertised rate?

You can find out at any of several Web sites that offer tools for testing your Internet connection speed. These sites typically upload and download large files between the Web site and your computer and time how long transfers take. They then provide you with an accurate assessment of how fast your Internet connection really is at any time of the day or night.

You can expect to see your connection speed fluctuate throughout the day as more or fewer people go online to surf the Web, but if you notice that your Internet speed is always significantly slower than what your service provider advertised, you need to do some troubleshooting on your end and possibly contact your ISP.

Test Internet Connection Speed

1. Type **bandwidthplace.com/speedtest/** in your browser's Address bar and press Enter.
2. Scroll down and click your connection type (○ changes to ◉).
   - Additional connection types appear here.
3. Click Start.

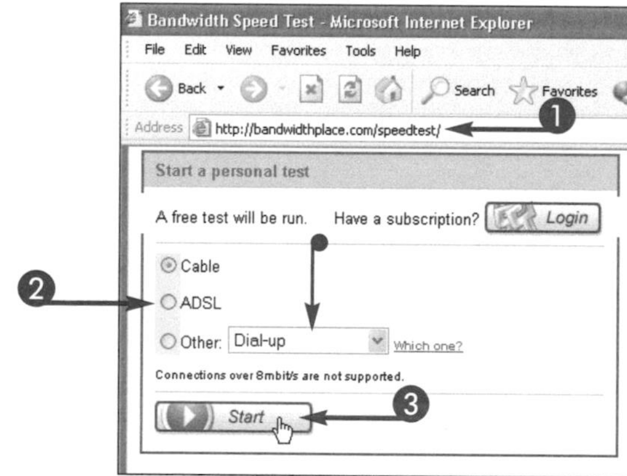

This screen prompts you to specify your geographical location.

4. Click your country.
5. Click here and select your state.
6. Click Continue.

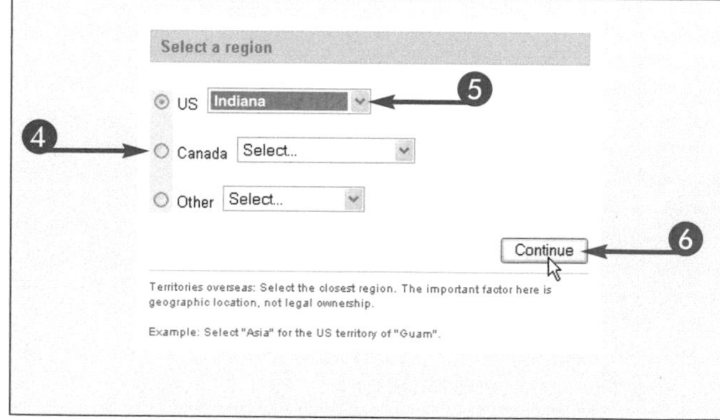

As the test runs, a progress message appears.

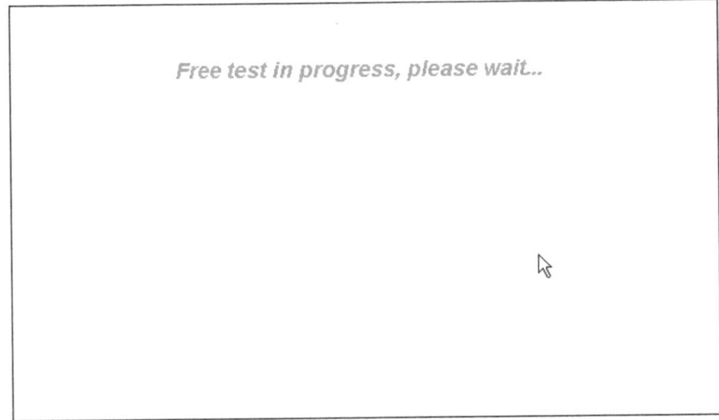

When the test is complete, personal test results appear.

- Your speed appears here.
- You can click here for additional details.
- You can find tools for improving your connection speed.

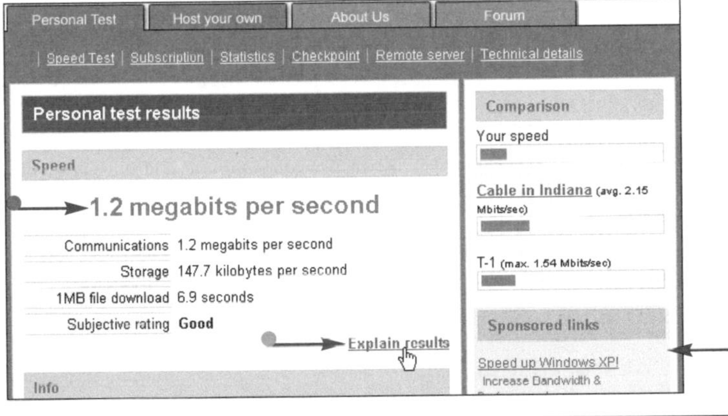

I cannot connect to the Bandwidth Place Web site. What other sites can test my connection speed?

▼ Many Web sites feature Internet connection speed tests. Check out these sites:

www.dslreports.com/stest

us.mcafee.com/root/speedometer.asp

www.pcpitstop.com/internet/default.asp

You can find more places to test your connection speed by going to www.testmyspeed.com and typing your area code. Most of these test sites chart your connection speed against several other types of connections, including 56 Kbps dial-up modem, cable modem, DSL, and T1.

If my computers are networked and I am testing from a PC that is not directly connected to the Internet, how does that affect the results?

▼ People and businesses who have more than one computer commonly network their computers to share resources, including an Internet connection. If your modem is connected to a router that all networked computers connect to to access the Intenet, you can run the test from any PC. However, if the modem connects to a central PC that all other PCs connect to, then run the test from the central PC. Otherwise, the test results may show a much slower connection than what you actually have.

The tests show that my cable modem is transferring data at about the same rate as a 56 Kbps modem. What should I do?

▼ Run the test again or try running a speed test at another test site. Sometimes the site may be too busy to provide accurate results. If you ran the test during a peak usage time, try running the test later. If the tests consistently show that your cable modem connection is slower than half the advertised speed, contact your cable Internet service provider.

Understanding PC Security Threats

By understanding and appreciating the potential threats to your PC and your online privacy, you can more effectively protect your PC and your personal information. Before the Internet became such a popular tool for distributing information and communicating globally, PC security threats were limited to viruses and other software that could damage the files on your PC. If you never shared programs or files with other users, your PC was completely safe.

As soon as you connect your PC to the Internet, it becomes vulnerable to various security threats. A program that you download and install from the Internet can place a virus on your PC or install a spyware application that collects data and passes it along to an interested party. A document attached to an e-mail message you receive may contain malicious software designed to destroy data. And without the proper security in place, a devious hacker, commonly called a *cracker*, can break into your PC to use its resources or to steal sensitive data, such as passwords or account numbers.

Although you cannot completely protect your computer from potential security breaches, you can employ some basic security utilities and techniques to ensure that your computer is not wide open to attacks.

Viruses and Worms

A *virus* consists of computer code that is designed to perform unauthorized activities on a computer. Many viruses do little or no damage; they are programmed simply to display a funny or frightening message or image or animation at a scheduled time. Other viruses are very destructive, wiping out files, reformatting a hard drive, or simply replicating themselves to the point at which they completely exhaust a computer's memory and disk space.

Viruses differ from other malicious software in two respects — they can replicate themselves and they can attach themselves to other files, which enables them to spread to other computers. A *worm* is a type of virus that also replicates itself but does not infect other files. Both viruses and worms can quickly spread through a network, infecting all computers on the network.

In the next section, "Scan for Viruses Online with Symnatec," you learn how to connect to a Web site that can scan your computer for most known viruses to determine if your PC is infected. In Chapter 27, you learn how to install and configure antivirus software to protect your PC. Some experts recommend that users follow safe computing practices to avoid virus infection, such as opening e-mail file attachments only from people you know and downloading programs only from reputable sites. However, e-mail messages and Web sites may not always be what they claim to be. Your best defense is a good, up-to-date antivirus utility that automatically scans all files coming into your computer.

Virus Hoaxes

A virus hoax is a false warning about a virus that usually does not exist. Most e-mail messages that warn of viruses are hoaxes, so the wise way to respond is to delete the message and not forward it to your friends and colleagues as most hoaxes suggest you do. If you think that a particular virus warning is legitimate, go to www.mcafee.com and check the virus hoax list before forwarding the warning to your friends, relatives, and colleagues. Forwarding a hoax simply adds more junk mail to a system that already has too much.

Trojan Horses

A *Trojan horse* is a program that masquerades as a useful or fun program but performs unauthorized, usually malicious activities on your computer. Unlike a virus, a Trojan horse does not replicate itself, but it can delete files, steal data, and disable PC security safeguards. You can protect your computer against Trojan horses using the same tools and utilities that protect it against viruses.

Spyware and *adware* are types of Trojan horses. They typically install themselves on your PC when you connect to a particular Web site or download and install a game or other program you want to use. Another type of Trojan horse is designed to attack computers that have dial-up modems; the program uses the modem to place expensive international phone calls. You may not know what is going on until you receive a phone bill for hundreds of dollars.

Hackers and Crackers

A *hacker* is an avid and knowledgeable computer user who loves to tweak programs in order to make them perform in ways that they were not designed to perform. A *cracker* is a hacker who breaks into systems, usually to steal data or cause damage.

Whenever your PC is connected to the Internet, it becomes part of a network and is susceptible to break-ins. Your PC is more susceptible if it has an always-on connection, such as a cable or DSL connection. If you use a modem to connect to the Internet and then you disconnect when you are done, your PC is fairly secure. Turning your computer off when you are not using it for an extended period of time is a good defense. Chapter 28 discusses some additional security tools and techniques.

Securing Your PC

No PC that is connected to the Internet is completely safe and secure. As soon as a developer announces a new security patch for one of its programs, a cracker finds another security flaw to exploit. As soon as a company identifies a pesky virus, someone modifies the virus to enable it to avoid detection.

Although you cannot make your PC completely secure, by combining safe computing practices with up-to-date security software, you can secure your PC enough to experience the full potential of the Internet with little worry.

Scan for Viruses Online with Symantec

If your PC does not have an up-to-date antivirus program installed, you can connect to a Web site that scans your PC for known viruses. If the scan detects a virus on your PC, it can provide you with instructions on how to remove the virus or you can order the company's antivirus software online, which can usually remove the virus for you automatically.

The two most popular antivirus software products are Norton AntiVirus and McAfee VirusScan. Both of these developers offer free virus scanning on their sites. You can run Norton's virus scan by visiting security.symantec.com. McAfee FreeScan is available at us.mcafee.com/root/mfs/default.asp. Both of these scans thoroughly examine your PC's memory and disk drives for known viruses.

Even if your PC is not infected with a virus, you should install an antivirus program on your PC, as explained in Chapter 27. Antivirus programs typically configure themselves to run in the background and prevent your PC from downloading and opening any infected files. The antivirus program also checks weekly or monthly for updated virus definitions so it has the data it needs to identify the latest viruses.

The steps in this section show you how to run Symantec to check for viruses. To avoid problems, please perform the steps in this section only if you do not have an antivirus program running on your PC.

Scan for Viruses Online with Symantec

1. Launch your Web browser.
2. In the address bar, type **security.norton.com** and press Enter.

   The Symantec Security Check page appears.
3. Click GO.

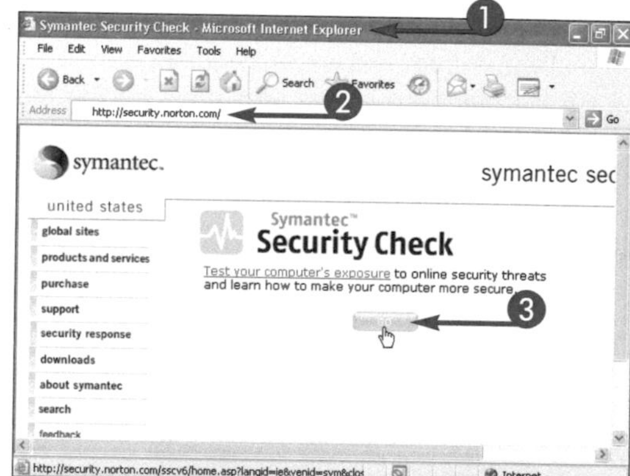

The Symantec Security Check page appears.

Note: *The screen may differ depending on the version of Windows you have.*

4. Under Virus Detection, click START.

   The Security Warning dialog box appears asking if you want to install and run Virus Detection.
5. Click Yes.

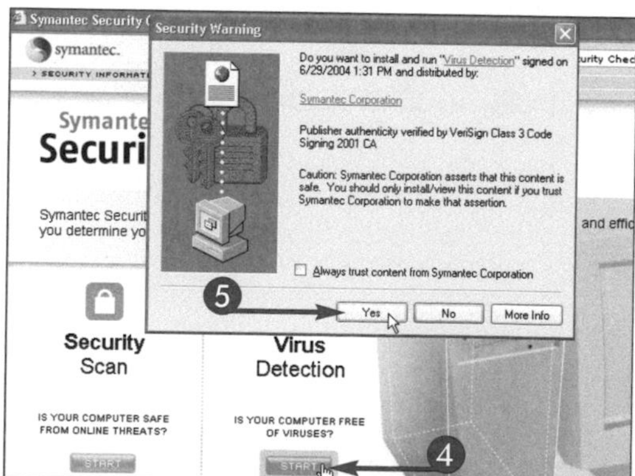

- Symantec Security Check displays its progress as it scans your computer for viruses.

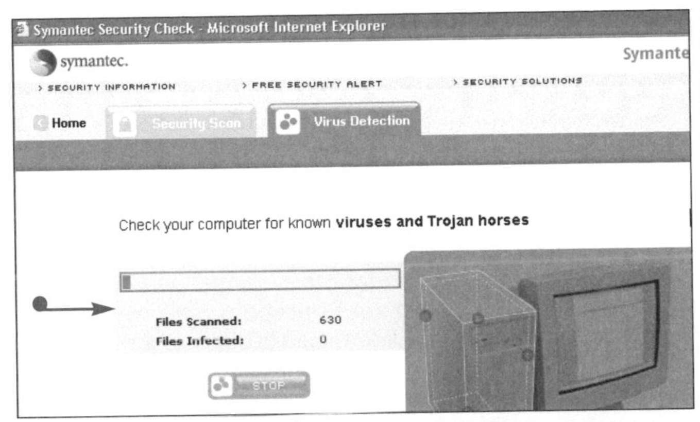

- When the scan is complete, Symantec Security Check displays its results.

6 Note any identified viruses.

- This PC is virus free.

If your computer is not virus free, you can install an anitvirus program to combat them.

Note: *See Chapter 27 for more on antivirus programs.*

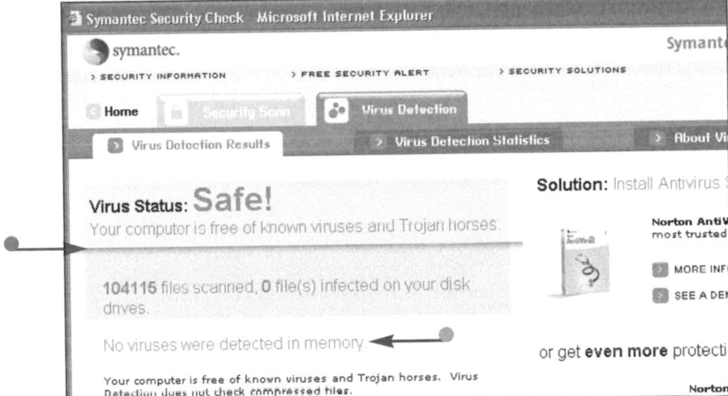

I found a free antivirus program on the Web that claims to be very effective. Can I save some money and use it instead of a commercial product?

▼ That depends. AVG AntiVirus, which you can download from www.grisoft.com, has a strong reputation and comes from a reliable source. However, other programs, though they may appear legitimate, may contain spyware, adware, or other types of malicious software that can cause more problems than they solve. Be very careful about downloading and installing software on the Web. Even software that you pay for can contain malicious components, so make sure you do a background check before installing any software on your computer.

The virus check identified a virus, but I really do not have the time to deal with it right now. What should I do?

▼ Save any documents that are currently opened, shut down programs that are running, and turn off your PC until you do have time to deal with the problem. If your PC starts up normally, you can start it later, install an antivirus program, and use the program to remove the virus from your PC. If your PC does not start normally, you can use the antivirus program's installation CD as an emergency disc to start your PC and scan it for viruses. Refer to the instructions included with the antivirus program and refer to Chapter 27 for additional information.

Test Your System Security with Symantec

The only computers that are completely secure are computers that never connect to other computers, via a network over the Internet or use files from other computers. That means that most computers are vulnerable to break-ins and/or virus infections. Still, many users give little thought to online security, often assuming that their Internet service provider is responsible for keeping the connection safe and secure. However, you really do not know how vulnerable your system is until you test your Internet connection yourself. You just might discover that your system is wide open to break-ins.

Several software companies on the Internet provide free diagnostics to test your computer's vulnerabilities. These diagnostics typically determine whether your computer is running an antivirus program and how visible your computer is on the Internet. If your computer is highly visible — that is, if it has a port number that a cracker can identify — then your computer is very vulnerable to break-ins. The steps in this section show you how to run Symantec's security check to determine if your computer is vulnerable. Chapter 28 discusses tools and techniques that can help you tighten security for your PC.

Test Your System Security with Symantec

1. Launch your Web browser.
2. Type **security.norton.com** and press Enter.

   The Symantec Security Check page appears.
3. Click GO.

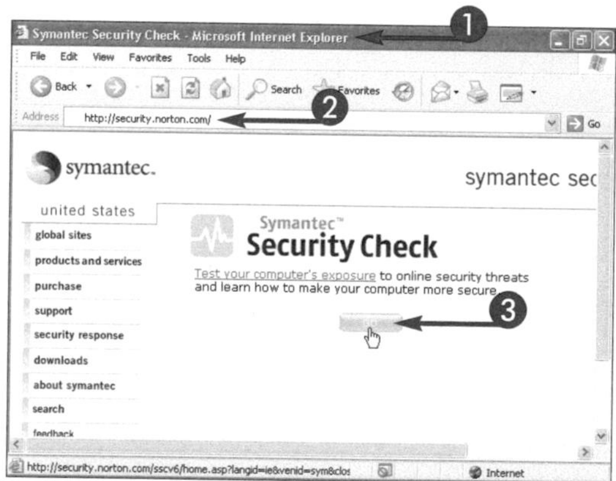

The Symantec Security Check page appears.

4. Under Security Scan, click START.

- Symantec Security Check displays its progress as it scans your computer and Internet connection.

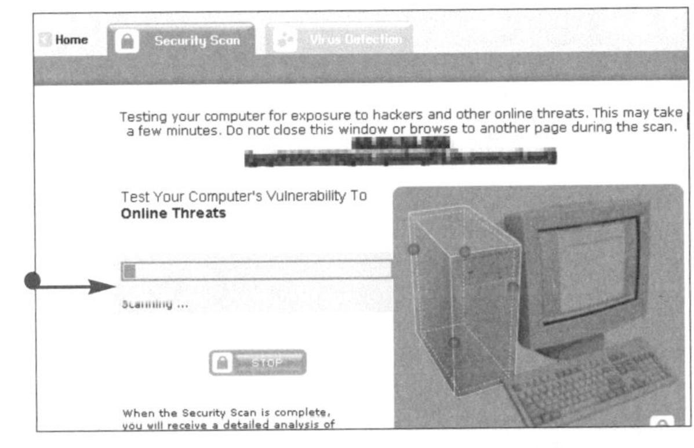

- When the scan is complete, Symantec Security Check displays its results.

5 Note any insecure areas that require attention.

- This computer is secure.
- You can click the Show Details link to view additional information.

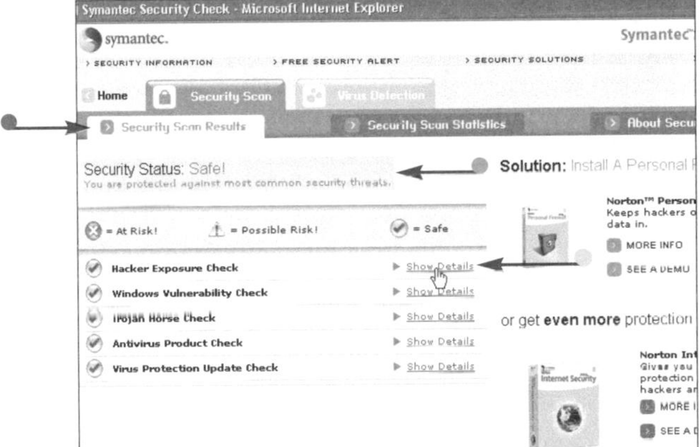

As I was browsing the Web, a warning popped up saying that anyone can easily break into my PC, and offering a program that can help. What should I do?

As you browse the Web, some sites display pop-up ads with exaggerated security warnings to sell you unnecessary software or services. The most suspect ads appear in windows that have no obvious way to close them. By responding to the ad, you reward the advertiser, so press Alt+F4 to close the window, and refer to Chapter 28 for more on securing your PC. Several programs on the market can help make your PC more secure, but do not look to these advertisements for reliable advice.

I have a dial-up modem connection. Do I need to be concerned about Internet security?

A dial-up modem connection is much more secure than an always-on connection, such as a cable or DSL connection. If you connect for an hour or less at a time simply to check your e-mail and browse the Web, you do not need to concern yourself with securing your PC against break-ins. You still need to be concerned about viruses, worms, and Trojan horses. You should also turn off your modem or your PC, or both, when not using them to prevent any programs from dialing out.

Understanding Your Backup Options

By understanding your backup options, you can develop a backup strategy that protects your valuable data without requiring you to spend an inordinate amount of time. Few people back up their data because it takes too much time or their PCs are not equipped with a backup drive and software that can make the job easier. Instead of selectively backing up their documents and essential settings and data, they choose not to back up at all.

Of course, a full system backup that copies everything on your system to one or more backup tapes or disks is ideal. But a complete backup can take more than an hour if your computer has more than a few gigabytes of data. If you think that your computer is unlikely to crash and destroy all of the files on your disk, you may conclude that the time you save each week outweighs the risk, especially if you do not use your PC to store essential documents and data.

However, most people have files on their computers that they consider indispensable. If you create documents for work or keep a journal or use your PC to store digital photos or home videos, you may have more to lose than you think. If you are reluctant to back up files because it takes too much time, consider creating a more reasonable backup strategy by following the advice in this section.

Backup Devices

One of the issues that discourages users from backing up their systems properly is the fact that few PCs come equipped with an efficient backup device. Backing up to recordable CDs or DVDs works, but the process can be time-consuming and usually requires you to keep track of multiple discs. Storing backups on traditional backup tapes is not ideal because you need to fast-forward or rewind to locate a file when you need to restore it.

Manufacturers are beginning to develop more practical backup drives. You can find several types of external hard drives that typically plug into a USB or FireWire port and can store more than 100GB. Iomega has a Rev35 drive that can store up to 90GB of data on a cartridge that is about the size of a credit card. With either of these devices, you can easily back up all of the files on a standard hard drive and have room to spare.

Backing Up Online

If your PC is connected to the Internet, you can back up your files online to a remote storage area. Several companies offer online backups, including iStorage at www.iomega.com/istorage/. You typically pay a monthly fee for a certain amount of storage space. Given the fact that your Internet connection uploads files much more slowly than it downloads them, backing up online can be very time-consuming, even over a cable or DSL connection.

Backup Utilities

Another issue that discourages users from backing up their files is the fact that most computers do not have a reliable and user-friendly backup utility. Most new computers include CD or DVD burner software that enables you to copy files to recordable CDs or DVDs, but you can record to a CD-R or DVD-R only once, and rewritable discs are not always reliable.

External hard drives and dedicated backup devices usually come with their own backup utilities, which are much easier to use and enable you to update your backups without having to back up all of your files every time.

Standard Backup Strategy

If you have a good backup program and a dedicated backup drive, such as a large external hard drive, the standard backup procedure is to perform a full backup once a week or once a month and an incremental backup every day. A full backup backs up all files on your computer, whether you have backed them up before. An incremental backup backs up only those files that have changed since the last backup. This ensures that you have up-to-date backups and are at risk of losing no more than a day's work.

Data-Only Backups

You can do data-only backups to back up only the documents you create. If you store all of your documents in My Documents, My Pictures, My Videos, and My Music folders, or other easily identifiable folders, you can quickly copy these folders to CDs or DVDs if you have a recordable CD or DVD drive. If the folders do not store more than can fit on a single disc, backing up is very easy. You should also back up your e-mail address book, which is fairly easy to do.

This strategy works well if you have the installation CDs for Windows and for all of the applications installed on your computer. If your PC's hard drive goes bad, you can reinstall Windows, reinstall the applications, and copy your document files to the new hard drive. You may lose some configuration settings for Windows and your applications, but the documents that you have trouble recreating are safe. You also lose any software updates you downloaded and installed to keep your applications up to date, but again, you can download and reinstall the updates.

Run Windows Backup Utility

Windows XP Professional, Windows 2000, Windows Me, and Windows 98 include Windows Backup, which you can use to back up files stored on your PC's hard drive. Windows XP Home edition includes Backup, but you have to install it separately or use a different backup utility; the first tip on the following page covers the installation. Most dedicated backup utilities, often included with backup drives, have advanced features that can automate your backups and help you keep your backup files up to date.

Windows Backup runs in two modes: Wizard or Advanced. The Backup Wizard can simplify your backups by leading you step-by-step through the process. However, the Wizard provides you with few options, so I recommend that you use the Advanced mode. With the Advanced mode, you can select the folders and files you want to back up, so you can see which files Windows Backup is copying. It also provides you with more control over the amount of data you back up, so you do not run out of space on your backup media. For example, if you try to back up 800MB of data to a drive that has only 600MB of free space, the backup operation aborts when the disk is full.

Run Windows Backup Utility

1. Click Start.
2. Click All Programs.
3. Click Accessories.
4. Click System Tools.
5. Click Backup.

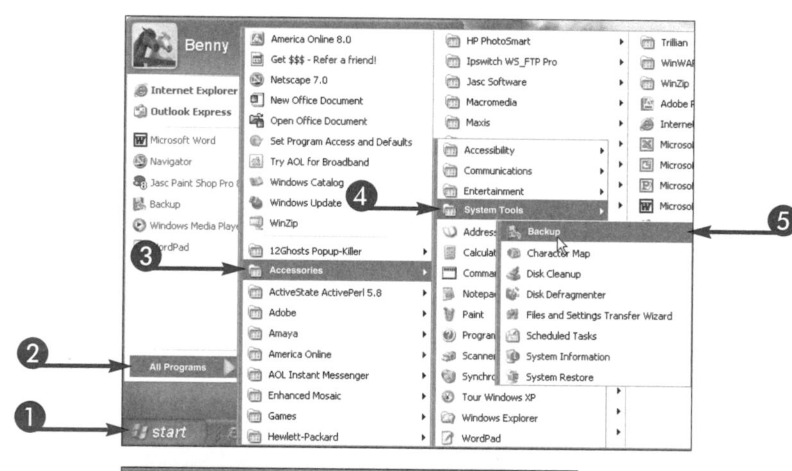

The Welcome to the Backup or Restore Wizard window appears.

6. Click the Advanced Mode link.

The Welcome to the Backup Utility Advanced Mode page appears.

7 Click the Backup tab.

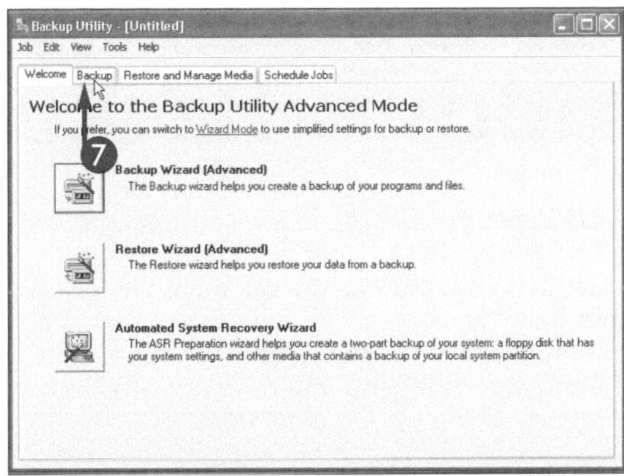

- Windows Backup displays a list of drives and folders you can back up.

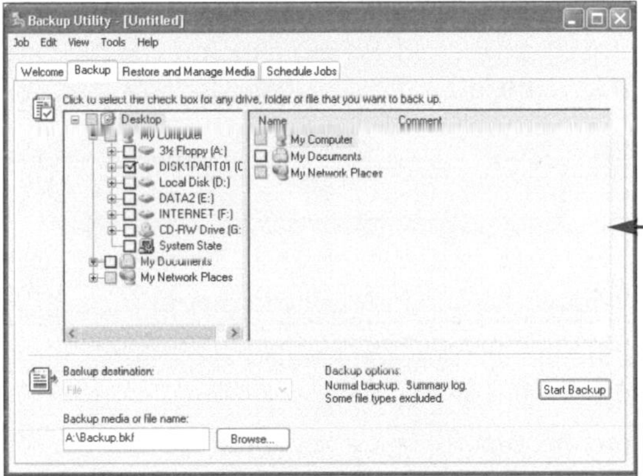

I have Windows XP Home edition. Can I back up my files?

Yes, but you must install Windows Backup from the Windows installation CD. Insert the Windows installation CD. If an installation screen appears, click Exit, Run My Computer, right-click the icon for the CD drive, and click Explore. Navigate to the VALUEADD\MSFT\NTBACKUP folder and double-click the Ntbackup.msi file. This runs the Backup Installation Wizard, which leads you through the process of installing Backup.

Can I try the Backup Wizard?

Yes. You can use the Backup Wizard to step through the backup process. You cannot harm any files by performing a backup. However, the Advanced option, which may take more time to learn, offers additional options that can help you take more control of your backups.

Windows Backup only backs up my files to my hard drive. What is the point in doing that?

Sometimes a section of a hard drive can fail, and if you have backups on a different section of the same drive, you can recover the files. However, it is always best to store files on a different drive, preferably on a removable storage medium, so you can store your backups in a remote location.

Back Up Files with Windows Backup

Using Windows Backup, you can duplicate selected files and folders to another disk so that if anything happens to the originals, you can restore them from the copies. Windows Backup gives you the option of running the Backup Wizard or running in Advanced mode. I recommend you run Windows Backup in Advanced mode, so you have more control over the backup operation.

When you run Windows Backup in Advanced mode, it displays a list of drives, folders, and files you can choose to back up. You can select a drive or folder to back it up. This instructs Windows Backup to back up all folders and files on the selected disk or in the selected folder. If you want to back up only selected folders or files on the disk or in the folder, you can select the plus sign next to the drive letter or folder name. This expands the list of items, so you can choose only the folders and files you want to back up. By being selective in marking backup folders and files, you can back up only the most important files and folders and limit the amount of time it takes to perform the backup.

Back Up Files with Windows Backup

1. Run Windows Backup in Advanced mode.

Note: *See the section "Run Windows Backup Utility" for more information.*

Windows Backup displays a list of drives and folders you can back up.

2. Click the plus sign (⊞) next to a drive letter or folder name to expand it.
3. Click the box next to a drive letter, folder name, or filename to select it (☐ changes to ☑).
4. Click Browse.

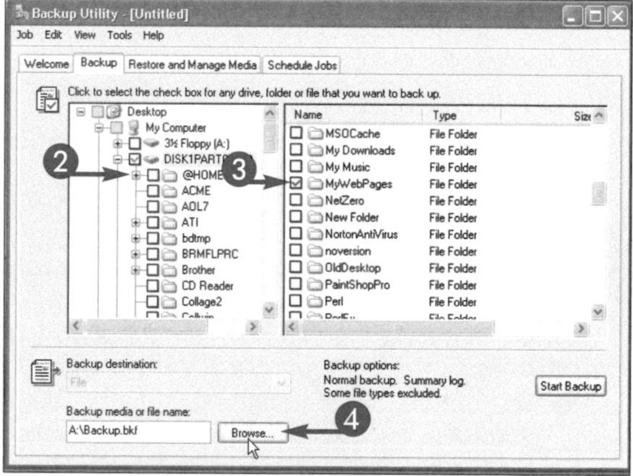

Backup prompts you to select the drive that you want to use to store the backup files.

5. Click here and select the drive you want to use to store the backup files.
   - You can type a different name for the backup file.
6. Click Save.

Note: *Windows Backup does not support recordable CD or DVD drives.*

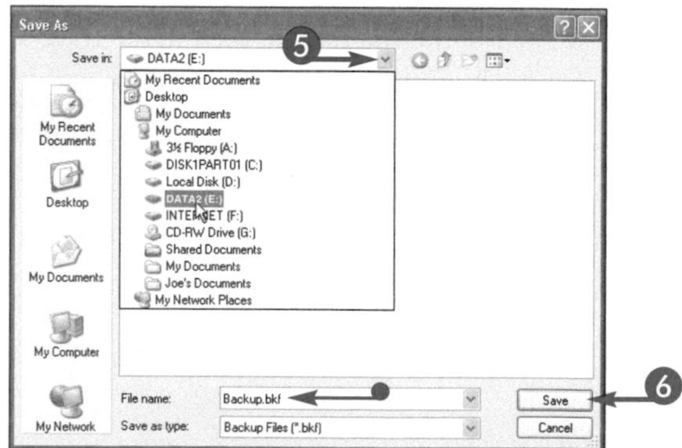

7 If you are backing up to a floppy drive or a tape backup unit, make sure that you have a disk or tape in the drive.

8 Click Start Backup.

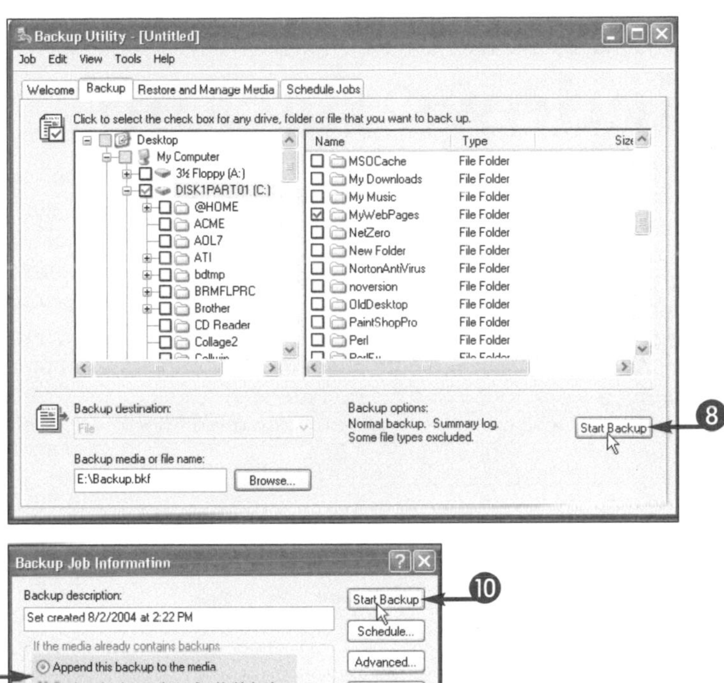

The Backup Job Information dialog box appears.

9 Click the Append this backup to the media option or the Replace the data on the media with this backup option (○ changes to ◉).

10 Click Start Backup.

The backup process begins.

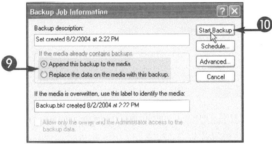

My only backup drive is a CD-R drive, so why would I use Windows Backup?

▼ You can back up your files to a backup file on your hard drive and then move the backup file from your hard drive to a CD-R in your PC's CD-R drive. When backing up in this way, make sure that you do not back up more data than can fit on a standard CD. Otherwise, you end up with a backup file that you cannot copy to a CD. This method works, but it is not an ideal way to back up files. If you want a system that is more practical, consider purchasing a dedicated backup drive or a more versatile backup utility.

Can I back up everything on my PC?

▼ Yes. If you choose to do a full system backup using the Windows Backup Wizard, Backup does a complete backup of your system, including the all-important Windows Registry file. This file contains all the settings that enable Windows to run on your PC, communicate with hardware devices, and run your other software. Run Windows Backup in Advanced mode, click the Welcome tab, click the Backup Wizard (Advanced) button, and follow the Wizard's instructions. You can also click the Automated System Recovery Wizard button on the opening Backup screen to create a floppy disk and backup file combination that you can use to recover and restore everything on your system in the event of a catastrophe.

Restore Files with Windows Backup

Rarely, if ever, do you need to restore your entire system. If you delete a file accidentally, you can restore it from the Recycle Bin and be assured that you have recovered the latest version of the file. If the Windows registry becomes corrupted, you can usually start your computer and restore a previous version of the registry to enable Windows to start up. You may lose a few configuration settings, but you have everything else intact. If you misplace or lose a file, you can restore that file from your backups without replacing other files.

If a file is missing, do not panic and restore all files on your disk. If your backup files are even a couple days old, you can lose much of your work by restoring everything when you only need to restore one or two files.

If your PC cannot run Windows, you may be able to repair your Windows installation, as discussed in Chapter 31. If you cannot repair the installation, you can reinstall Windows, as discussed in Chapter 32. You can then run Windows Backup, as shown in these steps, and restore your other files.

Restore Files with Windows Backup

1. Click Start.
2. Click All Programs.
3. Click Accessories.
4. Click System Tools.
5. Click Backup.

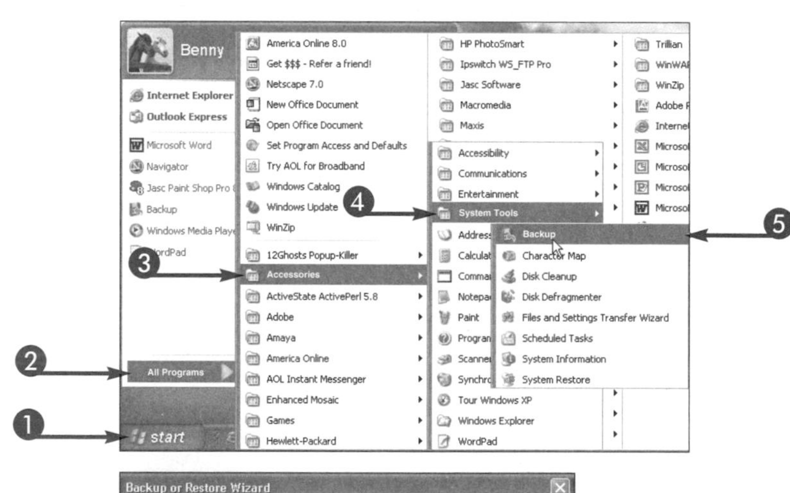

The Welcome to the Backup or Restore Wizard window appears.

6. Click Next.

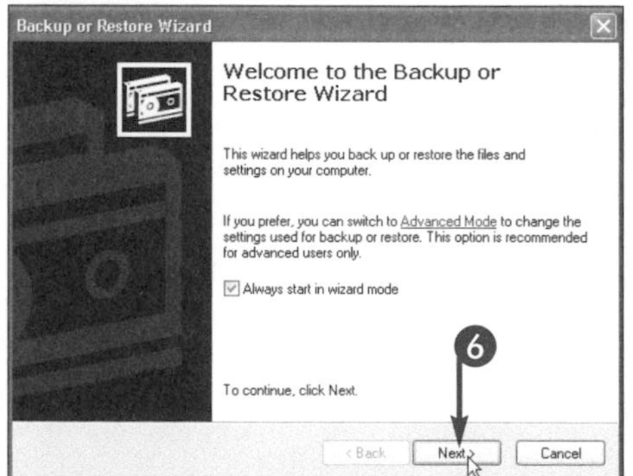

The Wizard prompts you to specify whether you want to back up or restore files.

7 Click the Restore files and settings option (○ changes to ◉).

8 Click Next.

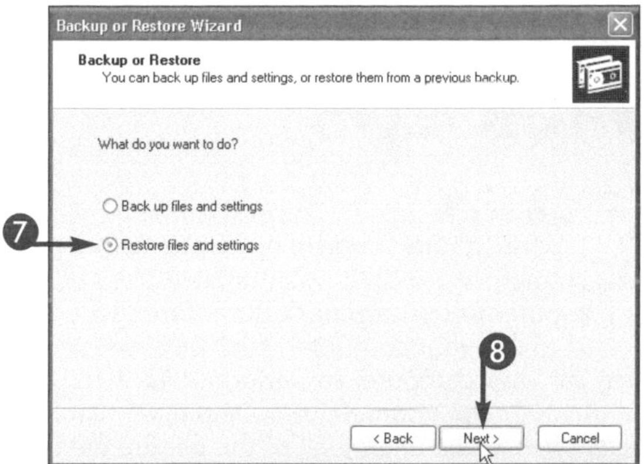

The Wizard displays a list of items you can restore.

9 Click ⊞ next to an item to expand the list.

10 Click the box next to each item you want to restore (☐ changes to ☑).

11 Click Next and follow the on-screen instructions to restore the selected items.

Windows Backup restores the items to your PC's hard drive.

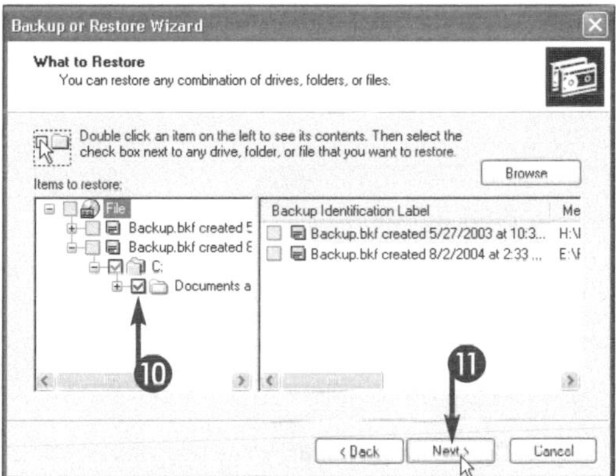

I tried to restore a file, but Windows Backup indicates that I have a more current version of the file on disk. What should I do?

▼ In most cases, you want to keep the newer version of the file, unless the newer version is corrupted. If you know that the file is corrupted, go ahead and replace it with the backed-up version. Otherwise, try to access the more current version of the file. If the file is fine, cancel the restoration. Another option is to restore the backup copy to a different folder, so you can compare the backed-up version to the current version; however, you need to close the Wizard and restore the file in Advanced mode.

I installed a program that messed up my PC. Can I restore Windows to a previous state?

▼ Yes, but try using System Restore first, as discussed in Chapter 19. This is the safest way to restore Windows to its prior condition. If that does not work, you can restore the *system state* if you have a backup of it, but do this only as a last resort. Run Windows Backup in Advanced mode. Click the Restore and Manage Media tab and click the System State option (☐ changes to ☑). The System State data that this restores includes the Windows registry, system boot files, and other key files and data.

Schedule Backups

You can schedule backups to run automatically at specified dates and times so you do not need to remember to back up your files. This also enables your computer to perform backups at times when you do not need to use your computer, such as overnight. Of course, for your computer to perform automated backups without your help, you need a backup drive that has sufficient free space to save all of the backup data to a single disk. You must also leave your PC turned on at the scheduled time.

To schedule backups, you must run Windows Backup in Advanced mode. You can then access a calendar that enables you to add *backup jobs*. Each backup job contains information about when and how to perform the backup and where to store the backups. For example, you can schedule a backup job to run on August 10 at 12 a.m. and back up all files, including your Windows system files to a disk in drive G. Or you can create a backup job that backs up only those files that have changed since the last backup. When you choose to add a backup job to the calendar, the Backup Wizard appears and leads you through the process of entering your preferences.

Schedule Backups

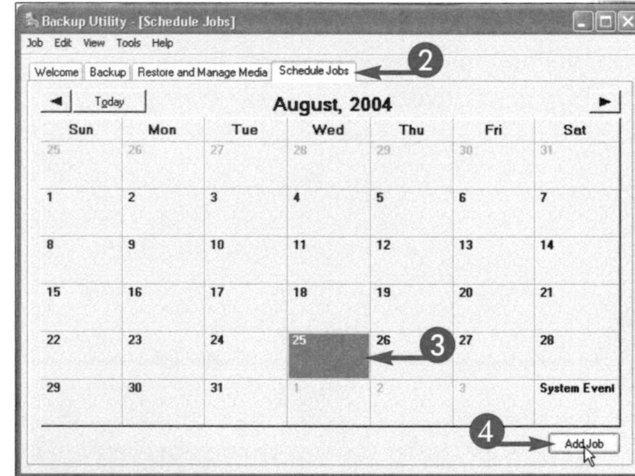

1. Run Windows Backup in Advanced mode.

Note: *See the section "Run Windows Backup Utility."*

2. Click the Schedule Jobs tab.

   A calendar appears displaying the days and dates of the current month.

3. Navigate to the day on which you want to schedule a backup.

4. Click Add Job.

   The Backup Wizard appears.

5. Click Next.

The Backup Wizard prompts you to specify what you want to back up.

6 Click the desired option (○ changes to ◉).

7 Click Next.

8 Follow the Wizard's instructions to enter your backup preferences.

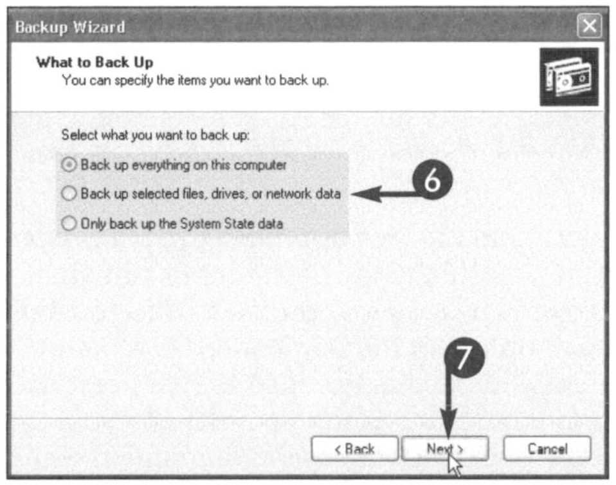

- The Wizard creates an icon for the backup job and displays it on the specified date.

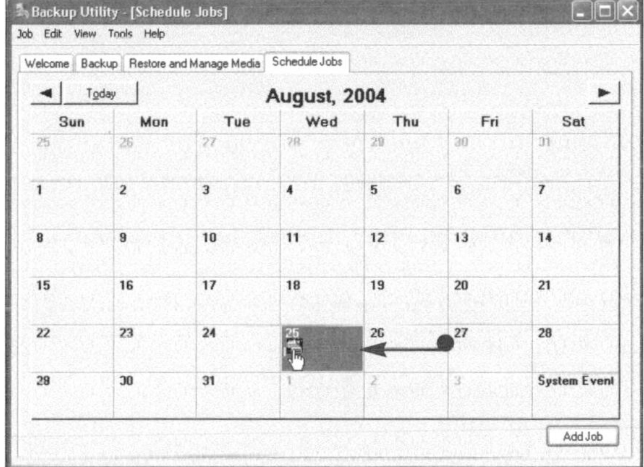

Can I schedule a backup using the Windows Task Scheduler?

▼ Yes. An advantage to using Task Scheduler is that you can schedule regular backups. For example, you can schedule an incremental backup to run every Saturday at 1 a.m. To run Task Scheduler, click Start, All Programs, Accessories, System Tools, and then Scheduled Tasks. You can then double-click the Add Scheduled Task icon to run the Scheduled Task Wizard, which leads you step-by-step through the process of scheduling a backup or other task. On the last page of the Wizard, click the "Open Advanced Properties for this task when I click Finish" option (☐ changes to ☑) and then click Finish. This enables you to set your backup preferences.

How do I replace an old full backup with a current full backup?

▼ When scheduling a backup job, the Backup Wizard prompts you to choose whether you want to append this backup to existing backups or replace the existing backups. Click the "Replace the data on the media with this backup" option (○ changes to ◉), and then follow the Wizard's instructions to enter additional preferences. You should always have two backup sets. When you replace a backup set, replace the older of the two sets. This approach prevents you from losing your new backup set if the current backup operation fails.

Record Settings Before Making Changes

The steps you take for optimizing your PC often require you to change hardware or software settings. You can avoid problems and recover from mistakes by writing down the original settings before changing them. A good practice is to keep a notebook next to your PC and log every change you make to your system. Include the date and time on which you made the change, so you can trace back any problems to the date on which they may have arisen.

The results of some changes are immediately evident. For example, in Chapter 28 you learn how to enable the Windows Firewall to prevent unauthorized access to your PC through the Internet. In some cases, enabling a firewall can prevent a PC from connecting to the Internet and accessing the Web. The negative effect is immediately evident, and you know instantly that you must change the setting back. However, you may not be aware of the effects of other changes until much later. If you make a mistake editing the Windows registry, for example, you may not notice the error until you try to run a program that the change affected.

Record Settings Before Making Changes

1. Display the dialog box that contains the setting you want to change.

   This example shows a display option that you can change.

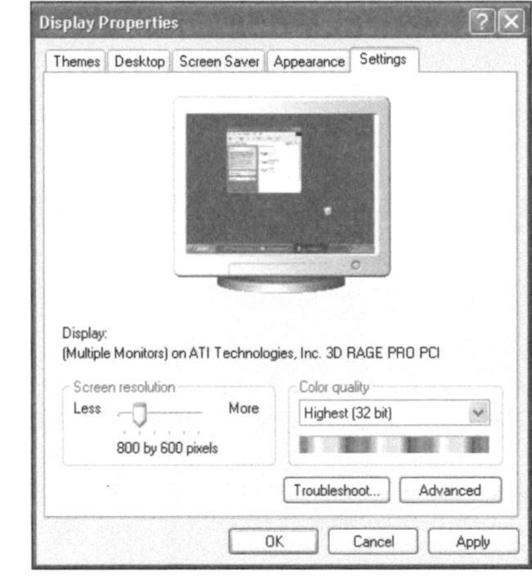

2. Write down the current settings.

Note: *You can press the Print Screen key to place a picture of the screen on the Windows Clipboard and then paste the screen into a Word document and print it.*

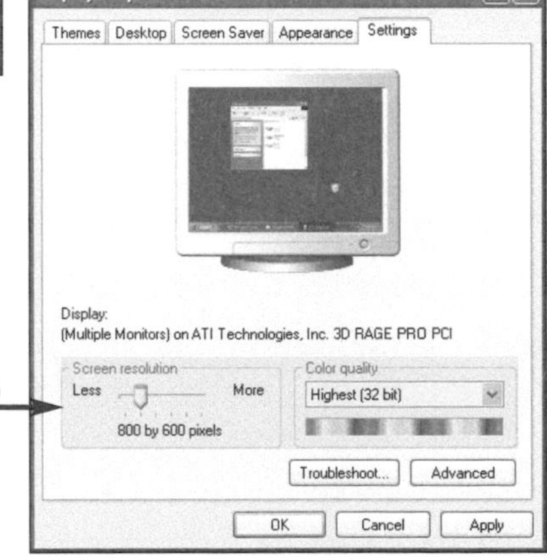

3 Change your preferences.

4 Click OK.

5 Note any problems with the new settings.

6 If your change caused a problem, return to the dialog box that contains the setting you changed.

7 Change the setting back to the original setting noted in step 2.

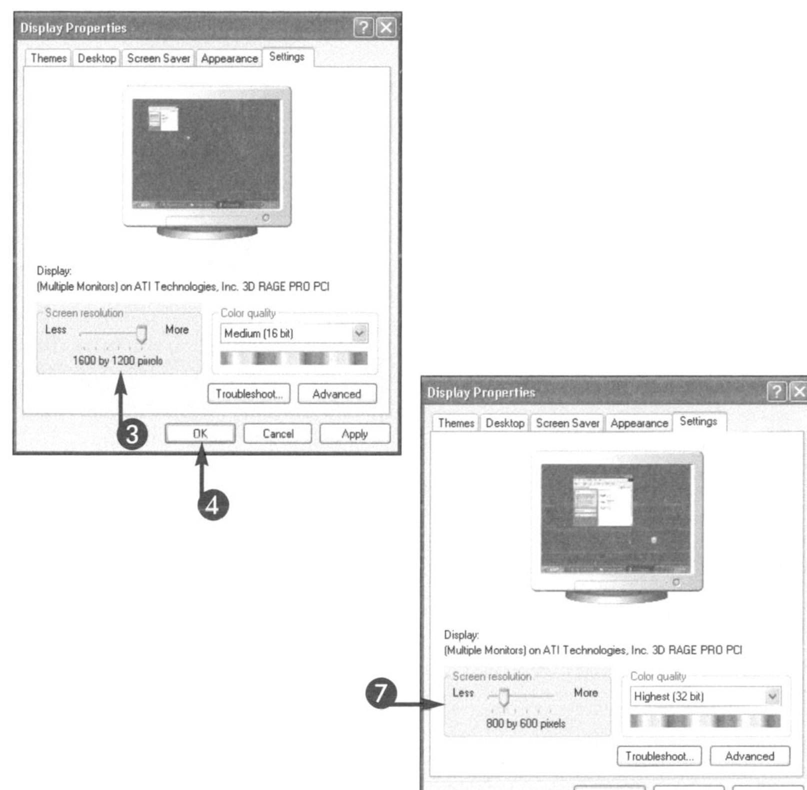

When optimizing my computer, can I make all of my changes at once?

▼ It is recommended that you change one setting at a time, especially when configuring hardware devices. By changing one setting and then testing the device before changing another setting, you can see the effect of each change and trace any problems that arise back to a specific change you made. If you are troubleshooting a problem, you should always change one setting at a time and record each change. A minor change can cause major problems, but if you have the original settings written down and you proceed methodically, you can usually recover.

Should I follow any other precautions before making changes to my system?

▼ Before you install a program, edit the Windows registry, or change any hardware settings, you should create a system restore point, as explained in Chapter 19. With a restore point, you can return Windows to its previous condition. Windows may already be set up to automatically create restore points, but refer to the instructions in Chapter 19 to make sure. You should also keep a record of any passwords stored on your computer in case these passwords are lost. Keep the passwords in a secure place.

Copy Downloaded Programs to CDs

More and more software companies distribute applications, utilities, and program updates on the Web. The company typically supplies you with an installation file and a registration number you must enter in order to install the program. This enables you to obtain programs without having to run out to a computer store, but it provides you with no disk or CD to reinstall the program if your hard drive fails or if you accidentally delete your installation file. Many users do not realize how many downloaded installation files and updates they have on their PCs until they need to reinstall an application.

If your computer has a recordable CD drive, you can copy these installation files to CDs and keep them on hand in case you need to reinstall the applications or program updates. If you purchased the program and received a registration number, write down the registration number and keep it with the disc. You can use a permanent marker to write the program's name and registration number on the print side of the disc — never write on the shiny side of a disc.

Copy Downloaded Programs to CDs

1. Click Start.
2. Click My Computer.

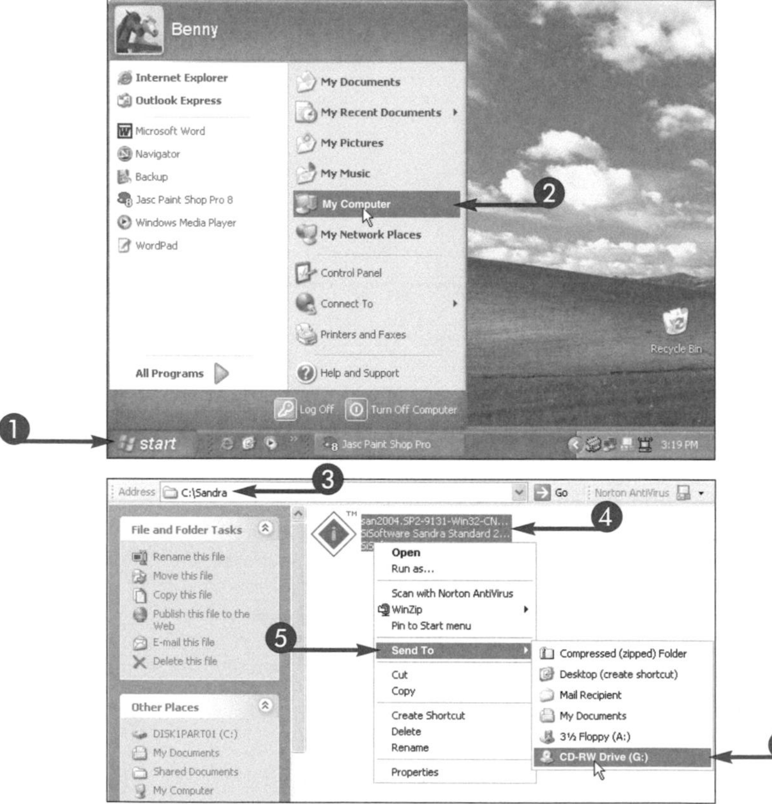

My Computer runs and displays icons for the disk drives on your computer.

3. Navigate to the folder in which the installation file is stored.
4. Right-click the installation file.
5. Click Send To.
6. Click the icon for the CD or DVD drive to which you want to copy the file.

- A window appears displaying an icon for the installation file that is ready to be written to the CD or DVD.

7. Load a blank recordable disc into the drive.

8. Click the Write these files to CD link.

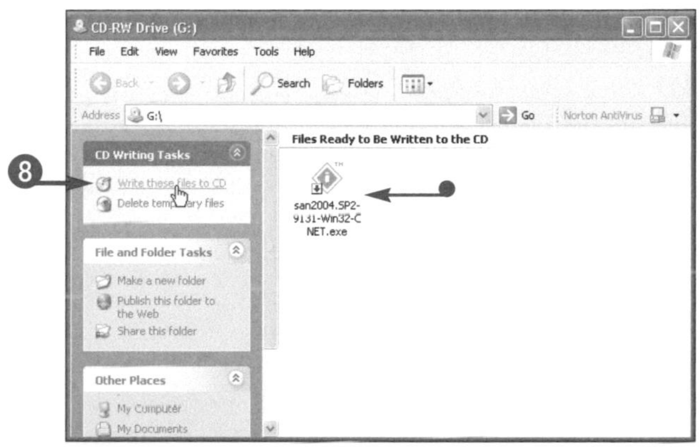

The CD Writing Wizard appears.

9. Follow the Wizard's instructions to copy the file to a CD or DVD.

The Wizard copies the installation file to the disc.

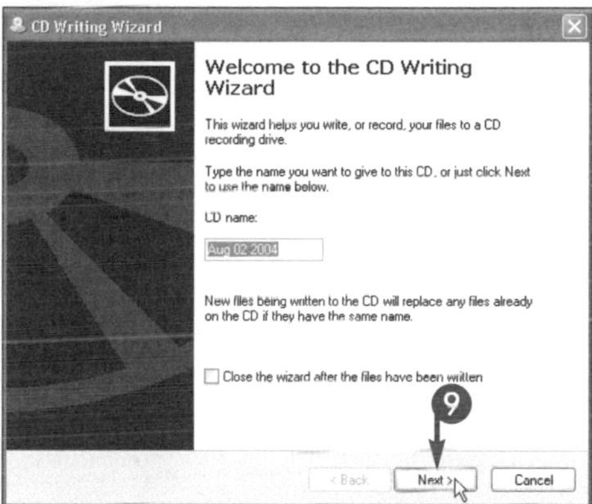

If I perform a full system backup, do I really need separate discs for my downloaded software?

▼ No. Your full system backup includes the installed program and the downloaded installation program. However, you can copy the installation file to a disc and then delete the installation file from your PC's hard drive to free up some disk space. This saves time during backups, as well, because your PC does not have to include the installation file in your backups. By having all of your software on CDs, you can perform data-only backups, as explained in the section "Understanding Your Backup Options," and be assured that you have a copy of everything on your PC.

Can I order programs and updates on CDs?

▼ Some software companies know that users like to have an installation CD for every program they purchase, so they make the CD available for an extra fee. For example, you can purchase Paint Shop Pro online from Jasc Software for $84 and pay an extra $17 for an installation CD and manual. This is approximately what you pay at a retailer for a boxed set, but you can obtain the program immediately online and then receive the CD and manual in a few days.

5 Automate File Removal with Disk Cleanup

6 Uninstall Programs You Never Use

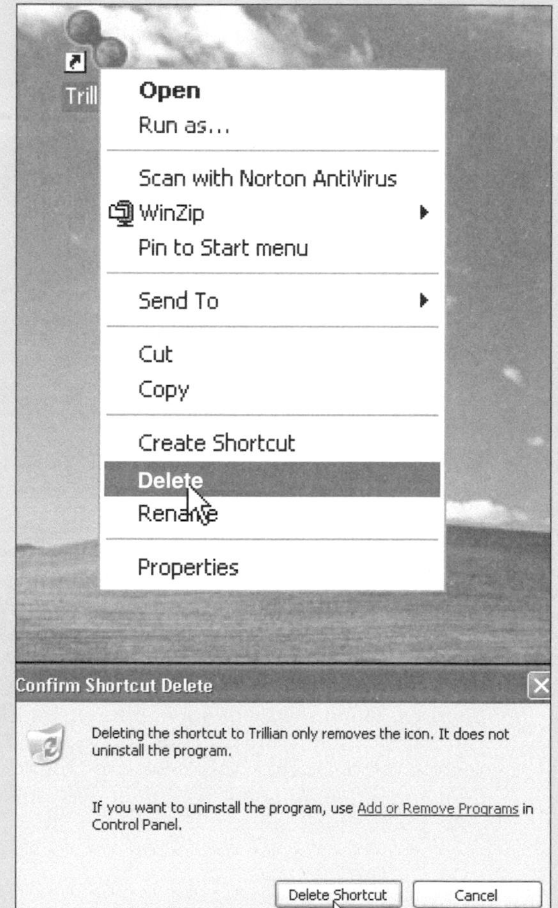

PART II
RECLAIMING DISK DRIVE SPACE

7 Find and Delete Other Useless Files

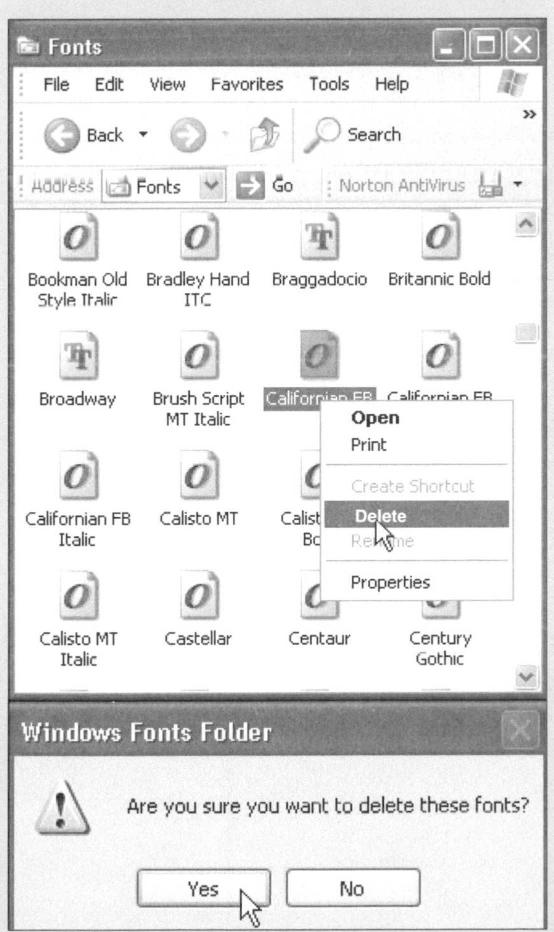

8 Clear Old E-mail Messages from Your System

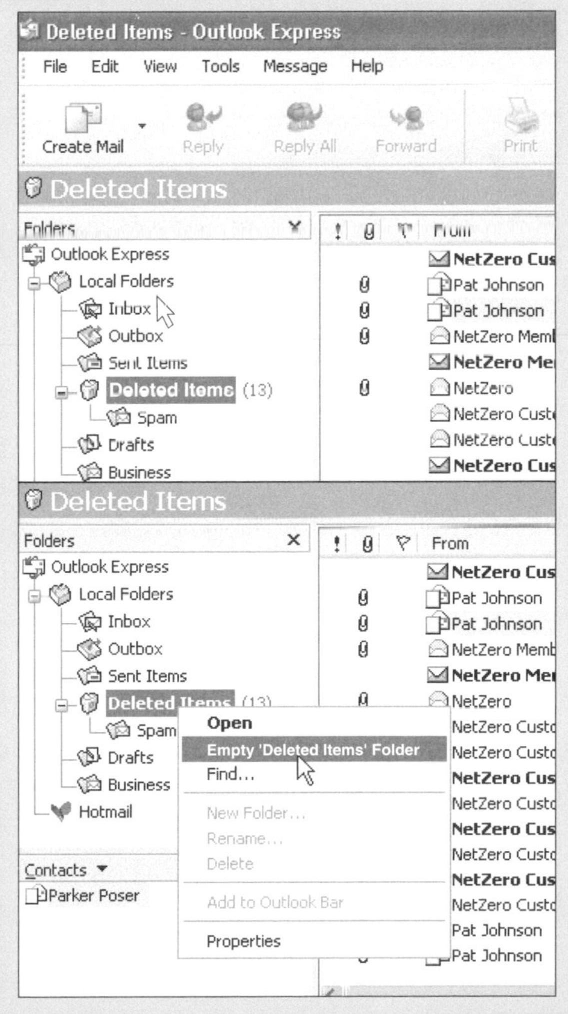

Run Disk Cleanup

You can remove temporary files and other working files that Windows and your applications leave behind by using the Windows Disk Cleanup utility. Disk Cleanup searches your computer for collections of files that you probably no longer use or need. These include temporary Internet files, which your Web browser uses to display Web pages faster when you reload them; files placed in the Recycle Bin when you choose to delete them; downloaded program files; and temporary files that applications create and use as you are working on documents.

When you run Disk Cleanup and select a drive to clean, Disk Cleanup displays a list of file types you can clear from the drive. You can click a check box to select or deselect any group of files. When you start the cleaning process, Disk Cleanup automatically removes the files from the disk, freeing up that space so you can use it to store other files or make it available to Windows for use as virtual memory.

Keep in mind that Disk Cleanup permanently removes files from a disk. If you decide to remove files stored in the Recycle Bin, you can no longer restore those files.

Run Disk Cleanup

1. Click Start.
2. Click All Programs.
3. Click Accessories.
4. Click System Tools.
5. Click Disk Cleanup.

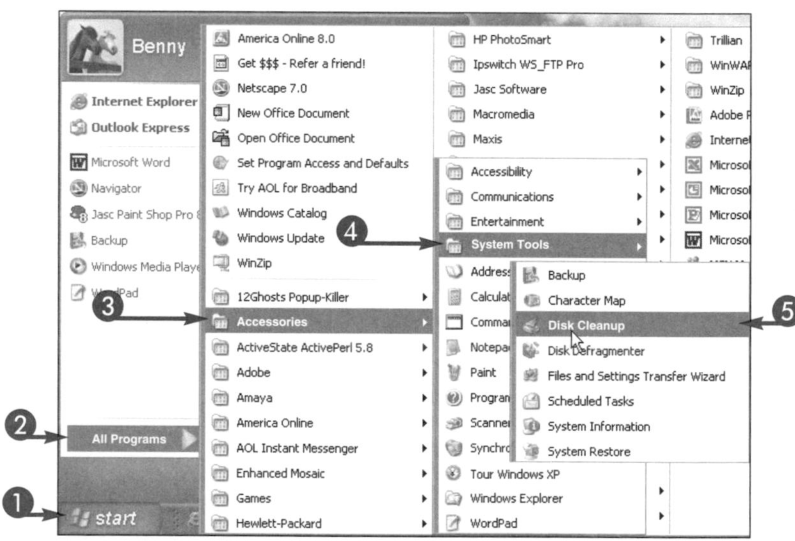

The Select Drive dialog box appears.

6. Click here and select the drive you want to clean.
7. Click OK.

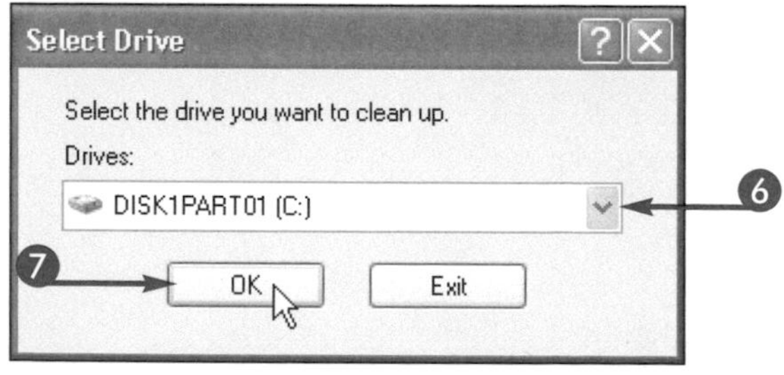

The Disk Cleanup dialog box appears.

8 Click the box next to each group of files you want to permanently remove from the drive (☐ changes to ☑).

9 Click OK.

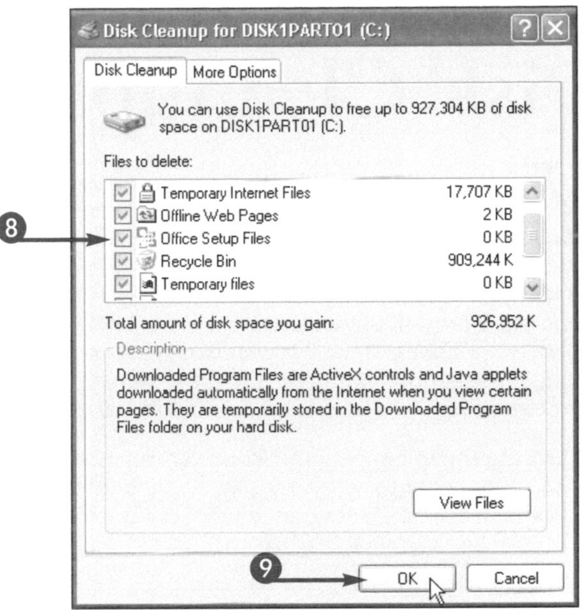

The Disk Cleanup dialog box appears, prompting you to confirm.

10 Click Yes.

Disk Cleanup removes the specified files from the drive.

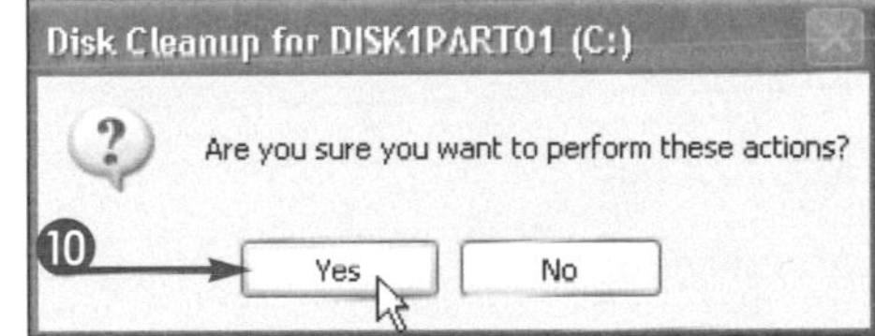

Can I run Disk Cleanup from My Computer or Windows Explorer?

▼ Yes. Run My Computer or Windows Explorer and display the icon for the disk drive you want to clean. Right-click the drive's icon and click Properties. This displays a dialog box that provides details about the disk drive, including the amount of free and used space on the disk. Click Disk Cleanup to run the utility.

Can I use Disk Cleanup to remove other files from the disk?

▼ Yes. The More Options tab in the Disk Cleanup dialog box features buttons that you can use to remove installed programs, Windows components you do not use, and old System Restore points. Chapter 6 shows you several ways to safely uninstall programs and Windows components. To remove System Restore points, refer to the section "Remove Old System Restore Points."

I have a Norton Protected Recycle Bin on my Desktop. Is that different from the Windows Recycle Bin?

▼ Yes. The Norton Protected Recycle Bin stores backup copies of deleted files that the Windows Recycle Bin does not protect. These include files that are overwritten by some applications when you choose to save a file. The Norton Protected Recycle Bin uses additional storage space. To reclaim this space, right-click the Norton Protected Recycle Bin icon or the Recycle Bin icon and click Empty Norton Protected Files.

Schedule Automated Disk Cleanups

You can schedule Disk Cleanup to run automatically to keep your PC's disk drives free of useless files. As you browse the Internet, create and edit documents, and delete files, your disk drives gradually fill with files you no longer use or need. You may not even notice that your disk drive contains several hundred megabytes of useless data. By scheduling regular disk cleanups, you ensure that your disk drives remain uncluttered even if you are too busy to notice the clutter.

You can use the Windows Task Scheduler to schedule the Disk Cleanup utility to run every day, week, or month on any day at any time. As long as your PC is turned on when the scheduled date and time arrives, Task Scheduler initiates Disk Cleanup, which then cleans the disk according to the disk cleanup preferences you entered. Although you can run Disk Cleanup daily, your PC's disk drive probably does not accumulate enough unnecessary files to justify a daily cleaning. It is recommended that you clean your PC's disk drive once a month or at least every other month.

In addition to scheduling a disk cleanup, consider following the instructions in Chapters 7 and 8 to remove additional files that Disk Cleanup does not remove.

Schedule Automated Disk Cleanups

1. Click Start.
2. Click All Programs.
3. Click Accessories.
4. Click System Tools.
5. Click Scheduled Tasks.

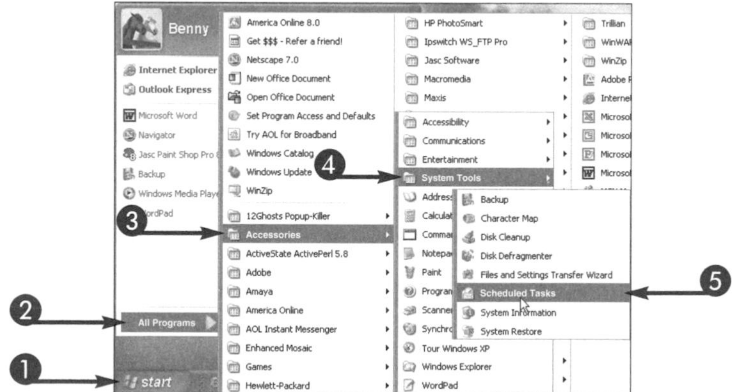

The Scheduled Tasks window appears.

6. Double-click the Add Scheduled Task icon.

   The Scheduled Task Wizard appears.

7. Click Next.

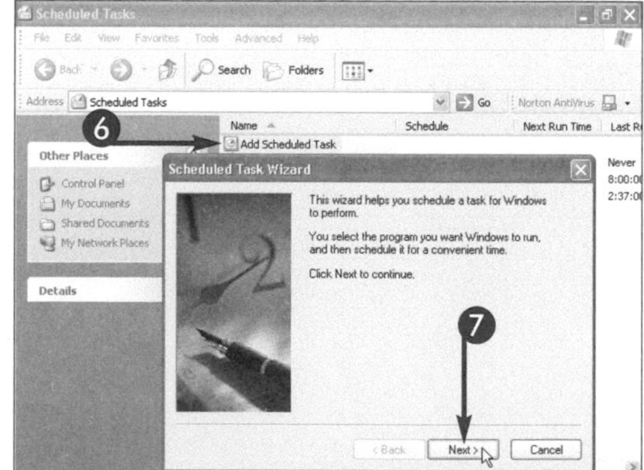

The Scheduled Task Wizard displays a list of programs you can schedule to run.

8 Click Disk Cleanup.

9 Click Next and follow the Wizard's instructions to enter your scheduling preferences.

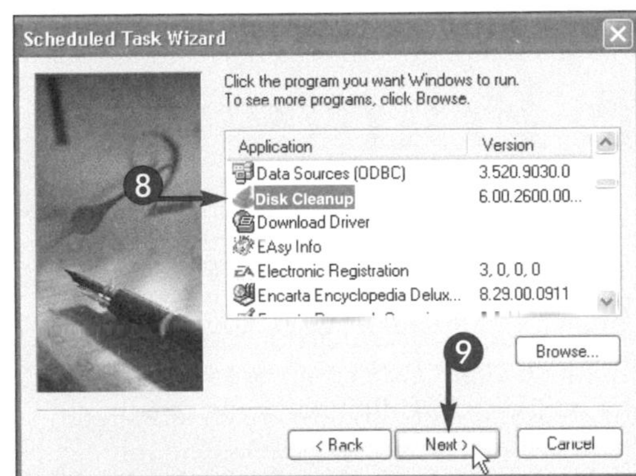

- The Wizard creates a new task in the Task Scheduler that runs Disk Cleanup at the times and on the days you specified.

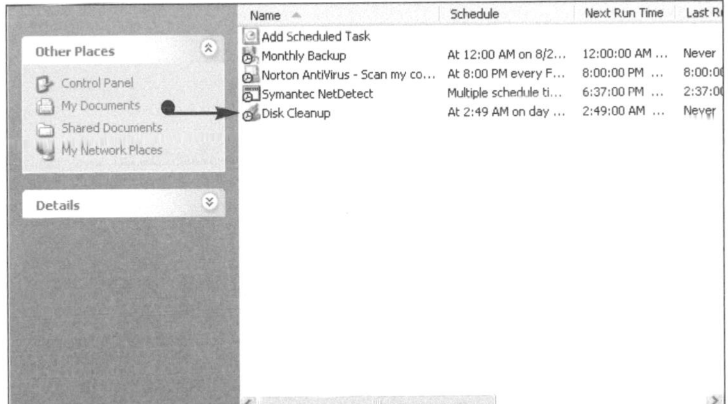

Can I change the settings for a scheduled task without creating a new scheduled task icon?

Yes. When you create a scheduled task, a new icon for the task appears in the Scheduled Tasks window. Double-click the icon for the scheduled task. A dialog box appears displaying the settings that control the scheduled task, including the days and times on which it runs. On the Task tab is a Run text box that displays the command line for running the program. You can often add one or more switches to the end of the command line to control the way the program runs. For example, you can type **/d c** after cleanmgr.exe to run the disk cleanup on drive C.

When I schedule Disk Cleanup, which files is it set up to clear from the disk drive?

When Task Scheduler runs Disk Cleanup, it uses the settings that were entered the last time you performed a disk cleanup. To change the settings without performing a disk cleanup, click the Windows Start button, click Run, type **cleanmgr /sageset:1**, and click OK. Change your preferences and click OK. Display the Task Scheduler and double-click the Disk Cleanup icon. Click the Task tab, and in the Run text box after cleanmgr.exe, type a space followed by **/sagerun:1**. Click OK. This tells Disk Cleanup to use the settings you entered with the sageset:1 switch. You can use any number between 0 and 65535.

Remove Old System Restore Points

You can reclaim additional storage space on your PC by deleting old *restore points*. Windows creates a restore point almost every day and whenever you significantly change your PC, typically by installing a new program or device driver. If a change causes problems with your PC's operation or the way Windows functions, you can restore your system to a previous condition by using any one of the system restore points. The restoration does not affect your e-mail or any documents you have changed or edited, so you do not lose any of your data.

When you create a system restore point or Windows creates one for you, it saves the Windows registry and critical application settings, which take up space on your PC's hard drive. If you are having no problems with your PC, other than the fact that it is running slowly, you can remove restore points to free up disk space.

Chapter 19 covers System Restore in detail, showing you how to run System Restore, create a restore point, restore your PC, and undo a system restoration when it fails to correct a problem.

Remove Old System Restore Points

1. Click Start.
2. Click All Programs.
3. Click Accessories.
4. Click System Tools.
5. Click Disk Cleanup.

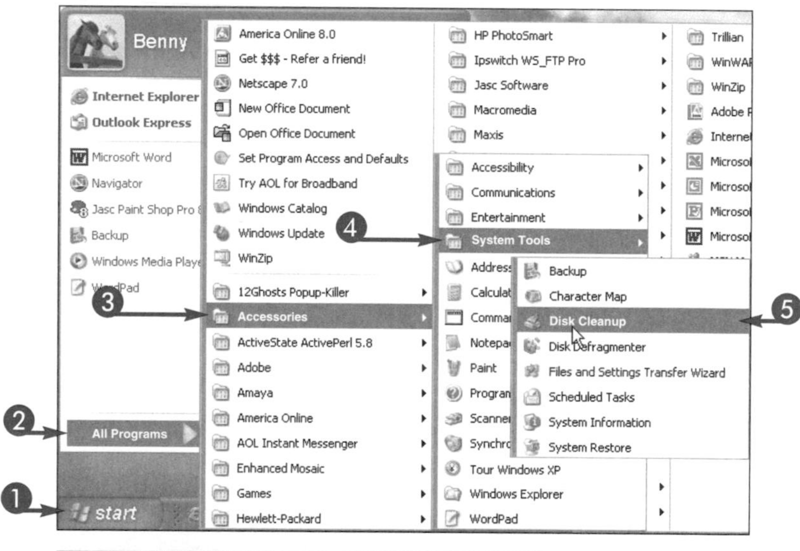

The Select Drive dialog box appears.

6. Click here and select the drive you want to clean.
7. Click OK.

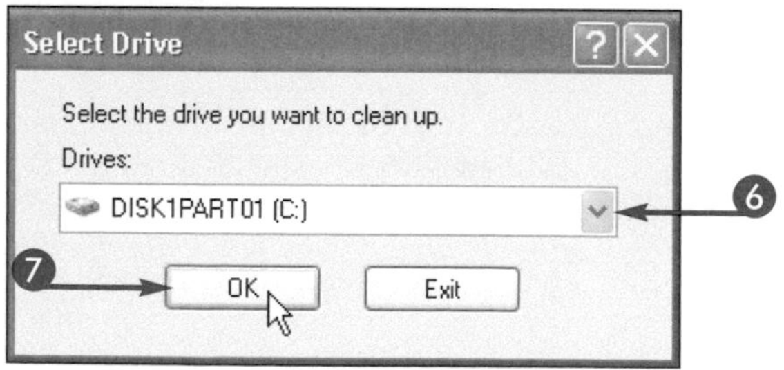

The Disk Cleanup dialog box appears.

8 Click the More Options tab.

9 Under System Restore, click Clean up.

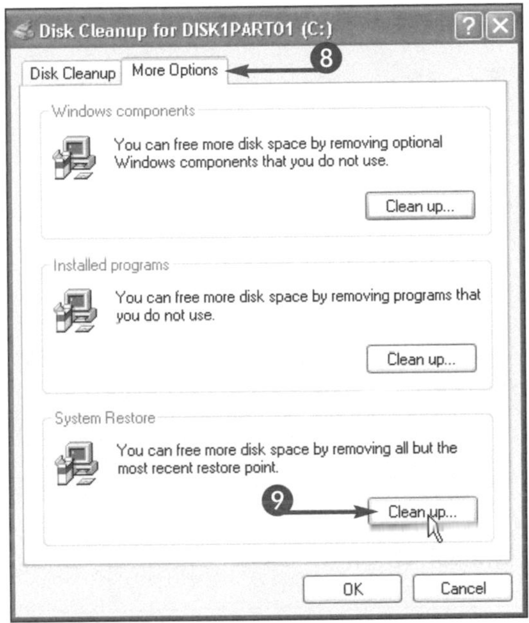

The Disk Cleanup dialog box appears, prompting you to confirm.

10 Click Yes.

Disk Cleanup removes all restore points except the most current one.

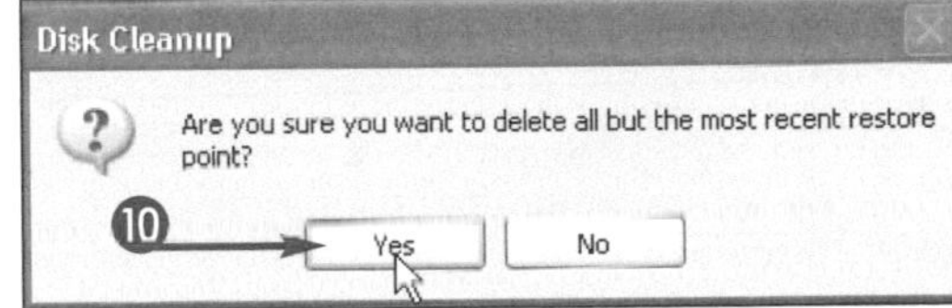

Can I remove only one or two restore points?

▼ No. You cannot selectively remove restore points. You must remove all restore points except the most current one or remove none at all. The reason you cannot delete individual restore points is that the restore points are incremental. If you delete a restore point, all restore points prior to it become useless. Keeping the last two or three restore points would be great, but that is not an option.

Can I disable System Restore for one of my drives?

▼ You can disable System Restore, but you must disable it for all of your PC's drives. Click Start, All Programs, Accessories, System Tools, and then click System Restore. Click the System Restore Settings link, click Turn off System Restore on all drives (☐ changes to ☑), and click OK. It is strongly recommended that you keep System Restore enabled on all drives. You can limit the space it uses by taking the steps in the next tip.

Can I limit the amount of disk space that System Restore uses?

▼ Yes. Click Start, All Programs, Accessories, System Tools, and then click System Restore. Next, click the System Restore Settings link. Click the icon for the disk drive whose System Restore settings you want to change and then click the Settings button. Drag the "Disk space to use" slider to the left to decrease the amount of disk space reserved for restore points. Click OK.

Run a Program's Uninstall Utility

You can reclaim additional space on your PC's hard drive by uninstalling programs that you do not use. When you install a program, the program places one or more files on the hard drive. It also places an icon on the Start, All Programs menu and sometimes on the desktop or in the Quick Launch toolbar to provide you with easy access. Most installations also modify the Windows registry to enable smooth operation in Windows.

If you try to remove a program simply by deleting its folder and all the files it contains, you can leave behind settings and files that take up system resources and may even cause problems later. To safely remove a program, you should use the program's uninstall utility. Most programs include an uninstall utility that removes all of the program's files and settings from your system, so no remnant of the program remains. Some uninstall utilities remove everything except the shortcut icons, which you must then remove separately.

You can usually find an icon for running the uninstall utility on the menu that contains the icon for running the program. If you cannot locate the icon, other sections in this chapter provide alternative methods for uninstalling programs.

Run a Program's Uninstall Utility

1. Click Start.
2. Click All Programs.
3. Click the submenu for the program you want to remove.
4. Click the icon for running the uninstall utility.

Note: *Sometimes, you must run an installation or setup utility that provides an option for uninstalling the program.*

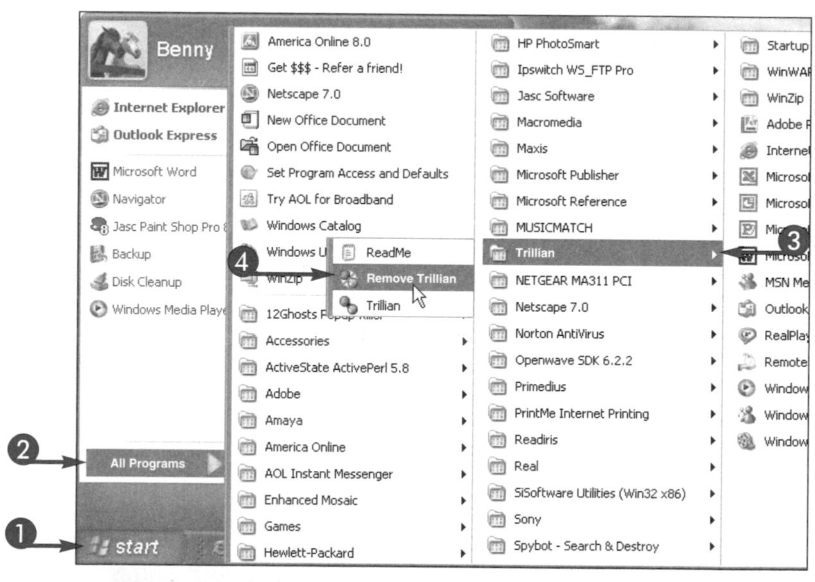

The install or uninstall utility starts.

5. Follow the on-screen instructions to uninstall the program.

The uninstall utility removes the program's files from your system.

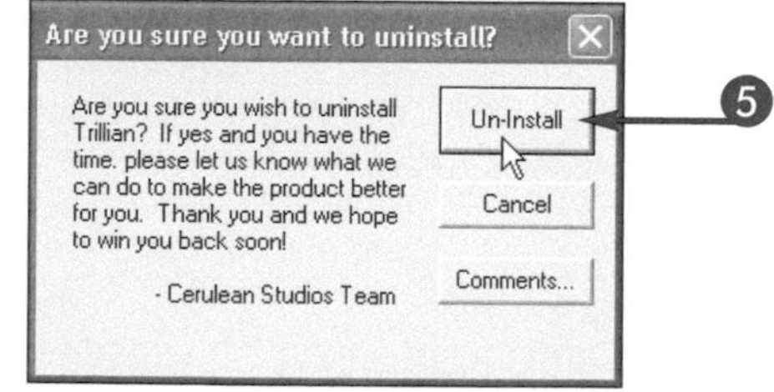

6 If a shortcut to the program remains, right-click the shortcut.

7 Click Delete.

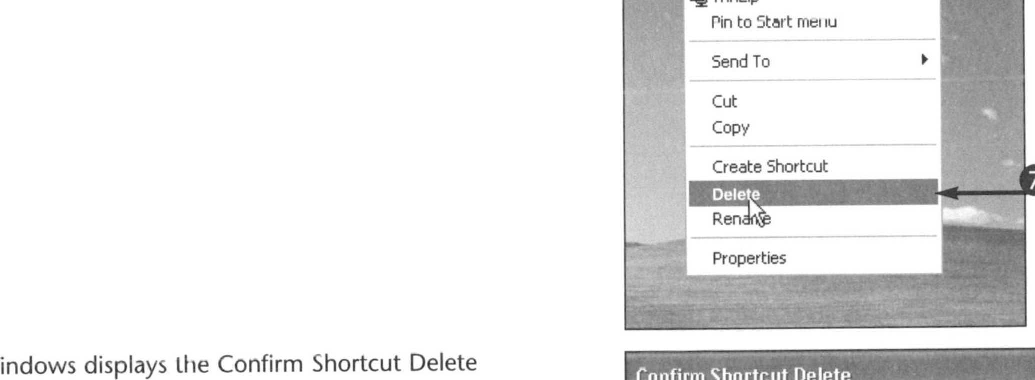

Windows displays the Confirm Shortcut Delete dialog box.

8 Click Delete Shortcut or Yes.

Windows removes the shortcut.

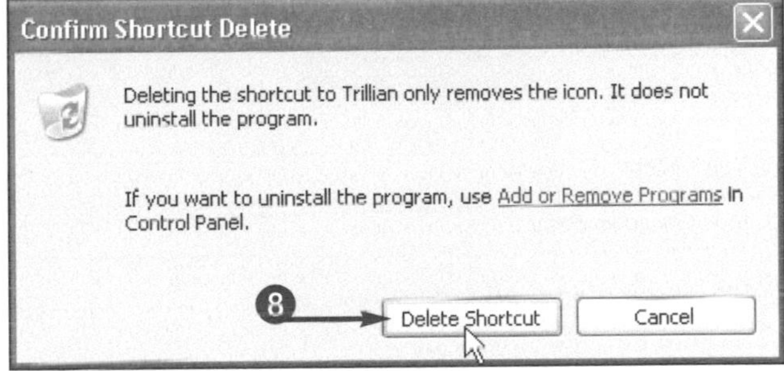

The uninstall utility displays a message indicating that a file is probably no longer needed but asking for my confirmation to delete it. What should I do?

- In most cases, the uninstall utility is being overly cautious in asking for your confirmation. To err on the side of caution, click the option to skip the file and leave it on the disk. Otherwise, click the option to confirm and proceed with the process of uninstalling the program. Some uninstall utilities provide you with an option to delete all program files without prompting for confirmation, so you do not need to deal with a series of annoying confirmation messages.

The program's submenu contains no icon for installing, uninstalling, or setting up the program. What should I do?

- Some programs include an uninstall command on the help menu or another menu in the program's window. Other programs provide access to the uninstall utility only through the Windows Add/Remove Programs utility. Others hide the uninstall utility in the folder that contains the files for running the program. If you cannot find an icon or command for removing the program, try one of the options in the section "Uninstall with the Add or Remove Programs Utility" or "Uninstall a Program from the Program's Folder." Do not simply delete the program's folder.

Uninstall with the Add or Remove Programs Utility

You can remove most programs by using the Windows Add or Remove Programs utility. Whenever you install a Windows program, it should add itself to the list of installed programs in the Add or Remove Programs window. For each program in the list, Windows displays a button labeled Change/Remove, Change or Remove, or Remove. You can use the button to run the program's uninstall or setup utility, which either automatically removes the program or displays options to customize or remove it. Some programs only provide an option for removing the program.

Uninstalling with the Add or Remove Programs utility features the added option of showing you how often you use a particular program. When you display the list of installed programs, Windows displays a brief message below each program, indicating whether you use the program frequently, occasionally, or rarely. It also shows you how much disk space the program occupies and the last time you ran the program. This helps you develop a clearer idea of whether you want to keep or remove a program. You may even notice that you have programs on your PC, such as adware, that you had no idea were installed.

Uninstall with the Add or Remove Programs Utility

1. Click Start.
2. Click Control Panel.

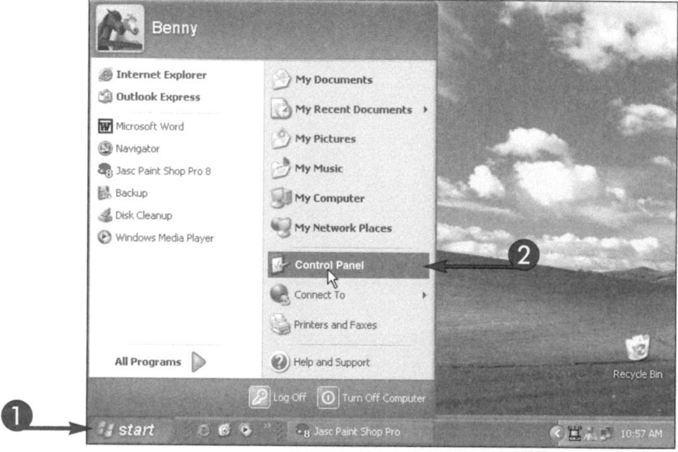

The Windows Control Panel appears.

Note: *If your Control Panel looks different, it may be displayed in Classic View. You can click Tools, Folder Options to access options for changing the view.*

3. Click the Add or Remove Programs link.

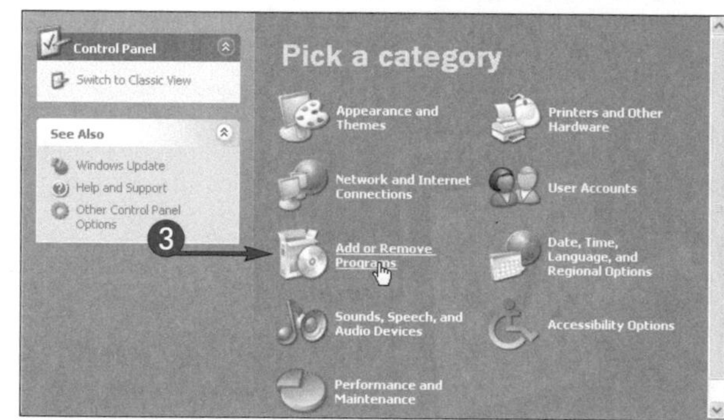

The Add or Remove Programs window appears.

4 Click a program's name.

Additional information about the program appears.

5 Click the Change/Remove, Change or Remove, or Remove button.

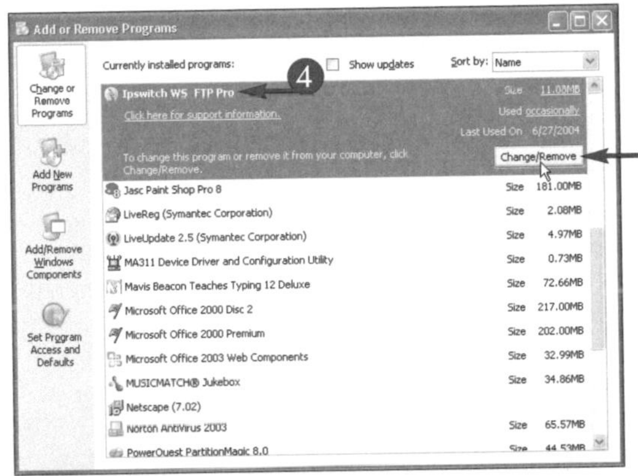

The uninstall or setup utility displays a dialog box instructing you on how to proceed.

6 Follow the on-screen instructions to uninstall the program.

The program is removed from your PC.

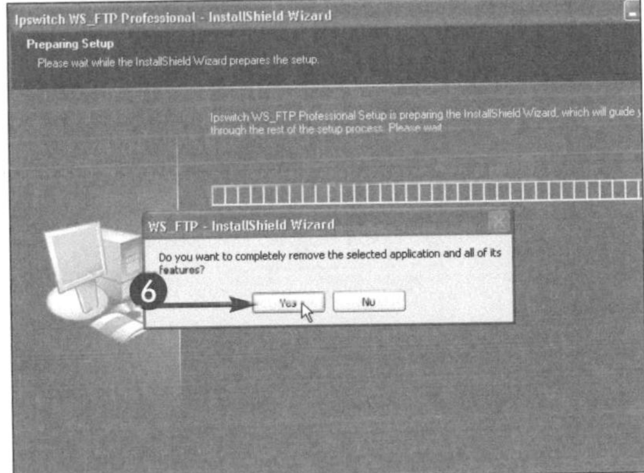

I tried to remove a program, but a dialog box appeared indicating that other users were logged on. What should I do?

▼ In most cases, you cannot remove a program entirely if more than one user is logged on to Windows. Click the Switch User button, log on to the other user's account, and log off that user. Then, return to Add or Remove Programs and try again to remove the program.

Can I uninstall programs from Windows Disk Cleanup?

▼ Yes. Disk Cleanup provides another way to run the Add or Remove Programs utility. Run Disk Cleanup, as explained in Chapter 5, click the More Options tab, and under Installed Programs, click Clean up. This opens the Add or Remove Programs window, and you can then remove the program by peforming the steps in this section.

Can I remove specific portions of a program without removing the entire program?

▼ In some cases, you can change or customize a program's installation. For example, if Microsoft Office is installed and you do not use the database, Microsoft Access, you can click the Change/Remove button to run the Office installation utility and then use it to remove Microsoft Access.

Uninstall a Program from the Program's Folder

If a program does not appear in the Add or Remove Programs window or display an icon for removing it on the Start, All Programs menu, you can look in the program's folder for an uninstall or setup icon. Most programs have an uninstall utility, but some developers discourage users from uninstalling their programs by placing the utility in a relatively inaccessible location. With a little detective work, you can usually find the icon for removing the program.

When you install most programs, the installation routine creates a new folder in the Program Files folder, which is usually located on drive C. It places most of the program files in this new folder and may include an installation or setup file. By opening this folder in My Computer or Windows Explorer, you can usually find the installation or setup icon you need to remove the program. You can then double-click the icon to launch the installation or setup routine and follow its on-screen instructions to uninstall the program.

If you do not find the file you need to remove the program, other options are still available.

Uninstall a Program from the Program's Folder

1. Click Start.
2. Click My Computer.

   My Computer appears, displaying icons for your disk drives.
3. Double-click the icon for the drive on which you install your programs.

Note: *This is usually drive C.*

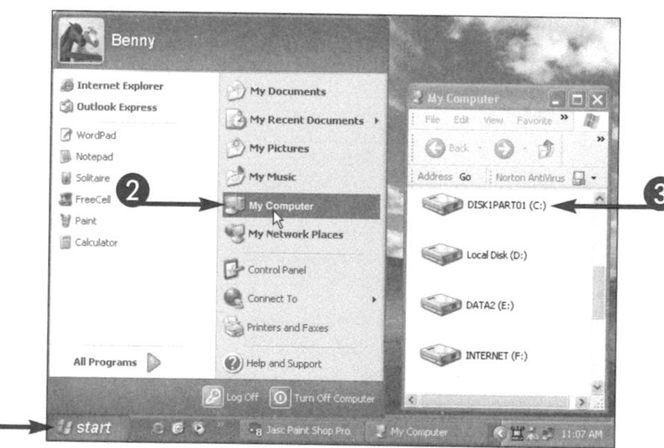

4. Double-click the Program Files folder.

   The Program Files folder displays its contents.
5. Double-click the folder for the program you want to remove.

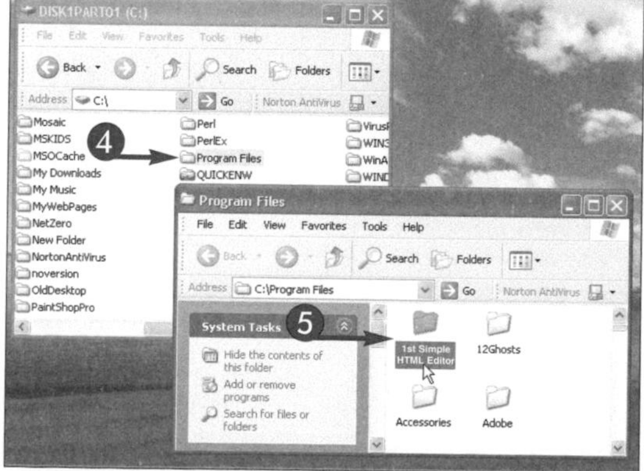

The program's files appear.

6 Double-click the icon for installing, setting up, or uninstalling the program.

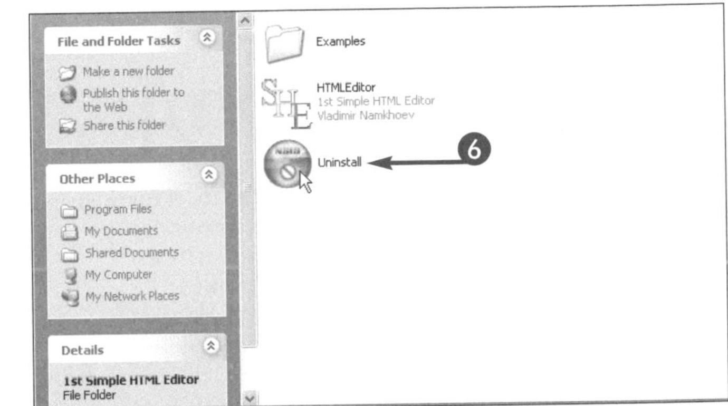

The program's uninstall utility displays instructions on how to proceed.

7 Follow the on-screen instructions to remove the program.

- The uninstall utility removes the program from your PC.

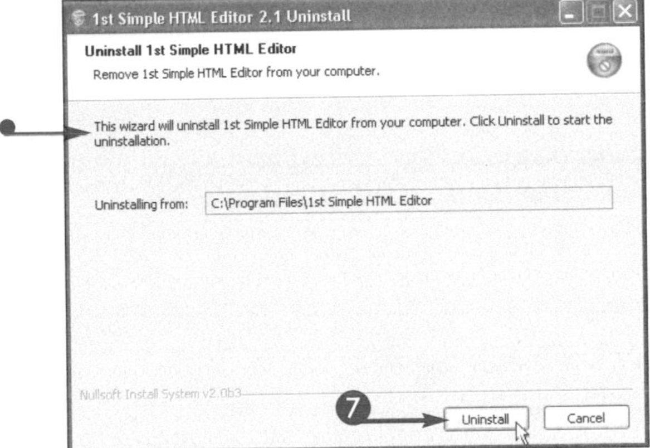

I cannot find an icon for removing the program in Add or Remove Programs, on the Start, Programs menu, or in the program's folder. Should I just delete the program's folder?

▼ Delete a program's folder only as a last resort. This can leave errant entries in the Windows registry, which can cause problems later. In some cases, you can use the program's Help system to obtain information about removing the program. You can also check the program's folder for a Readme file, which may contain instructions for removing the program. If you know the address of the developer's Web site, visit the site for additional information.

I still cannot find information on removing the program. Can I delete the program's folder now?

▼ Yes. You can remove a program by deleting the folder that contains the program's files. First, create a system restore point, as explained in Chapter 19. Open the Program Files folder, right-click the program's folder, and click Delete. When prompted to confirm, click Yes. You should clean the registry, as explained in Chapter 20. A registry cleaner typically removes registry entries that point to files that no longer exist. If you run into problems later, you can always restore your system and restore the program's folder from the Recycle Bin, as shown in Chapter 7.

Remove Unused Windows Components

When you install Windows, the installation routine installs the most commonly used components. These include Windows accessories such as Microsoft Paint and the Windows calculator; games, including FreeCell; networking services; and Windows Messenger. You can remove components selectively while keeping the rest of Windows intact.

The Add or Remove Programs window contains the Add/Remove Windows Components icon, which you can click to display a list of all Windows components. Some of the items in the list are actually groups of components. You can select or deselect all components in the group or select components individually. If the check box next to a component group appears gray, some of the items in the group are selected and some are not. After selecting which components you want to remove, you can have all of the components removed at once.

The steps in this section show you how to remove Windows components, but you can use the same steps to install additional components.

Remove Unused Windows Components

1. Click Start.
2. Click Control Panel.

   The Windows Control Panel appears.
3. Click the Add or Remove Programs link.

   The Add or Remove Programs window appears.
4. Click the Add/Remove Windows Components icon.

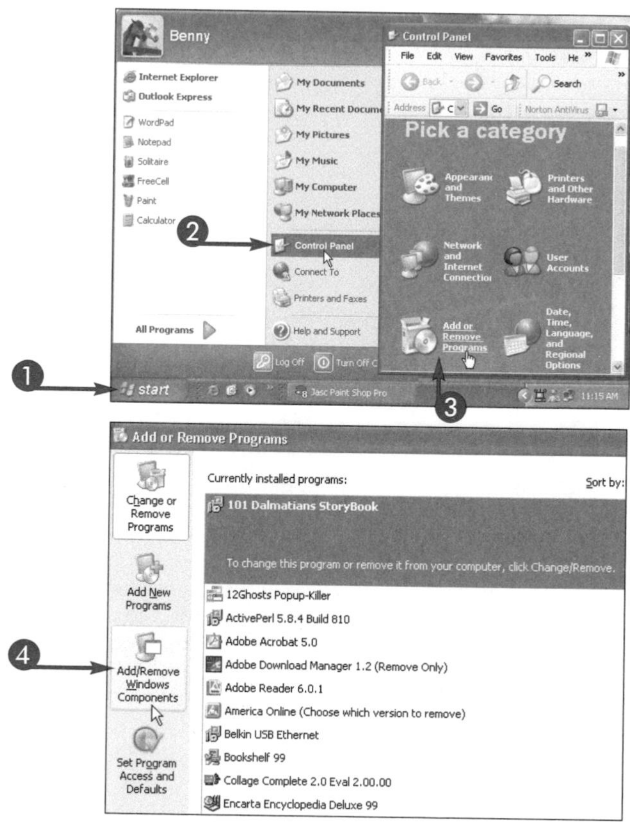

The Windows Components Wizard appears.

5 Click a component or component group.

- If the Details button is available, you can click it to display individual components in a group.

6 Click a check mark next to an item (☑ changes to ☐) to remove it.

7 Click Next.

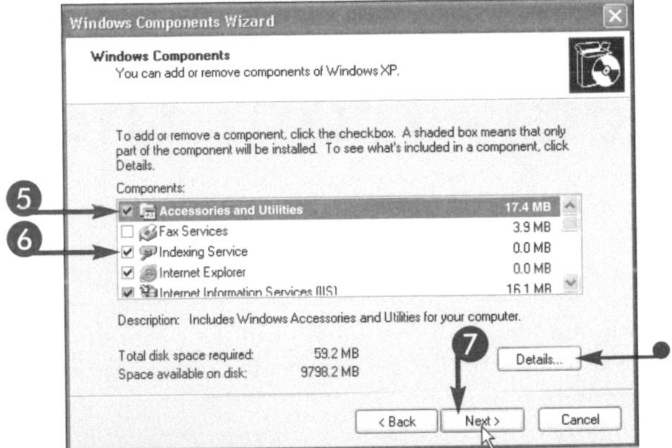

- The Wizard removes the Windows components you chose to remove and displays the Completing the Windows Components Wizard message.

8 Click Finish.

Windows closes the dialog box.

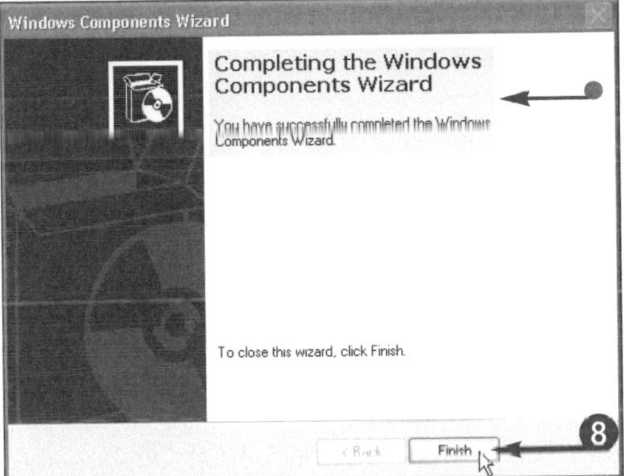

Can I reinstall a Windows component after deleting it?

▼ Yes. Run Windows Components Wizard again, select the component you want to reinstall, and follow the Wizard's instructions to complete the installation. In some cases, you may need to insert the Windows Installation CD to complete the process.

The check box next to a component group is gray. How do I install all the components in the group?

▼ A gray box with a check mark in it indicates that some, but not all of the components in the group are selected. To select all components in the group, click the check box (☑ changes to ☐) once to remove the check mark and then click the check box again to add the check mark (☐ changes to ☑).

I want to remove some components in a group, but not all of them. How do I do it?

▼ Display the Windows Components Wizard. Click the component group that includes the components you want to remove. Click Details to display a list of components in the group. If you click Accessories and Utilities and then click Details, the Windows Components Wizard displays two subgroups: Accessories and Games. You can click Accessories or Games and click Details to display individual accessories or games. Click a check box next to a component to toggle the check mark on or off (☐ changes to ☑). After removing the check marks next to the components you want to remove, click OK to return to the Wizard.

Remove or Unpin Program Items from the Start Menu

Sometimes you remove a program from your PC, but the program's submenu and icons remain on the Start menu. You can remove these items from the menu to reduce the clutter. You can also remove programs from the Start menu if you always run the program from somewhere else, such as the Windows desktop or the Quick Launch toolbar.

Windows displays programs on the Start menu, the All Programs menu, and on various submenus on the All Programs menu. If you frequently use a program, Windows automatically adds it to the Start menu to make it convenient to run. You can also choose to *pin* a program to the top of the Start menu or unpin programs that you rarely use.

The programs that appear on the Start menu are typically placed there during the program's installation. These are shortcuts that you can safely delete if you no longer use the program or if you removed the program from your PC. Removing a shortcut from the Start, All Programs menu does not remove the program from your PC. It only removes one of the shortcuts used to launch the program.

Remove or Unpin Program Items from the Start Menu

Remove a Start Menu Item

1. Click Start.
2. Click All Programs.
3. Right-click the item you want to remove.
4. Click Delete.

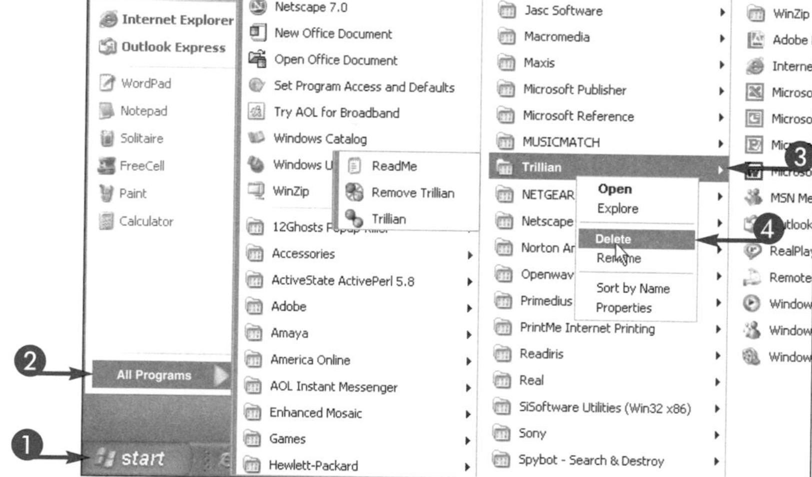

Windows displays a confirmation dialog box.

5. Click Yes.

Windows removes the item from the Start ⇨ All Programs menu.

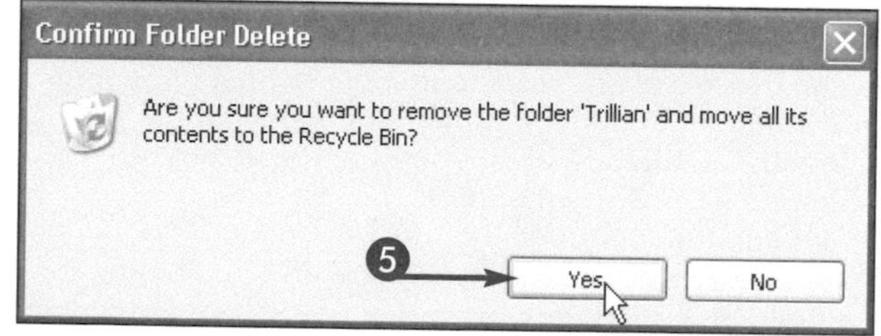

Unpin a Start Menu Program

1. Click Start.
2. Right-click the program you want to unpin.
3. Click Unpin from Start menu.

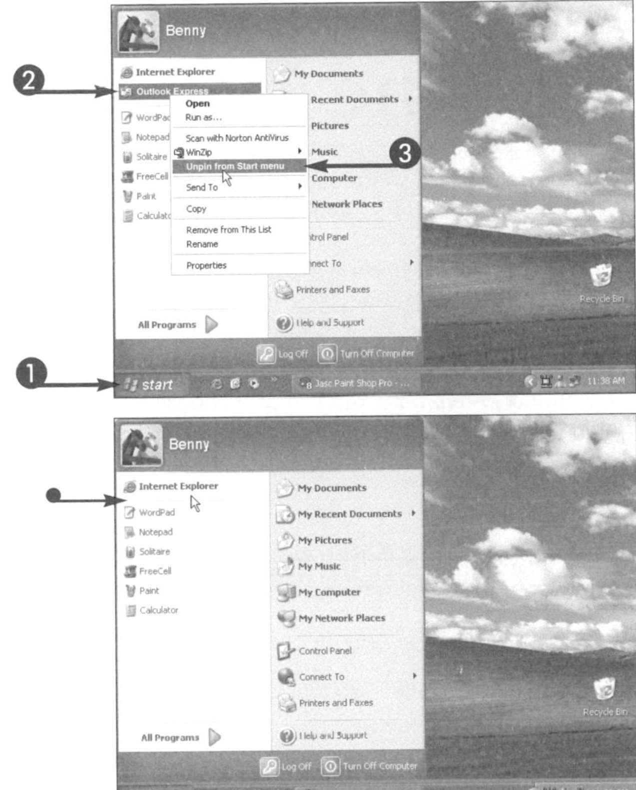

- Windows removes the program from the Start menu.

Can I remove the shortcuts that Windows automatically adds to the Start menu when I use a program?

▼ Yes. To remove a shortcut, click Start, right-click the shortcut you want to remove, and click Remove from This List. To clear all shortcuts from the list, right-click Start, and then click Properties, the Customize button, and then the Clear List button. To prevent Windows from adding shortcuts to the Start menu, set the "Number of programs on Start menu" box to 0 (zero). You can click the Advanced tab to access options for removing additional items from the Start menu, such as My Music or Printers and Faxes.

Can I move items on the Start menu?

▼ Yes. Open the Start menu and display the item you want to move. This can be a submenu or a shortcut icon. Click and drag the item where you want it to appear. As you drag, a horizontal line appears showing where Windows will place the item if you release the mouse button. You can drag the item over a submenu to open the menu, and then drag the item over the open submenu to place the item on the submenu. When the horizontal line is where you want the item moved, release the mouse button.

Clear Unused Shortcuts from the Windows Desktop

You can remove shortcuts you do not use from the Windows desktop to keep the desktop uncluttered and conserve system resources. A shortcut is a copy of the icon that runs a program or accesses a file or folder. Deleting a shortcut does not affect the original program or file in any way.

Some programs automatically place a shortcut on the desktop during installation. You can also choose to place shortcuts on the desktop for programs or utilities you frequently use and other items you often access such as documents or folders. Shortcuts provide easy access to programs, folders, and files, but if you no longer use a shortcut, it can get in the way and consume a tiny bit of memory that your PC can use for performing some other task. By removing these unused shortcuts, you can make the Windows desktop a more efficient work area.

You can identify shortcuts by the boxed arrow that appears in the lower left corner of the icon. Notice that the Recycle Bin does not have this boxed arrow, because it is not a shortcut; Windows provides no option for deleting it.

Clear Unused Shortcuts from the Windows Desktop

1. Display the Windows desktop.
2. Right-click the shortcut you want to remove.
3. Click Delete.

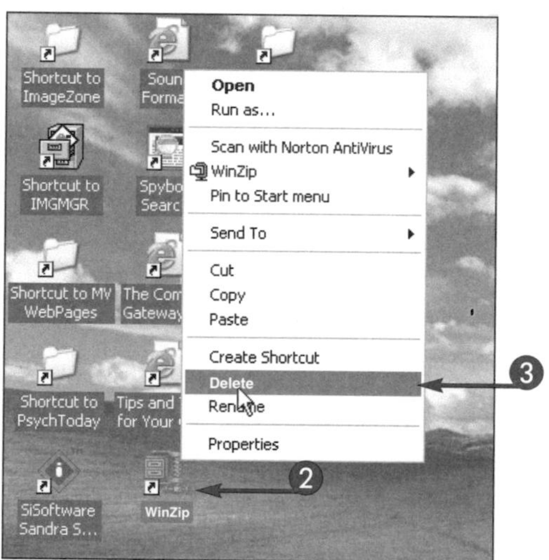

The Confirm Shortcut Delete or Confirm File Delete dialog box appears.

4. Click Yes or click Delete Shortcut.

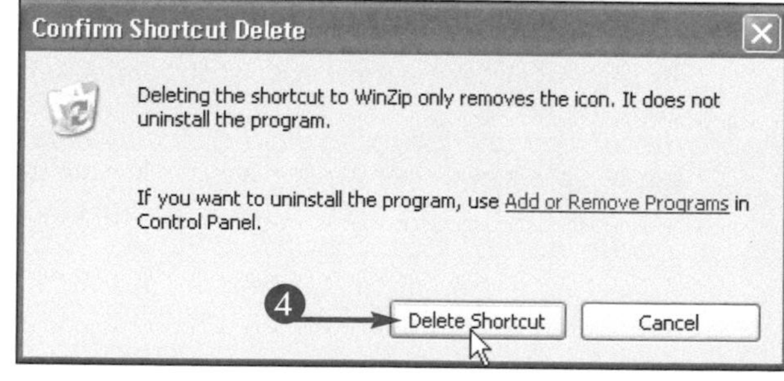

- Windows removes the shortcut from the desktop.

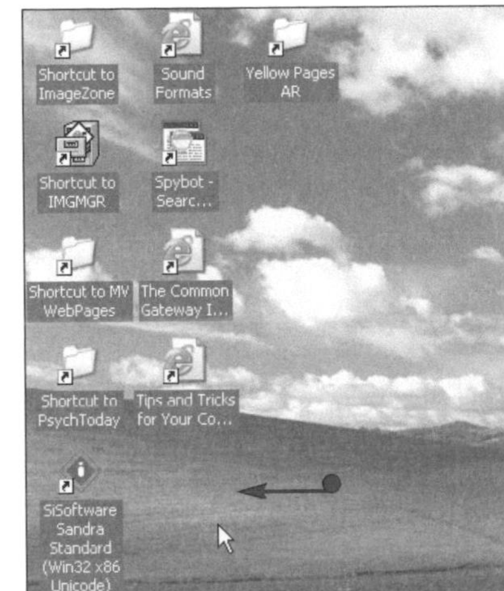

- You can right-click the desktop and click Undo Delete to restore the shortcut.

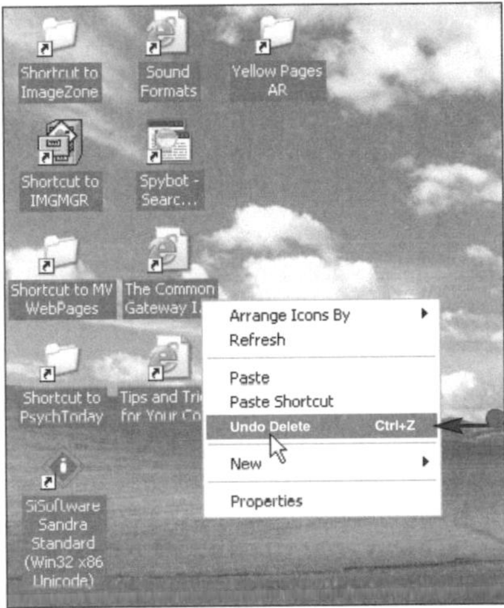

I have a couple shortcuts that I cannot delete. Is there any way to remove them?

▼ Yes. You can tweak the Windows registry to remove the shortcuts from the desktop. The Windows registry contains settings that control almost every aspect of Windows. Tweaking consists of editing the registry to change one or more settings. Refer to Part VI for instructions on how to safely tweak the registry.

Can I remove shortcuts without permanently deleting them?

▼ Yes. You can create a folder on the desktop and move shortcuts that you rarely use to the folder. To create a folder, right-click a blank area of the desktop, click New and then Folder. Type a name for the folder. You can then click and drag shortcuts to the new folder to move them off the desktop and into the folder.

Can I delete more than one shortcut at a time?

▼ Yes. First, select all of the shortcuts you want to delete. You can click and drag a selection box around the icons or hold down the Ctrl key while clicking each icon you want to delete. Then, right-click one of the selected icons and click Delete. If one of the selected icons is an icon that Windows does not allow you to delete, Windows may not delete any of the selected icons.

Display Filename Extensions

You can reclaim hard drive space by deleting unnecessary files that the Disk Cleanup utility does not identify for removal. These include documents you no longer need, duplicate copies of files, and a host of other files you do not want. Identifying file types is very helpful in deciding which files to delete and in grouping files so you can delete multiple files of the same type. You can also search for files using the filename extension to find all files of a given type.

You can identify a file's type by looking at the filename extension — the characters that follow the period at the end of the file's name. A file that has an .exe filename extension is an executable file, which you can double-click to run a program. A filename extension of .tmp marks a temporary file, which you can safely delete. A file that has the .doc filename extension is typically a Word document.

By default, Windows hides the filename extension, and relies on the appearance of the icon to indicate the file type. However, you can choose to have Windows display filename extensions.

Display Filename Extensions

1. Click Start.
2. Click My Computer.

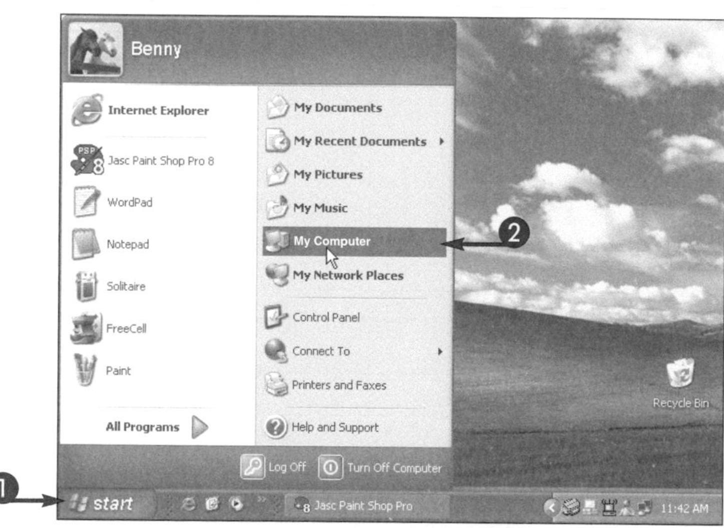

The My Computer window appears.

3. Click Tools.
4. Click Folder Options.

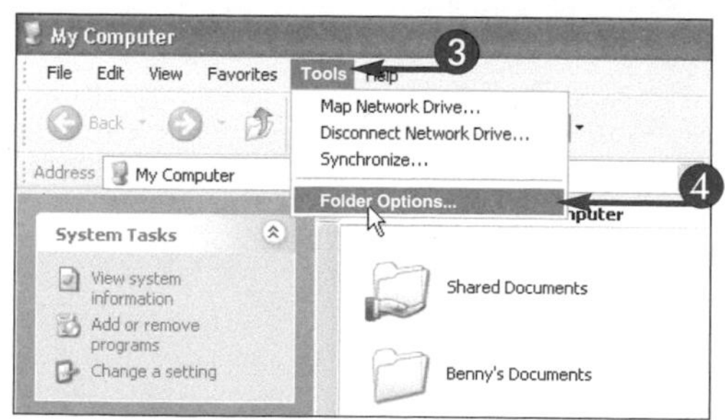

The Folder Options dialog box appears.

5. Click the View tab.
6. Click the Hide extensions for known file types option (☑ changes to ☐).
7. Click OK.

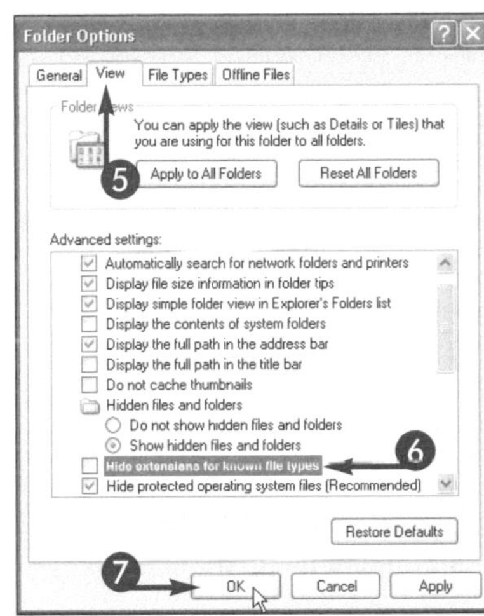

My Computer displays filename extensions for all files.

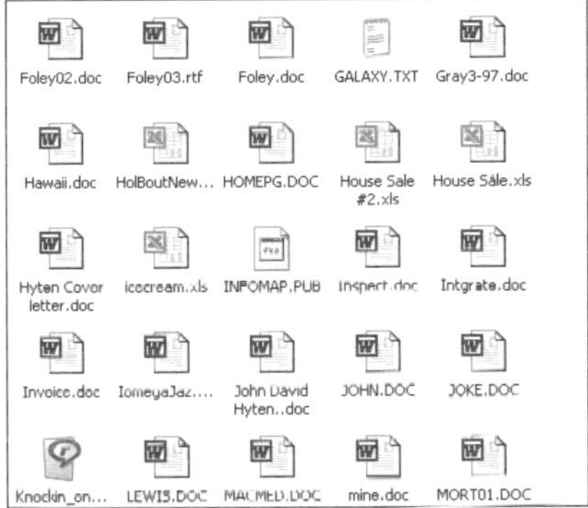

Why does my document file have an icon that represents a program?

▼ The icon that appears next to the filename represents the program that is associated with that file type. If you double-click the document icon, Windows automatically runs the associated program, which then opens the document. You can view a list of filename extensions and their associated programs by clicking the File Types tab in the Folder Options dialog box.

Are there any critical system files I should never delete?

▼ Yes. By default, Windows is set up to hide these files so you do not accidentally delete them. However, this can prevent you from accessing important files and folders. To change the settings for hiding system files and folders, open My Computer, click Tools, Folder Options, and then the View tab, and click the Hide protected operating system files and Do not show hidden files and folders options (☑ changes to ☐). System file names and icons appear ghosted; be careful not to delete these files.

How do I locate all of the temporary files on my PC?

▼ Use the Windows Search option to search for all files named *.tmp. In Windows XP, click Start, Search, and then All files and folders, type ***.tmp**, and press Enter. The entry *.tmp instructs Windows to find all files that have the .tmp extension. You may need to click the Search subfolders option (○ changes to ◉) to search all of the folders.

Delete Files from the Default Data Directories

If you save all of your files in the My Documents folder or one of its subfolders, you can easily locate most of the files you have created and saved. Although the documents and other files you create are probably the most valuable data on your PC, they can also be the most unnecessary files. Old letters and memos, out-of-focus digital photos, digital audio recordings you never listen to, and other old data files can pile up over time and consume valuable storage space. In addition, whenever you search for a file, Windows needs to search through all of these files; by removing unnecessary files, you can find and open files more efficiently.

When you are looking to reclaim hard drive space, the My Documents folder and its subfolders are prime areas to examine for useless data, because these are the default data folders that Windows uses to store documents and the other files you create. However, if you created your own folders for storing your files, look in those folders for unnecessary files, instead. And, if you share your computer with other users, encourage them to remove useless files from their default data directories, as well.

Delete Files from the Default Data Directories

1. Click Start.
2. Click My Documents.

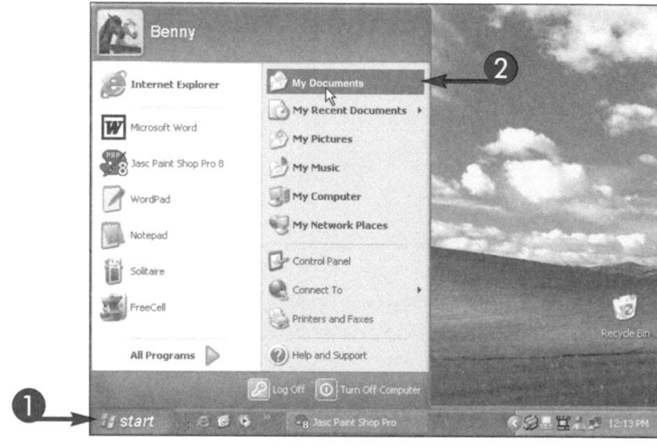

The My Documents window appears, displaying the contents of the My Documents folder.

3. Click a file you want to delete.
4. Hold down the Ctrl key while clicking additional files you want to delete.

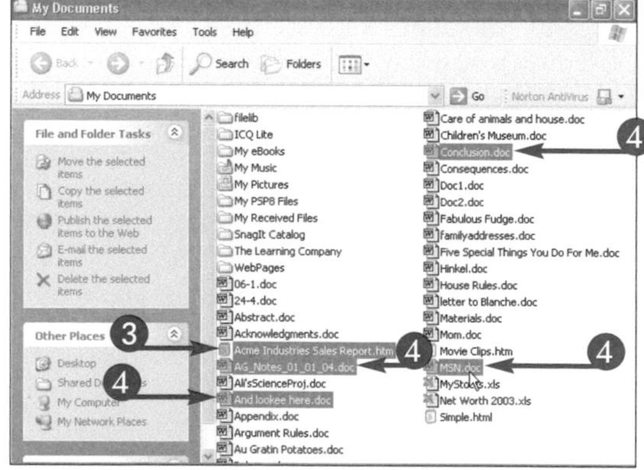

5 Right-click one of the selected files.

6 Click Delete.

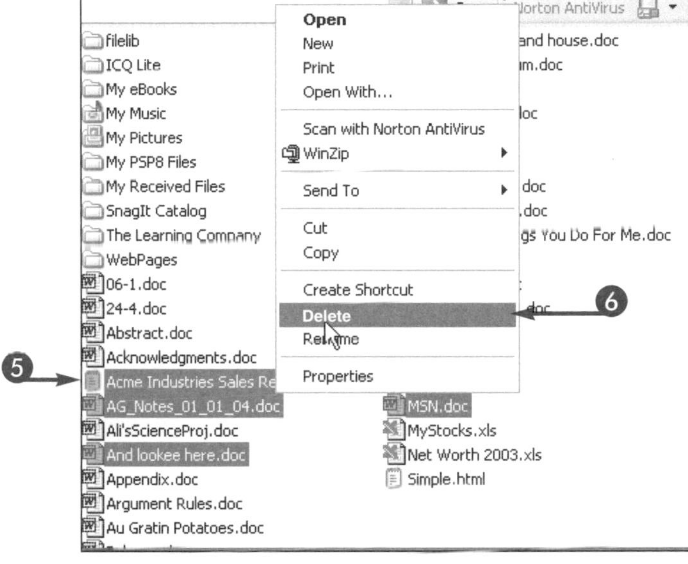

The Confirm Multiple File Delete dialog box appears.

7 Click Yes.

Windows moves the files from My Documents to the Recycle Bin.

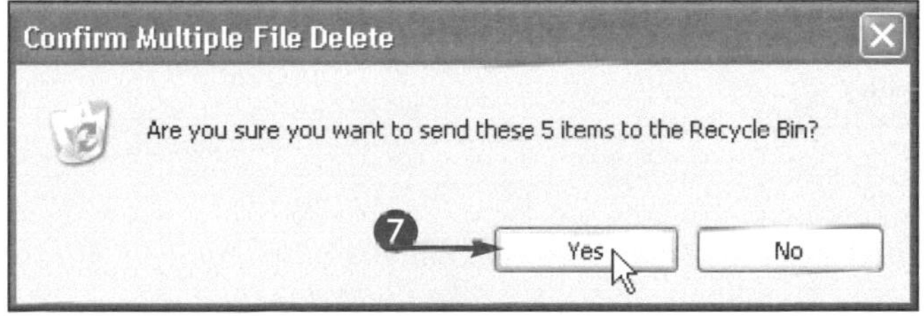

I accidentally deleted an important file. Can I get it back?

▼ If you recently deleted a file and have not yet emptied the Recycle Bin, you have a good chance of recovering the file. On the Windows desktop, double-click the Recycle Bin icon to open the Recycle Bin. Find the file you accidentally deleted. Right-click the file and click Restore. Windows moves the file from the Recycle Bin back to its original location. You can also restore items from the Recycle Bin by dragging them out of the Recycle Bin and onto the Windows desktop or into a folder where you want to store the file. For more information, refer to the section "Empty the Recycle Bin."

Where else should I look for files I can safely delete?

▼ Many programs create and use subfolders of the My Documents folder to store their files. Check the My Pictures, My Videos, and My Music folders for digital media files that typically require large amounts of storage. Check My Documents for other subfolders, as well. To find out where a program is storing the documents you create, launch the program and open a new file. Click File and then Save, and then look in the Save In text box for the name of the folder in which the program is about to save the file. You can usually delete a file from the Save As dialog box by right-clicking the file and clicking Delete.

Find Other Files You Created

Although most of the files you create are probably stored in your default data directories, you may occasionally save documents and files to other areas of your hard drive. You can locate these files by using the Windows search feature to search for files by file type. For example, you can search for all files that have the filename extension .doc to find all Word documents or you can search for files that have the extension .mp3 to find all MP3 audio recordings.

The Windows Search feature is an excellent tool for tracking down files by type. You can type settings that instruct Windows to search every disk drive on your PC and every folder and subfolder for a specified file type. When the search is complete, the Search feature displays all of the files it finds in a single list, making it easy to delete entire groups of files.

When searching for and deleting files in this way, you should be careful not to delete essential files that Windows or other programs need in order to function properly. For example, deleting all of the WAV files on your computer eliminates the sounds that Windows plays when certain events occur.

Find Other Files You Created

1. Click Start.
2. Click Search.

Note: *If your PC uses a version of Windows other than Windows XP, the steps for displaying the Search Results window may differ.*

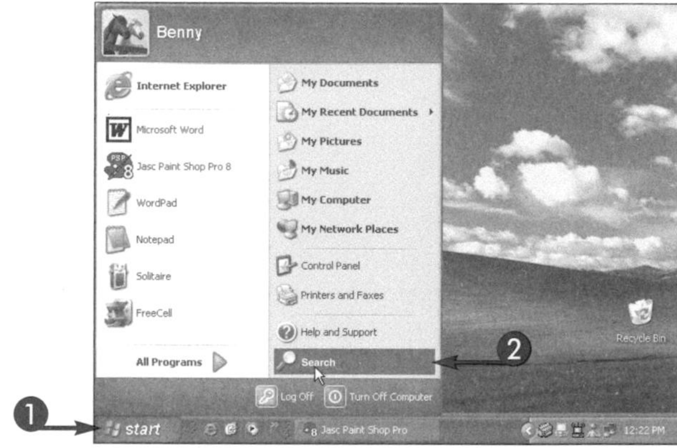

- The Search Results window appears and prompts you to specify the type of item to search for.

3. Click the All files and folders link.

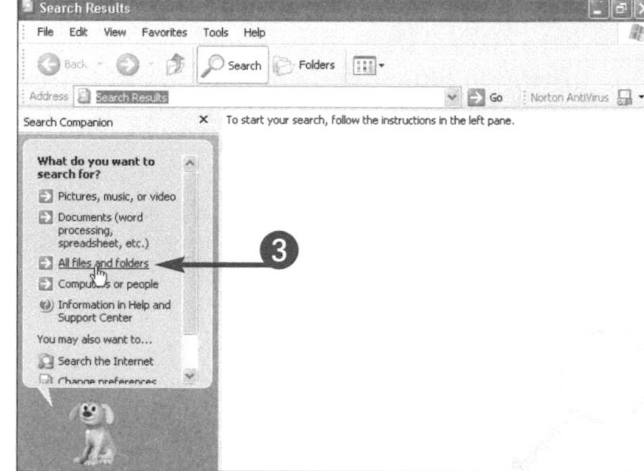

The Search page prompts you to enter your search criteria.

4. Type *. followed by the filename extension for the type of file you want to find.
5. Click here and click the drive or drives you want to search.
6. Click Search.

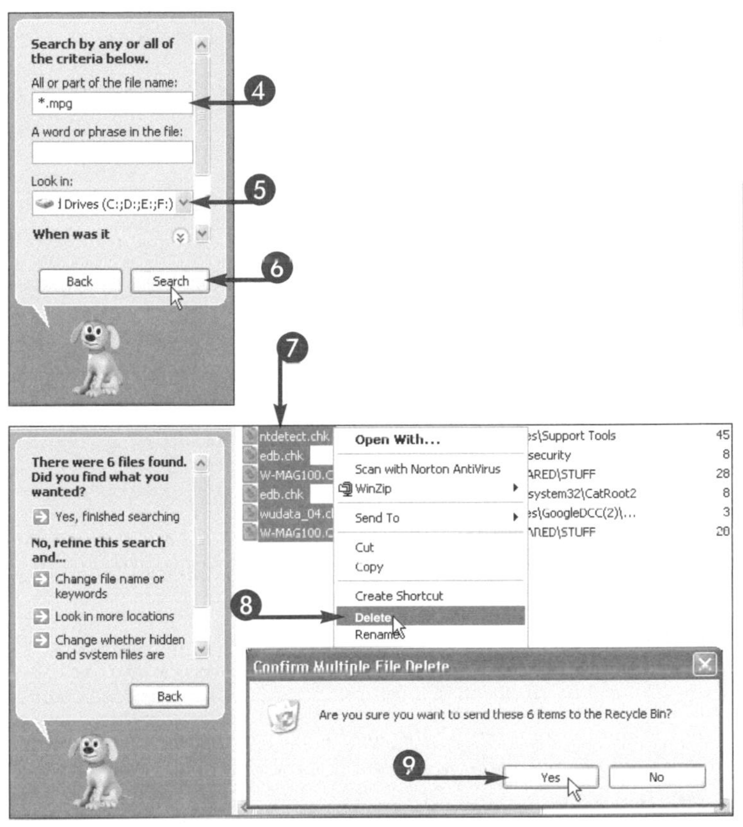

The Search feature looks for files with the specified filename extension and displays the names of any files with that extension.

7. Right-click a file you want to delete.
8. Click Delete.

   Windows displays a dialog box to confirm your deletions.

9. Click Yes.

   Windows deletes the file, placing it in the Recycle Bin.

Are there any common file types I should search for?

▼ Yes. The following table lists some of the more common file types you may want to delete. Be careful not to delete any files you need or any files that Windows or other programs need to function properly. If you think you may need these files later, consider copying them to a CD before deleting them.

File Type	*Extension*
Word document	.doc
Text files	.txt
Rich Text Format file	.rtf
Backup files	.bak, .old, .000, .001, .002, etc.
Log files	.log
Scandisk repair files	.chk
PDF files	.pdf
Temporary files	.tmp
Images	.jpg, .jpeg, .gif, .tif, .tiff, .bmp, .pcx, .png, .wmf
Audio files	.mp3, .wav, .wma, .midi, .ra, .ram, .aif, .aiff
Video files	.mov, .qt, .avi, .mpg, .mpg2, .mpg3, .mpg4, .mpeg, .mpeg2, .mpeg3, .mpeg4, m3u, .rm
Zip files	.zip

List Files by Size, Type, or Date

You can list files by size to help you decide which files you can delete to reclaim the most disk space. You can list files by type, so you can easily select a group of files that are the same type and delete them with a single command. You can also list files by date to find the oldest files on your PC's hard drive and determine whether or not you still need those old files.

Whenever you view a list of files or folders in My Computer, Windows Explorer, or the Search Results window, Windows provides several options for arranging the file list. You can arrange files by name, size, type, or the dates on which the files were most recently modified. In most cases, you want to arrange files by name to place them in alphabetical order, so you can easily locate a file. However, when you want to delete files, you may find that arranging files by size, type, or date modified is more useful. After you finish working with the files, you can then rearrange the files to list them by name.

List Files by Size, Type, or Date

1. Display a list of files in My Computer, Windows Explorer, or the Search Results window.
2. Click View.
3. Click Details.

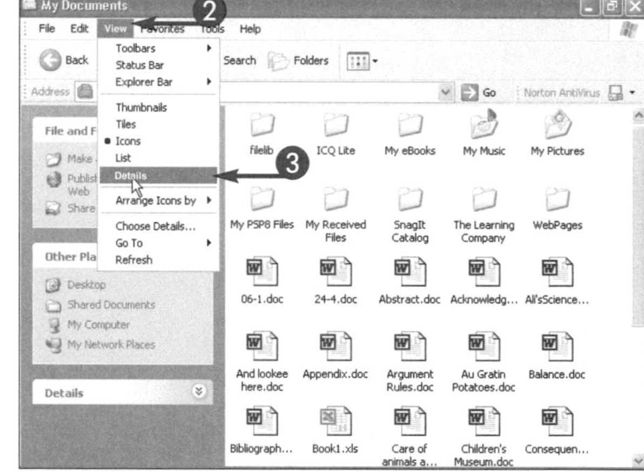

Windows displays the name, size, and type of each file, the date it was created, and other details.

4. Click View.
5. Click Arrange Icons by.
6. Click the criteria you want to use to arrange the icons.

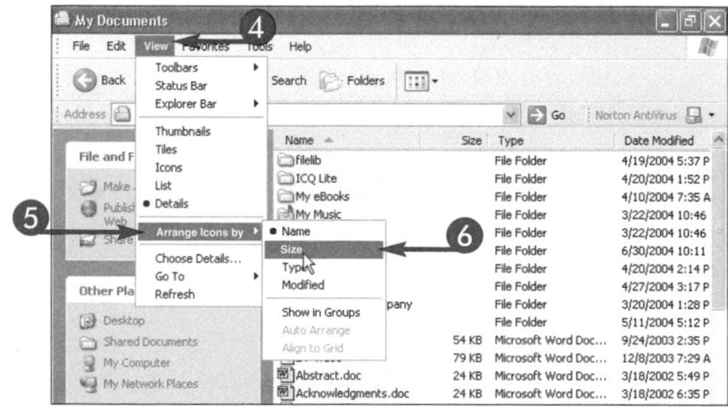

Windows rearranges the items according to the selected criteria.

- You can click a column heading to rearrange the list of items and click the same column heading to reverse the order in which the items are listed.

Name	Size	Type	Date Modified
filelib		File Folder	4/19/2004 5:37 P
ICQ Lite		File Folder	4/20/2004 1:52 P
My eBooks		File Folder	4/10/2004 7:35 A
My Music		File Folder	3/22/2004 10:46
My Pictures		File Folder	3/22/2004 10:46
My PSP8 Files		File Folder	6/30/2004 10:11
My Received Files		File Folder	4/20/2004 2:14 P
SnagIt Catalog		File Folder	4/27/2004 3:17 P
The Learning Company		File Folder	3/20/2004 1:28 P
WebPages		File Folder	5/11/2004 5:12 P
Simple.html	1 KB	HTML Document	6/2/2004 2:08 PM
Movie Clips.htm	3 KB	HTML Document	4/10/2001 2:14 P
MyStocks.xls	14 KB	Microsoft Excel Wor...	10/23/2002 1:23
Net Worth 2003.xls	14 KB	Microsoft Excel Wor...	9/18/2002 4:32 P
Doc2.doc	20 KB	Microsoft Word Doc...	3/18/2002 6:36 P
Mom.doc	23 KB	Microsoft Word Doc...	12/5/2001 5:55 P
Acknowledgments.doc	24 KB	Microsoft Word Doc...	3/10/2002 6:35 P
Appendix.doc	24 KB	Microsoft Word Doc...	3/18/2002 6:37 P
Balance.doc	24 KB	Microsoft Word Doc...	10/2/2001 6:22 P

Windows rearranges the icons according to the items in the selected column.

Name	Size	Type	Date Modified
Ali'sScienceProj.doc	303 KB	Microsoft Word Doc...	3/12/2002 7:31 P
Doc1.doc	84 KB	Microsoft Word Doc...	3/15/2001 7:08 P
24-4.doc	79 KB	Microsoft Word Doc...	12/8/2003 7:29 A
06-1.doc	54 KB	Microsoft Word Doc...	9/24/2003 2:35 P
[illegible]	32 KB	Microsoft Excel Wor...	10/21/2002 1:10
letter to Blanche.doc	26 KB	Microsoft Word Doc...	8/8/2001 11:21 A
familyaddresses.doc	26 KB	Microsoft Word Doc...	7/11/2001 10:02
Care of animals and h...	26 KB	Microsoft Word Doc...	6/4/2001 6:43 PM
House Rules.doc	25 KB	Microsoft Word Doc...	10/13/2002 5:08
Children's Museum.doc	25 KB	Microsoft Word Doc...	11/13/2001 8:37
Au Gratin Potatoes.doc	25 KB	Microsoft Word Doc...	5/28/2002 6:39 A
[illegible]	[illegible]	Microsoft Word Doc...	10/2/2001 6:24 P
Materials.doc	25 KB	Microsoft Word Doc...	3/19/2002 5:53 P
Argument Rules.doc	24 KB	Microsoft Word Doc...	10/12/2002 5:15
Abstract.doc	24 KB	Microsoft Word Doc...	3/18/2002 5:49 P
Hinkel.doc	24 KB	Microsoft Word Doc...	3/16/2002 1:30 P
Five Special Things Y...	24 KB	Microsoft Word Doc...	5/9/2002 3:36 PM
Fabulous Fudge.doc	24 KB	Microsoft Word Doc...	12/30/2001 9:25
Consequences.doc	24 KB	Microsoft Word Doc...	10/11/2002 11:31

In Details view, can I rearrange the columns?

▼ Yes. You can click and drag the line to the right of a column heading to change the column's width. You can drag a column heading to the left or right and drop it in the desired location. For example, you can drag the Name column heading to the right of the Size column heading and drop it in place.

Can I arrange icons in other views, such as Icon view?

▼ Yes, but other views provide little information about a file or folder. In Icon view, for example, Windows displays only the file's name and an icon that represents its type. You can position the mouse pointer on an item to display a screentip that provides additional information. The Explorer bar, which appears to the left of the file list, may also display details about the currently selected item.

Can I obtain additional information about a file or folder without opening it?

▼ Yes. You can right-click a file or folder icon and then click Properties to display additional information about a file or folder. The Properties dialog box displays the file's name, location, and size; the date on which it was created, last modified, and most recently opened; and the file's attributes.

Safely Delete Files

You can delete files from your PC's hard drive directory without actually removing them from the disk. Whenever you delete files, Windows automatically moves the files to the Recycle Bin. The Recycle Bin is a temporary holding area that helps you recover files in the event that you delete them by accident.

The Recycle Bin is configured to use a certain percentage of disk space. If you delete more files than the Recycle Bin can hold, files you deleted previously are permanently removed to make room for the newly deleted files. When you accidentally delete a file, you usually realize the mistake within a day or two of committing the error. As long as you do not empty the Recycle Bin daily or perform frequent disk cleanups, you have a good chance of recovering the file. You can simply open the Recycle Bin, right-click the deleted item, and click Restore to restore it to its original location.

If your PC has more than one hard drive, the Recycle Bin uses a percentage of each drive for storing deleted files. The Recycle Bin typically uses about 10 percent of a hard drive's total storage space.

Safely Delete Files

❶ Click a file or folder you want to delete.

- You press the Ctrl key while clicking additional files or folders to select multiple items.

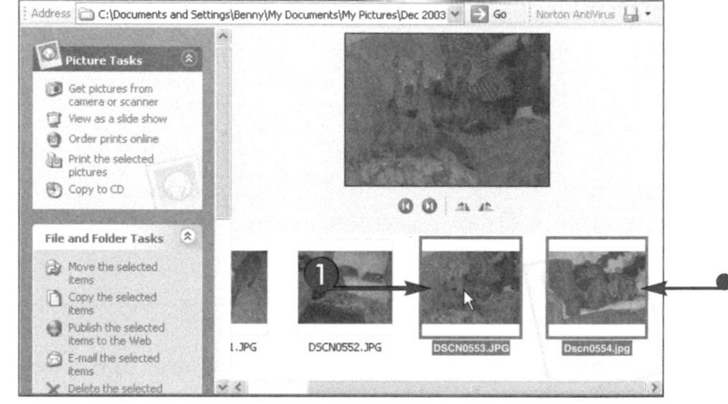

❷ Right-click one of the selected items.

❸ Click Delete.

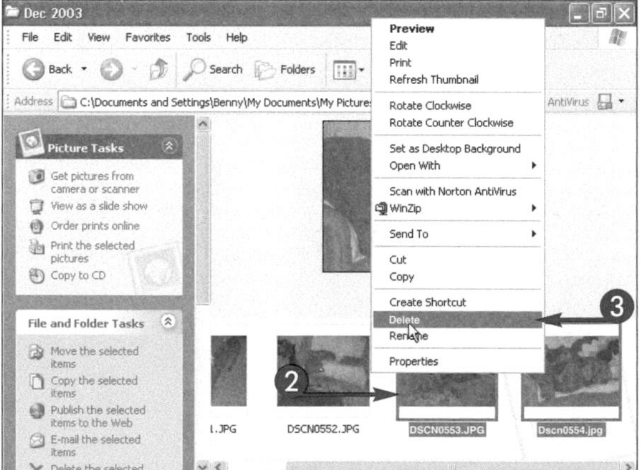

The Confirm Multiple File Delete dialog box appears.

4 Click Yes.

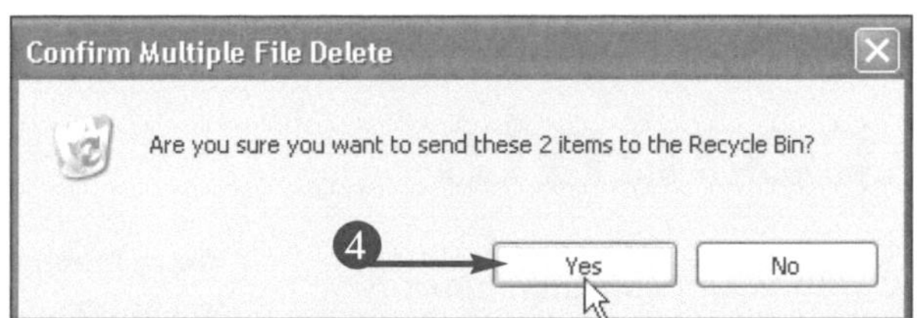

Windows moves the selected items from their original storage area to the Recycle Bin.

5 Double-click the Recycle Bin icon.

- The Recycle Bin displays the deleted item(s) it contains.

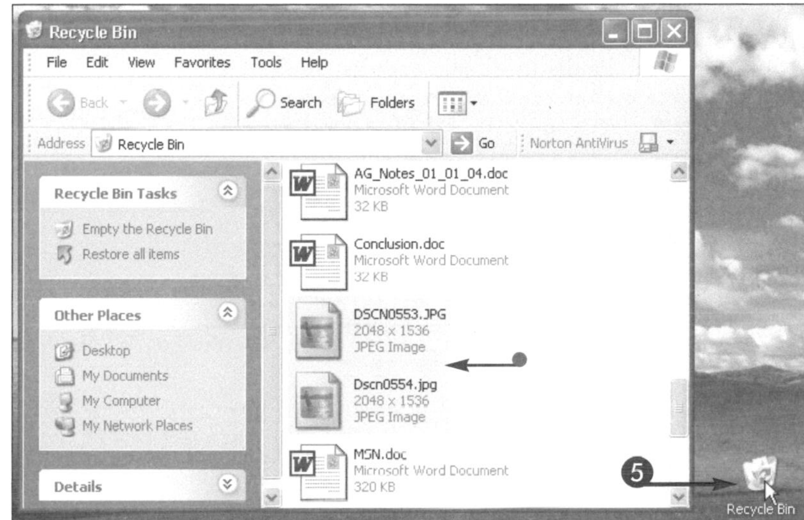

Can I permanently delete a file or folder?

▼ Yes. If you already deleted the item, double-click the Recycle Bin icon, right-click the item, and click Delete. A dialog box appears prompting you to confirm the deletion. Click Yes. If you have not yet sent the item to the Recycle Bin, you can bypass the Recycle Bin and permanently delete a file by holding down the Shift key when clicking Delete.

I shut down my PC before saving a document I had just created. Can I recover it?

▼ Usually not, but if the program you used to create the document has an auto-save feature, you can possibly recover some of your work. Check the program's help system to determine how to proceed.

I permanently deleted an extremely important file. Is there any way to recover it?

▼ You can possibly recover the file using a special undelete utility. Do not turn off your computer or perform any tasks, because any activity can permanently erase the data on the disk. You can download shareware and trialware versions of undelete utilities at www.download.com, but use a different PC to download the program and then run it from a CD or floppy disk. When you delete a file, the file's contents typically remain on the disk until your PC needs to use that storage space for another file. This makes it possible to recover accidentally deleted files.

Remove Inactive User Accounts

If you share your PC with other people, Windows XP enables you to create a separate user account for each person. Each user has his or her own set of "My" folders, including My Documents, My Pictures, and My Music. If a person no longer uses the computer, you can delete the person's user account. When you delete an account, Windows gives you the option of saving the person's user account files so you can transfer them to another PC or use them to reopen the account later. If the person does not need the files, you can delete them to reclaim some hard drive space.

These folders usually contain some very valuable data files, so consider copying them to a CD or other storage medium before deleting them, or at least check with the person before deleting them. If you decide not to delete the user account files when you delete an account, Windows places a folder for the deleted user account on the Windows desktop. This folder contains the user's My Documents folder and its contents. You can delete this folder at any time. Windows does not save the person's Outlook Express e-mail messages or Internet Explorer favorites.

Remove Inactive User Accounts

Note: *You must log on using an administrator account to remove user accounts.*

1. Click Start.
2. Click Control Panel.

The Control Panel appears.

3. Click User Accounts.

The User Accounts window appears.

4. Click the user account you want to delete.

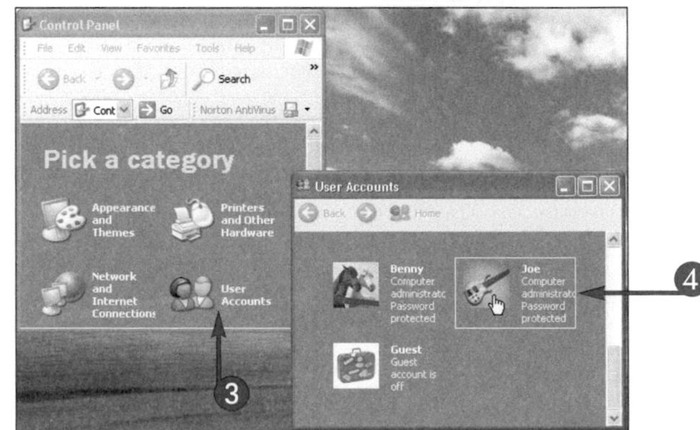

The options for the selected account appear.

5 Click the Delete the account link.

What do you want to change about Joe's account?

Change the name

Change the password

Remove the password

Change the picture

Change the account type

5 Delete the account

Joe
Computer administrator
Password protected

PART II

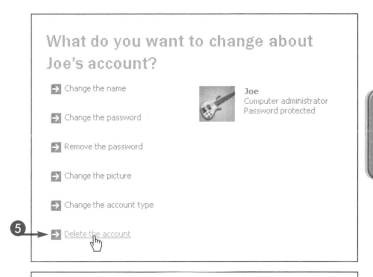

You are prompted to specify whether you want to delete or keep the user's files.

6 Click either Keep Files or click Delete Files.

Windows either retains a copy of the user's files and desktop settings, or deletes the files and desktop settings.

Do you want to keep Joe's files?

Before you delete Joe's account, Windows can automatically save the contents of Joe's desktop and "My Documents" folder to a new folder called "Joe" on your desktop. However, Windows cannot save Joe's e-mail messages, Internet favorites, and other settings.

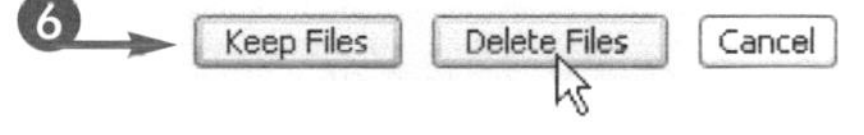

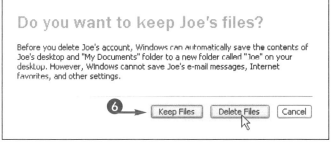

Can I remove an account simply by deleting the user's folders and files?

▼ No. When you create an account, Windows adds settings into its registry so Windows can identify users when they log on. If you delete a user's folder without deleting the account, the user's name continues to appear on the Windows logon screen.

Windows does not allow me to delete a user's account. What's wrong?

▼ You can delete a user's account only if the user is not currently logged on and if you are logged on as an administrator. If the user is logged on, switch to that account and log off. Log on using a user account that has administrator priveleges. You can then delete the account.

Can I restore a user account later?

▼ If you choose to keep the user account files, you can restore the account later. First, recreate the user account. This creates a subfolder that has the user's name on it in the Documents and Settings folder. For example, if you created an account for Jennifer, the location of the new folder is C:\Documents and Settings\Jennifer. This folder contains several subfolders, including Desktop and My Documents. You can copy the user account files that Windows saved when you deleted the account and paste them into the corresponding subfolders to restore the user account to its original condition. However, if the user had any Outlook Express e-mail or Internet Explorer favorites, those are permanently lost.

Identify and Delete Duplicate Files

If you copy and move files, you may have some duplicate files on your PC. Finding these files is difficult, but you can find utilities designed specifically to handle this task. If you have the Windows XP installation CD, you already have a utility that tracks down duplicate files for you. On this CD in the Support/Tools folder is a file named SUPTOOLS that you can run to install approximately 100 utilities for diagnosing and solving problems and improving system performance. When prompted, choose to do a complete installation rather than a typical installation. This installs a Windows program on your PC called DupFinder, which identifies duplicate files stored in different folders on your PC. This task shows how to run and use this utility.

If you do not have the Windows XP installation CD, you can download any of several similar utilities for identifying duplicate files. Visit Download.com at www.download.com or another shareware site, download one of the utilities, and install it on your PC.

Before deleting what appear to be duplicate files, examine the files carefully to ensure that their names, dates, and sizes are exactly the same. If you are unsure whether two files are exact duplicates, leave both files intact.

Identify and Delete Duplicate Files

1. Launch My Computer.
2. Navigate to the Program Files\Support Tools folder.
3. Double-click the dupfinder icon.

The DupFinder window appears.

4. Click here and type **?:** where *?* is the letter of the drive you want to search.
5. Ensure the Include subfolders option is selected (☐ changes to ☑).
6. Click Start Search.
7. Wait until the search is complete.

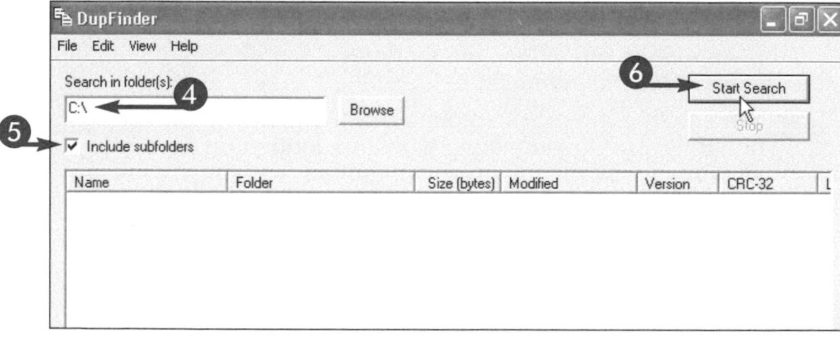

DupFinder displays a list of files that have identical names.

8 Compare the file sizes of two files that have the same name.

9 Compare the dates on which these same two files were modified.

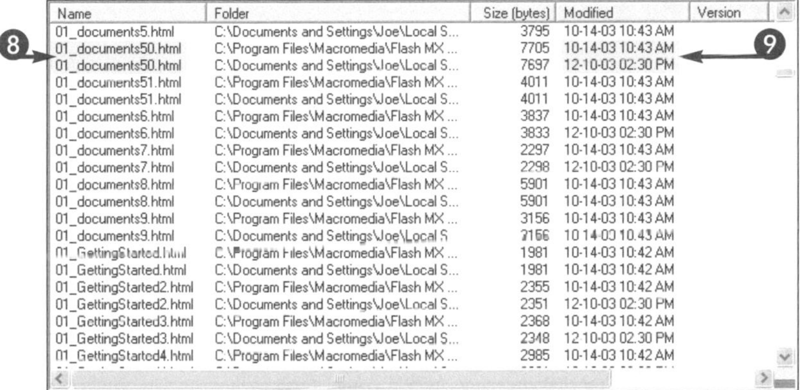

10 Right-click the undesired duplicate file.

11 Click Delete.

Windows asks if you want to delete the file.

12 Click Yes.

DupFile removes the file from the disk.

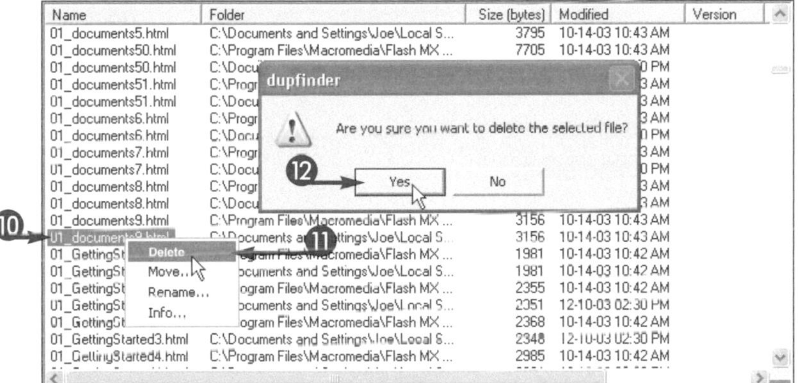

Is DupFinder available for other versions of Windows?

- DupFinder is included with Windows XP, the Windows 98 Resource Kit, and the Windows 2000 Server Resource Kit. If you have a different version of Windows, download and try Space Hound from www.fineware.com. Funduc software at www.funduc.com and CellarStone India at www.cellarstoneindia.com also offer a shareware version of their duplicate file finders.

Can DupFinder hide system files, so I do not accidentally delete them?

- Yes. Click View and then Options. The Options dialog box appears. Under Include in search, click Read-only files (☑ changes to ☐) and click Hidden files (☑ changes to ☐). With these two options unselected, the search does not display system files or hidden files, making it a little safer to delete duplicate files.

Can duplicate files cause problems other than cluttering my hard drive?

- Occasionally, a duplicate file can interfere with the operation of a program. If several copies of a device driver are installed, for example, Windows may have trouble identifying which driver to run, which may lead to system instability and possibly even cause your computer to crash. DupFinder and other similar utilities can help you locate and delete the extraneous copies.

Delete Unused Fonts

Windows and many of the applications you install on your PC include fonts to display and print text in various formats. You can save a great deal of disk space by removing the fonts that you never use. Of course, you must be careful not to delete system fonts that Windows and the applications use to display the desktop, title bars, and other objects that comprise the Interface. However, you can usually identify some of the more obvious fonts as fonts you have never seen or used, and safely remove them.

In Windows XP, you can open the Fonts folder, which stores most of the fonts installed on your PC. You can choose to list fonts by similarity, so you can have a clear idea of which fonts are completely different and which ones are nearly identical. If you have fonts installed that are very similar, you can often delete one of the fonts without limiting your font options too much.

When viewing a list of fonts by name, you may have trouble picturing a font's appearance. Fortunately, you can double-click the name of a font to preview it before deleting it.

Delete Unused Fonts

1. Click Start.
2. Click Control Panel.

   The Control Panel appears.
3. Click Appearance and Themes.

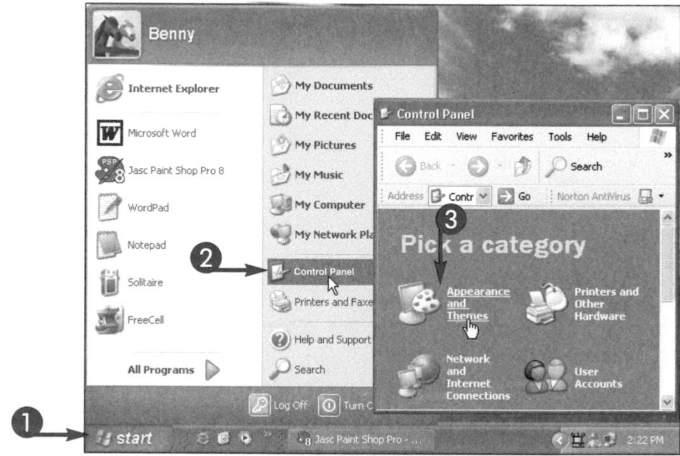

The Appearance and Themes window appears.

4. Under See Also, click Fonts.

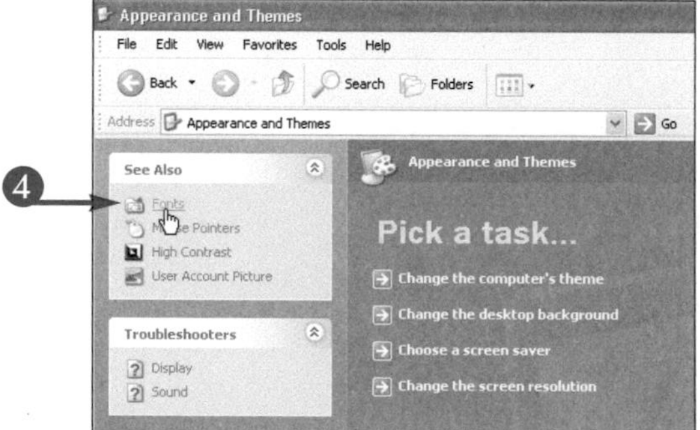

The Fonts window appears.

5 Double-click a Font's name.

- A window appears, displaying sample text in the selected font.

6 Right-click a font you do not want.

7 Click Delete.

The Windows Fonts Folder dialog box appears, prompting you to confirm.

8 Click Yes.

Windows deletes the font file.

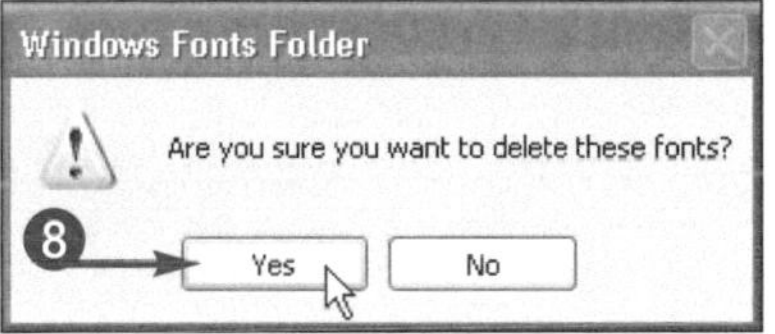

Are there any fonts that I should not delete?

▼ Yes. Do not delete any of the Arial fonts, Courier, MS or Microsoft Sans Serif or Serif, Roman, Script, Small Fonts, Symbol, Times New Roman, or Wingdings. Keep any font that has a red A icon and any font that starts with the letters MS. Several applications also have fonts that they require to display properly.

Can I delete fonts in other versions of Windows?

▼ Yes. Windows 98, Windows NT, and Windows 2000 have a font manager that you can use to preview and delete fonts. To run the font manager, click Start, Settings, and then Control Panel. Next, double-click the Fonts icon. You can select a font by clicking it, and select additional fonts by pressing the Ctrl key while clicking them. Click File and then Delete to remove the selected fonts.

I deleted a font, and now one of my programs does not display properly. Can I restore the font?

▼ Yes. You can restore the font from the Recycle Bin. Double-click the Recycle Bin icon on the Windows desktop and then right-click the font and click Restore. If you delete a Windows font that you cannot restore, you can repair your Windows installation, as explained in Chapter 31, to restore the font from the Windows installation CD.

Empty the Recycle Bin

As you delete files, you do not actually clear much space from your PC's hard drive because Windows only moves the files to the Recycle Bin. To reclaim the storage space, you can empty the Recycle Bin.

Emptying the Recycle Bin permanently deletes the files, so be careful. You may want to carefully examine the files in the Recycle Bin before emptying it to determine if it contains any files you might need later. If you see a file that you are not sure you want to delete, you can restore the file before you empty the Recycle Bin.

Another option is to leave the Recycle Bin alone for a week or two and then if you find that you do not miss any of the files, empty the Recycle Bin. Emptying it right after you have deleted a number of files is a little risky.

Keep in mind that the Recycle Bin uses a fixed amount of hard drive space, so emptying the Recycle Bin is optional. If the Recycle Bin needs more space, it automatically purges files to make room for the newly deleted ones.

Empty the Recycle Bin

1. Double-click the Recycle Bin.

   The Recycle Bin appears, displaying its contents.

2. Examine the contents to ensure that you do not permanently delete an item you need.

Note: *You can restore an item by right-clicking it and clicking Restore.*

3. Click the Empty the Recycle Bin link.

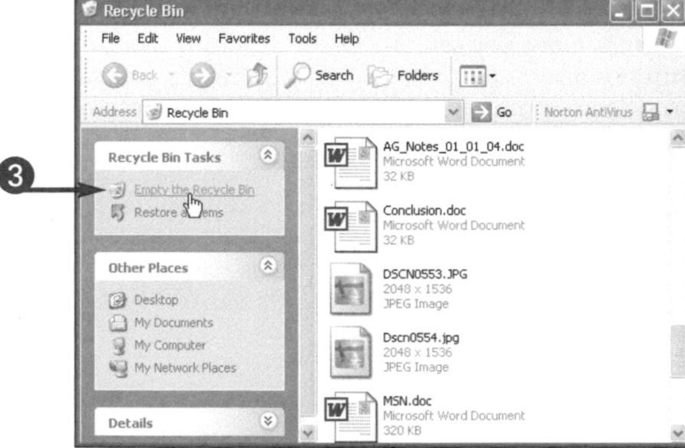

The Confirm Multiple File Delete dialog box appears.

4 If you are certain that you want to permanently delete the contents of the Recycle Bin, click Yes.

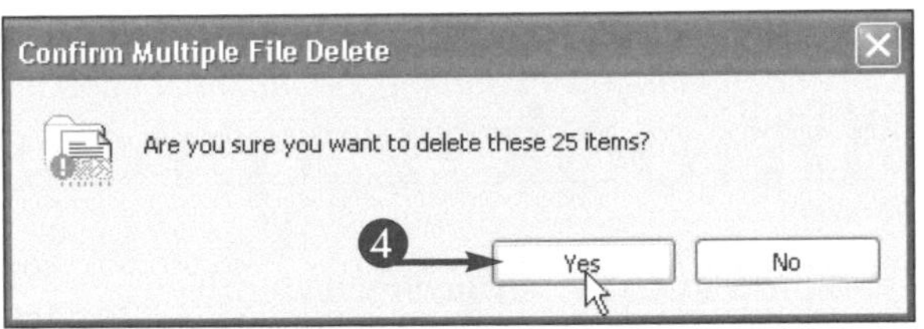

Windows empties the Recycle Bin.

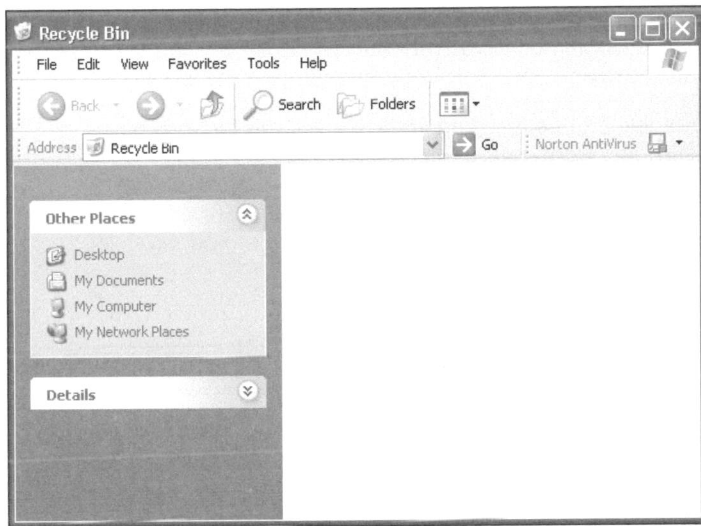

Can I prevent the Confirm Multiple File Delete dialog box from appearing every time I delete a file?

- Yes. Right-click the Recycle Bin icon and click Properties. Click the Display deleted confirmation dialog option (☑ changes to ☐). Click OK. Now, whenever you delete an item, Windows instantly moves it to the Recycle Bin. If you press the Shift key while deleting an item, Windows permanently deletes the file without prompting for confirmation.

Can I disable the Recycle Bin?

- Yes. You can disable the Recycle Bin so that items are permanently deleted whenever you click Delete. Right-click the Recycle Bin icon, click Properties, click the Do not move files to the Recycle Bin option (☐ changes to ☑), and click OK. A safer option is to configure the Recycle Bin to use less disk space. Display the Properties dialog box and click and drag the Maximum size of Recycle Bin slider to the left. Click OK.

Once a file is permanently deleted, can I be sure that no one else can view its contents?

- No. When you empty the Recycle Bin, the contents of the deleted files remain intact until your PC writes another file on the same area of the disk. If you want to make sure that nobody can access the file, you can use a shredder utility to destroy the file. You can find several freeware and shareware file shredders at www.download.com.

Archive E-mail Messages in Outlook Express

In most e-mail programs, you can archive old e-mail messages by copying them to a CD, DVD, or other removable storage medium. You can then delete messages from your e-mail program without worrying about destroying your only copy of an important message.

In Outlook Express, you can archive messages by copying the DBX files from your e-mail folders to a removable storage medium, such as a recordable CD. Each DBX file contains all of the messages stored in a folder. For example, Sent Items.dbx contains copies of all messages you have sent, including file attachments.

You can save time archiving your e-mail messages by compressing your Inbox and other folders first, as explained in the section "Compact Folders." This also reduces the size of the DBX files, so they take up less space. However, this is an optional step. After you archive your messages and delete the messages you no longer want, you can compress the folders to reclaim storage space on your PC's hard drive.

The steps in this section show how to archive e-mail messages in Outlook Express. If you use a different e-mail program, check its help system for instructions.

Archive E-mail Messages in Outlook Express

1. Launch Outlook Express.
2. Click Tools.
3. Click Options.

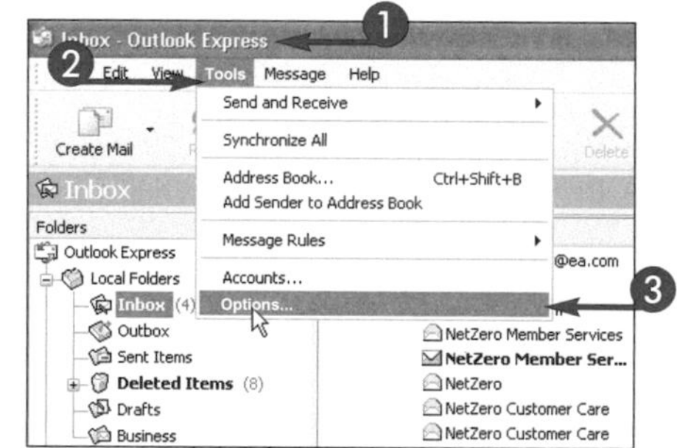

The Options dialog box appears.

4. Click the Maintenance tab.
5. Click Store Folder.

   The Store Location dialog box appears.

6. Click and drag over the pathname to highlight it.
7. Press Ctrl+C.

   Windows copies the mailbox folder path.

8. Exit Outlook Express.

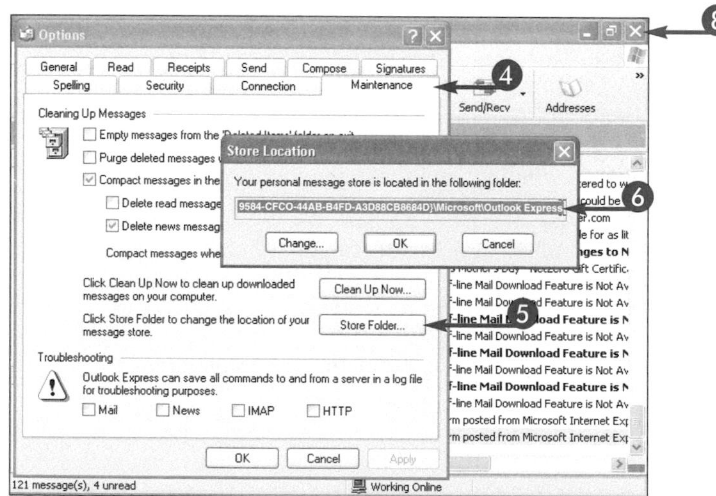

9. Open the My Computer window.
10. Click and drag over the entry in the Address field.
11. Press Ctrl+V.

    The path that you copied in step 7 is inserted.
12. Press Enter.
13. Click in the file list pane.
14. Press Ctrl+A.
    - All mailbox files are selected and highlighted.

Note: *You can Ctrl+click a file to deselect it.*

15. Right-click a folder that contains messages you want to archive.
16. Click Send To.
17. Click the drive that contains the disc on which you want the archives stored.
18. Follow the on-screen instructions to complete the process.

    Windows copies the archives to the selected disc.

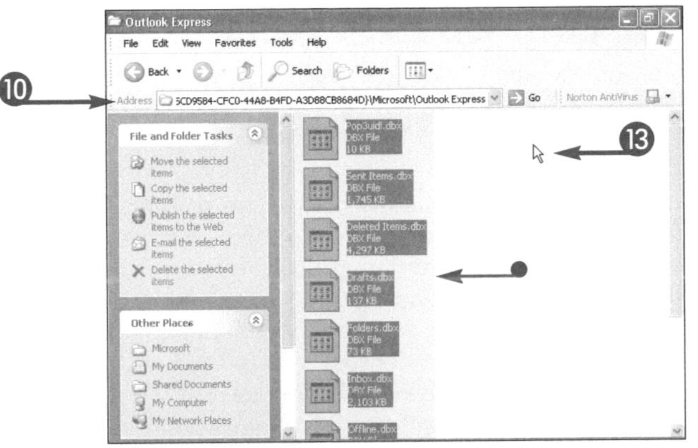

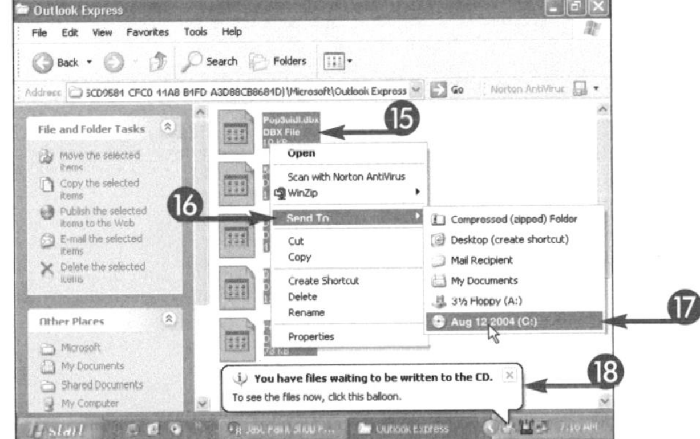

Can I use this same technique to move my e-mail messages to another PC?

▼ Yes. You can transfer your Outlook Express e-mail folders to another PC by copying the DBX files from the archive disk to the new PC's hard drive. Use the same steps shown here to locate the folder in which Outlook Express stores the DBX files on the new PC and copy the DBX files to that folder. If the new PC already has e-mail messages on it, do not overwrite the existing DBX files with the DBX files from the other PC. Import the messages instead, as explained in the next tip.

Can I import messages from a DBX file into an existing e-mail message folder that contains messages?

▼ Yes. First, create a new folder and copy the DBX files you archived to the new folder. Click File, Import, and then Messages. Follow the on-screen instructions to import the messages. You must specify the e-mail program and version number from which to import the messages and then navigate to the new folder, which contains the archive files. If you are importing messages from an Outlook Express archive, when prompted to import from an identity or store folder, select the option to import from the store folder and then follow the instructions to select the folder into which you copied the DBX files.

Delete Copies of Sent Messages

Unless you need copies of messages you sent for legal purposes or to keep a record of your replies, you can clear them from your PC to reclaim additional storage space. When you send an e-mail message, your e-mail program may save a copy of it in a Sent Items folder or a folder of a similar name. Most users rarely look inside this folder, because they are more interested in incoming messages — messages that they have received. Because of this, many users are unaware that their e-mail programs are cluttered with copies of old sent messages.

If you have copies of sent messages that are more than a month old and you never refer back to these messages, this is a good sign that you have sent messages that you can safely delete. If you archived these messages, as discussed in the section "Archive E-mail Messages in Outlook Express," you have copies of the messages already and can safely delete all of the copies on your PC's hard drive. This not only helps you reclaim storage space, but it makes your e-mail program run more efficiently.

If you use your e-mail to keep a record of invoices, bill payments, or other important business correspondence, you may want to archive these messages or print them before deleting them.

Delete Copies of Sent Messages

1. Launch your e-mail program.
2. Navigate to the folder that contains copies of sent messages.
3. Sort the messages by date.
   - In Outlook Express, you can click the Sent column heading to sort messages by date.

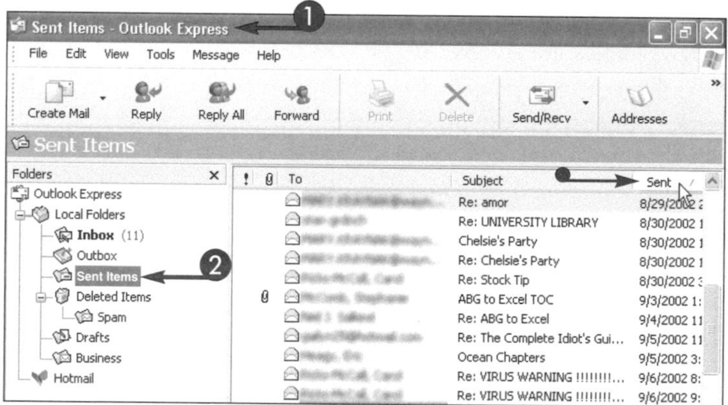

4. Click the oldest message.
5. Scroll down the message list.
6. Press the Shift key while clicking the most recent message you want to delete.

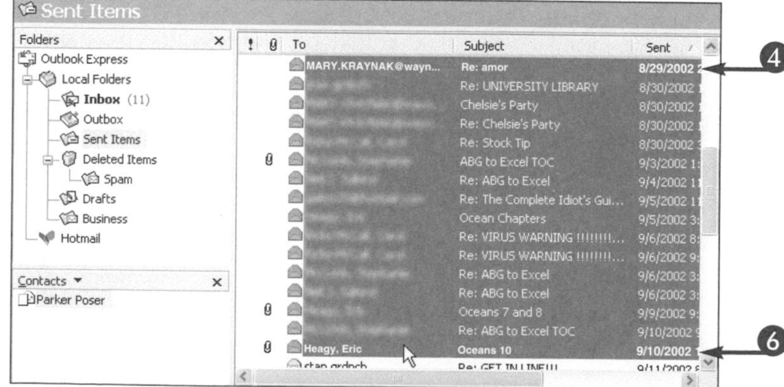

7 Right-click one of the selected messages.

8 Click Delete.

Note: *If prompted to confirm the deletion, click the button to confirm.*

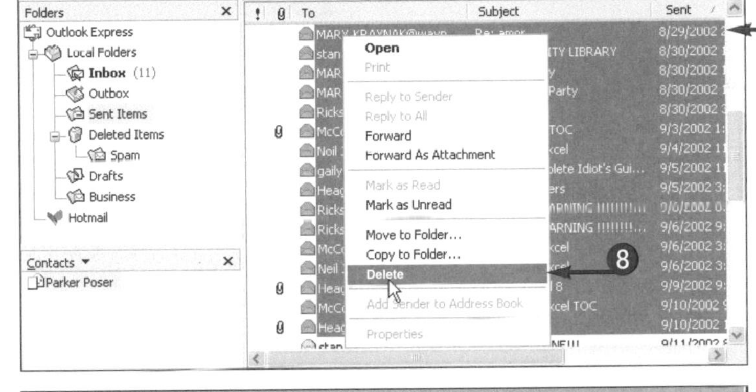

Your e-mail program removes the items.

- Outlook Express moves the items to the Deleted Items folder.

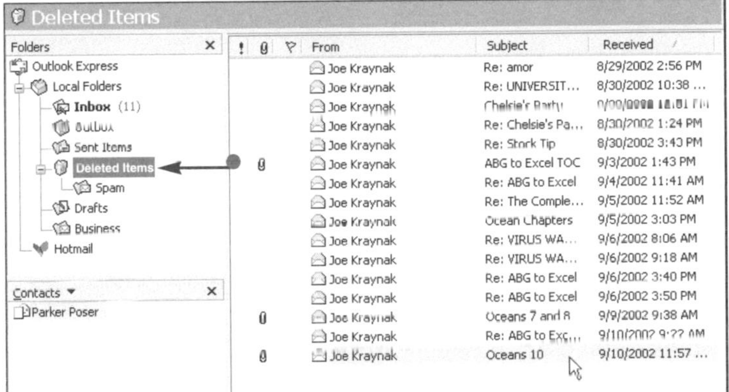

When I delete copies of sent messages, do I immediately reclaim that disk space?

▼ Not necessarily. Most e-mail programs move deleted items to a separate folder that acts as a recycle bin for the messages. To reclaim the space, you must empty the folder that contains the deleted items and then compress the Sent Items and Deleted Items folders. See the sections "Empty the Deleted Items Folder" and "Compact Folders" for more information.

Can I select all of my Sent Items with a single command?

▼ Yes. First, click in the pane that displays the list of sent items. Click Edit, and then Select All. In some e-mail programs, you must click Edit, Select, and then All. An alternative method that works in almost all e-mail programs is to click in the pane that displays the list of sent items and press Ctrl+A. You can also click the first item in the list and then press the Shift key while clicking the last item.

Can I prevent my e-mail program from saving copies of messages I send?

▼ Usually. In Outlook Express, click Tools, Options, and then the Sent tab. Click the Save copy of sent messages in the Sent Items folder option (☑ changes to ☐). In Netscape Mail, you can find the option by clicking Edit, Mail & Newsgroup Account Settings, and then Copies & Folders.

Delete Messages You Received

You can delete a message right after you read it by clicking the message and then clicking Delete. However, most people let old messages pile up in their inbox until some heavy-duty cleanup is required. If you archived the messages in your inbox, you can delete all of the messages knowing that you have a backup copy in case you need to refer to a message later. If you did not archive your inbox, you may want to be a little more selective in which messages you keep and which ones you delete.

When deleting messages you receive, a major concern is that you will delete the only record you have of a correspondent's e-mail address. When you reply to a message you receive, some e-mail programs add the recipient's e-mail address to your address book. If your e-mail program has this option and you use it, your address book probably has all of the e-mail addresses you need. However, you should always make sure the person's address is in your address book before deleting the message. You can then delete the message and still be able to contact the person later.

Delete Messages You Received

Save a Sender's Address

1. Launch your e-mail program.
2. Double-click a message from a sender whose e-mail address you want to store in your address book.

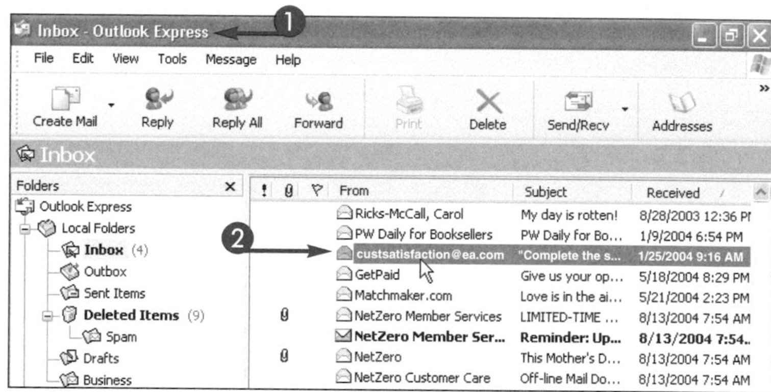

The Message appears in its own window.

3. Right-click the sender's name or address.
4. Click Add to Address Book.

Your e-mail program saves the person's e-mail address in your address book.

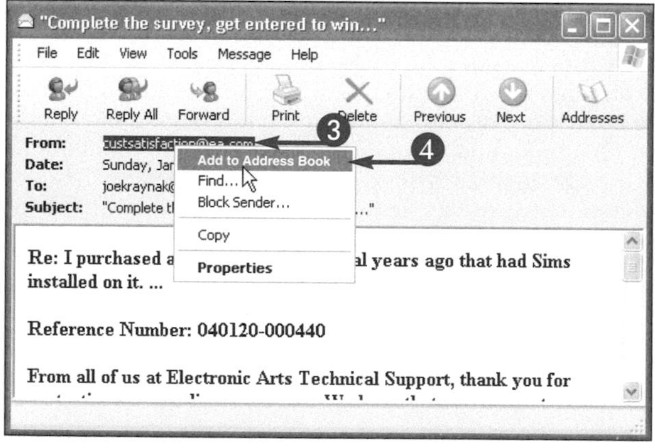

Delete Received Messages

1. Launch your e-mail program.
2. Click Inbox.
3. Click a message you want to delete.
   - You can press the Ctrl key while clicking additional messages to select more than one.

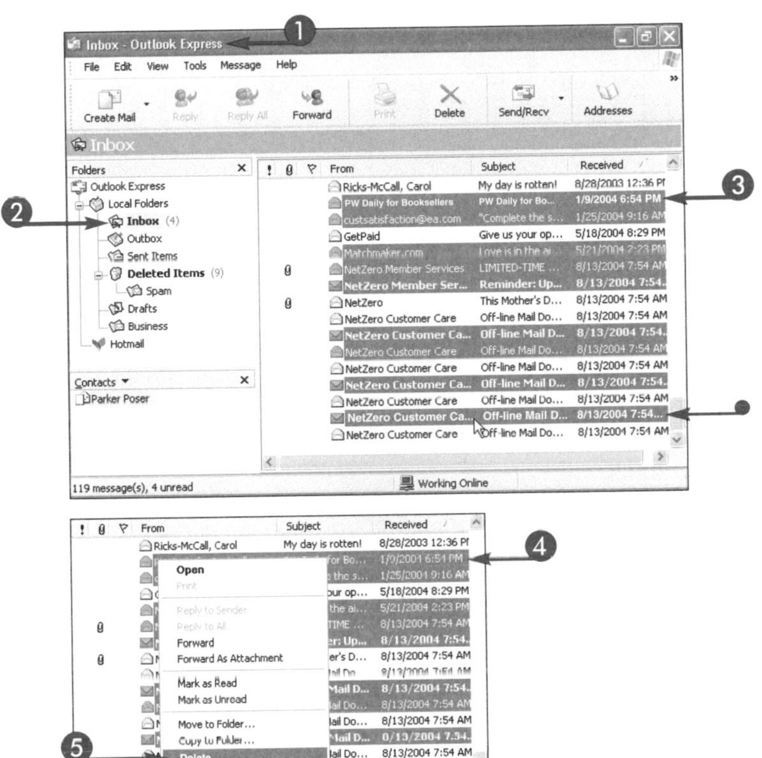

4. Right-click one of the selected messages.
5. Click Delete.

Note: *If prompted to confirm the deletion, click the button to confirm.*

Your e-mail program moves the selected messages to the Deleted Items folder.

Can I back up my address book to a CD?

▼ Many e-mail programs enable you to export your address book, so you can create a backup copy of it or transfer it to another PC. In Outlook Express, click File, Export, and then Address Book, and follow the on-screen instructions to save the exported address book as a separate file. In Netscape Mail, click Window, and then Address Book to display the Address book. Next, click Tools, and then Export to export it as a separate file. If you use a different e-mail program, refer to its help system for information on backing up or saving the Address Book.

I use my e-mail program for reading newsgroup messages, too. Can I delete those messages?

▼ Most newsgroup readers access messages from an NNTP (Network News Transfer Protocol) server, which typically synchronizes with the newsreader to expire old messages automatically, deleting newsgroup messages after a specified number of days. You can check your newsgroup reader's maintenance settings. In Outlook Express, click Tools, and then click Options. Next, click the Read tab and the Maintenance tab to explore the available options. In Netscape Mail, click Edit, Mail & Newsgroups Accounts Settings, click the triangle next to your newsgroup account, and then Offline & Disk Space. If you use a different newsgroup reader, refer to its help system for instructions.

Automatically Delete Undesirable Incoming Messages

If you receive unsolicited e-mail messages, which are commonly referred to as spam, you can have your e-mail program automatically delete incoming messages sent from a specific e-mail address. You may be tempted to reply to the sender to request that no additional e-mails be sent to your address, but, as discussed in Chapter 16, this often confirms the validity of your e-mail address and encourages the sender to send you even more spam. By having your e-mail program automatically delete unsolicited messages, you can prevent spam from building up in your inbox.

This may not reduce the amount of spam that your e-mail server receives, but it does reduce the amount of spam that you must deal with personally. To discourage advertisers from spamming you, you can try several techniques described in Chapter 16.

Almost all e-mail programs feature *message filters* that you can create and use to manage incoming messages automatically. For example, you can have all e-mail messages you receive from a friend placed in a separate folder. Message filters typically include an option to delete messages sent from a specific address or messages that have one or more key words in their description.

Automatically Delete Undesirable Incoming Messages

1. Launch your e-mail program.

   This example uses Outlook Express.

2. Click the option for displaying message rules for incoming mail.

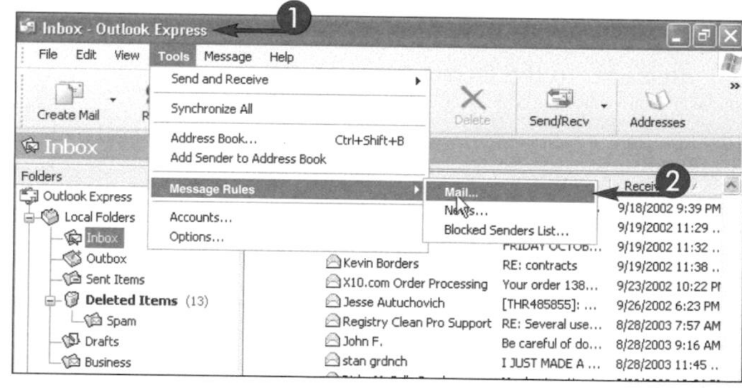

Your e-mail program displays a dialog box for creating and managing message rules.

3. Click the option for creating a new message rule.

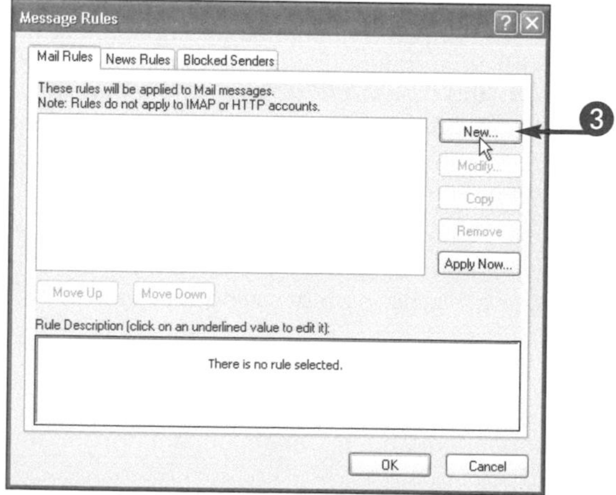

A new rule dialog box appears.

4 Click the criteria the message must meet to have the e-mail program perform a specific action to it.

5 Click the option for clarifying the criteria.

6 Type the specific data you want the e-mail program to look for in incoming messages.

7 Click the option to add the detail.

8 Click OK.

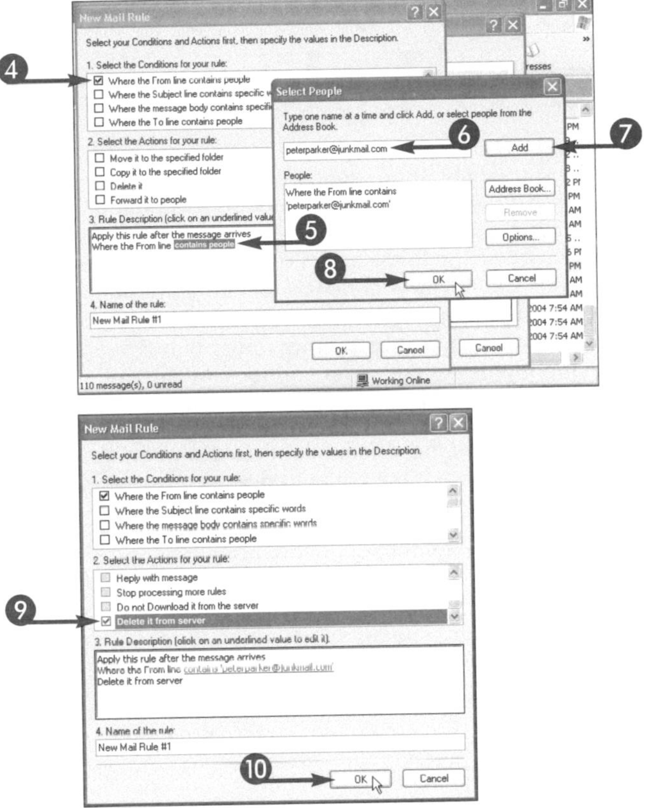

9 Click the action that you want the e-mail program to perform on messages that meet the specified criteria.

In this example, the message is removed from the mail server.

10 Click OK.

The new rule is added to the list of rules and you can click OK to close the message filters dialog box.

Can I use the Blocked Senders List in Outlook Express to automatically delete messages?

▼ Yes. In Outlook Express, you can add an e-mail address to the Blocked Senders List to have all messages from that address automatically moved to the Deleted Items folder on receipt. However, your PC must then spend time downloading those messages, and the messages remain in your Deleted Items folder until you empty it. If you are sure that you do not want to receive messages from a specific address, it is best to have them deleted from the server, so you do not have to download them. However, not all e-mail programs offer this option.

Do I need to type the entire e-mail address?

▼ No, you can type a portion of the e-mail address to block messages from a range of e-mail addresses. For example, if you receive unwanted messages from mulitple e-mail addresses that use the same domain, you can type the domain by itself. The domain is everything after the @ sign; for example, washington.gov. However, many spammers use tricks to hide their e-mail addresses or provide fake domains to prevent users from filtering out their messages. Your ISP may provide more powerful tools for blocking spam, or you can install a spam blocking utility. See Chapter 16 for more information.

Empty the Deleted Items Folder

As you delete items, your e-mail program may move them to a deleted items or trash folder rather than immediately removing them from the disk. The name of the folder varies depending on the e-mail program you use. If you accidentally delete a message, you can restore it by dragging it from the deleted items folder into the inbox folder or into another folder that is available. To permanently delete messages and reclaim the disk space that they take up, you can empty the deleted items folder.

Many users overlook the deleted items folder when they clean their hard drives. Disk Cleanup does not purge these files from the drive, and most e-mail programs do not inform you that the messages are being moved to a different folder rather than being deleted. Over time, the deleted items folder can become packed with old messages, including any file attachments they contain.

After deleting messages from the inbox and the sent items folder, you may want to wait a couple days to ensure that you no longer want the messages. Then, you can empty the deleted items folder to completely remove these messages from your PC.

Empty the Deleted Items Folder

1. Launch your e-mail program.
2. Click the icon for the folder that contains the deleted messages.

   The list of deleted messages appears.
3. Examine the list of messages to ensure that you do not need any of the messages in the list.
   - You can click and drag a message to the inbox, or another mailbox folder, to keep it.

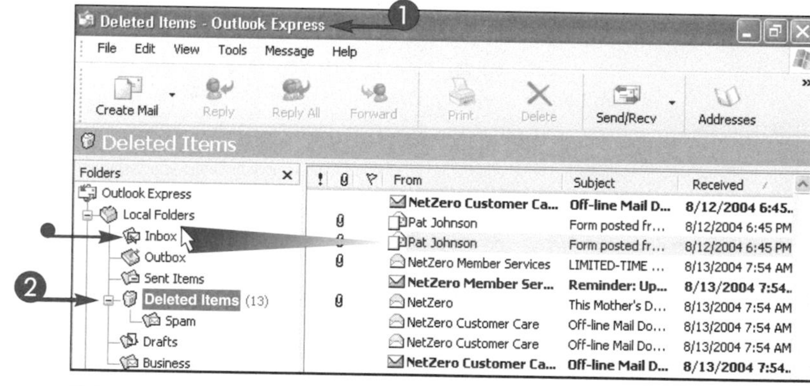

4. Right-click the icon for the folder that contains the deleted messages.
5. Click the command to empty the folder.

   In Outlook Express, you can click Edit and then click Empty 'Deleted Items' Folder. In Netscape Mail, you can click File and then Empty Trash.

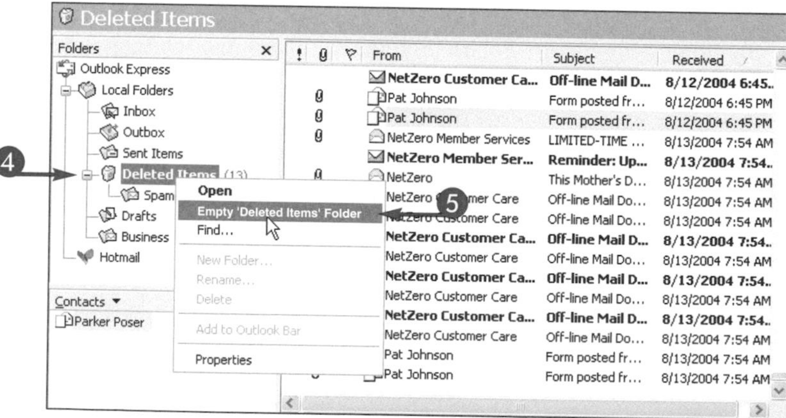

Your e-mail program may display a dialog box prompting you to confirm the deletion.

6 Click Yes.

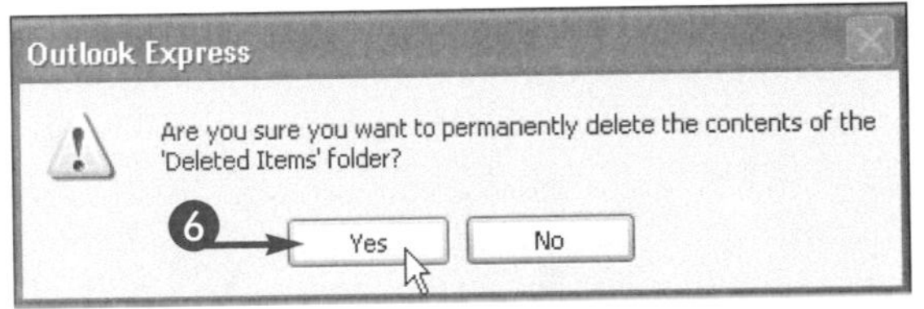

Your e-mail program empties the items from the folder and removes them from your PC.

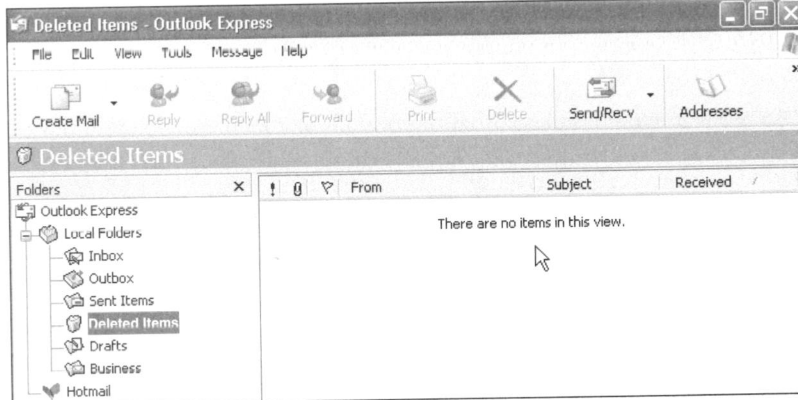

PART II

Can I prevent my e-mail program from storing messages I delete?

▼ Maybe. If you use Outlook Express, you can bypass the Deleted Items folder by pressing the Shift key while you click Delete. In Netscape Mail, you must use the key combination Shift+Del to delete the messages rather than moving them to the Trash folder. Other e-mail programs may have similar features; refer to your e-mail program's help system for more information. Bypassing the Deleted Items or Trash folder is especially useful if you receive a great deal of spam. You can permanently delete the unsolicited messages, without opening them, to remove them from your PC.

Can I automate the process of emptying the Deleted Items or Trash folder?

▼ Yes. You can have Outlook Express automatically empty the Deleted Items folder whenever you exit. Click Tools, Options, the Maintenance tab, and then the Empty messages from the 'Deleted Items' folder on exit option (☐ changes to ☑). Click OK. In Netscape Mail, click Edit, Mail & Newsgroups Accounts Settings, click the triangle next to your mail account, and then Server Settings. Click Empty Trash on Exit (☐ changes to ☑) and click OK. Other e-mail programs may have similar features. Be careful not to exit your e-mail program unless you are sure you do not need any items you deleted in the current session.

Compact Folders

When you delete messages, the message header and contents of each message are removed from the folder, but blank space remains where the message header was stored. You can compact the folders to remove any unused space. Compacting decreases the size of each folder and enhances the overall performance of your e-mail program. Each message folder is actually a separate file in which the e-mail program stores messages. Over time, this file can become large and more prone to becoming corrupted, so compacting it regularly is important. If your e-mail program seems slower than usual or you receive error messages when you attempt to display a message, this may be a sign that compacting is overdue.

Whenever you perform maintenance tasks in your e-mail program to remove messages, you should follow up by emptying the deleted items folder and then compacting all folders. Simply deleting messages does not completely free up the storage space they were using.

If you have deleted many messages without compacting your folders, the compacting operation can take several minutes to complete. You can compact each folder separately or compact them all at one time.

Compact Folders

Compact a Single Folder

1. Launch your e-mail program.
2. Click the message folder that you want to compact.

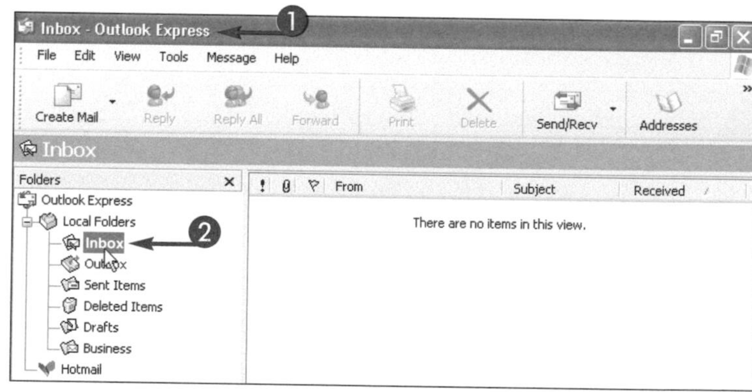

3. Click the command to compact this folder.

   In Outlook Express, click File, Folder, and then Compact; in Netscape Mail, right-click the folder and click Compact This Folder.

   Your e-mail program compacts the selected folder.

Note: *A dialog box may appear, displaying the progress of the compaction, and then close when the operation is complete.*

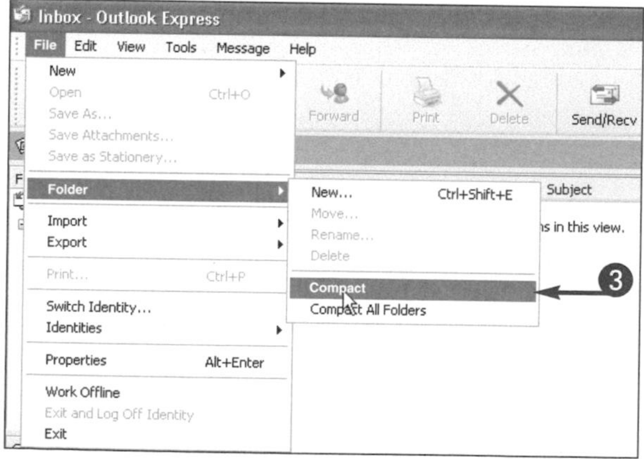

Compact All Folders

1. Launch your e-mail program.
2. Click File.
3. Click the command to compact the folders.

   In Outlook Express, click File, Folder, and then Compact All Folders; in Netscape Mail, click File, and then Compact Folders.

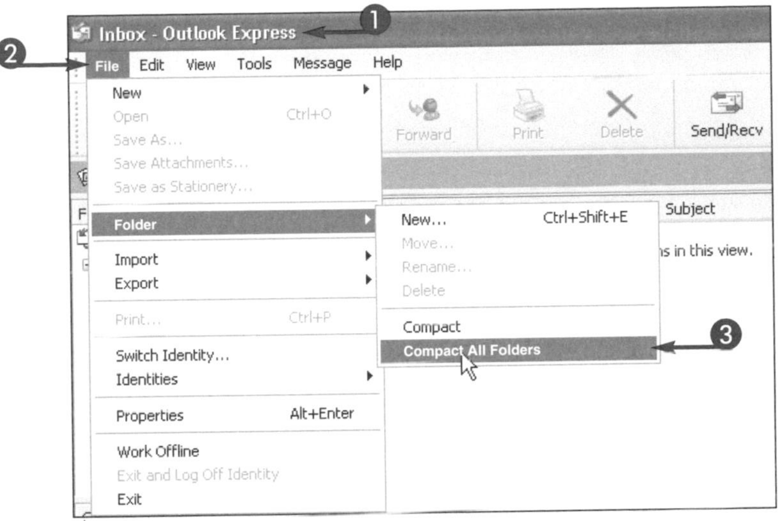

Your e-mail program compacts all message folders.

A dialog box may appear, displaying the progress of the compaction, and then close when the operation is complete.

Does compacting a folder compress the message content?

▼ No. It only removes space between the messages, which makes the file that stores the messages smaller. Compacting can help you reclaim a great deal of wasted space, especially if you have deleted many messages and have not compacted your folders for several weeks.

Why does my e-mail program report that I have 157 messages in a folder that contains only 20 messages?

▼ Your e-mail program may be counting message headers for messages that you have deleted. Compacting the folder may help your e-mail program determine a more accurate count. E-mail programs often display the total number of messages and total unread messages in the status bar at the bottom of the window, or in the left pane.

Can I make my e-mail program compact folders automatically?

▼ Most programs enable you to enter a preference to compact message folders automatically. In Outlook Express, click Tools, Options, the Maintenance tab, and then the Compact messages in the background option (☐ changes to ☑). You can also indicate the percentage of wasted space that initiates Outlook Express to compact a folder. In Netscape Mail, click Edit, Preferences, Offline & Disk Space, and then the "Compact folders when it will save over ___ KB" option (☐ changes to ☑). You can type a number in the blank. Enabling auto-compacting can slow down your e-mail program; if it does, then perform the same steps to disable the feature.

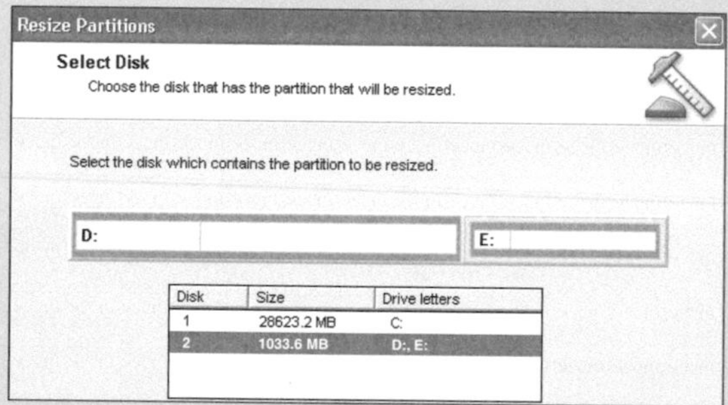

Resize Partitions
Select Disk
Choose the disk that has the partition that will be resized.
Select the disk which contains the partition to be resized.
D:
E:
Disk
Size
Drive letters
1
28623.2 MB
C:
2
1033.6 MB
D:, E:

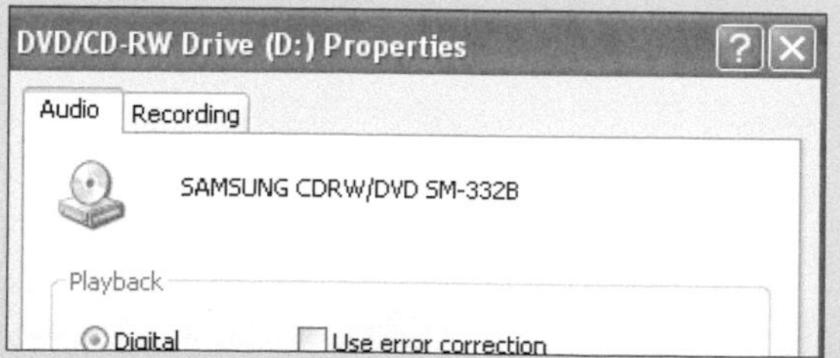

DVD/CD-RW Drive (D:) Properties
Audio
Recording
SAMSUNG CDRW/DVD SM-332B
Playback
Digital
Use error correction

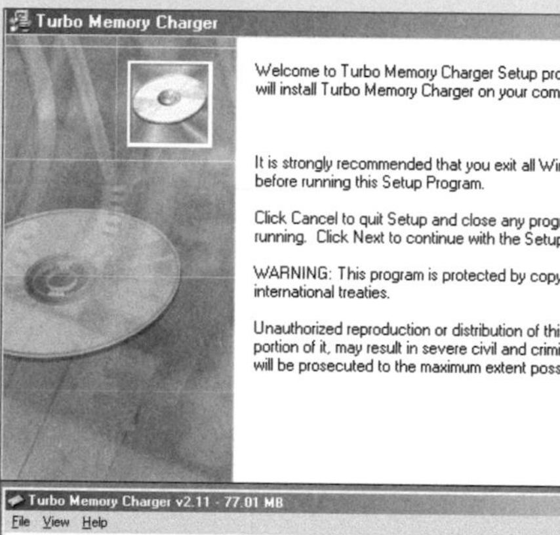

Turbo Memory Charger
Welcome to Turbo Memory Charger Setup program. This program will install Turbo Memory Charger on your computer.
It is strongly recommended that you exit all Windows programs before running this Setup Program.
Click Cancel to quit Setup and close any programs you have running. Click Next to continue with the Setup program.
WARNING: This program is protected by copyright law and international treaties.
Unauthorized reproduction or distribution of this program, or any portion of it, may result in severe civil and criminal penalties, and will be prosecuted to the maximum extent possible under law.

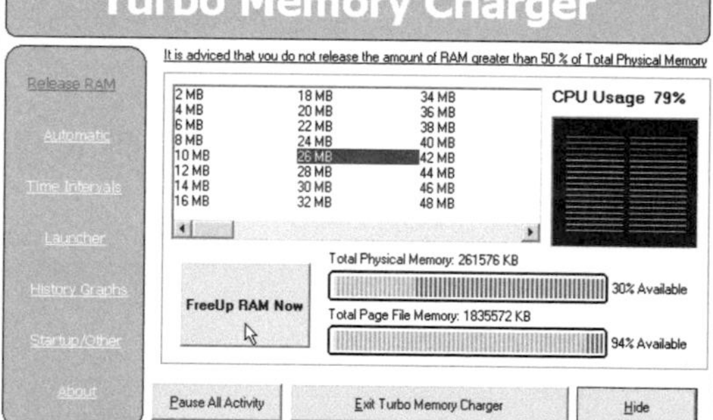

Turbo Memory Charger v2.11 - 77.01 MB
Turbo Memory Charger
It is adviced that you do not release the amount of RAM greater than 50 % of Total Physical Memory
CPU Usage 79%
FreeUp RAM Now
Total Physical Memory: 261576 KB
30% Available
Total Page File Memory: 1835572 KB
94% Available
Pause All Activity
Exit Turbo Memory Charger
Hide

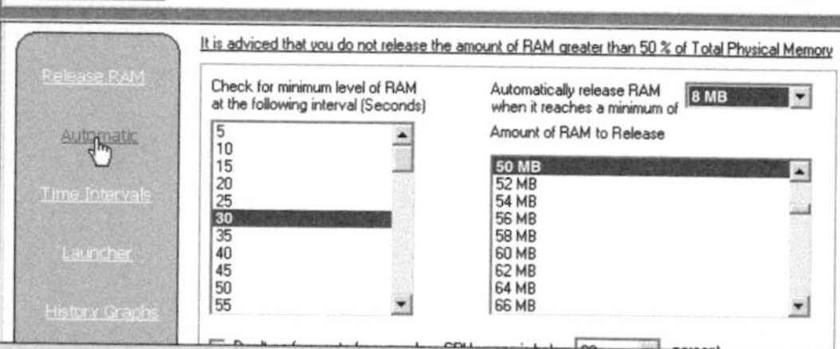

It is adviced that you do not release the amount of RAM greater than 50 % of Total Physical Memory
Check for minimum level of RAM at the following interval (Seconds)
Automatically release RAM when it reaches a minimum of
8 MB
Amount of RAM to Release

PART III
OPTIMIZING HARD DRIVE PERFORMANCE AND MEMORY

Identify Your Hard Drive's File System

You can identify your PC's file system to determine if the drive is formatted for optimal performance and security. Windows XP supports three file systems: FAT (File Allocation Table, which is rarely used), FAT32 (an improved version of FAT), and NTFS (NT File System, which was initially developed for Windows NT). The file system that a drive uses determines how data is mapped out on the disk so your computer can identify the various storage areas on the disk.

NTFS offers several advantages over FAT and FAT32. It improves the reliability of the drive, stores data more efficiently, enables Windows XP to manage larger drives and files, enables you to encrypt files and folders to keep their contents private, and provides you with the option of compressing data on the drive to conserve storage space.

The main disadvantage of NTFS is that older operating systems, including Windows 98, Windows Me, and DOS cannot access files stored on an NTFS drive. If you want to configure your PC to enable it to run more than one operating system, including one of the older operating systems, your drive should use the FAT32 file system. Otherwise, use NTFS. Before you make any changes, however, you should identify the file system that your PC uses.

Identify Your Hard Drive's File System

1. Click Start.
2. Click My Computer.

My Computer appears, displaying icons for your PC's disk drives.

3. Right-click the icon for the hard drive whose file system you want to check.
4. Click Properties.

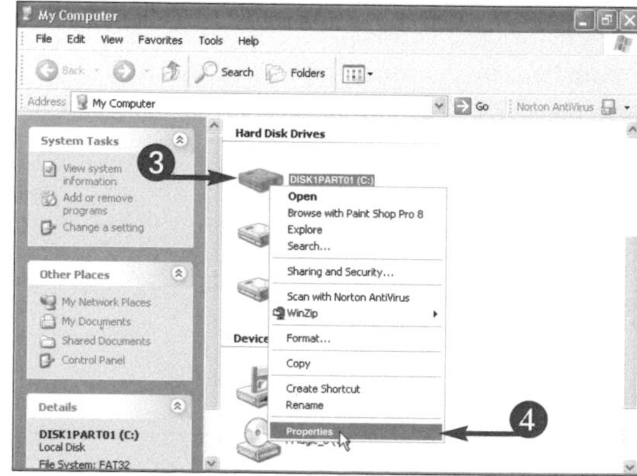

The Properties dialog box appears.

5 Note the file system currently in use.

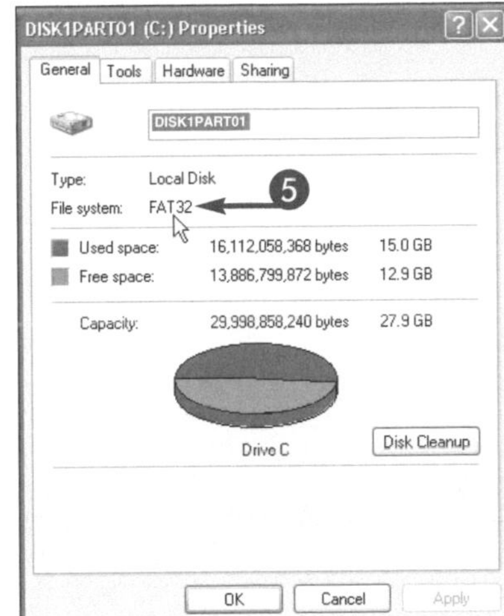

6 Click OK.

The Properties dialog box closes.

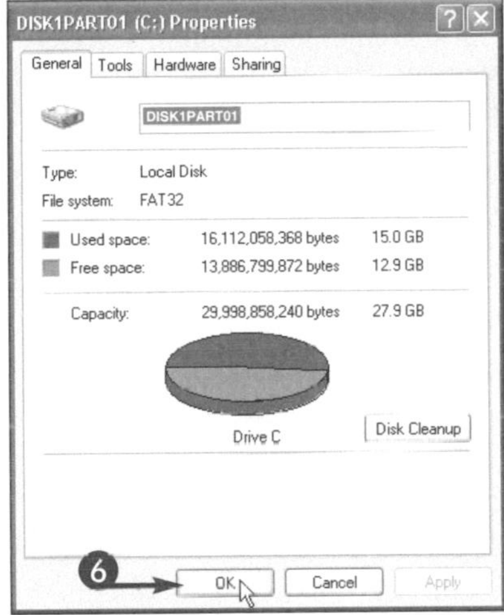

My PC has more than one drive. Do all of the drives require the same file system?

▼ No. Each drive can use a different file system. However, older operating systems, including Windows Me and DOS, cannot access any files stored on an NTFS drive. Windows XP, Windows 2000, and Windows NT can access files stored on FAT, FAT32, or NTFS drives.

Does Microsoft recommend using NTFS?

▼ Microsoft strongly recommends NTFS over FAT or FAT32, unless you plan on configuring your PC to run an older operating system that needs to access the files on the drive. Because FAT32 is limited to hard drives of 32GB or smaller, most new computers with large hard drives use the NTFS format.

My drive uses NTFS. Can I change it to FAT32 to determine which one works better?

▼ Windows provides no way to convert a hard drive from NTFS back to FAT32. You can purchase a third-party program, such as Partition Magic, and use it to attempt the conversion, but this is risky. Partition Magic may not be able to complete the task and it may even destroy data on your hard drive. If your drive is formatted with NTFS, then it is strongly recommended that you make no changes. If your drive uses FAT32, converting it to NTFS usually improves performance, but keep in mind that going back to FAT32 may not be an option.

Convert a Drive to NTFS

You can convert a drive from FAT32 to NTFS to make it more efficient and reliable. NTFS was developed for Windows NT to enable the operating system to manage larger disks and to support improved security features. If your PC's hard drive currently uses the FAT32 file system, you cannot use many of Windows' disk and file management utilities, such as setting file and folder permissions, encrypting files to prevent unauthorized access, or compressing drives to conserve disk space.

If you clear files that you do not need from the hard drive and you are still running low on unused disk space, you can install another hard drive or convert your existing drive to NTFS and then compress it or compress some of the folders, as explained in the next section, "Compress Contents of Disks, Files, or Folders."

Windows includes a conversion utility that can convert a drive from FAT32 to NTFS and leave existing files intact. After you convert a drive, you may not be able to convert it back to the FAT32 file system without losing your files, so make sure you want to perform the conversion before performing the steps in this section.

Convert a Drive to NTFS

1. Click Start.
2. Click All Programs.
3. Click Accessories.
4. Click Command Prompt.

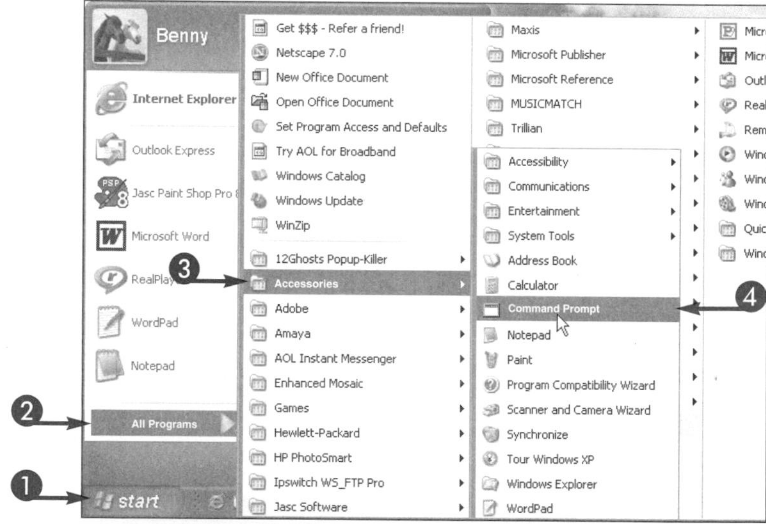

The Command Prompt window appears.

5. Type **convert *?*: /fs:ntfs** where *?* is the letter of the drive you want to convert.
6. Press Enter.

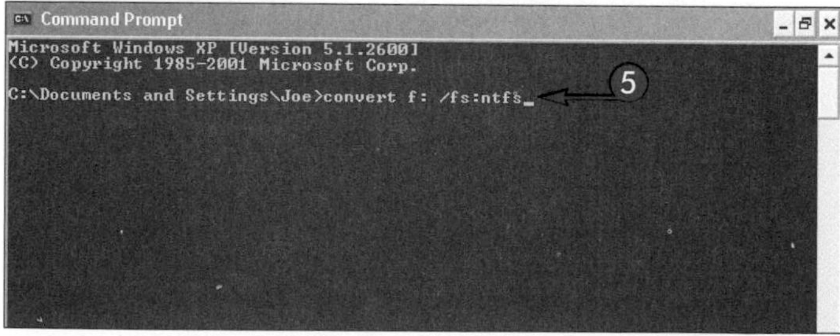

The conversion utility prompts you to type the volume's current name.

Note: *You can find the volume's name by right-clicking the drive's icon in My Computer and clicking Properties.*

7. Type the volume's current name.
8. Press Enter.

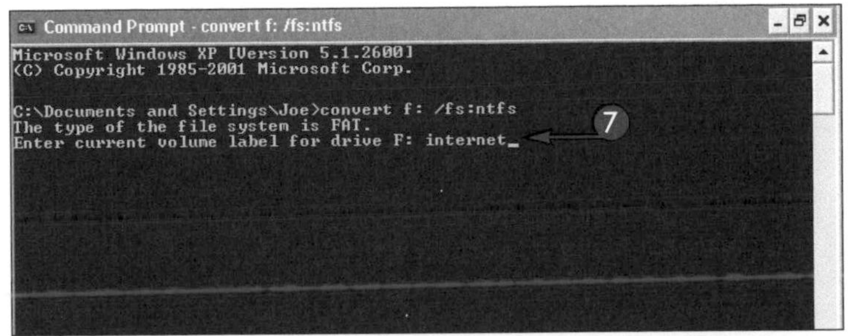

The conversion utility displays the progress of the operation.

9. Wait until a message appears, indicating that the conversion is complete.

The specified drive is now formatted using NTFS.

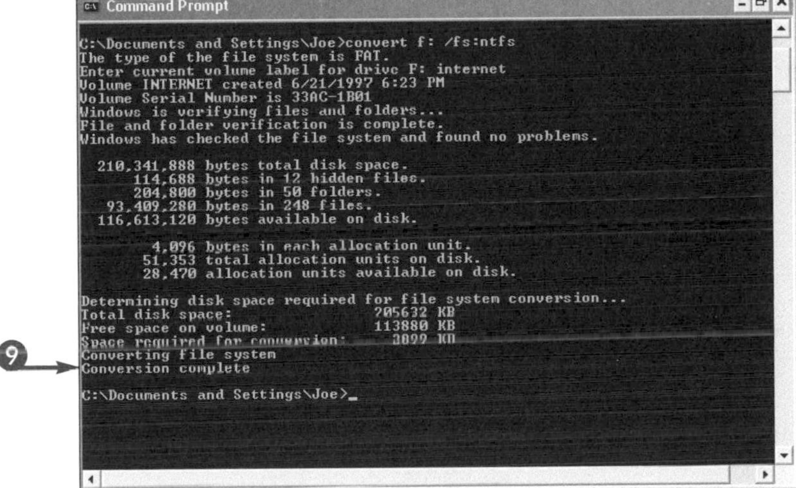

Are any other switches or options available for the convert command?

▼ Yes. To display a list of available options for the convert command, at the command prompt, type **convert /?**, and press Enter. The question mark instructs the convert utility to display a help screen. You can use the /v switch to run the conversion utility in verbose mode, which displays all messages during the conversion operation rather than just the most important messages. The /nosecurity switch enables anyone to access the converted files and the directory security settings for the drive. The /x switch dismounts the drive, if necessary, before converting it. The /cvtarea:filename switch is for advanced users only; it can help create a less fragmented file system, but the process is very involved.

A message appears indicating that the conversion utility cannot lock the drive. What happened? And what should I do?

▼ To convert a drive to NTFS without losing any data, the conversion utility must lock the drive to prevent any activity that can cause data loss. In such cases, the conversion utility usually provides the option of running the next time you start your PC.

I have a drive that contains files I no longer need. Should I convert it or reformat it?

▼ If a drive is empty or contains files you do not want, reformatting the drive provides better results. In My Computer, right-click the drive's letter and click Format. Open the File system drop-down list and click NTFS. Click Start.

Compress Contents of Disks, Files, or Folders

You can compress the contents of files, folders, and even an entire disk to conserve disk space on NTFS drives. The percentage of space you can free up by compressing items depends on the number of items you compress and the types of files. Some files are more compressible than others. If you compress an average hard drive, you can expect to reclaim about 10 to 25 percent of the space being used to store files and folders.

When you compress items, they appear and act as normal, and Windows compresses and decompresses files automatically when you open them. Files may take a little extra time to open and close. However, if your PC is running slowly because it has insufficient disk space to use as virtual memory, compressing the disk or several large folders can free up enough disk space to improve the overall performance of your PC.

If you compress a disk, folder, or file, and you are dissatisfied with the way it performs when compressed, you can always disable compression for that item. You can also compress all of a disk's contents and then disable compression for the files and folders you use most often.

Compress Contents of Disks, Files, or Folders

Compress Contents of Disk

1. Launch My Computer.
2. Right-click the icon for the drive whose contents you want to compress.
3. Click Properties.

   The Properties dialog box for the selected disk appears.

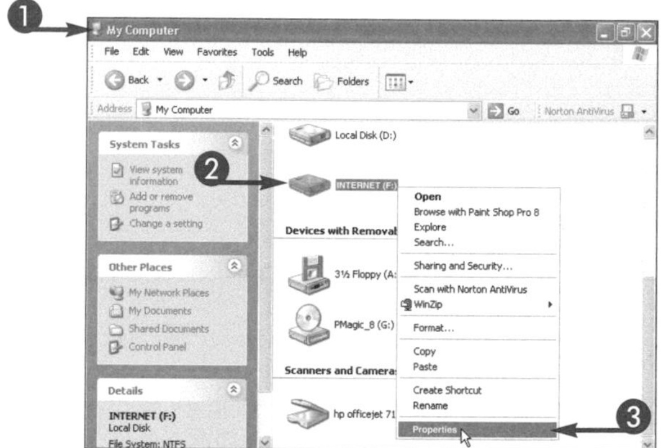

4. Click the "Compress drive to save disk space" option (☐ changes to ☑).
5. Click OK.

   The Confirm Attribute Changes dialog box appears.
6. Click the "Apply changes to *drive*, subfolders and files" option (○ changes to ◉), where *drive* is the drive that you want to compress.
7. Click OK.

   Windows compresses the contents of the disk.

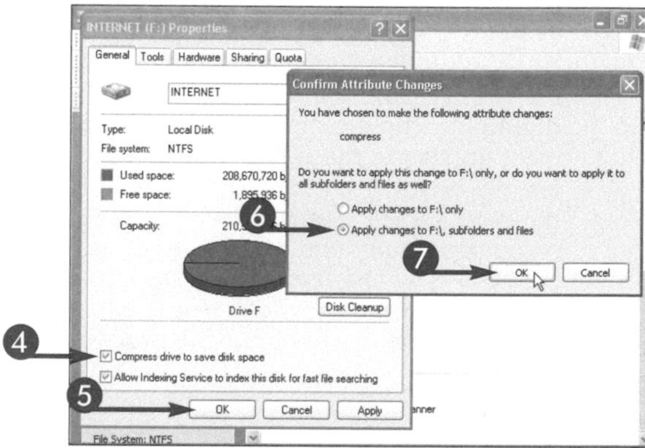

Compress a File or Folder

1. Launch My Computer.
2. Navigate to the drive and folder that contains the file or folder you want to compress.
3. Right-click the icon for the file or folder you want to compress.
4. Click Properties.

   The Properties dialog box for the selected item appears.

5. Click Advanced.

   The Advanced Attributes dialog box appears.

6. Click the "Compress contents to save disk space" option (☐ changes to ☑).
7. Click OK.

   You return to the folder's Properties dialog box.

8. Click OK.

   The Confirm Attribute Changes dialog box appears.

9. Click either the "Apply changes to this folder only" or the "Apply changes to this folder, subfolders and files" option (○ changes to ◉).
10. Click OK.

    Windows compresses the file or folder.

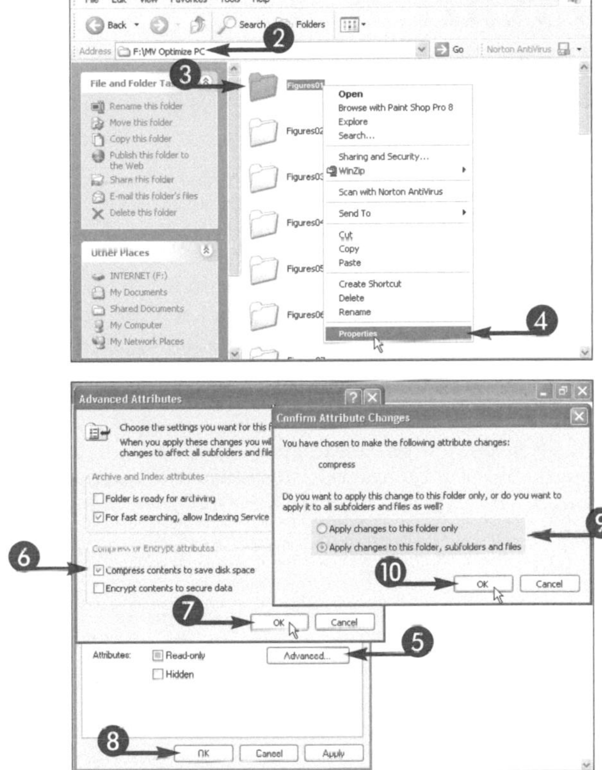

MASTER IT

Why does my disk drive's Properties dialog box not display an option for compressing the drive?

▼ The drive may be FAT or FAT32. The compression options are available only for NTFS drives. See the section "Identify Your Hard Drive's File System" to determine if it uses NTFS. If it uses FAT or FAT32, see the section "Convert a Drive to NTFS" for instructions.

Can I compress a file or folder and encrypt it?

▼ No. Windows does not allow you to encrypt a compressed file or folder. You must disable compression for the file or folder and then encrypt it. Encryption is available only on PCs running Windows XP Professional, not the Home edition.

Can I compress files and folders on a FAT32 drive?

▼ Yes. Windows XP features built-in Zip file compression that enables you to create compressed, Zipped folders. Any files or folders you place in a Zipped folder are automatically compressed. To create a Zipped folder, launch My Computer, navigate to the drive or folder in which you want the compressed folder, right-click a blank area inside the file list, click New, and then Compressed (zipped) folder. Type a name for the new folder and press Enter. You can identify a Zipped folder by the zipper on the folder's icon. You can decompress a file by clicking and dragging it out of the compressed folder into an uncompressed folder.

Install a Drive Management Utility

Using a drive management utility, you can divide a large hard drive into two or more *partitions*, each with its own drive letter, to make your folders and files more manageable and possibly improve performance. Each partition appears and functions like a separate hard drive. Some users prefer to keep their data on a separate drive to reduce the risk of data loss in the event that the system crashes. You must partition a drive that is larger than 32GB, if you plan on sticking with FAT32.

You can partition a drive using operating system commands, but you typically do this only when preparing a new hard drive to store data. Partitioning a drive that contains data can cause you to lose files and folders. A safer way to create and manage partitions on a drive that already contains data is to install and use a drive management utility, such as PartitionMagic.

Partitioning a drive that contains data is always risky and it may have a negative effect on PC performance, so partition a hard drive only if you need to run a second operating system on the same PC, or if you think that the file-management benefits outweigh the risks. Always back up your hard drive before partitioning it.

Install a Drive Management Utility

1. Load your drive management utility's installation CD onto your PC's CD drive.

   On most PCs, the installation routine runs automatically.

2. If the installation routine does not run, launch My Computer.
3. Double-click the icon for the CD drive in which you loaded the CD.
4. Double-click the icon for the installation file.

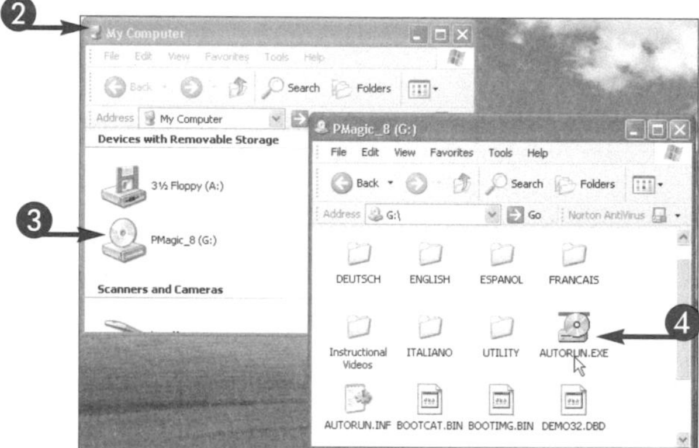

The opening installation screen appears.

5. If you have an option of utilities to install, click the partition utility.

The installation options appear.

6 Click Install.

The installation routine leads you through the process.

7 Follow the on-screen instructions to complete the installation.

The installation routine installs the drive management utility on your PC.

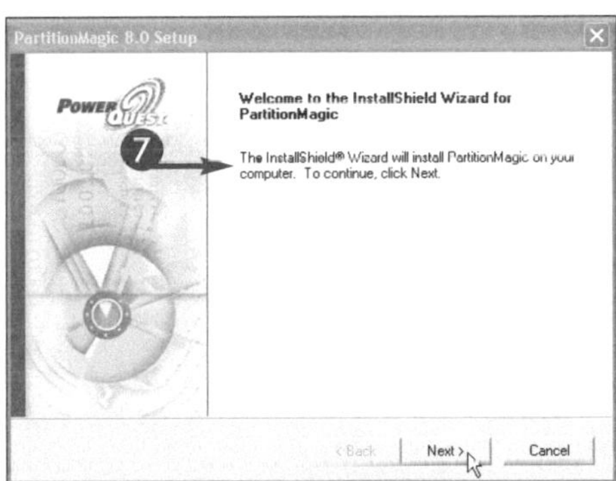

Does Windows XP include any utilities for managing drive partitions?

▼ Yes. You can use the Windows Computer Management utility to create and delete partitions, but the utility is not as intuitive or as powerful as a dedicated disk management program, such as PartitionMagic. To run the Computer Management utility, click Start, and then Run, type **compmgmt.msc**, and click OK. Click the plus sign (⊞) next to Storage, and then click the Disk Management icon. Computer Management displays all the hard drives and partitions on your PC. Be careful with making changes. If you delete a partition, which you can very easily do, you erase all data stored on that partition. Refer to the help system for specific instructions.

Is PartitionMagic the only utility available for managing disks and partitions?

▼ No. PartitionMagic is one of the more popular disk management utilities. You can learn more about it and order it at www.symantec.com. Partition Commander is another utility you can use to partition drives. You can check out its features and order it by visiting www.v-com.com. Both of these utilities provide tools to simplify the process of partitioning your drives and managing the sizes and locations of the partitions. They may also contain additional useful utilities. Partition Commander, for example, includes Copy Commander, which you can use to transfer the contents of one drive to another.

Partition Your Hard Drive

Using your disk management program, you can partition a hard drive into two or more separate storage areas. During the process, the program typically rearranges data already stored on the disk. Although most disk management programs have safety features that protect data in the event that your system crashes during the process or you experience a power outage, you should back up your hard drive before proceeding. Refer to Chapter 4 for instructions. If you do not want to back up the entire drive, at least back up any important documents stored on the drive.

Most disk management programs feature a wizard that leads you step-by-step through the partitioning process. However, the wizard prompts you to enter your preferences during the process. For example, a wizard usually prompts you to specify if you want to create a *primary* or *logical* partition. Your hard drive already contains a primary partition, which is used to store the Windows operating system. If you want to install another operating system, create a new primary partition. Otherwise, create a logical partition for storing data and other programs.

Partition Your Hard Drive

1. Launch your disk management program.

   This example uses PartitionMagic.

2. Click the letter of the drive that you want to partition.
3. Click the Create a new partition link.

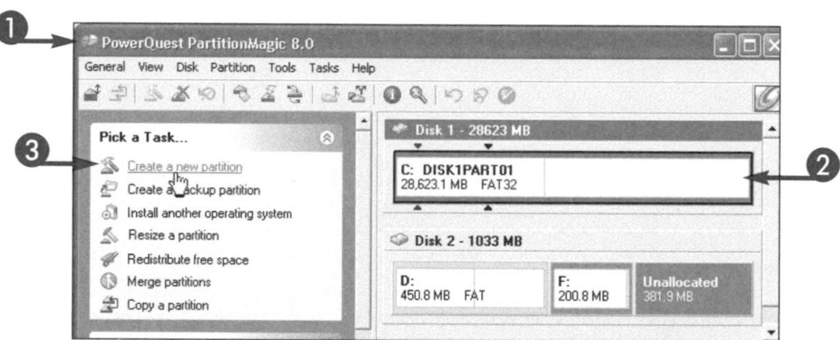

   The Create New Partition Wizard appears.

4. Click Next.

   The wizard prompts you to confirm the drive you want to partition.

5. Click the letter of the drive you want to partition.
6. Click Next.

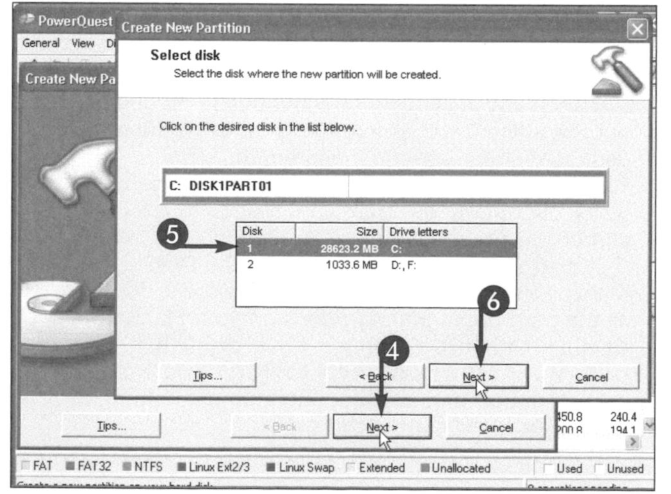

The wizard prompts you to specify the location for the new partition.

7 Click the option to specify if you want the partition placed before or after the existing partition.

Note: *If you are unsure, click the option marked "recommended."*

8 Click Next.

The wizard prompts you to specify the size and file system to use.

9 Click here to set the partition size.

10 Type a label for the new partition.

11 Click here and select a partition type.

12 Click here and select the file system.

13 Click here and select a drive letter.

14 Click Next and follow the on-screen instructions to complete the operation.

The disk management program creates a new blank partition and assigns it a drive letter.

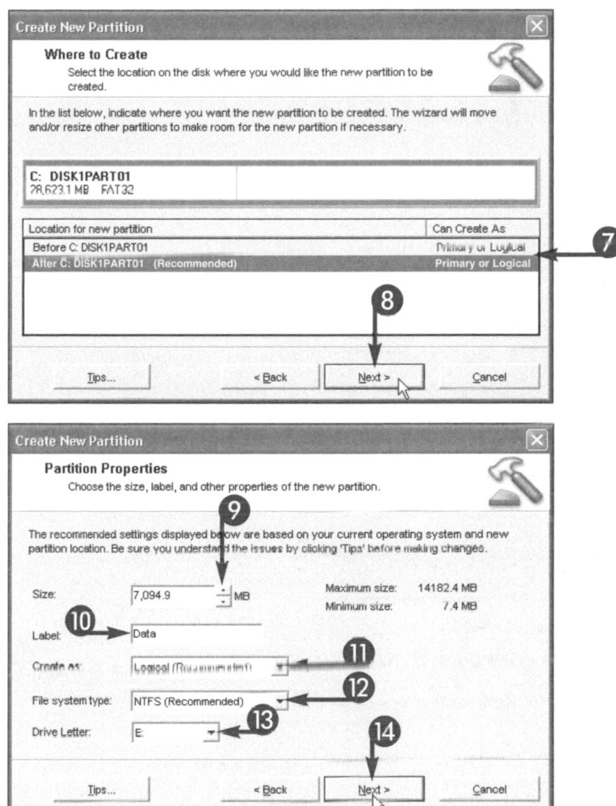

PART III

When asked if I want to create a FAT32 or NTFS partition, which should I choose?

▼ If your PC is running Windows XP or Windows 2000, you probably want to create an NTFS partition, as explained in the section "Identify Your Hard Drive's File System." If you want the contents of the drive to be accessible to an older operating system, such as Windows 98, Windows Me, or DOS, create a FAT32 partition.

How much space should I provide the new partition?

▼ Windows is usually installed on the original primary partition, and it needs room for temporary files, updates, and virtual memory. Leave some free space on the original partition. For example, if your PC has a 40GB hard drive and Windows and your other files occupy about 10GB of space, consider making the new partition 25GB and leaving at least 5GB of free space on the original partition.

I partitioned my hard drive, and now my CD-ROM drive is drive E instead of D. Is this normal?

▼ Yes. Windows typically assigns drive letters to the hard drives first and then it assigns the next letter or letters to the CD and DVD drives or to external drives. You may find this confusing if you are accustomed to working with a single hard drive. If it bothers you too much, most disk management programs provide an option to reassign drive letters.

Resize Partitions

If you underestimated the space needed on the original primary partition or on the new partition, you can resize the partitions to change their relative sizes. For example, if you have a primary partition C that is 10GB and a logical partition D that is 30GB and you want an extra 5GB for drive C, you can adjust the partition sizes so that C is 15GB and D is 25GB. This may require the disk management program to rearrange data on the disk, which is a little risky. Most disk management programs have built-in safeguards to prevent data loss, but it is still a good idea to back up your files before resizing partitions.

A disk management program, such as PartitionMagic, typically displays each partition as a rectangle that graphically displays the relative size of the partitions. When you create partitions, they are usually placed side-by-side, so to make one partition larger, you must make its neighboring partition smaller. In PartitionMagic, you can specify a target size for a partition and have PartitionMagic make the required adjustments for you.

Resize Partitions

1. Launch your drive management program.
2. Click the Resize a partition link.

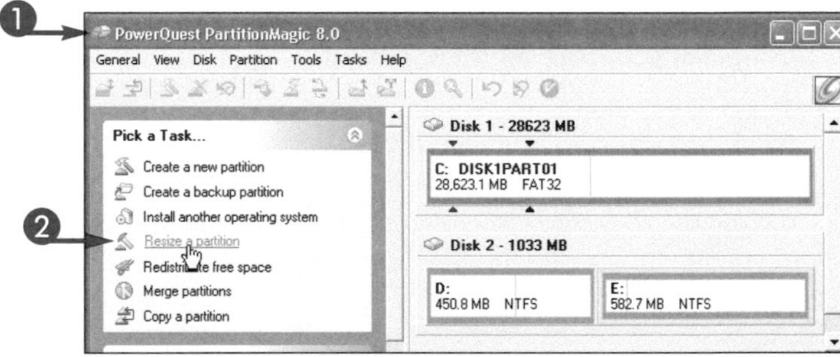

The Resize Partitions Wizard appears.

3. Click Next.

The wizard prompts you to select a drive.

4. Click the drive that contains the partitions you want to resize.
5. Click Next.

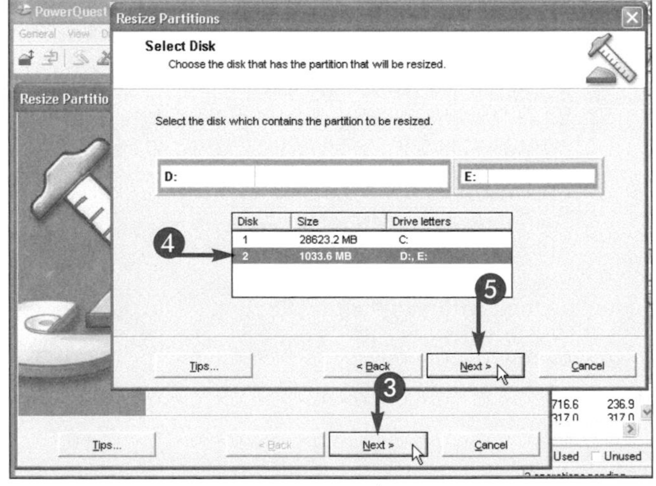

6 Click the partition that you want to enlarge.

7 Click Next.

8 Click here to specify the size you want for the partition.

9 Click Next.

10 Follow the on-screen instructions to complete the operation.

Your disk management program increases the size of the selected partition and decreases the size of adjacent partitions.

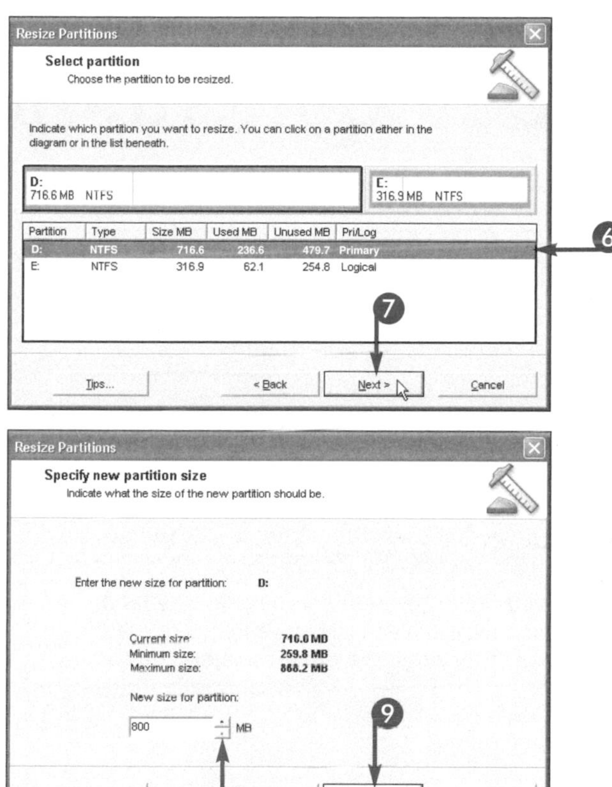

Do smaller partitions store data more efficiently?

▼ Smaller partitions can often store more data because they use smaller storage units, called *clusters*. If the cluster size is 16K, a file 1K in size requires only one cluster, but it takes up 16K of disk space, wasting the remaining 15K in the cluster. On a partition that uses 4K clusters, the file wastes only 3K of disk space. FAT32 drives use smaller cluster sizes for smaller drives, so dividing a FAT32 drive into partitions of 8GB or smaller reduces the cluster size to 4K, providing additional storage space. NTFS-formatted drives use 4K clusters no matter how large the drive.

Can I change a partition's size by using drag-and-drop techniques?

▼ Yes, but this method can be a little tricky. To display a window that lets you use the drag-and-drop technique, right-click a partition and click Resize. When resizing adjacent partitions, you must click and drag the right side of the partition on the left and the left side of the partition on the right to change their relative sizes. If you click and drag the left side of the left partition, you create unallocated space on the left that the partition on the right cannot use. Likewise, if you drag the right side of the partition on the right, you create unallocated space that the partition on the left cannot use.

Understanding File Fragmentation

As you delete files from and save files to your PC's hard drive, the files become more and more fragmented. Instead of depositing on neighboring storage areas of a disk, parts of the file scatter over the surface of the disk. To read a fragmented file from a disk, the hard drive must locate all of the file's parts and move the read-write head to different areas of the disk to gather all of the file's data. This adds to the time it takes your PC to run applications and open documents. It also makes your PC more likely to lose track of the various parts of a file, causing the file to become corrupt. You can make your PC's hard drive run more efficiently by defragmenting the files on the drive.

Understanding How Files Become Fragmented

Your PC stores each file in one or more *clusters* on its hard drive. A cluster is typically a 4K (kilobytes) unit of storage space, but it can be as small as 512 bytes or as large as 64K. On a drive that uses 4K clusters, a 32K file requires 8 clusters. A 1MB file requires 256 clusters.

Ideally, a hard drive stores an entire file in a series of neighboring clusters. When the drive needs to read the file, it can find all of its parts in a single location. This is how a drive functions when it is new. As you install programs and create files on a new drive, the drive records each file in neighboring clusters.

However, when you remove a program or delete a file, the deletion creates a blank storage area on the disk.

Instead of leaving this area blank, the drive uses it to store files. When you install a program or save a file to the disk, the drive writes as much of the data to the blank storage area as will fit there and then writes the rest of the data to other storage areas on the disk. Files that are stored on non-neighboring clusters are fragmented.

As you delete files, install and uninstall programs, and create and save files to the disk, it becomes more and more fragmented.

Negative Effects of Fragmentation

A hard drive consists of one or more platters — magnetic storage disks that spin inside the hard drive — and one or more read-write heads that record and read data from the disks as they spin. The read-write heads hover just above the platters, and they move back and forth over the surface of the disks to specific storage areas.

Each drive uses a file system that maps out the storage areas to help the drive identify the location's files or parts of files. When all the parts of a file are stored in a single location, the drive can quickly identify the location of all of the file's parts and move the read-write heads to the area where the file is stored. If a file is fragmented, the drive must move the read-write heads to different areas of the disk to read all of the file's parts. This not only makes your drive less efficient, but it also decreases its life span and makes your files more susceptible to becoming corrupted.

Fragmentation also interferes with the operating system's ability to manage virtual memory — disk space used as memory. Windows requires a dedicated area of disk space, preferably in a single location on the disk, to use as virtual memory. Fragmentation makes it more difficult to find a clear area to use.

Defragmenting a Drive

You can run a defragmentation utility on your PC's hard drive to evaluate the percentage of fragmentation that your drive is currently experiencing. You can then choose to defragment the drive. Windows includes a utility called Disk Defragmenter, which you can use to perform both tasks.

When defragmenting a disk, Disk Defragmenter moves files around on the disk to place each file in a contiguous — undivided — storage area. This improves the efficiency with which the drive can read the file and it reduces the risk of data loss. Disk Defragmenter also moves certain program files on the outside edges of the disk to improve the speed at which they can run.

An added benefit of defragmenting a disk is that the defragmentation process creates a contiguous blank area of the disk that is available to store any new files. This prevents newly added files from becoming fragmented, and it provides Windows with a wide-open storage area to use as virtual memory.

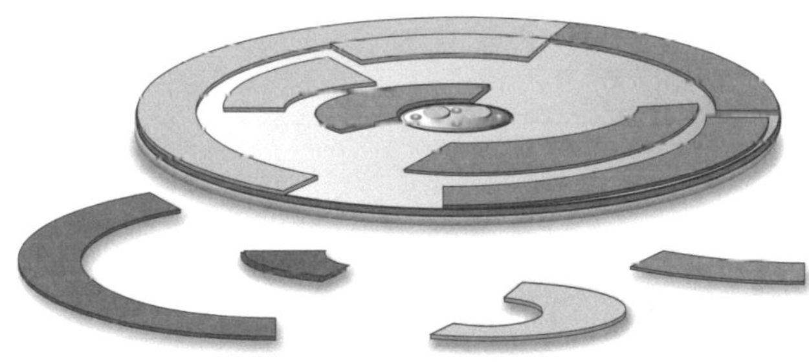

Analyze a Disk for Fragmentation

You can use Disk Defragmenter to analyze the degree of file fragmentation on your PC's hard drive and provide a recommendation on whether or not you need to defragment the drive. When you have Disk Defragmenter analyze a drive, it displays a chart that shows the amount of disk usage before defragmentation and displays a dialog box with its recommendation of whether you need to defragment the drive.

If your drive is fairly new and you have not removed any programs from it or deleted or moved any document files, your drive may have a low degree of fragmentation and may not require defragmentation. You may have most of the files stored in contiguous clusters, which means your drive is performing optimally.

If you have performed significant disk maintenance, as instructed in other chapters in this book, your drive very likely has a high degree of fragmentation. If this is the case, defragmentation can significantly improve hard drive performance.

Every week or so and after you perform heavy-duty disk maintenance, including removing programs and clearing temporary files from a disk, you should evaluate the fragmentation percentage to determine if defragmentation can enhance your hard drive's performance.

Analyze a Disk for Fragmentation

1. Click Start.
2. Click All Programs.
3. Click Accessories.
4. Click System Tools.
5. Click Disk Defragmenter.

Disk Defragmenter appears, displaying an icon (🖴) for each disk drive.

6. Click 🖴 for the drive you want to analyze for fragmentation.
7. Click Analyze.

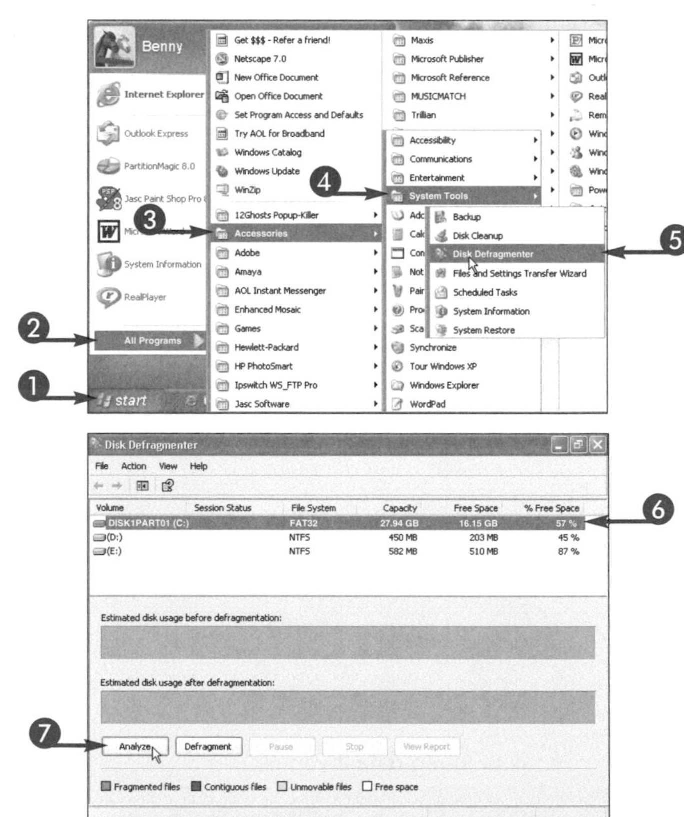

- Disk Defragmenter displays its progress in the status bar as it analyzes the disk.
- Disk Defragmenter displays a chart illustrating the estimated disk usage before file fragmentation.

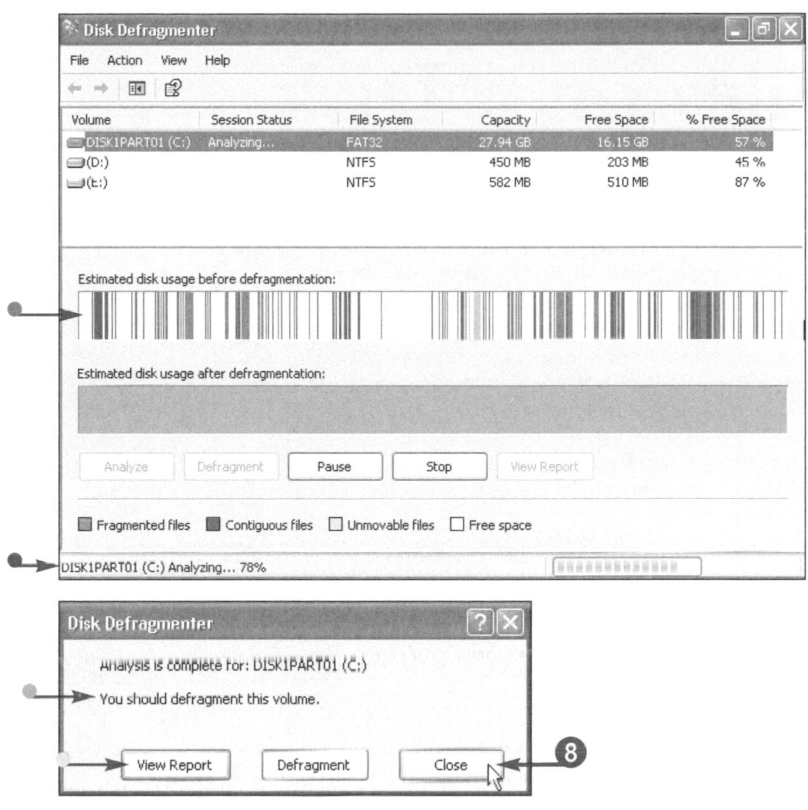

- When Disk Defragmenter is finished, it displays its recommendation.
- You can click View Report to review additional details.

8. Click Close.

The Disk Defragmenter dialog box closes and returns you to the main window.

Can I lose data by defragmenting a disk?

▼ Although moving data around on a disk may result in data loss, Disk Defragmenter is reliable. The biggest risk you run is if your PC crashes or experiences a power outage during the process. For complete safety, back up your data, as explained in Chapter 4. Because Disk Defragmenter rearranges data to store each file in a contiguous storage area on a disk, you run more risk of losing data if you do not defragment regularly.

I create documents, install programs, and browse the Web, but I rarely remove programs or delete files. Do I need to defragment my drive?

▼ Installing programs, creating and editing documents, and browsing the Web can all lead to file fragmentation. The only way to determine if you need to defragment a drive is to analyze it for fragmentation.

Does defragmenting the drive free up storage space?

▼ Not significantly. Disk Defragmenter does not help reclaim disk space. It consolidates files so that each file is stored in a contiguous storage area on the disk and it consolidates free space so storage space is readily available for additional files and folders. To reclaim disk space, refer to the chapters in Part II.

Defragment Files on a Disk

You can use Disk Defragmenter to defragment the files on a disk, significantly improve the performance and reliability of the disk drive, and reduce the wear and tear on the drive. Before you defragment the files on a disk, have Disk Defragmenter analyze the disk to determine the degree of fragmentation, as instructed in the previous section, "Analyze a Disk for Fragmentation." When the defragmentation is complete, you can analyze the disk again to compare the results.

Run Disk Defragmenter at a time when nobody needs to use the PC. The defragmentation process can take several hours on a large hard drive that is significantly fragmented. Many users start defragmenting just before they leave work or before going to bed at night.

If the hard drive that you want to defragment has less than 15 percent free space remaining, do some disk maintenance to clear files from the disk. Disk Defragmenter requires 15 percent of the disk to store data temporarily as it rearranges items on the disk. Refer to the chapters in Part II for instructions on how to reclaim disk space.

Defragment Files on a Disk

1. Click Start.
2. Click All Programs.
3. Click Accessories.
4. Click System Tools.
5. Click Disk Defragmenter.

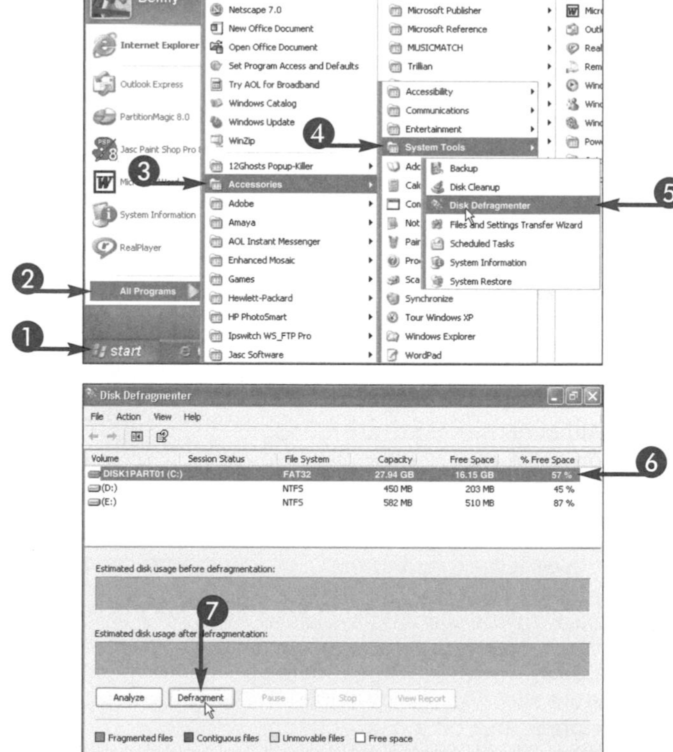

Disk Defragmenter appears, displaying an icon ( ) for each disk drive.

6. Click the icon for the drive you want to defragment.
7. Click Defragment.

- Disk Defragmenter displays its progress in the status bar as it defragments the disk.

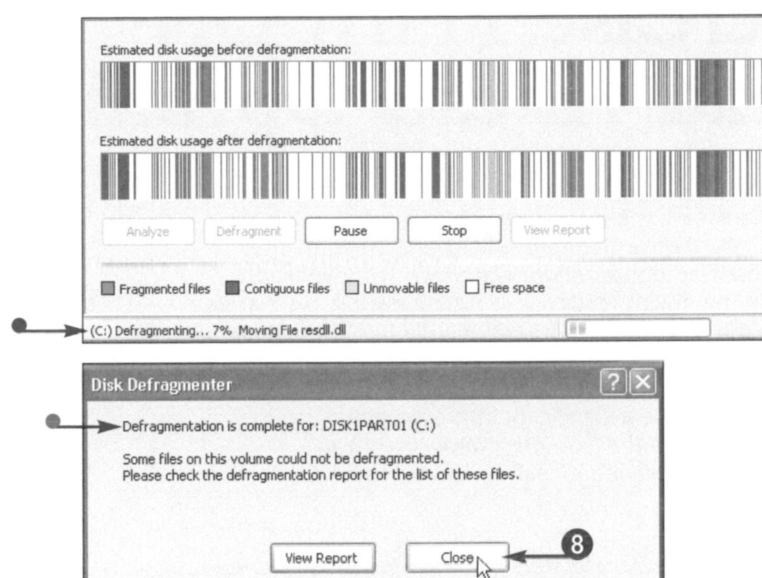

- When the defragmentation is complete, Disk Defragmenter displays a message indicating that the process has been successful.

8. Click Close.

   You are returned to the Disk Defragmenter window.

When I run Disk Defragmenter, it displays a message indicating that I need Administrator privileges to defragment a volume, and all the buttons in Disk Defragmenter are grayed out. What is wrong?

▼ To analyze a disk for fragmentation or to defragment a disk, you must log on to Windows as an administrator. You are probably logged on using a limited account. If you share your PC with others, the person in charge of setting up the PC may have created a limited account for you to prevent unauthorized changes to the PC's configuration. You can either log on using a different username or ask the person to give your account administrator privileges. Before running Disk Defragmenter, log on using an administrator account, and log off any other users who may be logged on.

Disk Defragmenter runs for awhile and then locks up or displays an error message. What should I do?

▼ Disk Defragmenter may have a conflict with another program that is running in the background. Try disabling your screen saver and any power-saving features that may be enabled. You can access these options by right-clicking a blank area of the Windows desktop and then clicking Properties and the Screen Saver tab. You may also need to exit programs that are running in the background, such as antivirus programs. Many of these programs display icons in the system tray at the right end of the taskbar. Right-click an icon to view available options. If you disable an antivirus program, re-enable it immediately after defragmenting the disk.

PART III

Increase Hard Drive Read-Ahead Optimization

If your PC is running Windows 98 or Windows Me, you can increase the read-ahead optimization setting for your hard drive to improve its overall performance. With read-ahead optimization, whenever the drive reads data from the disk, it reads a little additional data so that it needs to return to the disk less frequently to retrieve data. Increasing the read-ahead optimization setting for a hard drive can enhance a hard drive's performance. Although you may not notice a significant improvement in performance, even the smallest improvement can contribute to enhancing overall system performance.

When adjusting the read-ahead optimization setting, also pay some attention to the setting that enables you to define the primary role of this PC. You can select Desktop computer, Mobile or docking system, or Network server. The option you select controls the amount of memory set aside to cache — temporarily store — pathnames and filenames. You can sometimes improve a desktop PC's performance by defining its primary role as a network server, even if it is not a server, so that it can locate folders and files more quickly. You can try the setting, and if it does not improve performance, you can change it back.

Increase Hard Drive Read-Ahead Optimization

1. Right-click My Computer.
2. Click Properties.

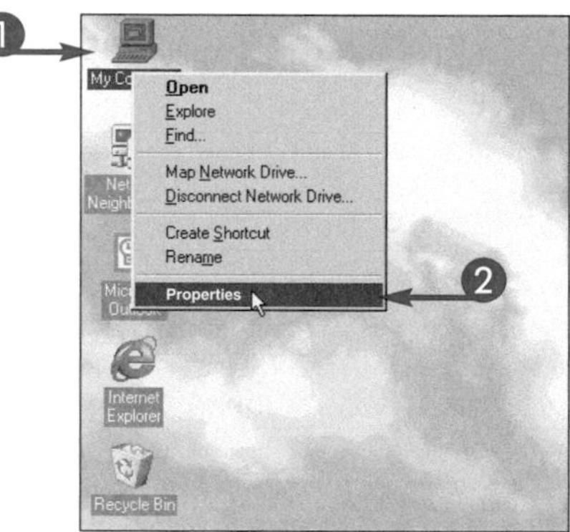

The System Properties dialog box appears.

3. Click the Performance tab.
4. Click File System.

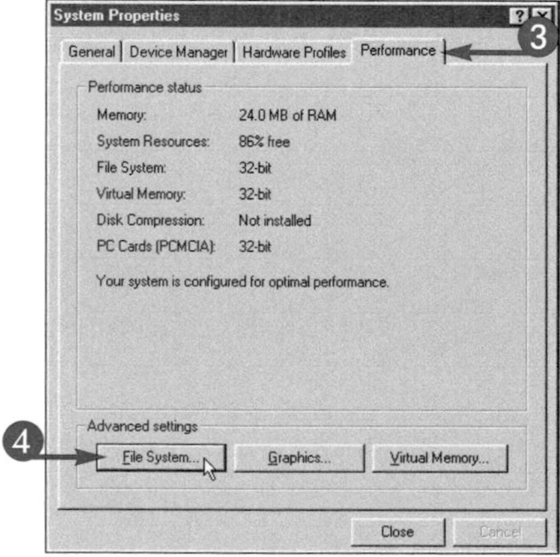

The File System Properties dialog box appears.

5 Click and drag the Read-ahead optimization slider all the way to the right.

6 Click here and click Network server.

7 Click OK.

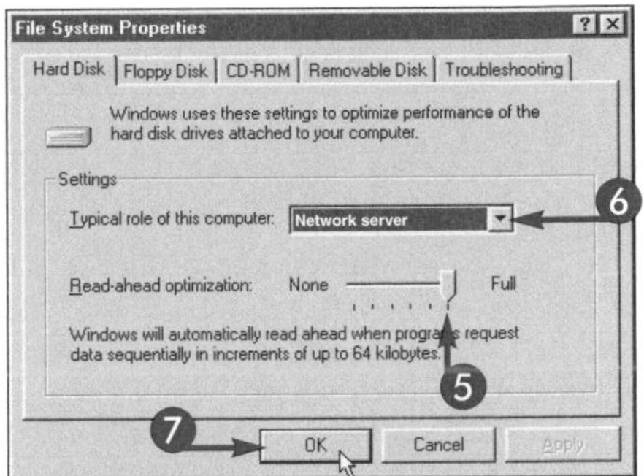

The File System Properties dialog box closes and returns you to the System Properties dialog box.

8 Click Close.

The System Properties dialog box applies your changes and closes.

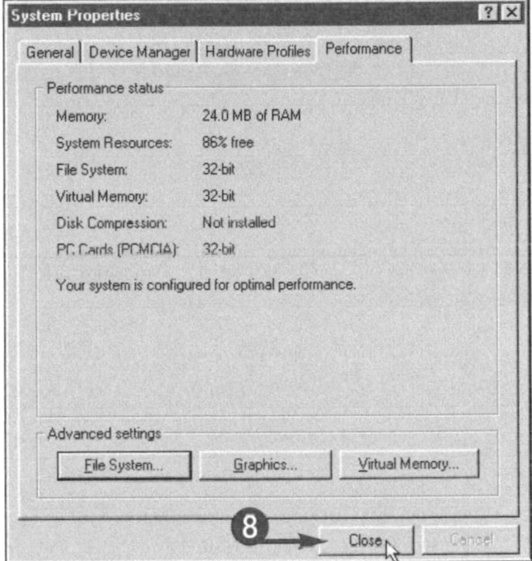

PART III

Does Windows XP or Windows 2000 have a setting that controls read-ahead optimization?

▼ No. Windows 2000 and Windows XP do not enable you to adjust the read-ahead buffer for your drives. You may possibly improve hard drive performance by enabling write caching, as explained in the next section, "Enable Write Caching." You should also ensure that DMA mode is enabled for your IDE (Intelligent Drive Electronics) controllers, as explained in the section "Enable DMA Mode."

Ever since I installed Windows XP, my drives seem slow. What happened, and what can I do about it?

▼ The original release of Windows XP caused problems with some hard drives that negatively affected their performance. Make sure you download and install all critical updates to Windows XP, as discussed in Chapter 22. You should also check for an updated driver for your hard drive, as explained in Chapter 23.

I increased the Read-ahead optimization setting to full, and now my system seems slower. What should I do?

▼ Try decreasing the read-ahead optimization to the next lower setting. The full setting causes the hard drive to read ahead in increments of 64K. The next lower setting is 32K. If you still experience problems, try the 16K setting. Defragmenting the drive can also help. For more on defragmenting your drive, see the sections "Analyze a Disk for Fragmentation" and "Defragment Files on a Disk."

Enable Write Caching

You can enable write caching for a drive to improve hard drive performance. Windows 2000 and Windows XP feature a write-caching option for all fixed storage devices, such as internal hard disk drives. With write caching, Windows stores data temporarily in memory before writing it to the disk, so the drive is not constantly writing small amounts of data to disk. This can improve the performance of the drive and free it up to perform other tasks, such as loading program files and data.

By default, Windows enables write caching for all internal hard drives, but you should check the setting to make sure it is enabled. Windows disables write caching for any removable drives, such as external hard drives, so that if the drive is disconnected without warning, you lose no data.

If your PC commonly crashes or you frequently experience power outages, you may want to disable write caching to prevent data loss. Because write caching delays the process of writing data to the disk, if the PC crashes or the power is interrupted before Windows has a chance to write the data to the disk, you may lose that data.

Enable Write Caching

1. Click Start.
2. Right-click My Computer.
3. Click Properties.

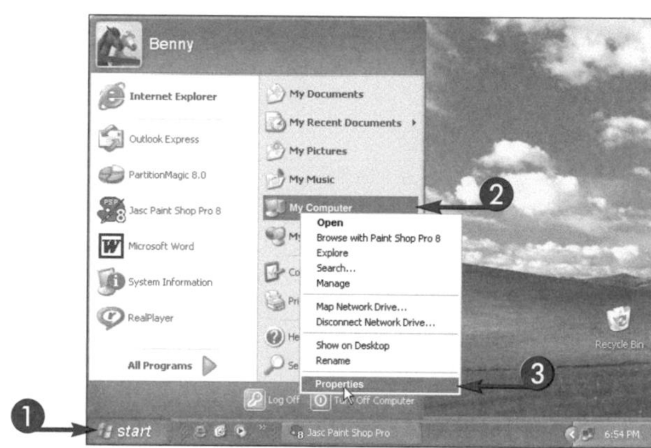

The System Properties dialog box appears.

4. Click the Hardware tab.
5. Click Device Manager.

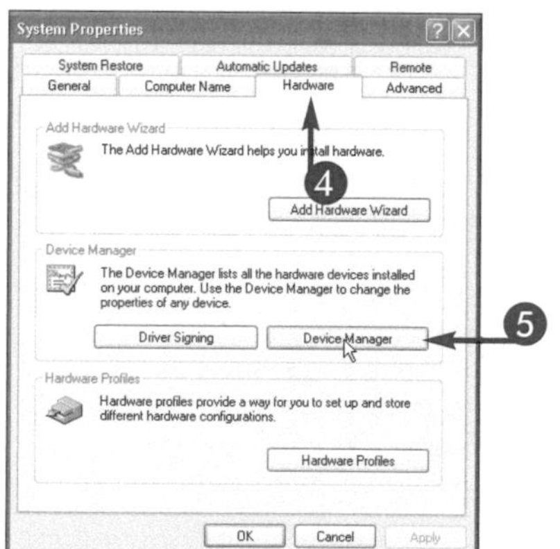

The Device Manager window appears.

6 Click the plus sign (⊞) next to Disk drives.

7 Right-click the disk drive for which you want to enable write caching.

8 Click Properties.

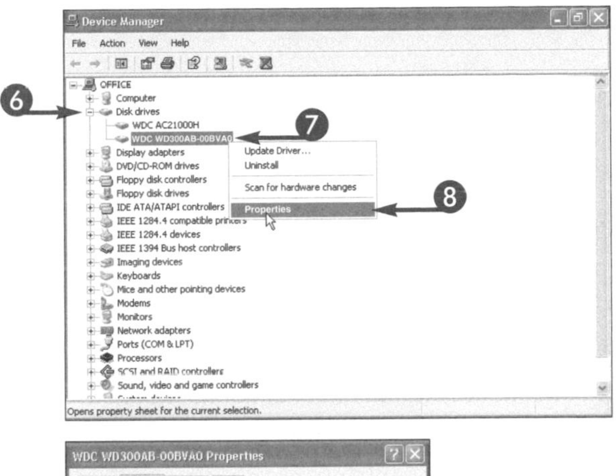

The Properties dialog box for the selected disk drive appears.

9 Click the Policies tab.

10 If the Enable write caching on the disk option is unchecked, click to select it (☐ changes to ☑).

11 Click OK.

Windows saves your changes.

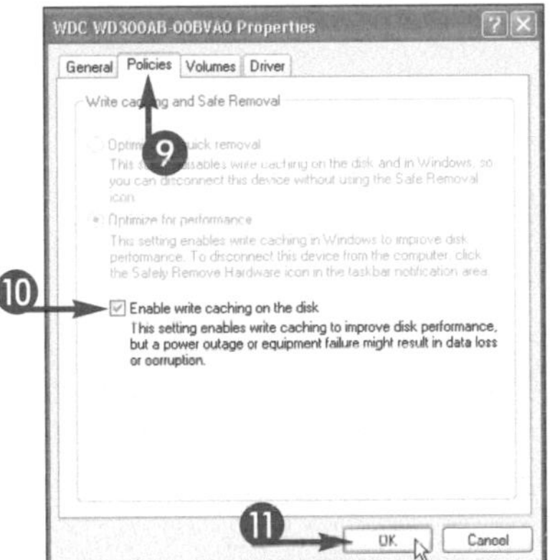

The Policies tab in the Properties dialog box for my disk drive has two options that are grayed out. Why?

▼ These options are available only for removable disk drives, such as an external hard drive that connects to a FireWire or USB port or a card reader. The Optimize for quick removal option (○ changes to ⦿) disables write caching for the device, so you can disconnect it without first clicking the Safe Removal button and be fairly certain that you will not lose data. The Safe Removal icon appears on the right end of the taskbar whenever Windows detects a device that uses disk caching. The Optimize for performance option (○ changes to ⦿) enables write caching for the device, but to avoid losing data, you must click the Safe Removal button before disconnecting the device.

Can disabling write caching for a drive improve system performance in other ways?

▼ Usually not, but it can improve performance for audio and video applications that need to write data immediately to disk. If you are working with audio or video clips and are experiencing data loss, try disabling write caching. In Windows 98 and Windows Me, the option is called write-behind disk caching. Right-click My Computer, click Properties, click File System, click the Troubleshooting tab, and then click the Disable write-behind disk caching for all drives option (☐ changes to ☑). A more common cause of data loss in video and audio data transfers is a slow drive or slow connection, such as USB1.

Optimize CD Drive Performance

If you have an older CD drive and your PC is running Windows 98 or Windows Me, you can potentially improve its performance by providing it with a larger supplemental cache size and optimizing the access pattern that Windows uses to read data from the disk. The supplemental cache size is PC memory that Windows uses, in addition to the drive's built-in cache, to make read and write operations proceed more smoothly. Newer CD drives are faster and have improved caching, so a supplemental cache is unnecessary.

Optimizing the access pattern indicates the preferred speed at which you want Windows to read and write data from the CD. You can try different speeds to determine the speed that works best for your CD drive. In most cases, you can optimize your CD drive's performance by selecting a speed that matches the top speed that your CD drive is rated and by maximizing the supplemental cache size. However, maximizing the supplemental cache size can sometimes diminish performance.

The steps in this section are for Windows 98 and Windows Me only. Windows XP and Windows 2000 have no comparable settings for improving CD drive performance.

Optimize CD Drive Performance

1. Right-click My Computer.
2. Click Properties.

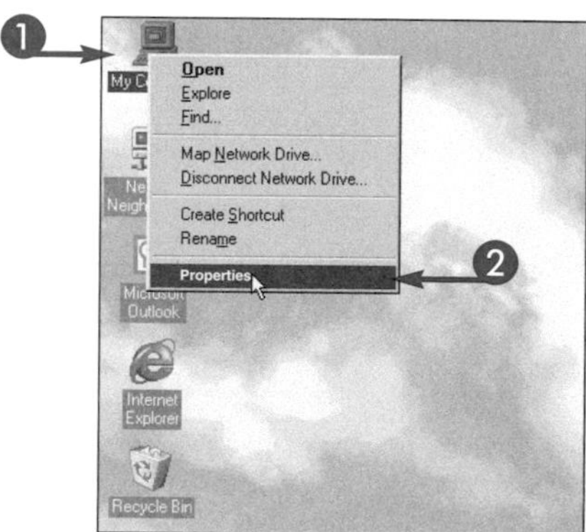

The System Properties dialog box appears.

3. Click the Performance tab.
4. Click File System.

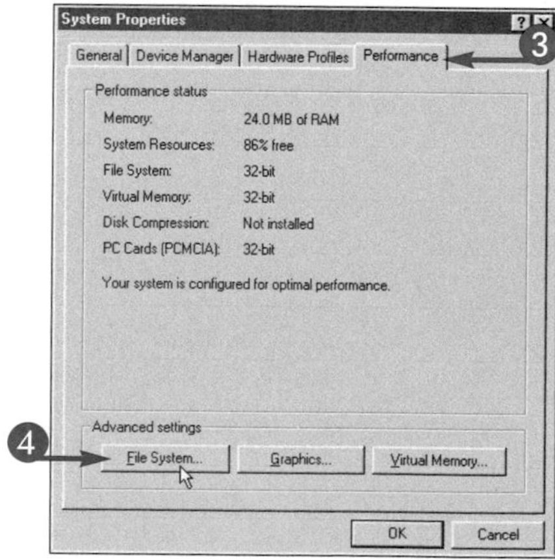

The File System Properties dialog box appears.

5. Click the CD-ROM tab.
6. Click and drag the Supplemental cache size slider all the way to the right.
7. Click here and click the top speed of your CD drive.
8. Click OK.

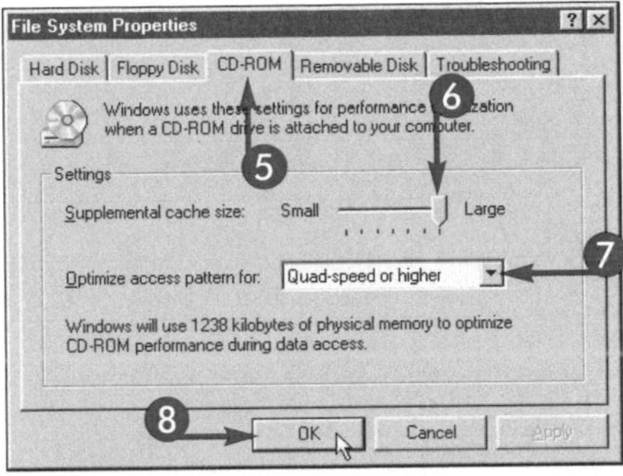

The File System Properties dialog box closes and returns you to the System Properties dialog box.

9. Click OK.

The System Properties dialog box applies your changes and closes.

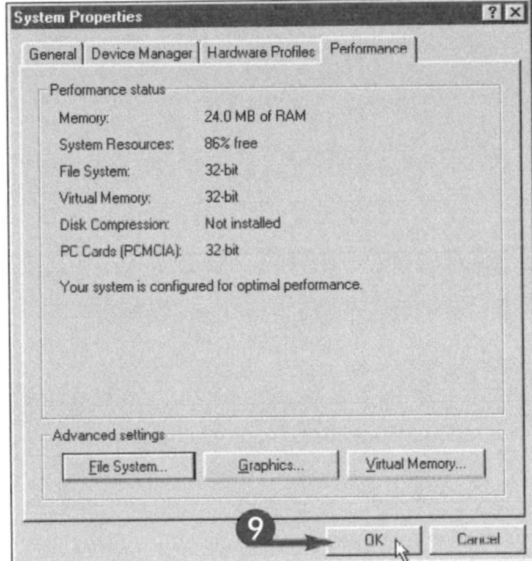

PART III

Is there anything I can do in Windows XP or Windows 2000 to improve my CD drive performance?

▼ No, but you may possibly enhance audio quality by enabling digital audio for the drive. Right-click My Computer, click Properties, click the Hardware tab, Device Manager, ⊞ next to DVD/CD-ROM drives, and then right-click the icon for your CD drive, and click Properties. Click the Properties tab, click the Enable digital CD audio for this CD-ROM device option (☐ changes to ☑), and click OK. This may enhance audio quality when playing audio CDs, but it may also cause problems. If your PC experiences problems playing audio CDs, disable the setting.

Can I increase the speed at which my CD-RW drive writes data to discs?

▼ Most CD-recording utilities enable you to adjust the recording speed. Select the highest speed setting that your CD drive supports. If you have problems writing at this speed, try a slower setting. To avoid problems, use high-quality recordable discs that have a speed rating that matches the highest speed that your CD drive supports. For example, if you have a 48X CD drive, use recordable CDs that have a rating of at least 48X. You may obtain better results by recording at a speed that is a factor of the media speed; for example, record at 24X on 48X media or 26X on 52X media.

Optimize DVD Drive Performance

You can optimize DVD drive performance to enhance audio and video portions of movies and other media. Because DVDs typically store audio and video files that are very large, playing DVDs places great demands on system resources, including RAM, processor power, and video capabilities. If DVDs play slowly on your PC or you notice that the playback is choppy or the screen occasionally freezes, you can analyze your system to determine potential bottlenecks and possibly free up enough system resources to correct the problem.

In many cases, you can solve the problem by enabling DMA mode, as explained in the following section, "Enable DMA Mode." This gives the DVD drive direct access to memory without having to go through your PC's processor.

If you enable DMA mode and DVD playback is still choppy, you can adjust the settings in your DVD player to optimize the display for video playback. These steps show you how to change DVD settings in Windows Media Player. If you are using a different DVD player, check its help system for instructions. You may have better results using a third-party DVD player, such as WinDVD or PowerDVD.

Optimize DVD Drive Performance

1. Click Start.
2. Click All Programs.
3. Click Accessories.
4. Click Entertainment.
5. Click Windows Media Player.

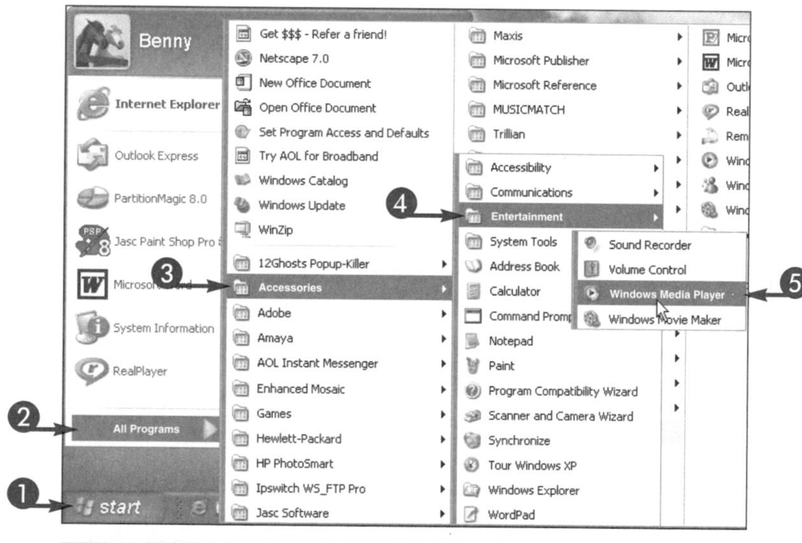

Windows Media Player appears.

6. Click Tools.
7. Click Options.

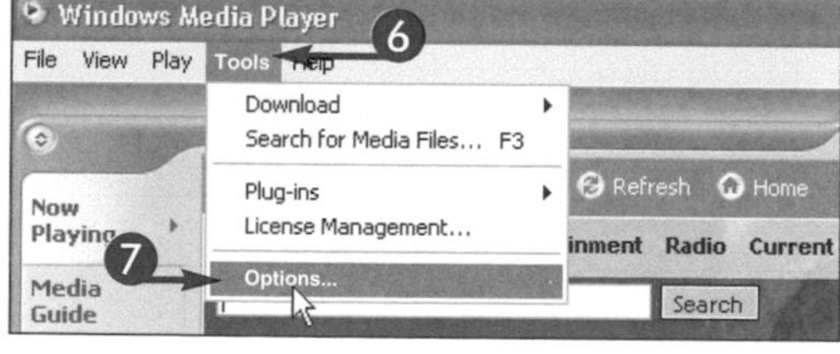

The Options dialog box appears.

8 Click the Devices tab.

9 Click the DVD drive you want to optimize.

10 Click Properties.

The DVD drive's Properties dialog box appears.

11 Click the Digital option under both Playback and Copy (○ changes to ◉).

12 If the Use error correction option is checked, click Use error correction to toggle it off (☑ changes to ☐).

13 Click OK to return to the Options dialog box.

14 Click OK in the Options dialog box.

Media Player saves the DVD playback and recording settings you entered.

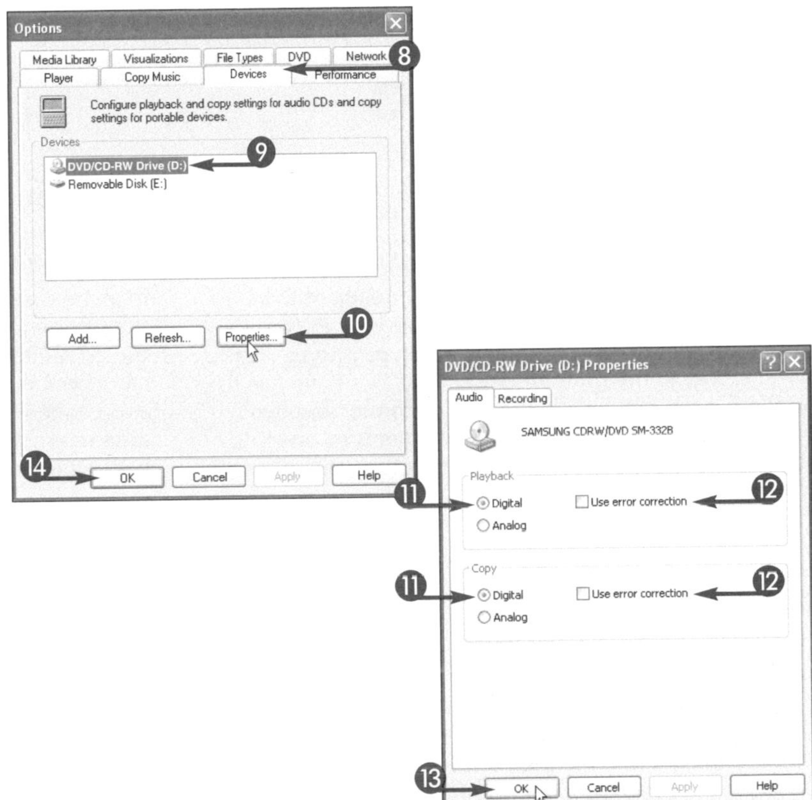

Can video settings affect my DVD drive's playback performance?

▼ Yes. DVDs play video through the video card — the display adapter. Your PC should have a display adapter that has at least 16MB of video RAM (VRAM) to ensure that it can handle the huge amounts of data that the DVD plays through it; 32MB is much better. To check the amount of video RAM on your display adapter, right-click the Windows desktop, click Properties, the Settings tab, Advanced, and then the Adapter tab. If your display adapter has less than 16MB of RAM, DVD video playback may be choppy or frames may freeze. You can improve the DVD video playback performance by installing a display adapter that has more VRAM.

I enabled DMA mode and adjusted the DVD settings in my DVD player, but the drive is still slow. Do you have any other suggestions?

▼ Check your system resources, as explained in Chapter 2, to ensure that your PC meets the minimum system requirements specified for the DVD drive. Try disabling the Windows screen saver and Windows power-saving options, as explained in the section "Defragment Files on a Disk." Remove other programs from memory that may interfere with your DVD player, as shown in Chapter 13. You can try updating the driver for your DVD drive and display adapter, as explained in Chapter 24. If the problem is with video playback, try optimizing the display settings, as recommended in Chapter 26.

Enable DMA Mode

You can enable DMA mode to provide your disk drives with direct memory access and take some of the burden off your PC's processor. Windows typically enables DMA mode by default for all IDE controllers that support DMA. The IDE (Intelligent Drive Electronics) controller is the connector on your PC's motherboard that the wide data cable plugs into to connect drives to the motherboard. Most PCs have two IDE controllers, each of which is capable of connecting two drives. On most PCs, the hard drive connects to one IDE controller and the CD-ROM drive connects to the other IDE controller.

Enabling DMA mode generally does not improve the rate of data transfer between the drive and memory, but it frees the processor from having to monitor the transfers, resulting in a slight performance boost.

In some cases, if you install Windows XP as an upgrade, it does not enable DMA mode for the IDE controllers, even if the controller and your hard drive support DMA mode. You can check which mode Windows XP is configured to use and change the mode to improve performance. If problems arise after you enable DMA mode, you can always change back to the original setting.

Enable DMA Mode

1. Click Start.
2. Right-click My Computer.
3. Click Properties.

- The System Properties dialog box appears.

4. Click the Hardware tab.
5. Click Device Manager.

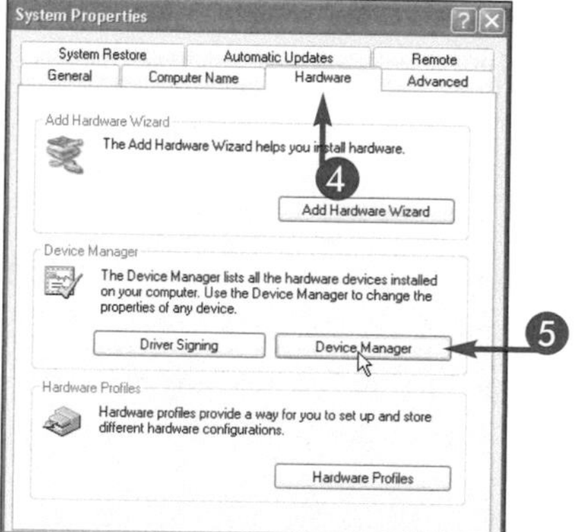

The Device Manager appears.

6 Click ⊞ next to the IDE option.

7 Right-click Primary IDE Channel.

8 Click Properties.

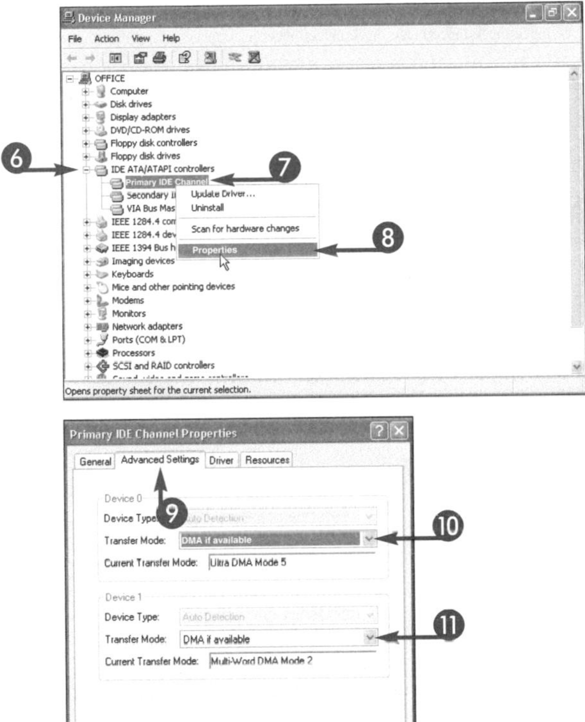

The Primary IDE Channel Properties dialog box appears.

9 Click the Advanced Settings tab.

10 Click here and click DMA if available.

11 Click here and click DMA if available.

12 Click OK.

Windows saves the settings and returns you to the Device Manager.

13 Repeat steps 7 to 12 for the Secondary IDE Channel.

I chose to enable DMA mode, but when I checked later, the option was no longer selected. What should I have done?

▼ In some cases, particularly if you upgraded to Windows XP rather than purchasing a new PC with Windows XP installed on it, Windows cannot enable DMA mode even if your drives support it. This is usually because the previous version of Windows installed on your PC did not support DMA mode for the IDE controllers. Update the device drivers for your IDE controller, as explained in Chapter 23. This usually corrects the problem. You can then perform the steps in this section to determine if DMA mode is enabled.

I just installed a new drive, and now my system seems sluggish. What happened?

▼ Each IDE connector on the motherboard supports two drives that are linked together with a single data cable. The IDE controller supports data transfers from only one drive at a time. Connecting a second drive can have a negative impact on the performance of the first drive. If you have two drives, connect each drive to its own IDE connector. If you have three drives, connect the main drive — the drive on which Windows is installed — to the primary IDE connector and plug the other two drives into the secondary IDE connector.

Optimize Processor Usage

You can instruct Windows to devote more processor time to the programs that you are currently using or to programs that are running in the background. By allocating more processor time to the program you are using, the program becomes more responsive.

As you know, one of the major features of the Windows operating system is that it enables you to multitask — to perform two or more tasks at the same time. You can, for example, work on one document while another document is printing. The program that you are currently using is called a *foreground* program. Any program working behind the scenes is a *background* program.

In Windows XP, you can allocate more processor time to the foreground program or divide the processor time equally between the foreground and background programs. When you divide the processor time equally, background programs run more smoothly, but you may notice that the foreground program does not respond as quickly.

You may prefer to divide processor time equally between foreground and background programs if your PC is on a network and shares resources with other users in the background.

Optimize Processor Usage

1. Click Start.
2. Right-click My Computer.
3. Click Properties.

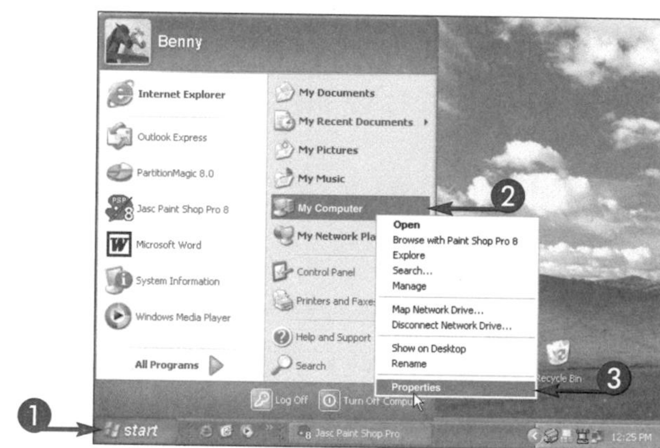

The System Properties dialog box appears.

4. Click the Advanced tab.
5. Under Performance, click Settings.

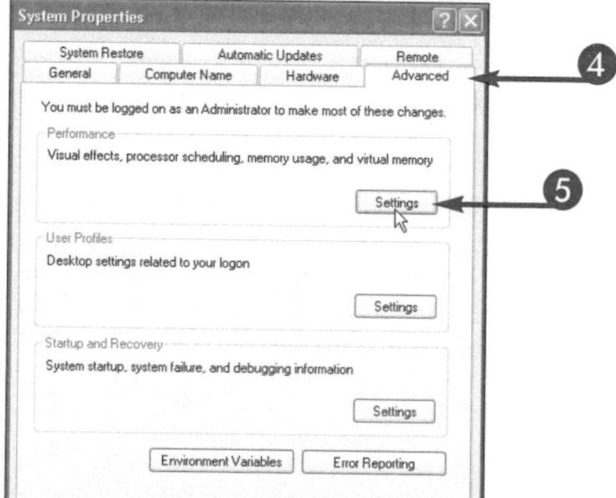

The Performance Options dialog box appears.

6 Click the Advanced tab.

7 Under Processor scheduling, click either the Programs or Background services option (○ changes to ◉).

Programs allocates more processor time to the foreground program while Background services allocates the processor time more equitably between the foreground programs and background programs and services.

8 Click OK.

The Performance Options dialog box closes and returns you to the System Properties dialog box.

9 Click OK.

The System Properties dialog box saves your settings and closes.

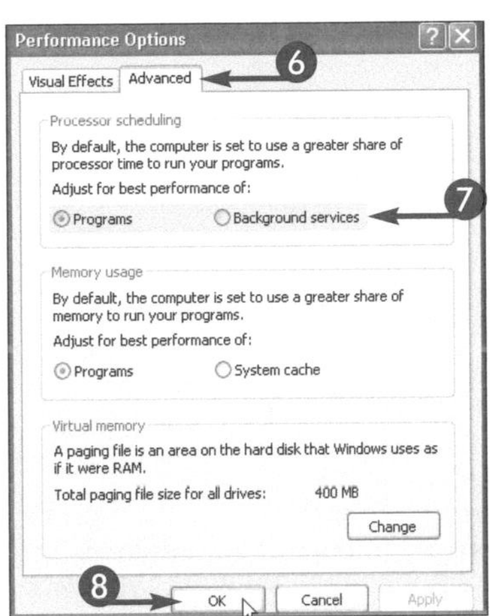

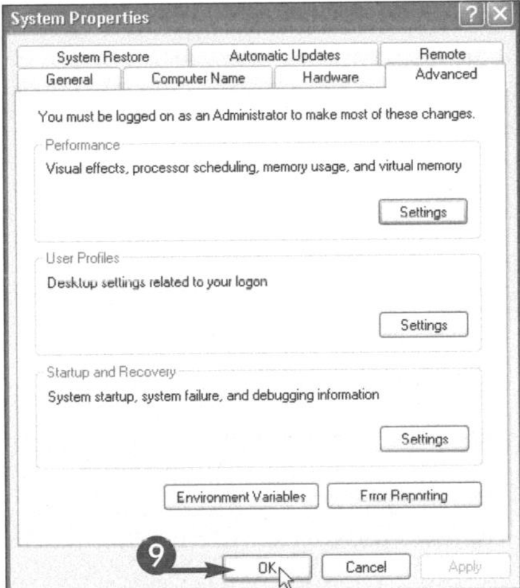

I noticed a Visual Effects tab in the Performance Options dialog box. Can I change those settings?

▼ Yes. Windows uses several special effects to make the display appear smoother and more visually appealing, but these effects require additional system resources. Chapter 25 shows you how to change these settings and others to make the display more efficient.

What types of services run in the background?

▼ Printing, virus-checking, pop-up blockers, schedulers, and several other applications and services commonly run in the background. In addition, if your PC is on a network, it may act as a server, enabling other users to access its resources in the background. You can press Ctrl+Alt+Del to display the Task Manager, which displays a list of applications and processes that are running both in the foreground and in the background.

Can I change the options under Memory usage and Virtual memory?

▼ Yes. You can reallocate memory usage to programs or system cache, as explained in the next section, "Optimize Memory Usage." You can reconfigure virtual memory to specify the amount of virtual memory to use and to instruct Windows to use a different hard drive for virtual memory if your PC is equipped with more than one hard drive. Refer to the section "Optimize Virtual Memory" for details.

Optimize Memory Usage

You can optimize your PC's memory usage by allocating more memory to the programs you use or more memory to system cache. By default, Windows is configured to assign more memory to the programs you use. However, if your PC is on a network and commonly acts as a server, you can improve its performance as a server by allocating more memory to the system cache. You can also improve the performance of programs that require a larger cache by assigning more memory to the system cache.

The System Properties dialog box provides easy access to Windows performance settings. You can use these settings to optimize processor usage, as explained in the previous section; optimize memory usage, as explained in this section; optimize virtual memory, as explained in the next section; or disable Windows visual effects for enhanced performance, as shown in Chapter 25.

Although these options are considered advanced, they are very easy to change and do not pose any risk to your PC or to Windows. You can try different settings to see which settings improve performance for the way you use your PC.

Optimize Memory Usage

1. Click Start.
2. Right-click My Computer.
3. Click Properties.

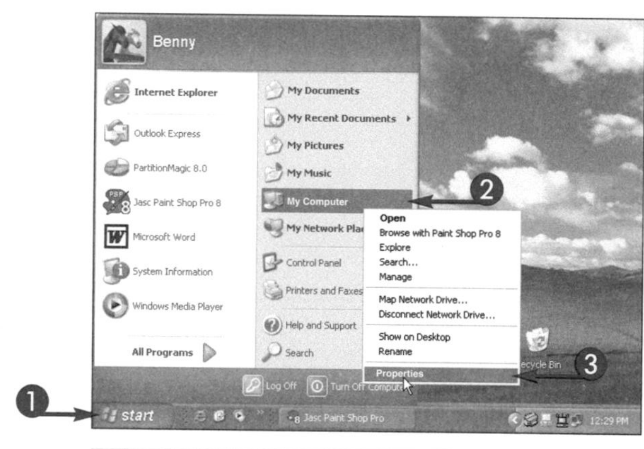

The System Properties dialog box appears.

4. Click the Advanced tab.
5. Under Performance, click Settings.

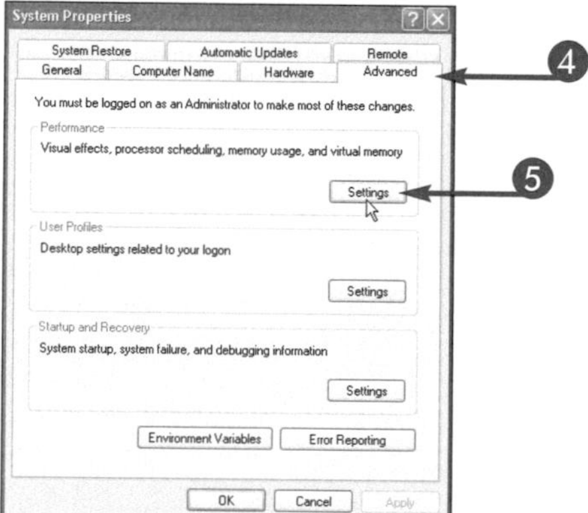

The Performance Options dialog box appears.

6 Click the Advanced tab.

7 Under Memory usage, click either the Programs or System cache option (○ changes to ◉).

The Programs option allocates more memory to your applications, while System cache allocates more memory to the system cache for network operations and processes, such as background printing, that require a larger cache.

8 Click OK.

The Performance Options dialog box closes and returns you to the System Properties dialog box.

9 Click OK.

The System Properties dialog box saves your settings and closes.

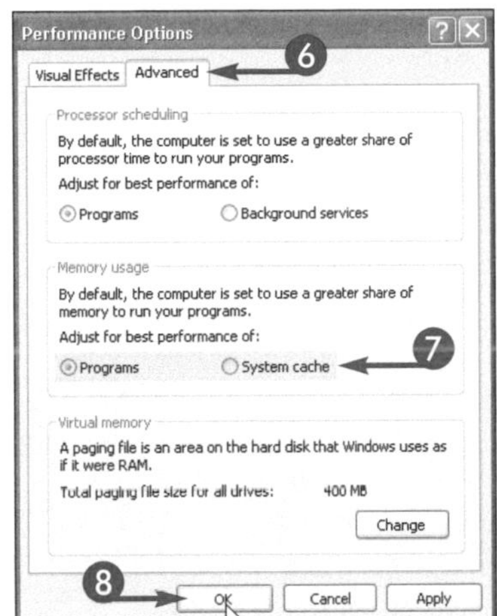

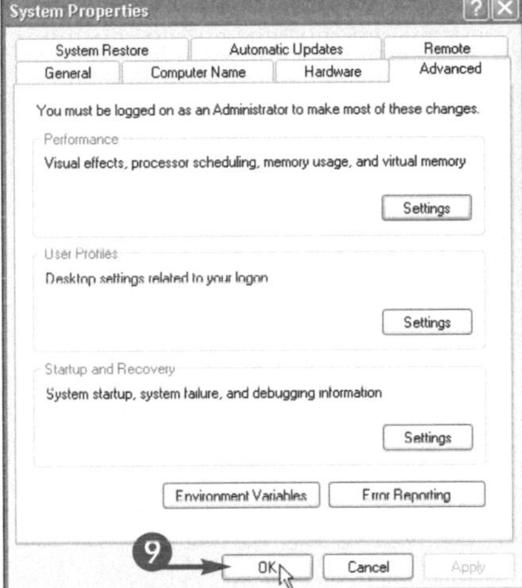

When I examine the amount of physical memory available, the amount is always very low. Why?

▼ Physical memory, or RAM, is a very valuable commodity, so Windows XP tries to find a way to use it. It may use memory to perform minor tasks or store additional data that may be needed to perform a task. In most cases, if you run an application that requires physical memory that Windows is using for some nonessential function, Windows clears the memory so the application can use it. Do not be surprised if your PC has 256MB RAM and shows only 30 or 40MB available even when you are not running any applications in the foreground. This is normal.

What exactly is the system cache?

▼ The system cache is an area of memory that acts as a buffer between the main memory and the processor. It stores data and makes it readily available to the processor when the processor needs it. This enables the processor to operate at full speed without having to wait for data. It also reduces the number of times the PC needs to go to the hard drive to read or write data. Network servers can benefit from a larger system cache. In addition, some applications, particularly those that create and manage large files, benefit from a larger system cache.

Optimize Virtual Memory

If your PC has more than one physical hard drive, you can divide the amount of virtual memory between the two drives to improve its performance. Windows uses two types of memory — physical memory in the form of RAM chips, and virtual memory in the form of disk space, which is much slower than RAM. When you install Windows, it creates a *paging file* on the same disk on which Windows is installed, and it swaps data between RAM and the paging file as needed.

Because the paging file is stored on the same drive on which Windows is installed, whenever you perform a task, the drive must not only read instructions from the hard drive but must also access data stored in the paging file on that same hard drive. By instructing Windows to allocate a portion of virtual memory to a different hard drive, you can have two hard drives working to keep up with your system's physical memory and processor.

Try this technique only if your PC has a second physical drive that is suitable for use. A slow hard drive, a separate partition of the same hard drive, or an external backup drive that is connected to a relatively slow USB port will not enhance performance.

Optimize Virtual Memory

1. Click Start.
2. Right-click My Computer.
3. Click Properties.

The System Properties dialog box appears.

4. Click the Advanced tab.
5. Under Performance, click Settings.

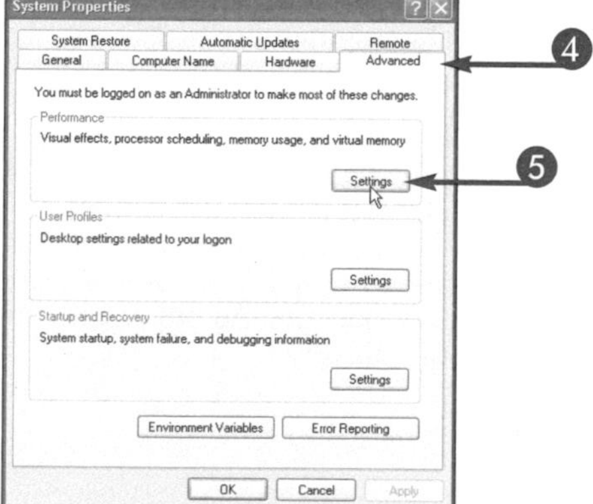

The Performance Options dialog box appears.

6. Click the Advanced tab.
7. Under Virtual memory, click Change.

The Virtual Memory dialog box appears.

8. Click a physical hard drive you want to use for virtual memory.
9. Click the Custom size option (○ changes to ◉).
10. Type the minimum size you want to use as the initial size in megabytes.
11. Type a maximum size in megabytes.
12. Click Set.
13. Repeat steps 8 to 12 for the second physical drive.
14. Click OK.

Windows saves your settings and may prompt you to restart your computer.

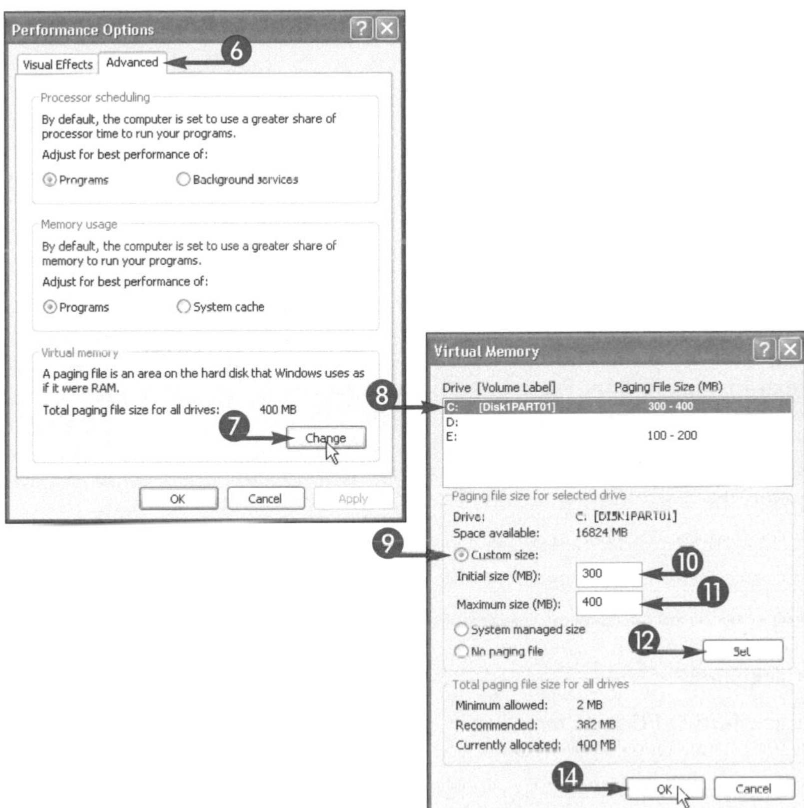

How do I know if my PC's two drives are different physical drives or two partitions of the same drive?

▼ Click Start, click Control Panel, click Performance and Maintenance, click Administrative Tools, and then double-click the Computer Management icon. Click ⊞ next to Storage and then click Disk Management. At the bottom of the pane on the right are graphic representations of your hard drives and partitions. This shows you each physical hard drive and each partition on each physical hard drive. If you have a third-party hard drive management program, as described in Chapter 9, you can use it to obtain information about your PC's physical drives and partitions.

My PC has a gigabyte of physical memory. Can I disable virtual memory to force Windows to use the faster physical memory?

▼ Yes, but this can cause serious problems. Windows and some applications need a minimum amount of virtual memory to function. You can set the virtual memory to 0 (zero) to delete the paging file and prevent Windows from attempting to access the drive for virtual memory, but I strongly recommend that you set virtual memory no lower than the minimum that Windows recommends. Enabling Windows to automatically control the amount of virtual memory usually delivers the best results.

Reclaim Memory with a System Restart

You can often free up a significant amount of memory by restarting Windows. Ideally, when you exit an application, the application completely removes itself from your PC's memory so that Windows can use that memory for other applications and to perform additional tasks. In reality, many programs leave behind remnants of computer code that occupy memory even after you exit the application. Restarting Windows clears applications completely from memory. If you notice that your PC is beginning to act sluggish, you can save your work, close all applications, and then restart Windows by following the steps in this section. If you prefer not to shut down your system, you can try a memory optimizer as discussed in the next section, "Download and Install a Memory Optimizer," which purges your PC's memory automatically. Logging out and logging back on may also help reclaim memory.

Before you restart your system, you should save any documents on which you have been working to prevent losing your changes. You should then exit any programs that are running. If more than one user is logged on to Windows, have those users log off to prevent losing any work. You can then safely restart Windows, as shown in these steps.

Reclaim Memory with a System Restart

1. Click Start.
2. Click Turn Off Computer.

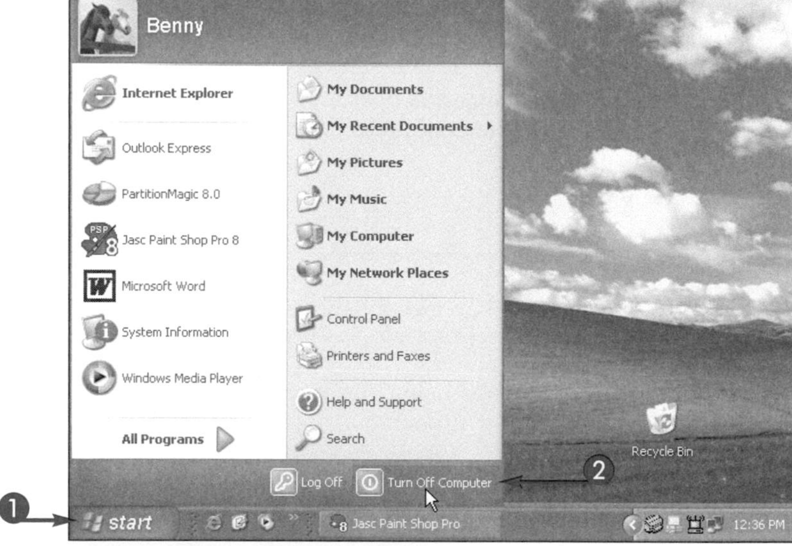

The Turn off computer dialog box appears.

3. Click Restart.

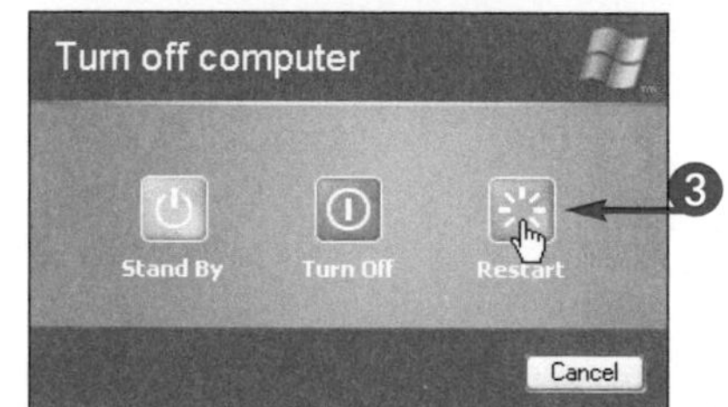

Windows shuts down.

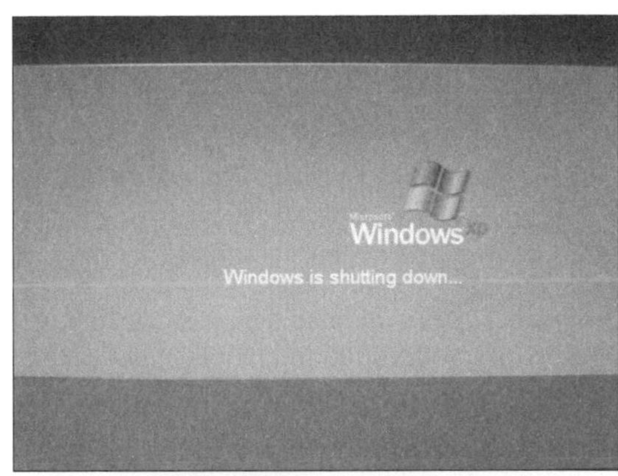

Windows restarts and displays the desktop.

You should notice a boost in system performance.

Can I tell how much memory I reclaimed by restarting my system?

▼ Yes. You can run the System Information utility, as discussed in Chapter 2, before and after you restart Windows. If you notice that the restart reclaims very little memory or shows that even more physical memory is being used, Windows is probably set up to run several programs on startup. Refer to Chapter 13 for instructions on how to streamline the Windows startup.

Is any version of Windows better at managing memory?

▼ Windows XP and Windows 2000 are much better than older versions of Windows at managing memory. Windows XP and Windows 2000 allocate memory separately to each application that runs, and they reclaim this memory from applications when you exit them. In older versions of Windows, programs remain in memory after you exit them. See the next section, "Download and Install a Memory Optimizer," for details.

Should I shut down my PC or let it run when I am done using it?

▼ Experts debate whether users should keep their PCs running or shut them down when not in use. One good reason to shut down a PC when you are not using it is to prevent unauthorized access to it over the Internet, if you have an always-on connection, or prevent it from dialing out without your permission, if you have a modem connection.

Download and Install a Memory Optimizer

You can download and install a utility for optimizing memory in Windows. If your PC is running Windows XP or Windows 2000, you already have an operating system that manages memory efficiently. You can install a memory optimizer, and it may provide your PC with a slight performance boost or it may simply consume system resources.

Older versions of Windows, including Windows 98 and Windows Me, manage memory less efficiently. In many cases, when you exit an application in an older version of Windows, the application no longer appears on-screen, but it continues to occupy memory. If you leave your PC on for an extended period of time, remnants of programs build up in your PC's memory leaving your PC with insufficient amounts of free memory to run applications. Applications may begin to freeze or crash, or Windows may eventually crash, displaying the dreaded blue screen that forces you to reboot your PC.

A memory optimizer automatically removes unused programs from memory to free up memory and reduce the risk of system crashes.

Download and Install a Memory Optimizer

1. Launch your Web browser.
2. In the address bar, type **www.download.com** and press Enter.
   - The Download.com home page appears.
3. Click the Utilities & Drivers link.

Links to shareware and trialware utilities and drivers appear.

4. Click the Optimizers & Diagnostics link.

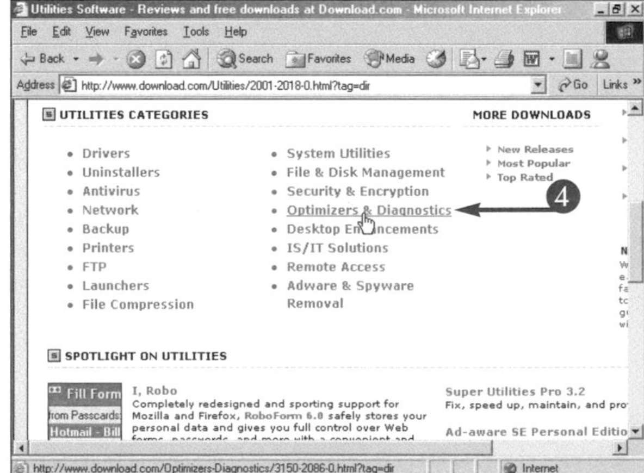

A list of system optimizers and diagnostic utilities appears.

5 Scroll down the list to find a memory optimizer you want to try.

6 Click the link to download the memory optimizer.

The File Download dialog box appears, prompting you to specify whether you want to open or save the file.

7 Click Open.

Your Web browser downloads the program and initiates the installation routine.

8 Follow the on-screen instructions to install the memory optimizer.

The memory optimizer is installed on your PC.

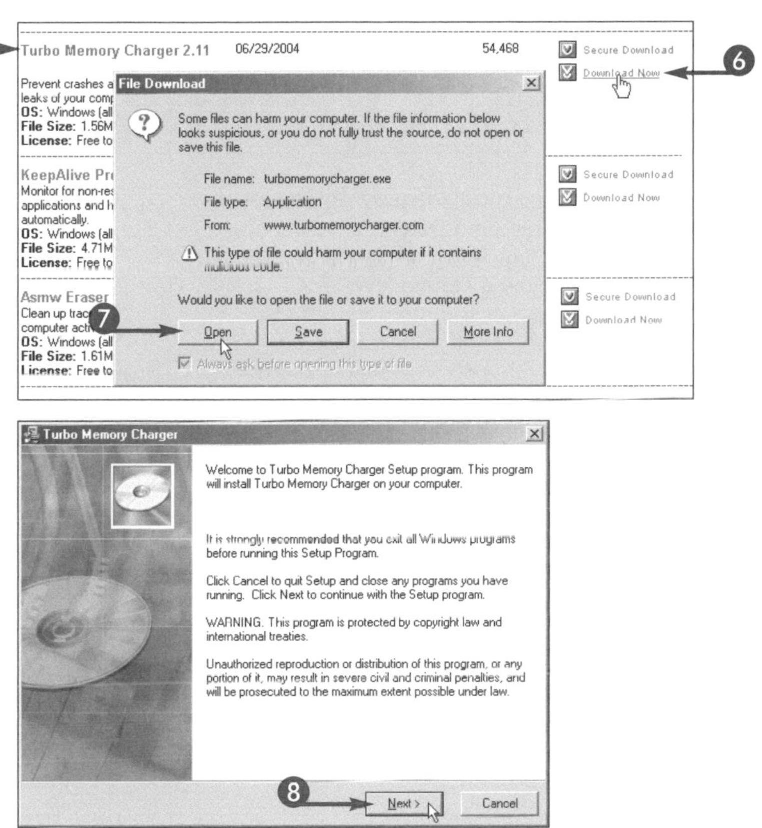

PART III

Can I run a memory optimizer in Windows XP or 2000 to see if it improves performance?

▼ Yes. A company called brentleim Software offers a freeware version of Memory Optimizer, which is specifically designed to run under Windows XP and Windows 2000. You can download a copy of the program at www.brentleimsoftware.com. The program provides a basic interface that shows you graphically how much physical and virtual memory is in use and provides single-click access to memory optimization.

Does the memory optimizer require a great deal of system resources?

▼ Most memory optimizers are fairly small programs that run in the background and optimize memory only when free memory dips below a certain level. You can usually configure the program to specify how aggressively you want it to manage memory, as explained in the next section, "Configure a Memory Optimizer." Memory optimizers typically free much more memory than they require to run.

Do I absolutely need a memory optimizer?

▼ If your PC is running a version of Windows prior to Windows XP or Windows 2000, and it has only 32MB of physical memory, a memory optimizer can significantly improve performance and help reduce the frequency of program crashes. If you cannot or do not want to install additional physical memory, a memory optimizer is an excellent option.

Configure a Memory Optimizer

You can configure most memory optimizers to automatically free up a specific amount or percentage of your PC's memory when the amount of free memory dips below a certain level. For example, you can enter settings to instruct the memory optimizer to reclaim 50MB of memory when your PC has only 2MB remaining. You can also choose to schedule memory optimization at certain intervals such as every two or three hours, for example. Turbo Memory Charger, which is highlighted in the steps in this section, can also free up memory whenever you launch a program.

Memory optimizers typically run in the background, monitoring the amount of memory. When a memory optimizer starts freeing up memory, it takes control of most of your system resources and briefly prevents you from working. The interruption can become annoying, so when configuring your memory optimizer, you need to decide how aggressively you want it to function. If your memory optimizer takes control of your computer every 15 minutes to free some memory, it may slow down your PC rather than speed it up. You can usually get by with one or two optimizations per day.

Configure a Memory Optimizer

1. Launch your memory optimizer.

   This example shows Turbo Memory Charger, which you can download at www.turbomemorycharger.com.

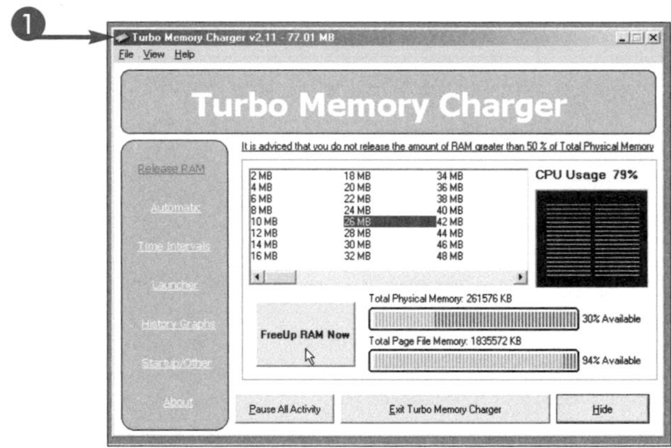

2. Click the option for automating memory optimization.
3. Click the interval at which you want the optimizer to check for low memory conditions.
4. Click here and select the level of free memory that initiates an optimization.
5. Click the amount of RAM you want the optimizer to release.

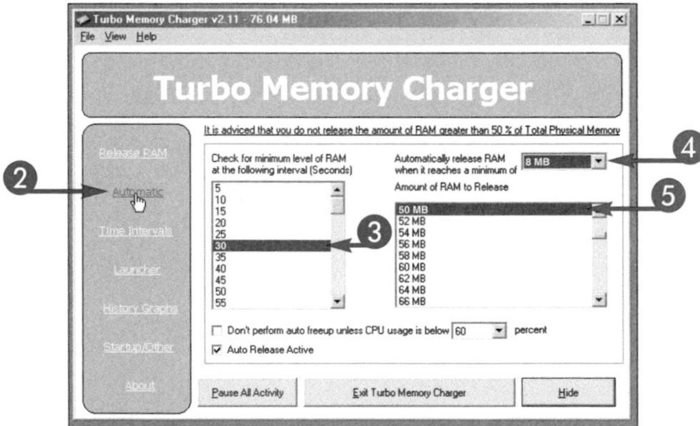

- You can click here to instruct the optimizer not to optimize memory if the processor is too busy (☐ changes to ☑).

6 Click here (☐ changes to ☑) to enable the optimizer to automatically release memory according to the settings you entered.

7 Click Hide.

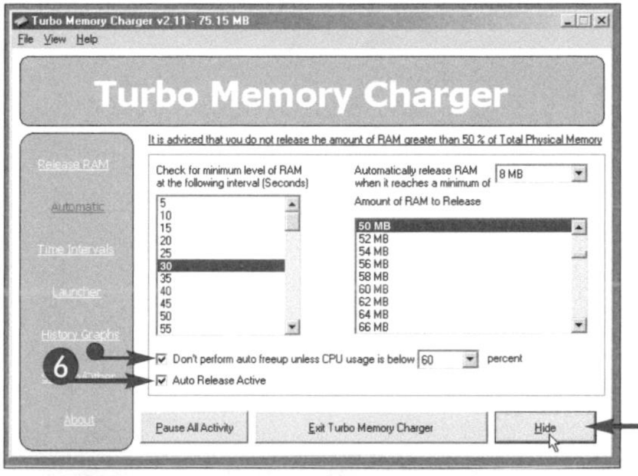

- The memory optimizer minimizes, but it remains running in the background.

You can double-click the memory optimizer's icon to check or change its settings.

How much memory should I have the optimizer release?

▼ Turbo Memory Charger recommends that you release no more than 50 percent of your system's physical memory, or RAM. If you instruct your memory optimizer to become too aggressive, it may try to release programs from RAM that need to be running. This can cause programs to crash or cause Windows to lock up. Your goal is not to free up as much memory as possible but to make the best use of it.

Do I need to keep a memory optimizer running in the background?

▼ No. You can clear memory at any time by running your memory optimizer and then clicking the button or selecting the option to optimize memory. You can then exit the program. This prevents your memory optimizer from trying to free memory at inopportune times. However, it places the burden of monitoring memory use on you.

Does a memory optimizer clear all of the programs that I do not use from memory?

▼ No. A memory optimizer typically ensures that any program you exit is completely removed from memory. Programs that you do not use may run on startup without your knowledge. Refer to Chapters 13 and 14 for techniques to deal with these programs.

12 Adjust the BIOS Startup Settings

13 Streamline the Windows Startup

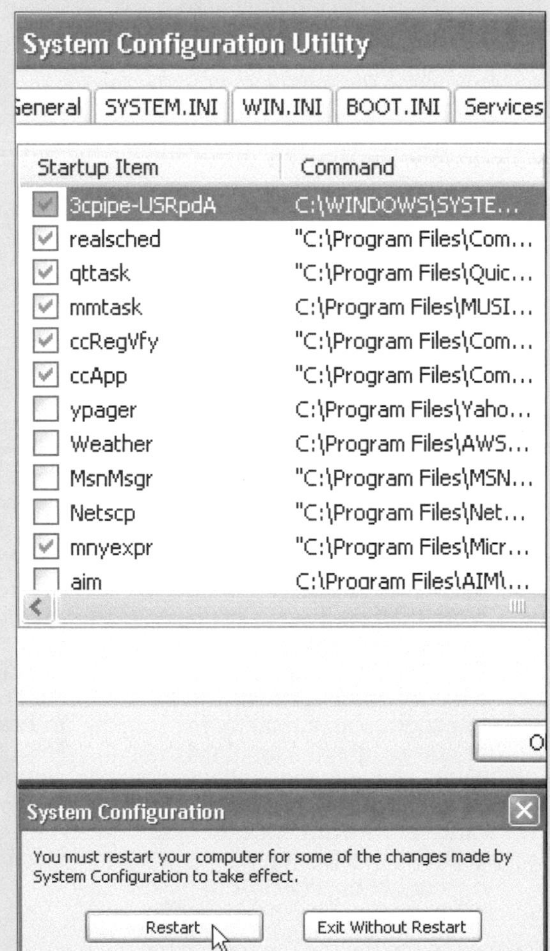

PART IV
MAKING YOUR PC START FASTER

Understanding Your PC's BIOS

You can make your PC start faster by adjusting its BIOS startup settings. *BIOS,* pronounced *buy-ose,* is an acronym for Basic Input/Output System. It is built-in computer code that provides information about your PC's components and instructions that enable the various components to communicate with one another. Your PC stores the BIOS on a ROM — read-only memory — chip, and the BIOS generally remains unchanged. However, your PC stores BIOS configuration settings and the current date and time in a separate area that you can modify.

PC manufacturers discourage users from accessing the BIOS configuration settings, because entering a wrong setting can cause serious problems. However, if you are careful and you record any setting before changing it, you can often tweak the settings to improve your PC's performance. For example, you can change the boot sequence, which is the order in which the PC examines your disk drives for an operating system, such as Windows, that it can load. If your PC is set up to check drive A first, you can change the setting to have your PC go directly to the drive on which Windows is installed. This chapter provides instructions on how to change some relatively safe settings to make your PC start a little faster.

CMOS

Your PC stores the BIOS on a separate ROM chip. Almost all new PCs use a *Flash ROM* chip, which enables you to upgrade the BIOS using software from the BIOS developer rather than having to physically replace the chip. The system date and the BIOS configuration settings that you can change are not stored on the ROM chip. They are stored on the CMOS, which is an acronym for Complementary Metal-Oxide Semiconductor.

A small battery feeds the CMOS a steady flow of current to enable it to store the system date and configuration settings even when you turn off your PC. If the battery runs out of power, the date and settings are lost, and the PC does not start up properly. This usually happens only on PCs that are more than three years old.

In this chapter, you learn how to back up your CMOS so you can restore it if you enter a wrong setting. An added bonus to backing up the CMOS data is that if the CMOS battery runs out of power, you can replace the battery and then restore the date and settings from your backup to get your PC up and running in minutes.

BIOS Versions

PC motherboards — the main circuit boards inside PCs — can have different versions of the BIOS. The BIOS version typically consists of the manufacturer's name, such as Phoenix or AMI, followed by a code that represents the BIOS version. As with any software, the BIOS can include bugs or may not provide support for newer technologies, so BIOS manufacturers commonly release upgrades that you can install, typically by running a BIOS upgrade utility from a floppy disk or CD when you boot your PC.

If your PC is having no problems, you do not need to be concerned about upgrading the BIOS, but if the BIOS has problems handling new hardware or device drivers, your PC's manufacturer may recommend that you install a BIOS upgrade. You can usually download the latest BIOS version from the PC manufacturer's or BIOS developer's Web site. The upgrades are often offered free of charge.

If you do need to upgrade the BIOS, follow the manufacturer's recommendations and instructions carefully. Installing the wrong version can render your system unusable, at least until you obtain and install the correct version.

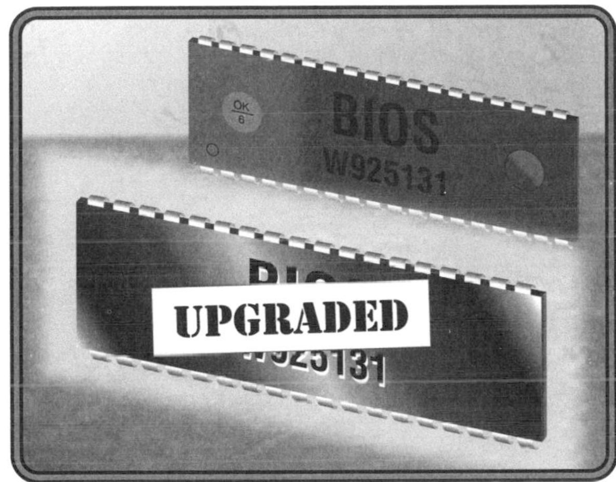

What to Expect When Changing BIOS Settings

This high-tech discussion of the BIOS, CMOS, and Flash ROM may lead you to think that changing the BIOS Settings is a complex task. Actually, the most difficult step is accessing the menu that enables you to enter your changes. Most PC manufacturers discourage users from changing BIOS settings by making the settings difficult to access. In some cases, a message appears on the screen indicating the keystroke you must press to display the setup screen. In other cases, the manufacturer lists the keystroke somewhere in the operator's manual or on the manufacturer's Web site.

Once you find the keystroke, you need quick fingers to press it before Windows starts. Once your PC launches its operating system, it locks you out of the BIOS settings.

Another challenge you face is learning how to navigate the BIOS settings menu. Because your PC does not load a mouse driver until after it launches Windows, you have no mouse control over the menu. You must use arrow keys, PageUp, PageDown, and other keystrokes to access options and change settings.

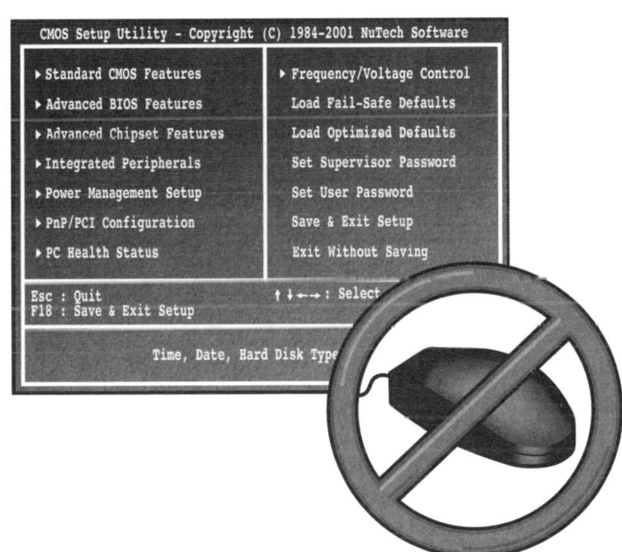

PART IV

Back Up Your PC's CMOS

You can back up your PC's CMOS so that if you change a BIOS setting that causes a problem, you can easily restore the setting and solve the problem. This also provides you with a record of the settings in case the CMOS battery runs out of power or a computer glitch deletes the settings.

Alternatively, you can back up the settings manually, by recording each setting on paper. You may find this a tedious process, but if you keep a log of your PC and the settings you change, a paper record of your PC's BIOS settings is a valuable addition to your log. Some users prefer not to write down all of the settings; instead, they record any settings before changing them. Doing this may help you recover if a setting you change causes a problem, but it does little to help you recover if you lose all BIOS settings.

Another way to make a backup is to use a utility to back up the settings to a floppy disk. PC management utilities, such as Norton SystemWorks, enable you to create rescue disks that include the contents of the CMOS. You can also find CMOS backup utilities on the Web, such as CMOSsave, presented in these steps.

Back Up Your PC's CMOS

Download CMOSsave

1. In your Web browser's address bar, type **mindprod.com/products.html** and press Enter.
2. Scroll down the page and click the link to download CMOSsave/CMOSrest.
3. Click Open.

   Your Web browser downloads the Zipped file and displays its contents.
4. Copy or extract the files to folder, floppy disk, or CD.

Back Up CMOS Settings

1. Click Start.
2. Click All Programs.
3. Click Accessories.
4. Click Command Prompt.

Note: *You can also display the command prompt by starting your PC with a bootable disk in the floppy disk drive.*

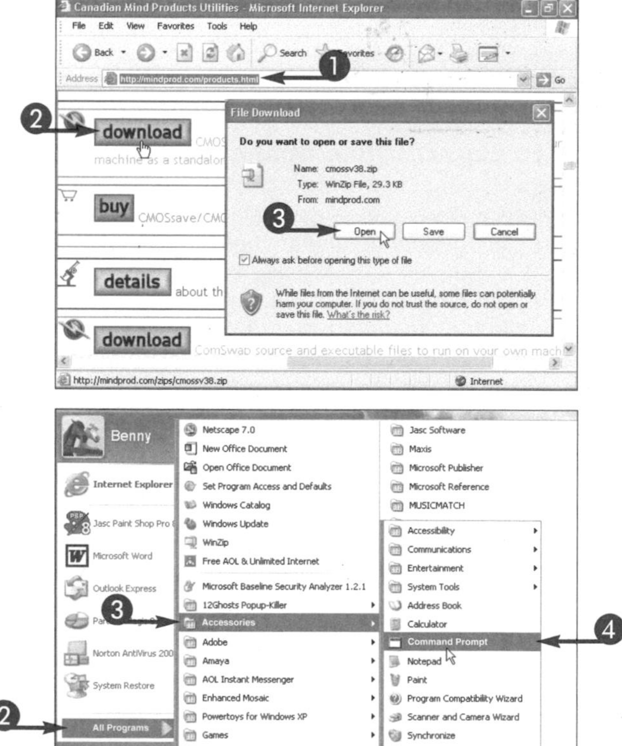

5 Type *c:* where *c* is the letter of the drive on which the CMOSsave files are stored and press Enter.

6 Type ***cd\foldername*** replacing *foldername* with the name of the folder in which the CMOSsave files are stored, and press Enter.

7 Type ***cmossave filename.sav*** replacing *filename* with the name of the file in which you want the CMOS settings saved, and press Enter.

- CMOSsave copies the CMOS settings to the specified file.

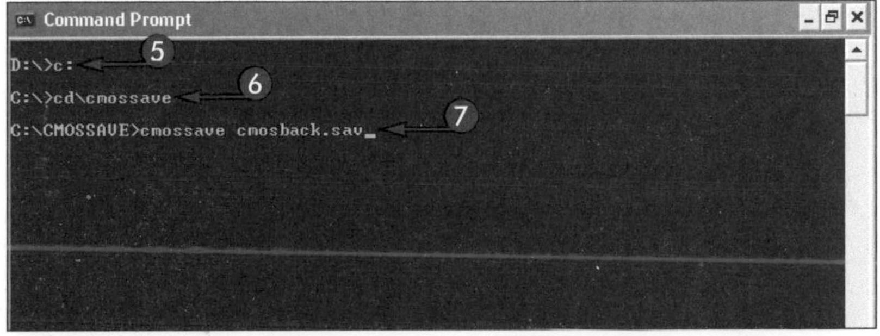


```
Command Prompt
D:\>c:

C:\>cd\cmossave

C:\CMOSSAVE>cmossave cmosback.sav
     CMOSSave 3.8

Saves contents of CMOS to a file on hard disk or floppy.
copyright (c) 1991-2004 Roedy Green, Canadian Mind Products
#327 - 964 Heywood Avenue, Victoria, BC Canada V8V 2Y5
tel:(250) 361-9093   mailto:roedyg@mindprod.com   http://mindprod.com
Shareware to freely distribute and use for any purpose except military.

CMOS successfully saved

C:\CMOSSAVE>
```

PART IV

I cannot find CMOSsave to download it. Do you have any other suggestions?

▼ Many backup programs and system utilities, such as Norton System Works, can help you create rescue disks or CDs that contain the CMOS contents. If you have such a program, check its help system for information. Your BIOS setup menu may also offer an option for backing up the BIOS. See the next section, "Access the BIOS Settings," and then examine the menu system for a backup option. You can find shareware or trialware versions of other rescue utilities on the Web; you may need to try several to find one that works on your system.

If I do not back up the BIOS settings and I lose the settings, what should I do?

▼ Some PCs include a built-in backup that contains the default BIOS settings. If you lose settings because of a CMOS battery failure, you can replace the battery, restart the PC, access the BIOS settings, and then press a special keystroke to restore the default settings. If you lost settings because the CMOS battery ran out of power, you should change the battery. The process is not very complicated, but it does require you to open the system and locate the battery on the motherboard. Check your PC's documentation or contact technical support and follow all recommended safety precautions when working inside your PC.

Access the BIOS Settings

You can press your PC's setup keystroke on startup but before Windows starts to access the BIOS settings. Most PC manufacturers display the setup keystroke as one of the messages on the startup screen that appears when you first turn on your PC. You may see a message such as "Press F2 to enter setup." As long as you have your monitor powered up, you should see the setup keystroke. However, not all PC manufacturers display the setup keystroke on startup, so you may need to refer to your PC's manual or contact technical support online or over the phone.

Many PCs use one of the function keys as the setup keystroke — F1, F2, and F10 are fairly common. Others use the Del key or a keystroke combination, such as Ctrl+Alt+Esc. If you cannot find the keystroke anywhere on the screen, in your records, or through the manufacturer's technical support, the screen may display the BIOS manufacturer and version number. Use this information to try to track down the setup keystroke online, or refer to the table of keystrokes on the next page. Without the correct keystroke, you cannot access the BIOS setup.

Access the BIOS Settings

1. Click Start.
2. Click Turn Off Computer.

   The Turn off computer dialog box appears.
3. Click the Turn Off button.

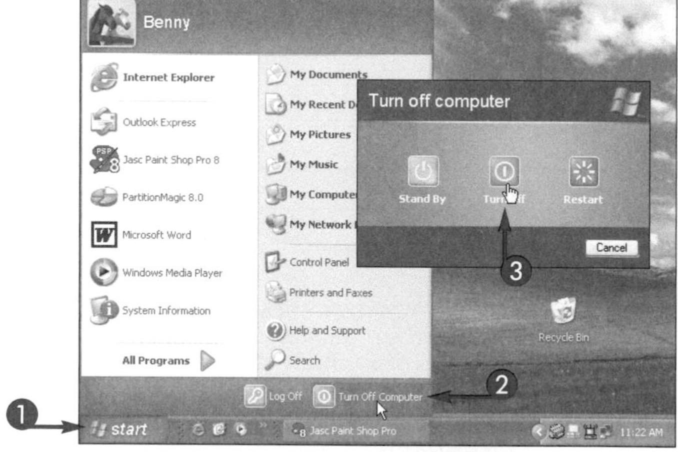

Windows shuts down and typically turns off the power to the PC.

4. If Windows does not power down your PC, press and hold your PC's power button until the PC turns off.
5. If your monitor is off, press its power button to turn it on.
6. Press your PC's power button to turn on your PC.

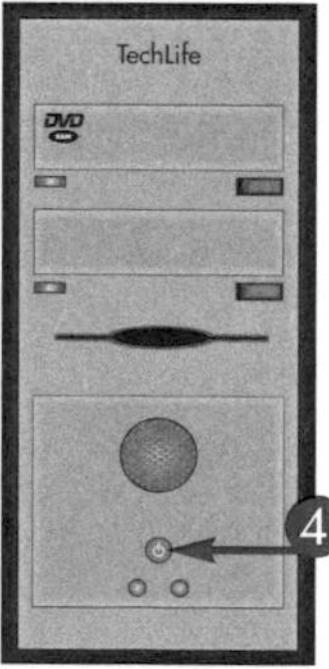

Your PC starts and startup messages appear on the monitor.

7. When a message appears instructing you to press the setup keystroke, press the specified keystroke.

Note: *If no message appears, press the setup keystroke several times as your PC starts up.*

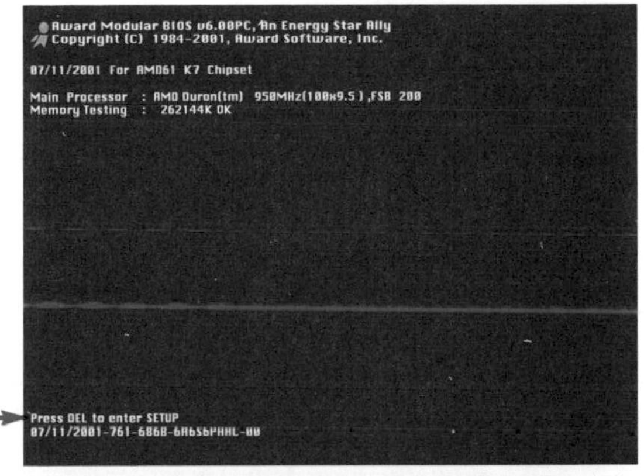

The BIOS settings menu appears.

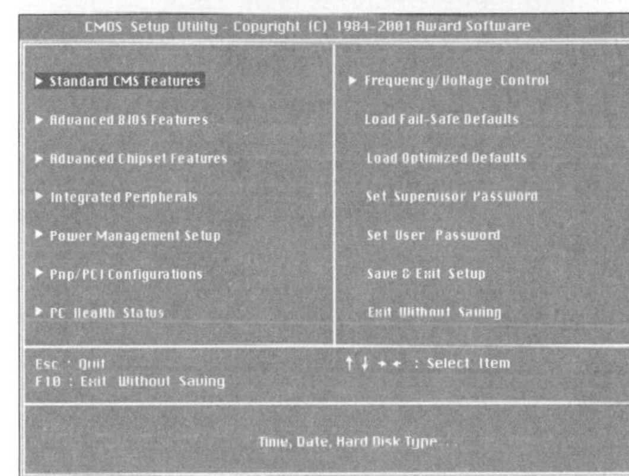

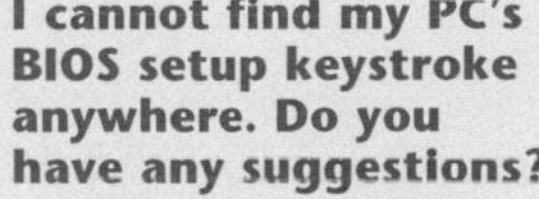

I cannot find my PC's BIOS setup keystroke anywhere. Do you have any suggestions?

Yes. Try the Del key first, and then F1, F2, or F10. Refer to the keystrokes in the following table.

Keystroke	PC or BIOS
F1	Older IBM PS/1 models, Gateway 2000 PCs, some Toshiba models, some versions of the Phoenix BIOS
F2	NEC, Micron
F10	Compaq
Del	AMI BIOS
Esc	Some Toshiba models
Insert	Some newer IBM PS/2 models
Tab	eMachines
Ctrl+Alt+[+]	Assorted PCs
Ctrl+Alt+?	Older IBM PS/2 models
Ctrl+Alt+Enter	Some Dells and other assorted PCs
Ctrl+Alt+Esc	AST, Tandon, and other PCs, some versions of the Award BIOS, some versions of the Phoenix BIOS
Ctrl+Alt+Ins	Some IBM PS/2 PCs and some versions of the Phoenix BIOS
Ctrl+Alt+S	Some versions of the Phoenix BIOS
Ctrl+Esc	Many assorted PCs, very common
Ctrl+Ins	Some IBM PS/2 models
Ctrl+S	Some versions of the Phoenix BIOS

Change the Boot Sequence for Faster Startups

You can change the *boot sequence* in your BIOS setup to have your PC start faster. The boot sequence is the order in which your PC examines its disk drives to find a disk from which it can load Windows. Many PCs examine the floppy drive first, and then the hard drive, and then the CD drive. If no bootable disk is in the floppy drive, the PC moves on to the hard drive to find the operating system. This configuration enables your PC to boot from an emergency floppy disk if it cannot boot from the hard drive. However, assuming your PC is running well, this configuration wastes time by checking the floppy drive every time you start your PC.

The BIOS setup menu enables you to change the boot sequence. You can place your hard drive at the top of the list, so your PC goes directly to it. Changing the boot sequence can also be useful if you need to run Windows Recovery from the Windows installation CD or run system diagnostics on startup. Instead of placing the floppy or hard drive at the top of the list, you can place the CD drive first.

Change the Boot Sequence for Faster Startups

❶ Start or restart your PC and access the BIOS setup screen.

Note: *See the previous section, "Access the BIOS Settings," for more information.*

❷ Navigate to the Boot options.

Navigation varies depending on the BIOS and version number.

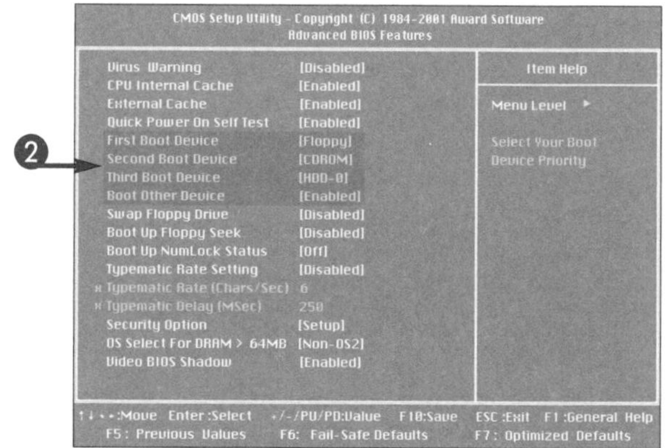

❸ Follow the on-screen instructions to move each drive to the desired position in the boot sequence.

- In this example, you select the First Boot Device option and then select the drive you want to use as the first boot device.

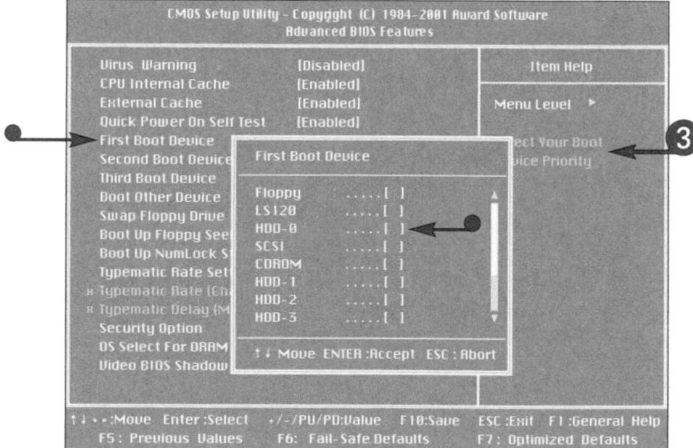

4 Navigate to the options for saving and exiting the BIOS Setup.

5 Select to highlight the option for saving and exiting.

6 Press Enter.

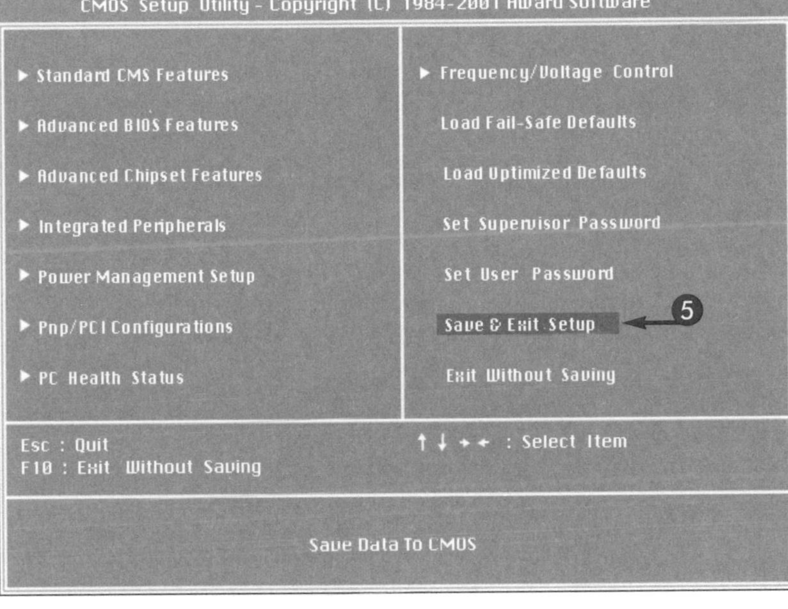

The BIOS setup may display a dialog box prompting you to confirm.

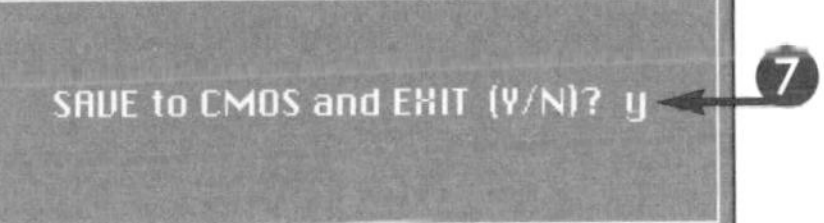

7 If a dialog box appears prompting you to confirm, select Yes or OK and press Enter.

The BIOS setup saves your settings in CMOS.

Can I look at the settings without changing them?

▼ Yes, but to be perfectly safe, when you are finished examining the settings, choose the option to exit without saving changes. If you inadvertantly changed a setting, this prevents the change from affecting your PC's performance. You can use this technique to examine and record BIOS settings so you have a backup on paper.

Can I experiment with different settings to optimize my PC?

▼ It is recommended that you change no setting unless you know the potential effects of the change. If you want to experiment, write down a setting before changing it and change only one setting at a time. By following this procedure, if you do encounter a problem, you can more easily trace the problem back to its cause and change the setting back.

I changed several settings and now my PC is not functioning properly. Can I choose the option for resetting the defaults?

▼ Sometimes, the setting for returning the defaults does not restore the manufacturer's settings; it only restores the original BIOS settings for the motherboard. The manufacturer may have changed the settings for an expansion card or drive that you ordered special. Changing back to the default settings can cause problems. If you have a backup, now is the time to use it.

Restore Your PC's CMOS

If you backed up the contents of your PC's CMOS, you can restore the BIOS settings in the event that you erred when changing a setting or the BIOS settings were deleted from the CMOS. If the CMOS battery runs out of power or a computer glitch erases or corrupts the contents of the CMOS, the BIOS remains safely stored on the ROM chip. However, any settings you entered are lost.

Your PC may store a backup of the BIOS settings automatically, in which case you can restore your settings from the backup by selecting a command from the BIOS setup menu. This usually restores the most recent version of the settings. If your PC does not store a backup, then you can restore the settings from the backup copy you created using your CMOS backup utility.

The procedure for restoring the BIOS settings varies depending on the recovery diskette or CD you made. However, in most cases, you need to boot your PC from the floppy disk or CD first. Refer to the previous section, "Change the Boot Sequence for Faster Startups," for instructions on how to change the boot sequence so you can boot from a floppy disk or CD.

Restore Your PC's CMOS

Note: *These steps use CMOSrest as an example.*

1. Load a bootable diskette or CD into your PC's floppy drive or CD drive.

2. Turn on the power to your PC.

   - Your PC boots up and displays the command prompt.

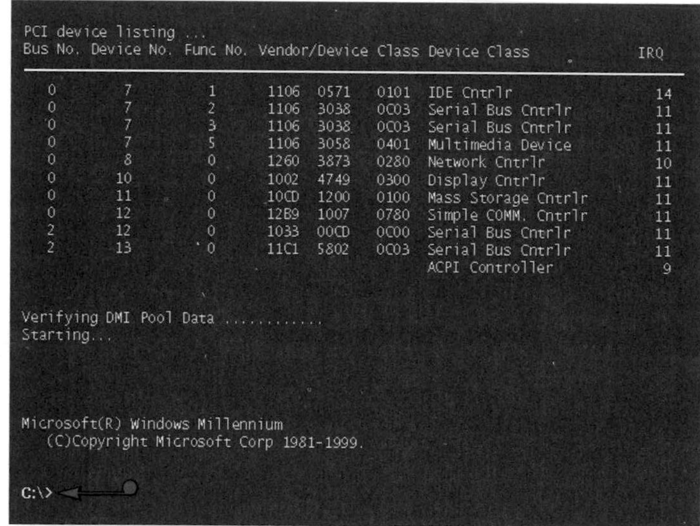

3. Type *a:* where *a* is the letter of the drive on which the CMOSrest files are stored, and press Enter.

   - If necessary, type *cd\foldername* replacing *foldername* with the name of the folder in which the CMOSrest files are stored, and press Enter.

4. Type **cmosrest** *filename*.**sav** replacing *filename* with the name of the file in which the CMOS settings are saved.

5. Press Enter.

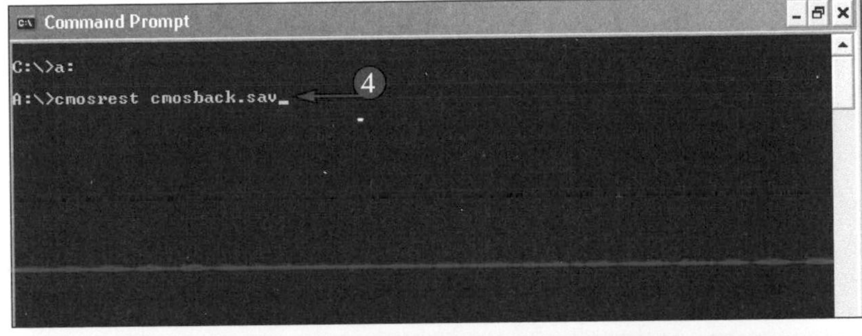

- CMOSrest restores the CMOS settings.

I have several backups of my BIOS settings. How do I know which one is most recent?

▼ You may need to examine your backup files on another PC to find the file that has the most current date. If you are checking files on a floppy disk, write-protect the disk first, so it does not pick up viruses if the other PC is infected. Insert the disk, and then use My Computer to display its contents. You can position the mouse pointer on a file to display the date when it was created, or you can click View, and then Details to display the date the file was created and modified and other information.

My PC does not boot from the backup disk I created. What should I do?

▼ You should have an emergency disk you created when you first installed Windows. You can boot from this disk and then run the CMOS recovery utility from another disk. If you do not have an emergency disk or if your PC has no floppy disk drive, try booting from the Windows installation CD, as discussed in Chapter 31. You may then be able to copy the CMOSrest files and the file that contains the CMOS settings to a folder on your hard drive and run the restore operation from the hard drive.

Run the System Configuration Utility

You can run the Windows System Configuration Utility to determine which programs automatically run when Windows starts. Windows runs many programs and Microsoft services on startup. These programs continue to run in the background, performing tasks behind the scenes, as you use your PC. In many cases, these programs are essential or at least very useful. For example, your printer may run several processes in the background to ensure that it is ready when you print a document.

However, many programs you rarely, if ever, use configure themselves to run in the background whether or not they are needed. Some may even display a dialog box occasionally to remind you to subscribe to a service or find out more about a product. These programs consume valuable system resources that your PC can use to perform important tasks.

The Windows System Configuration Utility can display a list of programs that Windows is set up to run automatically. Often, you can identify programs in the list that you rarely or never use, and disable them to prevent Windows from launching them at startup.

Run the System Configuration Utility

1. Click Start.
2. Click Run.

The Run dialog box appears.

3. Type **msconfig**.
4. Click OK.

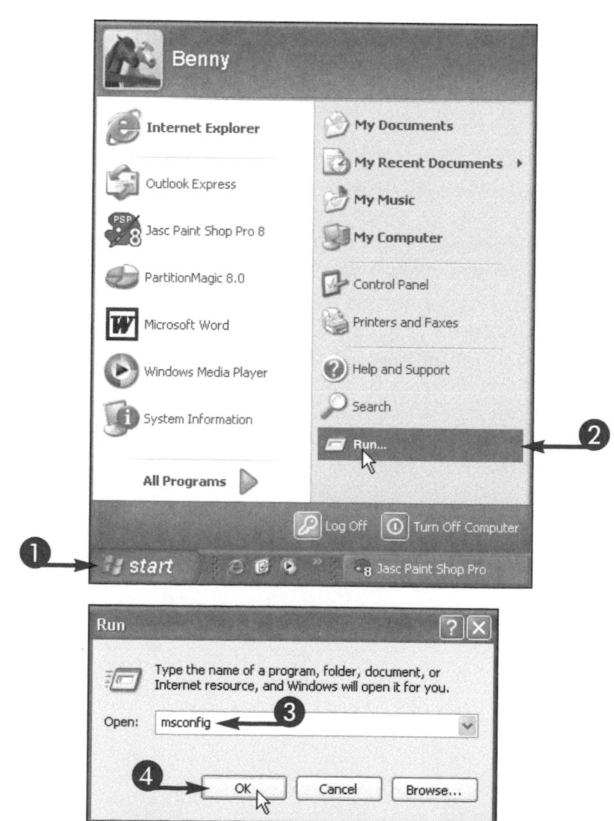

The System Configuration Utility appears.

- You can click the tabs to explore various options.
- You can click Help to obtain additional information.

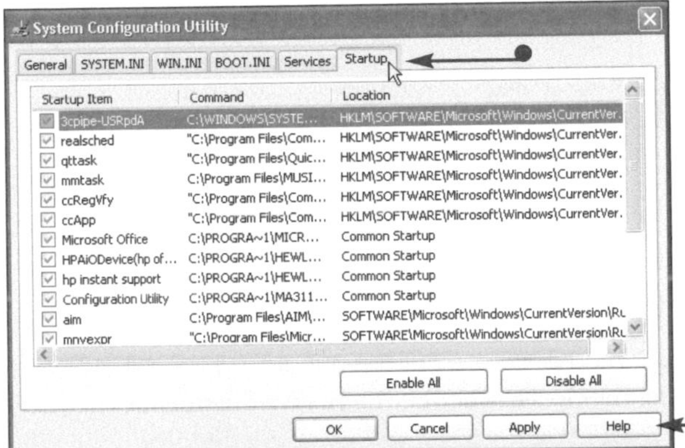

5 When you are done exploring the System Configuration Utility, click Cancel.

Windows closes the System Configuration Utility.

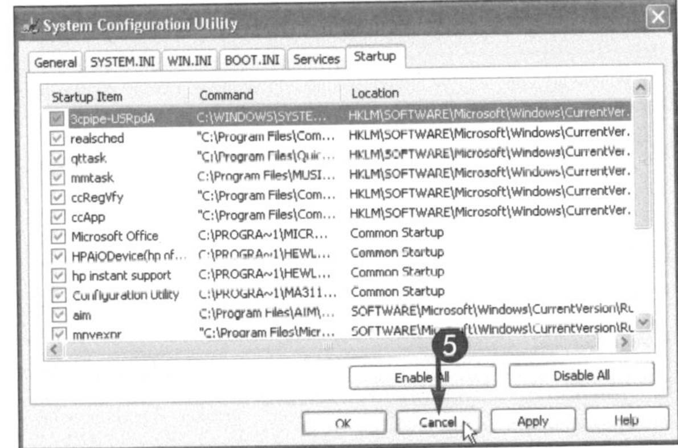

Can I use the System Configuration Utility to troubleshoot problems with Windows and my applications?

Yes. The System Configuration Utility is an excellent tool for troubleshooting all aspects of PC performance. Technicians commonly troubleshoot problems by disabling most of the items listed in the System Configuration Utility and then enabling items one at a time or in groups until the problem item is discovered. This methodical process of elimination allows the technician to focus on the cause of a problem. Before changing any settings in the System Configuration Utility, write down the original settings or back up the Windows system registry, as discussed in Chapter 19.

Is the System Configuration Utility available in all versions of Windows?

The System Configuration Utility is available in most recent versions of Windows, including Windows 98, Me, and XP. In Windows 98 and Me, you can access the utility by clicking Start, Programs, Accessories, System Tools, System Information, and then clicking the Tools menu and selecting System Configuration Utility.

Is there anything in the System Configuration Utility that I should avoid?

The System Configuration Utility contains a tab labeled BOOT.INI, which you should not edit unless specifically instructed to do so by a qualified technician. Entering the wrong setting in this file may make your PC unusable.

Perform a Diagnostic Startup

Using the System Configuration Utility, you can perform a diagnostic startup to determine if Windows is loading a program on startup that is causing a problem or negatively affecting your PC's performance. The diagnostic startup disables almost every program, process, and service that Windows runs on startup, providing you with a clean environment to troubleshoot problems. If you perform a diagnostic startup, and you find that the problem is still present, you can then switch back to a normal startup and examine other areas for possible causes.

One of the most beneficial features of the System Configuration Utility is that it allows you to enable and disable programs without permanently deleting their commands. You can easily reenable an item by placing a check mark next to it.

A diagnostic startup casts a wide net to search for problems. If you perform a diagnostic startup, restart Windows, and find that the problem is no longer present, your work has just begun. You must then proceed to enable individual items or groups of items, restarting Windows after each change, to narrow down the possible causes. The next section, "Disable Services and Programs on Startup," shows you how to enable and disable individual items.

Perform a Diagnostic Startup

1 Launch the System Configuration Utility.

Note: *See the section "Run the System Configuration Utility," for details.*

2 Click the Diagnostic Startup – load basic devices and services only option (○ changes to ◉).

3 Click OK.

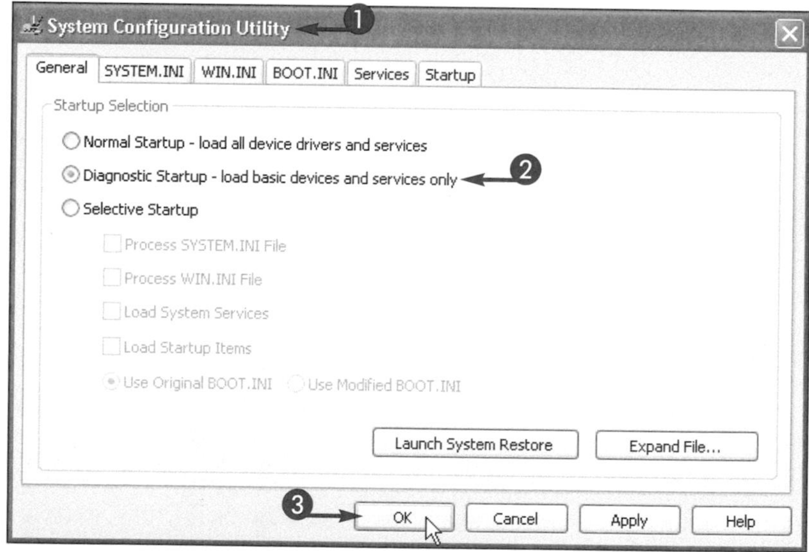

The System Configuration dialog box displays a message indicating that you must restart your PC for all changes to take effect.

4 Click Restart.

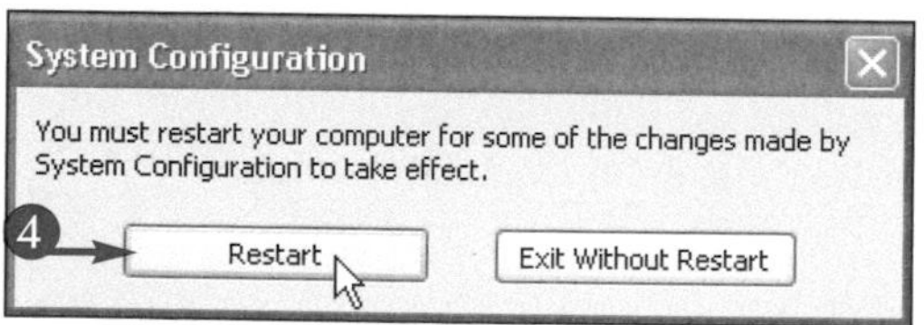

Windows shuts down and then restarts and displays a message indicating that Windows is running in diagnostic or selective mode.

5 Click OK.

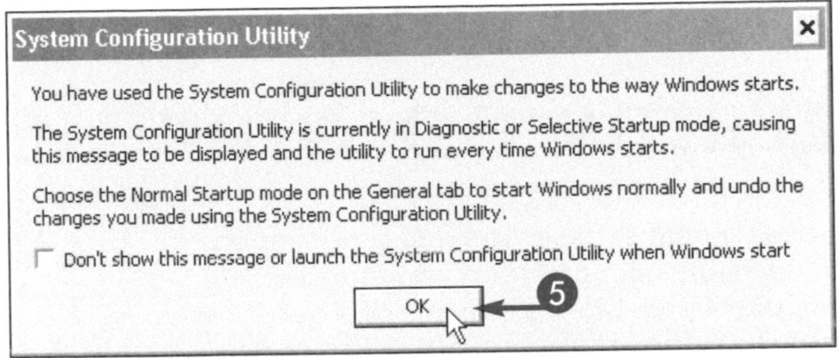

The System Configuration Utility window appears.

6 Click Cancel.

Note: *If you click OK instead of Cancel, Windows asks if you want to restart Windows.*

The System Configuration Utility window closes.

You can now test your PC's performance, as explained in Chapter 1, or use your PC as you normally do to determine if its performance has improved.

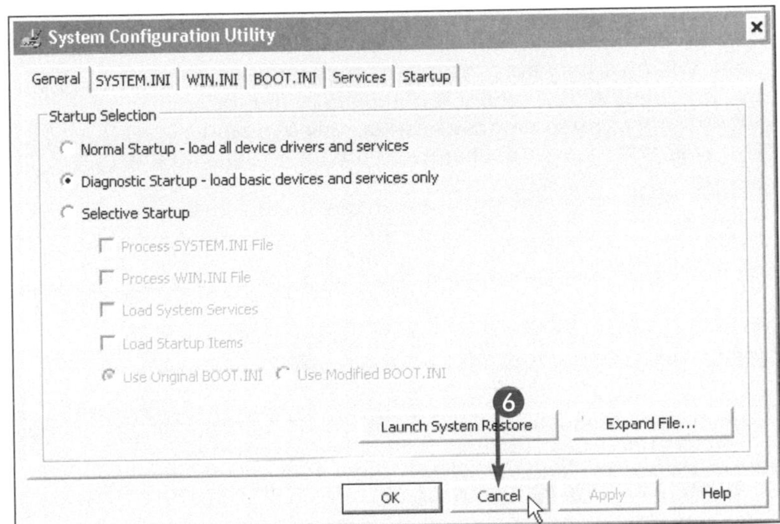

My PC runs great with the diagnostic startup. Can I keep it this way?

▼ The diagnostic startup is not intended to be a solution. It is a troubleshooting tool to help you find a permanent solution. On a diagnostic startup, several essential programs and services may not run, such as your antivirus software. Run in diagnostic mode only long enough to track down the cause of a problem or a performance issue.

I noticed the Selective Startup option. Can I use it instead?

▼ Yes. You can use the Selective Startup option, but merely selecting the option does little to streamline the Windows startup. You must then use the options on the Services and Startup tabs to disable items that you do not want Windows to run on startup. Refer to the next section, "Disable Services and Programs on Startup," for more information.

Can I re-enable everything that the diagnostic startup disabled?

▼ Yes. Run the System Configuration Utility again, click the Normal Startup – load all device drivers and services option (○ changes to ◉) and click OK. When the System Configuration Utility dialog box appears, informing you that you must restart Windows for all changes to take effect, click the Restart button. Windows restarts and runs all programs and services that it is set up to run on startup.

Disable Services and Programs on Startup

You can disable individual services and programs on startup to troubleshoot problems and to make Windows start faster. Many programs configure Windows to run them automatically on startup. Even if you uninstall a program, it may leave behind a command for running it. Windows then must spend time looking for the program. Windows may even display an error message on startup, indicating that it cannot find the file to run the program. Some of these programs can occupy a great deal of RAM, which Windows can allocate to programs that you actually use.

Using the System Configuration Utility, you can display lists of programs and services that run on startup. These lists often contain programs that you can readily recognize as programs that you have uninstalled or programs that display annoying messages that you have to spend time canceling. You might see a program, such as Netscape, that you were not aware was running taking up 18MB or more of RAM. By disabling these items, and then hiding the System Configuration Utility, as explained in the next section, "Hide the System Configuration Utility on Startup," you can make Windows start faster and run more efficiently.

Disable Services and Programs on Startup

1. Launch the System Configuration Utility.

Note: *See the section "Run the System Configuration Utility," for details.*

2. Click the Services tab.
3. Click the Hide all Microsoft Services option (☑ changes to ☐).

   This prevents you from accidentally disabling an essential service.

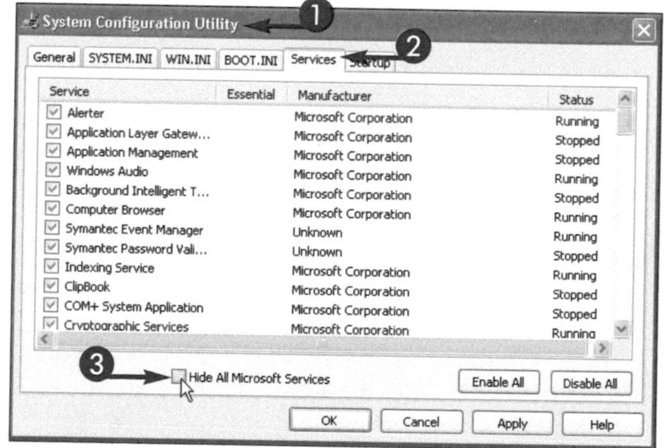

4. Examine the list of services for any easily recognizable services you want to disable.
5. If you see a service you want to disable, click it to remove the check mark (☑ changes to ☐).

Note: *Do not disable any services related to your antivirus program.*

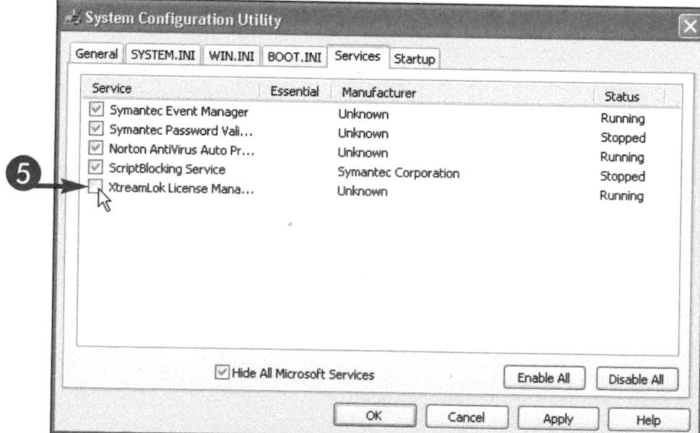

6 Click the Startup tab.

7 Examine the list of startup programs for any easily recognizable programs you want to disable.

8 If you see a program you want to disable, click it to remove the check mark (☑ changes to ☐).

9 Click OK.

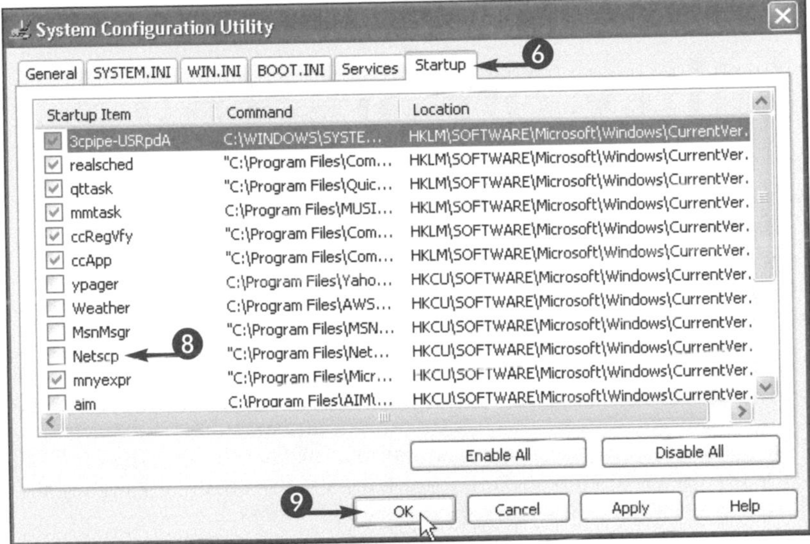

The System Configuration dialog box displays a message indicating that you must restart your PC for all changes to take effect.

10 Click Restart and follow the on-screen instructions to restart Windows.

Windows shuts down and restarts, but does not run any of the services or startup programs you disabled.

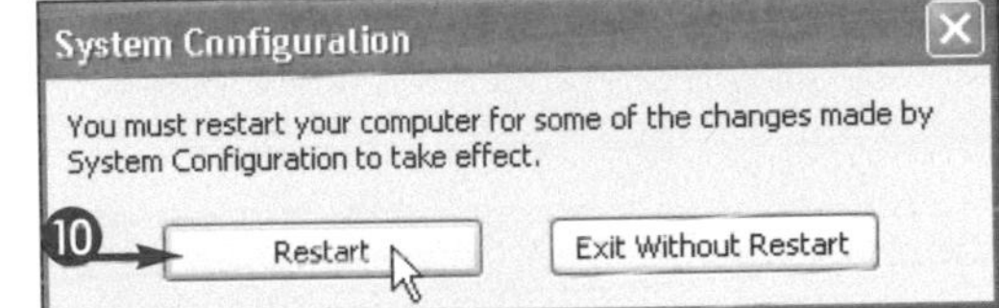

How can I identify the services and startup programs that are related to my antivirus program?

▼ The two most common antivirus programs are Symantec's Norton AntiVirus and McAfee's VirusScan. If you see anything labeled Symantec or McAfee, make sure the item is enabled. Disabling your virus protection, or a portion of it, leaves your system open to attack.

Can I disable the items on the WIN.INI or SYSTEM.INI tab?

▼ You can disable items on the WIN.INI tab or SYSTEM.INI tab, but you may run into problems if your PC has an older hardware device or 16-bit software installed. The items on these tabs enable Windows to manage older devices and software. Focus on the items that appear on the Services and Startup tabs.

Does the System Configuration Utility display all the programs that are running in Windows?

▼ No. If you press Ctrl+Alt+Del, you can see a more thorough list of applications and processes running in Windows. If you click an application or process and click End Task, Windows may give you the option of shutting down the application or process, but the next time you start your PC, it will run again. If you disable it using the System Configuration Utility, however, the application or process does not run the next time you start Windows.

Hide the System Configuration Utility on Startup

Although the System Configuration Utility is a great tool for configuring the Windows startup and preventing programs you do not use from occupying valuable memory, it can become annoying if it appears every time you start Windows. Fortunately, you can hide the System Configuration Utility on startup to prevent it from informing you that you are now running Windows in diagnostic or selective mode.

Whenever you run Windows in a mode other than Normal Startup, Windows runs the System Configuration Utility, which warns you that only selected programs and services are being run. This prevents users from making changes, restarting Windows, and then wondering what happened when they cannot use a particular service. However, if you intentionally disable several programs and services to streamline the Windows startup, you do not want to have to shut down the System Configuration Utility every time you start Windows, before you can start working.

When you restart Windows after making changes, the System Configuration Utility appears, and you can select an option to prevent it from automatically appearing on subsequent startups. If you need to use it, you can always launch it as instructed in the section "Run the System Configuration Utility."

Hide the System Configuration Utility on Startup

1. Launch the System Configuration Utility.

Note: *See the section "Run the System Configuration Utility," for details.*

2. Click check boxes next to programs or services to configure the Windows startup.

Note: *For complete instructions, refer to the section "Disable Services and Programs on Startup."*

3. Click OK.

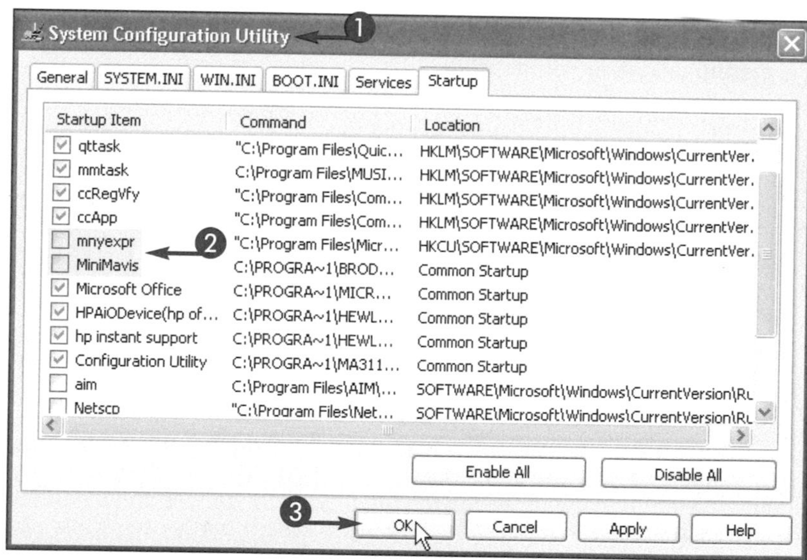

The System Configuration dialog box displays a message indicating that you must restart your PC for all changes to take effect.

4. Click Restart.

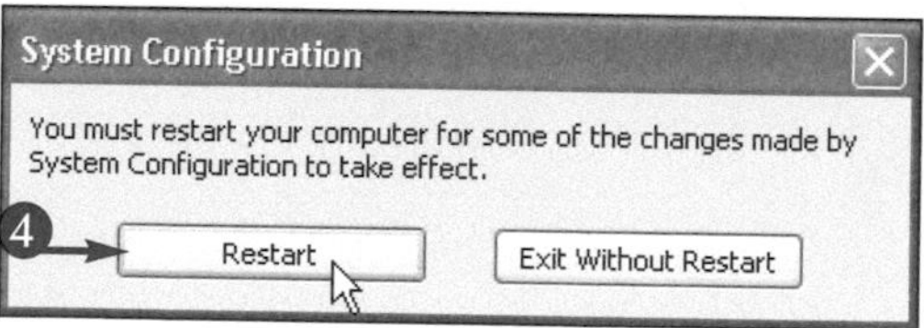

Windows shuts down and then restarts and displays a message indicating that you are running Windows in diagnostic or selective mode.

5 Click the "Don't show this message or launch the System Configuration Utility when Windows start" option (☐ changes to ☑).

6 Click OK.

The dialog box closes and does not appear the next time you start Windows.

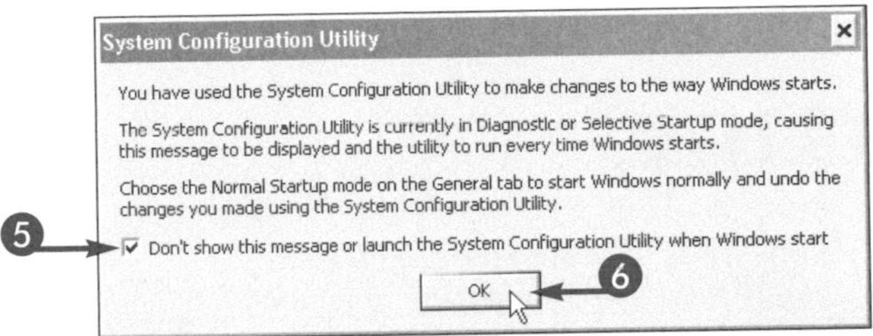

PART IV

If the System Configuration Utility does not appear on startup, do the programs and services I disabled remain disabled?

▼ Yes. All of the changes you make using the System Configuration Utility remain in effect until you change them again. The only difference is that when you start Windows, you are not warned that you are running Windows in diagnostic or selective mode.

How do I prevent programs from running on startup?

▼ Many programs that run automatically when you start Windows are on the Windows Startup menu. Click Start, All Programs, and then Startup to view a list of these programs. You can right-click a program's name and click Delete to remove it from this menu and prevent it from running on startup. Many programs add themselves to the Windows Registry, making them more difficult to remove. To tweak the Windows registry, see Chapter 21.

Is there any way to prevent a program from setting itself up to run automatically on startup?

▼ During the installation process, some programs give you a choice, but many do not. Some developers intentionally design their programs in such a way to prevent you from disabling them on startup. The best defense is to install programs only from reliable developers. The cost of many free programs is the patience you must pay to have them on your system.

Disable Error Reporting

You can disable the Windows error-reporting feature to suppress dialog boxes that prompt you to report software conflicts to Microsoft. The error-reporting feature is designed to inform Microsoft of software conflicts that prevent you from exiting programs properly and cause programs or Windows itself to crash.

Sometimes, you may need to press Ctrl+Alt+Del to display the Windows Task Manager and exit a program that is not responding. After Windows shuts down the program, a dialog box may appear prompting you to report the error to Microsoft. After you have encountered about a dozen of these dialog boxes, they can become annoying. You not only have to deal with an unresponsive program, but then you have to spend additional time reporting the errors.

Fortunately, Windows provides a way to disable error reporting so these dialog boxes no longer appear. You can disable the feature entirely or configure error reporting to report only Windows operating system errors or only program errors or to inform you of errors but not prompt you to report them to Windows. These options can help reduce the time you spend responding to error messages.

Disable Error Reporting

1. Click Start.
2. Right-click My Computer.
3. Click Properties.

The System Properties dialog box appears.

4. Click the Advanced tab.
5. Click Error Reporting.

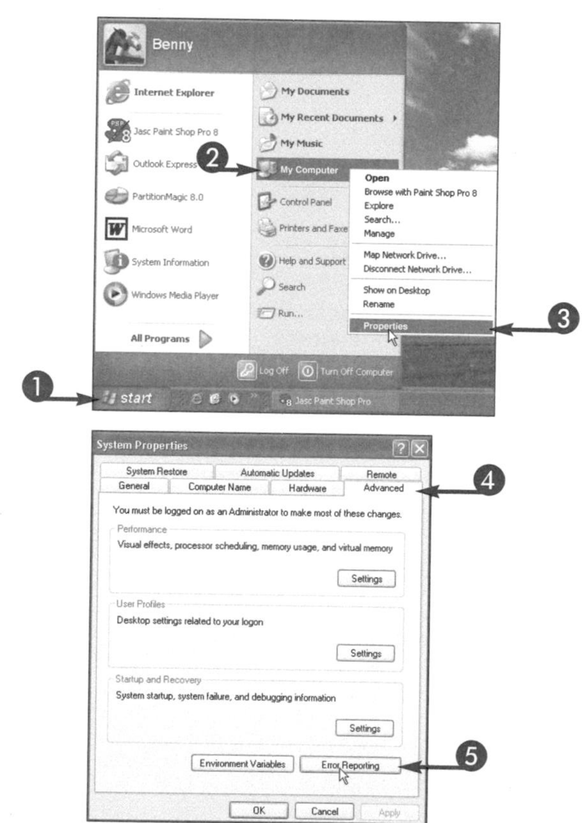

The Error Reporting dialog box appears.

6 Click the Disable error reporting option (○ changes to ◉).

- To prevent Windows from informing you of critical errors, you can click here (☑ changes to ☐).

7 Click OK.

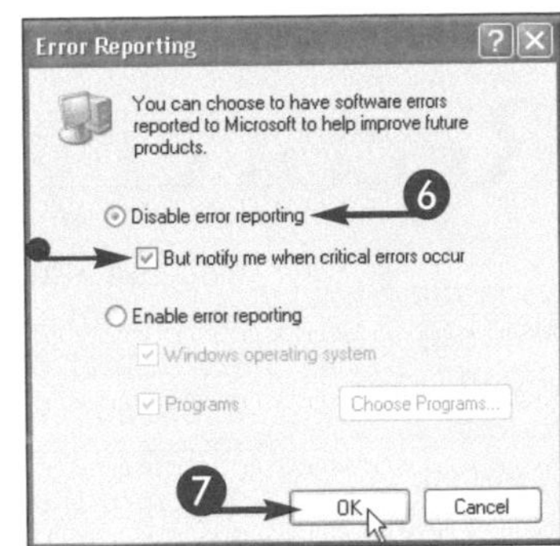

The Error Reporting dialog box closes, and you return to the System Properties dialog box.

8 Click OK.

Windows saves your settings.

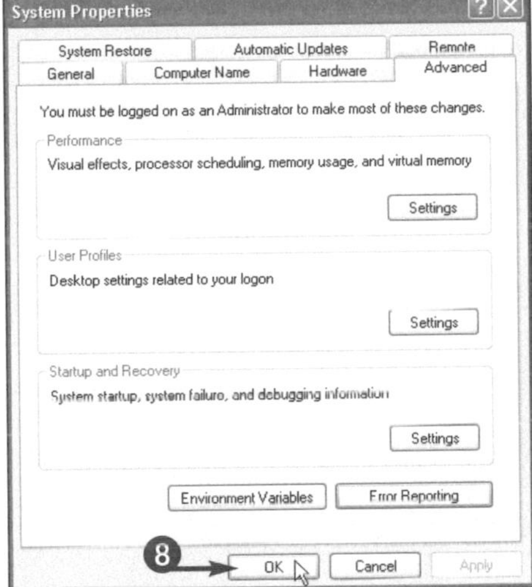

PART IV

Can I report only errors that occur in select programs?

▼ Yes. In the Error Reporting dialog box, instead of clicking the Disable error reporting option (○ changes to ◉), click the Enable error reporting option (○ changes to ◉). Click the Windows operating system option (☐ changes to ☑). Click Choose Programs. Then click the All programs option (○ changes to ◉) to enable error reporting for all programs in the list at the top, or click the All programs in this list option (○ changes to ◉) and then deselect a box next to the items you do not want Windows to check for errors (☑ changes to ☐). In the list at the bottom, add a check mark next to the programs that you want to exclude from error checking. You can click Add to add programs to this list.

When I add a program to the list of programs to exclude from error checking, what name should I use to identify the program?

▼ Windows requires that you enter the complete name of the executable program file, including its three-letter filename extension, which is usually .exe or .com. If you do not know the name of the executable program file, click Browse, navigate to the folder that stores the program's files, and double-click the file's name. It helps if you have Windows set up to display filename extensions, as discussed in Chapter 7. Most programs install their program files in a subfolder of the Program Files folder, typically stored on the same drive on which Windows is installed.

Optimize Windows Startup and Recovery

You can reduce or eliminate some delays in the Windows startup and streamline the Windows recovery to make Windows start and restart faster. Windows has two delays built into its startup routine. If your PC has more than one operating system installed, Windows waits 30 seconds for you to select the operating system to run. Windows also waits 30 seconds on startup if any errors occurred the last time you shut down Windows; this gives you time to choose whether to correct the errors or proceed with the startup. By reducing these waiting periods, you can often enable Windows to start faster.

You can also streamline the Windows recovery and restart process to save less information to your hard drive in the event that Windows crashes or shuts down unexpectedly. By default, Windows is set up to do a complete memory dump to your hard drive when a serious error occurs. Much of the information that Windows saves can help Microsoft technical support troubleshoot problems, but it is of little use to the average person. You can minimize the amount of reporting and recording that Windows performs when it shuts down unexpectedly, so that Windows restarts faster.

Optimize Windows Startup and Recovery

1. Click Start.
2. Right-click My Computer.
3. Click Properties.

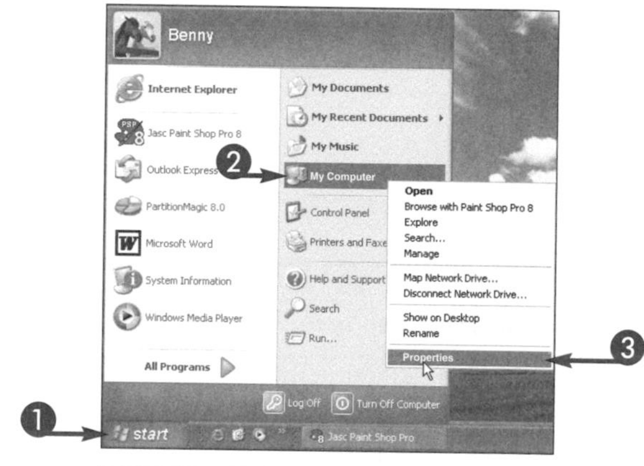

The System Properties dialog box appears.

4. Click the Advanced tab.
5. Under Startup and Recovery, click Settings.

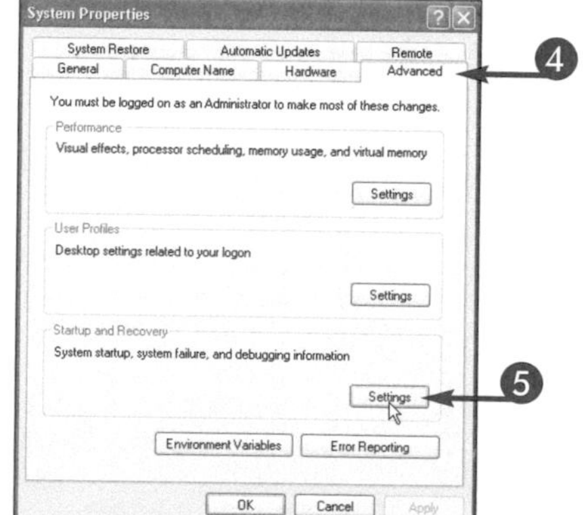

The Startup and Recovery dialog box appears.

6 Click here and click the operating system you want your PC to run at startup.

7 Click the "Time to display list of operating systems" option to deselect it (☑ changes to ☐).

8 Click here to decrease the amount of time Windows displays recovery options before starting Windows.

- You can click the Send an administrative alert option (☑ changes to ☐) if you have no administrator you need to alert.

9 Click here and select the amount of information you want to save from a memory dump.

10 Click OK to exit the Startup and Recovery dialog box and click OK in the System Properties dialog box.

Windows saves your changes and closes the System Properties dialog box.

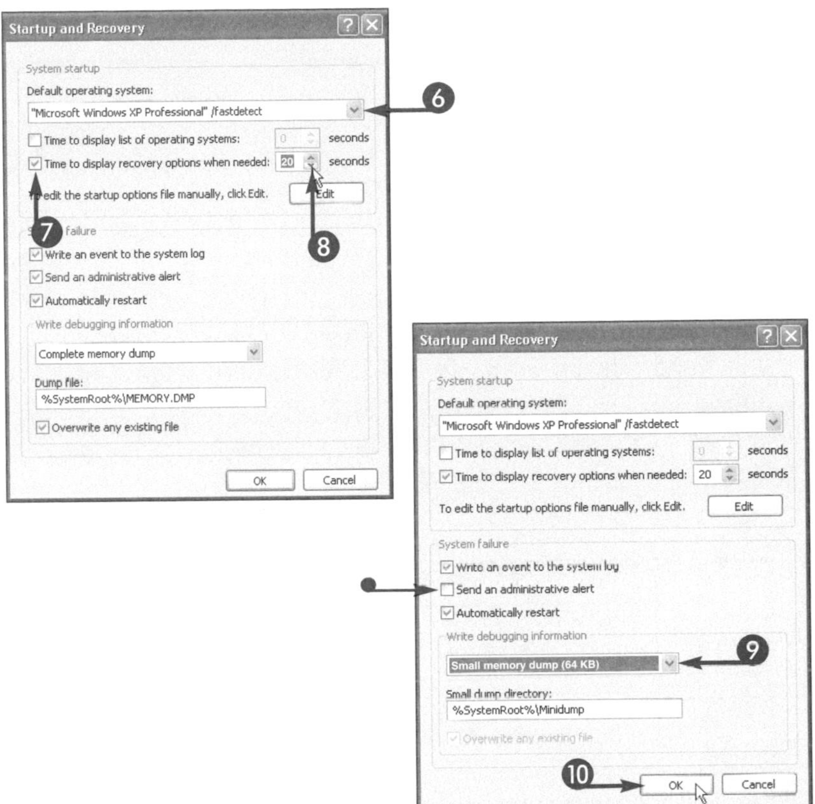

Which memory dump option should I choose?

The default option, Complete Memory Dump, is a little excessive, especially if your PC has more than 256MB of RAM. You can choose the (none) option to disable the memory dump, but that can be risky. The Small memory dump (64K) option saves the minimum amount of information needed to troubleshoot a problem. The Kernel memory dump option saves 50MB to 800MB of core Windows information, which is usually sufficient for troubleshooting most Windows problems. If your PC is running trouble-free, select the Small memory dump (64K) option. If your system begins to crash regularly, you can select the Kernel memory dump option to save additional information the next time Windows or one of your programs crashes.

When Windows dumps the memory, where does it store the dump?

Windows stores the memory dump in a file named MEMORY.DMP in the %SystemRoot% folder, which, on most PCs, is in the Windows folder. This is another typically huge file that you can safely delete from your PC's hard drive if your PC is currently not experiencing problems. If you choose the option to perform a Complete or Kernel memory dump, you can select the Overwrite any existing file option (☐ changes to ☑) to have Windows overwrite the information in the MEMORY.DMP file with information from the current memory dump. If you click the Small memory dump option, Windows creates a new memory dump file every time it shuts down unexpectedly.

14 Eliminate Spyware and Adware

15 Block Pop up Ads

16 Prevent Spam

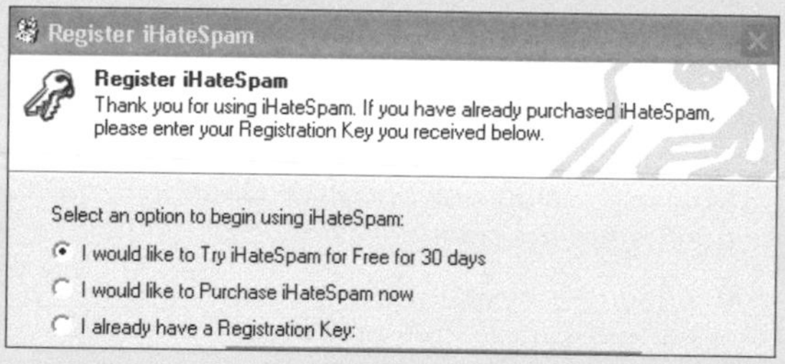

17 Optimize Internet Connection Speed

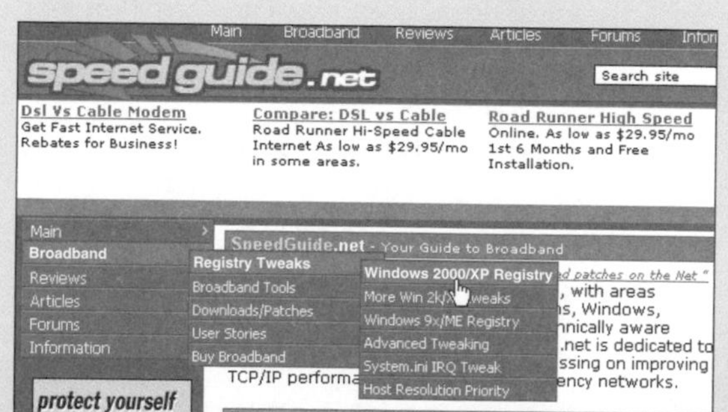

PART V
IMPROVING INTERNET PERFORMANCE

18 Optimize Your Web Browser

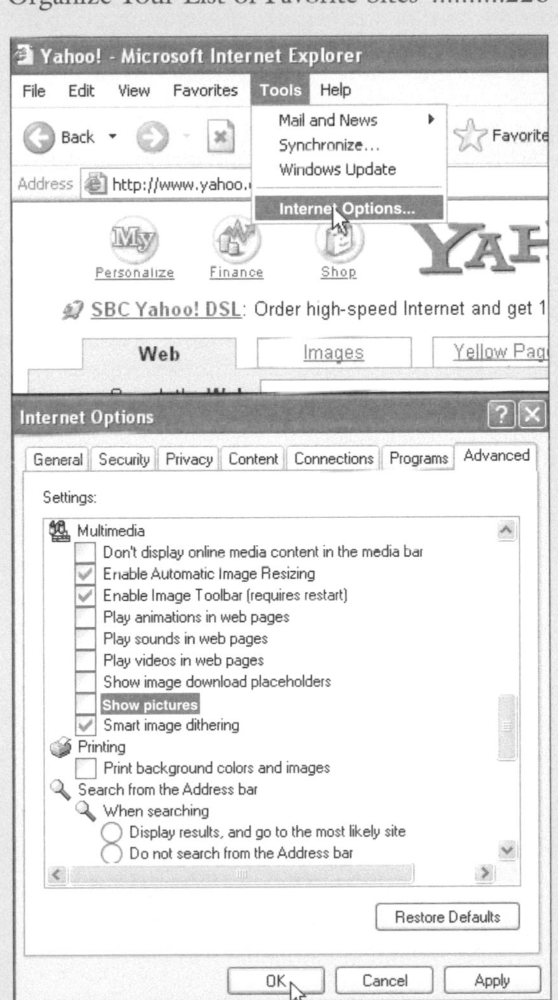

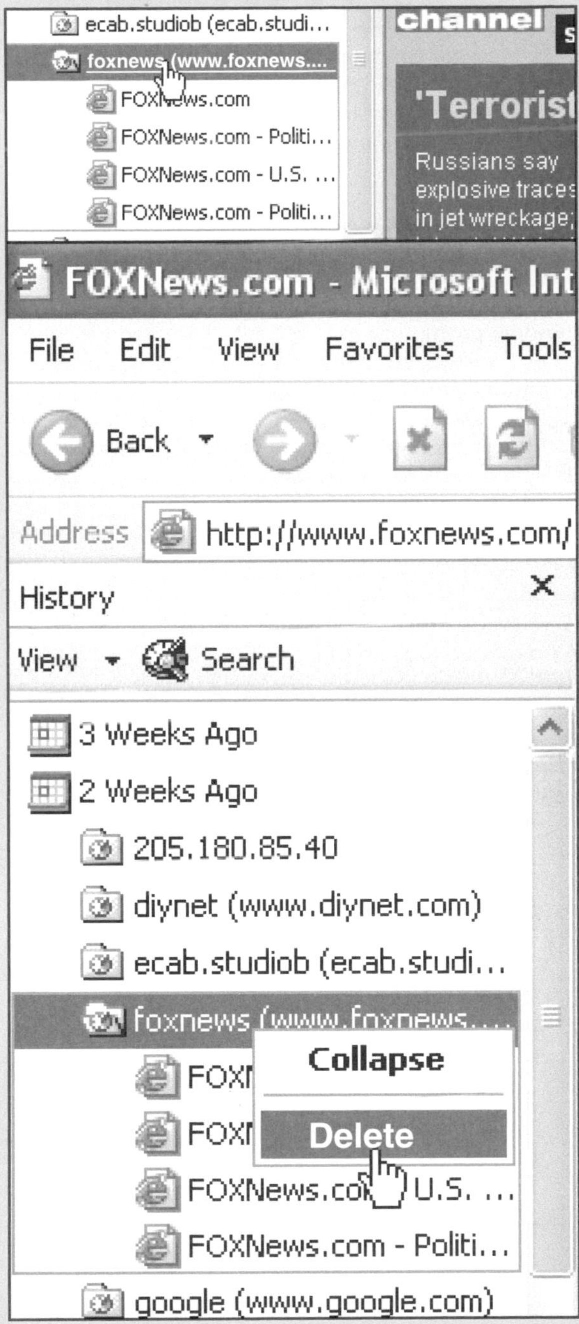

Understanding Adware and Spyware

By understanding the nature and sources of spyware and adware, you can begin to protect your system against them, improve the performance of your Internet connection, and enhance your experience on the World Wide Web.

Spyware poses the biggest threat to your privacy, while adware poses the biggest threat to Internet performance. Together, they can significantly slow down your Internet connection, negatively affect your productivity, compromise your privacy, and turn an otherwise pleasant Web browsing session into a frenetic advertising blitz.

Understanding Adware

Adware is software that contains built-in advertisements commonly promoting mail-order college degrees, low-cost mortgages, magazine subscriptions, prescription medications, and a host of other products and services. It can hijack your Web browser so your browser loads an advertising page whenever you launch it. It can cover your screen with advertisements even when you are not browsing the Web. And it can be nearly impossible to identify and remove.

Developers typically hide adware inside other, usually free programs, such as games, or shareware programs. You may click a button to install a program thinking that you are getting a great deal on some excellent software only to find that you have passively agreed to let a company advertise on your PC.

Understanding Spyware

Spyware is any software designed to monitor your activity and store a record of it or forward the information to a third party. Spyware can be a program that employers use to monitor their employees' computer use or that parents or teachers use to monitor student activity on the Internet. It can be used to collect e-mail addresses for spammers or acquire credit card numbers or passwords from a computer. However, spyware typically gathers information from Web searches you perform and other activity on your PC to help produce ads that are targeted to your needs and interests.

Spyware invades your privacy and uses your computer to do it. It steals bandwidth that your Internet connection uses to load Web pages faster. It occupies RAM, which your PC may use to run other programs more efficiently. And it consumes valuable storage space on your PC's hard drive.

Understanding Pop-up Ads

Most adware and spyware that infect your PC produce *pop-up ads*, commonly referred to as *pop-ups*. These ads typically appear in separate windows that cover the page you really want to view. The worst option, the option to order the product or find out more information, is usually positioned prominently inside the ad, while the option to cancel the ad often calls up another ad.

Not all pop-ups originate from adware or spyware, however. Many Web sites are designed to display one or more pop-ups whenever you open a particular page or click a link. These types of pop-ups are covered in Chapter 15.

Adware and Spyware Symptoms

Just because your PC displays pop-up ads whenever you browse the Web does not indicate that it is infected with adware or spyware. Web sites are capable of displaying advertising without the assistance of additional software. However, if you notice that your browser runs automatically and displays pop-up ads even when you are not browsing the Web, your PC may be infected. Additional symptoms include:

- Your PC is running a pop-up blocker, as discussed in Chapter 15, but pop-up ads still appear on your PC.
- Your Web browser's home page changes. Adware commonly *hijacks* a browser to redirect it to an advertising site.
- Your Web browser acquires a new toolbar that you cannot recall installing.
- Web sites mysteriously appear on your list of favorites.
- Your computer automatically becomes very active when you are not using it, and you cannot attribute the activity to a virus scan or other task you scheduled to run.

Defending Your PC

Because adware and spyware attack on two fronts, you must defend your PC on two fronts. You must defend it against Web-site-generated pop-up ads and against spyware and adware that are installed on your PC without your authorization.

You can prevent Web sites from automatically displaying pop-up ads by installing a pop-up blocker, as discussed in Chapter 15. A pop-up blocker intercepts pop-up ads and automatically shuts them down before they can appear on your monitor.

To protect your PC against spyware and adware, you can remove spyware and adware that is currently installed on your PC, tighten security settings in your Web browser, and avoid installing any suspicious freeware or shareware on your PC. This chapter shows you how to rid your PC of this malicious, annoying software and prevent it from infecting your PC again.

Identify Adware and Spyware

Sometimes, you can readily identify spyware and adware installed on your PC and remove it as easily as you remove other software — by running its uninstall utility.

If you frequently browse the Internet, play games, or download and install freeware or shareware, your PC is likely to be infected with spyware or adware. The only sign you may have is that ads keep popping up no matter which site you visit, or they pop up even when you are not browsing the Web. When your PC begins to exhibit any form of suspicious behavior, you should examine the list of installed programs to identify potential spyware or adware. You can then uninstall the malicious software, as explained in the following section, "Uninstall Adware and Spyware."

Many times, if you try to remove this malicious software by using a spyware or adware removal utility, the software leaves behind entries in the Windows registry that can cause problems. First, try to identify and then remove the software using its uninstall utility, as explained in this section and the next. If this does not work, then try using a spyware or adware removal utility, as explained in the section "Scan for and Remove Adware and Spyware."

Identify Adware and Spyware

1. Click Start.
2. Click Control Panel.

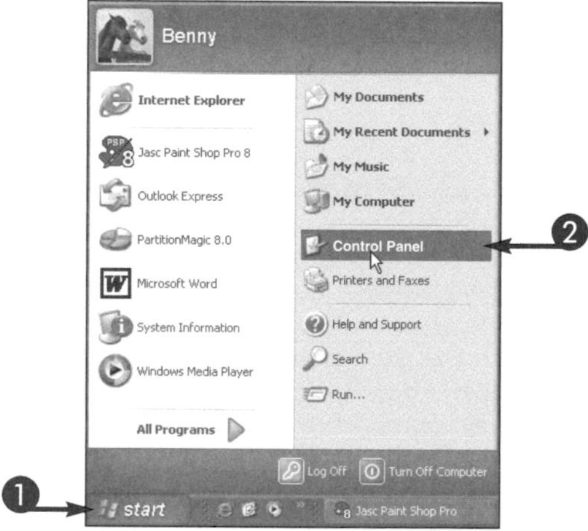

The Windows Control Panel appears.

3. Click the Add or Remove Programs link.

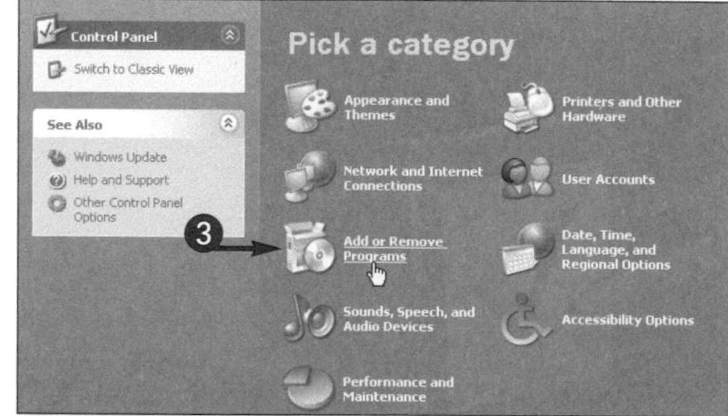

The Add or Remove Programs window appears, listing the names of installed programs.

4. Examine the list for the names of any suspicious software.

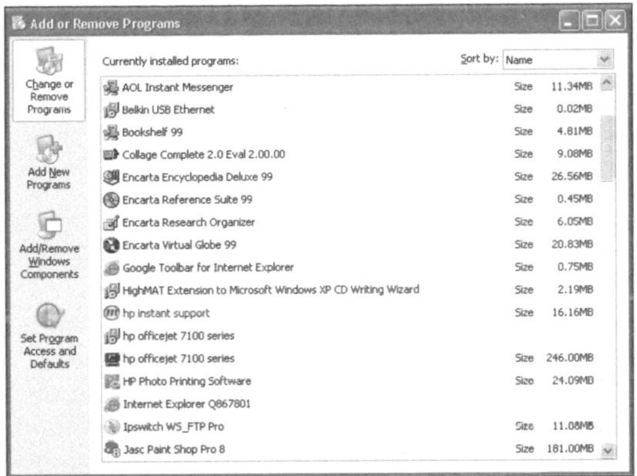

- In this example, Wild Tangent is identified.

Note: *To remove the suspicious software from your system, see the next section "Uninstall Adware and Spyware."*

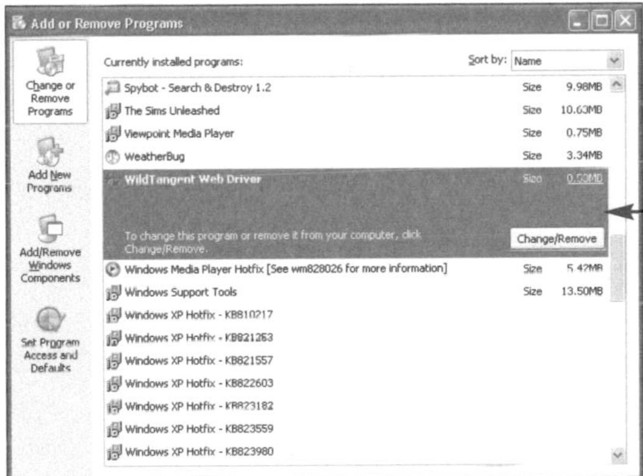

PART V

How can I tell if an installed program has a spyware or adware component?

▼ On the Web, you can find many lists of programs that are known to include spyware or adware components. Search for "known spyware" or "known adware" or check out www.spywareguide.com. Not all of these lists are completely accurate or current, so be sure to check several of them. Developers often modify program names to avoid detection.

Can I prevent spyware and adware from being installed on my PC?

▼ Many freeware and shareware programs contain an end user license agreement (EULA) warning users that the software includes an adware component. Read the EULA thoroughly before installing any program, and make sure you understand it. You often have the option of aborting the installation, in which case you cannot use the freeware or shareware, but at least you do not infect your computer with adware.

If I remove the adware or spyware, will I lose anything?

▼ If you install free software that includes adware or spyware and you delete the adware or spyware component, you often disable the free software as well. The price of using the free software is putting up with the advertising. You can install a special utility, such as Silencer, to redirect reports from spyware to different URLs and continue using the free software, but some of these utilities can have their own spyware or adware installed.

Uninstall Adware and Spyware

After you identify a program that is likely to include an adware or spyware component, you can often remove the program by running its uninstall utility. Some users enjoy a free program so much that they can tolerate the targeted advertising and are not concerned that the program may be collecting information about their activities and reporting it to a third party. Other users think that the pop-up ads are annoying and intrusive, and they value their privacy over the benefits of the free software, so they choose to uninstall the software. The choice is completely up to you.

In most cases, you cannot uninstall the adware or shareware without uninstalling or disabling the freeware or shareware program that is bound to it. During the removal process, the uninstall utility may display a message informing you that by removing the adware you can no longer use a particular program for free. It also asks you to confirm that this is what you want to do. At this point, you can continue uninstalling the program or abort the process and keep the program as well as the adware or shareware component.

Uninstall Adware and Spyware

1. Click Start.
2. Click Control Panel.

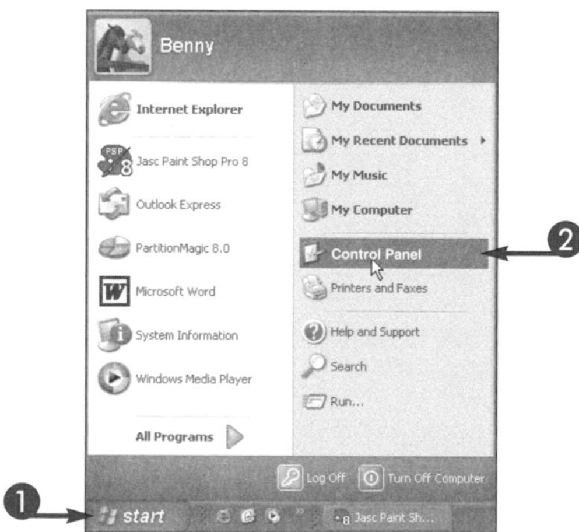

The Windows Control Panel appears.

3. Click the Add or Remove Programs link.

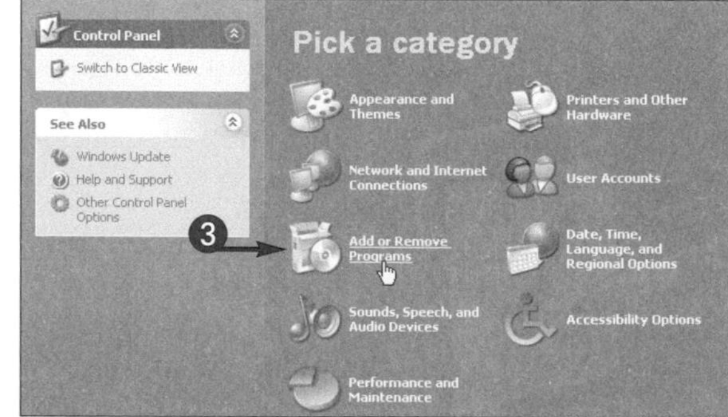

The Add or Remove Programs window appears.

4 Click the program that contains the spyware or adware component.

5 Click Remove or Change/Remove.

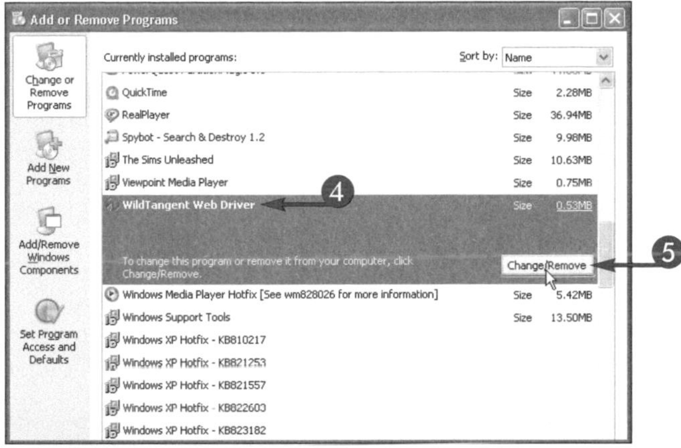

A dialog box may appear, prompting you to confirm or cancel the removal.

6 Click the option to continue uninstalling the program.

Windows removes the program from your PC.

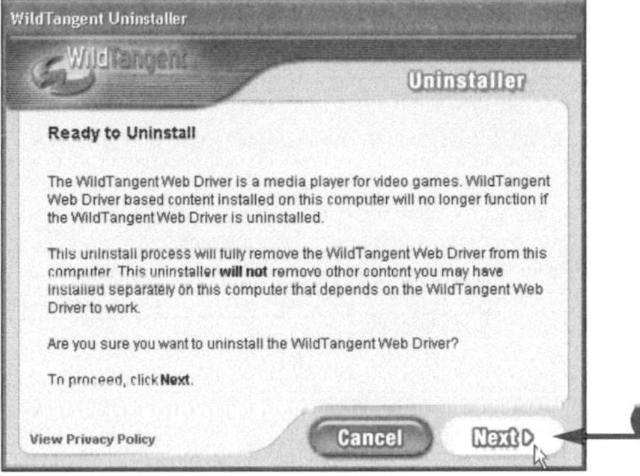

I followed these steps to remove the program, but it still seems to be on my PC. What should I do?

▼ By design, many spyware and adware programs firmly entrench themselves on a PC. They may even have their own hidden utilities that enable them to reinstall themselves after you uninstall them. If you follow the steps in this section and the adware or spyware remains on your PC, try removing it with a spyware or adware removal utility as discussed in the section "Download and Install Removal Utilities." If that does not rid your system of the malicious software, search for specific instructions on the Internet. A good place to go for help is the SWI Forums at forums.spywareinfo.com.

I have an antivirus program set up to automatically scan incoming files for viruses, so how did my PC become infected?

▼ Antivirus programs may or may not scan for adware and spyware. Most antivirus programs scan only for known viruses, Trojan horses, and worms, which are the more traditional forms of malicious software. Some antivirus tool developers, such as Symantec, are finally coming to realize that adware and spyware pose a threat of equal or greater significance to computer users and are producing products that support scanning for *expanded threats*, including adware, spyware, dialers that dial out from your PC without your permission, and hijackers that redirect your browser to a different home page.

Download and Install Removal Utilities

You can download and install special utilities to scan your PC for adware and spyware and automatically remove it from your PC. You must be careful, though. Many companies that create removal utilities are the same companies that create adware and spyware. Even worse, some removal utilities actually contain spyware or adware components, infecting your computer with even more malicious software.

This book recommends two utilities for removing spyware and adware: Ad-Aware by Lavasoft and Spybot Search and Destroy by Patrick M. Kolla. You can find dozens of other adware and spyware removal utilities on the Web, but these two are free and have proven themselves very reliable. They may not, however, be able to identify and remove every adware or spyware program in existence.

Although these two programs are designed to identify and remove many of the same programs, each is able to identify and remove some programs that the other overlooks, so installing and using both of them usually delivers the best results. This section shows you how to download and install both of these spyware and adware removal utilities. The next section, "Scan for and Remove Adware and Spyware," shows you how to use Spybot Search and Destroy.

Download and Install Removal Utilities

Download and Install Ad-Aware

1. Launch your Web browser.
2. In the address bar, type **www.lavasoftusa.com/software/adaware** and press Enter.
3. Click the Download link and navigate to the link for downloading the free version of Ad-Aware.
4. Click the link for downloading Ad-Aware.

Note: *You may need to follow a trail of links to find a link for downloading Ad-Aware.*

5. Click Open.

   Your Web browser downloads Ad-Aware and initiates the installation routine.

6. Follow the on-screen installation instructions.

   The installation routine installs Ad-Aware on your PC.

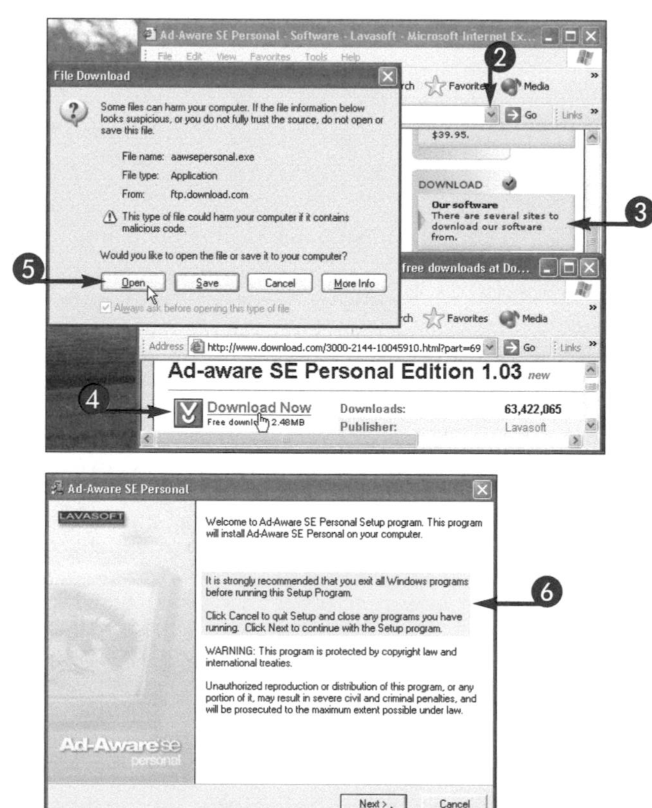

Download and Install Spybot Search and Destroy

1. Launch your Web browser.
2. In the address bar, type **www.safer-networking.org** and press Enter.
3. Click the Download link and follow the trail of links to the link for downloading the file.

Note: *You may need to click two or more links to reach a link for downloading the file.*

4. Click the link for downloading the file.

   The File Download dialog box appears asking if you want to open or save the file.

5. Click Open.

   Your Web browser downloads Spybot Search and Destroy and initiates the installation routine.

6. Follow the on-screen instructions.

   The installation routine installs Spybot Search and Destroy on your PC.

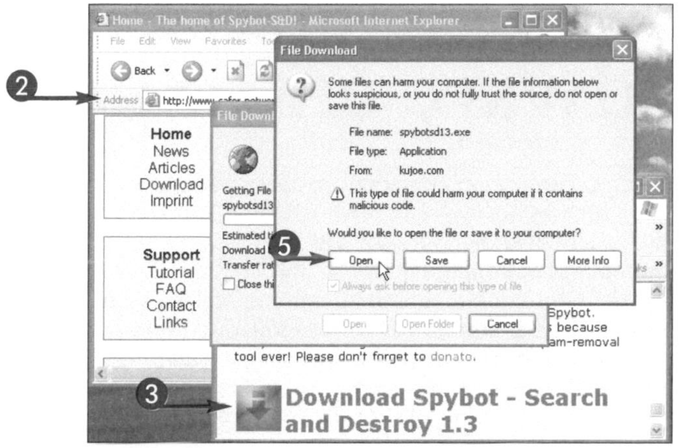

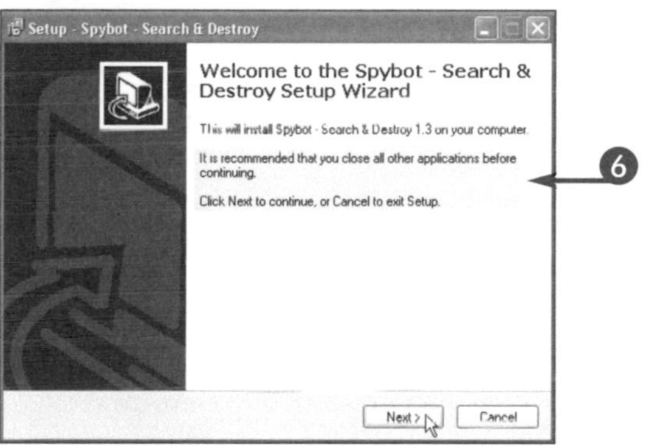

I was browsing the Web when this message popped up indicating that I may have spyware installed on my computer. What should I do?

▼ Pop-up ads that advertise programs to remove pop-up ads, spyware, or adware are all suspicious. Companies that are dedicated to protecting computers against adware and spyware generally do not advertise using a pop-up ad. If you are looking for a commercial utility for removing spyware and adware, try Pest Patrol. Also, if you search the Web for spyware or adware and advertised links appear, these links lead to commercial software that may or may not be legitimate. Some of these spyware and adware removal utilities are less useful than utilities you can obtain for free, and some may even be harmful.

Are there any other spyware or adware removal tools that you recommend?

▼ HijackThis is a great utility for tracking down hidden spyware and adware that many removal utilities cannot detect. However, using this tool requires a little more knowledge and intervention on your behalf. In many cases, using this tool with the help of some good advice in a spyware forum can enable you to rid your PC of the most stubborn spyware and adware. Check out Download.com at www.download.com for additional spyware and adware removal utilities and other tools. Because these utilities and tools work in different ways, a combination of them often leads to the best results.

Scan for and Remove Adware and Spyware

You can use an adware or spyware removal utility, such as Ad-Aware or Spybot Search and Destroy, to identify known adware and spyware on your PC and remove it automatically. These utilities typically search a hard drive for cookies, spyware, adware, dialers, Web browser hijackers, and other forms of software that operate secretly and without your authorization. They identify problem software and then either automatically remove it from your PC or display a list of the spyware or adware that you can choose to remove or retain.

Keep in mind that any spyware or adware you choose to remove may disable some functionality from installed programs. For example, if you delete all cookies, a site that you frequently visit may not present custom content for you the next time you visit. Also, removing spyware or adware may remove some games and other freeware or shareware that you frequently use.

The steps in this section show you how to use Spybot Search and Destroy to scan for and remove spyware and adware from your PC. Because no one program can identify and remove all known spyware and adware, you can use more than one removal utility to perform a more thorough cleaning.

Scan for and Remove Adware and Spyware

1. Double-click the icon for running your adware or spyware removal utility.

   These steps use Spybot Search and Destroy as an example.

Note: *To install the removal utility, which places the icon on your desktop, see the section "Download and Install Removal Utilities."*

- Your adware or spyware removal utility appears.

2. Click the option to scan your PC for adware and spyware.

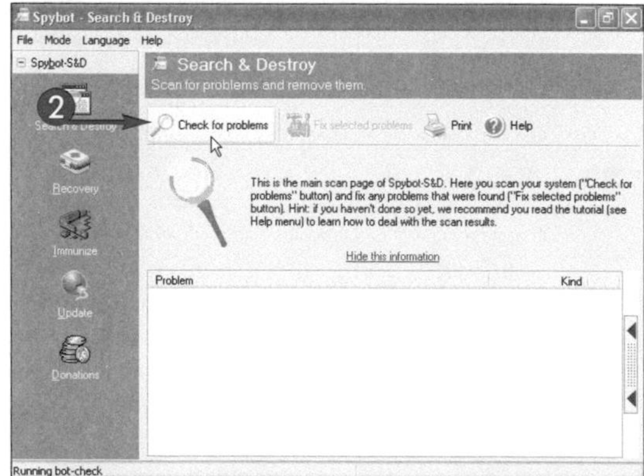

Your adware or spyware removal utility scans your PC for adware and spyware and displays a list of items it can remove.

3. Select the adware and spyware you want to remove.

   Some utilities automatically select all items, and you must click items to deselect them (☑ changes to ☐).

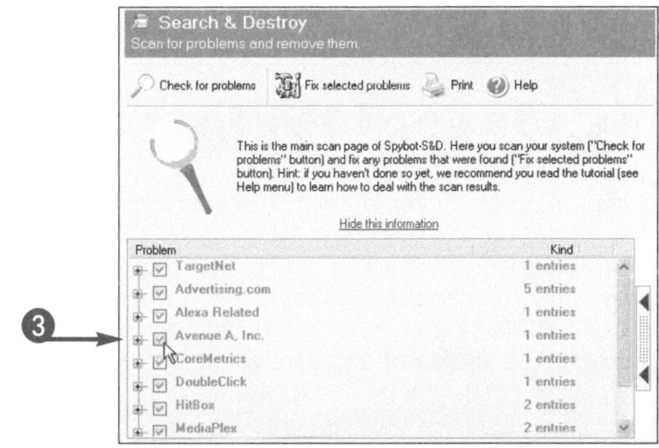

4. Click the option to remove the selected adware and spyware.

   The removal utility removes the selected items from your PC.

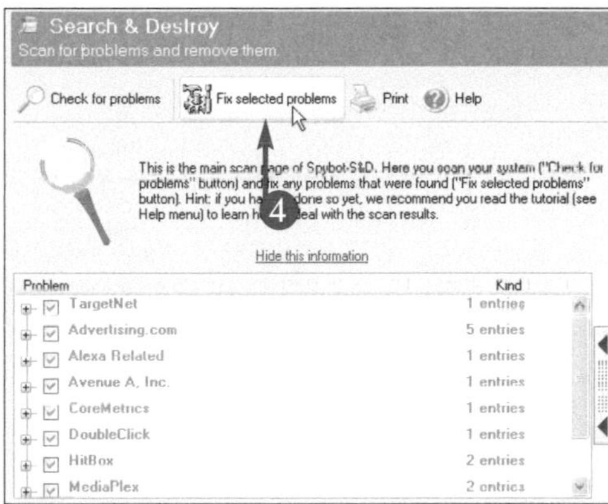

Do I need to update my adware or spyware removal utility?

▼ Yes. Developers constantly modify the names and components of their spyware and adware utilities to avoid detection, and they develop new software almost daily. To keep up with these changes, you should download and install any recommended updates for your removal utility. Most removal utilities display an option on the opening screen that you can click to download and install updates or obtain the latest version of the utility.

I removed the spyware, but it seems to come right back. What should I do?

▼ Try running Windows in safe mode, and then scan for and remove the spyware and adware. Restart Windows and keep tapping the F8 key at 2- to 3-second intervals as your PC boots up. When the startup menu appears, select the option for running in safe mode. Safe mode prevents the adware or spyware from running a program in the background that blocks attempts to remove the adware or shareware.

I tried running my scan with Windows in safe mode, but the problem remains. What should I do?

▼ Try running another adware or spyware removal utility in safe mode. If you used Spybot Search and Destory, for example, try using Ad-Aware to scan for and remove spyware and adware. If the problem persists, you may need further assistance. A good place to go for help is the SWI Forums at forums.spywareinfo.com.

Using Less Vulnerable Web Browsers

Internet Explorer is a powerful Web browser that enables you to experience the full power of the Web, but its openness makes your PC susceptible to adware and spyware. You can use a different Web browser, such as Opera or Mozilla Firefox, which sacrifices some functionality for improved security and less advertising.

One of the main problems with Internet Explorer is that it supports ActiveX components, which enable Web developers to add to the functionality of the Web browser by installing additional software on your PC. This added functionality often enhances your Web browsing experience. However, ActiveX components can also turn your Web browser into an advertising machine that spies on you.

Unless you tighten the security settings in Internet Explorer, as explained in the next section, "Tighten Security to Block Adware and Spyware," your PC is wide open to adware and spyware. Because of this, many users choose to use more secure Web browsers that do not enable sites to install ActiveX controls on their PCs.

Using Less Vulnerable Web Browsers

1. Launch your Web browser.
2. In the Address bar, type **www.download.com** and press Enter.

   The Download.com home page appears.
3. Scroll down the page and click Browsers.

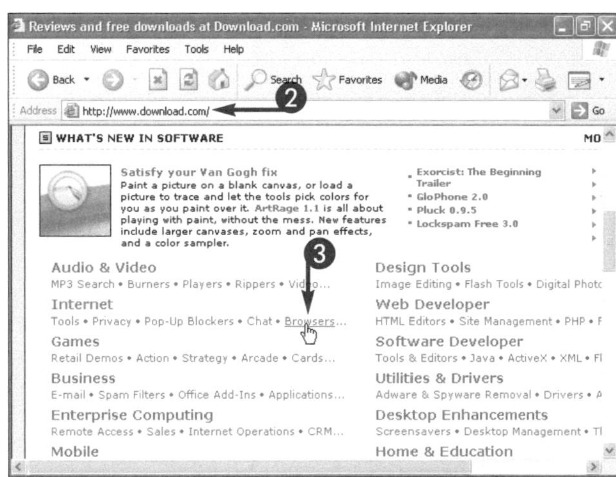

A list of Web browser categories appears.

4. Click Browsers.

A list of Web browsers appears.

5 Scroll down the list and click the Download Now link for the Web browser you want to try.

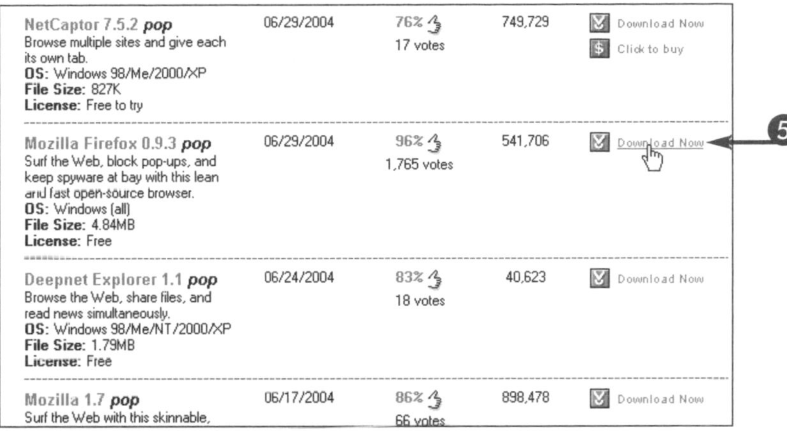

The File Download dialog box appears, prompting you to open or save the file.

6 Click Open and follow the on-screen instructions to install the browser.

The browser installs on your PC.

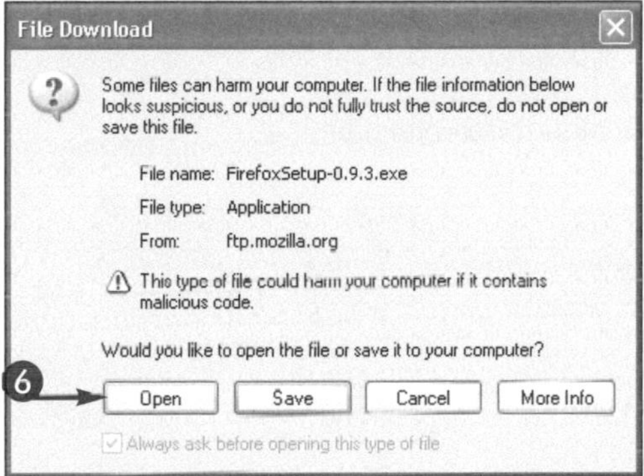

Why switch Web browsers?

- Opera and Mozilla Firefox offer additional features that many users find attractive, including tabbed Web browsing and a built-in pop-up blocker. Tabbed Web browsing keeps several pages open at the same time in a single window so you can quickly switch from one page to another by clicking a tab. A built-in pop-up blocker automatically shuts down Web-page-initiated pop-up ads. In addition, these alternative Web browsers often feature a more basic interface that some users find easier to navigate.

Why would I want to continue using Internet Explorer?

- If you have been using Internet Explorer for years, familiarity with the program may persuade you to keep using it, even if attractive alternatives are available. In addition, Internet Explorer is very powerful, and because it is the most common Web browser, Web developers commonly tailor their sites to appear and function best when viewed in Internet Explorer.

Why should I try a different Web browser?

- Mozilla Firefox is free, and you can download a shareware version of Opera to see what it has to offer. In other words, you can try an alternative Web browser for free, and you have not lost a thing. You may find that you prefer the alternative.

Tightening Security to Block Adware and Spyware

You can tighten security in Internet Explorer and other Web browsers to make them less susceptible to acquiring adware and spyware. Because Internet Explorer is particularly prone to acquiring adware and spyware, this section focuses on Internet Explorer's security settings.

One of the safest ways to browse the Web with Internet Explorer is to increase the security level for the Internet zone to High. This disables almost all active content, including safe and unsafe ActiveX controls, scripts, and file downloads. You can open and view pages that contain text, images, and audio and video clips, but you cannot view most interactive content, and you cannot download or install software from the Internet.

Setting the security level for the Internet zone to High can severely limit Internet Explorer's functionality and your ability to freely browse the Web. However, you can add your favorite Web sites to a list of trusted sites to enable Internet Explorer's full functionality for these sites. This is particularly useful if you typically visit only a few mainstream sites. In any case, you can try the tightened security settings, and if the settings restrict your browsing too much, you can change the security level back to its default setting of Medium.

Tightening Security to Block Adware and Spyware

1. Launch Internet Explorer.
2. Click Tools.
3. Click Internet Options.

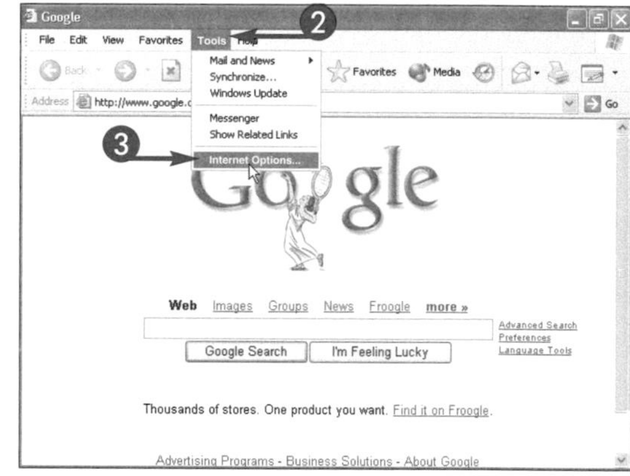

The Internet Options dialog box appears.

4. Click the Security tab.
5. Click the Internet button.
6. Click and drag the Security level for this zone slider up to High.

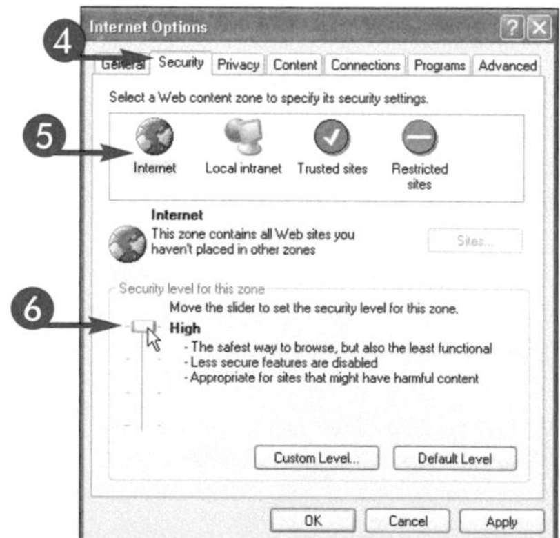

7. Click the Trusted sites button.
8. Click Sites.

   The Trusted sites dialog box appears.

9. Click the Require server verification (https:) for all sites in this zone option (☑ changes to ☐).
10. Click here and type the URL of a Web site you trust.
11. Click Add.
12. Repeat steps 10 and 11 for additional trusted sites.
13. Click OK in the Trusted sites dialog box.

   The Trusted sites dialog box closes.

   - You can click and drag the slider to set the security level for the Trusted sites zone.

14. Click OK.

   Internet Explorer saves the settings and closes the Internet Options dialog box.

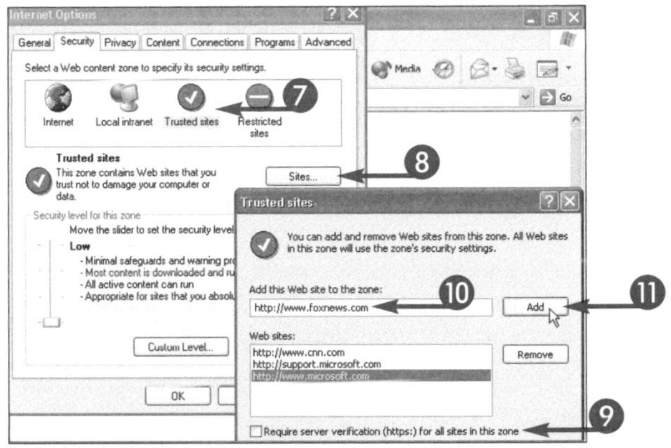

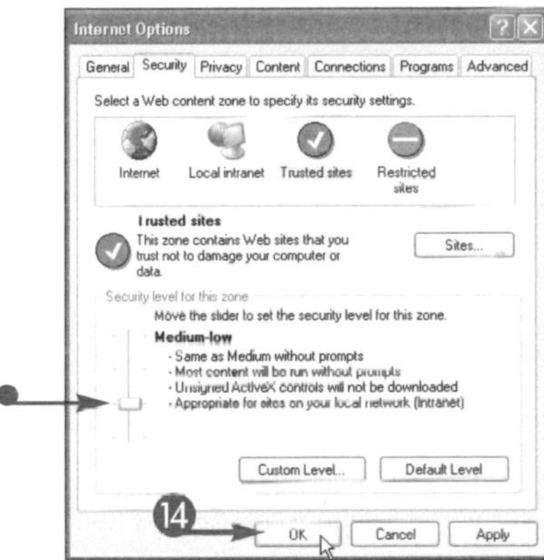

PART V

Can I set different security levels for different people who use my PC?

▼ Yes, but you must create separate user accounts in Windows. To create a user account, click Start, Control Panel, and then User Accounts. Click Create a new account and follow the on-screen instructions to create a user account. You must then log on as that user and change the security settings in Internet Explorer. These settings do not affect the Internet Explorer settings for other user accounts.

I set the security level for the Internet zone to high, but now I cannot place credit card orders online. What should I do?

▼ Repeat the steps to set the security level back to Medium or Medium-low, and then try accessing the site again. You may need to restart Internet Explorer. The other option is to add the site to your list of trusted sites, but this does not always enable you to access all features at the site.

Can I just add the sites that I do not trust to the list of restricted sites?

▼ Yes, but this blocks access only to those sites and does not provide protection when you visit sites you have not visited before. This book strongly recommends that you set the security level for the Internet zone to Medium or High, so that Internet Explorer can at least prompt you if a site attempts to install suspicious software on your PC.

Understanding Pop-ups and Pop-up Blockers

As you browse the Web, *pop-up ads*, or *pop-ups*, may accost you when you visit certain sites. By understanding the source of these pop-up ads and the tools you can use to block them, you can reduce their frequency and enhance your Web browsing experience.

Of course, some users appreciate the advertisements and even click them occasionally to learn more about products and services that can benefit them. If nobody used the ads to locate and order products or services online, merchants would quickly realize the ineffectiveness of the ads and stop using them. If you find value in the ads, this chapter is not for you. If the ads annoy you, this chapter shows you techniques for blocking them.

The Source of Pop-up Ads

Pop-up ads arise from two sources — adware, described in Chapter 14, and Web pages. Web pages can include tags or scripts that generate pop-up ads whenever you open or close a Web page, click a link, or perform some other action that acts as a trigger. Developers can even program delays into the Web pages, so that the ads appear after a specified time period.

Standard Pop-ups

A standard pop-up ad appears in a separate browser window on top of the window you are trying to view.

Pop-unders

A more sophisticated and polite form of pop-up ad appears in a window that is behind the window you are trying to view. These ads are sometimes referred to as *pop-unders*. They flash on your screen, but you only obtain a clear view of them after you close the windows behind which they appear.

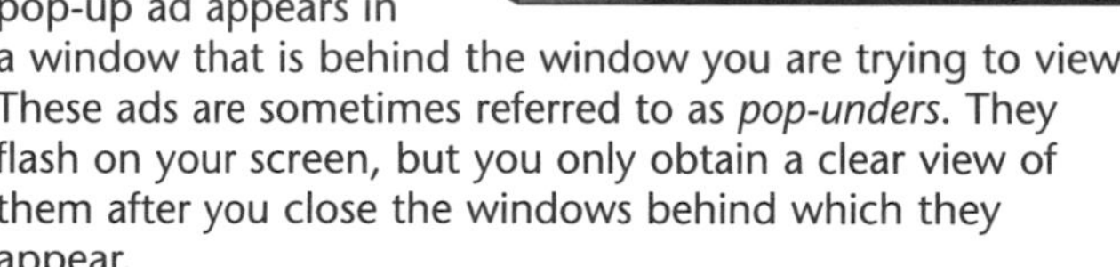

Layer Ads

An even more sophisticated form of Web advertisement is a *layer ad*, which typically appears inside the browser window on a layer above the page. It floats above the page, often moving across it. Layer ads, which are not strictly pop-ups, are very intrusive and often evade any pop-up blocking attempts.

Interstitial Ads

One of the most intrusive forms of Web advertising is the *interstitial ad*. You may think of an interstitial ad as a pop-up ad without a window; some interstitial ads do not even include a link or button to close them. Interstitial ads are often used on media Web sites to persuade a user to subscribe to the site or periodical.

Pop-up Blockers

Fortunately, most Web site ads are standard pop-up ads. Even more fortunate is that several companies have developed pop-up blockers that are highly effective at intercepting these ads and shutting them down before they appear on your PC.

Pop-up blockers run in the background and monitor Web activity on your PC. When they detect an incoming pop-up, they prevent it from loading. Most pop-up blockers are so unobtrusive that you may not even realize that they are running, except for the fact that you have far fewer ads popping up on your screen.

Types of Pop-up Blockers

Pop-up blockers generally come in three forms: as a Web browser feature, as a stand-alone program that is devoted entirely to blocking pop-up ads, or as a component of a toolbar. The version of Internet Explorer included with Windows XP Service Pack 2 includes a built-in pop-up blocker. The Google Toolbar, which you can obtain from toolbar.google.com, also contains a very effective pop-up blocker that keeps a running tally of the number of pop-up ads it has successfully intercepted. Yahoo! has a similar toolbar that you can download at companion. yahoo.com.

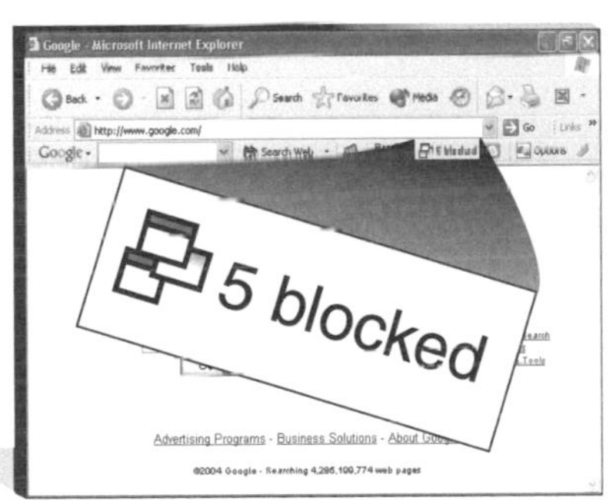

Many stand-alone pop-up blockers are also available, including 12Ghosts Popup-Killer and PopUpCop. Stand-alone pop-up blockers typically run automatically after Windows starts and remain running in the background as you use your PC. Most stand-alone pop-up blockers display an icon in the Windows system tray, at the right end of the taskbar, to indicate that they are running. They may also flash a message on your screen, typically for less than 1 second, every time they successfully intercept a pop-up ad.

The Downside to Pop-up Blockers

Advertisements are not the only content that appears in pop-up windows. Many Web developers use pop-up windows to display additional content unrelated to the content on the main page. For example, a developer may use pop-up windows to display definitions of important terms or to display a series of steps to complete a task. If you have a pop-up blocker installed and running, you may click a link and think that the link does not function, when in fact your pop-up blocker shut down the window. Likewise, if you receive an e-mail message that contains a link to a Web page, your pop-up blocker may prevent your browser from opening the page when you click its link. To view pop-ups, you can usually disable the pop-up blocker temporarily, as discussed in the section "Disable Pop-up Blocking Temporarily."

Download and Install 12Ghosts Popup-Killer

You can download and install a pop-up blocker to significantly reduce the number and frequency of pop-up ads on your PC. You can choose from more than 100 pop-up blockers, many of which are free or are offered as shareware — try before you buy. Most developers charge a nominal fee for their pop-up blockers — typically less than $20. Google, Yahoo!, and other companies offer pop-up blocking for free as part of their toolbars. If you choose to use the toolbar approach, make sure you download a toolbar that is designed to work with your Web browser.

Many pop-up blockers are stand-alone programs that run in the background and intercept pop-up ads before they can appear on your screen. You can visit nearly any shareware site and find links to dozens of stand-alone pop-up blockers. One very reliable and thorough pop-up blocker is 12Ghosts Popup-Killer, which is used as the example throughout this chapter. The 12Ghosts Popup-Killer, which is designed exclusively for Internet Explorer, has a very simple interface that enables you to configure the pop-up blocker to function the way you want it to. The steps in this section show you how to download and install the 12Ghosts Popup-Killer. The steps for downloading and installing other pop-up blockers are very similar.

Download and Install 12Ghosts Popup-Killer

1. In your browser's Address bar, type **www.12ghosts.com/ghosts/popup.htm** and press Enter.
2. Click the Download SuperGee link.

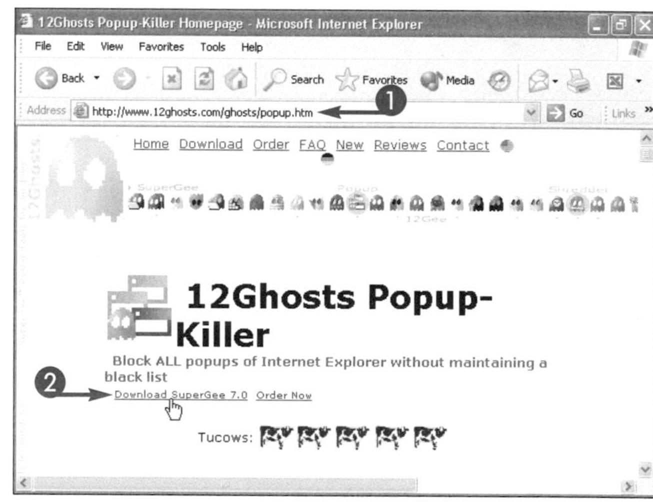

The File Download dialog box appears.

3. Click Open.

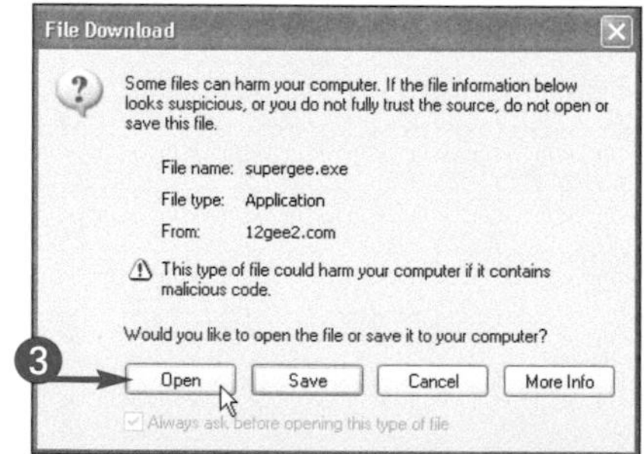

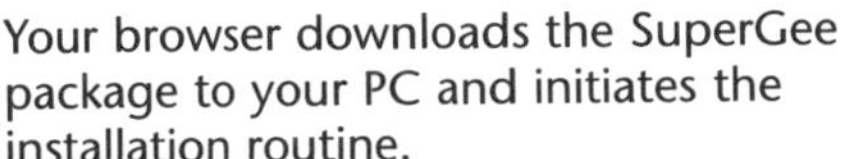

Your browser downloads the SuperGee package to your PC and initiates the installation routine.

4 Read the license agreement.

5 If you accept the terms of the agreement, click the I accept the agreement option (○ changes to ◉).

6 Click Next.

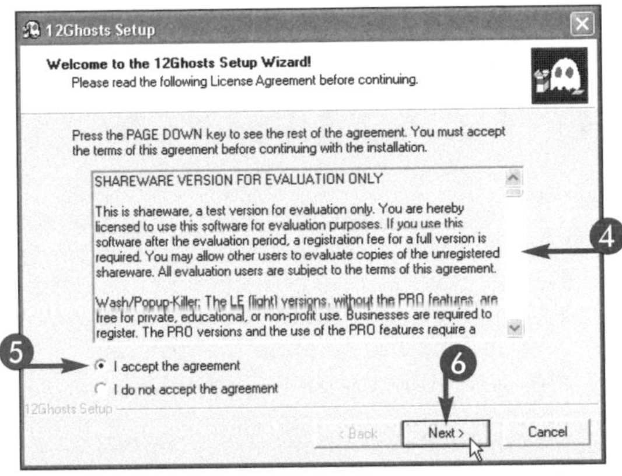

7 Follow the on-screen instructions to install 12Ghosts Popup-Killer.

12Ghosts Popup-Killer is installed and appears on the Start, All Programs, 12Ghosts Popup-Killer menu.

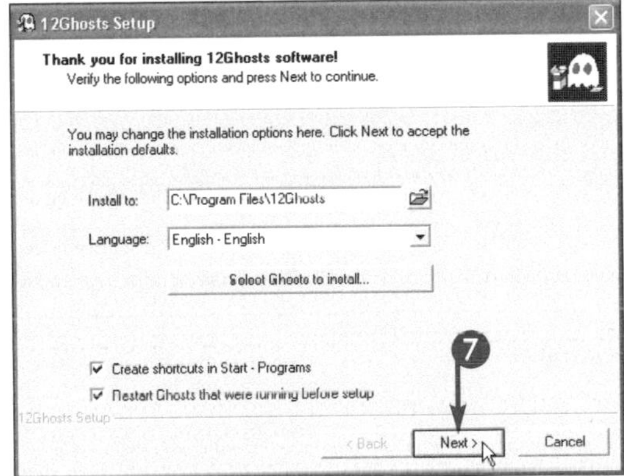

When I install 12Ghosts Popup-Killer, does it automatically start blocking pop-up ads?

▼ No. You must run 12Ghosts Popup-Killer and choose the option for enabling pop-up blocking, as explained in the next section, "Enable Pop-up Blocking in 12Ghosts." This instructs 12Ghosts Popup-Killer to run in the background and monitor your Web pages for any codes that call for displaying pop-up ads.

Does 12Ghosts Popup-Killer block the ads after my PC downloads them or before they are downloaded?

▼ 12Ghosts Popup-Killer blocks pop-up ads before your PC downloads them. It does this by examining the HTML source code that produces the Web page and disabling any codes that instruct the browser to open a new window. By blocking ads before your PC downloads them, 12Ghosts Popup-Killer conserves bandwidth as well as saving you the time and aggravation of having to close the pop-up windows.

Does 12Ghosts Popup-Killer block all unsolicited Web advertisements?

▼ No. No utility can block all unsolicited advertisements. Many Web pages have built-in banner ads that you cannot block. Other pages use layer ads or interstitial ads that are designed to evade detection. Web-based advertisers are constantly exploring ways to frustrate attempts to block ads. See the section "Understanding Pop-ups and Pop-up Blockers" for more information. For more on blocking adware and spyware, see Chapter 14.

Enable Pop-up Blocking in 12Ghosts

When you install most pop-up blockers, pop-up blocking is enabled by default. In some pop-up blockers, however, including 12Ghosts Popup-Killer, pop-up blocking is disabled by default. You must enable pop-up blocking to allow the program to start intercepting and shutting down pop-up ads.

When you enable a pop-up blocker, you instruct it to run in the background and start monitoring incoming Web pages to determine if the pages attempt to generate pop-up windows. Many Web pages contain source code that instructs the browser to open a page in a new window. The pop-up blocker typically intervenes to ensure that the new window does not open.

The steps in this section show you how to enable pop-up blocking in 12Ghosts Popup-Killer. The steps for enabling or disabling pop-up blocking in other programs differ, but typically consist of toggling an option on or off. You can check the pop-up blocker's help system for instructions. If you have a pop-up blocker that is part of a toolbar, it may have a down arrow icon next to it that you can click to display options for the pop-up blocker, including an option to enable or disable it.

Enable Pop-up Blocking in 12Ghosts

1. Click Start.
2. Click All Programs.
3. Click 12Ghosts Popup-Killer.
4. Click Popup-Killer.

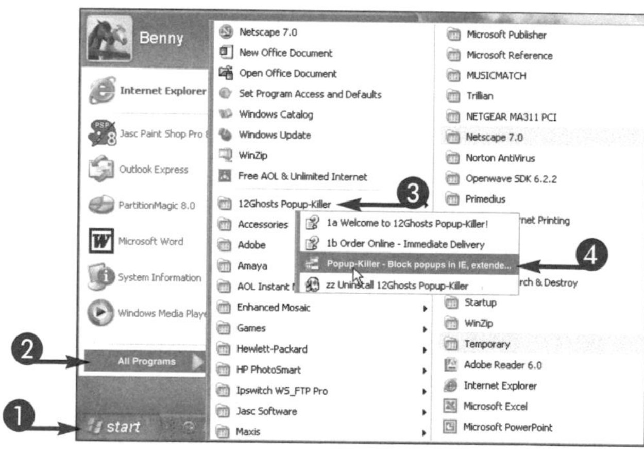

The 12Ghosts Popup-Killer dialog box appears.

5. Click the IE Popups tab.
6. Click the "Block secondary windows of Internet Explorer" option (☐ changes to ☑).
7. Click OK.

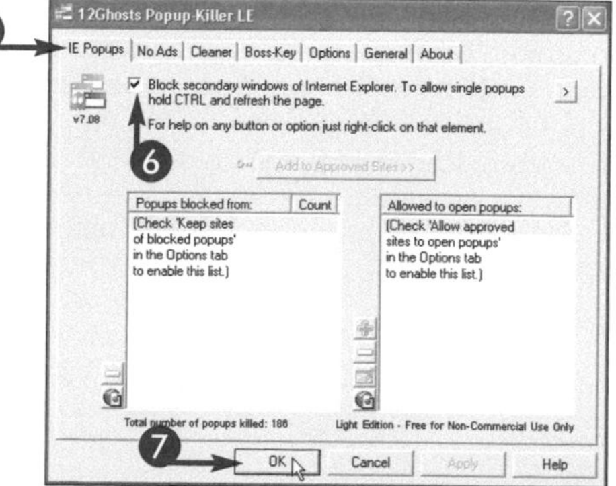

- The 12Ghosts Popup-Killer icon appears in the Windows system tray.

- When you open a page that generates a pop-up, 12Ghosts Popup-Killer displays a message indicating that it blocked the pop-up.

Note: *By default, the message appears for 100 milliseconds, but you can adjust its setting to display it as long as you want.*

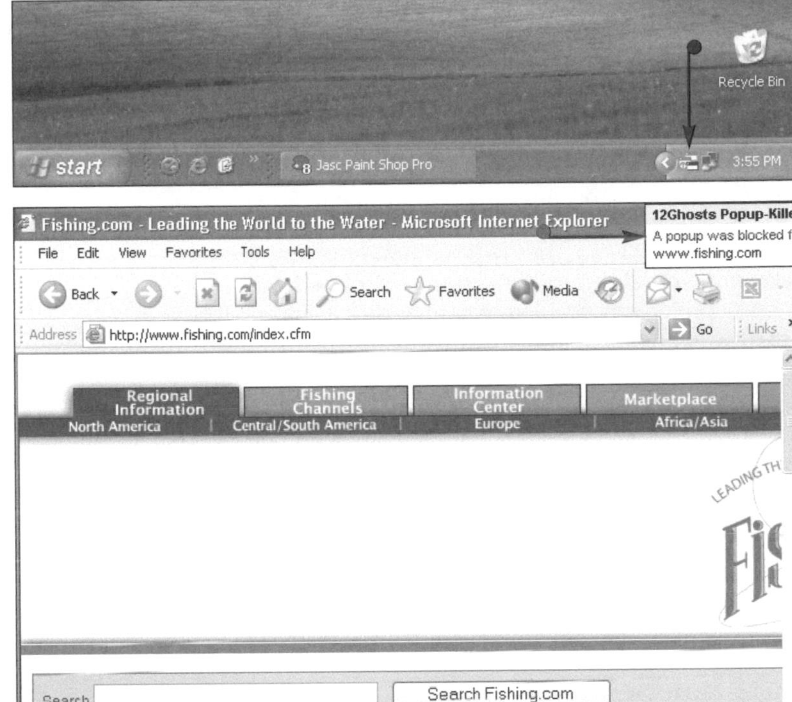

Can I disable pop-up blocking for certain sites?

▼ The free edition of 12Ghosts Popup-Killer does not allow you to disable pop-up blocking for specific sites, but if you pay for a licensed version, you can add sites to the Approved Sites list to enable the sites to display pop-up windows. The next section, "Disable Pop-up Blocking Temporarily" shows you how to enable pop-up windows for individual pages you load or links you click. Most pop-up blockers, including the pop-up blocker included in the Google Toolbar, provide an option to disable pop-up blocking for specific sites. This comes in handy for sites that use pop-up windows for purposes other than advertising.

I enabled pop-up blocking, but I am still receiving loads of pop-ups. What is going on?

▼ Your PC may have adware installed on it. Refer to Chapter 14 for information about adware and for instructions on how to identify it and remove it from your PC. 12Ghosts Popup-Killer has a feature that can help. Display its dialog box as instructed in the steps in this section, click the No Ads tab, and click the Block programs from starting Internet Explorer option (☐ changes to ☑). Some pop-up ads also use Windows Messenger to convey the ad. Open the 12Ghosts Popup-Killer dialog box again, click the Options tab, and click Stop Messenger Service Popups to disable the Windows Messenger.

Disable Pop-up Blocking Temporarily

Many Web pages contain links that open new windows for displaying Web content. Pop-up blockers rarely distinguish between new windows that display ads and new windows that display valuable content related to the currently displayed page. With pop-up blocking enabled, you may click a link and feel confused when nothing appears to happen. What is actually happening is that your pop-up blocker has prevented your browser from opening a new window. To view the content, you can temporarily disable pop-up blocking.

You can temporarily disable pop-up blocking in two ways. The first way is to follow the steps in the previous section, "Enable Pop-up Blocking in 12Ghosts," to toggle pop-up blocking off until you have accessed the content you want to view. You can then repeat the steps to toggle pop-up blocking on. Many pop-up blockers, including 12Ghosts Popup-Killer, feature an alternative. You can press and hold a specific key while clicking a link or typing a page's URL to temporarily disable pop-up blocking for this single instance. When you release the key, pop-up blocking is re-enabled. This works in your Web browser and if you click a link in an e-mail message to open a Web page. You can also try right-clicking the link and clicking Open in New Window.

Disable Pop-up Blocking Temporarily

1. Launch your Web browser.
2. Click a link for opening a page in a new window.
   - 12Ghosts Popup-Killer blocks the pop-up and briefly displays a message indicating that the pop-up was blocked.

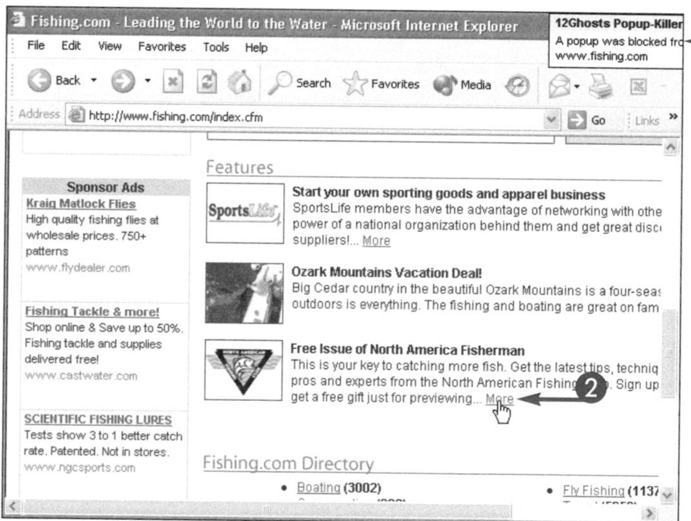

3. Press and hold down the Ctrl key while clicking the same link you clicked in step 2.

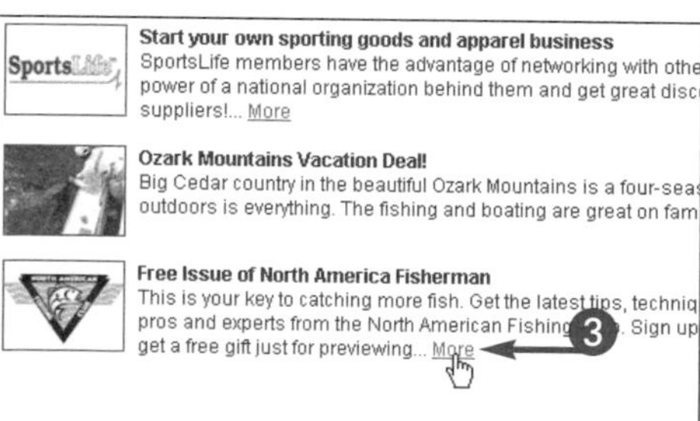

Your Web browser opens a new window that displays the content associated with the link.

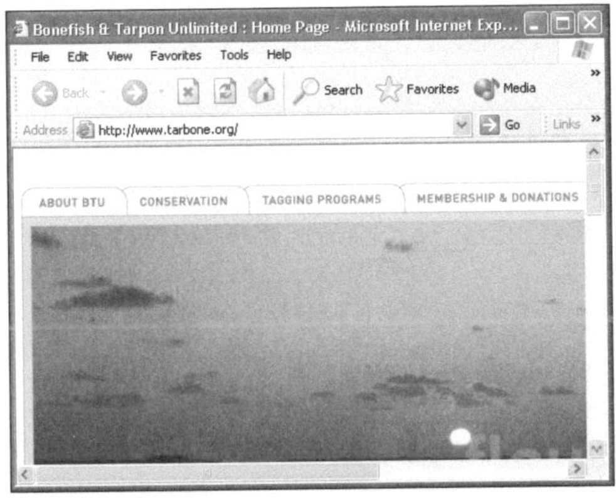

- You can toggle 12Ghosts Popup-Killer on or off by right-clicking its icon in the system tray and clicking Enable Popup Blocking.

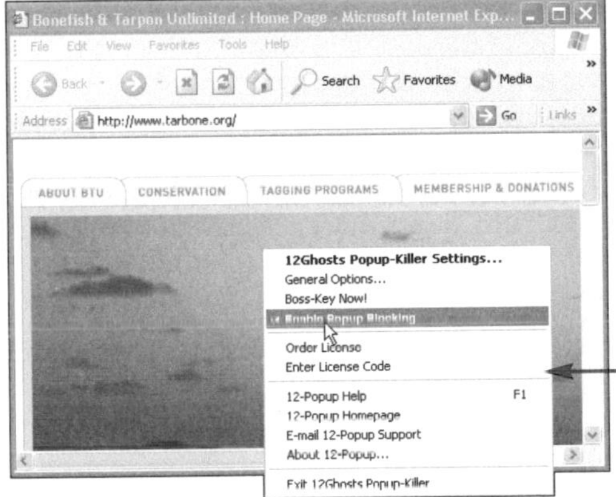

PART V

I am using the pop-up blocker in Google's Toolbar. Does it feature a hot key I can press to disable pop-up blocking temporarily?

Yes. Use the same keystroke as the keystroke that 12Ghosts Popup-Killer uses: Ctrl. When you want to allow a pop-up to pass through the pop-up blocker, press the Ctrl key while clicking its link or typing its address. To disable pop-up blocking for a site, click the blocked button ( ). The message on the button changes to Site popups allowed, and the pop-up blocker allows the site to display pop-ups. You can toggle pop-up blocking back on for this site by clicking the button again.

I am using the pop-up blocker in the Yahoo! toolbar. Does it feature a hot key I can press to disable pop-up blocking temporarily?

Yes. You can press the Ctrl key while clicking a link or typing a Web page address to temporarily disable pop-up blocking. You can also toggle pop-up blocking on or off by clicking the Popup Blocker button (59 blocked) and then clicking Enable Popup Blocker. The Yahoo! toolbar also contains an optional spyware blocker that you can download as part of the toolbar. For information about spyware and how to remove it from your PC, refer to Chapter 14.

Understanding Spam Sources

Spam is unsolicited e-mail, Internet junk mail that accounts for nearly half of all e-mail on the Internet. By knowing where and how spam originates, you can begin to take preventive measures to avoid being placed on mailing lists and to shut down spam that you are currently receiving.

Spam slows down your PC in several ways. It takes longer for your e-mail client to download the messages you want to read. It fills your e-mail server's inbox and your PC's hard drive with useless and often offensive content. And it requires your time to sort through and delete the junk messages.

Why Spam?

Companies spam because it is one of the most cost-effective ways to advertise products and services. Merchants can broadcast thousands of e-mail advertisements with a single command and have them reach their destinations in a matter of seconds. Other direct marketing methods, such as phone calls and paper mail, are much more costly and time-consuming. Companies also spam because it works; people actually purchase products and services because of e-mail advertisements they receive.

How Did They Get My Address?

Spammers employ many clever strategies to gather and confirm e-mail addresses. They may set up an engaging Web site and require you to enter your e-mail address to log on to the site. They may offer software for free — in exchange for your e-mail address. One of the more effective ways of obtaining e-mail addresses is to sponsor a contest in which users must supply an e-mail address to qualify for one of the fabulous prizes.

If you post messages in newsgroups and include your e-mail address so people can reply directly to you, spammers can obtain your e-mail address from your posted message. Spammers also search the Web for pages that contain e-mail addresses; many Web masters include an e-mail address so visitors can contact them directly. Sometimes unsuspecting friends or relatives pass your e-mail address along to a spammer thinking that they are doing you a favor.

Oftentimes, spammers simply send mass mailings to randomly generated lists of likely legitimate e-mail addresses and wait for the recipients to write back indicating that they want to be removed from the mailing list. The message may even have a link you can click to be removed from the list. However, if you respond to the message in any way, the spammers receive immediate confirmation that they have a valid e-mail address.

Can I Opt Out?

You may register at a company's Web site and click an option to specifically request that you be notified of any new products or special deals. This is called *opting in.* Legitimate companies typically let you opt out at any time, simply by sending an e-mail requesting to be removed from the mailing list.

Illegitimate companies do not allow you to opt out, even though, as of January 1, 2004, The Can Spam Act requires that companies include an opt-out link in their mailings or an address that recipients can reply to in order to opt out.

In many cases, if you try to opt out, you merely confirm your e-mail address, which tells the spammer that it has successfully contacted another potential customer. Once you confirm your e-mail address, the spammer can add your address to a list of confirmed addresses. Spammers often sell and exchange lists of confirmed addresses, so once your address is confirmed, having it removed from the list is nearly impossible.

What Is My ISP Doing to Stop Spam?

Many ISPs (Internet Service Providers) include their own spam filters, which are designed to block spam before it reaches your inbox. Some are highly effective and some are not. The major online services, including America Online and MSN, have traditionally been prime targets for spammers, but they are beginning to fight back. America Online 9.0 provides excellent protection against unsolicited e-mail, and MSN is working on its own system to block spam. If you are unsure what your ISP offers and how you can enable spam blocking for your account, log on to your ISP's Web site and do some research.

What Can I Do to Stop Spam?

Preventive measures are the best way to eliminate spam before you receive it. The next section, "Practice Spam Prevention," describes safe computing practices that can help you avoid having your e-mail address placed on a spam mailing list. If your e-mail address is already on one or more mailing lists, other sections in this chapter describe tools and techniques you can use to block spam, or at least filter it out automatically, so you will have less of it to manage directly. Of course, if everyone would boycott companies that advertised via spam, spam would disappear in a hurry, but that probably will not happen any time in the near future.

Practice Spam Prevention

The best way to live a spam-free existence on the Internet is to prevent your e-mail address from being added to a spam mailing list. The basic strategy is to provide your main e-mail address only to legitimate sites that do not pass your address on to other sites, and to never reply to spam, even to cancel it.

Of course, no spam-prevention strategy is 100 percent effective. Spammers can obtain your e-mail address simply by making a good educated guess. However, by practicing spam prevention, as instructed in this section, you can begin to stop the unrelenting barrage of spam.

Use Two or More E-mail Addresses

If you want to register for contests, download freeware or shareware, subscribe to sites, or perform other activity that places you at risk for receiving spam, consider obtaining additional, disposable e-mail addresses. You can then use your disposable e-mail addresses to register at sites and use your permanent e-mail address for correspondence with friends, relatives, and colleagues. See the section "Obtain an Alternative E-mail Address" for more information.

Ignore Unsolicited E-mail

Sometimes, the mere act of previewing or opening spam can confirm your e-mail address and make you more susceptible to receiving additional spam. Worse, an e-mail message may contain a Trojan horse that gathers e-mail addresses from your address book and forwards them to a third party, or uses your PC and e-mail to send spam.

To prevent this from happening, you can turn off the preview pane in your e-mail client, so that clicking a message description does not automatically open the message and display its contents. You can then delete any messages that arrive from unknown senders without opening them. Some e-mail clients, such as Thunderbird and The Bat, are less susceptible than others, such as Outlook and Outlook Express, to these problems, but by adjusting preferences, you can make any e-mail client more secure.

Do Not Unsubscribe to Spam

When you receive spam, the first impulse is to write back to the sender to request that the person stop sending you unsolicited mail. This is often the worst action to take.

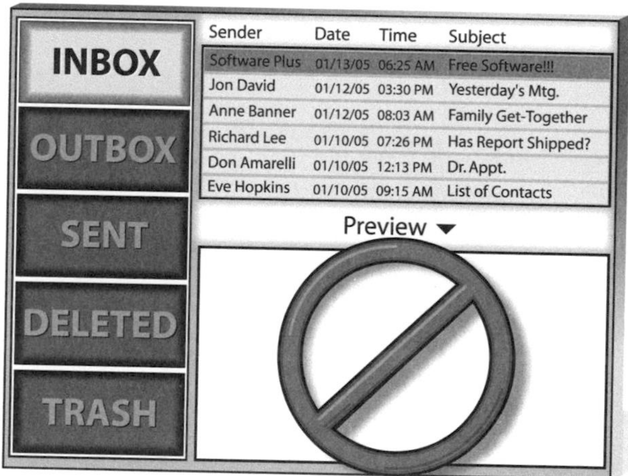

Replying to spam, even to unsubscribe from the mailing list, confirms your e-mail address, so the spammers know that they have hit their mark. This typically leads to an ever-increasing barrage of spam. Frequently, an unsolicited message contains a link you can click to unsubscribe; resist the temptation to click the link. Simply delete the message.

Guard Your E-mail Address

Because spammers can obtain your e-mail address from Web pages, blogs, and newsgroups, avoid posting your permanent e-mail address anywhere on the Internet. A blog, which is short for Web log, is a Web site that people commonly create to voice their opinions or keep a diary of events or thoughts that others can view.

You can use various *obfuscation* techniques to prevent your e-mail address from looking like an e-mail address, so search bots cannot identify your address. For example, when posting a message to a newsgroup, you can insert some text in place of the @ sign; for example, you may present your e-mail address as jdoeREplaCEinternet.com. Most newsgroup users will know to adjust the address to send you an e-mail message, or you can add a brief message telling the person how to decode your e-mail address. Using mixed case — REplaCE instead of REPLACE — prevents a spam bot from replacing a string of uppercase characters with @.

When it works, obfuscation causes search bots to skip over your e-mail address. However, many search bots are configured to identify obfuscation and retrieve the e-mail address, so omitting your e-mail address is the most effective option.

Read Privacy Policies

Before typing your e-mail address to register for anything, look for a privacy policy and read it thoroughly. Make sure that the privacy policy includes some language stating that the company does not share e-mail addresses with other companies. If you see no claim to this effect, do not submit your e-mail address. This company may not send unsolicited mail, but it may share your address with a company that does.

Do Not Forward Chain Letters

E-mail etiquette dictates that you should not forward chain letters, but many people still do, falsely believing that it can do no harm. Unfortunately, chain letters are pure gold to spammers. Most chain letters are packed with valid e-mail addresses that spammers love to get their hands on.

Inform Friends and Family

Unsuspecting friends and family members often think of you while they browse the Web. They encounter a joke or photo that they think will make you laugh or they see a story that they want to share with you. Many Web sites include links for such items that enable a person to forward the item to someone. All the person has to do is click the link, type your e-mail address, and click Send, and your e-mail address is added to a spam mailing list. Tell your friends and family that you would appreciate not receiving this material.

Check Your Sent Items Folder

Your PC and e-mail client may be spamming others without your knowledge. You may open an e-mail message or install a program on your PC that includes software that uses your e-mail client to broadcast advertisements to e-mail addresses in your address book. Check the Sent Items folder in your e-mail client to ensure that this is not happening. If you find messages that you did not send, you may need to run a virus check or spyware scan on your PC to remove the offending Trojan horse program.

Obtain an Alternative E-mail Address

You can direct spam away from your primary e-mail account by obtaining a second, disposable e-mail address and using it whenever you register freeware or shareware or sign up for contests or subscriptions. If you register using your alternative e-mail address, and a company starts spamming you, all of the junk mail goes to your alternative e-mail address. You can then safely ignore that e-mail account, because you receive all of your important e-mail through your primary e-mail account.

Many Internet companies, including Yahoo! and MSN Hotmail, offer free e-mail accounts. At the writing of this book, GMail from Google was still in the beta testing phase, but may be available by the time you read this. You can usually sign up for a free account by typing your name, city and state of residence, ZIP code, and other information, which may or may not be accurate, and by choosing a username, e-mail address, and password for the account.

In most cases, the e-mail account you create remains active only as long as you continue using it, so you may want to check it monthly. Of course, if the service automatically deletes your account because of inactivity, you can always create a new account.

Obtain an Alternative E-mail Address

1. Launch your Web browser.
2. In the Address bar, type the address of a Web site that offers free e-mail accounts.

   This example uses MSN Hotmail.
3. Click the option to sign up for a free e-mail account.

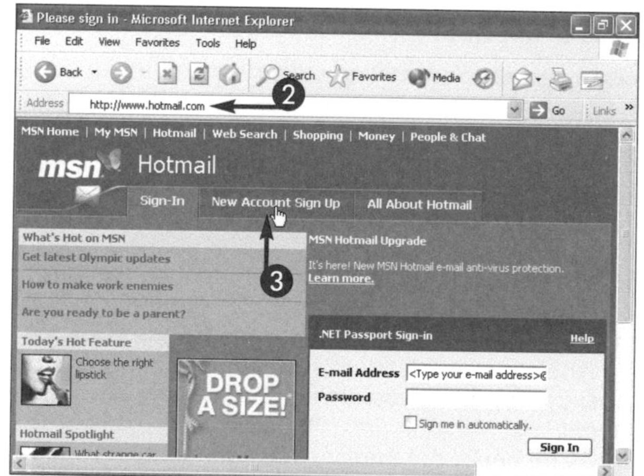

The Web site prompts you to type personal information.

4. Type the requested information.

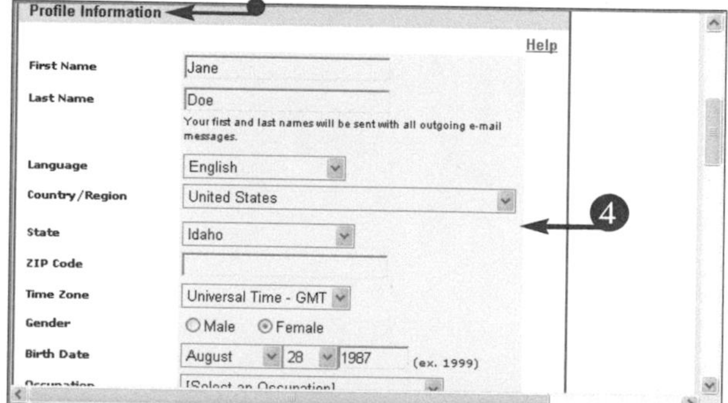

5 Scroll down the page to type additional information.

6 Type the e-mail address you want to use.

7 Type the password you want to use.

8 Type any additional information that the form requests.

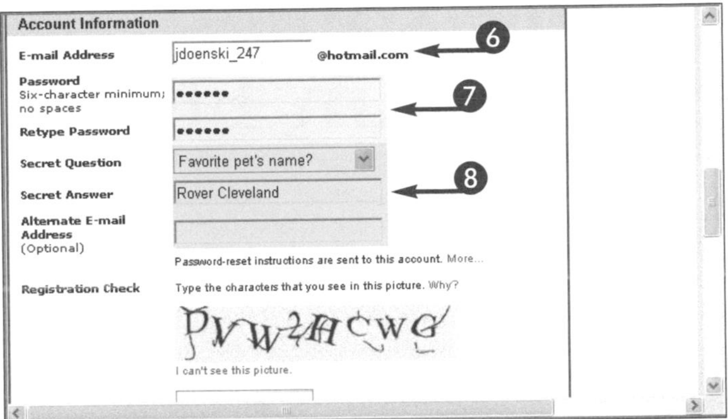

9 Scroll down the page.

10 Read the user agreements.

11 If you agree with the terms of use, follow the on-screen instructions to indicate that you agree.

The service creates your new e-mail account.

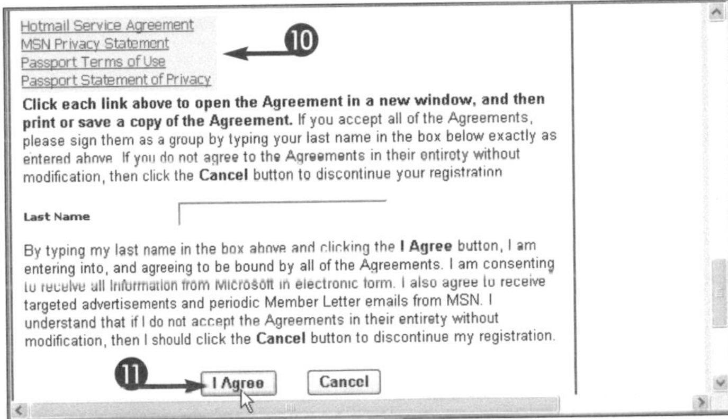

I typed the e-mail address but the service displayed a message indicating that the address was already in use. What should I do?

- Most common e-mail addresses are already in use, so you may need to modify your username. For example, you probably cannot use cutiepie@hotmail.com, but you can add a few characters to create a unique address that is not already being used, such as cutiepie_xyz12@hotmail.com. The service may recommend some options you can try.

How can these services support all of these alternative e-mail addresses?

- Most services place strict limits on the amount of storage space you can use for your free e-mail account. You may receive only a couple megabytes of storage, which is plenty for a disposable e-mail account. Also, if a person does not log on to the account for a prolonged period of time, usually a month or longer, the service automatically deletes the account.

When I register for a subscription that requires e-mail address confirmation, what should I do?

- Many sites require that you confirm your e-mail address to enable a free service or subscription. The site e-mails a confirmation message to the e-mail address you used when you signed up for the service. You must check your alternative e-mail account's inbox, find this message, and reply to it before you can use or access the free service.

Enable Your ISP's Spam Filter

Many ISPs feature their own spam-blocking capabilities, if you choose to use them. You can enable spam blocking to have your e-mail server automatically intercept and delete incoming messages from known or suspected spam sources. By blocking spam at the mail server, the ISP can conserve storage space on the mail server and save you the time it takes to delete spam. Some ISPs enable spam filtering by default; others require you to enable filtering for each e-mail account.

The steps in this section show how to enable spam filtering for a Comcast Internet e-mail account. The steps vary from one ISP to another, but if you know your username and password, you can usually log on to the ISP's Web site and click an option to obtain help entering your e-mail account preferences.

Many ISPs also enlist the aid of their members to help identify the sources of spam. If your ISP features Web-based e-mail, you may be able to click an option to report a message as spam and help the ISP more effectively identify spam.

Enable Your ISP's Spam Filter

1. Launch your Web browser.
2. In the Address bar, type the address to your ISP's Web site and press Enter.
3. Type your username.
4. Type your password.
5. Click the option to log on.

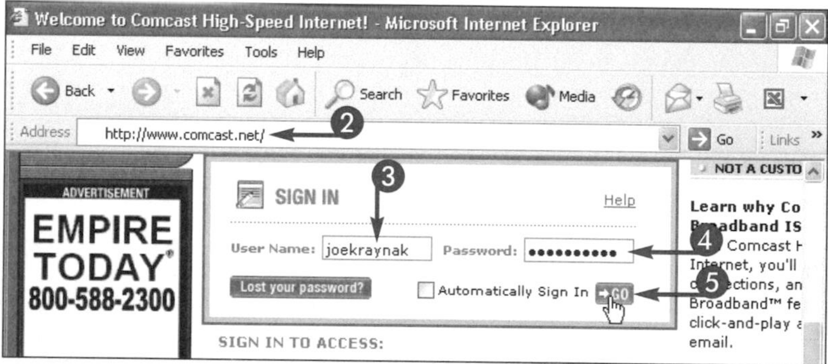

Your ISP displays the home page for your account.

6. Click the option for managing your account or setting preferences.

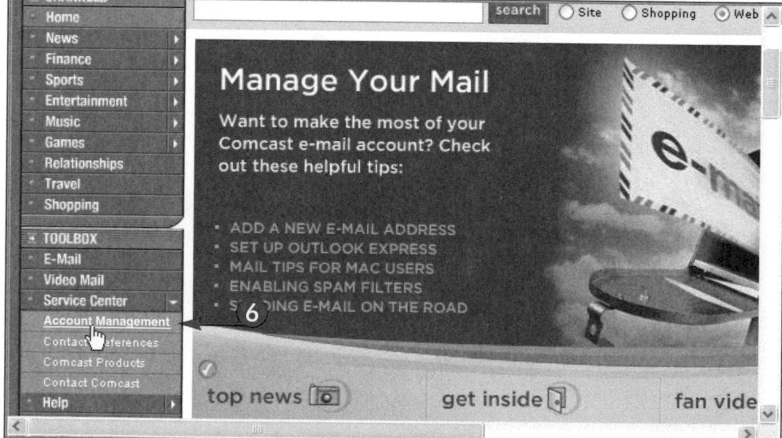

Your account options appear.

7 Click the option for setting spam filters.

Note: You may need to select a series of commands to locate the spam filter settings.

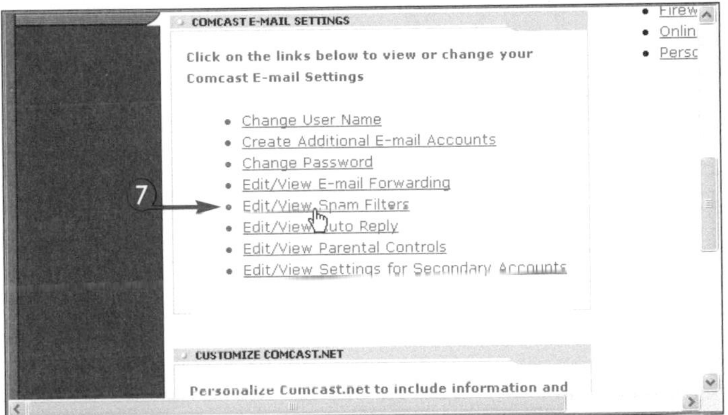

8 Click the option to enable spam filtering and select any other additional preferences.

- At Comcast Internet, you can save spam to a separate folder so you can review it before deleting the messages.

9 Click the option to update your settings.

Your ISP saves the spam filtering settings you selected.

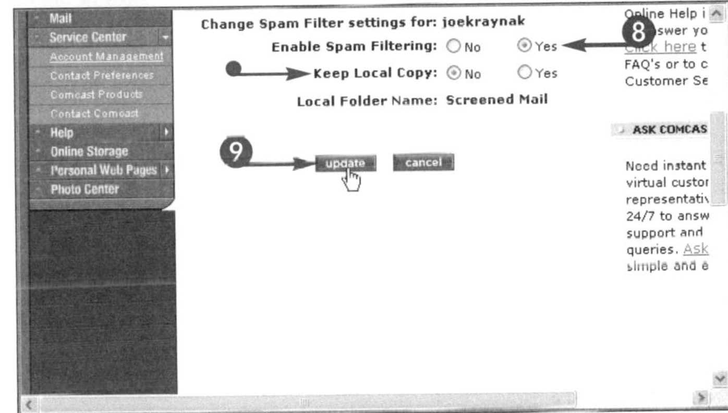

PART V

I cannot find the spam filtering options on my ISP's Web site. What should I do?

▼ Examine your ISP's home page for e-mail options, account management settings, or preferences. If you cannot find an area for managing your account, look for a help or FAQ (frequently asked questions) option and select it. Your ISP may provide e-mail filtering software that you must install or it may specify some other steps. As a last resort, call your ISP on the telephone.

I turned on the spam filter, but I am still receiving plenty of junk mail. Is this normal?

▼ Yes. Spammers constantly hone their skills and develop new methods to bypass spam filters, so you may keep receiving some spam. Filtering spam at the ISP is only one defense against spam. Refer to other sections in this chapter for additional options.

I keep getting the same spam from the same e-mail address. Can my ISP block e-mail coming in from that address?

▼ Maybe. Some ISPs can block e-mail by filtering out all messages from a particular address or by allowing e-mail that arrives only from one or more addresses. Check your account's e-mail preferences to determine your options. Even if an ISP provides no option you can change yourself, the ISP may be able to block e-mail from one or more addresses. Contact your ISP.

Obtain a Secure E-mail Client

You can choose a secure *e-mail client* — a program for sending and receiving e-mail messages — that more effectively prevents spammers from obtaining your e-mail address.

If you use Outlook or Outlook Express to manage your e-mail, your e-mail account may be susceptible to a technique for obtaining e-mail addresses called *spam beacons*. A spam beacon consists of an HTML tag that downloads an image from the spammer's image server to display in the e-mail message. The image can be a picture of anything or it can be a white box that does not even display, but the spammer associates your e-mail address with the image. When you open the message, your e-mail client downloads the image, which lets the spammer know that your e-mail address is valid and that it can add your address to an active mailing list.

You can make Outlook and Outlook Express more secure by disabling the display of images or by choosing to read all messages as text-only, but then you cannot view images or special text formatting used in messages from legitimate sources. By using a more secure e-mail client, you can view images in your e-mail messages and avoid falling victim to spam beacons.

Obtain a Secure E-mail Client

1. Launch your Web browser.
2. In the Address bar, type **www.download.com** and press Enter.
3. Click the Internet link.
4. Click the E-mail link.
5. Click the Clients link.

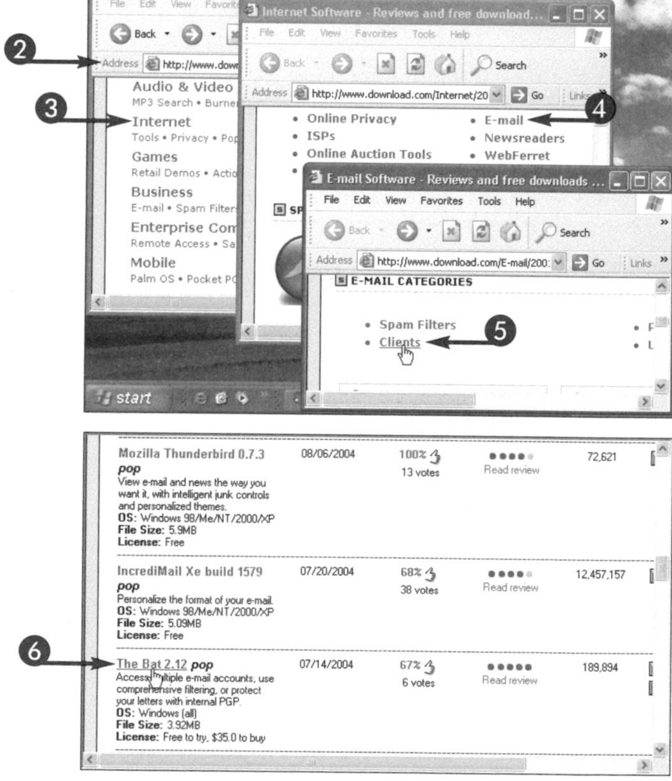

Download.com displays a list of e-mail clients.

6. Click the link for the e-mail client you want to try.

   This book recommends The Bat, Mozilla Thunderbird, Poco Mail, and Pegasus Mail.

Download.com displays a description and ratings for the e-mail client.

7 Click Download Now.

The File Download dialog box appears.

8 Click Open.

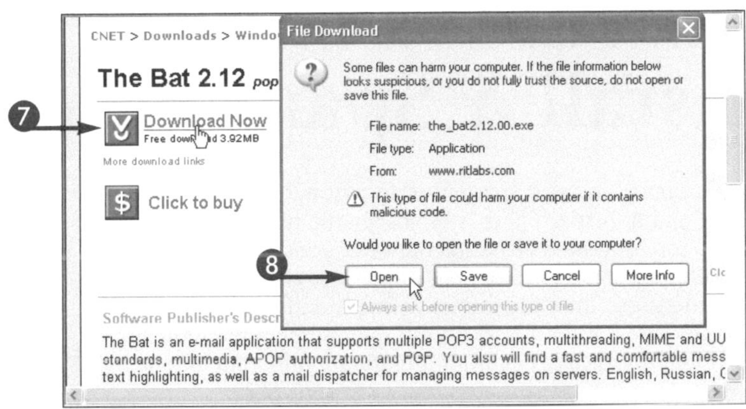

Your Web browser downloads the installation file and initiates the installation routine.

9 Follow the on-screen instructions to complete the installation.

The e-mail client installs on your PC.

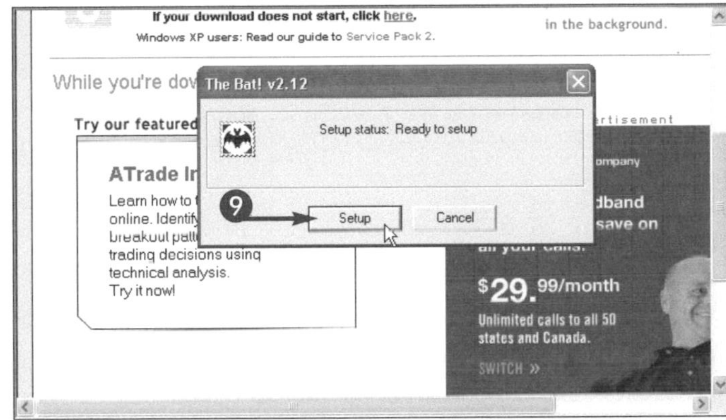

I like using Outlook Express. Can I configure it to be more secure?

▼ Yes. To increase security in Outlook Express, click Tools, Options, the Read tab, and then the Read all messages in plain text option (☐ changes to ☑). This prevents any HTML source code from loading and displays only the text portion of a message. You should also turn off the preview pane, if it is displayed. Click View, Layout, and then the Show preview pane option (☑ changes to ☐). To read a message with the preview pane hidden, double-click the message description. You can also use spam filters for Outlook Express, as explained in the next section, "Download and Install a Spam Filter."

Are these e-mail clients free?

▼ Some alternative e-mail clients, such as Thunderbird and Pegasus Mail, are free. If you want to try a solid e-mail client that features enhanced spam filtering without making an additional monetary investment, these are excellent candidates. Poco Mail offers a free trial version but costs $40 to register if you want to continue using it past the trial period. RitLabs also offers a free trial version of The Bat, but it costs $35 to continue using it after the trial period. Several other freeware and shareware e-mail clients are available, and you can learn more about them at Download.com.

Download and Install a Spam Filter

You can install a spam filter to automatically manage spam. A spam filter is typically an e-mail proxy server; that is, it stands between your e-mail client and your mail server and screens all incoming e-mail. It blocks messages that it identifies as spam and passes along messages that it identifies as acceptable. When you install a spam filter, it typically becomes integrated with your e-mail client, but you can set up preferences to control its function.

Some spam filters look for keywords in the message description or subject lines to identify spam. However, this technique often blocks acceptable messages and allows many unacceptable messages to pass through the filter. Most of the current spam filters employ *Bayesian filtering*, which looks at the entire message for a pattern of text and determines the probability of whether a message is spam. As you mark messages as spam or not spam, the Bayesian filter fine-tunes its ability to distinguish between spam and acceptable e-mail.

Many spam filters are available, and because Outlook and Outlook Express are the most commonly used e-mail clients, many filters are designed specifically for use with these clients.

Download and Install a Spam Filter

1. Launch your Web browser.
2. In the Address bar, type **www.download.com** and press Enter.
3. Click the Internet link.
4. Click the E-mail link.
5. Click the Spam Filters link.

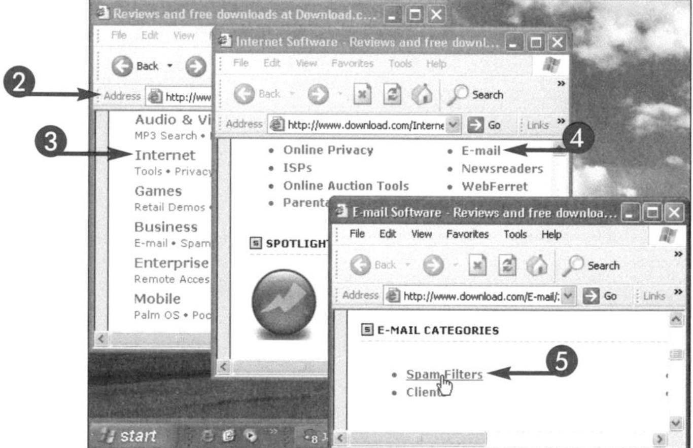

- Download.com displays a list of spam filters.

6. Click the link for a spam filter you want to try.

- This book recommends iHateSpam, POPFile, SpamBully, and ChoiceMail, although several other fine filtering programs are available.

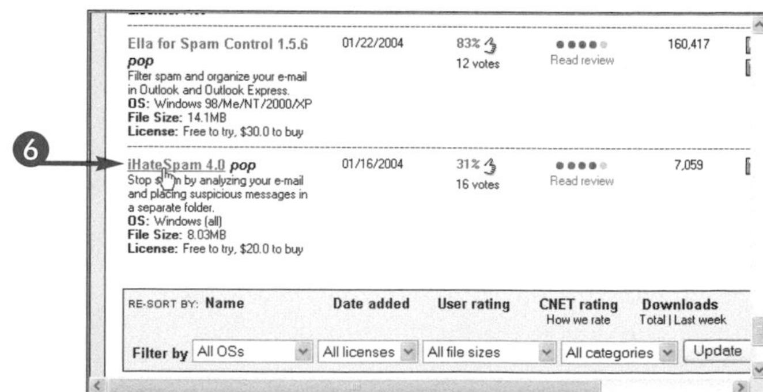

Download.com displays a description and ratings for the spam filter.

7. Click Download Now.

The File Download dialog box appears.

8. Click Open.

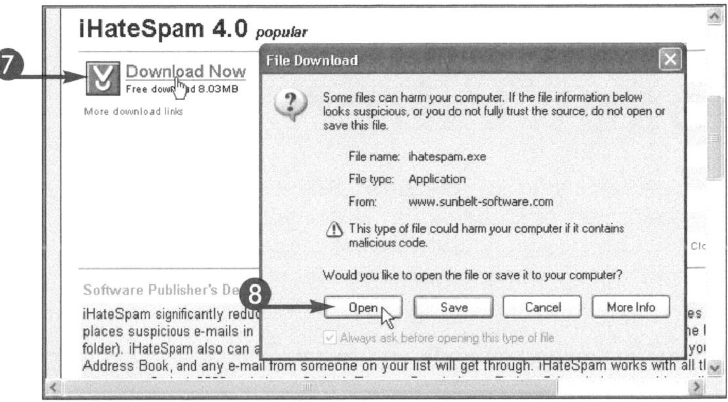

Your Web browser downloads the installation file and initiates the installation routine.

9. Follow the on-screen instructions to complete the installation.

The spam filter installs on your PC.

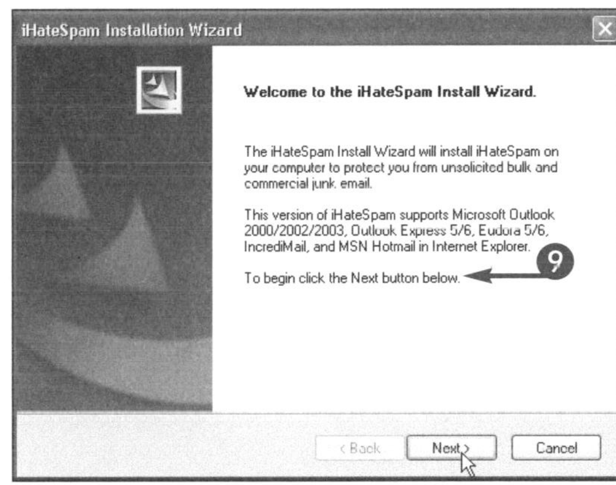

Do you recommend any other spam filters?

- Yes. One of the latest products that has received some excellent reviews is SpamBayes, which you can download from spambayes.sourceforge.net. The standard version works with Outlook, not Outlook Express, but a version is available for Outlook Express and other e-mail clients. As you can tell from its name, SpamBayes uses Bayesian filtering, but it uses modified Bayesian filtering and other approaches to enhance its effectiveness. SpamBayes is free, but you may not be able to find it at many of the freeware or shareware sites. Commercial spam filters include McAfee SpamKiller and Norton AntiSpam, which are both highly effective.

What other strategies do spam filters use to block spam?

- Traditional spam filtering uses either blacklists or whitelists, or a combination of the two, to filter e-mail. A blacklist blocks all e-mail that originates from a specified domain; for example, a blacklist may block all messages from junkmail4u.biz. A whitelist instructs the e-mail client to allow all e-mail messages that originate from a specific e-mail address or domain; for example, a whitelist may accept all e-mail from whitehouse.gov. Spam filters also commonly inspect the descriptions or content of incoming messages for words that commonly appear in spam. Some filters use a combination of whitelists, blacklists, and Bayesian filtering to more accurately distinguish spam from acceptable messages.

Configure Your Spam Filter

You can configure your spam filter by specifying addresses of senders from whom you want to accept messages, addresses of senders from whom you do not want to accept messages, and preferences for how you want blocked messages processed.

When you install most spam filters, they become integrated with your e-mail client. When you run your e-mail client for the first time after installing the filter, the filter typically runs a setup routine that configures the filter for your e-mail accounts and enables you to enter preferences for how the filter functions. The steps in this section use iHateSpam as an example. However, the steps vary a great deal depending on the spam filter you have installed and the e-mail client that you use.

iHateSpam runs a configuration wizard when it starts that leads you step by step through the setup process. The wizard prompts you to create a list of friends, specify any foreign language character sets to block, and select a learning preference. The learning preference enables you to join a network of other iHateSpam users to fine-tune iHateSpam's ability to distinguish spam from acceptable e-mail messages.

Configure Your Spam Filter

1. Launch your e-mail client.

Note: *The first time you run Outlook Express after installing a spam filter, the spam filter may prompt you to register.*

Note: *While this example uses iHateSpam, steps vary depending on the spam filter you install.*

2. Click the desired registration option.
3. Click OK.

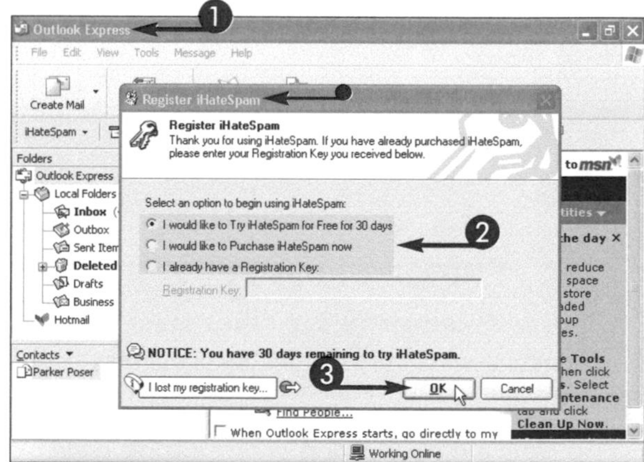

The Welcome screen appears offering to step you through the configuration process.

4. Click Next.

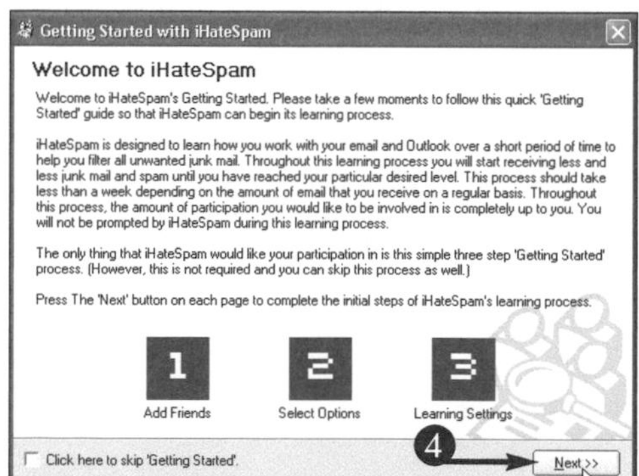

The spam filter displays a list of correspondents in your e-mail address book, so you can add them to your list of friends.

5 Click the box next to any names you do not want included in your list of friends (☑ changes to ☐).

6 Click Next.

The spam filter offers to block any incoming mail that contains foreign characters.

7 Click the option or options you want to use to filter out incoming mail from foreign sources (☐ changes to ☑).

8 Click Next.

9 Follow the on-screen instructions to complete the configuration process.

Your spam filter is configured to receive e-mail messages from acceptable sources and block messages from unacceptable sources.

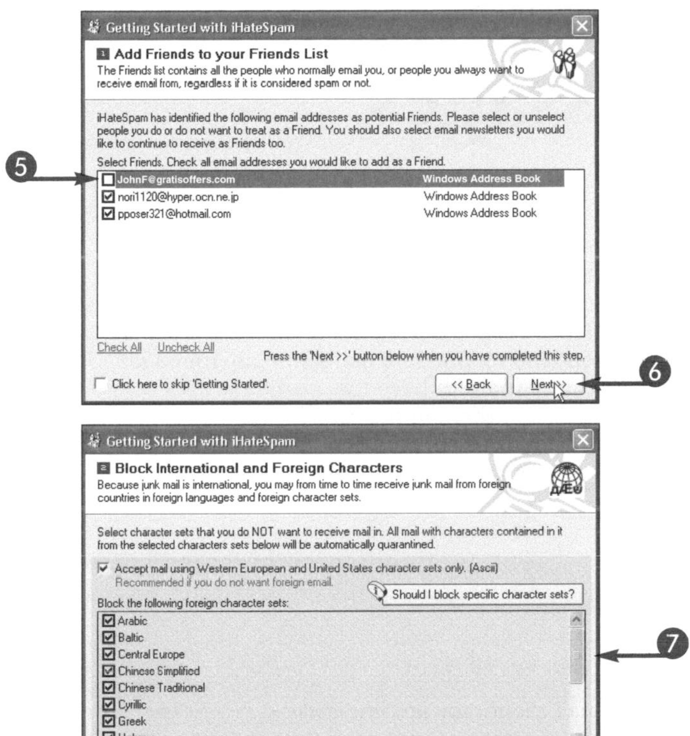

PART V

Do all spam filters lead you through the configuration process when you first run them?

▼ No. Many spam filters lead you through a setup process after you install them or the first time you run them, but you may need to select an option to run a configuration wizard or display a dialog box for entering your preferences. Spam filters commonly add a toolbar to your e-mail client that contains commands for marking incoming e-mail as spam or as acceptable messages. This toolbar usually contains an option or menu for configuring the filter. Configuring a filter typically consists of telling the filter what to block, what to accept, and how to treat blocked messages.

What purpose do the learning options serve?

▼ As discussed in the next section, "Mark Spam Messages," many spam filters keep a record of the types of messages you mark as spam and the types of messages you choose to read. It can then fine-tune its ability to identify spam, thus becoming more accurate the longer you use the filter. The learning options typically determine how and to what degree the filter obtains information from your selections. iHateSpam is somewhat unique in that it can obtain data from a community of users in order to learn not only from your choices but from the choices of many other users, as well.

Mark Spam Messages

When you receive messages, your spam filter typically sorts the messages, placing suspected spam in the Deleted Items folder or a special folder that it creates exclusively for spam. You can usually dump the suspected spam messages without looking at them, or you can review the messages and pick out any that are acceptable to you. You can also mark messages that you consider spam to have the spam filter automatically delete them in the future. When you mark a message as spam, most spam filters also add any keywords from the message to their database of words used to identify spam, and they use this information to fine-tune their ability to recognize spam.

You can also mark messages that are acceptable so that your spam filter does not question or block these messages or similar messages in the future.

The steps in this section show how to mark messages as spam in iHateSpam. The steps differ a great deal from one spam filter to another. Some spam blockers are more automated than others. However, the process of reviewing the messages before deleting them is similar in most spam blockers.

Mark Spam Messages

1. Launch your e-mail client.

   Your e-mail client may automatically retrieve new messages. If it does not, enter the command to retrieve new messages.

2. Click a message that is spam.
3. Click the button that marks the message as spam.

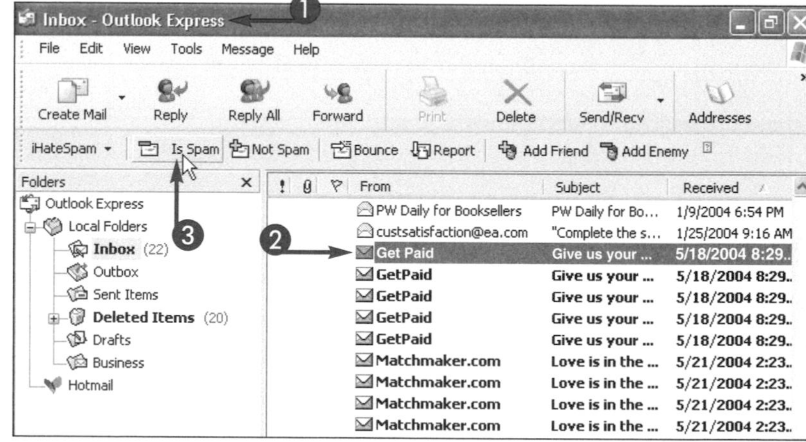

   A dialog box appears, prompting you to specify how you want the message processed.

4. Click the desired actions you want the spam filter to apply to this message.
5. Click OK.

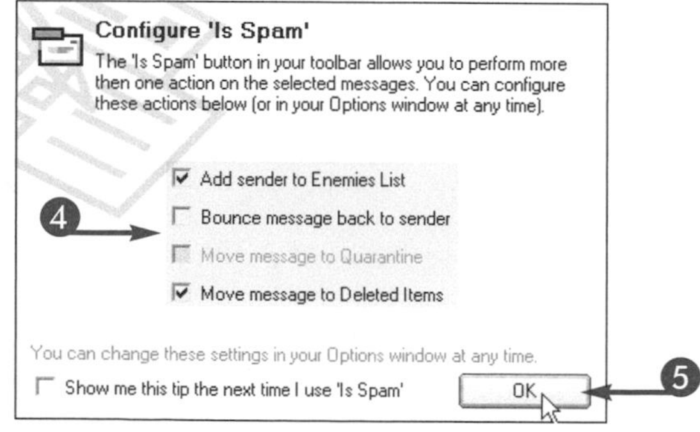

- A message appears indicating that the e-mail message has been marked as spam.

- You can click the iHateSpam icon in the system tray to access options for obtaining help, managing accounts, and viewing the quarantined messages.

Note: *For more on installing iHateSpam on your system, see the section "Download and Install a Spam Filter."*

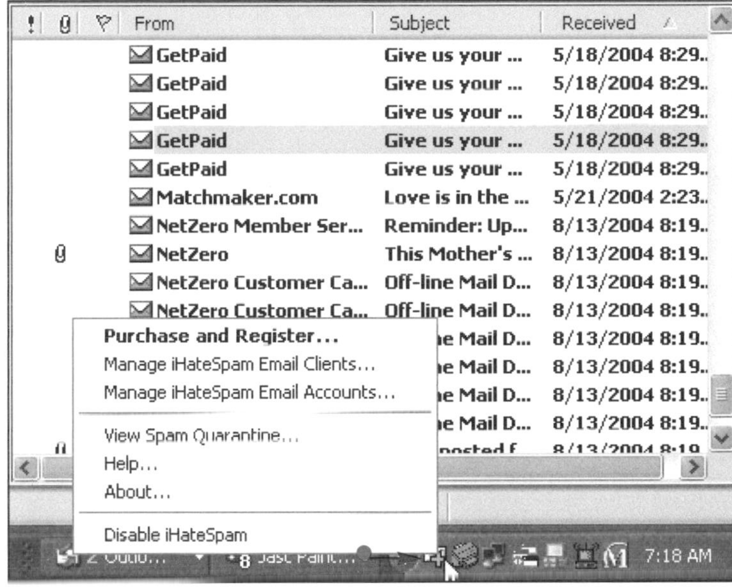

Do all spam filters allow me to mark incoming messages as spam?

▼ Most spam filters, especially those that use Bayesian filtering, not only allow you to mark spam and mark acceptable messages, but they recommend that you do so to help fine-tune the filter's ability to distinguish spam from acceptable messages. The more time you spend up front teaching the filter your preferences, the less time you need to spend later reviewing incoming messages.

In iHateSpam, I see an option to Add Friend or Add Enemy. What are those options for?

▼ You can click a message and then click Add Friend to have the sender's e-mail address added to a list of approved e-mail addresses so the filter does not block any incoming messages from that sender. You can click a message and click Add Enemy to add a sender's e-mail address to a blacklist, so that iHateSpam blocks all incoming messages from that sender.

Can I do anything to spammers to punish them?

▼ SpamBully is one of the few spam filters to include a feature to punish the spammer, but the punishment is pretty mild. Spam Bully loads any Web pages recommended in the spam message several times without purchasing anything, theoretically increasing the cost of bandwidth to the spammer. iHateSpam includes an option for bouncing the message back to the spammer or reporting the spammer, but these options are very ineffective because most spammers use fake e-mail addresses.

Troubleshoot Internet Connection Speed Problems

If your Internet connection seems slower than usual, you can often troubleshoot the problem yourself to identify the cause and address it. Several problems can slow down an Internet connection. Your modem or PC may have a loose cable; communications between your modem and ISP may be crossed; your ISP may be having problems with its system; your firewall software may be interfering with the data transfer; or, if you share a modem on a network, the Internet sharing system may be causing interference.

Before calling your ISP's technical support line and having a customer service representative place you on hold for several minutes only to lead you through a series of standard troubleshooting routines, you can run through the troubleshooting procedure first by following the suggestions in this section. Once you have a stable connection, you can refer to other sections in this chapter to further optimize your Internet connection speed.

Check the Cables

The first step in troubleshooting most PC problems is to rule out the hardware. Check the cable that leads from your modem to your PC to ensure that it is not damaged and that it connects securely to both the modem and the PC. Check the modem's power cable. Sometimes a loose power cable can cause as many headaches as a loose modem cable.

If you have a standard dial-up modem, plug a phone into the phone jack that you use for the modem, pick up the receiver, and listen. Make sure you hear a dial tone and that you do not hear static, which can signal a bad connection. If you hear static, you may need to contact your phone company for assistance. If you have a DSL line, you must connect a filter between the phone and the phone jack to test the line in this way.

If you use a cable modem, disconnect the cable from the modem and connect it to a TV set to determine if your cable service is working. Sometimes cable service is temporarily unavailable for a particular area. If cable TV service is unavailable, call your cable service to report the service interruption.

Disconnect the Router

If you have multiple PCs sharing a common Internet connection, typically a cable or DSL modem, the modem plugs into a router, a hub, or a switch, to which all of your PCs connect in order to use the modem. On the primary PC — usually the PC that is closest to the modem and router — disconnect the network cable from the modem, and instead of connecting the PC to the router, connect it directly to the modem. If your Internet connection is back up to speed, the problem is with your router or its software or settings, not with the modem or your ISP.

Disable the Firewall

As discussed in Chapter 28, firewalls are essential for securing your PC and network on the Internet. However, they are a common source of connection problems. If you cannot connect to the Internet or download files, or if the Internet seems slower than usual, try disabling the firewall, as shown in Chapter 28. If this fixes the problem, you may be able to adjust the firewall settings or install a different firewall that works better with your system.

Reset and Restart

One of the first troubleshooting steps a technician instructs you to do is to reset the modem, especially if you connect to the Internet using a cable or DSL modem. These modems have internal settings that the modem retains as long as the power is on. You can reset the modem by pressing the modem's reset button for 5 seconds — if it has a reset button — or disconnecting the power for 2 to 5 minutes and then reconnecting the modem.

If you have more than one PC connected to a router that connects to the modem, exit all programs that are running on the primary PC, and then shut down the PC. Disconnect the power to the router and to the modem. Leave everything off for at least 3 minutes. Turn on the modem and watch the indicator lights to ensure that it establishes a connection — usually the cable light appears green. Next, turn on the router and make sure the modem stays connected. Finally, turn on the PC.

This may fix the problem. If the modem cannot establish a DSL or cable connection even when the router and PC are off, call your DSL or cable provider. If turning on the router disconnects the modem from the ISP, contact technical support for your router. If you can connect, but the connection is still slow, continue troubleshooting.

Test the Connection

If you can establish a connection but the connection is slow, test the Internet connection speed, as explained in Chapter 3, to determine just how slow the connection is. You can also test the connection as shown in the next section, "Ping the Connection." Pinging provides detailed information about the speed of your connection and any data lost between your PC and a remote PC, which can be very valuable information in case you need to contact technical support.

Contact Your Service Provider

Internet connections have many variables that can affect their performance. After you rule out problems with the connection on your end, contact your service provider to determine if the service is experiencing problems. With cable and DSL modems, your service can run a test on your connection from a remote location and often diagnose the problem or inform you of service interruptions in your area.

Ping the Connection

You can ping a remote Web server to determine the amount of time it takes for a small packet of information to travel from your PC to the server and back, and to determine if any data is lost along the way. When you call your ISP's technical support department, a technician often leads you through the process of pinging a server to discover how well or poorly your Internet connection is performing. By performing this test before you contact technical support, you can save yourself some time on the phone and perhaps rule out any problems between your modem and your ISP.

Windows has a ping utility that you can run from the command prompt. The utility typically runs multiple pings and displays its progress and results. It displays the time it takes each packet of data to reach the remote Web server and return to your PC in milliseconds (ms). If you have a ping time that is 200ms or less and the test shows no packet loss, the results are acceptable. If the results consistently show packet loss at any speed or if ping times consistently exceed 200ms for several different servers, contact your ISP to help track down the problem.

Ping the Connection

1. Click Start.
2. Click All Programs.
3. Click Accessories.
4. Click Command Prompt.

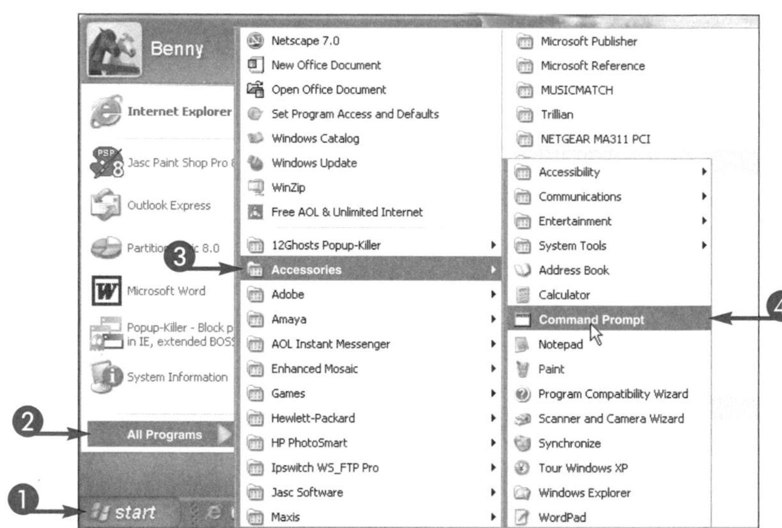

The Windows Command Prompt appears.

5. Type **ping** followed by the address of a Web server that is typically reliable and fast.

   This example uses Google.

6. Press Enter.

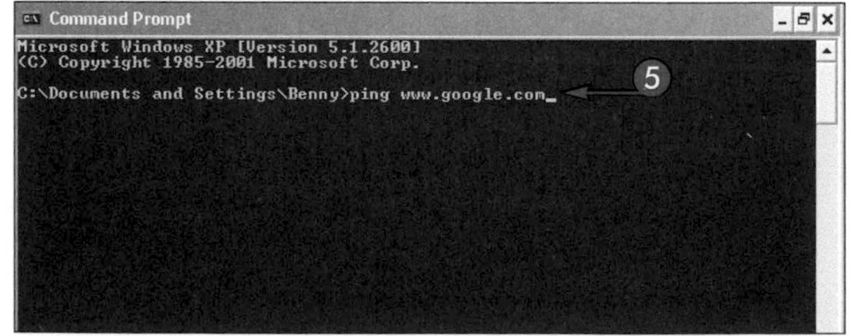

- Windows pings the remote Web server and displays the results.

```
Command Prompt
Microsoft Windows XP [Version 5.1.2600]
(C) Copyright 1985-2001 Microsoft Corp.

C:\Documents and Settings\Benny>ping www.google.com

Pinging www.google.akadns.net [64.233.167.104] with 32 bytes of data:

Reply from 64.233.167.104: bytes=32 time=77ms TTL=243
Reply from 64.233.167.104: bytes=32 time=17ms TTL=243
Reply from 64.233.167.104: bytes=32 time=20ms TTL=243
Reply from 64.233.167.104: bytes=32 time=17ms TTL=243

Ping statistics for 64.233.167.104:
    Packets: Sent = 4, Received = 4, Lost = 0 (0% loss),
Approximate round trip times in milli-seconds:
    Minimum = 17ms, Maximum = 77ms, Average = 32ms

C:\Documents and Settings\Benny>_
```

7. Repeat steps 5 and 6 to ping another reliable remote Web server.
   - Windows pings the remote Web server and displays the results.
8. Write down the results.

   You now have ping results that you can use to help troubleshoot a connection problem.

```
Command Prompt
Microsoft Windows XP [Version 5.1.2600]
(C) Copyright 1985-2001 Microsoft Corp.

C:\Documents and Settings\Benny>ping www.google.com

Pinging www.google.akadns.net [64.233.167.104] with 32 bytes of data:

Reply from 64.233.167.104: bytes=32 time=77ms TTL=243
Reply from 64.233.167.104: bytes=32 time=17ms TTL=243
Reply from 64.233.167.104: bytes=32 time=20ms TTL=243
Reply from 64.233.167.104: bytes=32 time=17ms TTL=243

Ping statistics for 64.233.167.104:
    Packets: Sent = 4, Received = 4, Lost = 0 (0% loss),
Approximate round trip times in milli-seconds:
    Minimum = 17ms, Maximum = 77ms, Average = 32ms

C:\Documents and Settings\Benny>ping www.yahoo.com

Pinging www.yahoo.akadns.net [216.109.118.70] with 32 bytes of data:

Reply from 216.109.118.70: bytes=32 time=100ms TTL=49
Reply from 216.109.118.70: bytes=32 time=180ms TTL=49
Reply from 216.109.118.70: bytes=32 time=39ms TTL=49
Reply from 216.109.118.70: bytes=32 time=37ms TTL=49

Ping statistics for 216.109.118.70:
    Packets: Sent = 4, Received = 4, Lost = 0 (0% loss),
Approximate round trip times in milli-seconds:
    Minimum = 37ms, Maximum = 180ms, Average = 89ms

C:\Documents and Settings\Benny>_
```


MASTER IT

Do I need to ping more than one remote Web server?

▼ Yes. Although pinging can provide you with valuable information, the information is very general. It only indicates the speed at which your overall Internet connection runs. If pinging indicates that the connection is slow or is losing data, the remote Web server, your ISP, or your modem or PC may be experiencing problems. If you ping two or more remote Web servers and receive similar results, you know that the remote server is not the problem, and you can focus on issues between your PC and your ISP's server.

What can my ISP do to help if the ping results reveal a problem?

▼ An ISP can run additional tests to pinpoint the location of the problem. The ISP may be able to test your modem from a remote location and determine if any line problems are slowing down the connection. If the ISP is experiencing service interruptions or other problems, its technicians can inform you of those issues. With DSL service, the problem is often traced to line problems or the central office to which you connect. Cable service often slows down during busy periods, especially if many people in your area use the same service.

Optimize Your Cable or DSL Connection

Your computer's operating system contains settings that control the speed at which your system transmits and receives data over network connections. When you have a cable modem, satellite connection, DSL hookup, or other broadband Internet connection, your computer becomes part of a network, and the network settings that are built into your operating system govern that connection. Unfortunately, these settings are often optimized for Ethernet networks and dial-up modem connections, not for broadband Internet connections.

You can tweak the settings yourself or you can use a utility, as explained in the section "Install and Run a Web Accelerator," that optimizes your operating system automatically. If you decide to tweak the settings yourself, you can find several Web sites that offer suggestions and instructions on which settings to change and how to change them. This section shows you how to navigate to one of the best Web sites devoted to optimizing broadband connections.

Each operating system uses different settings and stores them in different places, so the instructions differ depending on the operating system. SpeedGuide.net, highlighted here, focuses on various versions of the Windows operating system. Some instructions call for installing software or making changes to the Windows registry, so back up the registry as explained in Chapter 19 before making changes or installing tweaks.

Optimize Your Cable or DSL Connection

1. Launch your Web browser.
2. In your Web browser's Address bar, type **www.speedguide.net** and press Enter.
3. Click Broadband.
4. Point to Registry Tweaks.
5. Click your operating system.

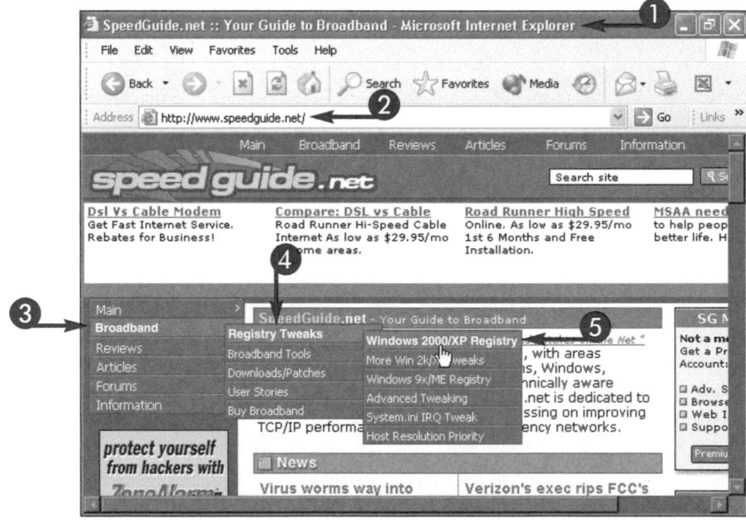

Articles related to tweaking your operating system appear.

6. Click the link for downloading patches and tweaks.

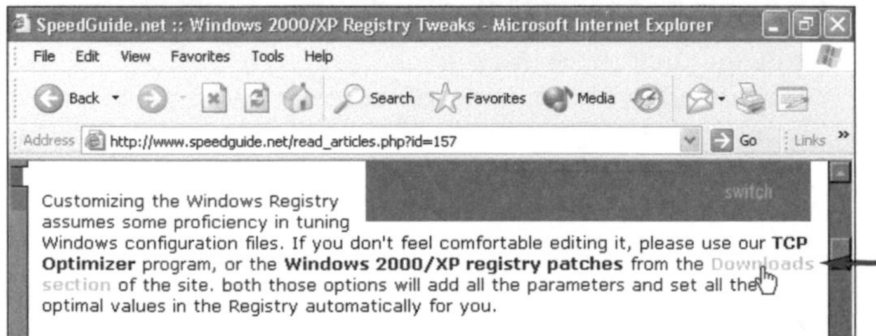

The links and patches page appears.

7. Read about available tweaks and patches.
8. To download a tweak utility or patch, click its link.

Note: *Some tweaks instruct you on how to enter changes while others install software patches that make the changes for you.*

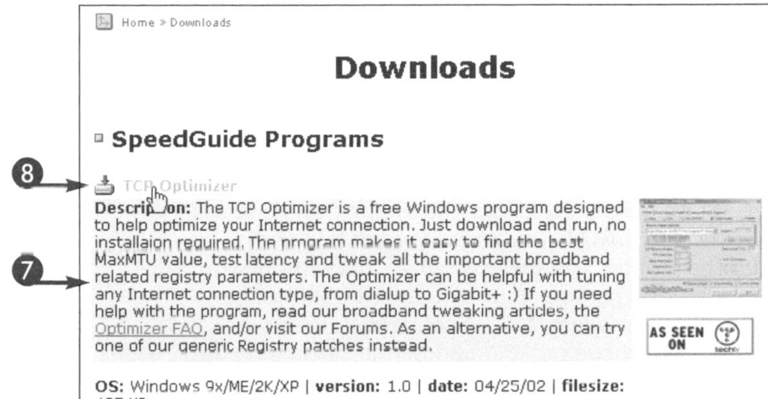

If you clicked a link for a software tweak or cpatch, the File Download dialog box appears.

9. Click Save, save the file to your computer, and run the installation.

Note: *Steps for installing and running patches and tweaks vary depending on the download and on your operating system.*

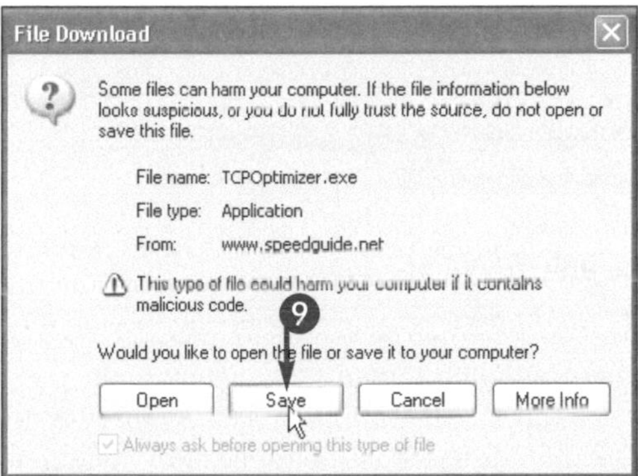

Can I manually tweak the Windows registry myself?

▼ Yes. Many tweaking sites recommend changes to the Windows registry that you can make yourself. However, you should always back up the registry before tweaking it. The Chapters in Part VI provide instructions on how to back up the registry, find specific entries in the registry, and enter your changes. If problems arise after you tweak the registry, you can refer to Chapter 19 to restore a previous version of the registry.

Can I obtain a utility that makes all of the optimization tweaks for me?

▼ Yes. You can download and install a Web accelerator, as instructed in the section "Install and Run a Web Accelerator." Most Web accelerators tweak the operating system and modem settings for you to optimize the connection. Other Web accelerators use different techniques to increase your Internet connection speed.

My connection is extremely slow. Will tweaking it help bring it up to speed?

▼ If your modem is connecting at less than half the speed at which your ISP advertised, your connection may be experiencing a more serious problem. Run through the troubleshooting steps in the section "Troubleshoot Internet Connection Speed Problems." A loose connection or other hardware problem can be slowing down your connection or the ISP may be experiencing service interruptions.

Optimize a Dial-Up Modem Connection

Most people assume that their modems are set up to transfer data over the Internet at the fastest rate possible, but that may not be the case. Settings that control the speed at which data can pass between the Internet and your computer might not be optimal for your modem. If your connection seems slow, you might benefit by checking and perhaps changing the *port speed* settings, which control the rate at which data passes through your computer's COM (communications) port.

Buffer settings can also affect the speed of a connection. A buffer stores data in memory, where the computer can access it more readily. In many cases, increasing the buffer size can help feed data at a more consistent rate to ensure that any data exchange proceeds smoothly without your modem having to wait to send or receive data. Generally, maximizing the buffer size increases speed, while decreasing it can help reduce communication errors that can result in lost data. When optimizing a dial-up modem connection, start high and then decrease the buffer size incrementally until the problem no longer persists.

Optimize a Dial-Up Modem Connection

1. Open the Windows Control Panel.
2. Click Printers and Other Hardware.

   The Printers and Other Hardware screen appears.
3. Click Phone and Modem Options.

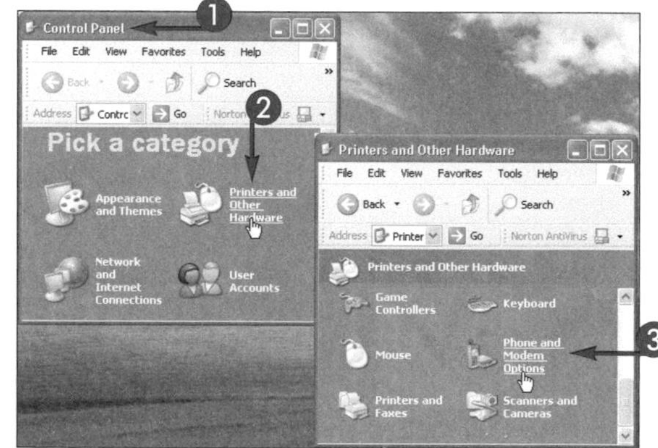

   The Phone and Modem Options dialog box appears.
4. Click the Modems tab.
5. Click the modem that you use to connect to the Internet.
6. Click Properties.

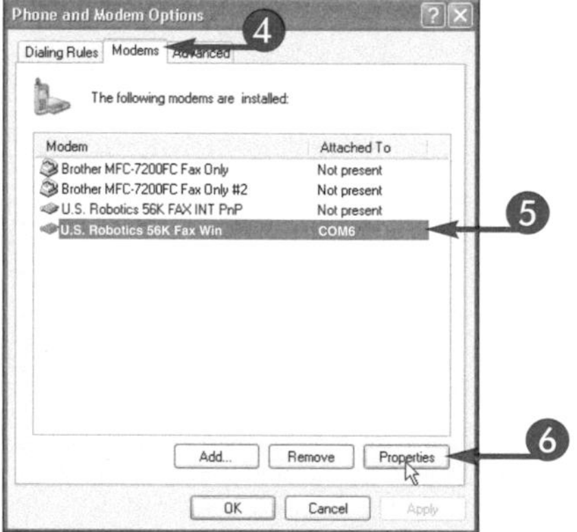

The Properties dialog box appears.

7 Click the Advanced tab.

8 Click Change Default Preferences.

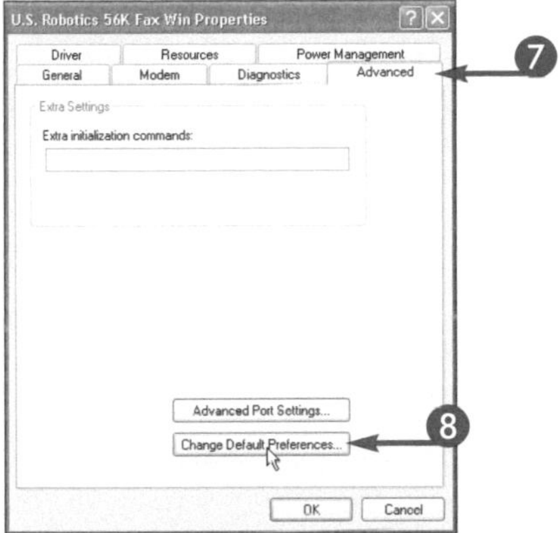

- The Default Preferences dialog box appears.

9 Click here and click the highest setting.

10 Click here and click Enabled.

11 Click here and click Hardware.

12 Click OK in the Default Preferences dialog box and again in the Properties dialog box.

Windows saves your settings.

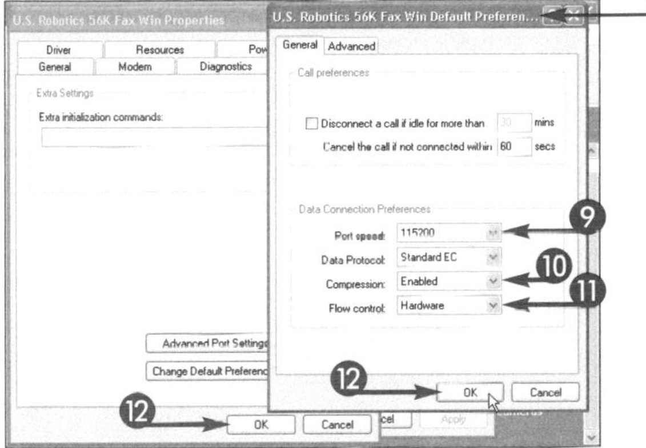

What else can negatively affect the speed of my dial-up modem?

▼ Interference from other devices can have a negative effect on the performance of your modem. If you have multiple phone jacks in your home or business that share the same line as your modem, try disconnecting phones or fax machines that are plugged into those jacks and retest your Internet connection speed, as discussed in Chapter 3. If a phone or fax machine is plugged into your modem, disconnect it and retest your Internet connection speed. Try using a different phone cord to plug your modem into the phone jack. A line filter or repeater can also help reduce interference.

Can I adjust other modem settings to improve my dial-up modem performance?

▼ Yes. In your modem's Properties dialog box, click the Advanced tab, Advanced Port Settings, and select Use FIFO Buffers (☐ changes to ☑). Click and drag the slide controls to maximize the buffer sizes for optimal performance. If you experience intermittent connection problems, try decreasing the buffer size.

This modem connection still is not as fast as I want it to be. What should I do?

▼ The best way to increase Internet connection speed is to upgrade to a broadband Internet service such as cable or DSL. If dial-up modem service is all you have available in your area, try installing a Web accelerator, as explained in the next section, "Install and Run a Web Accelerator."

Install and Run a Web Accelerator

You can speed up your Internet connection by using a Web accelerator. Two types of accelerators are available: *optimizers*, which are utilities that tweak your operating system settings for optimal performance, and *proxy servers*, which help your system load pages faster.

In this section, you install and use a shareware optimizer called TweakMASTER to adjust the system settings in your computer that control data transfer. Many other such utilities are available, and you can find them simply by searching the Web for "web accelerator." TweakMASTER is easy to use and has delivered positive results for many users. TweakMASTER can help optimize your Internet connection whether you use a dial-up, cable, or DSL modem.

Other Web accelerators work on different principles. Some are utilities that run in the background on your computer and optimize caching by "learning" your browser habits and trying to anticipate which pages you might want next. Others are proxy services, such as NetZero Hi-Speed, that are designed to be more responsive to your requests for pages than the Web servers on which the original pages are stored. You can use these services in addition to installing an optimizer.

Install and Run a Web Accelerator

1. Launch your Web browser.
2. In the Address bar, type **www.tweakmaster.com** and press Enter.
3. Click Download.
4. Click the link for downloading TweakMASTER.
5. Click Save.

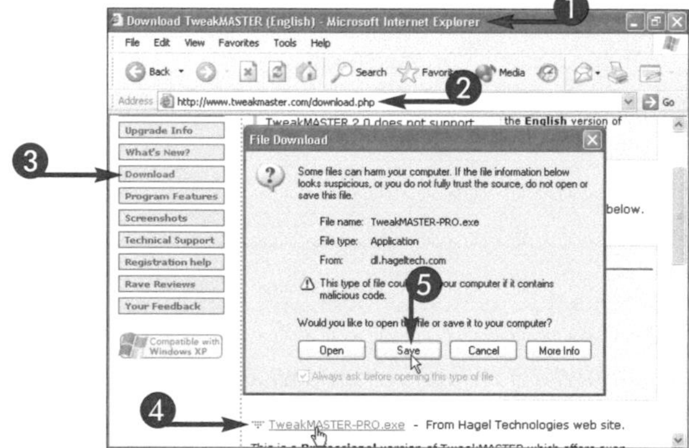

6. Open the folder that contains the TweakMASTER installation file.
7. Double-click the TweakMASTER installation file.
8. Follow the on-screen instructions to install TweakMASTER and run it.

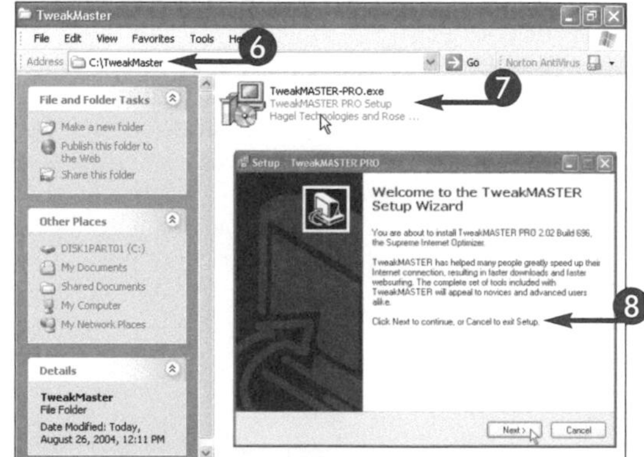

TweakMASTER's opening screen appears.

9 Click Connection Optimization Wizard.

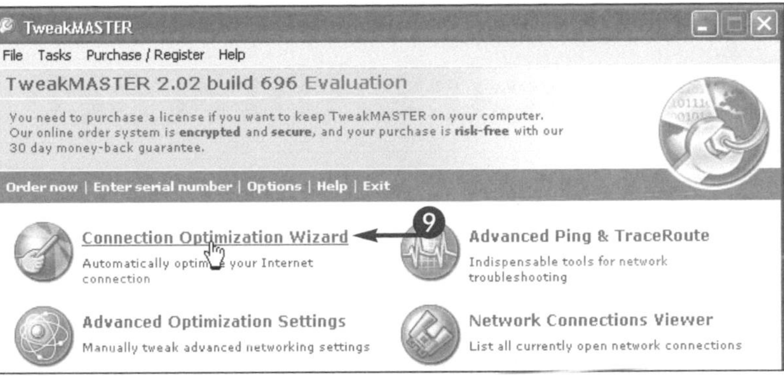

The Optimization Wizard appears.

10 Follow the wizard's instructions to optimize your system.

TweakMASTER's Optimization Wizard configures Windows to optimize your Internet connection.

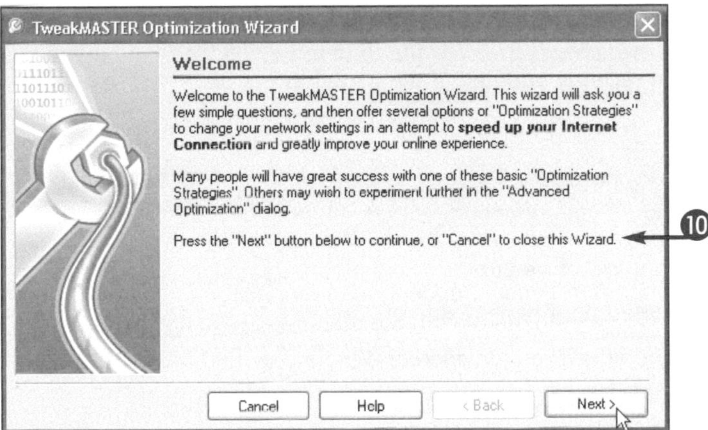

Should I use TweakMASTER's recommended settings or should I adjust them?

▼ The easiest way to optimize your Internet connection is to have TweakMASTER's wizard make all of the system changes for you, but it might not make full use of your system's potential. Take note of the settings the wizard uses and then try different settings to see if you can obtain better results. You can run TweakMASTER as often as you like to experiment with the settings. TweakMASTER has several additional features that you can also use and configure, including a clock synchronizer that can keep your system time current. On TweakMASTER's opening screen, click the Clock Snyc link.

TweakMASTER has a DNS Optimizer option. What is a DNS Optimizer and what effect does it have on my Internet connection speed?

▼ The DNS (Domain Name System) optimizer or DNS accelerator can help your PC quickly load the Web sites that you visit most frequently. It does this by storing the IP address — the numerical address — of the Web server on your PC, so that your Web browser can bypass the DNS server when you enter a Web page address and go directly to the specified Web server. TweakMASTER's DNS optimizer is designed to work automatically with Internet Explorer, but if you use a different Web browser, you can add IP addresses manually to the hosts list.

Optimize the Use of Temporary Internet Files

When you open pages in your Web browser, it automatically saves the pages and files associated with those pages, including image files, to a temporary storage area on your PC's hard drive. You can increase the amount of disk space that your Web browser uses to store temporary Internet files, so your Web browser can load more pages faster.

When you open a page that you have previously visited, your Web browser checks the Web site to determine if the page has been recently updated. If the page has not been updated, your Web browser loads the page from your PC's hard drive, which delivers the page content very quickly. If the page has been updated, your Web browser downloads the page from the Web, which is slower, especially if you have a dial-up modem connection.

The more space you provide on your PC's hard drive for temporary Internet files, the more pages your Web browser can store locally, and the faster your Web browser can load the pages. If your PC has several gigabytes of free disk space, you can increase the amount of space available for temporary Internet files.

Optimize the Use of Temporary Internet Files

1. Launch your Web browser.

   This example uses Internet Explorer.

Note: *The steps differ if you use another Web browser.*

2. Click Tools.
3. Click Internet Options.

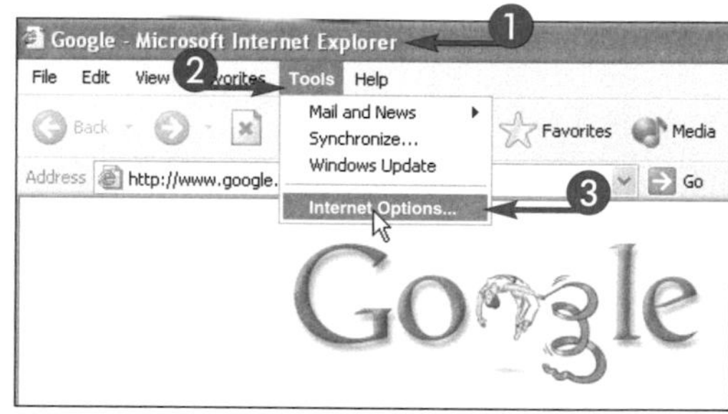

The Internet Options dialog box appears.

4. Under Temporary Internet files, click Settings.

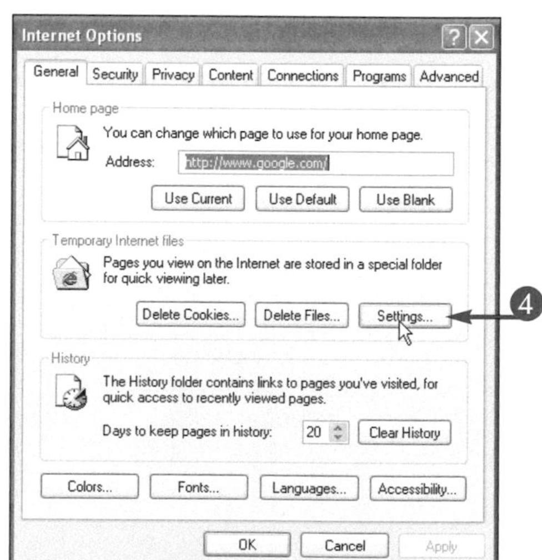

The Settings dialog box appears.

5 Click and drag the "Amount of disk space to use" slider to the right to increase the amount of space used for temporary Internet files.

- You can click Move Folder to move the folder to a faster hard drive that has more free space if your PC has a second hard drive.

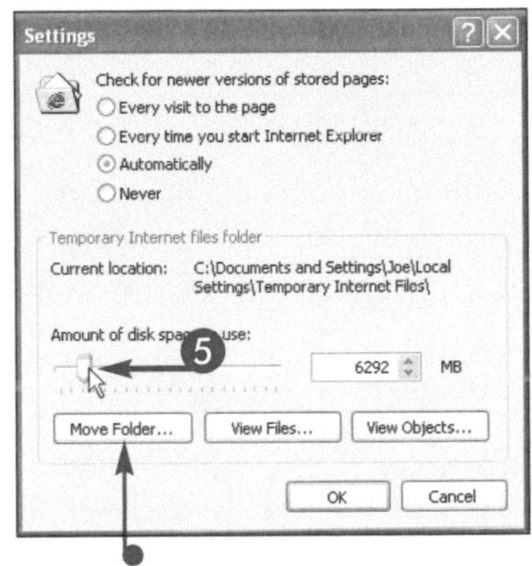

6 Click the option to specify how frequently you want to check Web sites for updated content.

The less frequently you have your Web browser check for updated content, the faster it loads pages.

7 Click OK in the Settings dialog box.

8 Click OK in the Internet Options dialog box.

Your Web browser saves your preferences.

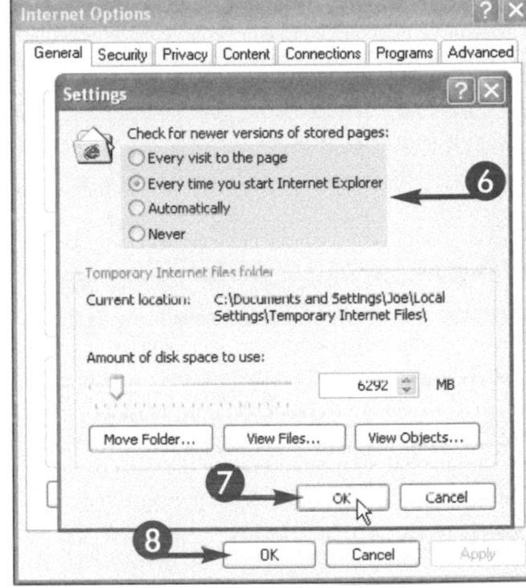

PART V

Can I delete the temporary Internet files?

▼ Yes. You can delete temporary Internet files in Internet Explorer by clicking Tools, Internet Options, and then Delete Files. Deleting the files may take 15 seconds or more, depending on the number of temporary files. When prompted to confirm the deletion, click OK. If you use a different Web browser, refer to its help system for instructions on how to delete temporary Internet files or *clear the cache*. A cache is a temporary storage area; many Web browsers refer to temporary Internet files as *cached pages*.

Can I have Internet Explorer delete temporary Internet files whenever I exit?

▼ Yes. You may want to delete temporary Internet files for security purposes — so someone else cannot access the content you were viewing. To have Internet Explorer automatically delete temporary Internet files when you exit, click Tools and then Internet Options. Click the Advanced tab and scroll down to the Security options. Click the Empty Temporary Internet Files folder when browser is closed option (☐ changes to ☑). Click OK.

Can too many temporary Internet files slow down my connection?

▼ Some experts claim that an overabundance of temporary Internet files can actually slow down an Internet connection because the browser must check all of these files to determine if more current versions of the files are available. If your Internet connection seems slower than usual, you can try clearing the cache, but generally more cached pages result in pages that reload faster.

Optimize the History List

Your Web browser keeps a record of the sites you visit and the Web pages you open at those sites. If you found a valuable Web site and cannot remember its address, you may spend hours searching for it. Fortunately, if you visited the site in the last week or so, your Web browser probably has a record of it. You can quickly return to the site by displaying the history list and clicking a link to the site.

When you find a valuable Web page, you should create a bookmark for the site or add it to your list of favorites, as explained in the section "Bookmark Your Favorite Sites."

Sometimes, however, you are so caught up in checking out different Web sites that you do not realize the value of a site until after you leave it. When this occurs, you may be able to find the Web site on your Web browser's history list.

By default, Internet Explorer keeps pages on its history list for 20 days; other browsers may limit the list to a specific number of pages. You can raise the limit to create a more comprehensive history list. You can also delete individual items from the history to reduce clutter.

Optimize the History List

Save More Pages in History List

1. Launch your Web browser.

   This example uses Internet Explorer.

Note: *The steps for other Web browsers may differ.*

2. Click Tools.
3. Click Internet Options.

   The Internet Options dialog box appears.

4. Click here to increase the number of days Internet Explorer keeps pages in the history list.
5. Click OK.

   Internet Explorer saves your settings.

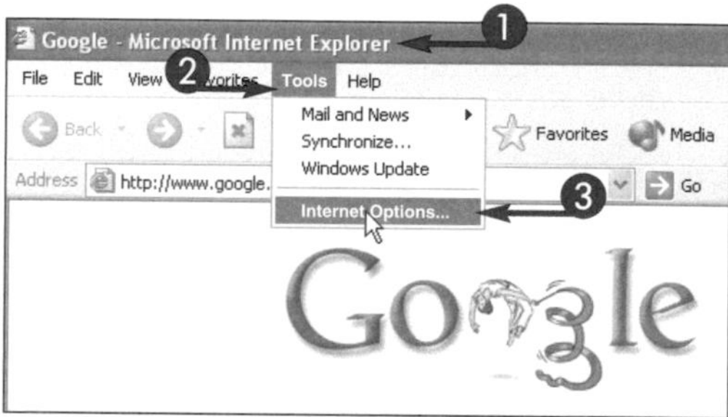

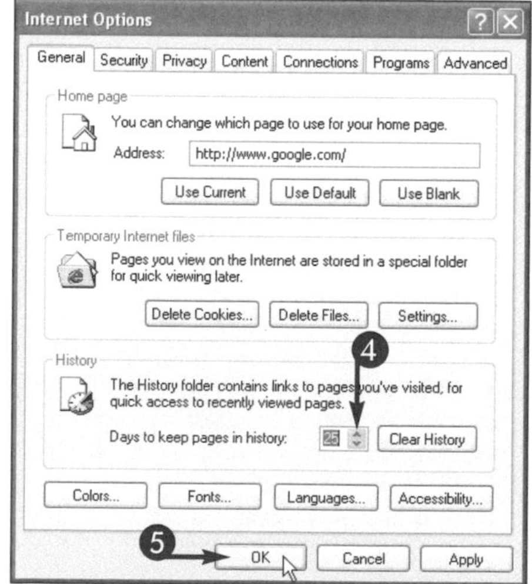

Delete Items from History List

1. Launch your Web browser.

   This example uses Internet Explorer.

2. Click the History button ( ).

   - The history list appears.

3. Click a week or day to expand the list.

4. Click a Web site icon to expand the list of pages you visited at the site.

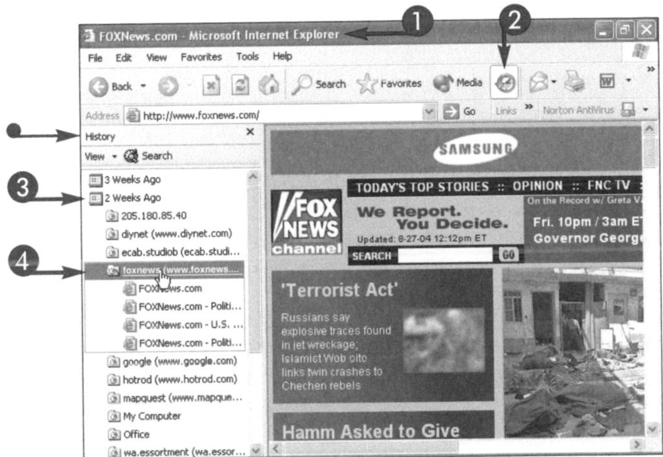

5. Right-click an item you want to delete.

6. Click Delete.

   Your browser removes the item from the history list.

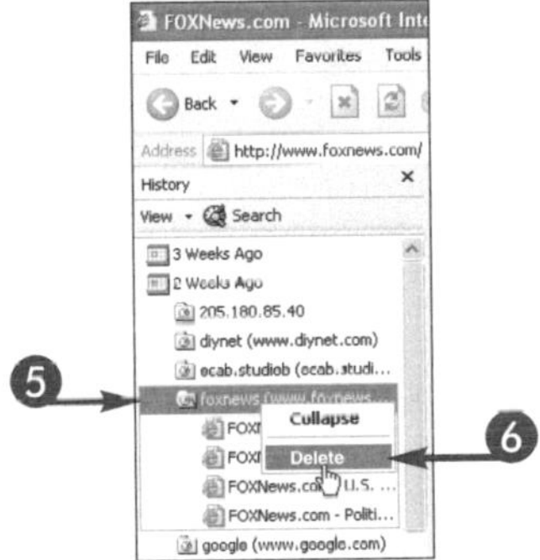

Can I clear the entire history list?

▼ Yes. Click Tools, Internet Options, the General tab, and then Clear History. The Internet Options dialog box appears, prompting you to confirm. Click Yes. This removes all items from the history list and from the list of sites in the address drop-down list.

How can I ensure that the browser successfully cleared the history list?

▼ Click the History button ( ) to view the list. Sometimes another program may temporarily lock the history list, in which case pages you visited during the current session may remain on the list. You can usually clear the list by restarting Windows and then clearing the history list again.

If I clear the history list and want to revisit pages later, can I restore the list?

▼ No. Once you clear the history list, the only way to place a page back on the list is to reopen the page. If you want to save a record of a page so you can revisit the page later, you should bookmark the page or add it to your list of favorite pages as discussed in the section ""Bookmark Your Favorite Sites." In Internet Explorer, you can add an item from the history list to your list of favorites by right-clicking the item in the history list and clicking Add to Favorites.

Browse without Pictures and Video

You can prevent your Web browser from displaying pictures, video, and other large media files so that your Web browser can download and display pages much faster.

Audio, video, animation, and graphics transform the Web from a static, text-only medium into a dynamic, multimedia resource. However, media files, including audio clips, video clips, animations, photographs, and illustrations can be very large and require additional time to download. If you research a topic and are concerned primarily with accessing articles, you can enter settings to prevent your browser from downloading images and audio and video clips.

Surfing the Web without its accompanying audiovisuals might not appeal to most people, but if you have a relatively slow dial-up connection and you need some additional speed, this can provide a big boost. Even if you choose to keep pictures on and disable audio, animations, and videos, you can see an increase in speed for those pages that use these types of media.

The steps in this section show you how to disable audio, video, animations, and pictures in Internet Explorer. If you use a different Web browser, consult its help system for instructions.

Browse without Pictures and Video

1. Launch your Web browser.

   This example uses Internet Explorer.

Note: *The steps for other Web browsers may differ.*

2. Click Tools.
3. Click Internet Options.

   The Internet Options dialog box appears.

4. Click the Advanced tab.
5. Scroll down to the Multimedia options.
6. Deselect any media options you want to disable (☑ changes to ☐).
7. Click OK.

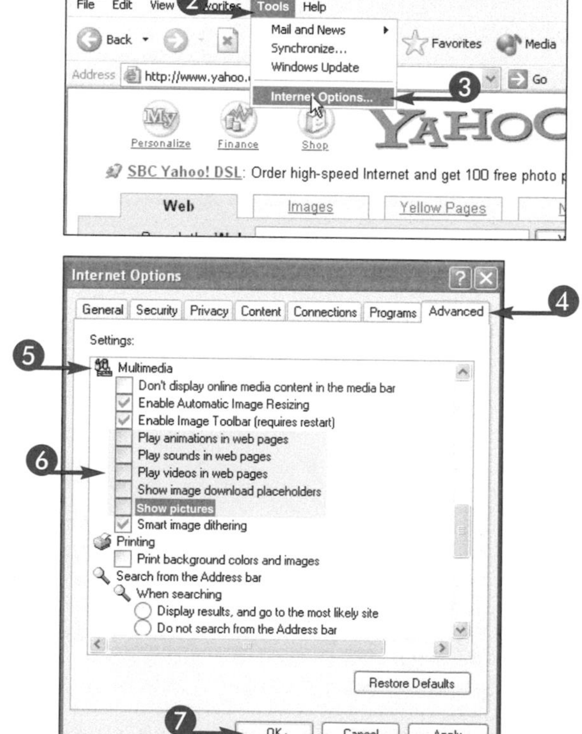

- If you disable pictures, when you load a page that contains pictures, placeholders appear.

8 To view a picture, right-click its placeholder.

9 Click Show Picture.

- The picture appears.

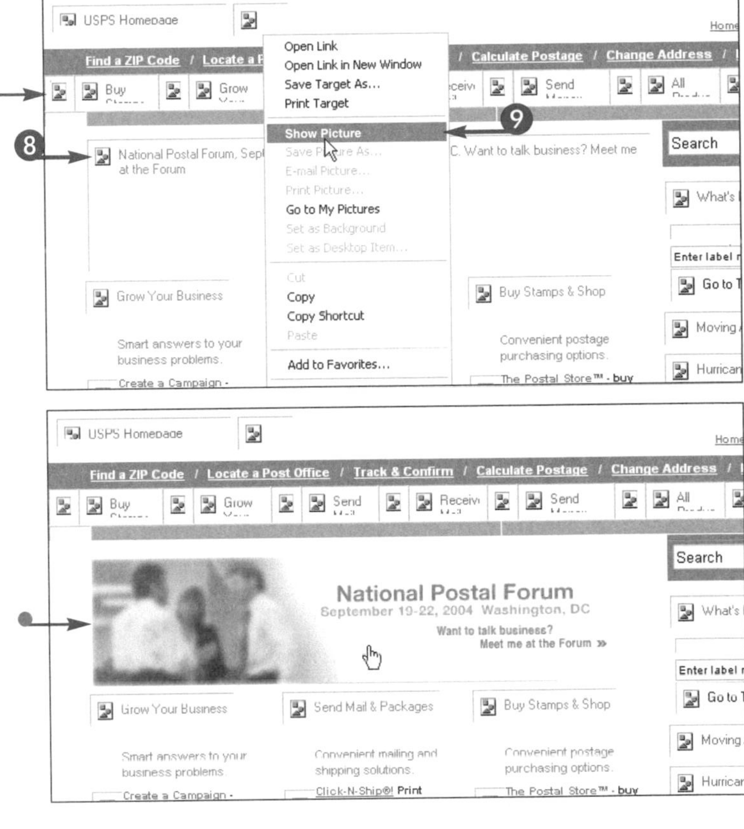

I changed several settings in the Internet Options dialog box. Can I change all of the settings back to their defaults?

Yes. Anything you change in the Internet Options dialog box, you can change back. To change all options back to their original settings, click Tools, Internet Options, the Advanced tab, and then click Restore Defaults. You may want to verify the settings before you click OK to save your changes.

The Advanced tab has many interesting options. How can I learn more about an option?

The Internet Options Advanced tab is packed with options that many users choose to ignore. Check them out. If the purpose of an option seems unclear, click the option's name, right-click it, and click What's This? A ToolTip appears displaying a brief description of the selected option.

Under Multimedia is an option for turning on an image toolbar. I clicked the option and clicked OK, but I do not see a picture toolbar. Where is it?

Internet Explore 6 features an Enable Image Toolbar option. With this option on, whenever you rest the mouse pointer on an image, a toolbar pops up with buttons to save, print, or e-mail the image or open your My Pictures folder.

Bookmark Your Favorite Sites

The Web is a disorganized collection of more than 4 billion sites and pages that you may find very difficult to successfully search and sort. When you do happen to find sites that answer your questions and that you probably want to return to in the future, you can bookmark those sites so that you can quickly return to them later. All browsers have a way of adding sites to a menu or toolbar so you can quickly return to those sites by selecting them from a list rather than having to type their addresses.

Netscape popularized the bookmarking of Web sites, which enables users to easily return to sites. Internet Explorer refers to its bookmarks as Favorites, but they essentially do the same thing — save the page's address (URL, or uniform resource locator) and provide you with an entry to click to quickly return to the page. And if the page or a portion of it is stored in the cache, it loads even more quickly. Several techniques are available for bookmarking pages. This section shows you two quick techniques for adding Web sites to your Favorites menu.

Bookmark Your Favorite Sites

Add Current Page to Favorites

1. Open a Web page you want to add to your Favorites menu.
2. Right-click a blank area of the page.
3. Click Add to Favorites.

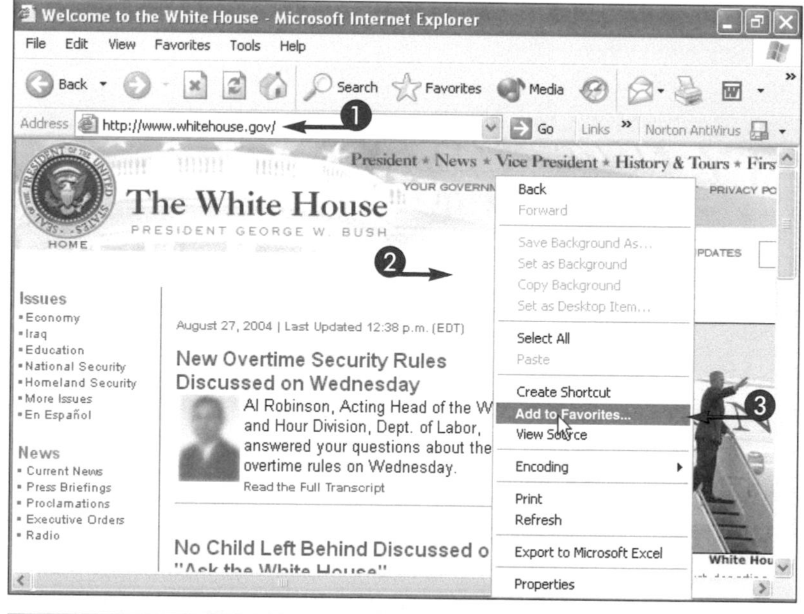

The Add Favorite dialog box appears.

4. Click OK.

Internet Explorer adds the site to your Favorites menu.

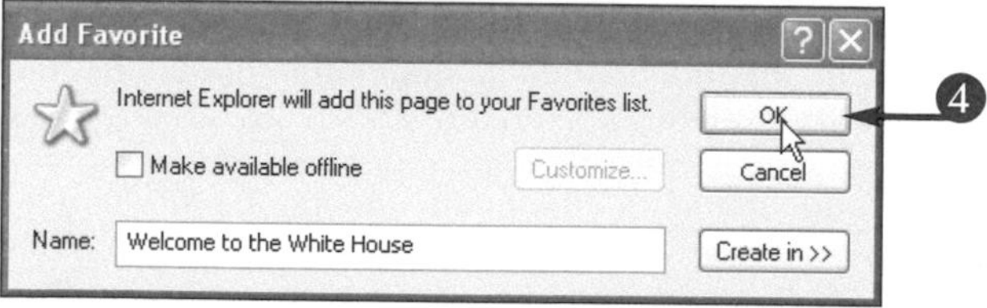

Add Linked Page to Favorites

1. Open a Web page that contains a link you want to add to your Favorites menu.
2. Right-click the link.
3. Click Add to Favorites.

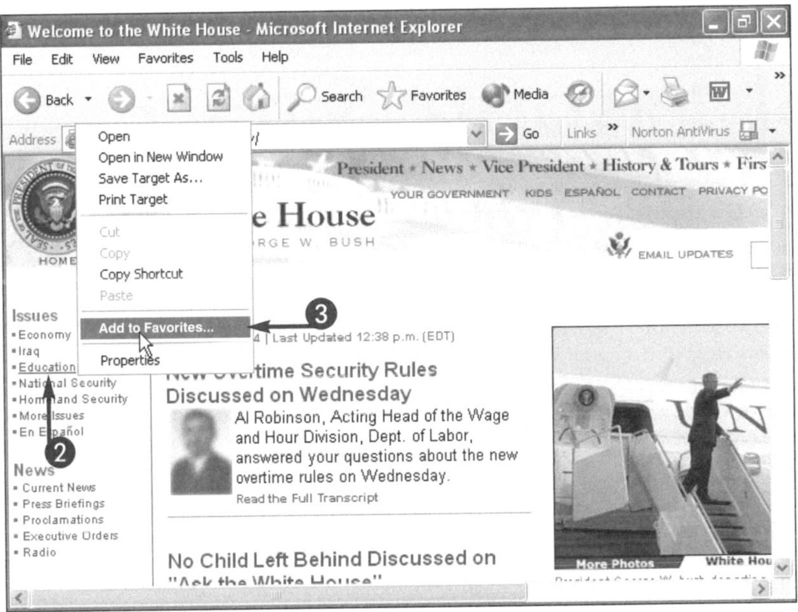

The Add Favorite dialog box appears.

4. Click OK.

The Add Favorite dialog box disappears and adds the linked site to the Favorites menu.

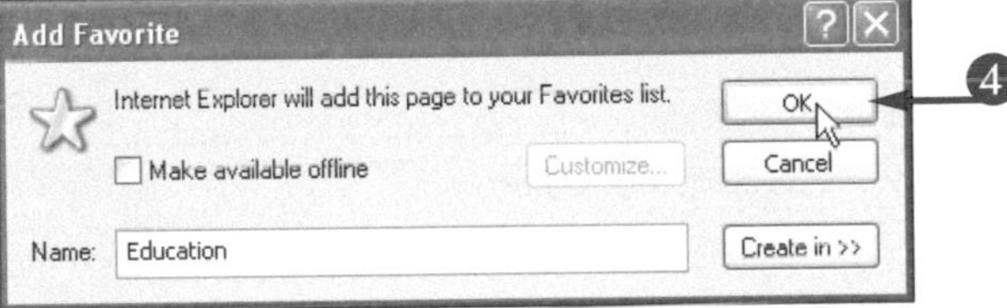

I want to add some items in my history list to my list of favorites. Do I need to open those pages first?

No. To add items directly from the history list to your list of favorites, right-click an item in the history list and click Add to Favorites. The Add Favorite dialog box appears. You can edit the name of the page or choose a folder in which to store it. Enter your preferences and then click OK.

In the Add Favorite dialog box, what does the Make available offline option do?

You can click this option (☐ changes to ☑) to view a page even when you are not connected to the Internet. Internet Explorer saves the page to your hard drive so it does not need to load the page from its Web server. If you select Make available offline, you can click the Customize button to control how frequently Internet Explorer updates the page.

Can I transfer the list of favorites on my work computer to my home PC?

Yes. Launch Internet Explorer on your PC at work and then click File, Import and Export. The Import/Export Wizard walks you through exporting your list of favorites as a file. You can then copy the file to removable storage or e-mail it as an attachment to your home PC. At home, run the Import/Export Wizard and follow its instructions to import the list of favorites.

Organize Your List of Favorite Sites

If you have many favorites, you can store them in separate folders that appear as submenus on the Favorites menu. This organizes your favorites so they are more easily accessible. For example, you can create folders for News, Health, Family, Games, and so on. When you choose to organize favorites, Internet Explorer displays a dialog box that enables you to create separate folders and to move favorites from one folder to another. It also provides options for renaming favorites and folders and deleting items.

Organizing your list of favorites does not make your favorite pages load any faster, but it does improve your efficiency. Instead of searching through a long list of pages to find a specific page, you can group related favorites on submenus. This can also make your Favorites menu easier to navigate, especially if your list of favorites is so long that they scroll off the screen.

While organizing your favorites, you may also want to edit their names. When Web developers name their pages, they try to be as descriptive as possible, but these names can be much too long for displaying on a menu.

Organize Your List of Favorite Sites

1. Launch your Web browser.

   This example uses Internet Explorer.

Note: *The steps for other Web browsers may differ.*

2. Click Favorites.
3. Click Organize Favorites.

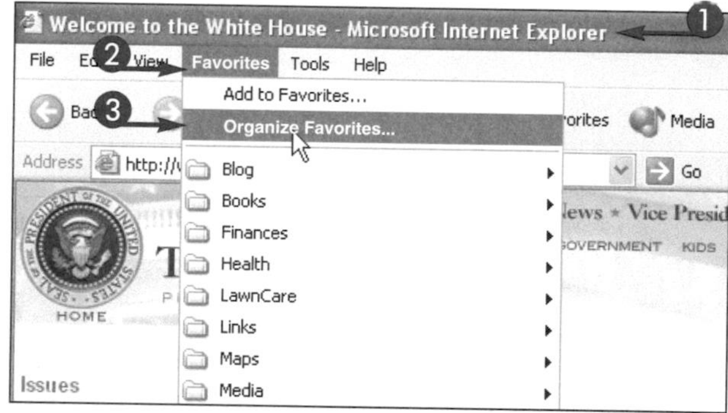

   The Organize Favorites dialog box appears.

4. Click Create Folder.

   A new folder appears.

5. Type a name for the new folder.
6. Press Enter.

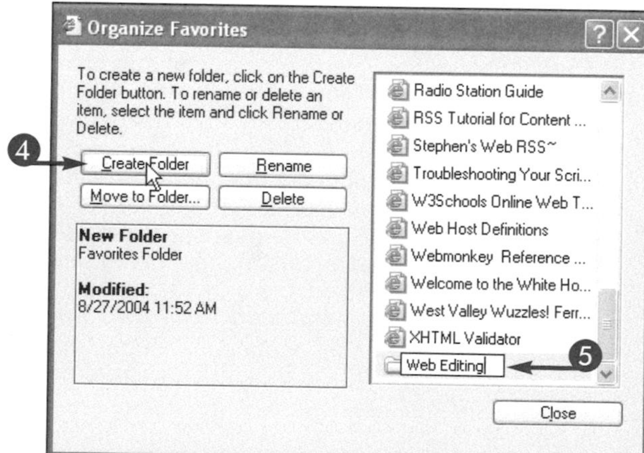

The new folder is assigned the name you typed.

7 Drag and drop a favorite onto the folder in which you want it moved.

The favorite moves to the selected folder.

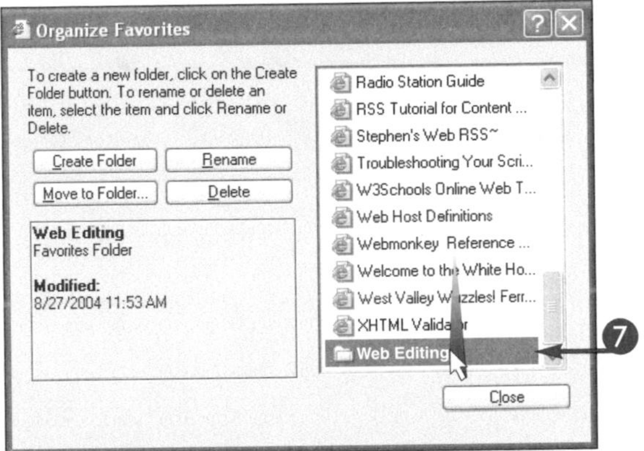

- You can drag favorites or folders up or down and drop them in place to move them.
- You can click Close to close the Organize Favorites window.

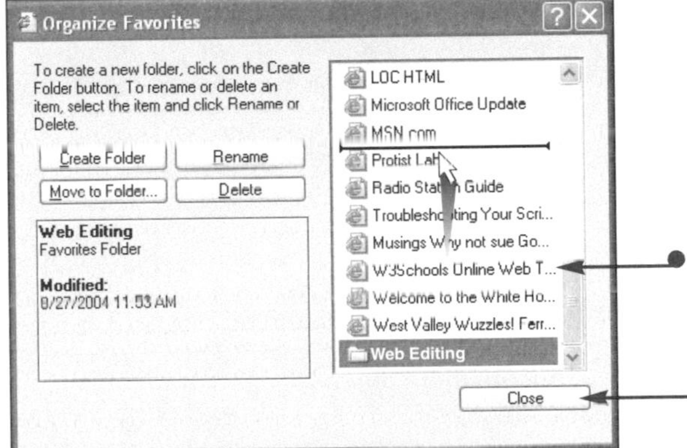

PART V

MASTER IT

Can I quickly rearrange items on the Favorites menu by dragging and dropping them where I want?

▼ Yes. You can rearrange your favorites by dragging them right on the Favorites menu. As you click and drag a favorite, a horizontal line appears showing where it will be placed. Drag a favorite over a submenu of the Favorites menu, and the submenu opens so that you can drag the item onto the submenu and drop it where you want it to appear.

Do Web browsers other than Internet Explorer offer similar features?

▼ Yes. Netscape Navigator features bookmarks instead of favorites, but they perform the same function. Click Bookmarks, Manage Bookmarks to display a window for organizing your bookmarks. In this window, you can drag and drop bookmarks and folders, create new folders, insert separators between unreleated sets of bookmarks, and delete and rename items.

Is there any way to make a page I frequently visit even more accessible?

▼ Yes. You can place a shortcut icon on the Windows desktop. Right-click a blank area of the page you want to quickly access and click Create Shortcut. Click OK to confirm. You can also drag an icon up to the Links toolbar (or Personal toolbar in Navigator) and drop it on the toolbar to create a button you can click to quickly open the page.

19 Back Up and Restore the Windows Registry

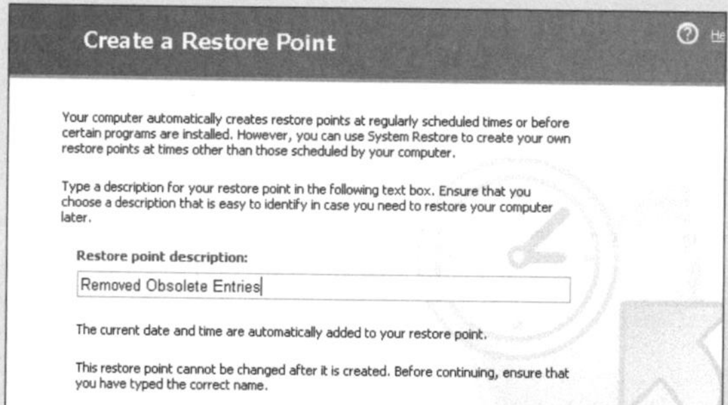

20 Remove Unnecessary Registry Entries

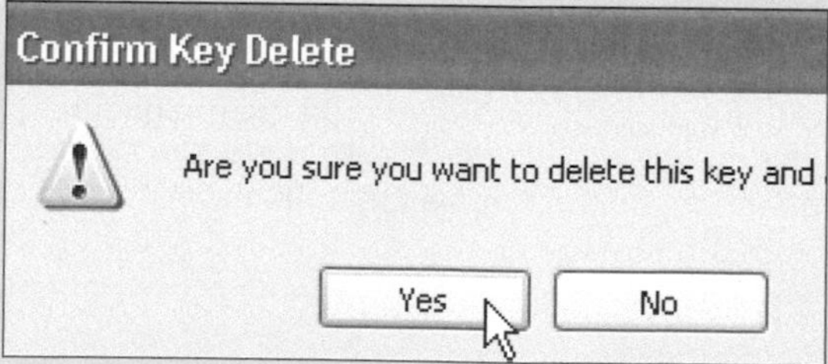

21 Tweak the Windows Registry

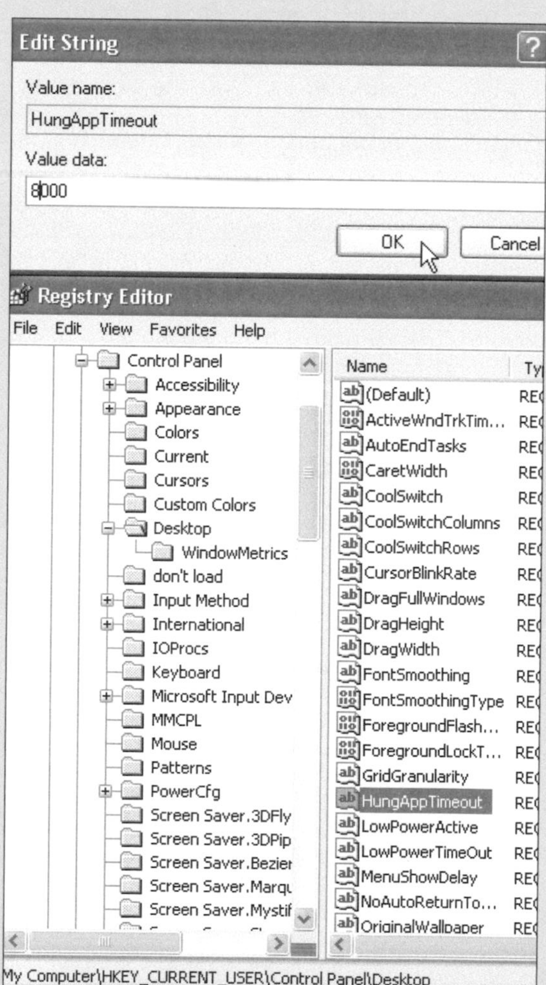

PART VI OPTIMIZING THE WINDOWS REGISTRY

Understanding the Windows Registry

By understanding the Windows registry, its function, and some of the problems inherent in its design, you can safely and confidently optimize the registry to make it more efficient and, in some cases, improve the performance of Windows and of your applications and hardware.

Microsoft discourages users from editing the Windows registry because a small editing error can cause serious problems. However, if you back up the registry before editing it and you use care when making changes, you can avoid major catastrophes and significantly enhance your PC's performance. This chapter shows you how to use the System Restore utility to back up and restore the registry and undo a restoration.

Exploring the Windows Registry

The Windows system registry contains the settings that control Windows and enable it to manage your PC, including its hardware and software. It contains information about user profiles and preferences, hardware configurations, and installed programs. Windows reads the registry on startup and constantly refers to it as you perform tasks.

You can open the registry to view its contents by clicking Start, Run, and then typing **regedit** and pressing Enter. The registry has five *hives*, which appear as folders. Each hive contains several folders and subfolders that you can open to display individual keys. Think of each key as a property for which you can enter a setting that controls the property. You can navigate the registry using the same techniques you use to navigate folders in Windows Explorer or other file-management utilities.

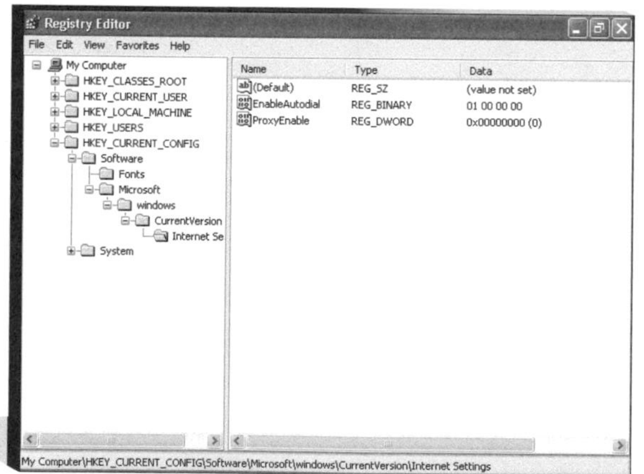

Changing Registry Entries

Although Microsoft recommends against opening the registry and editing it, Windows provides many ways to change the registry entries safely. Whenever you install an application or hardware device, Windows updates the registry to include new settings for that application or device. Whenever you configure Windows by changing the background or entering other preferences, you indirectly alter the registry in some way. You also change the registry whenever you enter a setting in one of your applications, such as resizing a window or specifying the default folder for your documents.

The Windows registry is very complex, so Microsoft tucks the registry behind the scenes and provides less complicated ways for you to modify it. However, Windows and some of the hardware and software that is available do not always modify the registry in a way that optimizes performance. Occasionally, you must edit the registry directly or use a special registry editor to access settings that Windows does not otherwise enable you to change. Chapter 20 provides instructions on how to use the Windows Registry Editor to open and edit the registry.

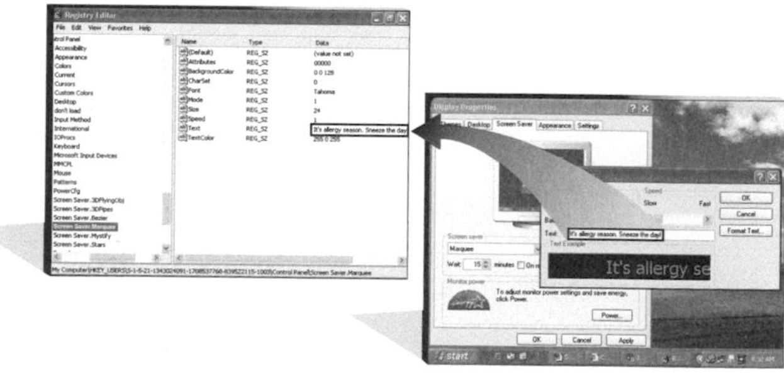

Backing Up the Registry

Because the registry is one of the most critical files on your PC, current versions of Windows, including Windows Me and Windows XP, back up the registry regularly. Whenever you install a program or a new hardware device, Windows creates a *restore point* that contains a copy of critical system files, including the Windows registry. If the registry file becomes corrupt or if you install an application or hardware device that causes problems, you can then perform a system restore, which replaces the new versions of the system files with the previous versions. This returns your PC to its previous condition, which usually solves the problem. Before you modify the registry in any way, you should create a restore point so you can recover the registry if you damage it. For more on creating a restore point, see the section "Create a System Restore Point." For more on recovering your registry, see the section "Restore Your PC to a Previous Condition."

Cleaning the Registry

The longer you use Windows, the larger the registry becomes. When you uninstall some programs or hardware devices or delete files from your hard drive, settings that apply to these programs, devices, and files may be left behind in the registry. Eventually, the Windows registry becomes bloated, fragmented, and inefficient. It may even start to cause intermittent errors, which you may find difficult to trace.

Every so often, you should clean the Windows registry, as discussed in Chapter 20. You can download, install, and run a utility that automatically deletes obsolete entries from the Windows registry and streamlines its operation. If you have Norton System Works or a similar PC management suite, you may already have a Windows registry cleaner installed on your PC. If you have not cleaned the registry for some time, you may not believe the number of obsolete entries it contains.

Tweaking the Registry

Windows contains dozens of configuration options that you can access through utilities in the Control Panel and by entering your preferences in various dialog boxes. However, many settings are unavailable, such as the settings that control data transfer over network connections. To adjust these settings, you must *tweak* — edit — the registry. You can tweak the registry by opening it in the Windows registry editor, and then manually editing entries. Alternatively, you can have special utilities tweak the registry for you.

Chapter 17 introduces TweakMASTER, which is a utility that tweaks the registry for you to optimize Internet performance. Other utilities may provide check box options or radio button options that you can click instead of having to type settings in the registry editor. These utilities can help you make changes and reduce the possibility of introducing errors into the registry.

Run System Restore

You can use the Windows System Restore utility to back up important system files before you install a program or hardware device or reconfigure Windows. System Restore can create a restore point that takes a snapshot of your current configuration settings. If a change you make results in diminished performance or prevents Windows from running properly, you can restore your PC to a previous condition by choosing any of the restore points from the System Restore calendar. If you restore your PC to its previous condition and are not satisfied with the results, you can undo the restoration and try a different system restore point. System Restore has helped numerous users recover from catastrophes.

System Restore backs up and restores only critical system files. It does not back up and restore any documents you create, so your documents remain in their current condition. In other words, if you create a document today, and you restore your system to the condition it was in two weeks ago, the document you created today is not affected in any way.

The steps in this section show you how to run System Restore. Other sections in this chapter discuss using System Restore to back up and restore the Windows system files.

Run System Restore

1. Click Start.
2. Click All Programs.
3. Click Accessories.
4. Click System Tools.
5. Click System Restore.

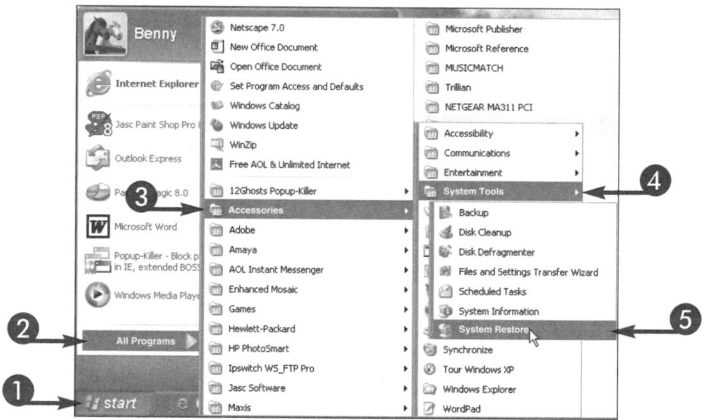

The System Restore Wizard appears.

- You can click here to access options for disabling System Restore or allocating disk space for restore points.

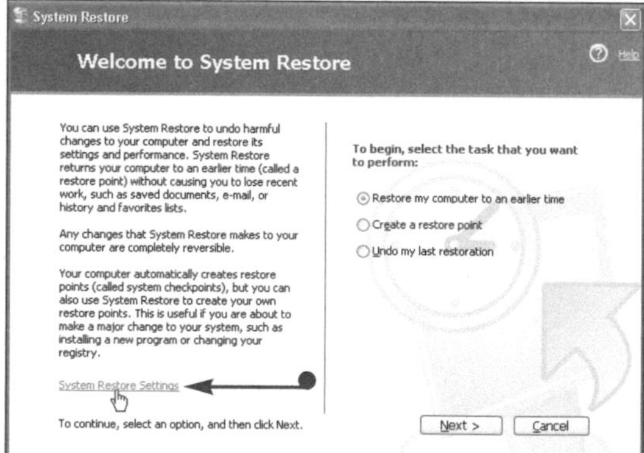

System Restore is a wizard that can step you through various tasks.

- You can choose the task you want to perform here.

- You can click Help to obtain additional information.

6 To exit without backing up or restoring system files, click Cancel.

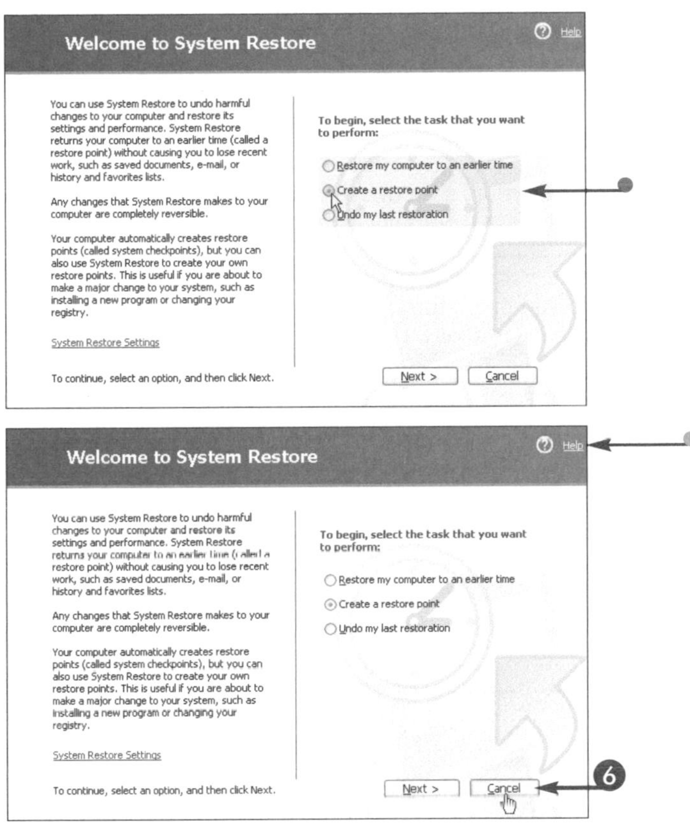

Can I disable System Restore if I do not use it?

▼ Yes, but this book strongly recommends against disabling System Restore. A safer option is to limit the amount of disk space that System Restore uses for restore points. Run System Restore, as instructed in steps 1 to 5 in this section and then click System Restore Settings. Click Settings and then drag the Disk space to use slider to the left or right to allocate the amount of disk space you want System Restore to use.

When I back up files using Windows Backup, does it back up the system files, too?

▼ If you back up only selected folders and files, Windows Backup does not back up the critical Windows system files. However, if you back up everything on your PC or back up the System State data, then Windows backs up its critical system files. You should always have at least one backup of the Windows system files in case the registry or another system file becomes corrupt.

Which versions of Windows feature System Restore?

▼ Windows XP Home and Professional editions, Windows Me, and Windows 2000 feature System Restore. If your PC is running Windows 98, you can restore a previous version of the registry by starting your PC in DOS mode, typing **scanreg /restore** at the DOS prompt, and pressing Enter. This provides a list of registries from which to choose along with the dates on which they were created.

Create a System Restore Point

Before you install a hardware device or a new program or make significant changes to Windows, you should create a system restore point. A system restore point saves the Windows registry and other critical system files, so you can return your PC to its previous condition in the event that a change causes undesirable results. If a change makes Windows unable to start normally, Windows can automatically return your PC to its previous condition, so you can continue using it.

Creating a system restore point is easy. The System Restore Wizard leads you step by step through the process. System Restore stamps the system restore point with a date and time so it can display the system restore points on a calendar. If you need to restore your PC to a previous condition, you simply select the date and time you want from a calendar of options.

Windows typically creates a system restore point for you every day and whenever you install a new device or program, so restore points are available even if you do not create them. However, before you edit the Windows registry, you should create a restore point.

Create a System Restore Point

1. Launch the System Restore Wizard.

Note: *Refer to the section "Run System Restore" for instructions.*

2. Click the Create a restore point option (○ changes to ◉).
3. Click Next.

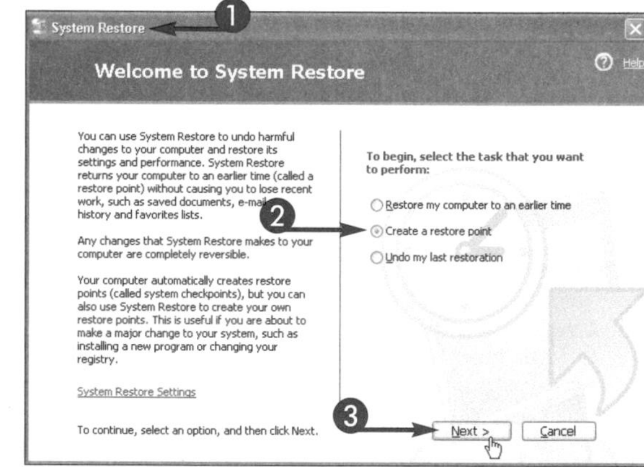

The System Restore Wizard prompts you to type a description of the restore point.

4. Type a brief description of the restore point.
5. Click Create.

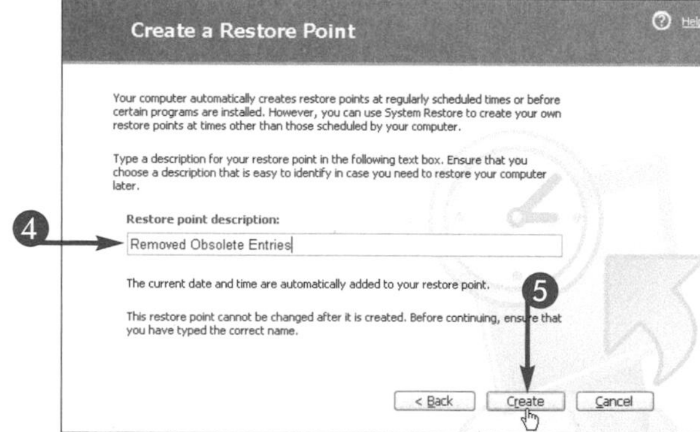

- The System Restore Wizard creates a new restore point and displays the date and time on which it was created.

6 Click Close.

Windows closes the System Restore Wizard.

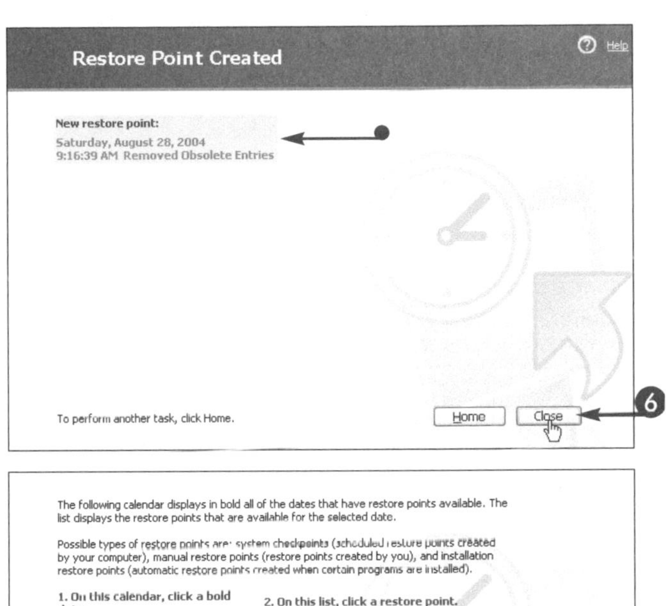

- When you choose to restore your PC to a previous condition, the new restore point appears on the calendar.

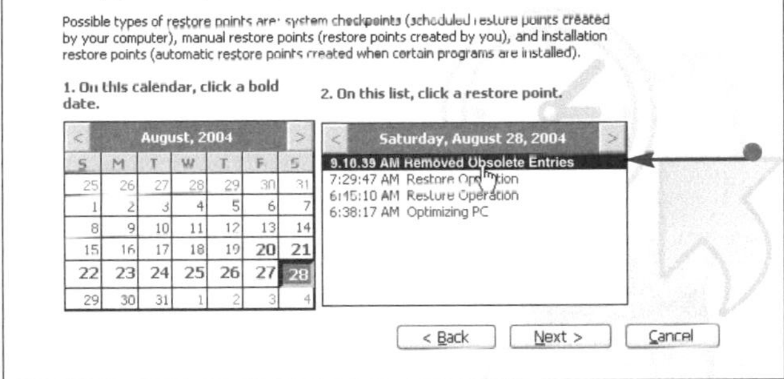

My PC has more than one hard drive. Can I disable System Restore for individual drives?

▼ To disable System Restore for the drive on which Windows is installed, you must disable System Restore for all drives. However, you can disable System Restore for individual drives on which Windows is not installed. On the opening page of the System Restore Wizard, click System Restore Settings. Click the drive for which you want to disable System Restore and click Settings. Click the Turn off System Restore on this drive option (☐ changes to ☑), and then click OK. This can save you some time when creating system restore points.

I cannot create a system restore point. What am I doing wrong?

▼ You must be logged on as an administrator to run System Restore or create system restore points. If you log on to a limited user account, you cannot create system restore points. Log off and then log on as an administrator. System Restore may not be able to create restore points if your free disk space dips below a certain threshold. Check to ensure that the hard drive on which Windows is installed has plenty of free disk space — at least 200MB, preferably more. Chapter 2 provides instructions on how to check the free space on your PC's disk drives.

Restore Your PC to a Previous Condition

Assuming that your computer has sufficient free disk space, Windows creates and stores several system restore points for your PC. When something goes wrong that prevents Windows or one of your applications from running normally, and you cannot correct the problem through other means, you can use the System Restore Wizard to return your PC to one of its previous working conditions.

When you restore your PC to one of its previous conditions, the restoration does not affect any documents you recently created or edited, e-mail you sent or received, or Web pages you bookmarked as favorites. The restoration affects only system files and configuration settings. For example, if you restore your PC using a system restore point from two weeks ago, any documents you created or edited in the past two weeks remain in their current condition. However, if you rearranged items on the Start menu or changed your desktop background, those changes are lost, because Windows configuration settings are stored in the registry.

If System Restore causes problems, you can always undo the most recent restoration and try restoring your PC using a different restore point. See the section "Undo a System Restore" for more information.

Restore Your PC to a Previous Condition

1. Launch the System Restore Wizard.

Note: *Refer to the section "Run System Restore" for instructions.*

2. Click the "Restore my computer to an earlier time" option (◯ changes to ◉).
3. Click Next.

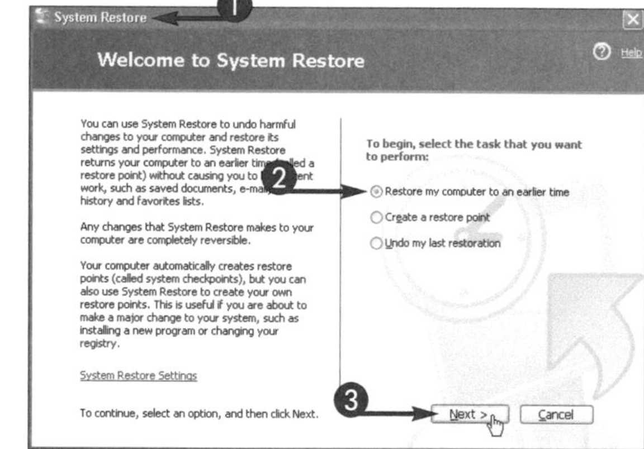

A calendar appears that contains the dates and times of available restore points.

- You can click these arrows (<, >) to switch months.

4. Click the date of the restore point you want to use.
5. Click the restore point you want to use.
6. Click Next.

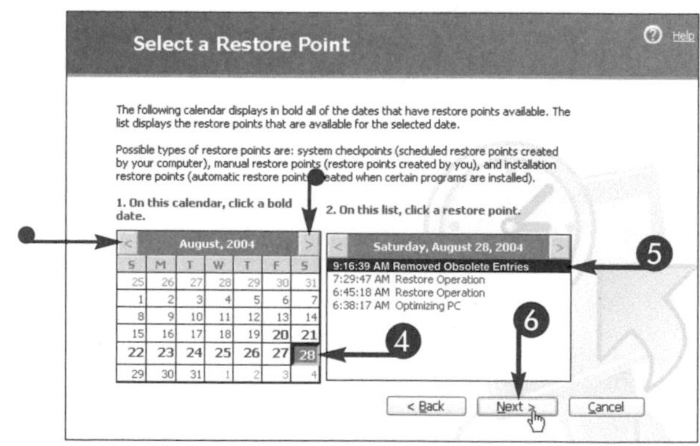

- A message appears assuring you that System Restore does not affect your documents and asking for your confirmation.

7 Click Next.

The System Restore Wizard gathers information about your PC, so it can undo the restoration, if needed, and then it restarts your PC.

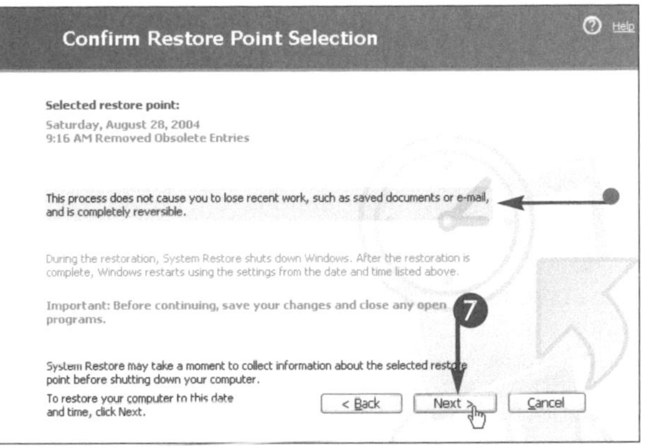

- The System Restore Wizard indicates that the restoration is complete.
- The System Restore Wizard informs you that you can undo the restoration or choose a different restore point.

8 Click OK.

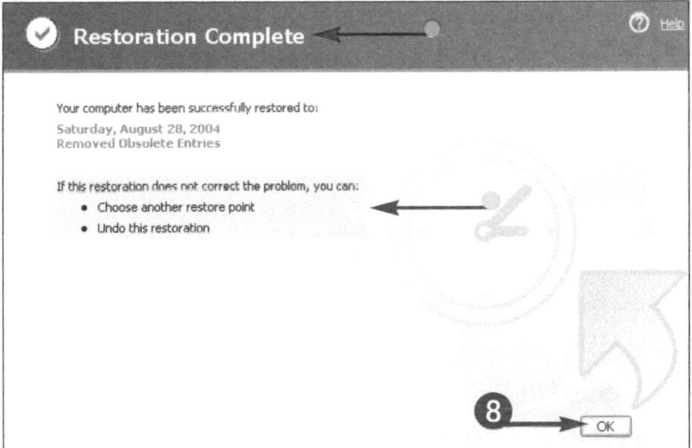

The System Restore Wizard does not display any restore points on the calendar. What happened?

▼ Windows has several built-in policies to deal with system restore points. If your PC is running low on disk space, Windows automatically deletes restore points to reclaim disk space for other operations. Windows also automatically deletes system restore points after 90 days. Another possibility is that you disabled System Restore or severely limited the amount of disk space allocated for storing system restore points; run System Restore, click System Restore Settings, and adjust the settings to enable System Restore and to allocate more disk space for system restore points. A computer virus or spyware may also delete system restore points.

Why are some dates on the calendar missing restore points?

▼ If you do not use your PC on a given day, Windows does not create a restore point, because nothing on your PC has changed. When Windows automatically creates a restore point, it names the restore point System checkpoint or gives it a name that matches the software or driver you installed at the time.

I click the back arrow button (<) to go back to the previous month, but nothing happens. What is wrong?

▼ Nothing is wrong. If Windows does not have a system restore point for a previous month, you cannot go back to that month to select a system restore point. You must choose one of the restore points that is available for the current month.

Undo a System Restore

When you restore your PC to a previous condition, System Restore automatically creates a new restore point. If you restore your PC to a previous condition and are unhappy with the results, you can undo the most recent system restoration or choose a different restore point.

After Windows restores your PC to a previous condition, it restarts Windows, and the System Restore Wizard appears, indicating that you can undo the restoration. You can click OK and then use your PC as you normally would to determine if it performs as well as you expect. You may want to use the current configuration for several days to ensure that everything is running properly. If Windows or one of your applications or hardware devices is not performing as well as you expect, you can run the System Restore Wizard again and try a different restore point.

Because you can undo only the most current system restore, this book recommends that you undo a system restore before you try a different system restore point. This ensures that you can return your PC to the condition it was in before you began experimenting with different system restore points.

Undo a System Restore

1. Launch the System Restore Wizard.

Note: *Refer to the section "Run System Restore" for instructions.*

2. Click the Undo my last restoration option (○ changes to ◉).
3. Click Next.

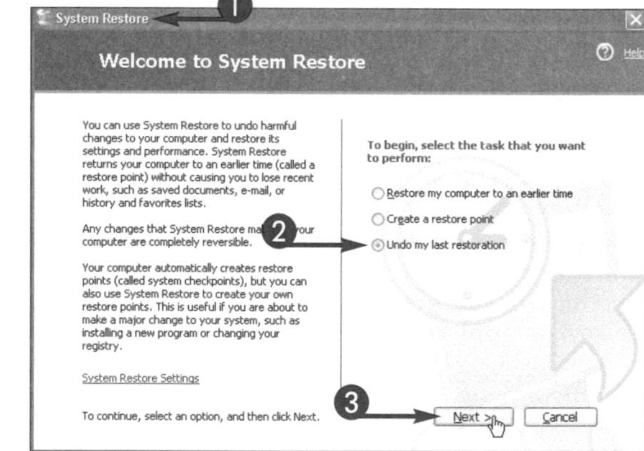

- A message appears assuring you that System Restore does not affect your documents and asking for your confirmation.

4. Click Next.

The System Restore Wizard reverses the most recent restoration, and then it restarts your PC.

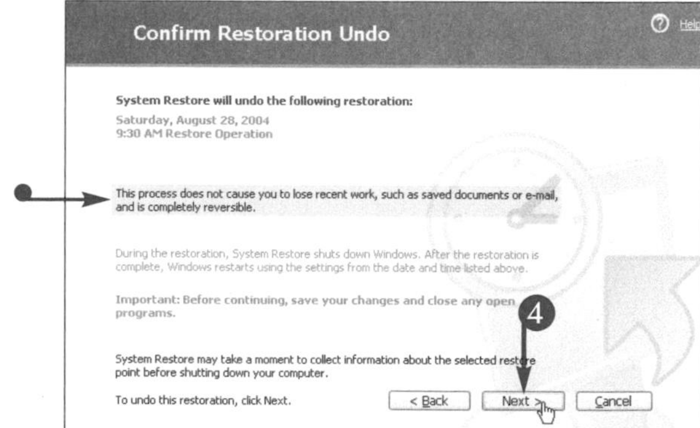

- The System Restore Wizard appears, displaying the Undo Complete message.

5 Click OK.

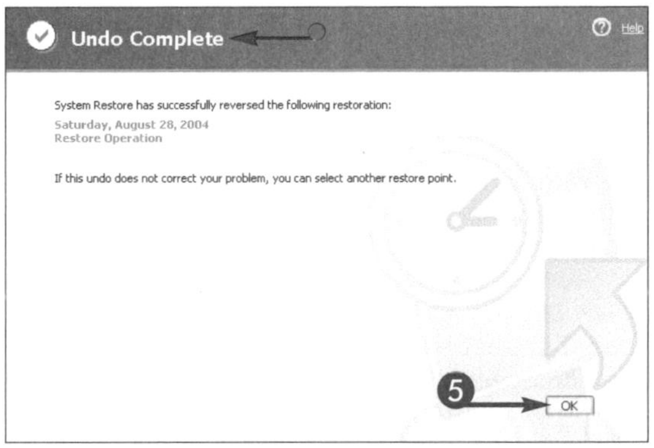

The System Restore Wizard closes and returns you to the Windows desktop.

You can run the System Restore Wizard again and try a different restore point.

Note: *See the section "Restore Your PC to a Previous Condition" for more on trying a different restore point.*

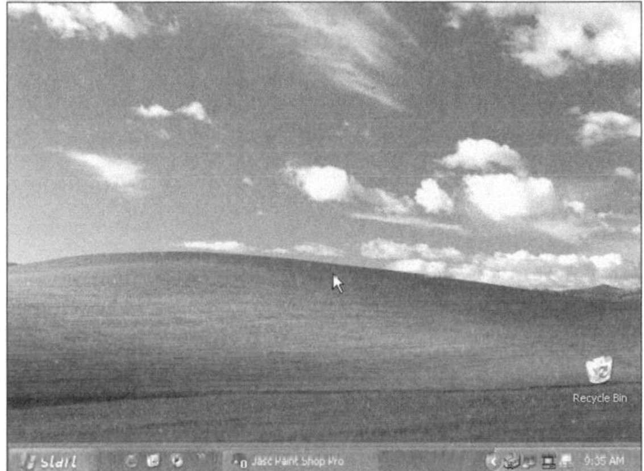

If my PC has a virus, can System Restore restore the virus after I remove the virus from my PC?

▼ Yes. If you use an antivirus utility such as Norton AntiVirus to remove a virus from your PC, and one of the Windows system files that System Restore copies is infected with the virus, restoring your system to a previous condition can reinfect your PC with the virus. If your PC has a virus, you may want to disable System Restore, remove the virus, and then enable System Restore. Disabling System Restore deletes all restore points from your PC. Refer to the tips in the section "Run System Restore" for information on how to disable System Restore.

Windows does not start, so how can I run System Restore?

▼ If you make changes to your PC that prevent Windows from starting, you can run System Restore from a command prompt. Restart your PC and press F8 at 2- to 3-second intervals as it boots. Windows displays a menu of startup options. Select the option for starting in Safe mode with a command prompt. Choose the option to log on as an administrator. At the command prompt, type **%systemroot%\system32\restore\rstrui.exe** and press Enter. Then, follow the on-screen instructions to restore your PC to an earlier date and time.

Download a Registry Cleaner

The Windows registry can become cluttered with obsolete settings for programs and hardware that your PC no longer uses. Over time, the buildup can bloat your registry, causing it to take longer to load and making it more difficult for Windows to find the information it needs. Moreover, obsolete settings can conflict with useful settings, causing Windows or your applications to crash. You can use a registry cleaner to automatically remove obsolete entries from the Windows registry.

A registry cleaner typically provides a safer way for cleaning the registry than trying to edit the registry manually. Most registry cleaners back up the registry before they clean it, and they automatically search for entries in the registry that point to files or folders that do not exist. Most serious errors that people make when editing the registry consist of removing entries that point to files or folders that do exist.

If you already have PC maintenance utilities such as Norton SystemWorks installed on your PC, you may have a registry cleaner. If your PC does not have a registry cleaner installed, you can find several shareware registry cleaners on the Web. This section shows you where to go to download TweakNow RegCleaner.

Download a Registry Cleaner

1. Launch your Web browser.
2. In the Address bar, type **www.download.com** and press Enter.
3. In the Search box, type **registry cleaner**.
4. Click here and click In Windows.
5. Click Go.

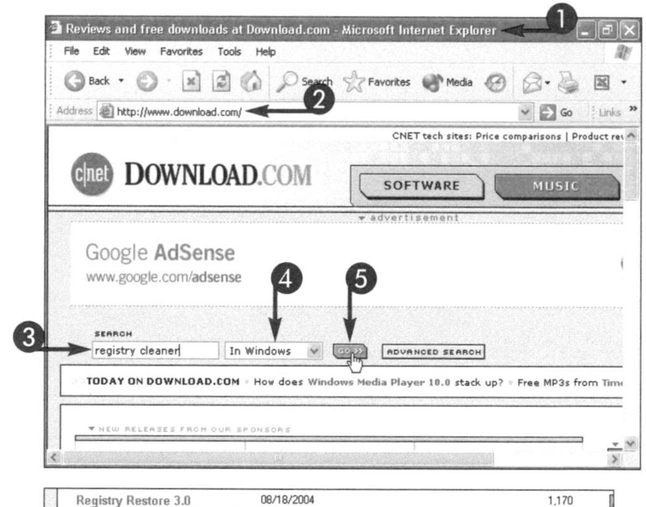

6. Scroll down to the desired registry cleaner.

   This example uses TweakNow RegCleaner.

7. Click the link for the registry cleaner you want to download.

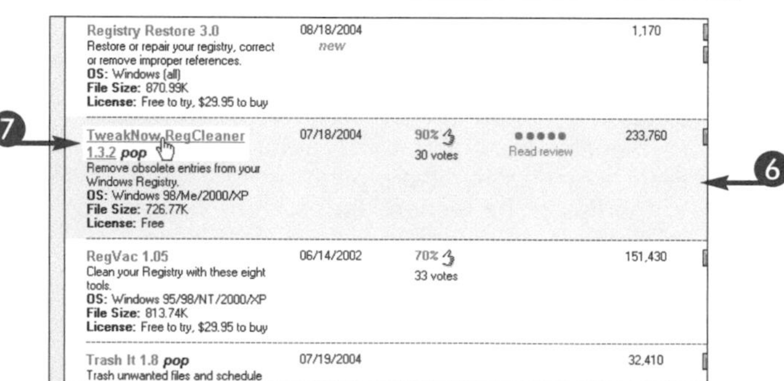

A description of the registry cleaner appears.

8 Click Download Now.

The File Download dialog box appears.

9 Click Open.

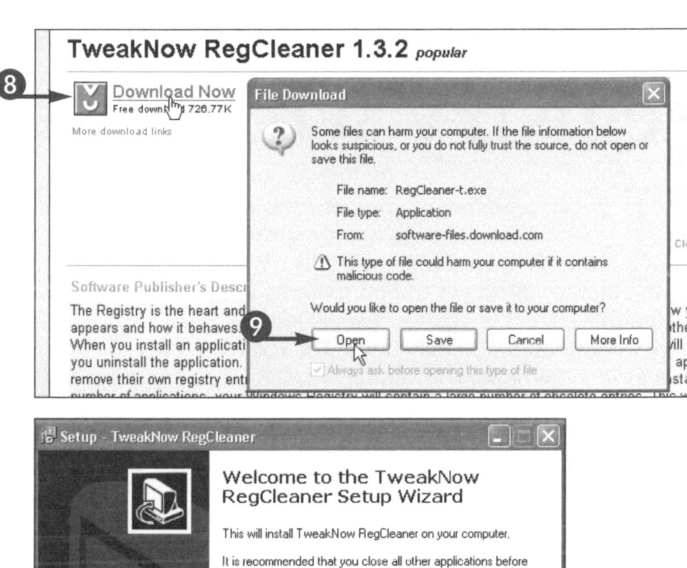

Your Web browser downloads the registry cleaner and initiates the installation routine.

10 Follow the on-screen instructions to install the registry cleaner.

The installation routine installs the registry cleaner on your PC.

Why should I use TweakNow instead of another registry cleaner?

▼ TweakNow is free, easy to use, and has a good reputation for making safe changes. If you already have a registry cleaner installed on your PC — for example, as part of Norton SystemWorks — you can use it instead. Other registry cleaners, including Registry Mechanic and Ashampoo WinOptimizer, are also excellent utilities.

I cannot find the registry cleaner I want to use at Download.com. Can I look somewhere else?

▼ Yes. This book uses Download.com in many of its examples because it provides an excellent selection of freeware, shareware, and trialware, and because it provides CNET reviews as well as user reviews of the software. However, you may prefer other popular shareware sites such as Tucows at www.tucows.com, Hotlib at www.hotlib.com, and Version Tracker at www.versiontracker.com.

Where can I learn more about TweakNow RegCleaner?

▼ TweakNow has its own Web site, where you can learn more about TweakNow RegCleaner and other TweakNow utilities. For about $14, you can purchase the commercial version of TweakNow RegCleaner, which includes the ability to scan applications. The free version scans for obsolete registry entries that point to fonts, ActiveX components, .com executable program files, help files, and many other file types that leave entries behind in the registry.

Clean the Windows Registry with TweakNow

Using TweakNow or another registry cleaner of your choice, you can remove obsolete entries from the Windows registry to trim its size and make it easier for Windows to find the entries it needs. Most registry editors, including TweakNow, back up the registry for you before modifying it. The registry cleaner then searches the registry for entries that point to files that no longer exist on the PC, and it deletes those entries.

Whenever you install an application, it usually registers itself with Windows by adding several entries to the Windows registry. These entries contain information that controls the program's appearance and performance. When you uninstall a program, it is supposed to remove all of its entries from the Windows registry, but programs frequently leave these entries behind. Over time, these obsolete entries can negatively affect the overall performance of Windows. If you have never cleaned the Windows registry, you may be surprised at the number of obsolete registry entries that your registry cleaner discovers.

The free version of TweakNow searches the Windows registry for entries that point to deleted files and folders, including ActiveX controls, help files, and startup files.

Clean the Windows Registry with TweakNow

1. Double-click the TweakNow RegCleaner icon on the Windows desktop.

Note: *For more on downloading this program, see the section "Download a Registry Cleaner."*

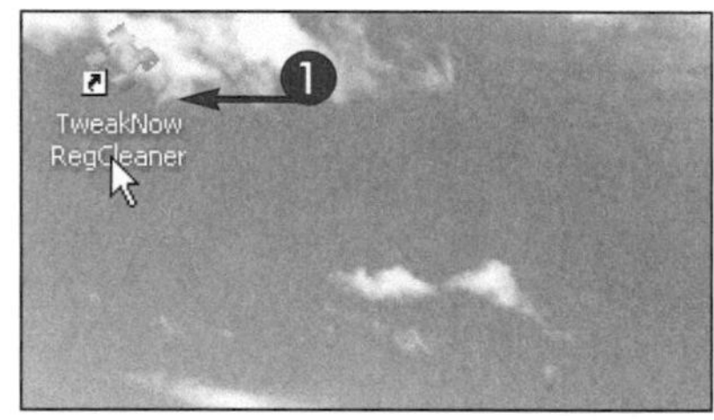

TweakNow's opening screen appears, indicating the areas of the registry it will scan.

2. Click Scan Now.

TweakNow backs up the registry and then displays a list of obsolete entries that are safe to delete.

- You can click the box next to an entry to exclude it from the cleanup (☑ changes to ☐).

Note: *You may want to exclude an entry from the cleanup if you know that it refers to a currently installed program.*

3 Click Delete.

TweakNow clears all obsolete entries from the registry and displays the Info dialog box indicating that the operation is complete.

4 Click OK.

The Info dialog box closes and returns you to TweakNow RegCleaner.

Does TweakNow remove any files that should have been deleted when I uninstalled a program?

▼ No. TweakNow does not delete any files on your PC. It typically deletes entries in the registry that point to files or folders that no longer exist or are no longer being used. TweakNow is conservative in choosing entries to delete. If it does not have 100 percent certainty that a registry entry is no longer needed, it displays a warning prompting you for confirmation.

After running TweakNow, one of my applications does not run properly. Can I undo what TweakNow did?

▼ Yes. Run TweakNow again, and click Restore. The Restore dialog box appears, displaying a list of registry backups. Click the backup file you want to restore and then click Restore. You can run TweakNow again and adjust its settings to perform a less aggressive registry cleanup. For example, you can exlude certain branches of the registry from the scanning operation.

Do I need the commercial version?

▼ For a thorough cleaning of the registry, you should purchase the commercial edition of TweakNow or another registry cleaner. Although the free version is capable of identifying and removing hundreds of obsolete entries from the registry, the applications you uninstall can leave behind hundreds more. When shopping for a registry cleaner, always make sure it has a recovery feature, just in case it cleans a little too aggressively.

Run Windows Registry Editor

Windows Registry Editor is a utility included with Windows that you can use to view and edit the contents of the registry. Sometimes, you must edit the registry to fix a problem with Windows or one of your applications. During a troubleshooting routine, for example, one of Microsoft's technicians may instruct you to edit or delete a registry key. In such cases, you can use Registry Editor to find the key and edit or remove it. In addition, many tweaks for improving PC performance require that you edit registry settings.

Microsoft recommends against making changes to the Windows registry, because even a minor typo in the registry can negatively affect Windows performance. It can even prevent Windows from running. Before making changes, refer to Chapter 19 for instructions on creating a system restore point.

When you run the Windows Registry Editor, a two-paned window appears. In the left pane is a list of *hives*, which appear as folders. Each hive contains several keys and subkeys that you can open to display individual values. Think of each value as a property for which you can enter data that controls the property.

Run Windows Registry Editor

1. Click Start.
2. Click Run.

The Run dialog box appears.

3. Type **regedit**.
4. Click OK.

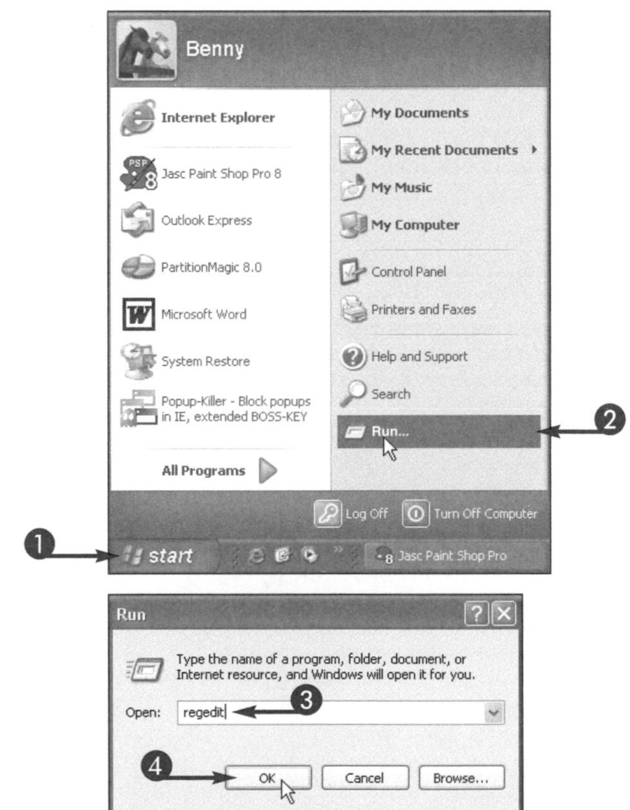

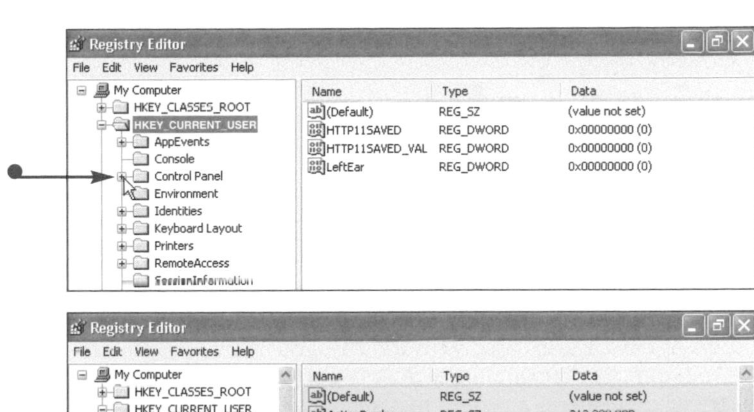

The Registry Editor appears.

- You can click the plus sign (⊞) next to a hive, key, or subkey to expand it.

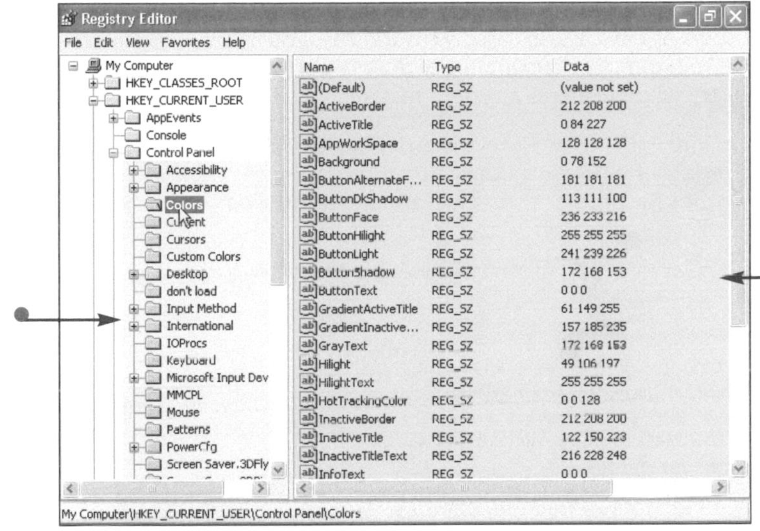

- The expanded key's subkeys appear.
- When you select a subkey, its values and corresponding data appear here.

The Registry Editor seems pretty complicated. Are any tools available that make the settings more understandable?

▼ Yes. You can download utilities that provide a more graphical interface for editing the Windows registry. Many of these utilities enable you to edit the registry by selecting options rather than typing specific settings. Others provide third-party registry editors that include instructions and tips for tweaking settings yourself. Chapter 21 provides additional details on where to obtain tweaking utilities and demonstrates how to use them.

Can I edit the registry and then exit without saving my changes?

▼ Unlike other applications that enable you to edit files, Registry Editor does not enable you to make changes and then exit without saving. As soon as you delete a folder or key or edit a setting, Registry Editor automatically executes the change. You can explore the Windows registry without making changes, but once you make a change, Registry Editor saves it.

Is the Windows registry a single file?

▼ No. The Windows registry is a collection of keys and values that are stored in several files, including files called USER.DAT, SYSTEM.DAT, and CLASSES.DAT. You cannot open and edit these files directly. You must use a registry editor, such as Windows Registry Editor, or a utility that enables you to tweak the registry.

Back Up Registry Keys

You can use Windows Registry Editor to back up the entire registry or any portion of it, such as individual keys. You can back up a key by exporting it and saving it as a file with the .reg filename extension. If you edit a key and then have problems using an application or device associated with the key, you can import the key from the backup rather than restoring the entire registry or performing a system restore.

Backing up individual registry keys is especially useful if you clean the registry by deleting duplicate entries or by deleting entries for programs that are no longer installed. You can delete an entry, reboot Windows, test to see if the deletion caused a problem, and then restore the key if problems arise.

When you back up an individual registry entry, carefully consider the name you assign each backup file. Use a name that accurately describes the change you made or the purpose for deleting a key. If you make several changes to your registry and then run into problems later, these descriptive filenames can help you decide which registry keys you need to restore.

Back Up Registry Keys

1 Launch Windows Registry Editor.

Note: *See the section "Run Windows Registry Editor" for details.*

2 Navigate to the key that you want to back up.

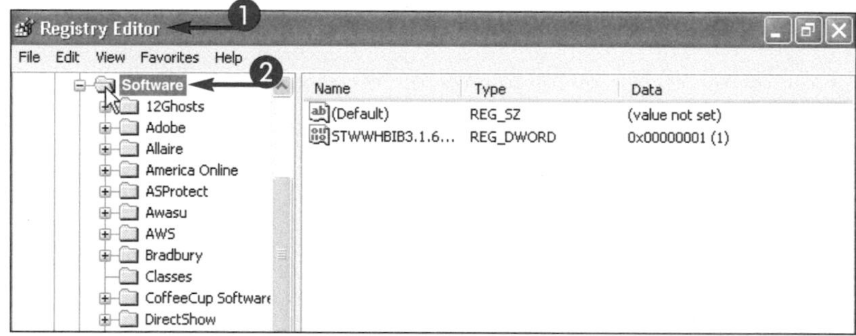

3 Click the key that you want to back up.

The selected key and all of its subkeys are included in the backup.

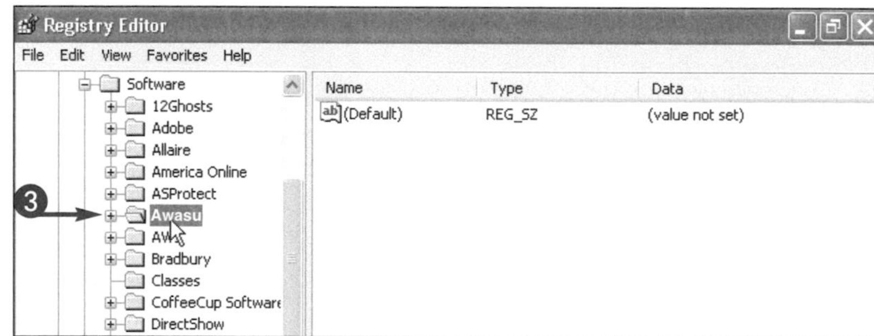

4 Click File.

5 Click Export.

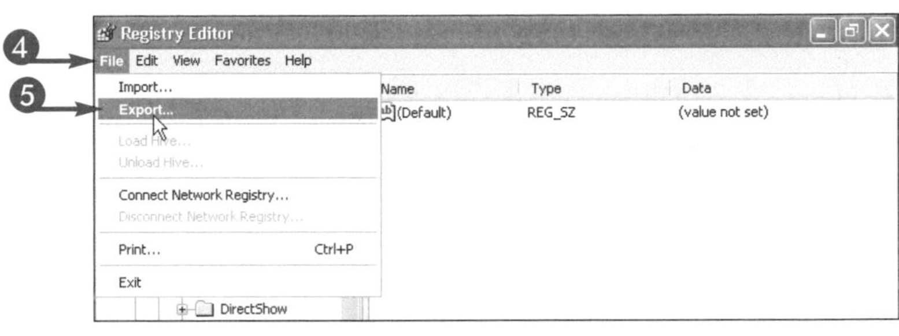

The Export Registry File dialog box appears.

6 Navigate to the folder in which you want to save the backup file.

7 Type a name for the backup file.

8 Click Save.

Registry Editor saves the selected key and all of its subkeys in a file in the folder you selected.

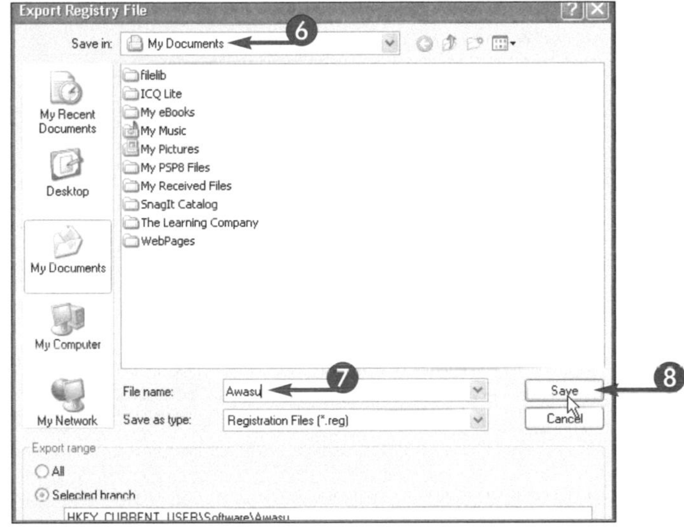

How do I back up the entire Windows system registry?

▼ Click File, and then Export. When the Export Registry File dialog box appears, under Export range, click the All option (○ changes to ◉). This tells Registry Editor to back up the entire registry rather than just the selected key and its subkeys. Navigate to the folder in which you want the file saved, type a name for the file, and click Save.

Can I lock the system registry to prevent other users from editing it?

▼ You can lock individual keys. Click the key you want to lock, click Edit, and then Permissions. The Permissions dialog box for the selected key appears, displaying a list of users and groups who are authorized to use this PC. Click the user or group to specify permissions and then click the desired options. You can click Allow or Deny to permit or prevent users from reading or editing specific keys.

Can I print the registry or a specific key?

▼ Yes, but this book does not recommend printing the entire registry because it is so large. Click the key that you want to print, click File, and then Print. In the Print dialog box, click the Select branch option (○ changes to ◉). Click Print. Registry Editor prints the selected key and all of its subkeys, including the key name, class name, last-write date and time, and the data for each value.

Restore Registry Keys

If you backed up a registry key, you can easily restore the key to the system registry. Before you delete or edit a registry key, you should make a backup of it, as explained in the section "Back Up Registry Keys." This saves the key in a file that has the .reg filename extension. You can open the system registry in Windows Registry Editor and then restore the key using the backup file. The backup file contains the information that Registry Editor needs to restore the key to its proper location. If you restore a key that is a subkey of another key, for example, Registry Editor restores the key inside its parent key.

Be careful when restoring registry keys. Registry Editor cannot determine which key has the correct settings. A good procedure to follow is to change only one registry key at a time and then test the change before making additional changes. If a change causes a problem, then restore the key you changed and try a different adjustment. If the change produces the desired results and causes no problems, you can delete the backup registry key later so it does not get mixed up with other backup files.

Restore Registry Keys

1. Launch Windows Registry Editor.

Note: *See the section "Run Windows Registry Editor" for details.*

2. Click File.
3. Click Import.

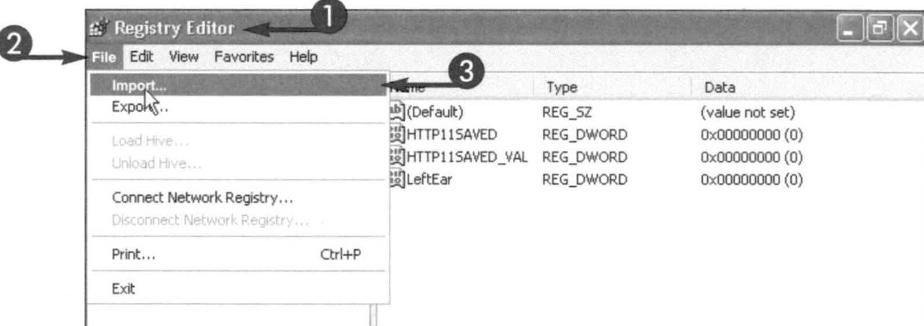

The Import Registry File dialog box appears.

4. Navigate to the folder in which you saved the file containing the backup key.
5. Click the file that contains the backup key you want to restore.
6. Click Open.

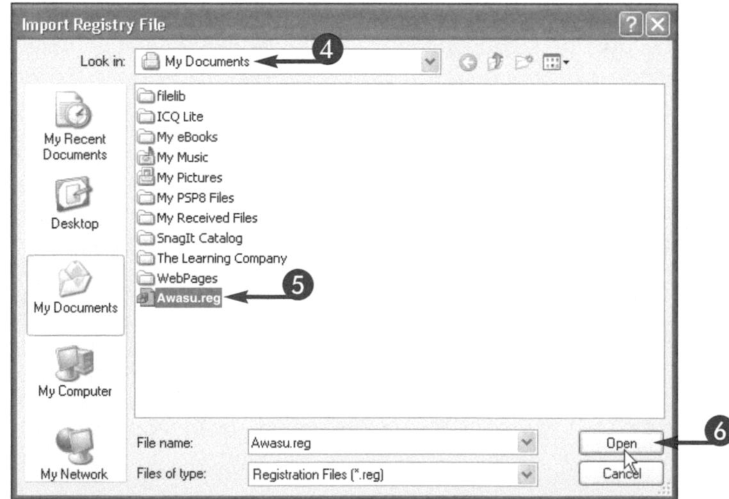

The Registry Editor dialog box appears, indicating that the Registry Editor successfully imported the information from the selected file.

7. Click OK.

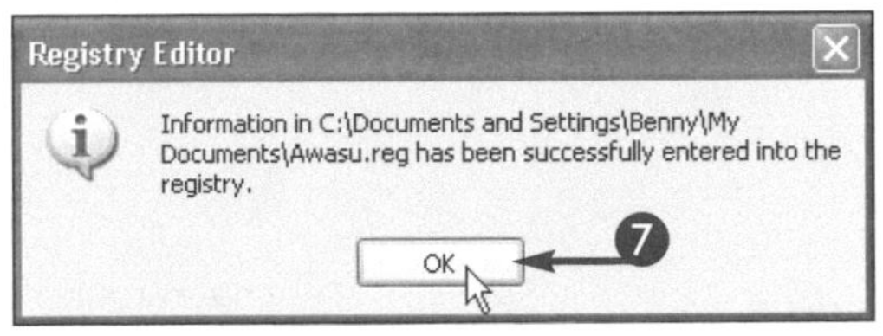

The Registry Editor dialog box closes, returning you to the Registry Editor.

- You can click a key to ensure that the Registry Editor imported the key.

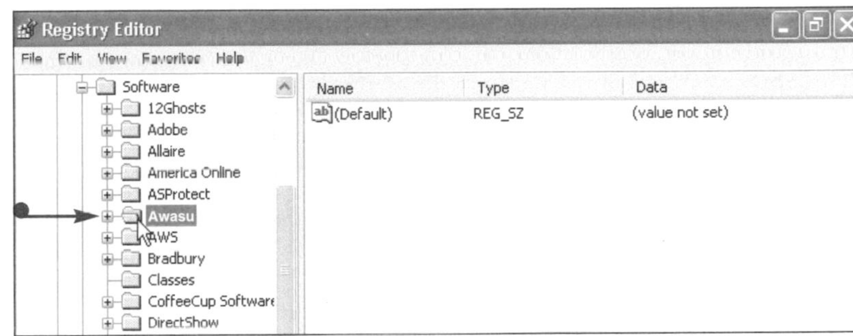

Do I need to launch Registry Editor to restore a key?

▼ No. You can double-click a backup file, a file that has the .reg filename extension, in Windows Explorer or My Computer, to automatically add the information from the file to the system registry. Always be careful when restoring registry keys, because Registry Editor does not prompt you for confirmation. When you click the option to import the backup key, Registry Editor automatically imports it, no questions asked.

Can I restore subkeys contained in a branch that I backed up?

▼ No. When you choose to import a key, Registry Editor imports the key and all of its subkeys. The import operation proceeds very quickly, so you would see no real benefit from restoring a subkey or an individual value even if it were possible. However, instead of backing up a key, you can jot down any settings before changing them and then manually restore individual settings.

Can I import a key that I exported on another PC?

▼ Yes, but this book recommends that you import only keys that you backed up on the same PC. If you import keys from other PCs, you run the risk of importing settings that point to folders or files that do not exist on this PC, which can cause serious problems.

Search the Registry

The Windows system registry is a huge database containing hundreds of keys and subkeys. When you need to delete or edit a specific key, you can use the Registry Editor's Find command to locate it. The Find feature searches every folder in the system registry to find the item you specify. A similar search, performed manually, can easily take several hours and turn up nothing.

The Find feature enables you to search for specific character strings in keys, values, or data. Values are specific properties, whereas data are settings for each value. For example, if Windows has a blue background, the value is background and the data entry is a numerical entry that represents blue. By default, Registry Editor performs a broad search, looking for all entries that contain the character string you specify; however, you can choose the Match whole string only option to have Registry Editor locate only those entries that exactly match the string you type.

Although the search is automated and proceeds much more quickly than a manual search, the search may take several seconds. If several entries contain the character string you specify, you may need to continue the search several times to find the correct entry.

Search the Registry

1. Launch Windows Registry Editor.

Note: *See the section "Run Windows Registry Editor" for details.*

2. Click Edit.
3. Click Find.

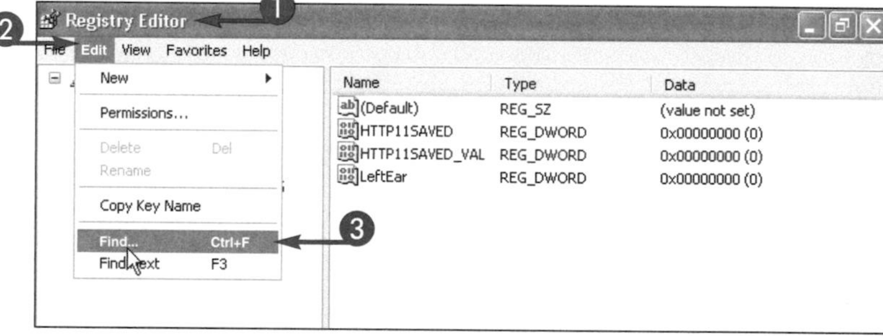

The Find dialog box appears.

4. Type the character string you want to find.

- You can click any of these options to exclude items from the search (☑ changes to ☐).
- You can click here to find only those items that exactly match the character string you type (☐ changes to ☑).

5. Click Find Next.

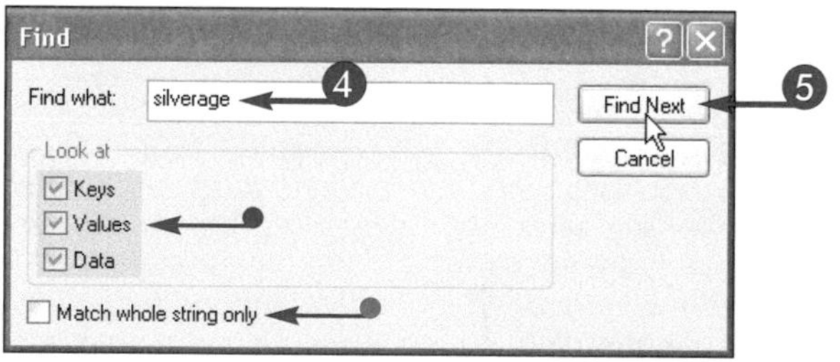

- If Registry Editor finds an item that matches the character string you typed, it highlights the first occurrence of the item.
- To find the next occurrence of the item, you can click Edit, and then Find Next.

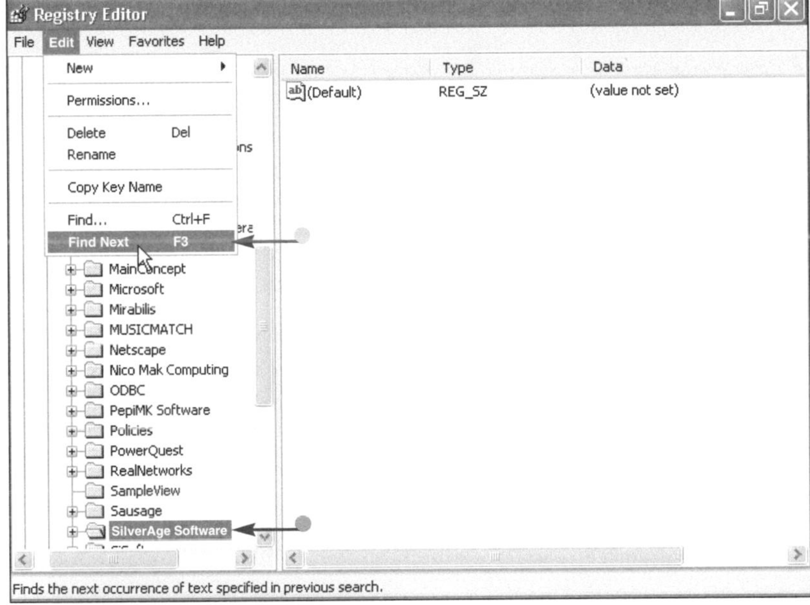

When Registry Editor reaches the end of the registry, the Registry Editor dialog box appears indicating that the search is complete.

6 Click OK.

The Registry Editor dialog box closes.

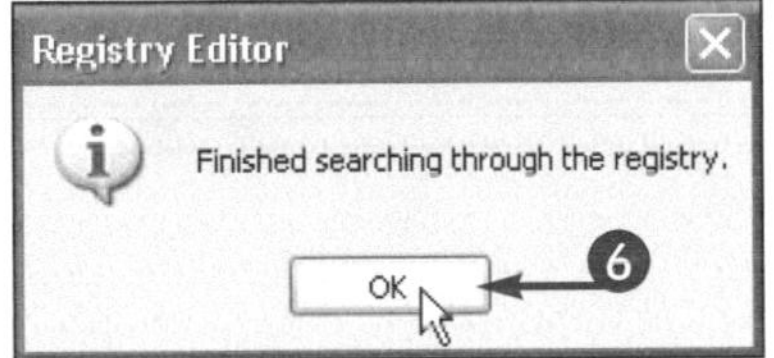

The Find dialog box gets in the way when I am trying to search. Can I hide it?

▼ Yes. After Registry Editor finds the first occurrence of the item that matches the character string you typed, click Cancel. This closes the Find dialog box. You can then press F3 to search for the next item that contains the character string. You do not have to have the Find dialog box open to continue searching. You can use a shortcut keystroke to start searching, as well. Press Ctrl+F to start a search. This displays the Find dialog box, which you can use as instructed in this section to search for an item.

I am trying to delete all references to a program I already uninstalled. Can I just delete the program's subkey under Software?

▼ No. Most programs insert subkeys and settings throughout the system registry, so deleting one key that appears to be the program's main key typically does not remove all references to the program's files. In some cases, you can visit the program's technical support area on the Web and find a list of entries you must delete or a character string that is unique to all of the program's registry settings. You then search for these items and remove them, as explained in the next section, "Delete Registry Keys."

Delete Registry Keys

Using a Windows registry cleaner, as instructed in the section "Clean the Windows Registry with TweakNow," is the safest way to remove registry entries that Windows no longer uses. A registry cleaner typically backs up the registry before proceeding and deletes only those keys that are no longer in use. It automates the process, so you do not accidentally delete critical registry keys. However, if your registry cleaner does not remove a key that is causing problems, you can delete the key using Windows Registry Editor.

Often, when you uninstall a program, the uninstall utility removes all of the program's files from your PC, but it leaves the registry entries untouched. In some cases, you can visit the program's technical support area on the Web to find a list of registry entries you must delete. Some instructions for removing viruses, adware, and spyware from your PC also specify registry entries you must delete. Knowing how to delete specific entries can often help you streamline the registry and regain control of your PC.

Before you proceed, create a system restore point, as explained in Chapter 19. You can also back up individual keys before deleting them as discussed in the section "Back Up Registry Keys."

Delete Registry Keys

1. Launch Windows Registry Editor.

Note: *See the section "Run Windows Registry Editor" for details.*

2. Click the key you want to delete.

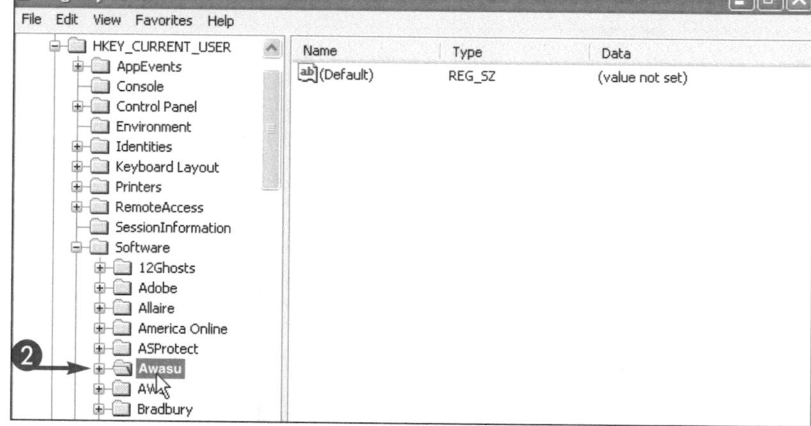

3. Click Edit.
4. Click Delete.

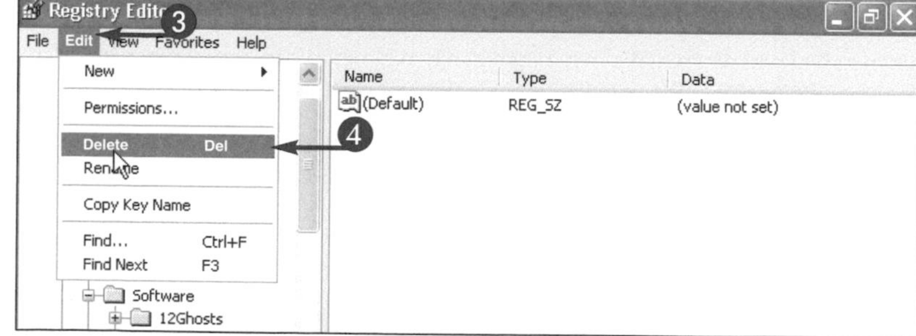

The Confirm Key Delete dialog box appears, prompting you to confirm the deletion of the selected key and all of its subkeys.

5 Click Yes to confirm.

- Registry Editor removes the selected key and all of its subkeys.

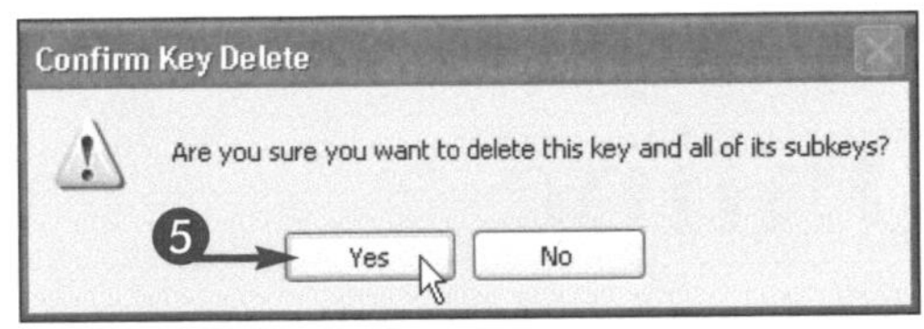

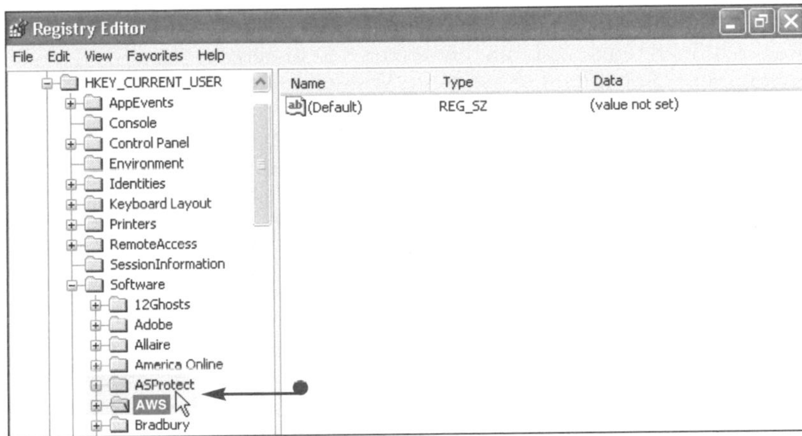

I accidentally deleted the wrong key. Where can I find the Undo option?

- Windows Registry Editor provides no Undo option. If you created a system restore point, as discussed in Chapter 19, you can restore the registry and the critical system files by restoring Windows to a previous date. If you backed up the registry key or the individual key you deleted, you can restore it, as instructed in the section "Restore Registry Keys."

When I try to delete a key, a message appears indicating that I cannot delete the key. Why not?

- You may not have permission to delete the key in Windows. Try logging off Windows and then logging on using an administrator account. Then, run Registry Editor, right-click the key you want to delete, and click Permissions. Select the option to provide yourself with full access to the key. Now try deleting the key.

Can I delete individual values without deleting an entire key?

- Yes. You can delete keys or values. The only items Windows prohibits you from deleting are predefined keys, such as HKEY_CURRENT_USER. To delete a value, right-click the value and click Delete. When prompted to confirm, click Yes.

Find Registry Tweaks Online

You can find hundreds of Windows registry tweaks for all versions of Windows online. Tweaking the Windows registry, sometimes referred to as *hacking Windows*, consists of editing or removing Windows registry entries and other settings to enhance Windows performance or modify its appearance or functionality in some way that Windows does not normally enable you to do. For example, you cannot remove the Recycle Bin icon from the Windows desktop as you can remove other desktop shortcuts, but you can tweak the registry to prevent Windows from displaying the Recycle Bin.

Tweaking is a hobby, an art form, and an obsession. People post tweaks in newsgroups, exchange them via e-mail, and devote entire Web sites and books to distributing them to as many users as possible. Some avid hackers, who know a little programming, even package their tweaks in executable program files, so you can simply download and install the tweak. In most cases, however, the hacker publishes the tweak as a set of changes that you must make to one or more keys in the Windows registry.

Before making any recommended changes, always create a system restore point, as explained in Chapter 19, or back up the registry or the keys you plan to edit, as instructed in Chapter 20.

Find Registry Tweaks Online

1. Launch your Web browser.
2. In the Address bar, type the address of your favorite search tool.

   This example uses Google.
3. Type **windows *??* tweaks** where *??* is the version of Windows that your PC is running.
4. Click the button to start the search or press Enter.

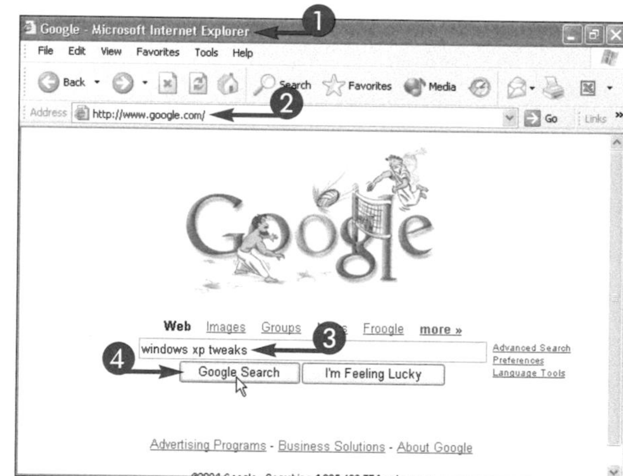

A list of links to Web sites that contain information about tweaking Windows appears.

5. Click the link for the Web site you want to explore.

- You can right-click a link and click Open in New Window to explore a tweak and then close the window to return to the list of tweaks.

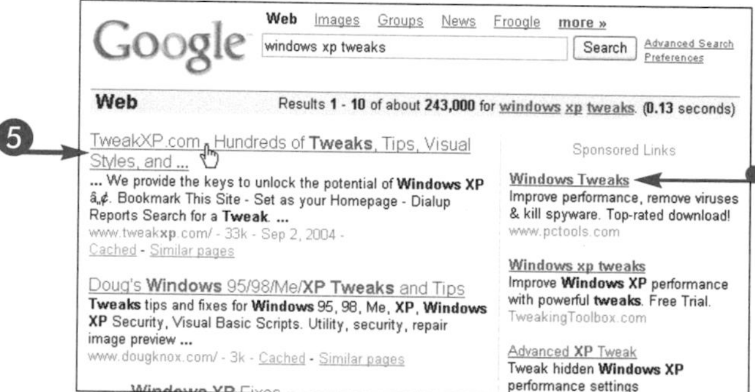

Your browser loads the linked Web page, which typically displays links to available tweaks.

6 Click the link for the tweak you want to learn.

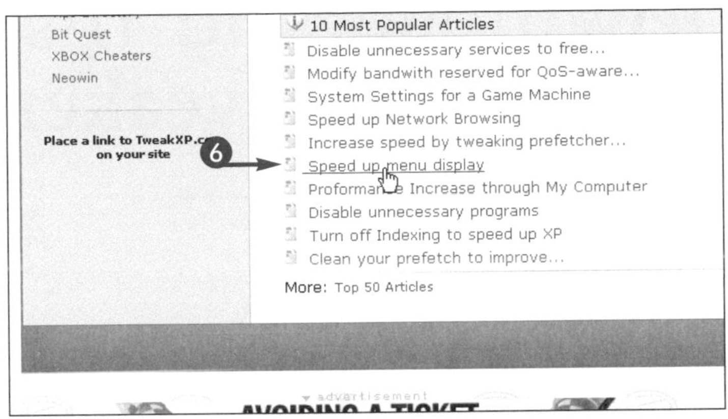

- A description of the tweak, or instructions on how to tweak the Windows registry, appears.

Note: *See the section "Tweak the Registry with Registry Editor" for instructions on how to tweak the Windows registry.*

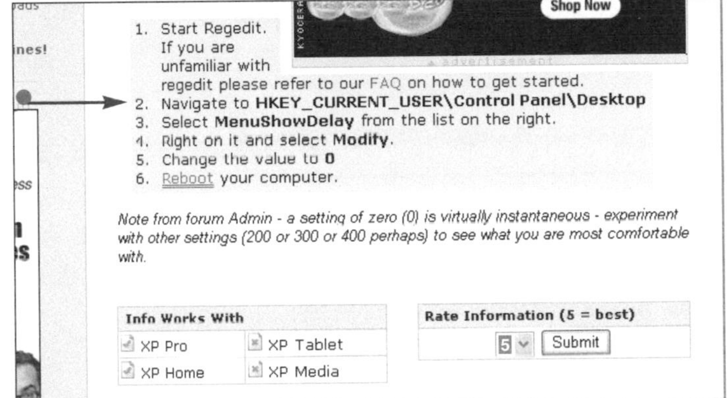

Are most tweaks safe?

▼ Yes. Most tweaks are safe, but you should always create a system restore point or back up the registry or the keys you plan to edit before modifying the registry. You should also carefully read the description of the tweak to make sure that the changes that the tweak recommends have the potential to produce the desired result. If a tweak recommends that you relax Windows security settings to make your PC run faster, for example, you may want to question the motivations of the person who is recommending the tweak.

Do you recommend any Windows tweaking Web sites?

▼ This book cannot guarantee the safety or effectiveness of any tweaks. However, many users have found that the following sites feature good collections of valuable Windows tweaks: TweakXP.com at www.tweakxp.com, Windows XP Tweak Guide at www.winguides.com/windowsxp, and Axcel216's MaxSpeeed WinDOwS site at www.mdgx.com. Several Web sites focus on tweaks that are designed to speed up your Internet connection; see Chapter 17 for more information. No one Web site contains a comprehensive collection of tweaks. One of the thrills of tweaking is to find tweaks on relatively obscure Web sites, so search the Web.

Download and Install a Registry Tweaker

You can tweak the registry using Windows Registry Editor, as explained in the section "Tweak the Registry with Registry Editor," but utilities designed specifically for tweaking the registry are often easier to use. Tweaking the registry with Registry Editor often requires you to locate specific keys and then edit complex values to achieve the desired result. Most of the time, you do not completely understand the keys or their values, so you edit blind, which can often lead to errors. Even a minor error in the registry can disable Windows or one of your applications. Utilities that are designed to tweak the registry often present the changes in a more understandable format; for example, you can use a wizard or dialog box to indicate your preferences, and then the registry tweaker makes the required adjustments.

Microsoft offers its own registry tweaker, called Tweak UI, which you can obtain from Microsoft's Web site, as shown in the steps in this section. For Windows XP, Tweak UI is one tool in a collection of tools that Microsoft calls PowerToys. Windows PowerToys include a CD slide show maker, a taskbar magnifier, a power calculator, and several additional utilities.

Download and Install Tweak UI

1. Launch your Web browser.
2. In the Address bar, type **www.microsoft.com/windowsxp/downloads/powertoys/xppowertoys.mspx** and press Enter.

Note: *Windows 98 or Me users should type **www.microsoft.com/ntworkstation/downloads/PowerToys/Networking/NTTweakUI.asp** and press Enter.*

The PowerToys page appears.

3. Scroll down the page.
4. Click the link for downloading Tweak UI.

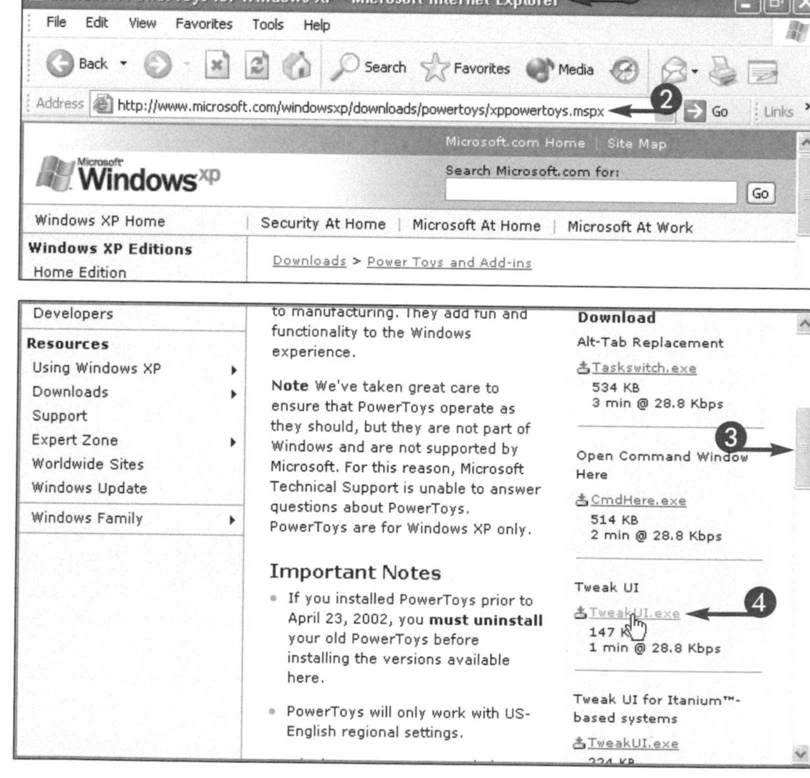

The File Download dialog box appears, prompting you to save the file or open it.

5 Click Open.

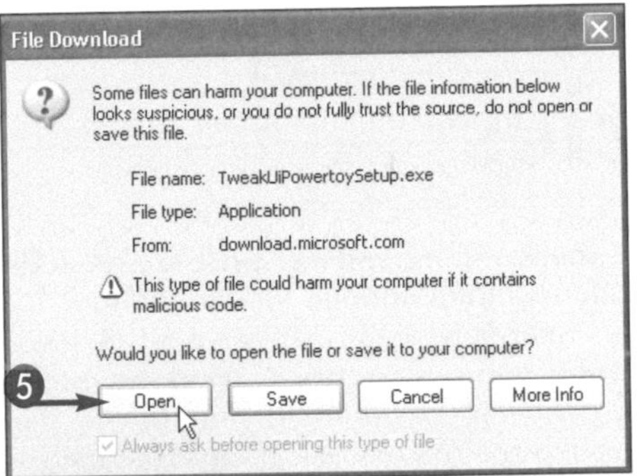

Your Web browser downloads the file and initializes the installation routine.

6 Follow the on-screen instructions to install Tweak UI.

Windows installs Tweak UI on your PC.

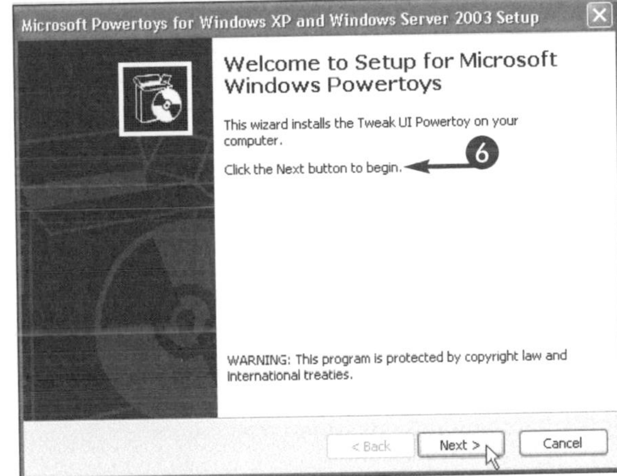

Where can I go to find third-party registry tweakers?

▼ You can go to www.download.com, www.tucows.com, or any of several other popular shareware sites to check out and download third-party utilities for tweaking the registry. Some notable utilities are Advanced System Optimizer, which also provides a registry cleaner, spyware remover, and system cleaner; WinBoost; Tweak Manager; and TweakXP Pro. By sticking with Microsoft's Tweak UI, you know that the utility has Microsoft's seal of approval. However, some of these third-party utilities provide more powerful features. Try more than one utility to see which you prefer, and always create a system restore point before making any changes.

I never knew about these Windows PowerToys. Is Microsoft hiding any other useful add-ons that I do not know about?

▼ Maybe. Microsoft is constantly updating Windows XP to remove bugs, fix security holes, and enhance peformance and compatibility. Chapter 22 shows where to go to download and install Windows updates. In addition, you can go to the Windows XP Downloads page at www.microsoft.com/windowsxp/downloads/default.mspx to determine if Microsoft has any additional freebies available for its operating system. At the time of writing of this book, the Download site featured a new service pack for Windows, security updates, a new version of Media Player, additional desktop accessories, PowerToys, and Tablet PC tools and updates.

Tweak Registry Entries

You can use a registry tweaker such as Tweak UI to indirectly edit the Windows system registry. The registry tweaker typically displays a list of various objects or behaviors you can control in Windows, such as how the mouse pointer behaves when you position it over an object on the screen. You can select an object or behavior, enter your preferences for it, and then save your settings, just as if you were entering preferences in a dialog box. When you save your settings, the registry tweaker automatically edits entries in the registry to modify the object's appearance or behavior according to your preferences.

This section uses Microsoft's Tweak UI to demonstrate a registry tweaker in action. Tweak UI provides access to many settings that Windows does not allow users to change through its standard collection of Control Panel options and dialog boxes. With Tweak UI, you can control the behavior of the mouse wheel, the appearance of shortcut icons, the color-coding that Windows Explorer uses for filenames, the appearance and behavior of the taskbar, and the appearance and function of dozens of other objects.

Tweak Registry Entries

1. Click Start.
2. Click All Programs.
3. Click Powertoys for Windows XP.
4. Click Tweak UI.

- Tweak UI appears, displaying brief instructions on how to use it.

5. Click the plus sign (⊞) next to a feature to view a list of its properties.

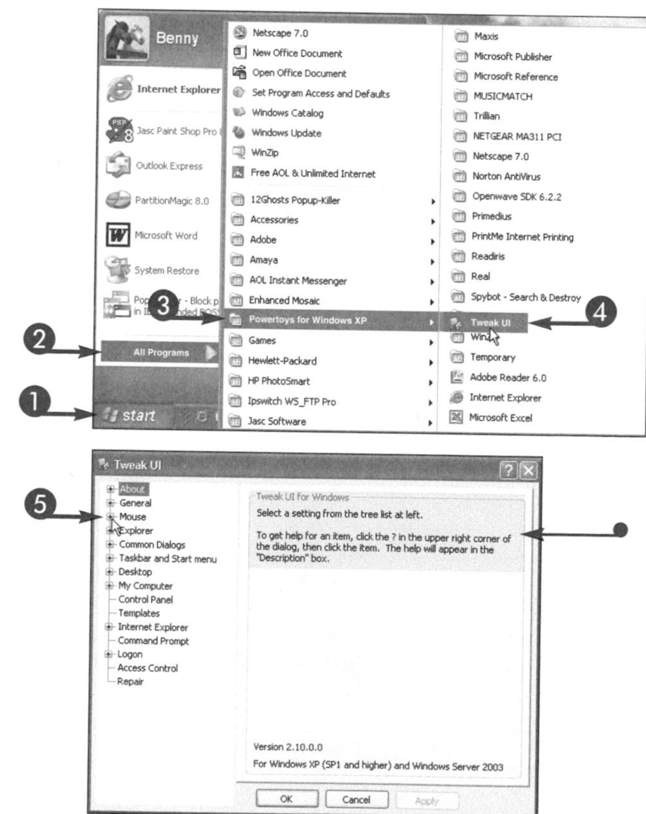

The list expands to display properties you can tweak.

6 Click a property you want to tweak.

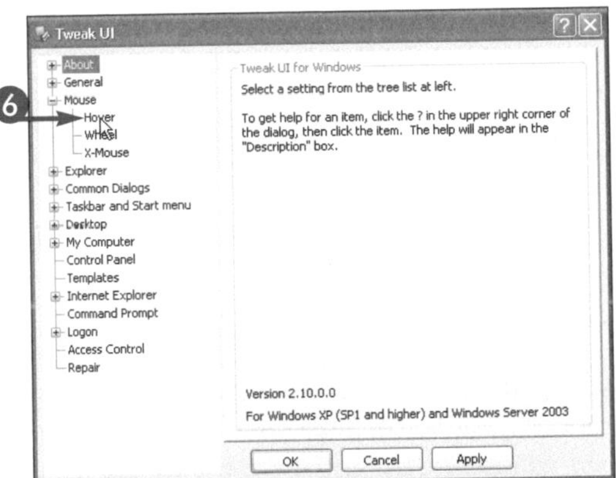

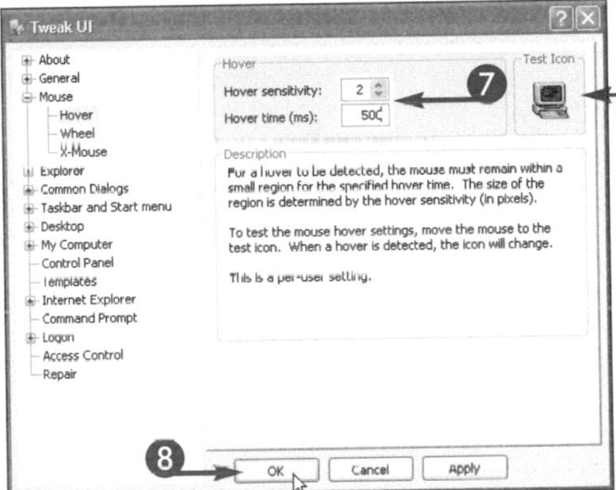

- The property's settings appear.

7 Type your preferences.

8 Click OK.

Tweak UI saves the settings you entered and adjusts the Windows registry accordingly.

Some of the settings for a property do not make sense to me. Can I obtain additional information?

▼ Yes. In the upper-right corner of the Tweak UI window is a help button (?) that you really do not need. Simply click the item about which you want more information. You can click a feature or property in the list on the left or click the name of a property in the pane on the right, but do not click a setting in the pane on the right, but do not click a check box (☐ changes to ☑) or radio button (○ changes to ◉), or you will change the setting. When you click an item, a Description box appears on the right near the bottom of the pane providing additional information about the selected item.

Can I cancel my changes without making any permanent changes to the registry?

▼ Until you click OK, Tweak UI makes no adjustments to the Windows registry. You can click Cancel to exit Tweak UI without making changes. If you already clicked OK, simply run Tweak UI again, and change the options back to their original settings. Of course, if you created a system restore point or backed up the registry before changing it, you can restore the registry to its previous condition. See Chapters 19 and 20 for additional details about backing up and restoring the registry. Tweak UI does not provide access to any settings that can disable Windows or cause problems with your Windows applications.

Tweak the Registry with Registry Editor

Tweak UI and similar utilities provide access to many settings that you cannot otherwise change in Windows, but they do not provide access to all registry keys that you may need to change to fix problems or enhance performance. To make additional adjustments, you can open the registry in Windows Registry Editor and enter the changes directly. Chapter 20 provides instructions on how to run Windows Registry Editor and delete individual keys. This section shows you how to display values and enter data for those values.

The registry is a database that contains a collection of keys. Each key has subkeys or values. A value is a property or feature that represents the appearance or behavior of a specific Windows component or some other aspect of the software or hardware installed on your PC. When you double-click a value, Registry Editor displays a dialog box in which you can enter or edit data for the value. The data you enter functions like a setting, controlling some aspect of a component's appearance or behavior. For example, you can change the mouse speed value to control how fast the mouse pointer travels across the screen.

Tweak the Registry with Registry Editor

1. Launch Registry Editor.

Note: *Refer to Chapter 20 for instructions on running the Windows Registry Editor.*

2. Navigate to the key that contains the value you want to change.

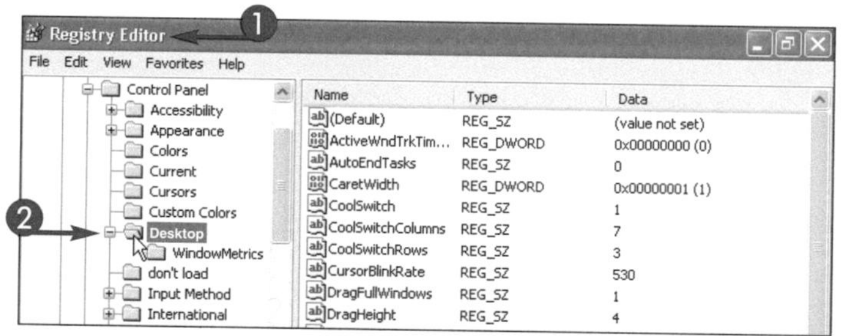

- The selected key's values appear here.

3. Double-click the value you want to edit.

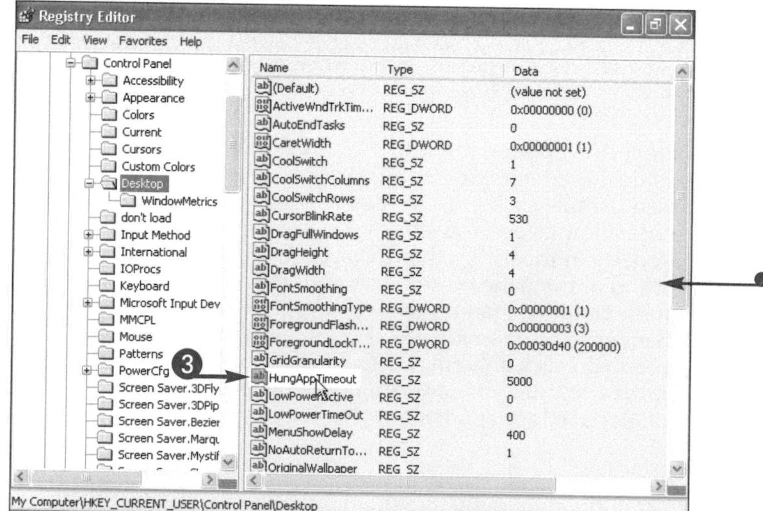

The Edit String dialog box appears, displaying the value name and value data.

4 Type the desired data here.

5 Click OK.

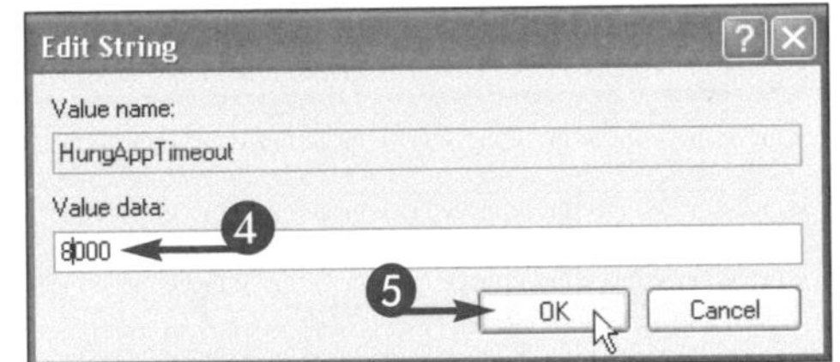

- Registry Editor displays the new data for the value.

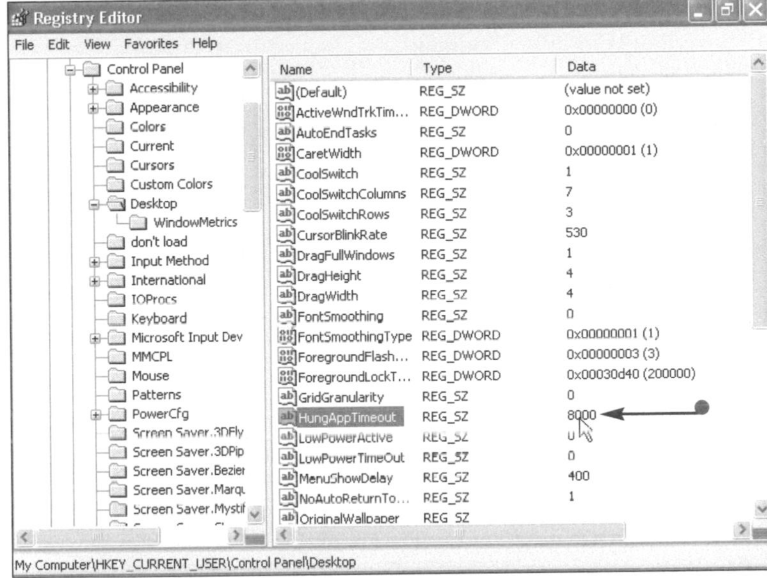

Does tweaking only consist of modifying value data?

▼ No. Tweaking consists of making any changes necessary to bring about the desired results in Windows. This includes deleting values or keys, editing value data, or even creating new values. Many tweaks can be very complicated, requiring you to edit several keys. Others may require you to delete a single key or edit only one value. Some users consider any change to the Windows default settings a tweak, even if you can make the changes using readily accessible Windows configuration tools. For example, at TweakXP.com, you can find some tweaks that require registry edits and many that do not.

Where can I obtain information about acceptable value data?

▼ You must rely on what you read at various Windows tweak Web sites and in books about acceptable value data entries. Value data can consist of anything from a drive letter to a numerical equivalent for a color to a number of seconds. The value data varies depending on the nature of the value. Most Windows tweak Web sites contain very specific instructions on the value data to enter. One of the benefits of using a tweak utility to make your changes is that it provides only valid data entries to limit your options. This prevents you from typing an unacceptable entry.

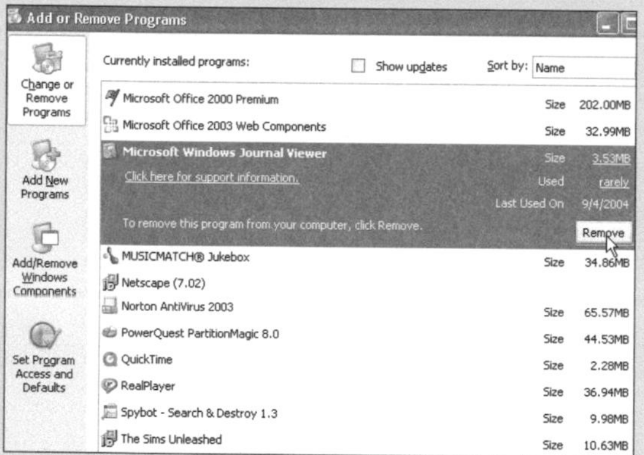

Add or Remove Programs
Change or Remove Programs
Add New Programs
Add/Remove Windows Components
Set Program Access and Defaults
Currently installed programs:
Show updates
Sort by: Name
Microsoft Office 2000 Premium Size 202.00MB
Microsoft Office 2003 Web Components Size 32.99MB
Microsoft Windows Journal Viewer Size 3.53MB
Click here for support information.
Used rarely
Last Used On 9/4/2004
To remove this program from your computer, click Remove.
Remove
MUSICMATCH® Jukebox Size 34.86MB
Netscape (7.02)
Norton AntiVirus 2003 Size 65.57MB
PowerQuest PartitionMagic 8.0 Size 44.53MB
QuickTime Size 2.28MB
RealPlayer Size 36.94MB
Spybot - Search & Destroy 1.3 Size 9.98MB
The Sims Unleashed Size 10.63MB

System Properties
System Restore
Automatic Updates
Remote
General
Computer Name
Hardware
Advanced
Device Manager
The Device Manager lists all the hardware devices installed on your computer. Use the Device Manager to change the properties of any device.
Device Manager

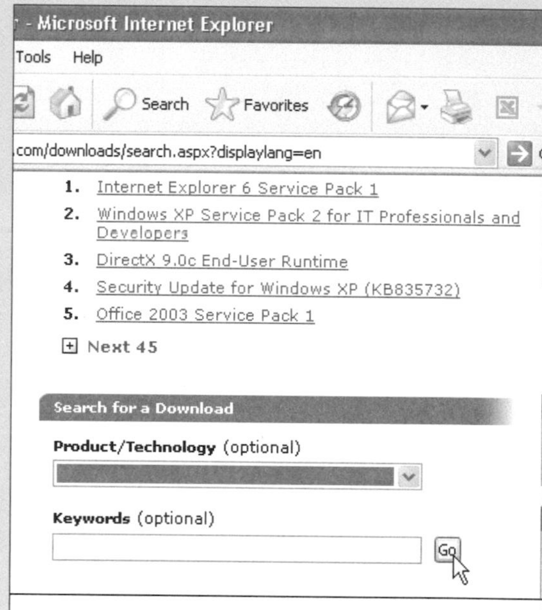

- Microsoft Internet Explorer
Tools Help
Search Favorites
.com/downloads/search.aspx?displaylang=en
1. Internet Explorer 6 Service Pack 1
2. Windows XP Service Pack 2 for IT Professionals and Developers
3. DirectX 9.0c End-User Runtime
4. Security Update for Windows XP (KB835732)
5. Office 2003 Service Pack 1
Next 45
Search for a Download
Product/Technology (optional)
Keywords (optional)
Go
2. MechWarrior 4: Vengeance Trial Version
Date: 12/6/2000 Popularity: #714 English download
3. MechWarrior 4: Mercenaries Update
MechWarrior 4: Mercenaries.
Date: 3/10/2003 Popularity: #1697 English download
4. MechWarrior 4: Vengeance Update v3.0
issues.
Date: 6/12/2003 Popularity: #2294 English download
5. MechWarrior 4: Mercenaries Trial Version

PART VII
UPDATING AND OPTIMIZING YOUR SOFTWARE

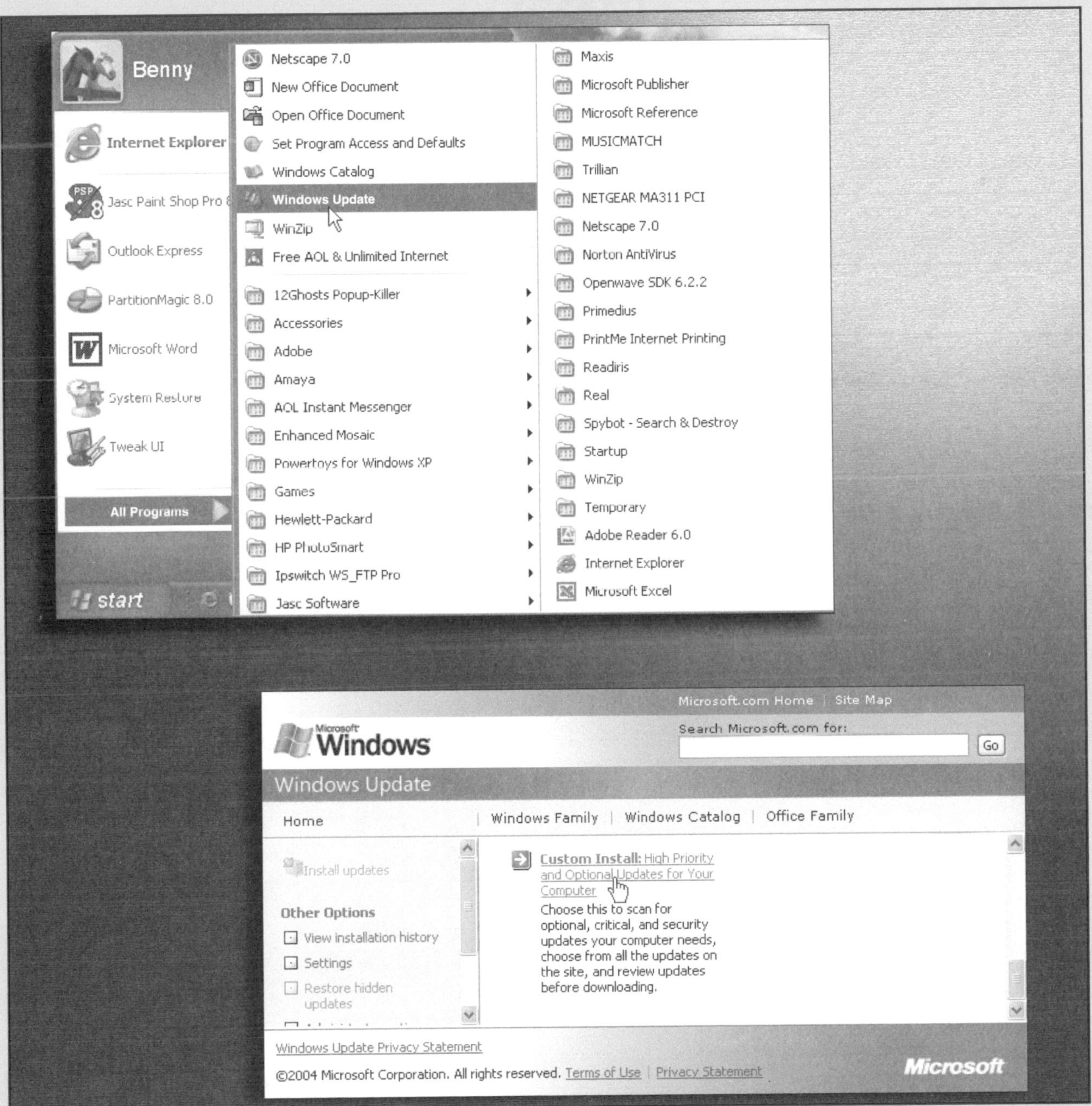

Install Critical Windows Updates

After releasing a version of its Windows operating system, Microsoft continues to develop it to remove bugs, enhance performance and security, and keep it current with the latest technical developments. Microsoft frequently releases critical Windows updates that you can install to keep your version of Windows current. Assuming your PC is connected to the Internet, you can check Microsoft's Web site for critical updates, download them to your PC, and install them for free. The steps in this section show you how to check for and install critical updates. The next section, "Install Optional Windows Updates," shows you how to download and install additional updates that add to or enhance Windows functionality.

Windows critical updates typically correct Windows bugs and security issues that make Windows vulnerable to viruses and allow unauthorized access to Windows PCs. Whenever your PC is connected to the Internet, it is not completely safe, but by installing security fixes, you can ensure that your system has the most secure version of Windows that is available.

All recent versions of Windows, including Windows 98, Windows Me, Windows 2000, and Windows XP, include a Windows Update feature that can help you locate, download, and install Windows updates.

Install Critical Windows Updates

1. Click Start.
2. Click All Programs.
3. Click Windows Update.

Note: *Your version of Windows may include the Windows Update command on the Accessories, System Tools menu.*

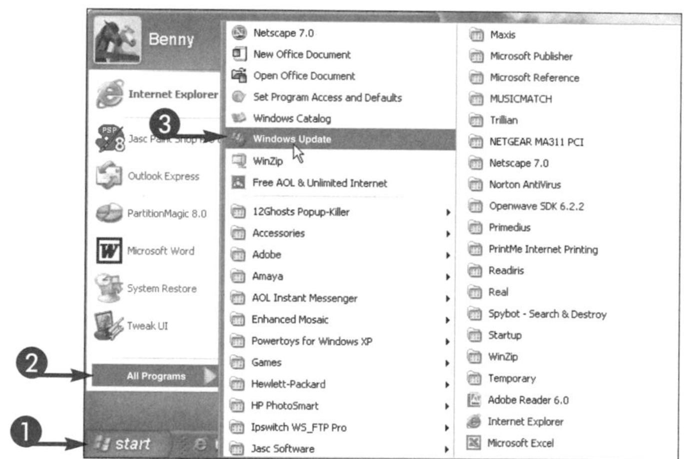

Windows runs Internet Explorer, which connects to the Internet and displays the opening Windows Update page.

4. Click the option to download and install only critical updates.

Note: *Microsoft often changes the options on its Web site, so the steps may differ from those given here.*

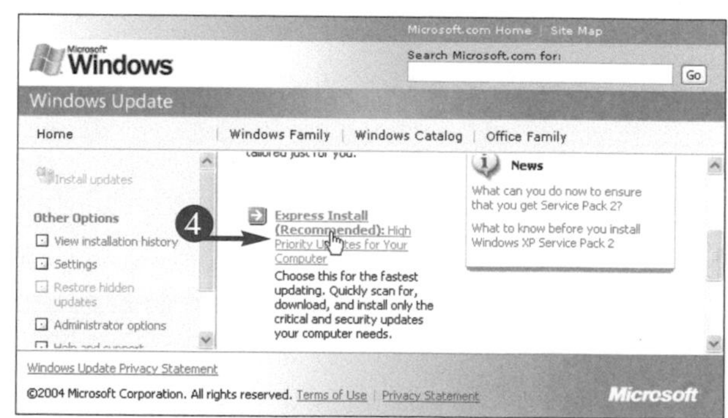

The update feature checks your PC to determine if critical updates are available.

If updates are available, an Install button appears.

5 Click Install.

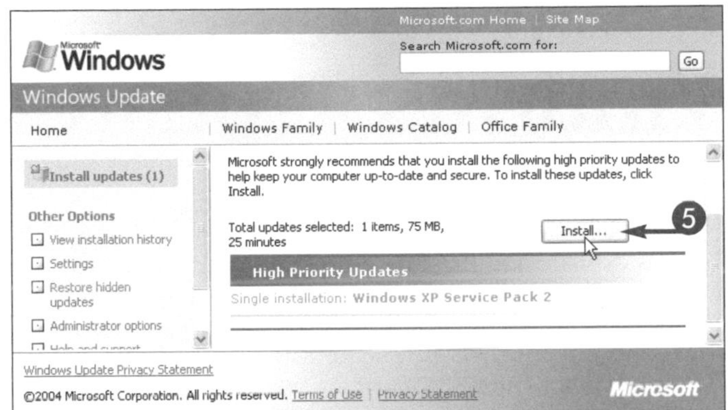

A user license agreement appears.

6 Read the license, and if you agree with its terms, click I Accept and follow the on-screen instructions to install the updates.

Windows downloads the updates and installs them on your PC.

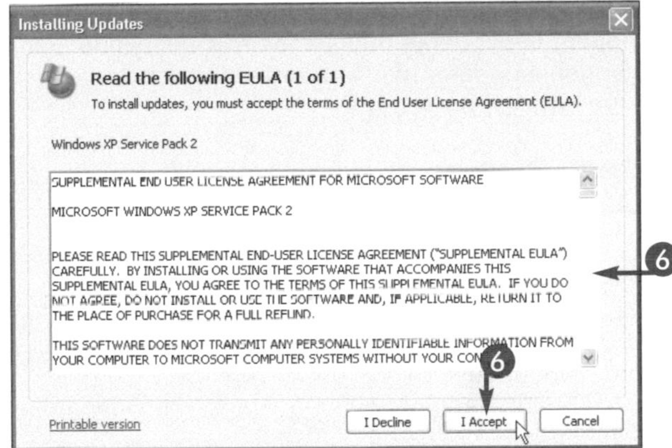

I installed the update and restarted Windows, and the screen now displays a message asking if I want to enable automatic updates. Should I enable automatic updates?

▼ Users often forget to check for updates. The Automatic Updates feature checks for updates and can usually download the updates when you are not using your PC so the download does not interfere with your PC use. This book recommends that you enable Automatic Updates. If you choose not to enable Automatic Updates now, you can do it later, as explained in the section "Schedule Windows Updates." Keeping the Windows software up to date is an important step in keeping your PC secure and performing optimally.

This is taking forever, and I need to get some work done. Can I cancel the Windows update and finish it later?

▼ Some Windows updates may require you to download huge files; for example, Microsoft offers Windows XP Service Pack 2 as a 75MB file. Over a cable modem or DSL connection, this may not be a problem, but over a standard modem connection, this file can take several hours to download. You can cancel the download and then resume it at a time when you do not intend to use your PC. When you return, you can complete the installation. Most updates do not require you to download large files.

Install Optional Windows Updates

To optimize PC performance and keep your PC secure, you should install critical Windows updates, as explained in the previous section. Microsoft also offers high-priority updates and optional updates that you do not need to install, but that can also improve your PC's performance and enhance its functionality. For example, Microsoft offers a Windows XP update that enables standard PCs to display documents created for viewing on Tablet PCs. In this case, the update is not essential, but it adds a component to Windows that some people may find very useful. Optional updates may also include drivers for devices that are installed on your PC.

When you choose to update Windows, Windows Update provides you with the option of installing critical updates or installing high-priority and optional updates. If you choose to install high-priority and optional updates, Windows Update displays a list of the available updates that you can choose to install. You can install them all at once or pick one or more updates to install now and then run Windows Update again later to install additional updates you may want.

Install Optional Windows Updates

1. Click Start.
2. Click All Programs.
3. Click Windows Update.

Note: *Your version of Windows may include the Windows Update command on the Accessories, System Tools menu.*

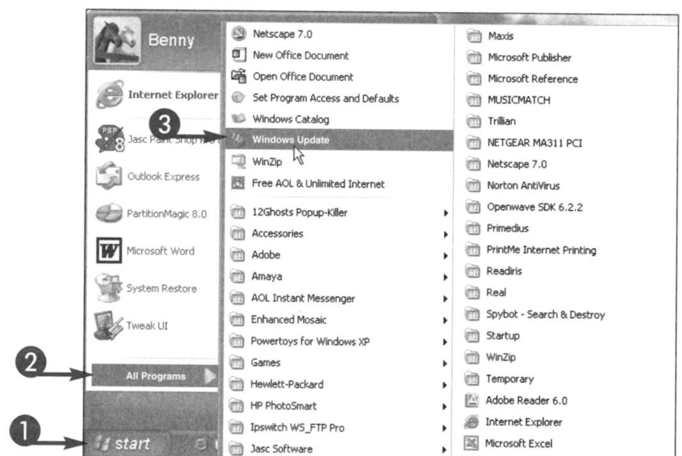

Windows runs Internet Explorer, which connects to the Internet and displays the opening Windows Update page.

4. Click the option to download and install high-priority and optional updates.

Note: *Microsoft often changes the options on its Web site, so the steps may differ from those given here.*

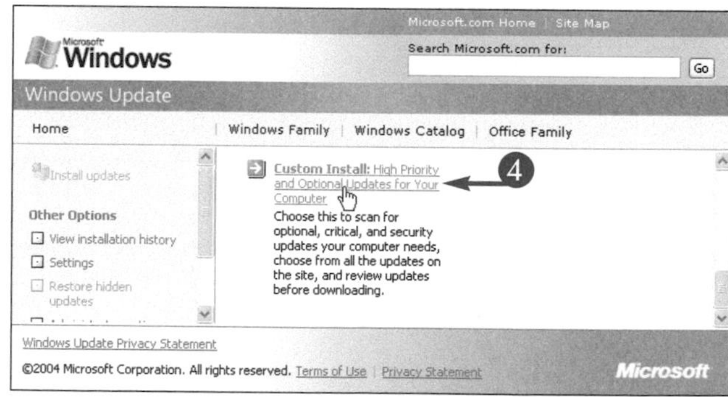

Windows Update displays a list of high-priority and optional updates.

5 Navigate to the category of updates from which you want to select.

6 Click the box next to each update you want to install (☐ changes to ☑).

7 Click the Go to Install updates link.

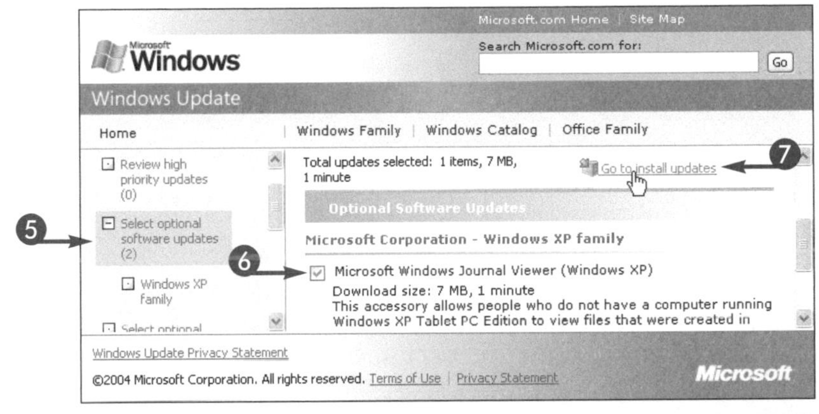

- Windows Update displays the number of updates selected and the total file size.

8 Click Install.

9 Follow the on-screen instructions to complete the installation.

Windows Update downloads and installs the selected updates on your PC.

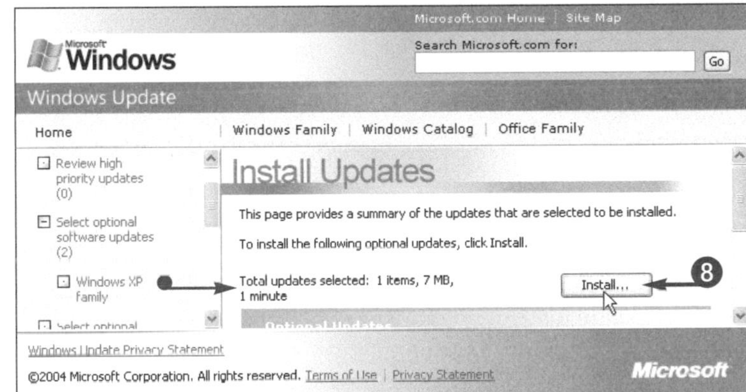

How can I learn more about an update before installing it?

▼ Windows Update displays two panes in Internet Explorer. In the left pane are links for each category of updates, such as software updates and hardware updates. When you click a link, the right pane displays links to the available updates. Click an update's link to display a brief description of it. Following the description is the Details link, which you can click to obtain additional information.

Should I just install all available updates to ensure that I do not miss out on anything?

▼ No. Install only the updates that provide components or features that you plan on using. Whenever you add functionality to Windows, you add to the Windows registry and consume additional hard disk storage space that your PC can use for other files. This contributes clutter that can negatively affect your PC's performance.

Can I view a list of updates I installed?

▼ Yes. You can view a list of updates in the Add or Remove Programs window. Click Start, Control Panel, and then click Add or Remove Programs. Scroll down to the bottom of the list to view Windows updates. If you install an update and find out later that you do not need it, you can uninstall it, as discussed in the section "Uninstall Windows Updates."

Schedule Windows Updates

You can schedule Windows updates so that Windows automatically checks for, downloads, and optionally installs updates while you are away from your PC. This enables Windows to perform this time-consuming chore without your assistance at a time when you do not need to use your PC. You can check for updates by performing the steps in the sections "Install Critical Windows Updates" and "Install Optional Windows Updates."

Windows Update provides four automatic update options:

Automatic (recommended) automatically downloads and installs updates every day or one day each week at a specified time.

Download updates for me, but let me choose when to install them automatically downloads the updates and displays an icon in the Windows system tray indicating that updates are available for installation.

Notify me but don't automatically download or install them checks for updates and notifies you when updates are available, so you can choose to download and install them at your convenience.

Turn off Automatic Updates disables automatic updates, so you need to remember to check for updates.

Schedule Windows Updates

1. Click Start.
2. Right-click My Computer.
3. Click Properties.

The System Properties dialog box appears.

4. Click the Automatic Updates tab.

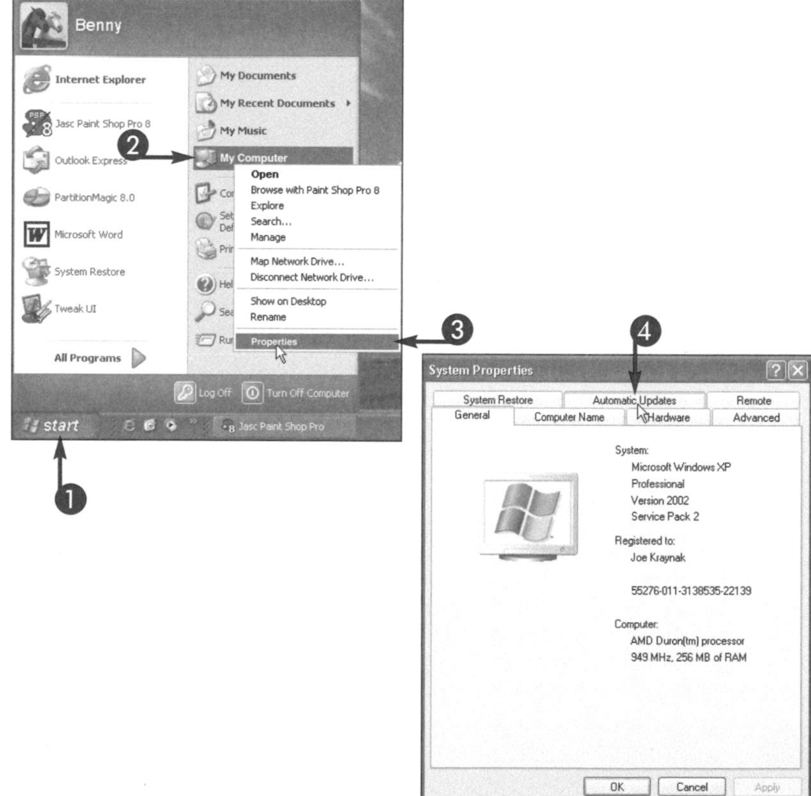

The Automatic Updates options appear.

Note: *This example uses the screen that appears for Windows XP Pro; options differ for different Windows versions.*

5 Click the desired update option (○ changes to ◉).

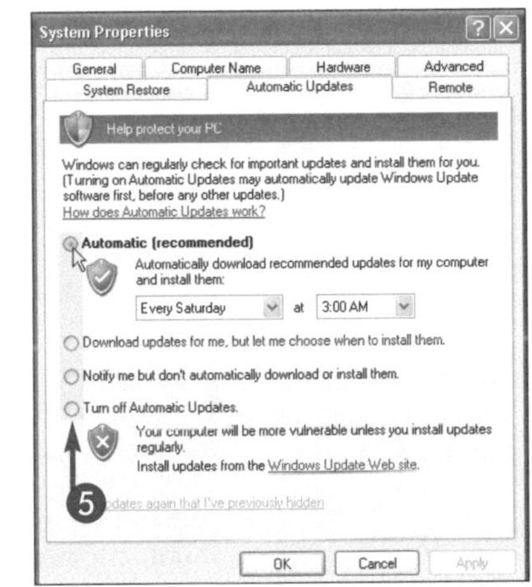

- If you selected Automatic (recommended), click here and click Every day or click the day of the week you want Windows Update to check for available updates.

6 Click here and select the time of day you want to check for updates.

7 Click OK.

Windows Update saves your preferences.

Note: *Your PC must be on at the scheduled time to have it download and install the updates.*

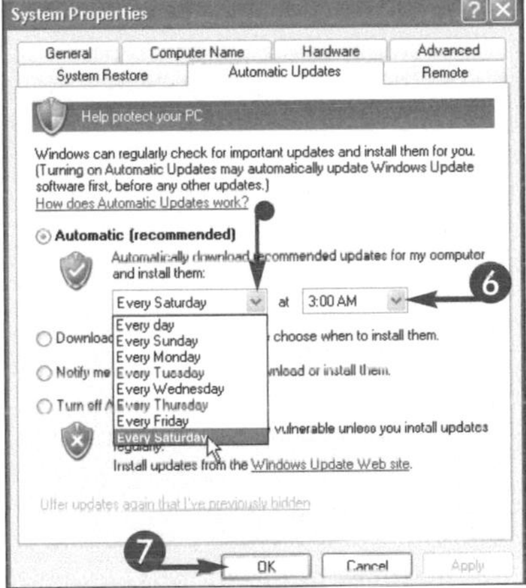

Are any other options available for installing updates automatically?

▼ Yes. If you choose the option to have Windows Update automatically download updates but not install them, Windows can install the updates when you shut down Windows. When you click Start, Turn Off Computer, and click Turn Off, Windows initiates the installation. When the installation is complete, Windows automatically shuts down your PC.

Can I learn more about automatic updates?

▼ Yes. In the System Properties dialog box, click the "How does Automatic Updates work?" or "Learn more about automatic updating" link. This opens the Windows Help window, which displays a description of the Automatic Updates feature and provides links to additional Automatic Updates topics. To learn more about Windows Security options, click Start, click All Programs, click Accessories, click System Tools, and then click Security Center.

A message appears indicating that I am not logged on as an administrator and cannot install the updates. What should I do?

▼ To install updates, you must log on using an administrator account. Log off Windows using the Start, Log Off command and then log on using an administrator account. Microsoft strongly recommends that you log on as an administrator only to configure Windows and install updates and other software. Otherwise, you can log on using a limited user account. See Chapter 28 for details.

Uninstall Windows Updates

Sometimes a Windows Update can cause problems. Other times, you may realize that you do not use an optional component that Windows Update installed. In either case, you can usually uninstall the Windows update to return your PC to its previous condition. You may also need to uninstall a Windows update if Windows Update installs a corrupt file. You can uninstall the update and then reinstall it to repair the installation.

When you install an update, Windows typically stores uninstall information, which contains previous Windows settings and a backup copy of any software that was replaced. As with other software you install, Windows adds the update to the Add or Remove Programs list. You can select the update, click the button for removing it or changing it, and then follow the on-screen instructions to uninstall the update.

If an update consists of installing a new version of a Windows component — for example, a new version of Internet Explorer — uninstalling typically replaces the new version with the previous version. Before installing an update, Windows usually creates a system restore point. If you encounter problems after uninstalling an update, you may need to restore your system, as discussed in Chapter 19.

Uninstall Windows Updates

1. Click Start.
2. Click Control Panel.

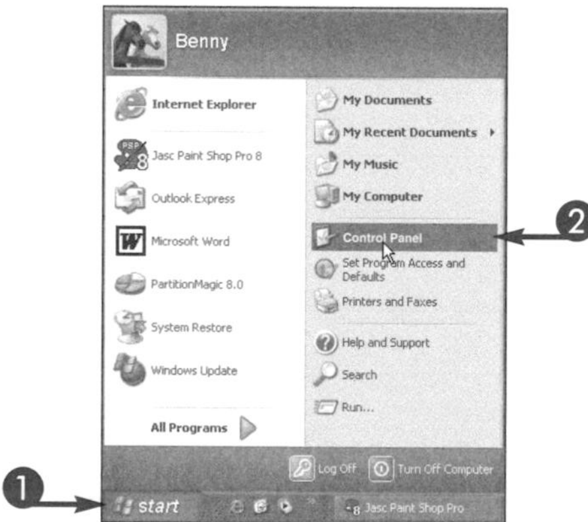

The Windows Control Panel appears.

3. Click Add or Remove Programs.

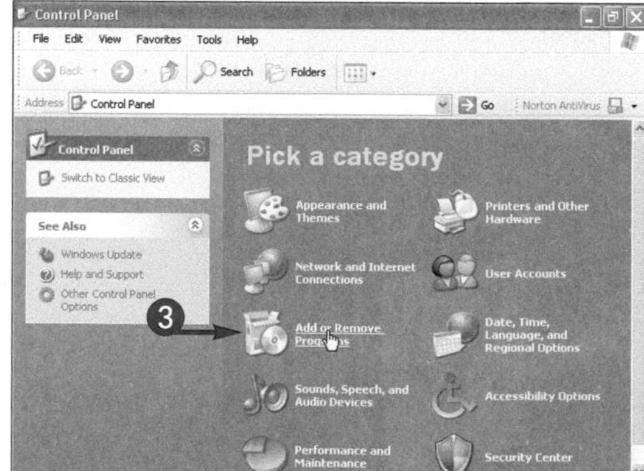

The Add or Remove Programs window appears, displaying a list of installed programs and Windows updates.

4. Scroll down to the list of Windows updates.
5. Click the update you want to uninstall.
6. Click Remove.

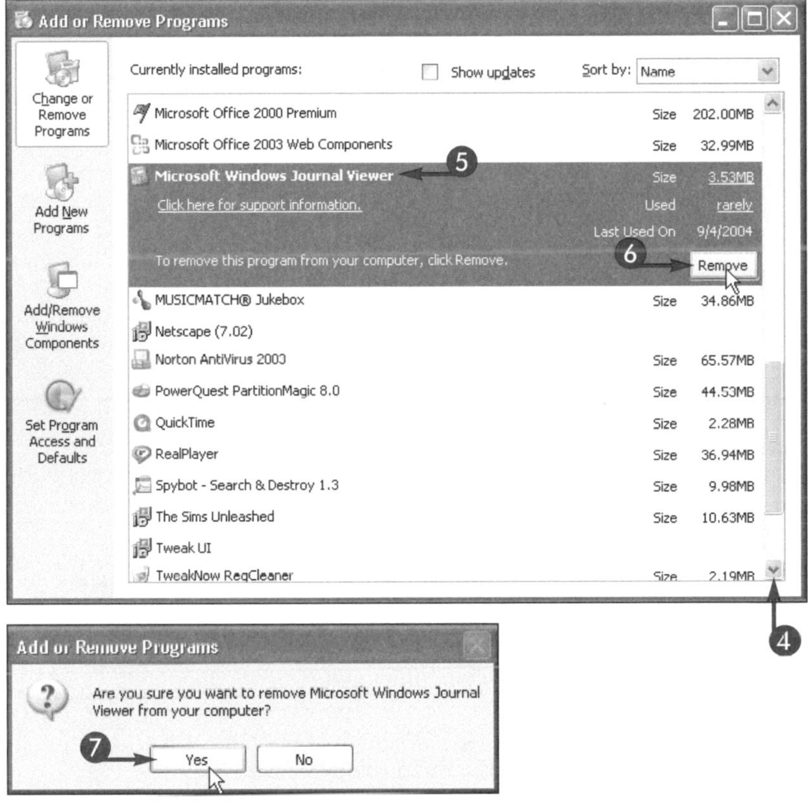

A dialog box appears, prompting you to confirm the deletion or providing instructions on how to proceed.

7. Follow the on-screen instructions to complete the removal process.

Windows uninstalls the update and returns your PC to its previous condition.

Can I view a list of all of the Windows updates I installed on my PC?

▼ Yes, but you must connect to the Internet in order to do so. Once connected, click Start, click All Programs, and then click Windows Update. Windows runs Internet Explorer, which loads the Windows Update page. In the left pane, click the View installation history link. A list of installed updates appears in the pane on the right. Scroll down to see a complete list of updates that are installed on your PC.

Add or Remove Programs had a long list of Windows updates before I installed Service Pack 2. Now it lists only Windows Service Pack 2. What happened to the other updates?

▼ If Windows Update installs an update that makes the other updates obsolete, it removes those previous updates from the Add or Remove Programs list. You do not need these items anymore, because the latest update makes them obsolete.

My installation history contains multiple updates, but I see only the Windows Service Pack in the Add or Remove Programs list. Where did the other updates go?

▼ If you install a service pack, such as Windows Service Pack 2, it may include multiple updates that Windows treats as a single update. When you choose to view the installation history, Windows Update shows all of the updates included in the service pack, but Windows does not enable you to uninstall individual updates.

Understanding Hardware Device Drivers

Each hardware device installed on your PC requires a device driver — software that enables Windows and your applications to communicate with the device. By understanding the role that device drivers play on your PC, how to check on them, and how to obtain updated device drivers, you can optimize the performance of each hardware device and enhance the overall performance of Windows.

Windows provides several features and utilities that enable you to inspect the device drivers installed on your PC, check their compatibility with Windows, and track down any device conflicts that may prevent one or more devices from functioning properly. Throughout this chapter, you learn how to use these tools to troubleshoot and repair any problems and make sure that Windows has the most current device drivers installed.

Installing Device Drivers

Your PC has several built-in hardware devices that are integral parts of the PC, including printer ports, USB ports, and disk drives. Windows typically installs drivers for these devices when Windows is installed on your PC. Whenever you connect a new device to your PC, such as a printer, mouse, external drive, or a new display adapter or monitor, Windows runs the Add New Hardware Wizard, which steps you through the process of installing a driver for the new device.

The Windows installation CD contains drivers for hundreds of Windows-compatible devices including printers, mice, keyboards, modems, network cards, display adapters, and monitors. In addition, a device may include its own drivers on a disk or CD.

When you install a new hardware device or connect a device to your PC, the Add New Hardware Wizard runs and searches Windows to determine if a compatible device driver is available. If it does not find a compatible driver on your system, it checks the CD and floppy disk drives for a disk or CD that includes the drivers and, if your PC is connected to the Internet, it checks Microsoft's Windows Web site for a compatible device driver. If the Add New Hardware Wizard locates an appropriate driver, it automatically installs it on your PC.

Signed and Unsigned Device Drivers

Microsoft tests device drivers to determine if they are Windows-compatible before approving their use and before including them on the Windows CD or on its Web site. Device drivers that Microsoft approves are called *signed* device drivers. Drivers that Microsoft has not approved are referred to as *unsigned*. To ensure trouble-free operation, Microsoft recommends that users install only signed drivers, although many unsigned drivers work fine.

The "Designed for Windows" Logo

To ensure that any new hardware you purchase is fully compatible with the version of Windows installed on your PC, Microsoft encourages you to look for hardware that has its seal of approval. For example, hardware that Microsoft approves for use with PCs running Windows XP has the Designed for Windows XP logo printed on the box and displayed in the Windows catalog.

However, some hardware that works perfectly well with your version of Windows may not have the Designed for Windows logo. In such cases, you can visit the manufacturer's Web site or contact the manufacturer to determine if the hardware and the device driver provided are compatible with the version of Windows installed on your PC. The installation instructions included with many devices include specific information indicating that it is safe to proceed with the device driver installation even if the Add New Hardware Wizard warns that the device is unsigned.

Obtaining Updated Device Drivers

Just as Microsoft continues to develop its Windows operating system after releasing it, hardware manufacturers continue to develop their device drivers after placing a device on the market in order to improve performance and address any compatibility issues. Manufacturers commonly make new drivers available on their Web sites. They may also provide Microsoft a copy of the new device driver to include in Windows Update.

To ensure that you have the most current device driver, you should run Windows Update, as discussed in Chapter 22. However, because manufacturers do not always provide Microsoft with updated drivers, you should also visit manufacturers' Web sites at least once a year and whenever a problem arises with a particular device. The section "Locate Updated Device Drivers" shows you where to look for updated device drivers. The section "Install an Updated Device Driver" shows you how to run the Add New Hardware Wizard to install updated drivers you obtain from a manufacturer or other source.

Obtaining and Installing Flash Updates

Some hardware devices, including modems, have built-in instructions that are stored on a flash ROM (read-only memory) chip. The instructions are called *firmware* because it is software that is built in to a hardware device. The device retains the firmware even if you turn off the power to the device. A flash ROM chip enables you to update the instructions by installing a flash upgrade, which typically consists of downloading and running a utility that updates the firmware. The flash upgrade burns new instructions into the flash ROM chip. The section "Install Flash Upgrades" demonstrates the process.

Check a Driver's Signature

The Windows Device Manager displays a list of all of the hardware devices that are installed on your PC. If you suspect that a device is not operating optimally or that it is causing problems with Windows or one or more of your applications, you may want to verify that the device has a signed device driver. Using Windows Device Manager, you can check the device driver to determine if the driver is signed. If the driver is not signed, then you may want to run Windows Update, as explained in Chapter 22, or download an updated, preferably signed, device driver from the manufacturer's Web site, as explained in the next section, "Locate Updated Device Drivers."

If you find a device driver that is unsigned, do not immediately remove the driver. An unsigned driver may be the only available driver for a device, particularly if the device is old and the manufacturer provides no updated driver for the current version of Windows or the device is new and Microsoft has not yet approved the driver. Removing a device driver disables the device. Make sure you have an updated driver available before removing the current driver.

For more on signed and unsigned drivers, see the section "Understanding Hardware Device Drivers."

Check a Driver's Signature

1. Click Start.
2. Right-click My Computer.
3. Click Properties.

The System Properties dialog box appears.

4. Click the Hardware tab.
5. Click Device Manager.

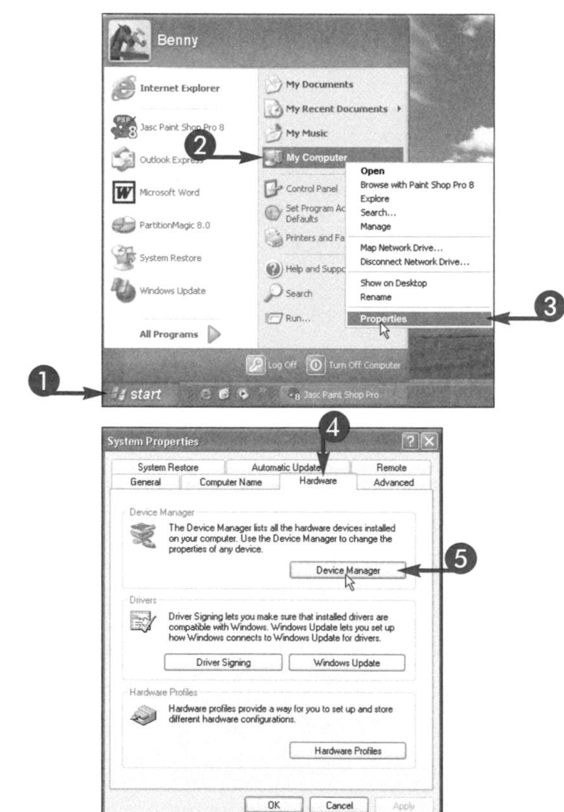

The Device Manager appears, displaying a list of installed hardware devices.

6 Click the plus sign (⊞) next to a hardware category to expand it.

7 Right-click a device.

8 Click Properties.

The Properties dialog box for the selected device appears.

9 Click the Driver tab.

- The Properties dialog box displays driver details, including information about the signature.
- You can click Uninstall to remove the driver, but make sure you have an updated driver available.

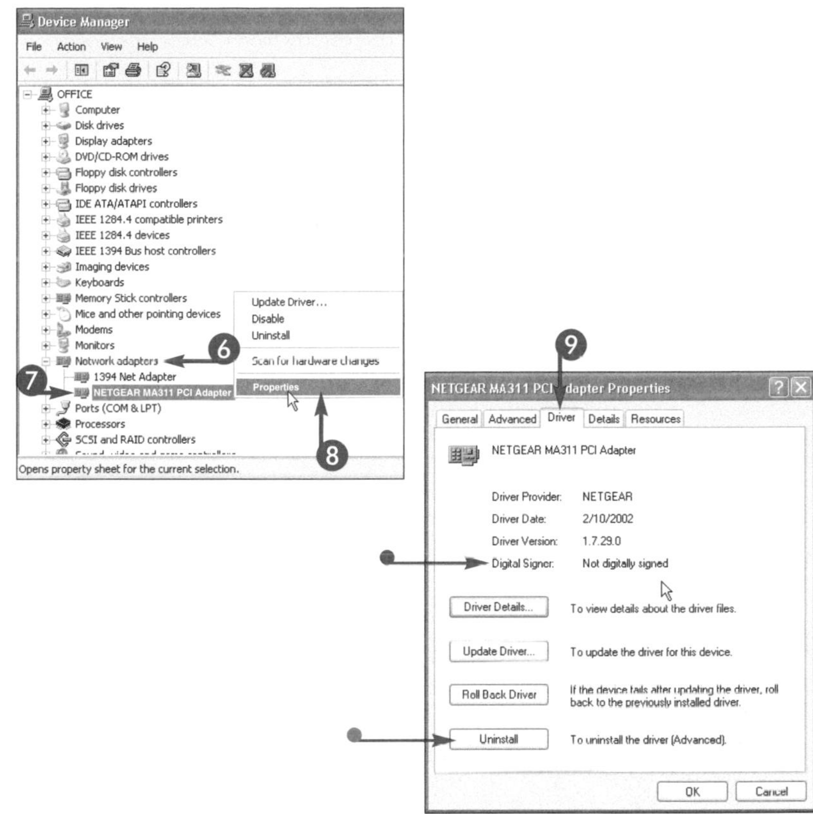

Can I prevent Windows from installing unsigned device drivers?

Yes. By default, Windows displays a warning whenever you attempt to install an unsigned device driver, but you can enter a setting to have Windows refuse to install unsigned drivers. Right-click My Computer and click Properties. Click the Hardware tab and then click Driver Signing. To prevent Windows from installing unsigned drivers, click the Block — Never install unsigned driver software option (○ changes to ◉). Click OK to save your changes.

Can I verify the signatures of Windows system files?

All Windows system files are digitally signed to help Windows determine if someone has tampered with the files. If you suspect that someone has gained unauthorized access to your PC and has tampered with the Windows system files, you can run File Signature Verification and check the files. Click Start, click Run, and then type **sigverif** and press Enter. When the File Signature Verification dialog box appears, click Start.

Can I verify the signatures of other application files?

Windows can check all of the files on your PC for a digital signature, but it does little good. Verification produces a long list of unsigned files, including files you created and application program files that developers rarely sign. However, if a technician suggests that you check a group of files, you can run File Signature Verification, as instructed in the previous tip, and click Advanced to enter preferences for checking all files in a particular folder.

Locate Updated Device Drivers

You can run Windows Update, as instructed in Chapter 22, to check for updated device drivers. Windows Update may find one or two device drivers that a manufacturer has updated and supplied to Microsoft. However, most manufacturers post their updated drivers on their own Web sites first. These drivers may not be available through Windows Update, so you should check the manufacturer's Web site.

Of course, all manufacturers set up their Web sites differently, so no set of instructions can cover the process of locating updated device drivers for all manufacturers. However, the process is similar for most manufacturers. You can use your Web browser to open the manufacturer's home page and then follow the links to the device that is installed on your PC. You may need to specify the product's name and model number. You can then click a link for technical support or a link specifically for obtaining updated device drivers. You can then download the device driver to your PC and follow the instructions in the next section, "Install an Updated Device Driver," to upgrade the device driver.

Locate Updated Device Drivers

1. Launch your Web browser.
2. Type the address of the manufacturer's Web site and press Enter.

   This example uses NETGEAR, a manufacturer of wireless networking hardware.

3. Click the link for technical support.

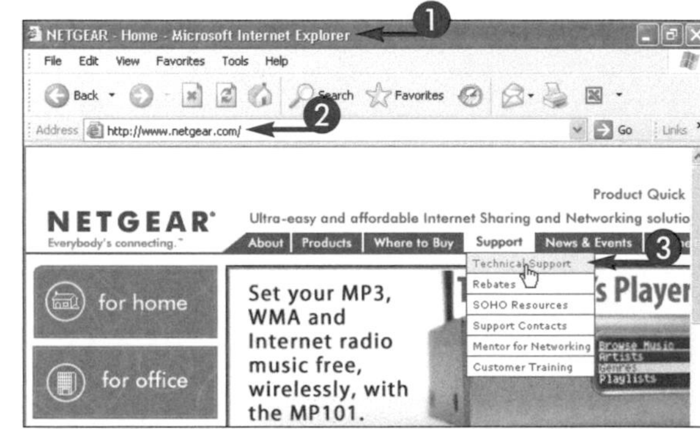

4. Select the product name and model number of the device for which you want an updated driver.
5. Click the link for the device driver version you want.

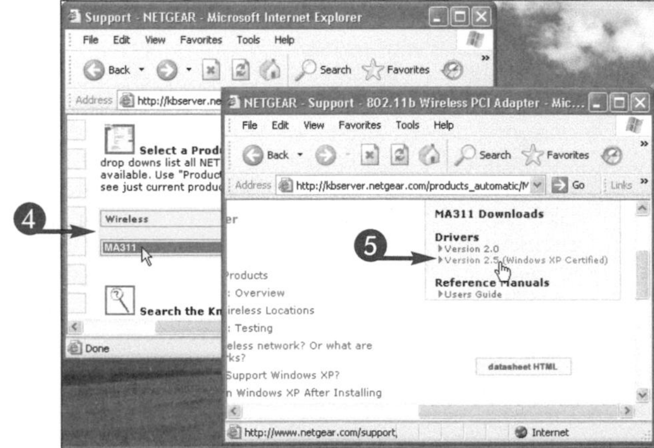

6 Click the link for the updated device driver.

The File Download dialog box appears.

7 Click Save.

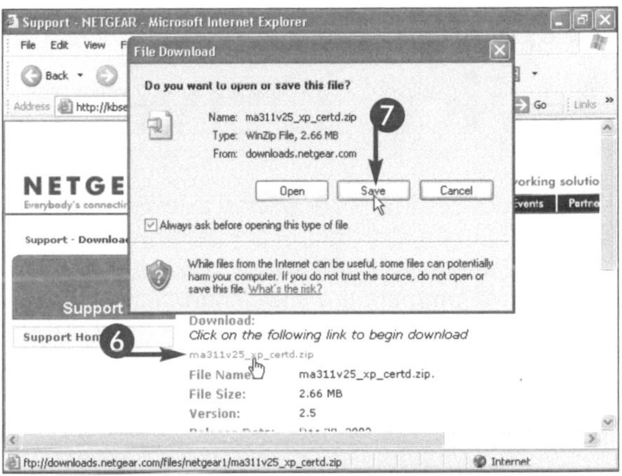

The Save As dialog box appears.

8 Navigate to the folder in which you want to save the updated device driver.

- You can click the New folder button (▢) to create a new folder inside the current folder.

9 Click Save.

Your Web browser downloads the updated device driver and saves it in the selected folder.

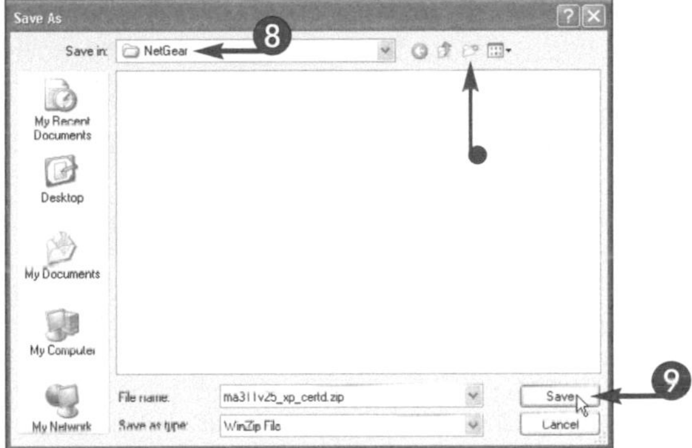

Is any Web site available where I can find updated device drivers for the most popular hardware?

▼ Yes. Several Web sites feature updated device drivers for a wide range of hardware. Drivers Headquarters at www.drivershq.com can even scan your PC and determine which devices have updated drivers available. To update your drivers, you must subscribe to the service for about $30. WinFiles.com also features updated Windows drivers and other utilities, although tracking down updated drivers can be a little difficult. WinGuides at www.winguides.com/drivers/ also provides a good collection of updated drivers. Many of these sites, however, require that you know what you need. A manufacturer's Web site often provides better guidance to help you pick the right driver.

Can I request that a manufacturer notify me of updated device drivers?

▼ Many manufacturers provide update notifications via e-mail, but you must register your hardware and sign up to receive the updates. Before registering for update notifications, read the manufacturer's privacy policy carefully to ensure that the manufacturer does not share your e-mail address with other companies and that you can opt out of receiving the e-mail notifications at any time. You do not want to register for e-mail notifications if by registering you agree to receive spam. Most manufacturers let you choose to receive only product updates and recalls, so the e-mail you receive from them is minimal.

Install an Updated Device Driver

Some device drivers are offered as executable program files that you can run like any installation routine; you can double-click the file and follow the on-screen instructions to complete the installation. Some drivers are distributed in zipped files that you must extract before you can install the drivers. Others are distributed as INF files that you can install by using the Windows Add New Hardware Wizard or by choosing to update the device driver.

If you obtain a device driver from a manufacturer's Web site, explore the page that describes the driver to determine if instructions are available, and then follow the manufacturer's instructions. If the manufacturer offers an executable program file that you can run to install the driver, you need little in the way of instructions. Simply double-click the file and follow the on-screen instructions. If the file is a compressed zip file, double-click the file and extract its contents; if it contains an executable program file, you can double-click the file to install the driver. If the file does not contain an executable program file, then take the steps in this section to replace the current driver with the updated driver.

Install an Updated Device Driver

1 Display the Properties dialog box for the device for which you want to install an updated driver.

Note: *Refer to the section "Check a Driver's Signature" for details.*

2 Click the Driver tab.

3 Click Update Driver.

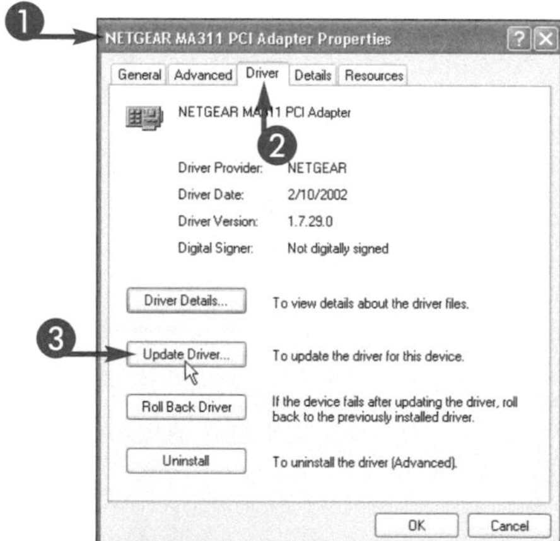

The Hardware Update Wizard appears, asking if you want to connect to Windows Update to check for updated drivers.

4 Click the No, not this time option (○ changes to ◉).

3 Click Next.

The wizard asks if you want to install the software automatically or specify a location where the driver is stored.

6 Click the Install from a list or specific location (Advanced) option (○ changes to ◉).

7 Click Next.

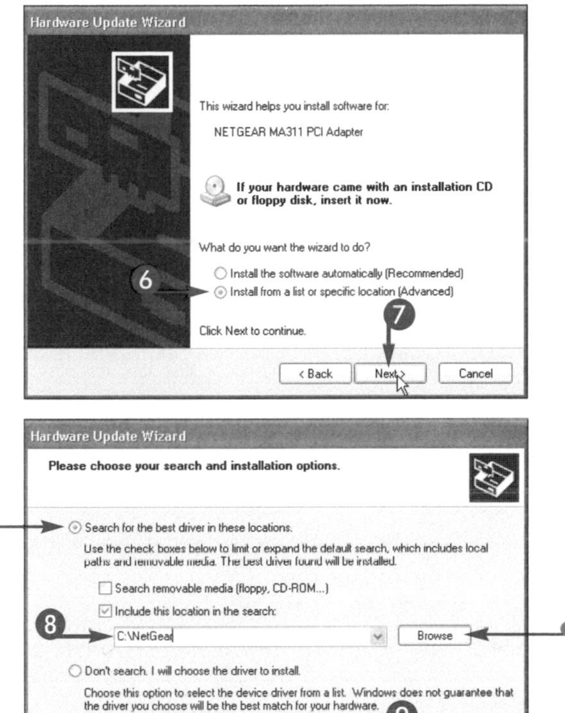

- The Wizard prompts you to specify where you want it to search for a driver.

8 Click here and type the location of the driver files.

- You can click Browse to select the folder from a list.

9 Click Next and follow the on-screen instructions to complete the installation.

The Hardware Update Wizard installs the driver from the specified location.

Can I just click the option to have the Hardware Update Wizard install the software automatically?

▼ No. The Hardware Update Wizard does not search your PC thoroughly for updated drivers. It can search a disk in the floppy disk drive or a CD, but it does not search the folders on the hard drive. You must specify the location of the folder in which the driver files are stored. If you choose the option to install the software automatically, the Hardware Update Wizard displays a message indicating that it cannot locate a newer version of the software. Click Back, and then click the Install from a list or specific location option (○ changes to ◉).

I installed the most current device driver, but the previous driver seemed to have worked better. Can I return to using the previous driver?

▼ Yes. Windows provides a rollback option for device drivers. Right-click My Computer and click Properties. Click the Hardware tab and then click Device Manager. Click the plus sign (⊞) next to the hardware category that contains the device. Right-click the device and click Properties. Click the Driver tab and then click the Roll Back Driver button. You may notice that the Driver tab also includes an Update Driver button. This button offers another way to run the Update Hardware Wizard to update drivers.

Check for Device Driver Conflicts

If two hardware devices are set up to use the same resources, the devices conflict, disabling one or both devices, or causing Windows or applications that use one of the devices to crash. The Device Manager gives a complete list of hardware devices installed on your PC. Next to any conflicting devices, Device Manager displays a warning icon indicating that you must take some action to resolve the conflict.

If two devices conflict, you can adjust the settings for one or both devices to ensure that they use different resources. *Resources* consist of areas of memory reserved for the device and interrupt requests (IRQs). An IRQ is a channel that the device uses to request the attention of the processor. If too many devices use the same reserved portion of memory or the same interrupt, communications become crossed, resulting in communications errors.

Adjusting the system resources for a device can often lead to conflicts with other devices, so the best course of action in most cases is to remove one of the devices and then let Windows reinstall the device, as explained in the next section, "Reinstall Device Drivers."

Check for Device Driver Conflicts

1. Click Start.
2. Right-click My Computer.
3. Click Properties.

The System Properties dialog box appears.

4. Click the Hardware tab.
5. Click Device Manager.

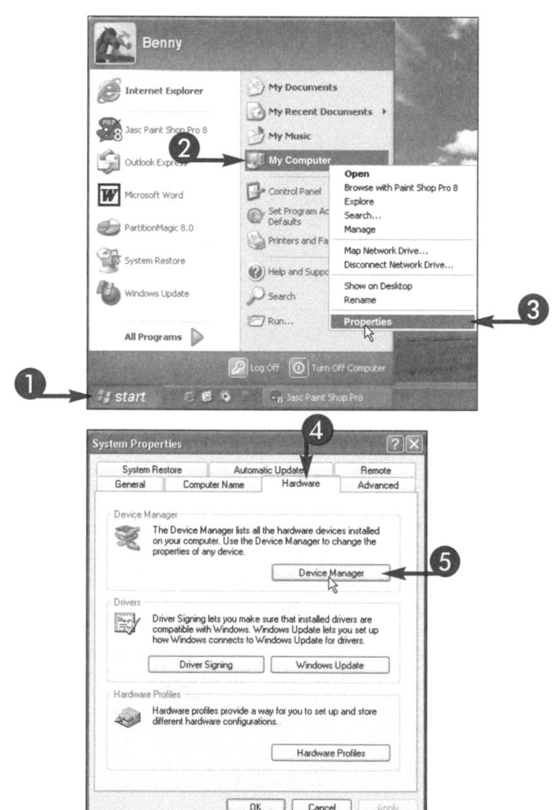

The Device Manager appears, displaying a list of hardware categories.

- If a device is not operating properly because of a conflict or other problem, a caution icon ( ) appears next to one or both devices.
- You can right-click a device and click Properties.
- In this example, the device cannot start.

In some cases, the Properties dialog box contains a Resources tab that displays the memory addresses and IRQ used for the device.

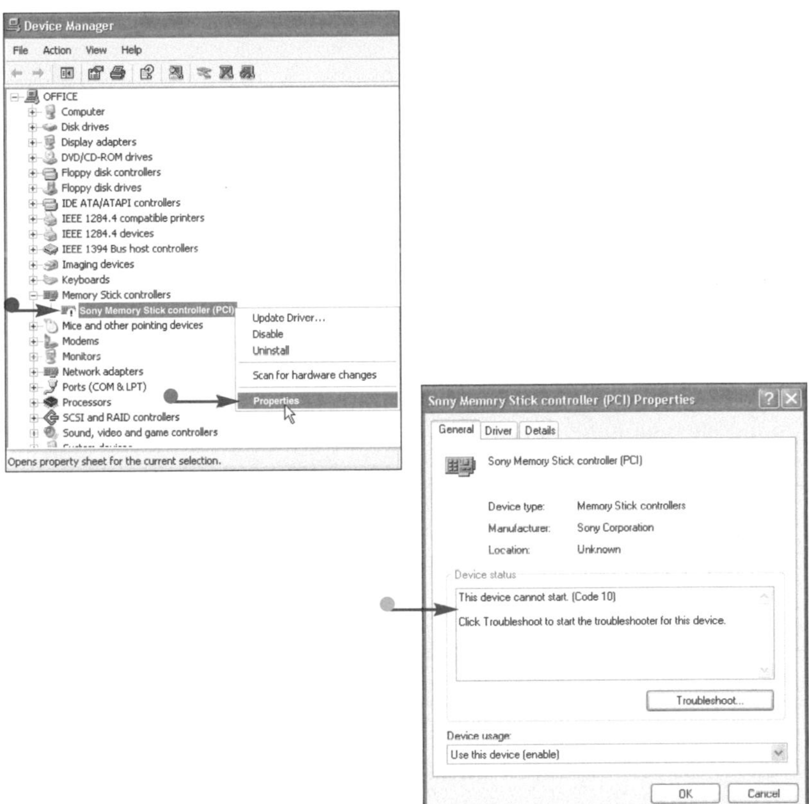

I have three devices that use the same IRQ. Should I try a different IRQ for one of the devices?

▼ Most PCs manufactured in the past five years enable several devices to share the same IRQ without conflict. Your PC and Windows are probably set up to automatically assign IRQs to devices in a way that avoids conflicts. You may be able to resolve a conflict by assigning a different IRQ to a device, but this may also cause conflicts with other devices. You may have better luck removing the device and reinstalling it. To remove a device, you do not physically disconnect it from the PC. You simply reinstall its device driver, as explained in the section "Reinstall Device Drivers."

I connected a device and then installed its driver, but the device is not working properly. Did I do something wrong?

▼ Perhaps. In some cases, you can plug in a device, start Windows, follow the on-screen instructions to install the device driver, and the device works fine. In other cases, the manufacturer may suggest that you install the device driver before connecting the device. If you connected the device first, and then installed the driver, try installing the driver first and then connecting the device. The next section, "Reinstall Device Drivers," shows you how to remove and replace a nonfunctioning driver.

Reinstall Device Drivers

When Windows Device Manager has a conflict between two devices, it displays a caution icon next to one or both of the devices. You can reinstall the driver for one of the devices to eliminate the conflict in most cases.

Reinstalling a device driver consists of removing a device from the list of devices in Device Manager and then allowing Windows to reinstall the device. Removing a device usually does not require that you disconnect the device from your PC. When you remove a device in Device Manager, Windows deletes its device driver. You can then use the Add New Hardware Wizard to search for the device and reinstall its device driver, which frequently resolves the conflict.

Some manufacturers recommend that you install the device driver before connecting the device to your PC. In these cases, the manufacturer usually supplies a program file that you can run to install the driver when the device is disconnected. You can then shut down your PC, connect the device, and restart your PC to install the device.

The steps in this section show how to reinstall a device driver with the Add New Hardware Wizard.

Reinstall Device Drivers

1. Click Start.
2. Right-click My Computer.
3. Click Properties.

- The System Properties dialog box appears.

4. Click the Hardware tab.
5. Click Device Manager.

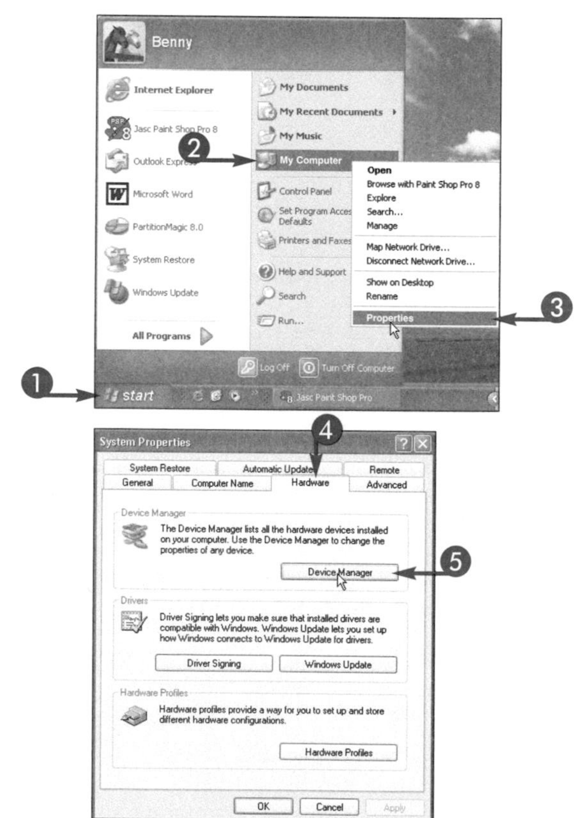

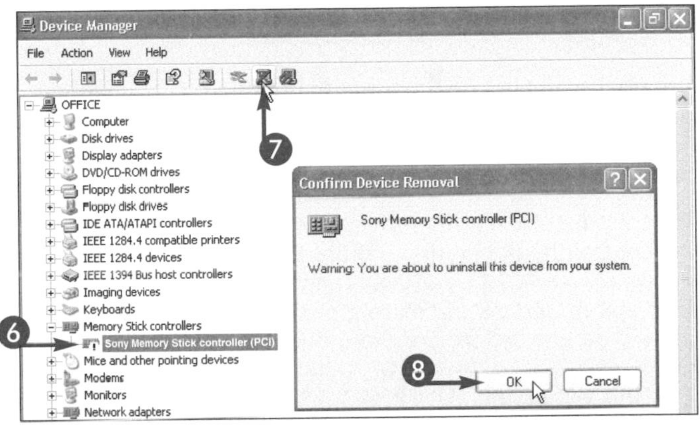

The Device Manager appears.

6 Click the device that has a [icon] next to it.

7 Click the Uninstall button ([icon]).

The Confirm Device Removal dialog box appears.

8 Click OK.

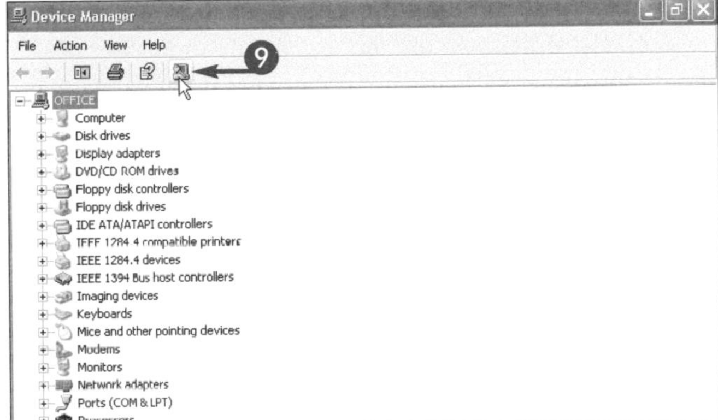

Device Manager removes the device from its list.

9 Click the Scan for hardware changes button ([icon]).

Windows scans your PC for uninstalled hardware devices and automatically installs the required device drivers.

I uninstalled the driver for a device that is connected to my PC and then scanned my PC for new hardware, but Device Manager did not identify the device. What should I do?

▼ Check the device to ensure that it is properly connected to your PC and that it is turned on, if necessary, and then run the scan again. If Device Manager does not identify the device, shut down Windows, turn off your PC, and restart your PC. When Windows starts, it scans your PC for new hardware and typically leads you through the process of installing a new driver. If that does not work, run the Add New Hardware Wizard. To run the wizard, click Start, Control Panel, Printers and Other Hardware, and then Add Hardware.

Can I disable a driver to determine if it is conflicting with another driver or causing other problems?

▼ Yes. One of the most useful features in Device Manager is that it allows you to temporarily disable a device without uninstalling its driver. Disabling a device is a very useful technique for troubleshooting conflicts. To disable a device, display its icon in Device Manager, and then right-click the icon and click Disable. A red X appears ([icon]) on the icon indicating that the device is disabled. To enable the device, right-click its icon again and click Enable. Do not disable critical components, such as the processor or disk drive controllers. When troubleshooting conflicts, focus on peripherals, such as modems, network adapters, and USB ports.

Install Flash Upgrades

Some devices, such as modems and network adapters, include their own built-in instructions that control their operation. Often, these instructions are stored on a flash ROM (read-only memory) chip, which enables you to update the instructions by installing a flash upgrade. The instructions are often referred to as *firmware.*

If a manufacturer offers a flash upgrade for one of the devices installed on your PC, you can install the flash upgrade to fix bugs and often improve the performance of the device. Many modems use flash upgrades to enable you to take advantage of new communications technologies without having to replace the modem. Installing a flash upgrade essentially provides you with a new modem that is capable of communicating at higher speeds.

Many devices support flash updates, including CD and DVD burners, MP3 players, and USB2 and FireWire hard drive controllers. To determine if flash ROM updates are available, visit the manufacturer's Web site for each device you own and search the technical support area for flash ROM updates. Flash ROM updates are usually offered as compressed ZIP files or executable program files. You simply run the update utility as you run any program, and it leads you through the process of installing the update.

Install Flash Upgrades

1. Launch your Web browser.
2. Navigate to the page that contains the flash ROM upgrade.
3. Click the link to the flash ROM upgrade file.

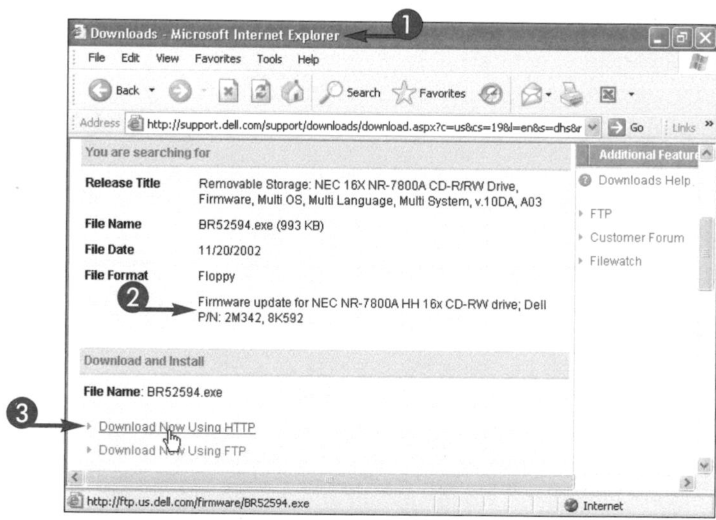

The File Download dialog box appears.

4. Click Save.

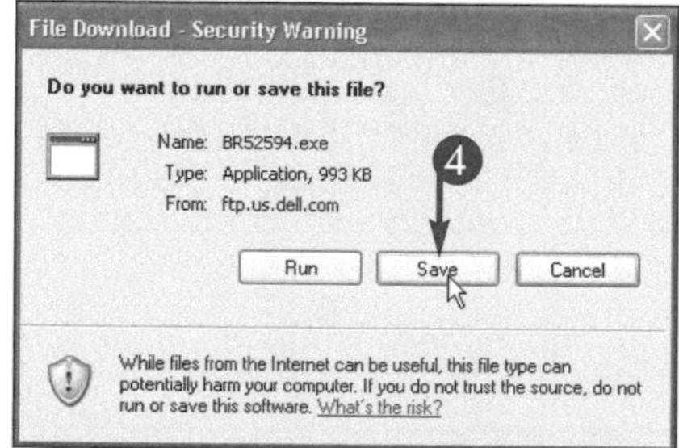

The Save As dialog box appears.

5 Navigate to the folder in which you want to save the flash ROM upgrade file.

- You can click [new folder icon] to create a new folder.

6 Click Save.

Your Web browser downloads the file and saves it in the selected folder.

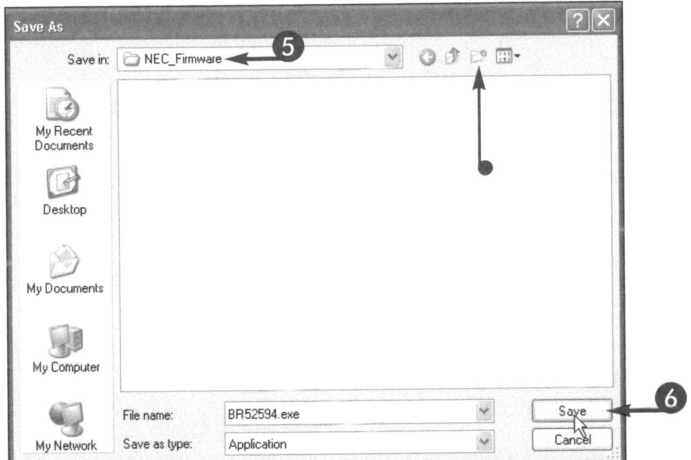

7 Navigate to the folder that contains the flash ROM upgrade file.

8 Double-click the file and follow the on-screen instructions to install the flash ROM upgrade.

The flash ROM upgrade utility upgrades the device by installing a new set of instructions on the ROM chip.

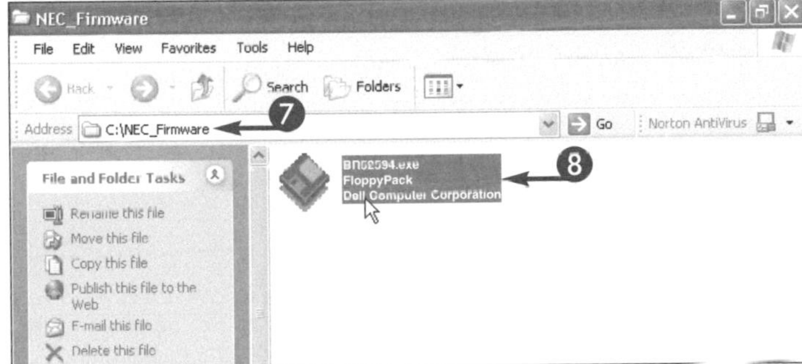

How can I find out if a flash ROM upgrade is available for a device installed on my PC?

▼ You need to do some detective work. If you purchased a PC from a major PC manufacturer such as Dell, Gateway, or IBM, you may be able to obtain information about available flash ROM updates on the manufacturer's Web site. For example, at Dell's Web site, you can enter the service number that is printed on the side of the PC to view a complete list of driver updates and flash ROM (firmware) upgrades for devices that are commonly installed on the model you own. You need to carefully select updates and upgrades, however, because the list may include devices that are not installed on your PC.

I found a flash BIOS for my PC. What is a flash BIOS, and should I install it?

▼ A flash BIOS installs firmware for a PC's motherboard. The BIOS (Basic Input/Output System) controls all communications among the processor, memory, and the devices installed on your PC. Installing the wrong BIOS update can cause serious problems, so before installing a flash BIOS, make sure you know your PC's current BIOS name and version number and make sure you have the correct BIOS update for your motherboard. Refer to Chapter 12 for additional information about the system BIOS and your system's CMOS settings.

Check for Updates Through Menus

Software manufacturers continue to develop their software long after they release it to the market to remove imperfections and improve performance. You can optimize your PC by ensuring that you have the latest updates for the software installed on your PC. Chapter 22 provides instructions on downloading and installing Windows updates. You can also download and install updates for the applications, games, utilities, and other programs that you commonly use.

Although some programs automatically check for updates, via the Internet, most programs include an option on one of their menus for obtaining software updates or for connecting to the developer's Web site where you can obtain information about the program. The Web site often includes one or more links for obtaining updates or add-ons. Most manufacturers offer updates free to registered users.

The steps you take to update your software over the Internet vary depending on the software and on how the manufacturer configures the update procedure. In most cases, you download an executable update file and run it on your PC. The installation routine automatically detects the location of the current version of the software and updates it for you. However, steps vary, so follow the manufacturer's instructions.

Check for Updates Through Menus

1. Launch the software you want to update.
2. Click the menu that contains an option for obtaining software updates or visiting the developer's Web site.

Note: *In most programs, you click Help.*

3. Click the option to check for updates or to visit the developer's Web site.

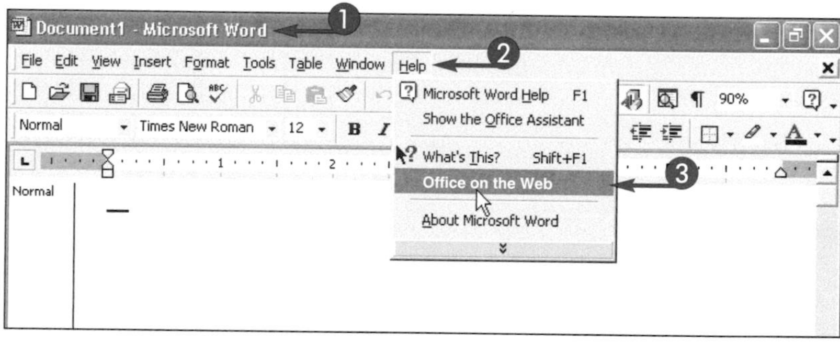

In this example, the program launches your Web browser and connects you to the developer's Web site.

4. Click the link to check for program updates.

Note: *You may need to click a series of links to reach an area that provides program updates.*

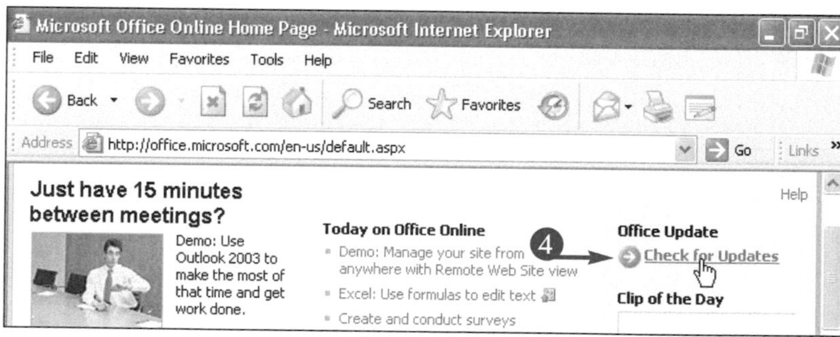

The Web site displays information about available updates.

5 Click the link for downloading the update.

The File Download dialog box appears.

6 Click Run or Open.

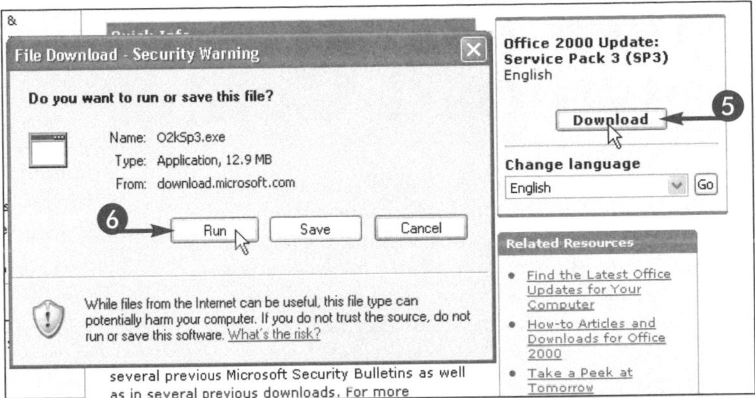

Your Web browser downloads the update file and initiates the installation routine.

Note: *If the file is a compressed ZIP file, you may need to extract the files first and then run the installation routine.*

The installation routine updates your program.

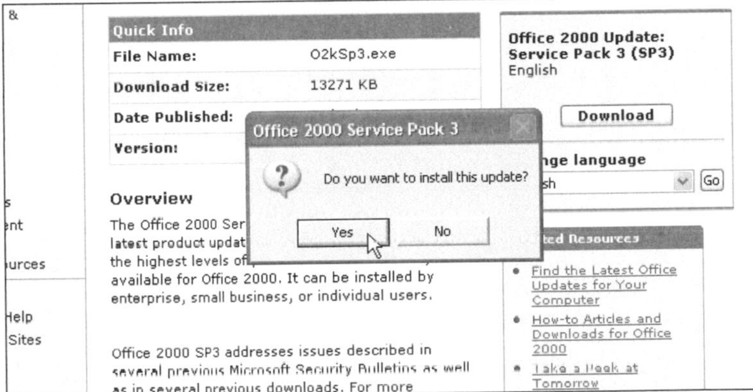

The program I want to update has no Help menu option for updating the software. What should I do?

▼ First, check the other menus for software update or technical support options or for connecting to the developer's Web site. Some programs have a Tools or Options menu that contains such commands. You can also go directly to the manufacturer's Web site, as shown in the following section, "Check Microsoft's Download Center."

When I checked for updates, the Web site indicated that I must order a new version of the program. What should I do?

▼ Some programs feature a menu option that leads you to a page for the latest version of the program, where you can usually order the current version online. However, if you are satisfied with the version currently installed on your PC, look for a technical support page for your version of the program to determine if any free updates are available.

Do I need to check for program updates for my antivirus software?

▼ Most antivirus utilities have an automatic update feature that downloads virus definition updates and program updates on a regular basis, typically once a week. This ensures that the antivirus utility can protect your PC against the most current viruses and other threats. Chapter 27 discusses antivirus utilities in greater detail and shows you how to enable automatic updates.

Check Microsoft's Download Center

Some software developers have Web sites that typically feature product information, technical support, and program updates. At these sites, you can often download program updates for free. Some manufacturers also offer add-ons, such as additional templates or tools that add functionality or make the program more useful.

Although Microsoft includes a command in most of its programs for obtaining updates, it also provides a separate area on its Web site called the Microsoft Download Center, which functions as a central location for obtaining all Microsoft program updates. The steps in this section show how to search for program updates at the Microsoft Download Center.

You can find program updates on most other software developer sites, but you may need to do a little searching to locate the updates. In most cases, you can go to a technical support area and select the program and version number to visit an area that provides technical support for the program along with any available program updates. If you have trouble tracking down a developer's Web site, use your favorite Web search tool to search for the developer or the program name.

Check Microsoft's Download Center

1. Launch your Web browser.
2. In the Address bar, type **www.microsoft.com/downloads** and press Enter.
3. Click here and select the software for which you want to locate updates.
   - You can type keywords here, such as a version number, to limit the search.
4. Click Go.

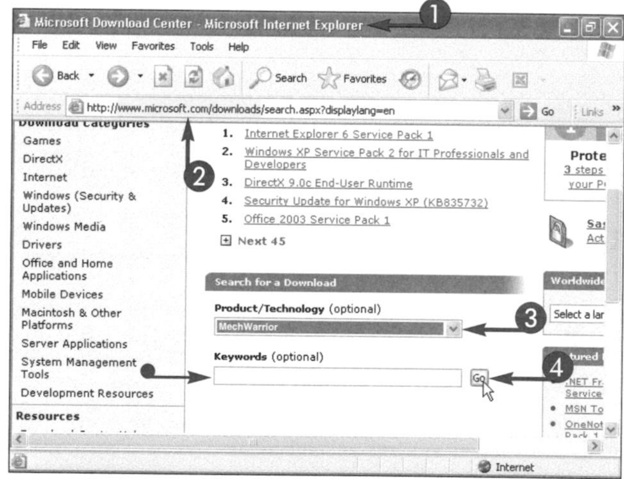

Microsoft Download Center displays a list of available software updates.

5. Click the link for the software update you want to download.

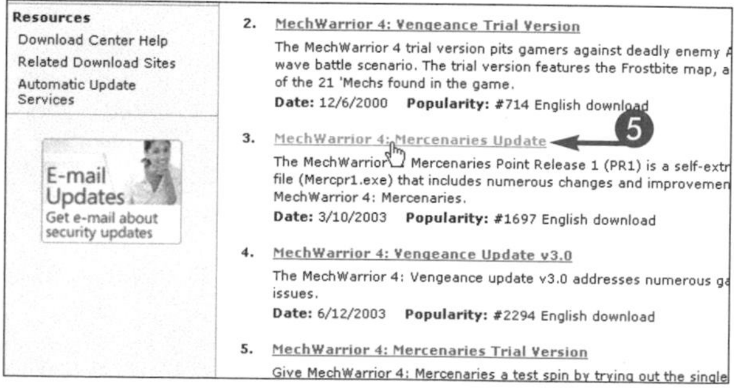

Microsoft Download Center displays an overview of the update and notes about the installation.

6. Click the button for downloading the update.

   The File Download dialog box appears.

7. Click Save.

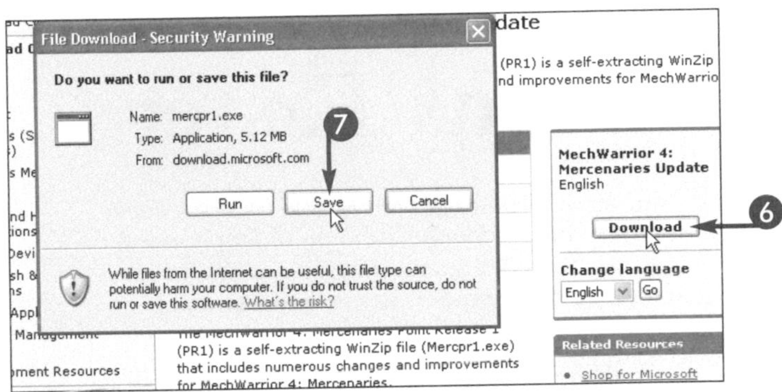

The Save As dialog box appears.

8. Navigate to the folder in which you want the downloaded file stored.

9. Click Save.

   Your Web browser downloads the file and saves it to the selected folder.

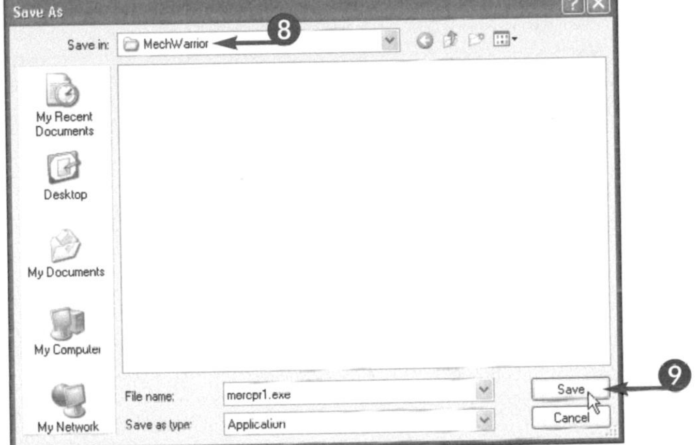

Is there a site where I can obtain software updates for popular programs?

▼ Yes. Some Web sites, including the Software Patch at www.softwarepatch.com, provide links to software patches and other updates for Windows and popular games and applications. They also feature updated device drivers. When you register your software, many developers offer you the option of receiving e-mail notification of software updates. This is another good way to stay informed and keep your software current.

The download site prompts me to enter the version number of the program. How can I determine the version number?

▼ In most programs, you can click Help and then click the About option to display a dialog box that includes the version number. In some cases, the About dialog box also includes the license or registration number. This number can come in handy if you registered a product that includes a lifetime of free upgrades.

I connected to a site that claims it has a patch for a program installed on my PC. What is a patch?

▼ A patch is a software update designed to repair a known problem, or bug, in a program or enhance program security. If a patch is available for a program installed on your PC, you should install the patch to ensure that your program does not crash, conflict with other programs, or enable unauthorized access to your PC or the data stored on it.

Run Older Programs Faster

Windows XP is much more capable than previous versions of Windows at running older programs commonly called *legacy programs*. If you have trouble running an older program, or you want to try making it run faster, you can adjust the program's compatibility settings in Windows XP. Older versions of Windows do not offer this option.

Compatibility settings enable you to select a version of Windows you want Windows XP to emulate when running the program. For example, you can choose to run the program in Windows 95, Windows 98/Me, or Windows NT/2000 mode. If you upgraded from one of these versions of Windows and the program ran better under that version, try selecting the version that ran it best.

Windows XP's compatibility settings also enable you to specify the number of screen colors and the screen resolution you want to use for the program's display. You can also disable visual themes and turn off advanced text services for a program to simplify the program's operation. The steps in this task show you how to adjust compatibility settings in Windows XP, but you may need to experiment with different configurations to find the optimal configuration for a particular program.

Run Older Programs Faster

1. Launch My Computer.
2. Navigate to the folder that contains the program's executable file.
3. Right-click the program's executable file.
4. Click Properties.

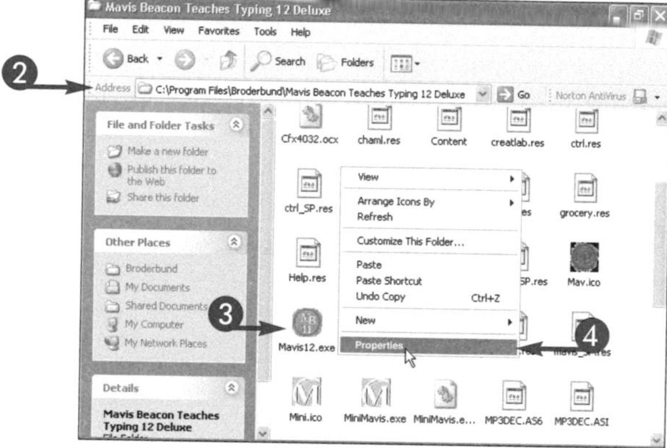

The Properties dialog box for the selected program file appears.

5. Click the Compatibility tab.
6. Click the Run this program in compatibility mode for *?* option, where *?* is the program name (☐ changes to ☑).
7. Click here and click the Windows version you want Windows XP to emulate when running the program.

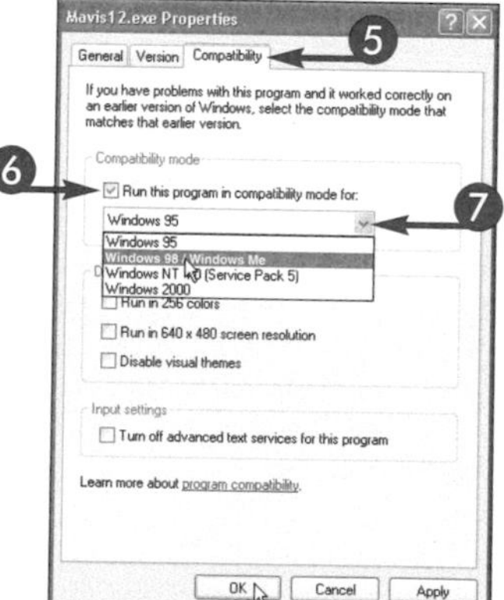

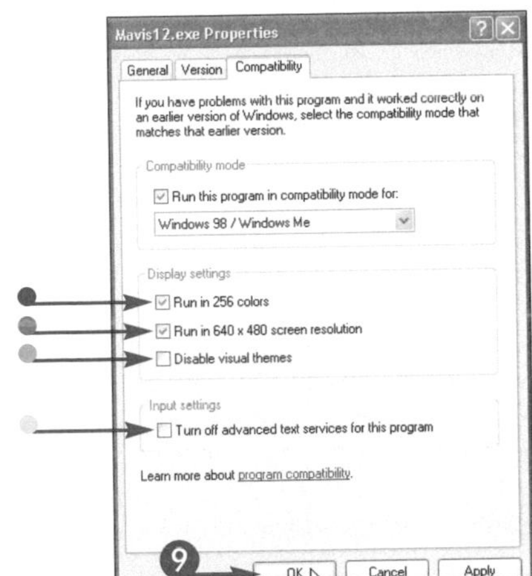

8 Click the settings that apply to your situation (☐ changes to ☑).

- This option displays the program in the minimal number of colors.
- This option runs the program in the lowest screen resolution.
- This option disables visual themes, which may cause problems with menus or buttons.
- This option disables any text services that may cause problems with the program's display.

9 Click OK.

Windows saves the settings and returns you to My Computer.

- You can double-click the program icon to test the program with its new settings.

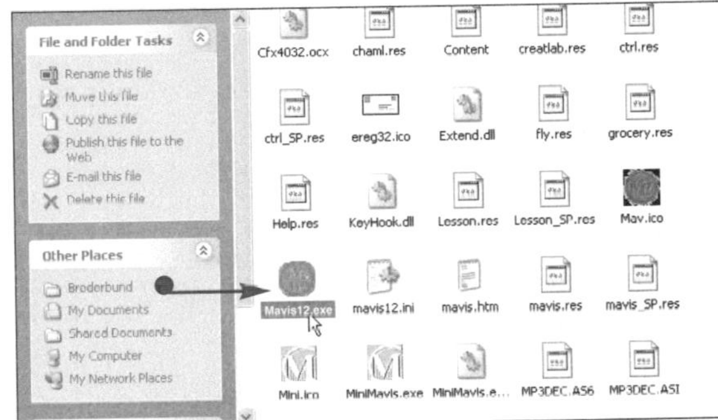

Does Windows 98 or Windows Me provide similar options for older programs?

Windows 98 and Me do not feature a Compatibility tab for program files. However, if you have trouble running an older program that was designed to run in DOS rather than Windows, you can choose to run it in MS-DOS mode. Right-click the program file, click Properties, the Program tab, and then the Advanced button. In the Advanced Program Settings dialog box, click the MS-DOS mode option (☐ changes to ☑). If you still have trouble running the program, you may need to create a custom MS-DOS configuration. Consult the program's technical support for help.

Can I obtain additional information about program compatibility in Windows XP?

Yes. You can search the Windows Help system for additional information. Even better, you can run the Program Compatibility Wizard and let it step you through the process of configuring a legacy program. Click Start, click All Programs, click Accessories, and then click the Program Compatibility Wizard. The Program Compatibility Wizard is part of the Windows Help system. It enables you to pick the program you want to configure and then test it with different configurations to find the optimal settings for the program. If you have trouble installing a legacy program, you can run the Program Compatibility Wizard on the installation file.

Optimize Multimedia Applications

Windows supports DirectX, a technology that enables multimedia applications to take full advantage of the high-end multimedia hardware installed on your PC. You can ensure that your PC has the latest version of DirectX installed by installing available Windows updates, as discussed in Chapter 22. In addition, you can use Windows DirectX Diagnostic Tool to ensure that all of your multimedia hardware is working properly and that acceleration is enabled for all of those devices that support it.

When you run Windows DirectX Diagnostic Tool, it goes online to obtain information about your multimedia hardware and checks to make sure that the device drivers are digitally signed. The DirectX Diagnostic Tool displays several tabs full of options for testing your multimedia hardware and adjusting the settings. If you know DirectX terminology and understand the technology, you can use the information to troubleshoot problems and fully optimize your system. If you have no knowledge of DirectX, the DirectX Diagnostic Tool can help you learn. It also provides some tools that require little knowledge to use, including a More Help tab that features several automated DirectX troubleshooters.

Optimize Multimedia Applications

1. Click Start.
2. Click Run.

The Run dialog box appears.

3. Type **dxdiag**.
4. Click OK or press Enter.

The DirectX Diagnostic Tool dialog box appears, asking if you want to check DirectX files for digital signatures.

5. Click Yes.

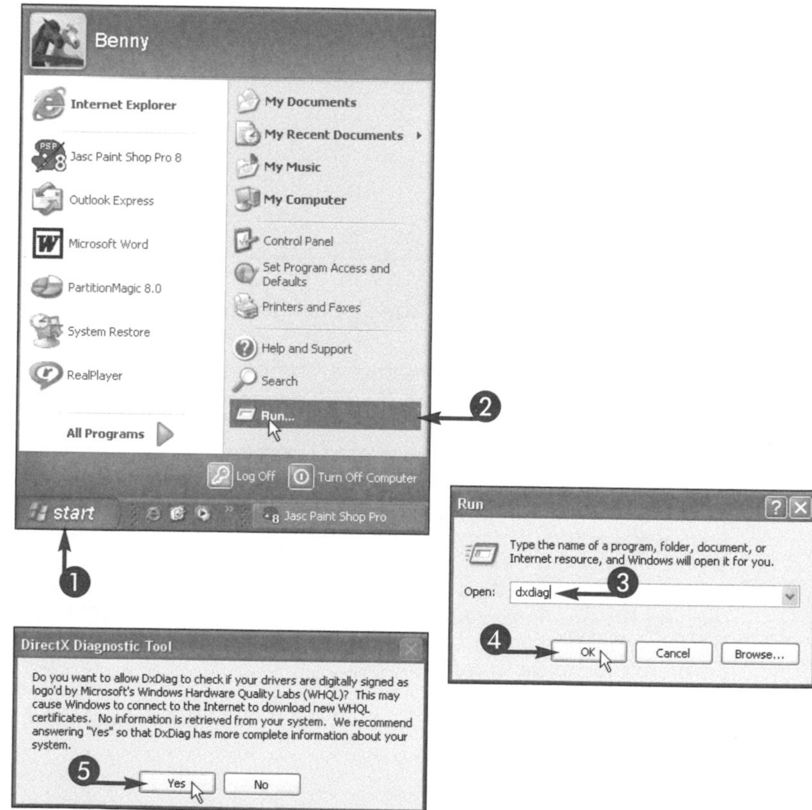

The DirectX Diagnostic Tool appears.

6 Click the tab for a device you want to examine.

- You can click a Test button to test the performance of a device.
- If the device fails a test, you can disable or decrease the acceleration and try testing the device again.

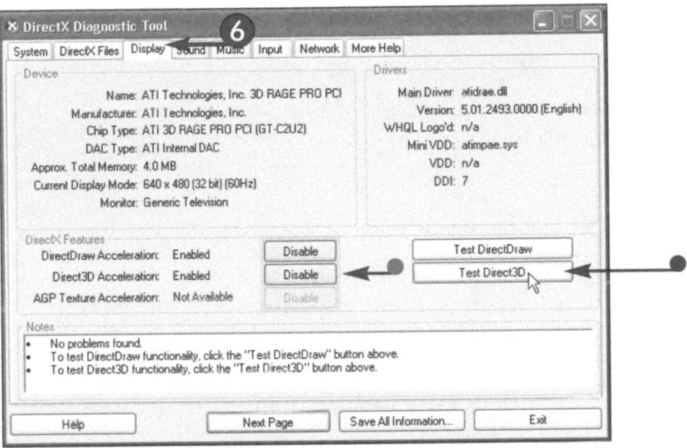

7 Click the More Help tab.

- You can click a button to run one of the automated troubleshooters.

8 When you are done, click Exit.

The DirectX Diagnostic Tool closes.

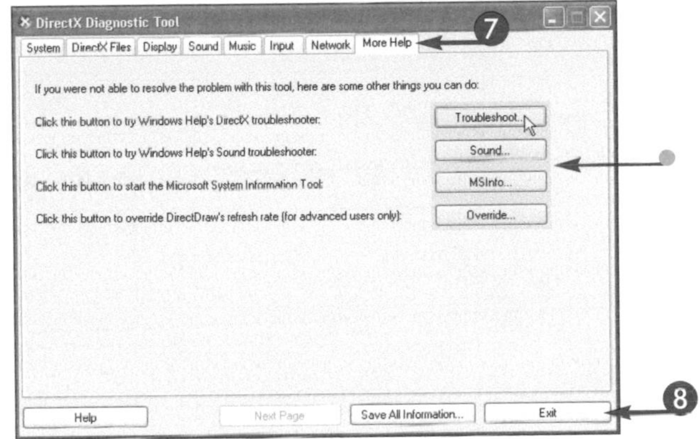

Which options should I focus on in the DirectX Diagnostic Tool?

Focus on any option that has a control for enabling or regulating acceleration. In most cases, you want to maximize the acceleration setting, unless problems arise. For example, on the Display tab under DirectX Features, enable all acceleration options and then click the buttons for testing the acceleration. If your PC passes the tests, leave the acceleration options enabled.

Some of my acceleration options are grayed out. What does that mean?

Grayed-out options are unavailable for the hardware installed on your PC. That is, your hardware does not support the DirectX feature to which the option refers. If you run games or other programs that support DirectX, you may improve performance for these programs by installing hardware that fully supports the latest version of DirectX.

I use my PC mostly for running a word processor and checking my e-mail. Do I need to worry about DirectX settings?

You rarely need to concern yourself with the DirectX settings unless a problem occurs when running a multimedia program. Windows enters the settings that it deems most effective for the hardware installed on your PC. As long as the DirectX Diagnostic Tool reports "No problems" for all devices, you can leave the settings as they are.

25 Streamline the Windows Desktop

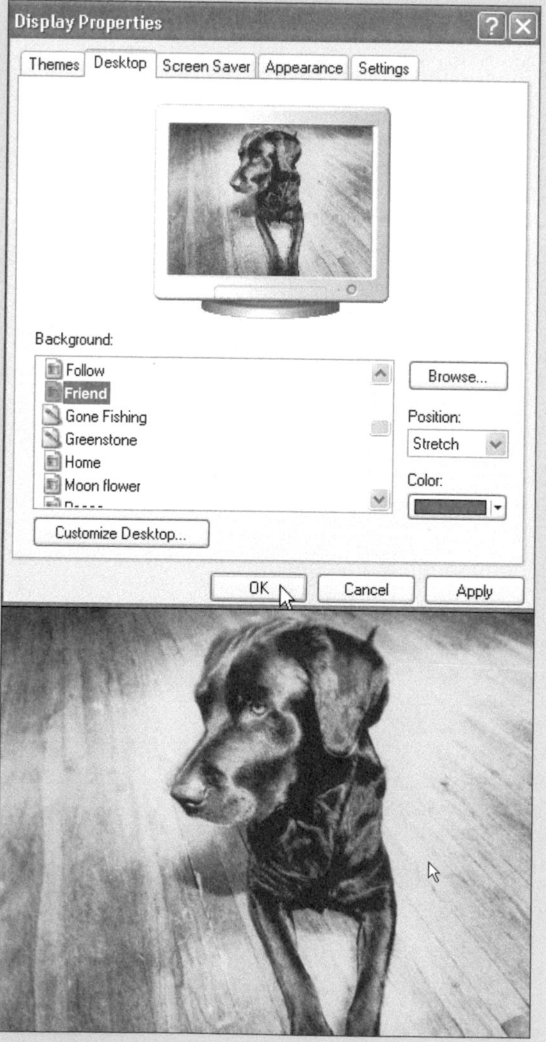

26 Optimize the Display Settings

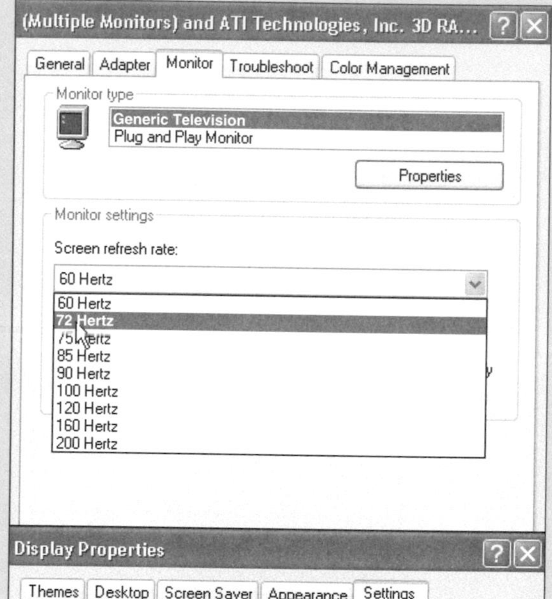

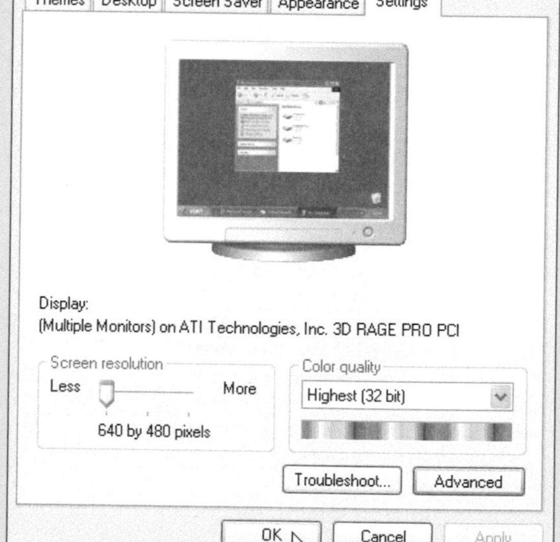

PART VIII
OPTIMIZING YOUR PC'S DISPLAY

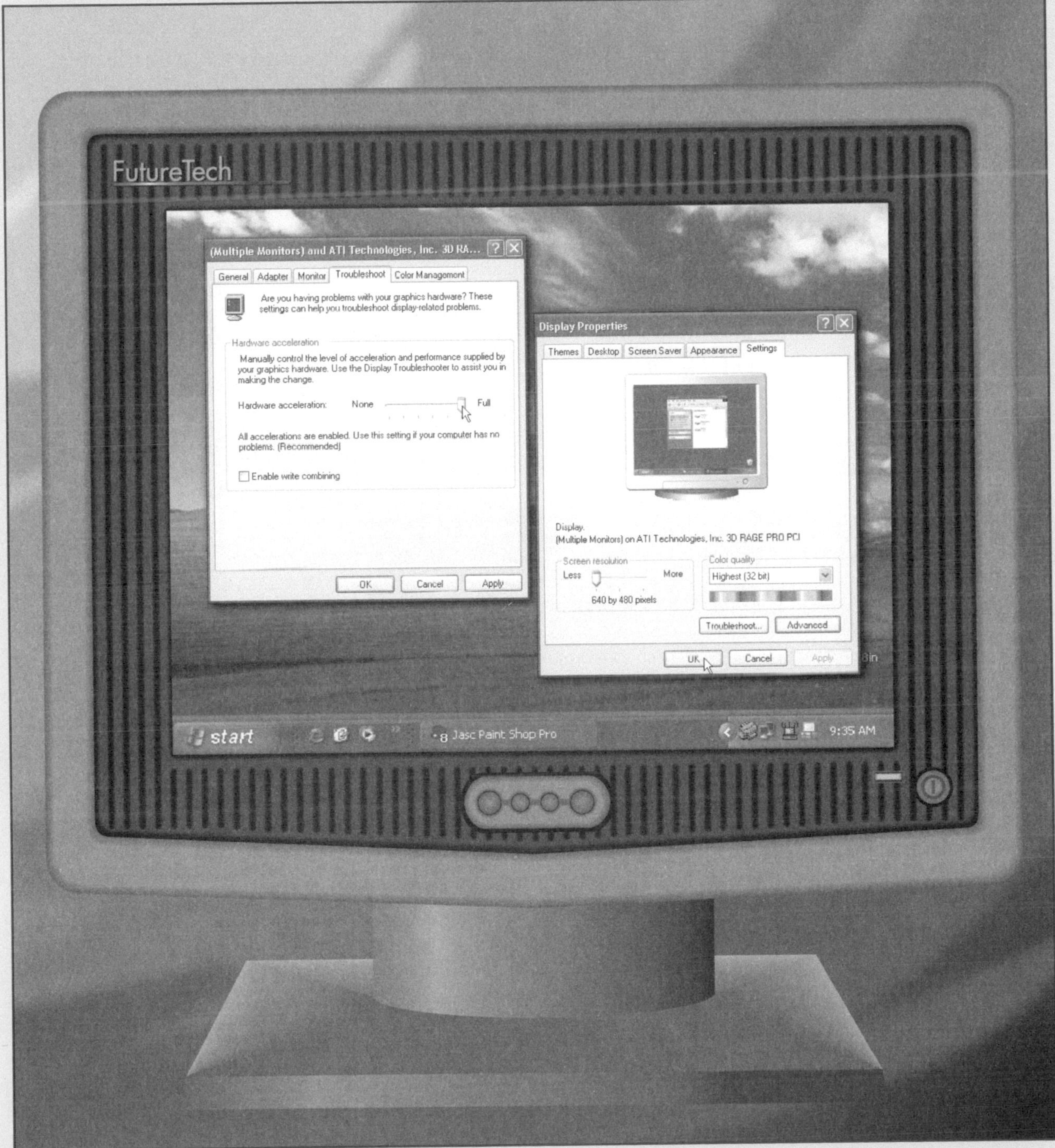

Remove Desktop Themes

Windows features themes that control the overall look and feel of Windows, including the appearance of the Windows desktop mouse pointers as well as the sounds that Windows emits when you perform various actions, such as running a program or clicking OK in a dialog box. The basic themes require few additional resources, but fancier themes require additional memory and disk storage and make your PC's display adapter work a little harder. If you can tolerate the boredom of a basic theme, you can conserve system resources by using a basic theme and removing the fancy themes from your PC.

Windows XP includes only two desktop themes: Windows Classic and Windows XP. Unless you download and install additional themes from the Internet, or purchase themes as part of Microsoft Plus! for Windows or another Windows add-on package, you are using one of the basic themes already.

The steps in this section show you how to choose a desktop theme and delete themes you do not use in Windows XP. If your PC is running an earlier version of Windows, refer to the second tip on the following page for instructions on how to access desktop themes.

Remove Desktop Themes

Choose a Basic Desktop Theme

1. Right-click a blank area of the Windows desktop.
2. Click Properties.

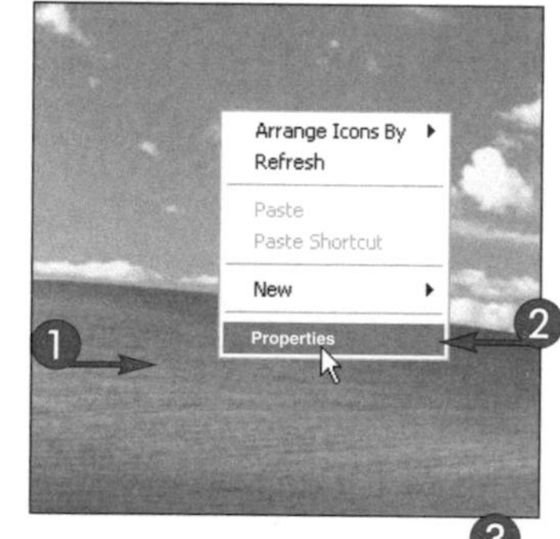

The Display Properties dialog box appears.

3. Click the Themes tab.
4. Click here and click a basic desktop theme.
5. Click OK.

Windows activates the basic theme.

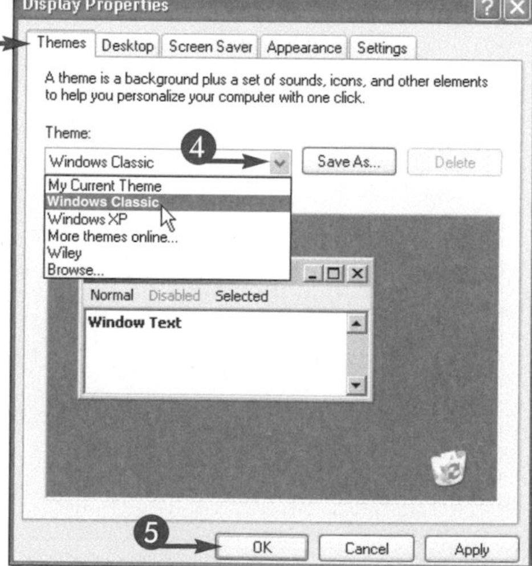

Delete a Theme

1. Right-click a blank area of the Windows desktop.
2. Click Properties.

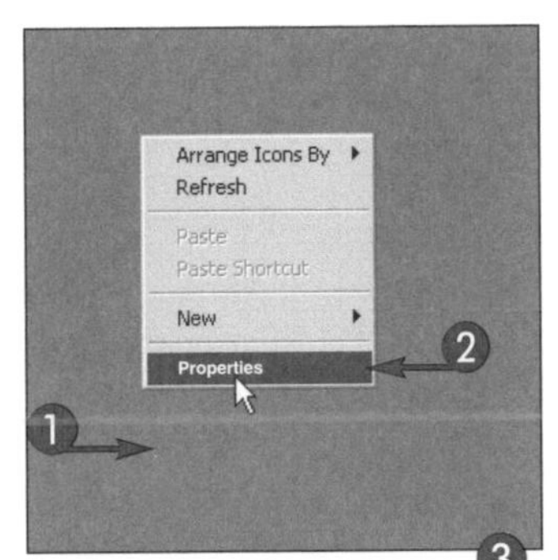

The Display Properties dialog box appears.

3. Click the Themes tab.
4. Click here and click the theme you want to delete.

Note: *You cannot delete the Windows Classic or Windows XP theme.*

5. Click Delete.

Windows removes the theme from your PC.

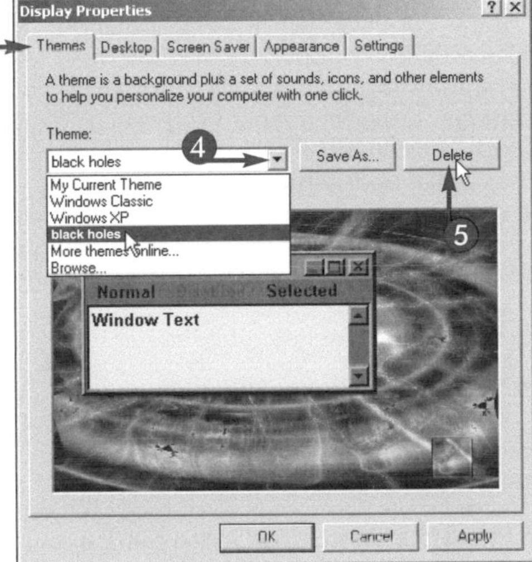

I like themes and am not concerned that they require some additional system resources. Where can I obtain additional themes?

▼ Some versions of Windows include additional themes on the Windows installation CD. You can use the Add or Remove Programs utility to add Windows components and install additional themes. If your PC is running Windows XP, you can purchase Microsoft Plus! for Windows, which is a popular add-on package that includes additional themes, games, and tools to enhance your Windows experience. You can also find free desktop themes online by searching for "windows desktop themes." Shareware sites, including www.download.com and www.tucows.com, feature themes as well.

My PC is running Windows 98. Where can I find my desktop themes?

▼ First, you must install the desktop themes. Insert the Windows CD into your PC's CD drive. Open the Windows Control Panel, double-click Add/Remove Programs, click the Windows Setup tab, and click the check box next to Desktop Themes (☐ changes to ☑). You can click Details to deselect any themes you do not want to install. Click OK to install the selected themes. The installation routine adds a Desktop Themes icon to the Windows Control Panel. Double-click the Desktop Themes icon to display the Desktop Themes window, which enables you to select the desktop theme you want to use.

Disable Desktop Web Pages

You can display Web pages on the Windows desktop to keep abreast of sports scores, weather reports, headline news, stock prices, and any other information that is available on the Web. The capability of displaying Web page content on the Windows desktop is part of the Windows Active Desktop feature that was introduced with Windows 98 and Internet Explorer 4 and is a fairly interesting and useful feature. However, Web content can slow down your PC, particularly if the Active Desktop components frequently download updates, your PC uses a dial-up Internet connection, or the page contains large graphics, video clips, or animations. Web content can also consume valuable desktop space that you can use for displaying shortcut icons.

You can disable these items to prevent them from appearing on the desktop and free up some additional system resources. Of course, if your desktop Web pages are indispensable to you, you may choose to keep them, but if they run in the background and you rarely look at them, disabling them may provide your PC with an added performance boost.

The steps you take to disable desktop Web pages vary depending on the version of Windows installed on your PC. However, you can access the options by way of the Display Properties dialog box.

Disable Desktop Web Pages

1. Right-click a blank area of the Windows desktop.
2. Click Properties.

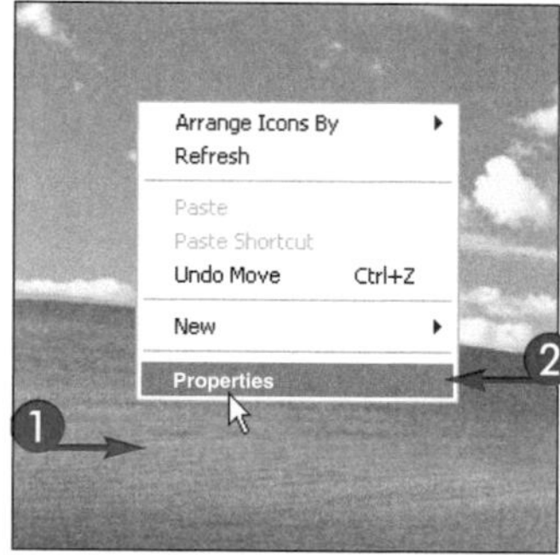

- The Display Properties dialog box appears.

3. Click the Desktop tab.

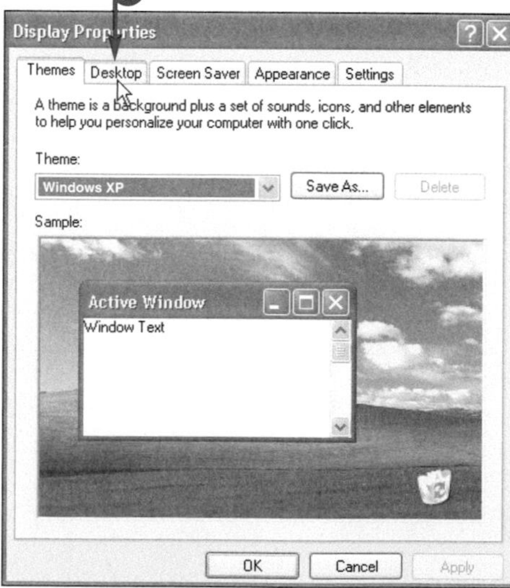

4 Click Customize Desktop.

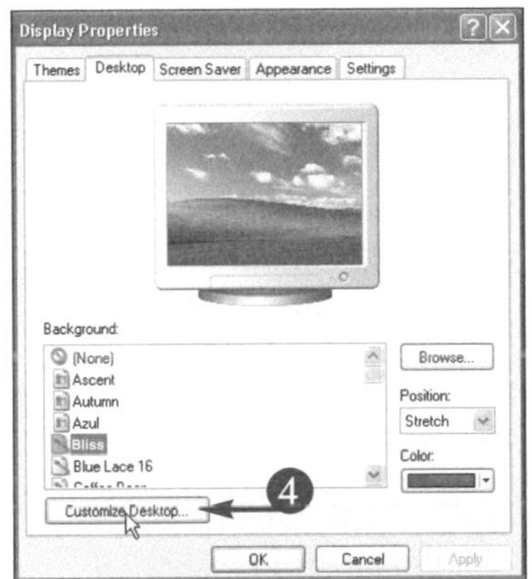

The Desktop Items dialog box appears.

5 Click the Web tab.

6 Click the check box next to each item you want to disable (☑ changes to ☐).

- You can click an item and click Delete to permanently remove it.

7 Click OK.

8 Click OK.

Windows saves your settings and disables the selected desktop Web pages.

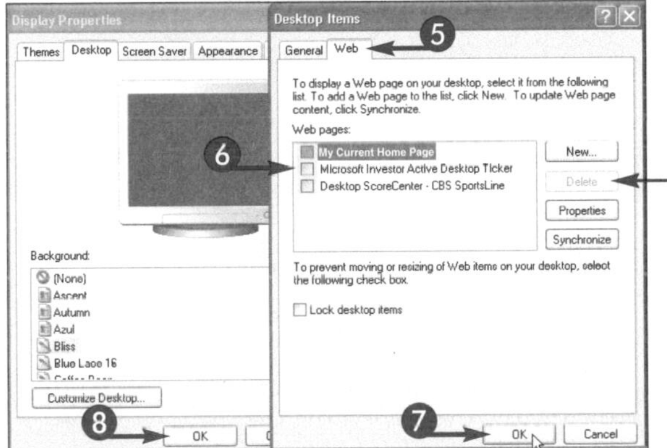

Can I control how often Windows updates the content for a Web-based desktop item?

▼ Yes. Display the list of desktop items. Click the item you want to schedule for updates and click Properties. Click the Schedule tab, click Add, and use the options in the resulting dialog box to enter your preferences, including the frequency of the updates.

Is there an easy way to use an image from the Web as a desktop item?

▼ Yes. Display the image in Internet Explorer. Right-click the image and click Set as Desktop Item. The Internet Explorer dialog box appears, prompting you to confirm. Click Yes. You can remove the item from the Windows desktop by performing the steps provided in this section.

I like the idea of adding Web-page content to the desktop. How do I add an item?

▼ Right-click the desktop, click Properties, the Desktop tab, Customize Desktop, the Web tab, and then New. The New Desktop Item dialog box appears. You can click Visit Gallery to add items from Microsoft's old Active Desktop Gallery. The Gallery features an investment ticker, CBS SportsLine, and an MSNBC weather map. You can add a specific Web page to the desktop by typing its URL, starting with http://, in the Location text box. Or, if you have an image you saved as a JPG or GIF file, or you saved a Web page, you can click Browse to select the file.

Change Graphic Backgrounds

The default background for Windows XP, which is called Bliss, displays a valley of green with a blue sky above it. This is one of Windows' larger background files consuming approximately 1.5MB. Windows features a collection of additional graphic backgrounds that consume much less memory — in most cases, less than 100KB of RAM. Some of the backgrounds are low-resolution photos, while others are small graphics that Windows tiles to fill the screen. You can select one of these smaller images, so that the Windows background does not require so much memory.

You can change backgrounds in the Display Properties dialog box, but if you want to use a background that requires less memory, be careful not to select a large photo that requires even more memory than the default Windows background. When Windows displays a list of backgrounds from which you can choose, it displays any JPG, GIF, PNG, or BMP graphics that are stored in your My Photos folder in addition to the standard Windows backgrounds. Some of these files can be quite large if you shot them in high resolution with a digital camera.

Change Graphic Backgrounds

1. Right-click a blank area of the Windows background.
2. Click Properties.

The Display Properties dialog box appears.

3. Click the Desktop tab.
4. Scroll down the list of backgrounds.

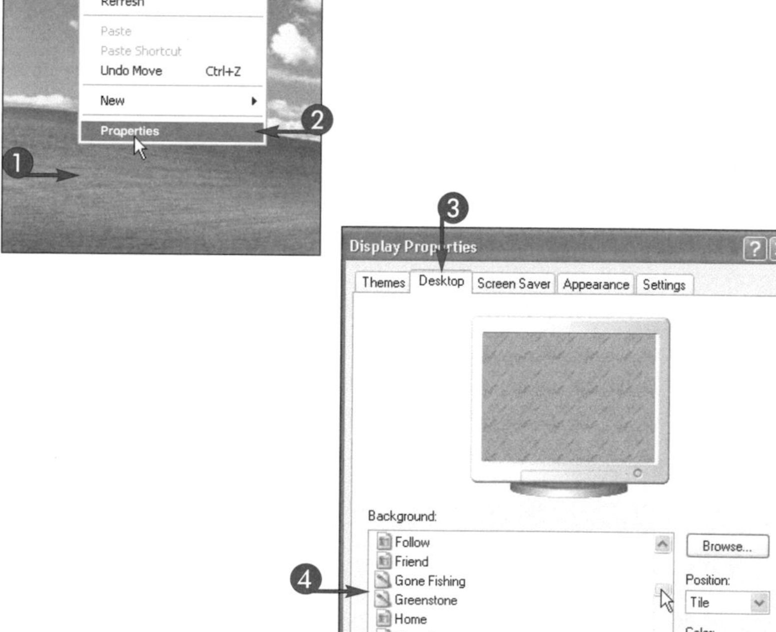

5 Click a background that you want to use.

- The selected background appears in the preview area.

6 Click OK.

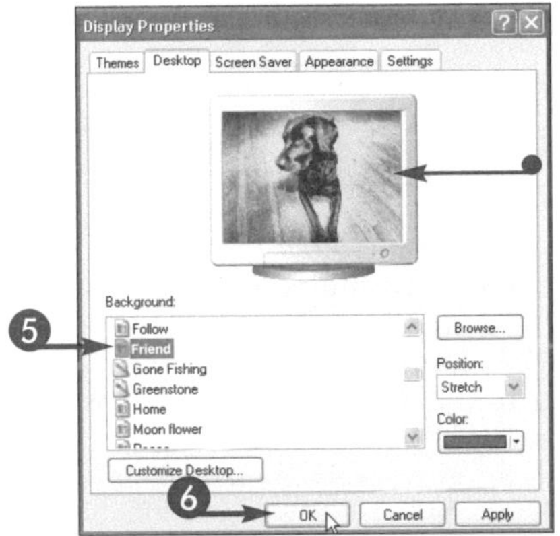

The Display Properties dialog box closes, and Windows displays the selected desktop background.

How can I tell the size of the file used for the background?

▼ Launch My Computer and then navigate to the Windows\Web\Wallpaper folder. Click View and then Details to display information about the files, including the size of each file. Most of the background images are between 50K and 80K.

Can I use any image that is stored on my PC?

▼ You can click the Browse button and use the resulting dialog box to select any image on your PC that is saved in the JPG, GIF, PNG, or BMP format. You can use an image from a Web page by right-clicking the image and clicking Set as Background. Most Web pages contain images that are stored in a format that Windows requires for use as wallpaper.

Can I use a photo I took as my Windows background image?

▼ Yes. If you save the file as a JPG, GIF, PNG, or BMP file, you can use it as a Windows background. However, if you use a photo from a high-resolution digital camera, the background image might require more than a megabyte of RAM. Try reducing the size of the image by opening it in a photo-editing program and decreasing the image resolution, the number of colors, or the physical size of the image. You can usually resize an image to match the size of the desktop by adjusting the size in pixels.

Optimize the Windows Taskbar

You can hide the Windows taskbar to provide additional space for displaying program windows when you are not using the taskbar. You can enter settings to have the taskbar come into view whenever you move the mouse pointer to the edge of the screen where the taskbar normally appears.

Hiding the Windows taskbar does not optimize the Windows desktop by making it run faster, but it can reduce desktop clutter and help you work more efficiently. The taskbar typically displays the Start button; one or more toolbars, including the Quick Launch toolbar; and the system tray, on the right end of the toolbar, which displays a clock and icons for programs that run in the background. This can leave little room for displaying buttons that you can use to switch between active programs and documents.

You can enlarge the taskbar to provide additional space and then hide it to create a custom taskbar that displays all of the tools you need and stays out of your way. If you find yourself scrolling inside the taskbar to access buttons that it is too small to display, this toolbar configuration can significantly enhance your desktop.

Optimize the Windows Taskbar

Note: *You may need to right-click the taskbar and click Unlock the Taskbar before performing these steps.*

1. Position the mouse pointer at the edge of the taskbar.
2. Click and drag the edge of the taskbar toward the center of the screen.
3. When the taskbar is the size you want, release the mouse button.

Windows resizes the taskbar.

Note: *You can drag the taskbar to the top, left, or right edge of the screen.*

4. Right-click a blank area of the taskbar.
5. Click Properties.

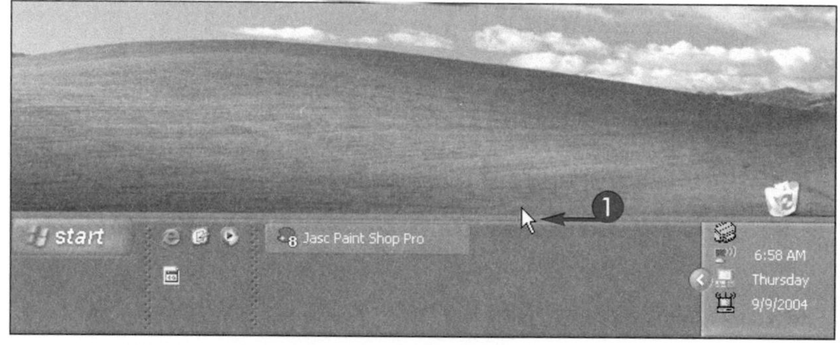

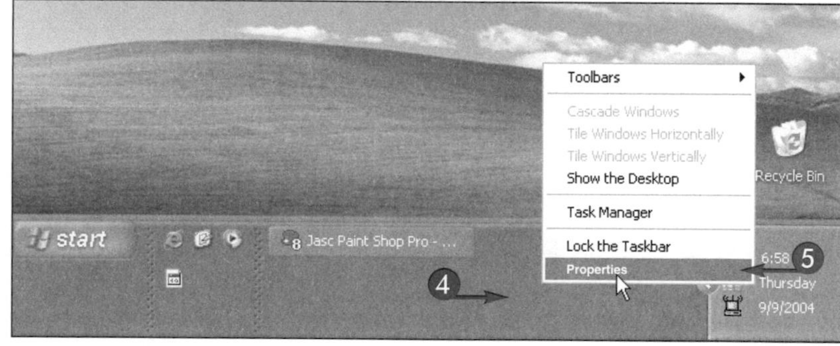

The Taskbar and Start Menu Properties dialog box appears.

6 Click the Taskbar tab.

7 Click the Auto-hide the taskbar option (☐ changes to ☑).

- Ensure that the Keep the taskbar on top of other windows option is selected.

8 Click OK.

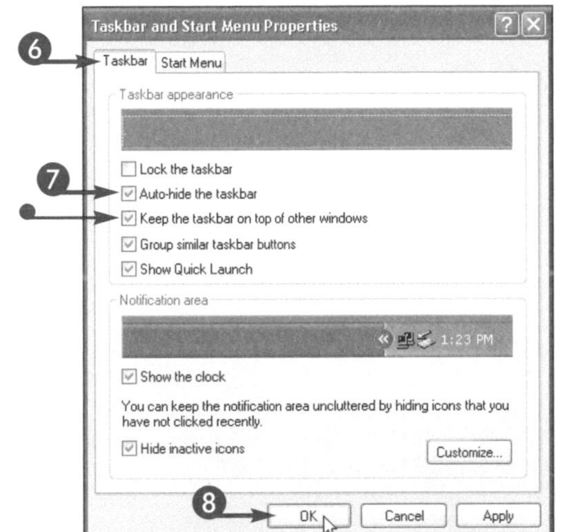

When the desktop or a window is active, Windows hides the taskbar.

9 Move the mouse pointer to the edge of the screen where the taskbar normally appears to bring the taskbar into view.

Windows displays the taskbar.

Can I display other toolbars like the Quick Launch toolbar in my taskbar?

▼ Yes. Right-click a blank area of the taskbar, click Toolbars, and click the toolbar you want. The Address toolbar, for example, displays a text box in which you can type a Web page address to open the page in your Web browser. You can click New Toolbar to select a folder to use as a toolbar; the contents of the folder appear as toolbar buttons. You can click and drag any folder onto a blank area of the toolbar to transform the folder into a toolbar. You can also drag individual items from folders or from the Start menu and drop them on a toolbar to create buttons for those items.

My toolbar disappeared. How do I get it back?

▼ If your toolbar is hiding, move the mouse pointer to the edge of the screen where it normally appears, and the toolbar should appear. If it does not appear, you may have made it too small. Move the mouse pointer to the edge of the screen where the toolbar normally appears, so the mouse pointer appears as a double-headed arrow. This indicates that the mouse is positioned over the inner edge of the taskbar. Hold down the left mouse button while dragging the edge of the taskbar toward the center of the screen. This makes the toolbar larger, bringing it into view.

Disable Fancy Visual Effects

You can optimize the way Windows displays menus and other components by disabling the fancy visual effects that Windows uses. By default, the Windows display is configured to balance appearance and performance. Each option that is designed to enhance Windows' appearance has a slight negative effect on Windows' performance.

The visual effects that Windows uses typically enhance the display to make the desktop, windows, toolbars, and text more attractive and to smooth transitions between screens and menus. Effects include drop shadows for menus and for the mouse pointer, smooth screen fonts, smooth edges of drop-down menus, and fade in or out and slide in or out of menus. All of these effects make Windows appear smoother and friendlier, but they also require additional memory and processor power.

Fortunately, Windows enables you to adjust the visual effects in a way that establishes the balance you want. You can disable all visual effects to optimize Windows performance, enable all visual effects to optimize appearance, or pick and choose the visual effects that you want to use. By default, Windows determines the trade-offs for you that it deems are best for your PC.

Disable Fancy Visual Effects

1. Click Start.
2. Right-click My Computer.
3. Click Properties.

The System Properties dialog box appears.

4. Click the Advanced tab.
5. Under Performance, click Settings.

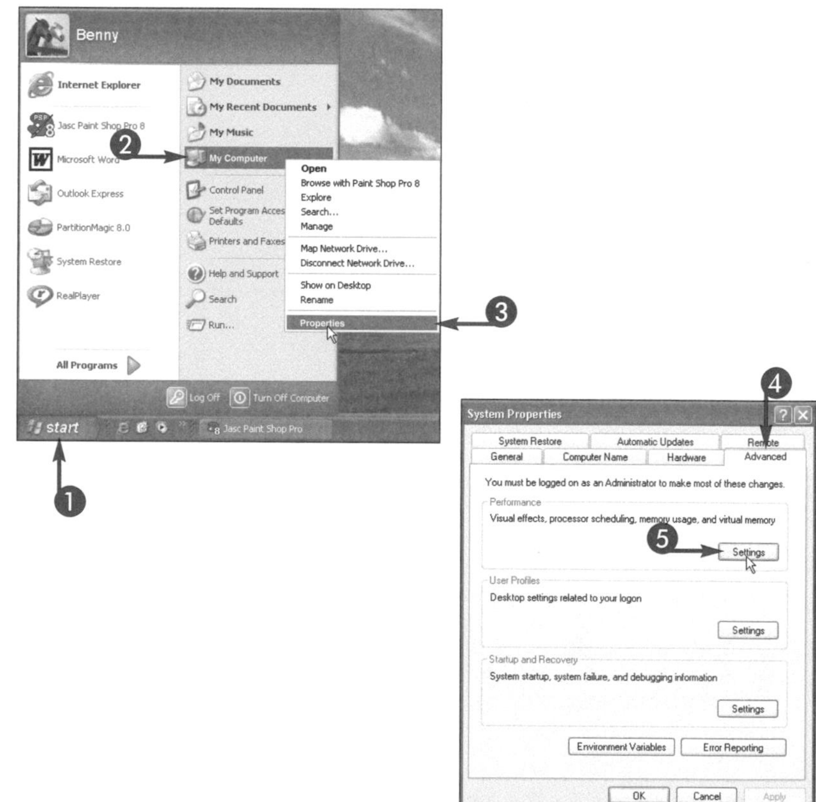

The Performance Options dialog box appears.

6 Click the Visual Effects tab.

7 Click the Adjust for best performance option (○ changes to ◉).

8 Click OK.

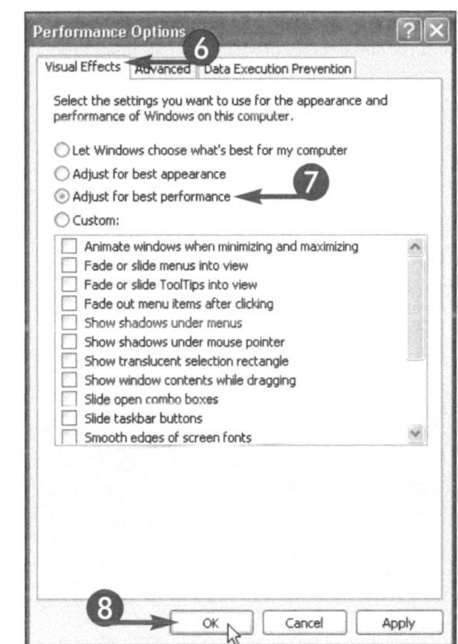

The Performance Options dialog box closes and returns you to the System Properties dialog box.

9 Click OK.

Windows saves your Visual Effects settings, configuring Windows for optimum performance.

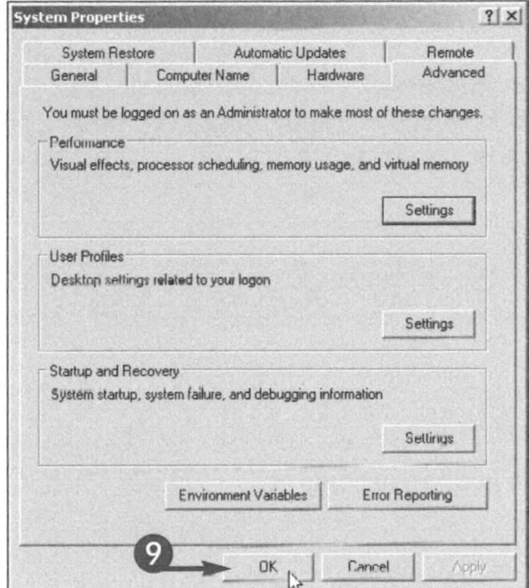

Can I adjust the visual effects using the Display Settings dialog box?

▼ You can adjust some visual effects using the Display Settings dialog box, including the transition effect used for menus, menu shadows, and smooth screen fonts, but the visual effects options in the Display Settings dialog box are very limited. By adjusting the settings in the Performance Options dialog box, as recommended in the steps in this section, you have complete control over every Windows visual effect.

Can I adjust any other settings in the Performance Options dialog box to improve Windows performance?

▼ Yes. You can click the Advanced tab for additional options that enable you to allocate processor and memory usage in favor of the programs you actively use or those that are running in the background. The Advanced tab also provides an option to control virtual memory — hard drive space used as memory. Refer to Chapter 11 for additional information and instructions.

I disabled all of the visual effects, but now Windows and my program windows seem flat. What should I do?

▼ Disabling visual effects creates a flatter, jerkier interface that responds more quickly to your actions. After a day or two, most people become accustomed to the change and appreciate the improved performance. However, if you prefer a more attractive, smoother interface, adjust the visual effects to create the balance of appearance and performance that appeals to you.

Disable the Windows Screen Saver

You can disable the Windows screen saver or at least adjust its settings to make it less intrusive, so that the screen saver does not interrupt your workflow throughout the day.

In the past, screen savers were essential tools in helping to prevent damage to the monitor. A screen saver blacks out the monitor or displays a moving picture on it, so that a static image does not permanently burn itself into the inner surface of the monitor. Monitors produced in the last 10 years or so are not susceptible to this type of damage, but many people use screen savers as a decorative diversion. Screen savers also provide some degree of privacy, preventing passers-by from seeing what you were working on when you stepped away from your PC.

However, if your screen saver is configured to start whenever your PC is inactive for a short period of time or if it returns you to the Windows welcome screen whenever you start using your PC, you can adjust the screen saver settings to disable the screen saver or prevent it from interrupting your work.

Disable the Windows Screen Saver

1. Right-click a blank area of the Windows desktop.
2. Click Properties.

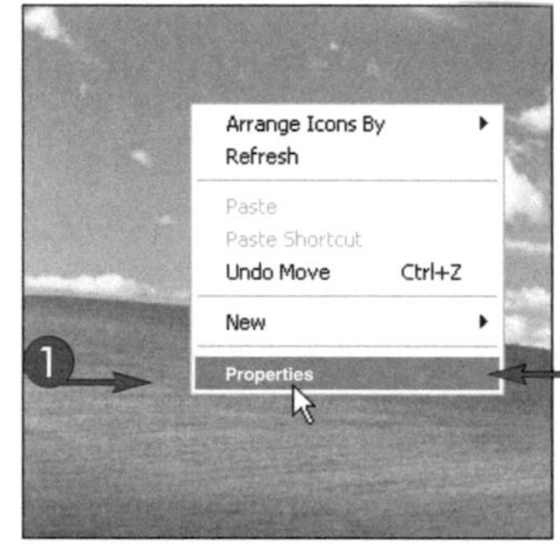

The Display Properties dialog box appears.

3. Click the Screen Saver tab.

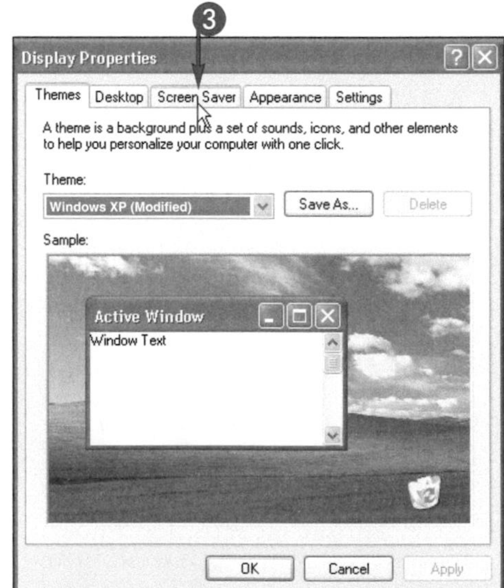

The Screen Saver properties appear.

Note: *Screen Saver properties vary depending on the developer.*

- You can disable the screen saver by clicking here and selecting (None).

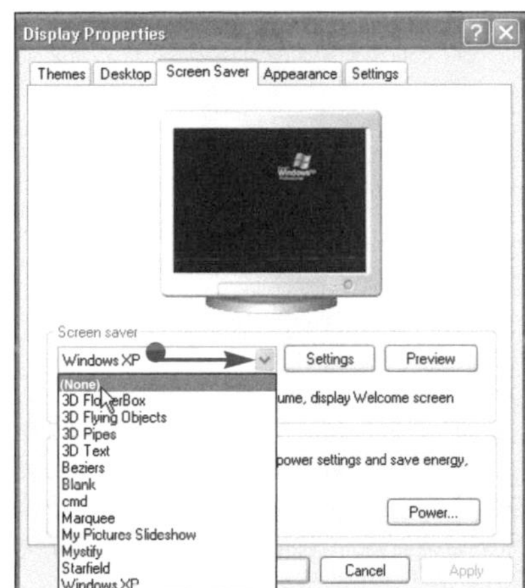

- You can click here to adjust the amount of time your PC is inactive before the screen saver starts.
- You can click here to deselect the option so that Windows does not display its welcome screen when you return (☑ changes to ☐).

4 Click OK.

Windows saves your screen saver settings.

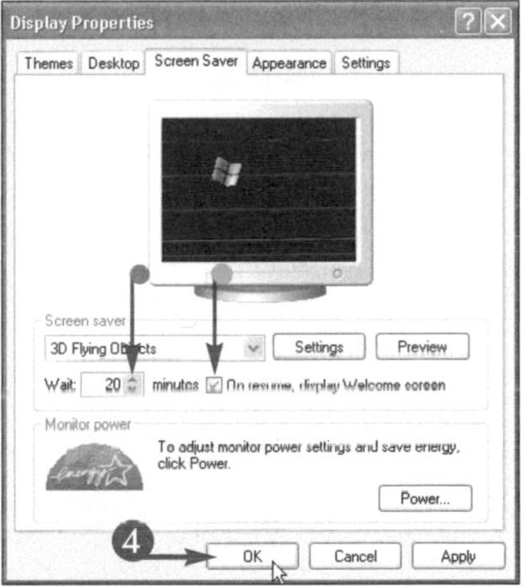

Can I adjust settings to control the way a particular screen saver appears on my PC?

▼ In most cases, you can configure a screen saver to run faster or display its animated objects in a different way. After you select the screen saver you want, click Settings and enter your preferences. Settings typically include the speed at which the animation plays and the number of objects it presents, but the settings differ significantly for different screen savers.

Can I obtain additional screen savers?

▼ Yes. You can find additional screen savers online. Screen savers are also commonly included as components of Windows desktop themes. For more information about desktop themes, refer to the section "Remove Desktop Themes."

My monitor blacks out and then takes awhile to start up when I return to work. What causes that?

▼ In addition to the screen saver settings, your system has power-saving settings that automatically shut off the monitor and power down the hard drive usually after about 20 minutes. These settings may be partially shutting down your PC to conserve energy. When you start using your PC again, it must restart your monitor and disk drives, which can cause a small delay. To prevent this from happening or prevent it from happening as often as it does, you can adjust the power-saving settings. Open the Display Settings dialog box, click the Screen Saver tab, and click the Power button to access the settings.

Configure Folder Options for Speed

You can adjust folder options to increase the speed at which folders open to display their contents and to improve your own efficiency in performing file-management tasks. For example, if Windows is set up to open each folder in a separate window, you may find that closing all of those windows when you are finished is an inefficient way to work. You can change the folder options to enable you to navigate folders in a single window.

Choosing the single-click option for activating folders and files can also save you some time. For example, if you normally need to double-click a folder to open it, you can enable the single-click option so that you need to click a folder only once to open it. Of course, this requires some retraining on your part to learn that you must point to files and folders to select them rather than clicking to select.

Windows also includes several view options for folders that you can adjust to make folders and their contents appear faster on-screen. For example, if you do not work on a network, you can disable the Automatically search for network folder and printers option to save time.

Configure Folder Options for Speed

1. Click Start.
2. Click My Computer.

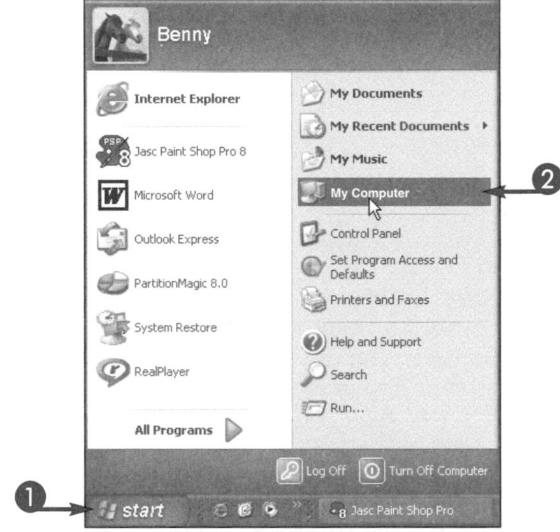

The My Computer window appears.

3. Click Tools.
4. Click Folder Options.

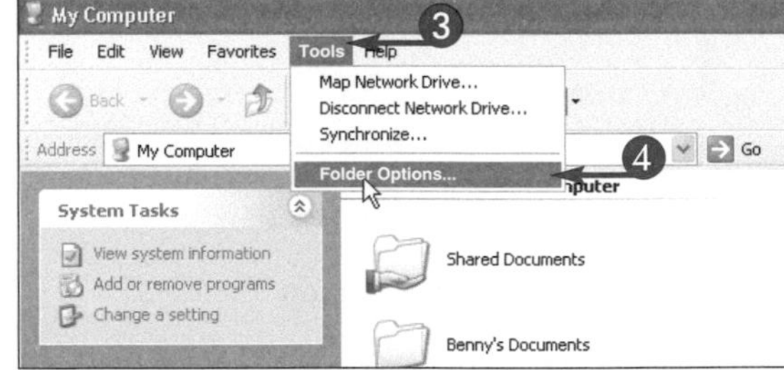

The Folder Options dialog box appears.

- You can click the Open each folder in the same window option (○ changes to ◉) to browse folders in one window.
- You can click the Single-click to open an item option (○ changes to ◉) to open files and folders with a single click.

5 Click the View tab.

6 Under Advanced settings, click to select or deselect options.

For more information about an option, right-click the option and click What's This?

7 Click OK.

Windows saves your settings.

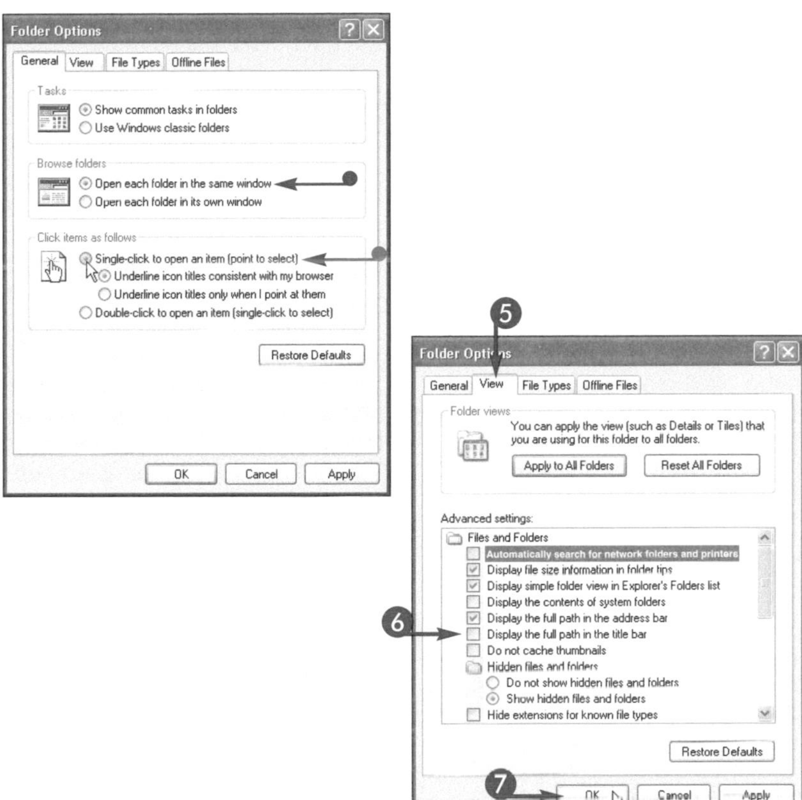

Which View options have the most positive effect on performance?

▼ By default, Windows caches thumbnail images of folders so it does not need to recreate the thumbnails every time you display a folder's icon, so leave the Do not cache thumbnails option deselected. Turning on the "Launch folder windows in a separate process" option (☐ changes to ☑) can improve stability but may impair performance slightly. When configuring Windows, the three Hide options can slow you down. Click the "Do not show hidden files and folders" option (◉ changes to ○), the Hide extensions for known file types option (☑ changes to ☐), and the Hide protected operating system files option (☑ changes to ☐). This gives you access to all files on your PC.

I prefer using Windows Explorer to manage files and folders. Is there a quick way to access it?

▼ Windows Explorer displays a two-paned window, displaying drives and folders in the left pane and the contents of the currently selected folder in the right pane. The standard way of displaying Windows Explorer is to click Start, All Programs, Accessories, and then Windows Explorer. A quicker way is to right-click an object and then click Explore. You can right-click the Start menu and click Explore, right-click My Computer, and click Explore, or right-click any folder and click Explore. To view the folder list in My Computer, click View, Explorer Bar, Folders or click the Folders button (Folders) in the toolbar.

Optimize Display Settings

You can optimize the display settings in Windows for appearance or performance. Two components of your PC contribute to creating the display — the display adapter and the monitor. When you enter display settings in Windows, you change the settings for the display adapter, and the monitor adjusts automatically to accommodate the changes.

Windows provides access to two display settings that control display quality and performance: screen resolution and color quality. *Screen resolution* defines the number of colored dots that comprise the display and is expressed in width x height; for example, a resolution of 800 x 600 creates a display that is 800 dots wide by 600 tall. At higher resolutions, the dots are smaller and packed more tightly on the screen, usually resulting in a sharper display. However, flat panel monitors have an optimal resolution; the display quality suffers if you use a resolution setting that is lower or higher than the optimum setting.

Color quality is determined by the number of colors used in the display and typically ranges from 256 colors up to 32-bit color — over 4 billion colors. When adjusting settings, you make trade-offs between performance and appearance. For example, if you are playing a multiplayer video game across a network or Internet connection, you may want to decrease resolution and color depth to make the game more responsive.

Optimize Display Settings

1. Right-click a blank area of the Windows desktop.
2. Click Properties.

The Display Properties dialog box appears.

3. Click the Settings tab.
4. Click and drag the Screen resolution slider to the left or right to set the resolution you want.
5. Click here and select the color depth you want.
6. For additional resolution options, click Advanced.

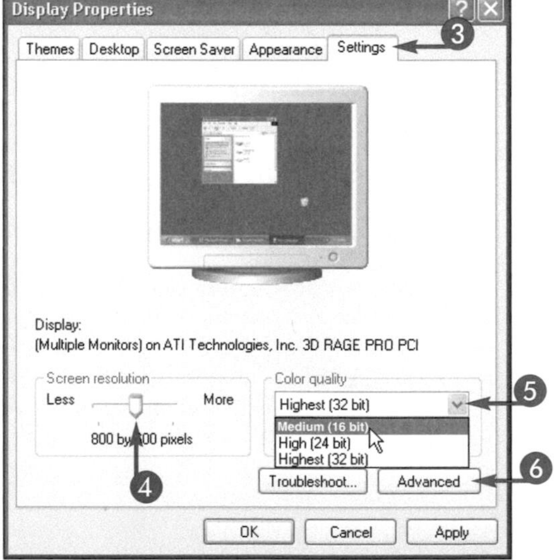

The advanced display settings appear.

7. Click the Adapter tab.
8. Click List All Modes.

The List All Modes dialog box appears.

9. Click the display mode you want to use.
10. Click OK.
11. Click OK.

The Display Properties dialog box reappears.

12. Click OK.

Windows saves your settings and refreshes the screen according to the new settings.

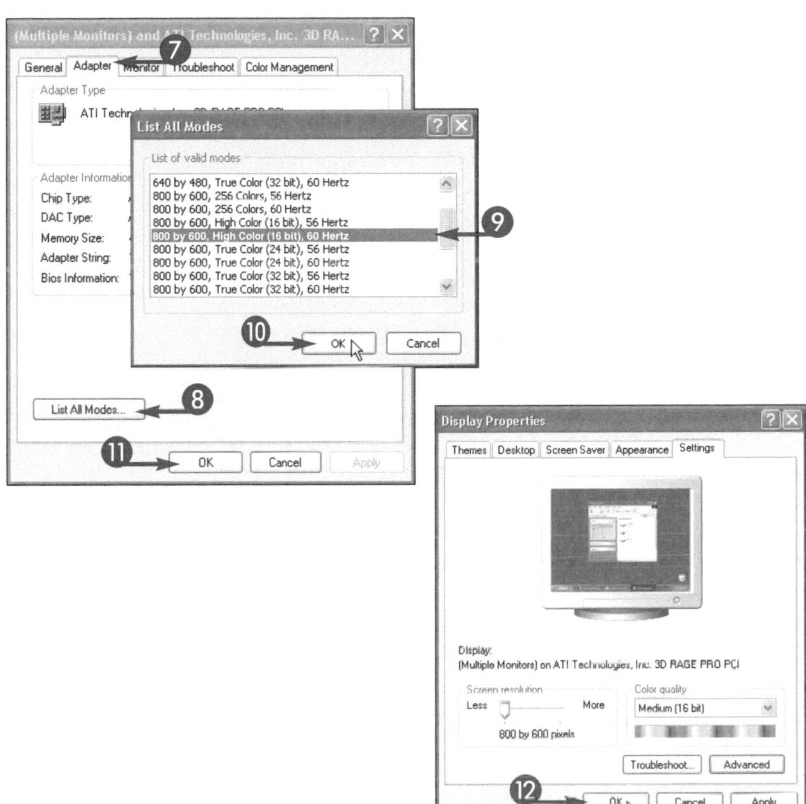

I have one game that I need to run in 256 colors. Can I run it in 256 colors without modifying the display settings for my other programs?

▼ If you have Windows XP, you can use its Compatibility Mode feature to run the game in 256 colors without affecting the display for your other applications. Click Start, All Programs, Accessories, and then Program Compatibility Wizard, and follow the Wizard's instructions to set up the game to run in 256-color mode. If you play a multiplayer game over the Internet or over another network connection, decreasing screen resolution and color quality often increases the game's frame rate — the number of frames the game displays per second — which makes the game more responsive.

When I decrease the screen resolution, everything looks larger. Why?

▼ When you decrease the screen resolution, the display uses fewer colored dots spaced farther apart to create the display. This makes objects larger, and sometimes more fuzzy, especially on LCDs (Liquid Crystal Displays). Conversely, when you increase screen resolution, objects appear smaller. If the objects are too small, you can adjust other display settings to use larger icons and fonts. To increase the font size and icon size for your display, right-click a blank area of the desktop, click Properties, and click the Appearance tab. Select the font size you want from the Font size menu, and click Effects to access options for changing the icon size.

Optimize Screen Refresh Rate

You can optimize your monitor's screen refresh rate to reduce flicker and improve the display quality. A monitor's refresh rate is the frequency at which the monitor illuminates the dots on the screen to create the display; unlike CRT (cathode ray tube) monitors, LCDs, such as those used in flat-panel displays, do not refresh the display. The refresh rate is commonly expressed in hertz (Hz). A refresh rate of 60 Hz indicates that the monitor refreshes the display 60 times per second.

If your monitor is working fine and you perceive no flicker, you can safely leave the refresh rate setting alone. However, if you notice a slight flicker, you may be able to reduce or eliminate the flicker by increasing the refresh rate.

When adjusting the refresh rate, you must be careful not to exceed the maximum refresh rate for your monitor. Check your monitor's specifications either in its manual or on the manufacturer's Web site. Exceeding the maximum refresh rate can permanently damage the monitor. In most cases, you want to choose a refresh rate that is somewhat lower than the maximum. If your monitor supports a refresh rate of 100 Hz, for example, a setting of 80 Hz is usually sufficient to reduce flicker to an imperceptible level.

Optimize Screen Refresh Rate

1. Right-click a blank area of the Windows desktop.
2. Click Properties.

The Display Properties dialog box appears.

3. Click the Settings tab.
4. Click Advanced.

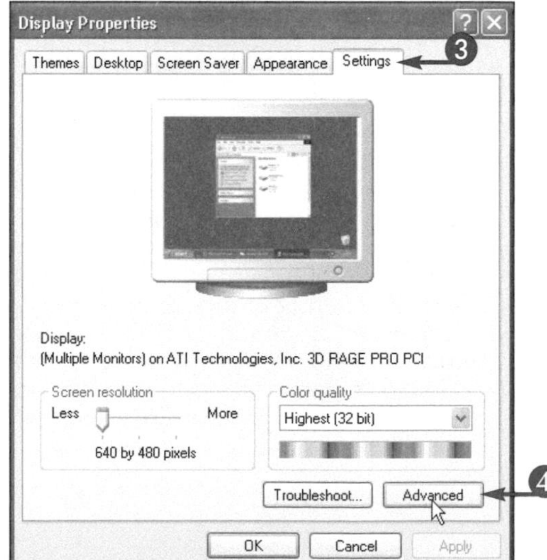

The advanced settings appear.

5. Click the Monitor tab.
6. Click here and select the refresh rate you want to use.

Note: *Do not select a setting that exceeds the maximum refresh rate for your monitor.*

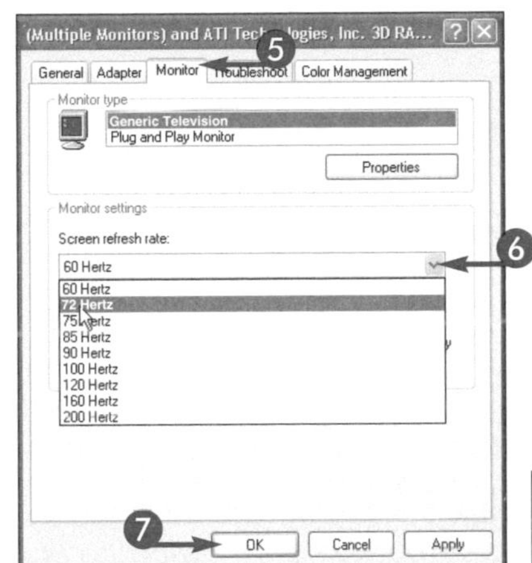

7. Click OK.

The Display Properties dialog box reappears.

8. Click OK.

Windows saves your settings and uses the new refresh rate you selected.

My display is not flickering, but it is very blurry. Does Windows have any settings I can adjust to fix it?

▼ No, but do not make the common mistake of automatically assuming that your monitor is damaged. Often a small adjustment is all it needs. Unfortunately, making adjustments is rarely an intuitive process. Refer to the monitor's owner's manual for information about various settings or visit the manufacturer's Web site. Some manufacturers provide utilities that can help you adjust the settings. For example, Sony has a utility that displays test screens complete with instructions about which adjustments to make if the test screen does not appear a certain way.

Windows has my monitor or display adapter listed as a generic type. Should I be concerned?

▼ You should be concerned enough to check it out. If you know the make and model of your adapter and monitor, visit the manufacturer's Web site to locate the correct device drivers for your hardware and your version of Windows and install those drivers. Using device drivers designed specifically for your display adapter and monitor typically provide the best results. However, if a specific driver is unavailable and you are not experiencing any difficulties with your display, the Windows generic device drivers are the best option. Do not try installing a device driver that is not designed for your display adapter or monitor.

Optimize the Hardware Acceleration Setting

You can maximize the hardware acceleration setting for your display adapter to make full use of its resources. Windows typically maximizes the hardware acceleration setting for a display adapter during installation. This enables the display adapter to run at full speed and use any advanced features it has built into it to optimize the display. However, Windows may have entered a lower acceleration setting to start, or you or someone else may have decreased the setting to troubleshoot a problem and then neglected to maximize acceleration after resolving the problem.

In any case, you can check the hardware acceleration setting for your display adapter and adjust it, if necessary, to optimize the display for Windows and all of your other applications, games, and utilities.

The most effective approach is to start with the highest setting and then decrease the acceleration as needed until your PC runs all programs without problems. If your PC experiences no problems at the highest setting, you can safely run your PC with maximum acceleration. If the PC experiences problems running a particular application or game, you can then try the next lower setting. Continue bumping down the setting until your PC runs without problems.

Optimize the Hardware Acceleration Setting

1. Right-click a blank area of the Windows desktop.
2. Click Properties.

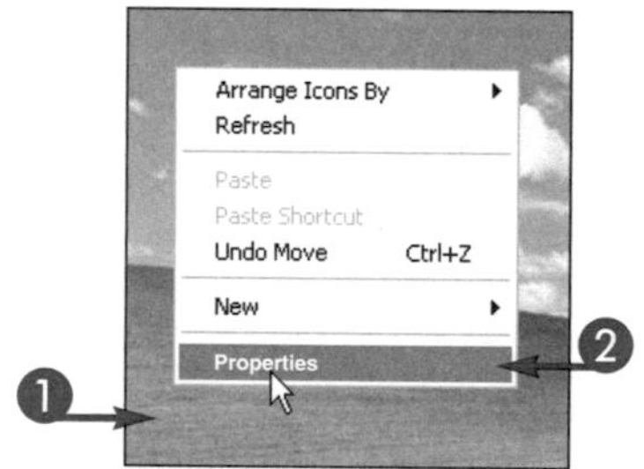

The Display Properties dialog box appears.

3. Click the Settings tab.
4. Click Advanced.

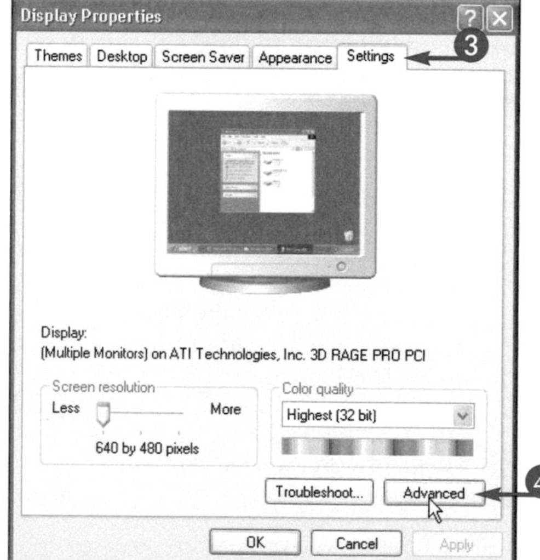

The advanced options appear.

5 Click the Troubleshoot tab.

6 Click and drag the Hardware acceleration slider to the left or right to select the setting you want to use.

- You can click the Enable write combining option to improve performance (☐ changes to ☑).

7 Click OK.

The Display Properties dialog box reappears.

8 Click OK.

Windows saves your settings and runs your display adapter according to the preferences you entered.

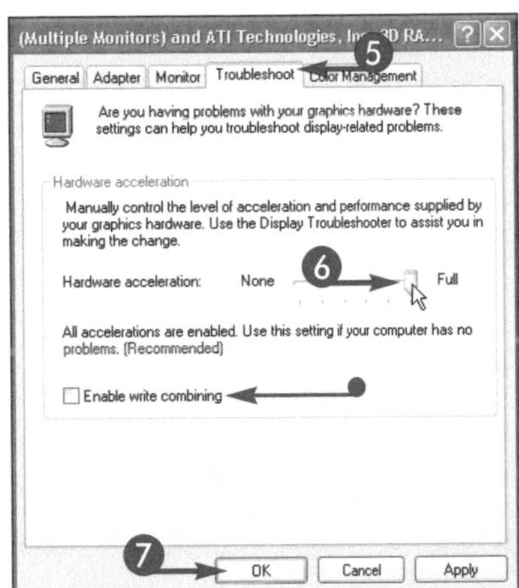

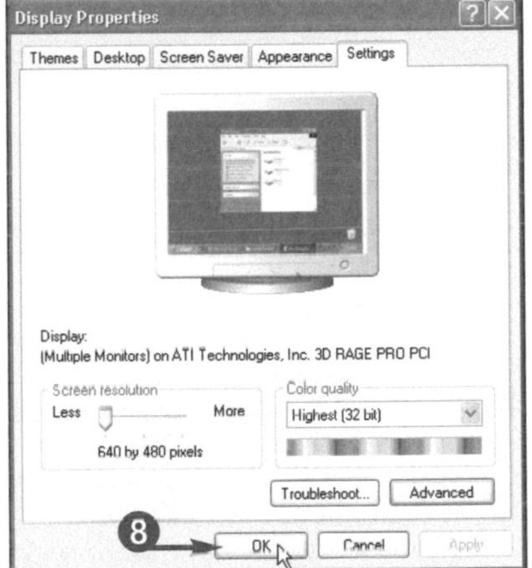

The only way I can get my game to run is to set the Hardware acceleration to None. What else can I try?

▼ Games frequently test your display adapter's limits and commonly reveal problems with device drivers. The first step you should take is to make sure that you have a correct and up-to-date display driver installed. Refer to Chapter 23 for instructions on how to locate, download, and install updated device drivers. Also, many games communicate to the display adapter indirectly through the Windows DirectX layer, so update Windows, as explained in Chapter 22, making sure you have the current version of DirectX. You can learn more about DirectX in Chapter 24.

The video playback in Windows Media Player is choppy. Do you know of any fix?

▼ Media Player has its own video acceleration setting. In some cases, the video acceleration setting in Media Player can become out of sync with the Windows video acceleration setting, which can cause problems with the video playback. Try adjusting the video acceleration setting in Media Player. Open Media Player's Tools menu, click Options, and then the Performance tab. Click and drag the Video acceleration slider all the way to the right. You can also try increasing the Buffer setting to ensure that Media Player has a consistent stream of data to play. You can also try using a different media player.

27 Install and Configure an AntiVirus Program

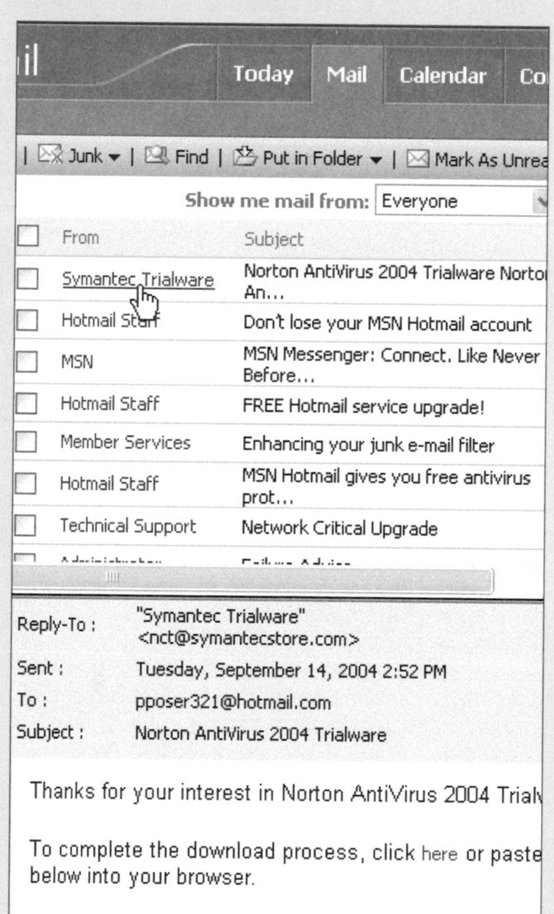

28 Prevent Unauthorized Access to Your PC

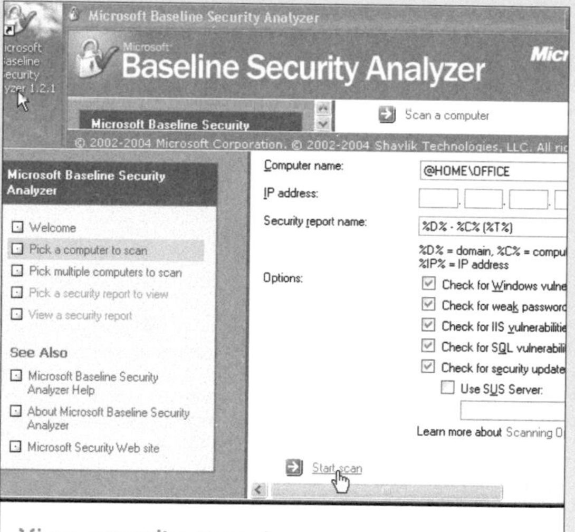

PART IX PROTECTING YOUR PC FROM VIRUSES AND CRACKERS

29 Configure a Browser's Security Settings

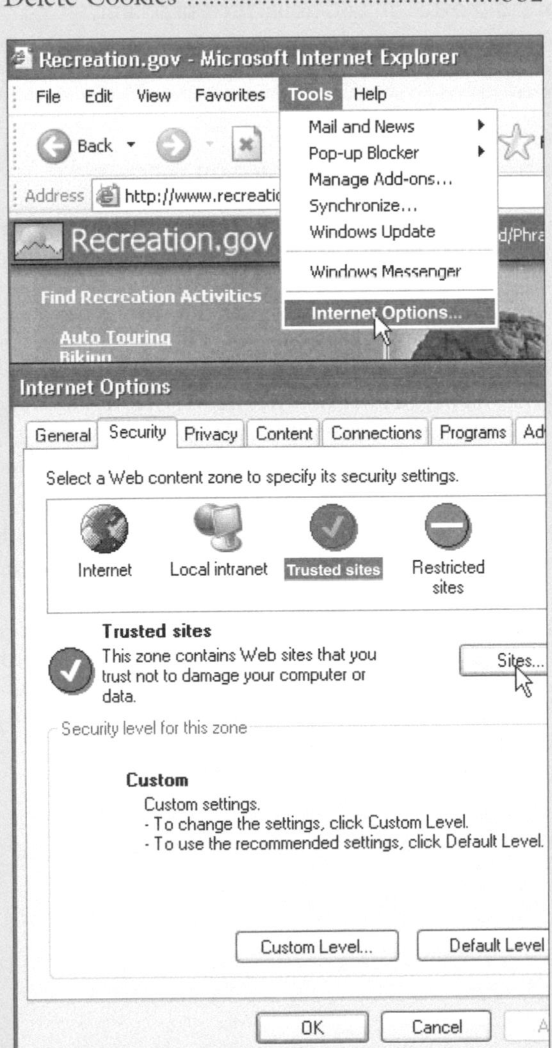

30 Censor Sites That Contain Offensive Content

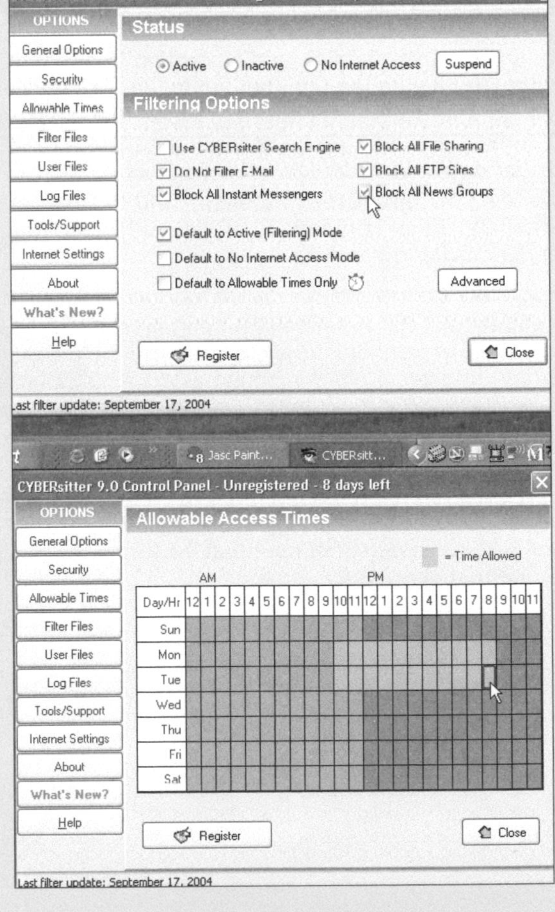

Understanding Virus Risks

A virus is replicating programming code that runs on your PC without your permission, and is specifically designed to vandalize your PC, compromise security, or perform a prank. Viruses often disable Internet connections, destroy files, use the host's e-mail program to spread the virus, and perform other unauthorized acts of destruction and mayhem. If your computer has contact with another computer — over the Internet, a network connection, or by exchanging files on disks — it is at risk of catching and spreading a computer virus.

By understanding the nature of viruses, the methods they use to spread to other computers, and the risks they pose to your PC, you can develop a strategy to defend your PC against infection and minimize the negative effects of a virus by detecting and removing it before it can perform significant acts of destruction. In this chapter, you learn some techniques for preventing viruses from infecting your PC, and you learn how to install and configure antivirus software to provide an additional level of security.

Virus Creators

People who create viruses are not necessarily motivated to cause destruction. Some people develop viruses out of curiosity — to learn how a virus works and to find out whether they are capable of creating a virus of their own. Others do it for fun — to perform a prank that causes a funny message to pop up on other users' screens on a particular date and time. Every virus, however, can be modified to perform acts of vandalism and to steal personal information from computers, so all viruses have at least the potential for doing harm.

In many cases, virus creators create informal clubs in which they exchange ideas and programming code and challenge one another to develop viruses that are more effective at spreading undetected and infecting as many computers as possible. Because of this, viruses commonly evolve over time into different versions of the same virus and different viruses altogether. To effectively defend against viruses, antivirus software developers must constantly update their software so that it can identify as many existing viruses as possible. Some experts estimate that 15 to 20 new viruses are unleashed every week.

Types of Viruses

Viruses are designed to attack the most critical and vulnerable areas of your PC and exploit their weaknesses. In the past, almost all viruses were *file viruses* that spread via program files, or *boot sector viruses* that spread when users shared disks. As long as you did not insert an infected floppy disk into your PC's floppy disk drive or run an infected program on your PC, it was pretty safe. Now, different types of viruses are becoming much more common:

- *Macro viruses* are commonly attached to documents, including Word documents, Excel Worksheets, and PowerPoint presentations. Macros enable users to record a series of commands and play them back with a single keystroke or a click of the mouse, but they can be designed to automatically delete data, as well.
- *Script viruses* are commonly used on Web pages and in e-mail messages to automatically execute whenever the user performs an action that runs the script. In some cases, a script can run as soon as you open an e-mail message or Web page. This makes script viruses particularly difficult to defend against.

How Viruses Spread

Viruses spread by infecting files that are then passed from one computer to another. They can infect your PC in any number of ways:

- From infected floppy disks, CDs, DVDs, or memory cards
- From e-mail messages that include script viruses
- From infected e-mail file attachments — either program files or documents that contain macro viruses
- From Web sites that are designed to automatically install programs on your PC, with or without your permission
- From files you download and install on your PC or infected documents you open

Knowing the common ways that viruses spread from one computer to another, you can understand the precautions you must take to prevent your PC from becoming infected.

Protecting Your PC

The most important step in preventing your PC from becoming infected by a virus is to download and install an antivirus utility, enable its auto-protect features so that it can scan all files that your PC receives, and update the virus definition list at least once a week. You can help protect your system by taking a few precautions, as well:

- Before turning on your PC, make sure no disk is in the floppy drive. Boot sector viruses can infect a PC from a disk.
- Do not open any e-mail messages from people whom you do not know.
- Do not open or run e-mail file attachments from unknown sources.
- Scan e-mail attachments from known sources before opening or running them.
- Download files only from known, reliable sources.
- Keep Windows and your other software updated with the latest security patches, as explained in Chapters 22 and 24.
- Back up important files in case you need to recover files after removing a virus.
- Secure your PC to prevent unauthorized access, as explained in Chapter 28.
- Adjust your Web browser's security settings, as explained in Chapter 29, to prevent pop-ups, unauthorized software installations, and unauthorized running of scripts.

Install an AntiVirus Program

The Internet is a dangerous place for a computer, especially when it comes to viruses. Any program you download and install can carry a virus. Nearly any e-mail attachment can infect your computer. Even ActiveX controls embedded in Web pages can carry destructive computer code. And once a virus infects your system, it usually acts as a tenacious bug, making itself extremely difficult to remove.

Before you connect to the Internet, you should install an antivirus program on your PC and learn how to use it. An antivirus program protects your system in two ways: It scans incoming files to prevent infection, and it scans files already on your computer to rid your computer of any infection it might already have. Most antivirus programs also scan outgoing messages to prevent spreading viruses.

If you have never checked your computer for viruses, it may already be infected, making it even more urgent to install an antivirus program and scan your PC immediately. This section leads you through the process of downloading and installing Norton AntiVirus. You may also purchase a boxed copy of Norton AntiVirus, McAfee VirusScan, or another antivirus program, and install it from an installation CD.

Install an Antivirus Program

1. Type **www.symantec.com/downloads** in Internet Explorer's Address box and press Enter.

   Symantec's downloads page appears.

2. Scroll down and click the Download NOW! button for the antivirus program you want.

   This example uses Norton AntiVirus.

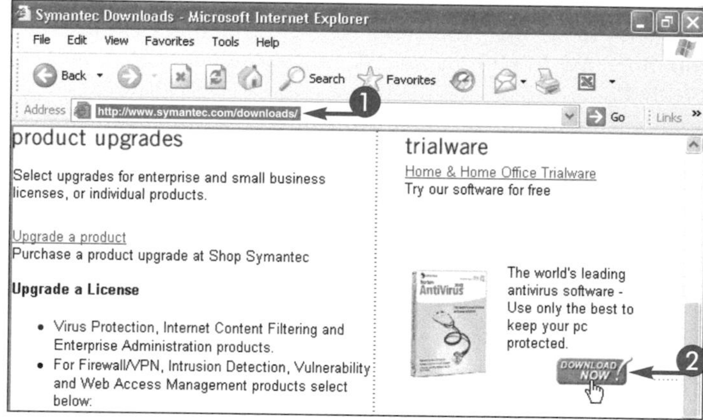

The Web site prompts you to specify your country of residence and your e-mail address.

3. Click here and select your country of residence.
4. Click here and type your e-mail address.
5. Click SUBMIT.

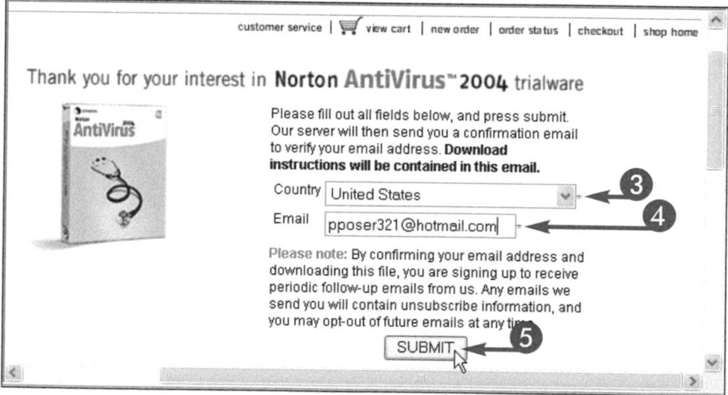

Symantec sends you an e-mail message to ensure that the e-mail address is valid.

6 Launch your e-mail program.

7 Click or double-click the message you received from Symantec.

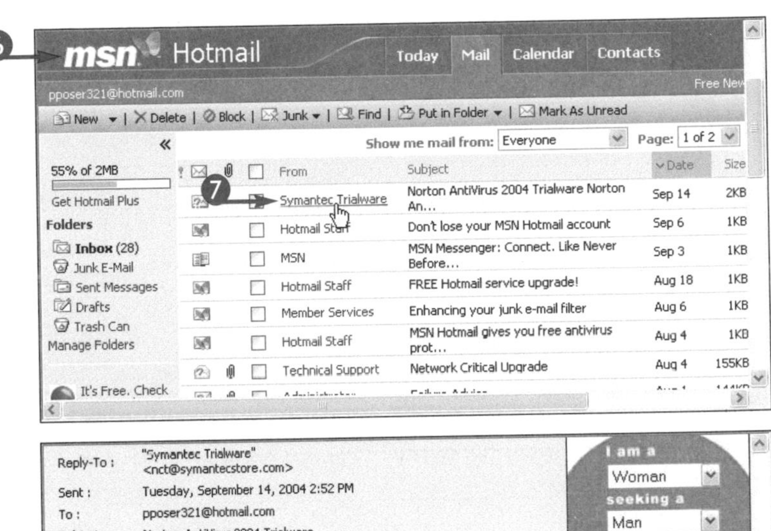

8 In the message that appears, follow the instructions to download and install the trial version of Norton AntiVirus.

The antivirus program is installed on your PC.

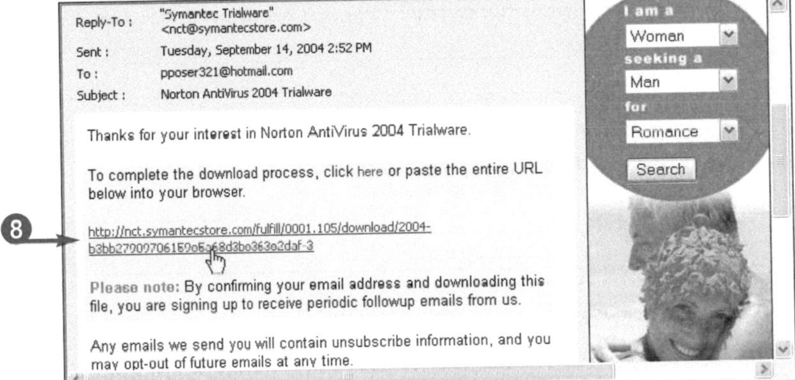

I downloaded and installed the Norton AntiVirus trialware. How long can I keep using it for free?

▼ The Norton AntiVirus trialware works for 15 days. After that, you must pay for the program to continue using it. You can order the product online. Symantec typically offers one or two years of free virus definition and program updates. Be sure to register for the updates so Norton AntiVirus can protect your PC from the latest viruses.

Where else can I go to obtain trialware or shareware versions of antivirus software?

▼ McAfee VirusScan is another excellent antivirus utility. You can obtain a 15-day free trial version of the program from download.mcafee.com. You can obtain AVG Anti-Virus from free.grisoft.com. AVG Anti-Virus is freeware for home users. Business users must pay for the utility, but special licensing deals are available for schools and nonprofit organizations.

How many different viruses are there?

▼ Nobody knows exactly, but at the writing of this book, McAfee's AVERT (Anti-Virus Emergency Response Team) reported the existence of more than 94,000 distinct viruses. McAfee's Security Headquarters at www.mcafeesecurity.com/us/security/home.asp is a great place to go to learn more about viruses and to determine whether information you receive about a virus is a valid warning or a hoax.

Scan Your System for Viruses

You can scan your entire PC, including its memory and all files on its disk drives, for known viruses or for any suspicious activity that may be a sign of a virus. To identify viruses, an antivirus program searches your system for identifiable programming code, commonly called *signatures*, contained in thousands of known viruses. If it finds a file that contains a virus signature, it displays the name of that file and provides options for removing the virus or deleting the file. In some cases, you have the option to quarantine the file, so that you cannot run it or open it.

In addition to scanning files for virus signatures, antivirus utilities commonly scan for any suspicious activity that may be a sign of a virus. For example, if a system file that never changes size suddenly becomes larger, the antivirus program can alert you of the change and help you identify the program that changed the file. It may also provide a way of restoring the file to its original condition.

When scanning for viruses, your antivirus program does not take action without your confirmation. However, you usually want to follow its recommendations in order to rid your PC of existing viruses.

Scan Your System for Viruses

1. Click Start.
2. Click All Programs.
3. Click the folder that contains your antivirus utility.
4. Click the name of your antivirus utility.

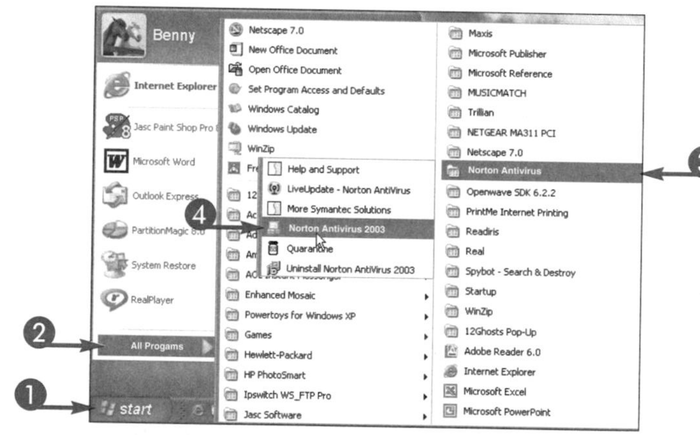

The antivirus utility's program window appears.

5. Click the option to scan for viruses.
6. Click the option to scan your entire computer.
7. Click the option to start scanning.

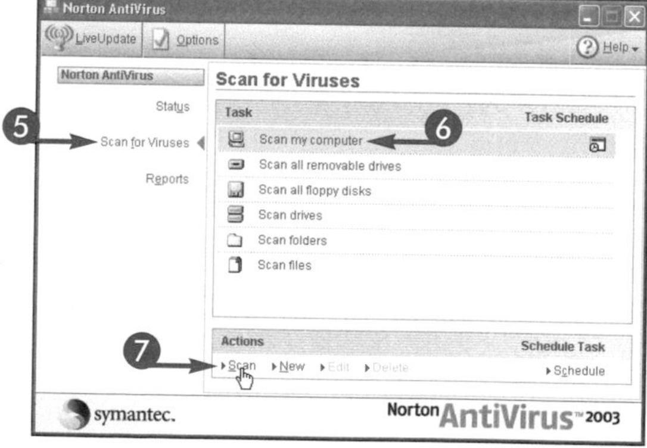

- Your antivirus program scans your PC's memory, disks, and files for viruses.

Note: *The time required to scan all files depends on the speed of your PC and the number and size of files on the disks.*

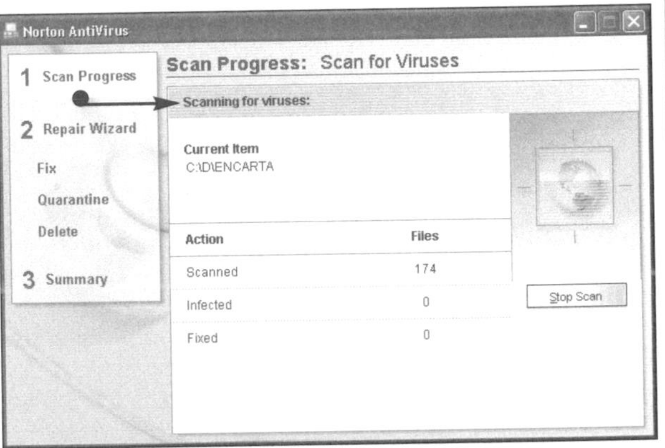

When the scan is complete, your antivirus utility displays the results.

- In this example, the antivirus utility detected no viruses.

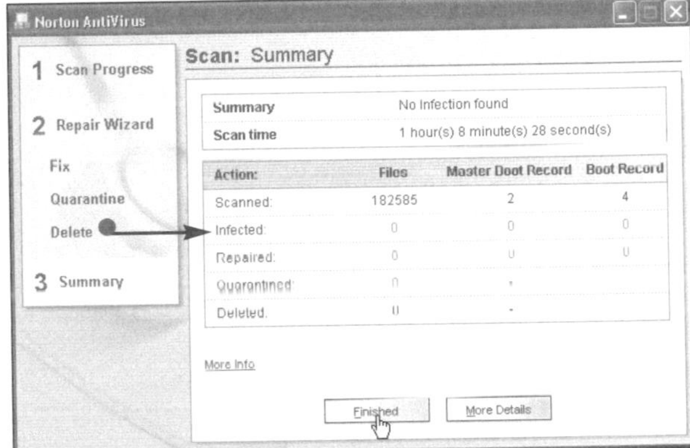

Can I scan individual drives, files, and folders?

Yes. In Norton AntiVirus, you can click Scan drives, Scan folders, or Scan files. A dialog box appears, prompting you to select the drive(s), folder(s), or file(s) you want to scan. Make your selections (☐ changes to ☑) and then click the option to start scanning. Your antivirus program may add a command to the context menu that appears when you right-click a disk, file, or folder in My Computer, making it even easier to scan individual items. You can simply right-click the disk, folder, or file you want to scan and then click the option to scan the selected item for viruses.

I ran Norton AntiVirus, and it detected a virus. What are my options for removing the virus?

Norton AntiVirus features a Wizard that leads you step-by-step through the process of removing the virus from your PC. The Wizard proceeds through three stages, from the safest option to the most drastic. First, it tries to remove the virus without harming the file it has infected. If AntiVirus cannot do that successfully, it tries to quarantine infected files. If it cannot effectively quarantine the files, it offers to delete them for you. Although the Wizard gives you the final decision on how to deal with infected files, you should follow its recommendations to ensure that the virus is removed safely.

Enable Auto-Protect Features

In most antivirus programs, you can enable an auto-protect feature that runs automatically whenever you start your computer and continues to run as you use your computer to perform various tasks. On startup, the auto-protect feature scans your computer's boot directory for viruses, a common point of attack. Whenever you download a file from the Internet, auto-protect scans it and reports potential viruses, so you can take immediate action before you open or run the file. In addition, auto-protect can scan incoming and outgoing e-mail messages and attachments for known viruses.

When you install most antivirus programs, the program enables the auto-protect feature by default. However, you should make sure auto-protect is on and is configured to provide your system with optimum protection. This section shows you how to enable auto-protect in Norton AntiVirus for Windows and enter your protection preferences. For more on installing Norton AntiVirus, see the section "Install an Antivirus Program."

You can also follow the steps in this section to disable auto-protect for times when a program does not install or run properly when an antivirus program is running in the background. Some CD and DVD burners, for example, conflict with antivirus software, so you must disable the auto-protect feature to burn discs. You may also want to selectively disable some auto-protect features to improve performance; for example, you can send e-mail faster by disabling auto-protect for outgoing messages.

Enable Auto-Protect Features

1. Click Start.
2. Click All Programs.
3. Click Norton AntiVirus.
4. Click Norton AntiVirus.

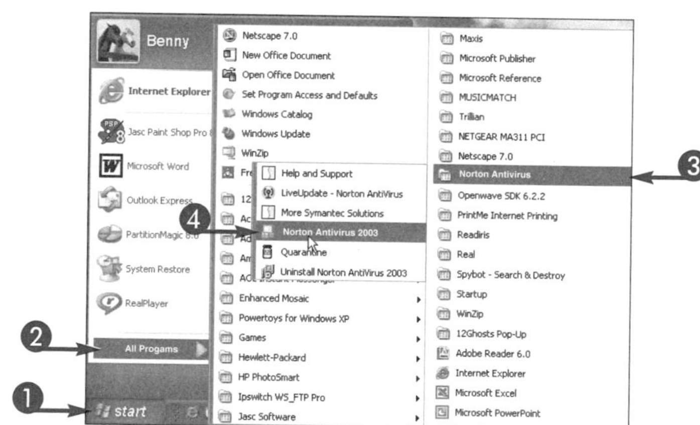

- Norton AntiVirus appears and indicates whether auto-protect is on or off.

5. Click the Options button.

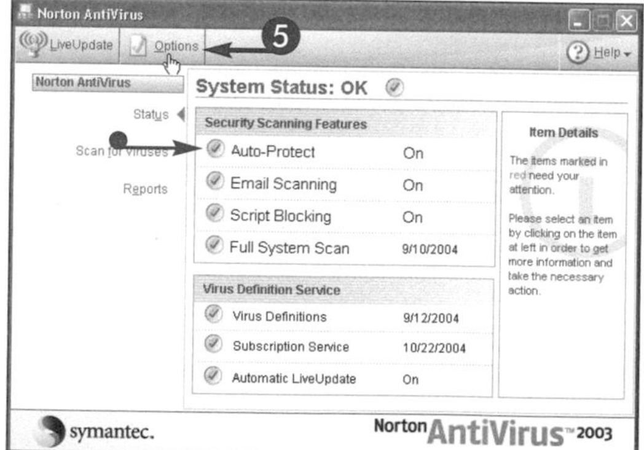

The Norton AntiVirus Options dialog box appears.

6 Click Auto-Protect.

- You can click the Enable Auto-Protect option to enable auto-protect (☐ changes to ☑).
- You can click the Start Auto-Protect when Windows starts up option to run auto-protect at startup (☐ changes to ☑).
- You can click the Show Auto-Protect icon in the tray option to display the Norton AntiVirus icon in the Windows system tray (☐ changes to ☑).

7 Click Email.

- You can click the Scan incoming Email option to have Norton AntiVirus scan e-mail you receive for viruses.

8 Click OK.

Norton AntiVirus saves your settings and returns you to its main program window, which you can now exit.

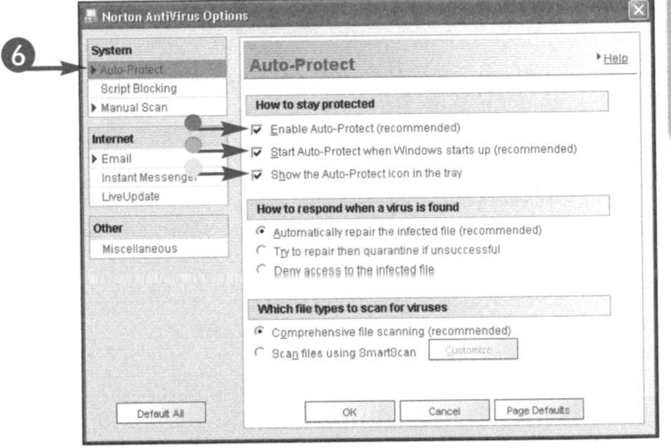

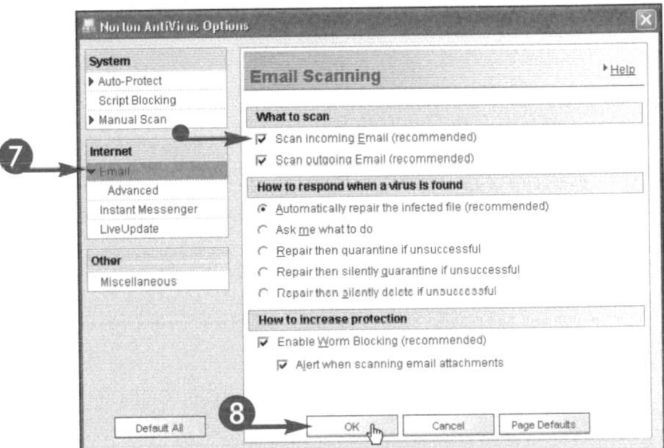

Do I really need to scan all outgoing e-mail messages?

After you do a full system scan to ensure that your PC is free of viruses, you have little reason to scan outgoing e-mail messages for viruses, even though Norton AntiVirus recommends it. Enabling scanning of outgoing messages adds significantly to the time it takes to send messages that contain attachments. If you disable this option, make sure you perform a full system scan weekly.

My PC is much slower now that I enabled auto-protection. Can I disable some automatic scans?

You can adjust the auto-protect settings to scan files less aggressively, but you must make trade-offs. Increasing security typically slows down your PC, because your antivirus utility must scan a wider range of files. If you limit the types of files that your antivirus utility scans, you place your PC at a greater risk of becoming infected.

I noticed options for protecting my instant messaging software. Are these necessary?

In the past, instant messaging programs only allowed users to exchange text messages. Now, they enable users to exchange files and share control of their computers. You should enable virus scanning for your instant messaging programs. In addition, you should check the security settings in your instant messaging programs, so other users cannot gain unauthorized access to your PC.

Enable Norton Automatic Updates

An antivirus utility is only effective if its list of virus definitions is accurate and complete. If you scan for viruses using an antivirus utility that has an old virus-definition list, it is not capable of identifying current viruses or removing them from your system.

Fortunately, the companies that develop antivirus utilities provide updates to their virus definition lists. Typically, you receive a 1- or 2-year subscription to virus updates when you purchase an antivirus utility. You can then download updates for free. Most programs display a button or link on the opening screen that you can click to download and install the updates. The subscription may also include program updates that you can download and install.

Norton AntiVirus and McAfee VirusScan also enable you to schedule automatic updates, so you do not need to remember to download and install updates. For example, you can schedule Norton AntiVirus to check for and install updates every Friday at 8:00 p.m. to ensure that you have definitions of the most current viruses. You can also schedule your antivirus program to perform a full system scan after installing the updates.

Enable Norton Automatic Updates

1. Click Start.
2. Click All Programs.
3. Click Norton AntiVirus.
4. Click Norton AntiVirus.

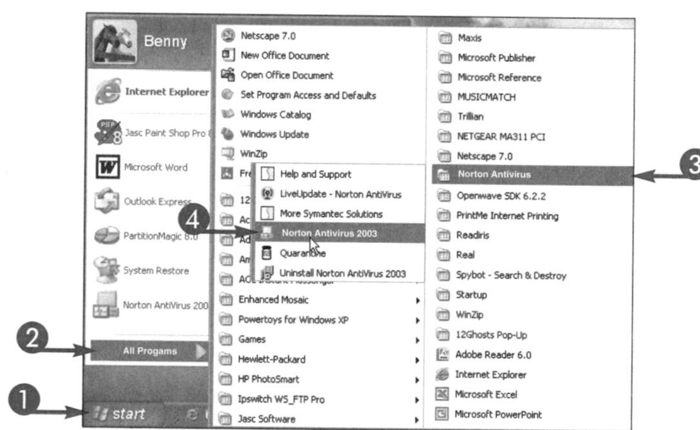

Norton AntiVirus appears.

5. Click the Options button.

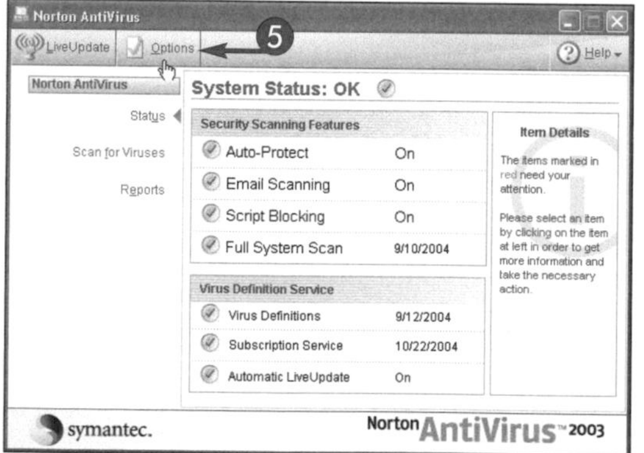

The Norton AntiVirus Options dialog box appears.

6 Click the Live Update link.

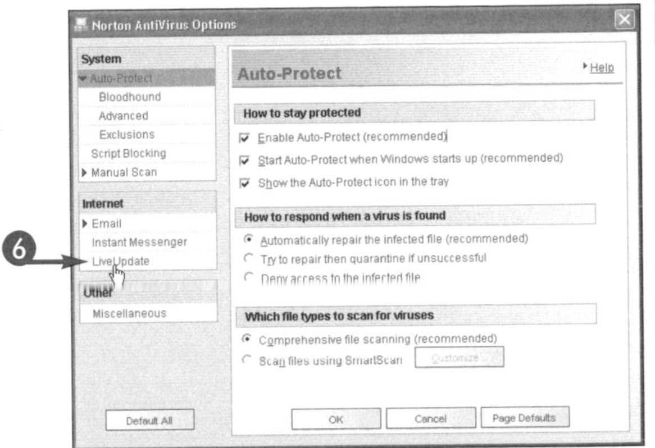

- The Automatic LiveUpdate options page appears.

7 Click the Enable automatic LiveUpdate option (☐ changes to ☑).

8 Click the Apply virus protection updates option (☐ changes to ☑).

9 Click the Notify me of Norton AntiVirus program updates option (☐ changes to ☑).

10 Click OK.

Norton AntiVirus saves the settings.

Note: *You must turn on your computer and connect it to the Internet at the scheduled time in order to download updates.*

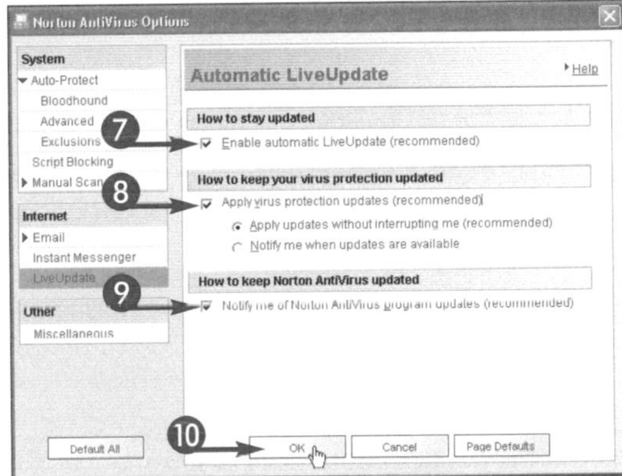

If I do not enable automatic updates, can I check for updates myself?

▼ Yes. Norton AntiVirus displays a button on its opening screen labeled LiveUpdate. Click LiveUpdate to view a list of components that require updates. Click Next and follow the on-screen instructions to download and install the updates. This ensures that you have the latest virus definition list and available program updates.

What happens if my PC is turned off when my antivirus program is scheduled to check for updates?

▼ If your PC is off at the scheduled time, your antivirus program checks for updates the next time you turn on your computer, log on to Windows, and connect to the Internet. It downloads and installs the updates in the background and then displays a pop-up message indicating that the updates were successfully downloaded and installed.

Should I renew my subscription for updates or purchase a new version of the antivirus utility?

▼ When your subscription expires, the antivirus developer may provide an option for you to renew your subscription for an additional fee. In some cases, you can purchase a new version of the utility complete with a new subscription for less than the cost of a subscription renewal. Check prices before renewing your subscription.

Understanding Internet Security

Whenever your PC connects to the Internet, it becomes part of the largest network in the world. Although it may not be as visible a target as a Web server at a large corporation, it is still vulnerable to being accessed without your permission. With the proper know-how, other people can log on to your computer, copy files and passwords, and freely use your computer's resources.

How vulnerable your PC is depends on the security measures you take. If you have an always-on Internet connection and you leave your PC on all the time without taking any steps to secure the connection, it is wide open for public access. However, if you connect to the Internet through a firewall-enabled router and you take a few additional steps to secure your operating system, you can lock out most users who may want to break into your system.

Is Your PC at Risk?

If you connect to the Internet over the phone line using a dial-up modem, and you immediately disconnect after using the Internet, your connection is fairly secure. The biggest threat your connection faces is Trojan horse software designed to automatically dial pay phone services at times when you are likely to be asleep. Scanning your PC regularly for viruses and keeping your PC turned off when you are not using it can prevent it from dialing out without your knowledge.

If your PC has a cable modem or DSL connection — commonly referred to as an always-on connection — it is at greater risk for attack, because it provides a stable target. A *cracker* — a person who breaks into computers — can more easily locate your PC among the many thousands on the Internet and try various techniques to gain access to it.

If you have an always-on connection, you can make your Internet connection much more secure by following the recommendations and instructions presented in this chapter.

Securing Your Connection: Firewalls and Routers

The first line of defense against computer break-ins is a firewall or router. A firewall is software that hides your computer's Internet address and filters traffic to prevent unauthorized or suspicious data transfers between your computer and other computers on the Internet. A firewall follows various rules to determine which data transfers to allow and which ones to prohibit.

Corporations and other large businesses are particularly susceptible to break-ins, and they need to control the types of data allowed to enter and leave the network, so firewalls are essential for business networks. However, home and small-business networks are also vulnerable, especially to unauthorized remote logins, so if your PC has an always-on connection, you should install and enable a firewall, as discussed in the section "Enable the Windows Firewall."

A *router* is a device that controls traffic between two or more networks. Many home networks use a wireless router that serves two functions — it provides a central hub through which all computers on the internal network connect to one another, and it acts as a gateway through which all traffic between the home network and the Internet passes. The router connects directly to the cable or DSL modem; all computers on the network connect to the router to obtain e-mail and to browse the Web rather than connecting directly to servers on the Internet. The router functions as a buffer between the network and the Internet. Most routers that serve this function have their own built-in firewall software that you can configure to filter traffic.

Securing Your PC

In order to receive e-mail and browse the Web, your PC cannot shut down traffic completely and remain isolated; as long as it is connected, it is vulnerable. However, by installing and using antivirus and security software and practicing safe computing, you can make your PC as secure as reasonably possible. You can also:

- Install and enable a firewall to help prevent unauthorized access, as explained in the section "Enable the Windows Firewall."
- Disable file and printer sharing for Microsoft Networks, as explained in the section "Disable File and Printer Sharing."
- Encrypt folders that contain sensitive data, as instructed in the section "Encrypt a Folder."
- Install an antivirus program, keep it updated, and enable its auto-protect features, as explained in Chapter 27. Antivirus software can identify and remove Trojan horse software designed to enable remote access to your PC.
- Keep your operating system software and application software up to date, as explained in Chapters 22 and 24. This ensures that you have the latest security patches installed.
- Scan for and remove adware and spyware, which can compromise your privacy, as explained in Chapter 14.
- Tighten your Web browser's security settings, as discussed in Chapter 29.

Microsoft Security Center

Chapter 22 contains instructions on how to update Windows to ensure that you have the latest security patches and other Windows updates installed. If you install Windows Service Pack 2, Windows automatically connects you to the Microsoft Security Center, which tests your PC to ensure that it has a firewall installed and running, that it has antivirus software installed and set up to protect your PC, and that the Windows automatic updates feature is enabled. To visit the Microsoft Security Center, click Start, All Programs, Accessories, System Tools, and then Security Center. If Security Center does not appear on the menu, you have not yet updated to Microsoft Windows XP Service Pack 2.

Test Windows Security

The Microsoft Security Center, introduced in the section "Understanding Internet Security," can test three major security areas: the firewall, antivirus protection, and Windows XP software updates, but it does not test for security issues with your software, such as missing software patches and macro vulnerability. It also does not test other potential vulnerabilities, such as whether you have a file server installed without your knowledge.

To overcome these limitations, Microsoft offers a free utility called MBSA (Microsoft Baseline Security Analyzer) that you can use to thoroughly scan your PC for areas where you can tighten security. MBSA analyzes Windows and Microsoft Office applications to ensure that all critical security updates are installed, that a firewall is installed and enabled, that Internet Explorer's security zones are enabled for all uses, and that other potential security holes are plugged.

MBSA analyzes your PC, your Internet connection, and your network configurations, and then displays a report showing a list of all of the items it checked. MBSA marks any areas that pose a high security risk with a red X and provides instructions on how to correct problems and tighten security.

Test Windows Security

Download and Install MBSA

1. In your Web browser's Address bar, type **www.microsoft.com/technet/security/tools/mbsahome.mspx** and press Enter.

Note: *If the MBSA page has moved, run Windows Help, search for MBSA, and click the link to connect to the MBSA page.*

2. Click the link for downloading the language version of MBSA that you want.

The File Download dialog box appears.

3. Click Run and follow the on-screen instructions to download and install the MBSA utility.

Your Web browser downloads and installs the MBSA utility and adds an icon for running it on the Start, All Programs menu.

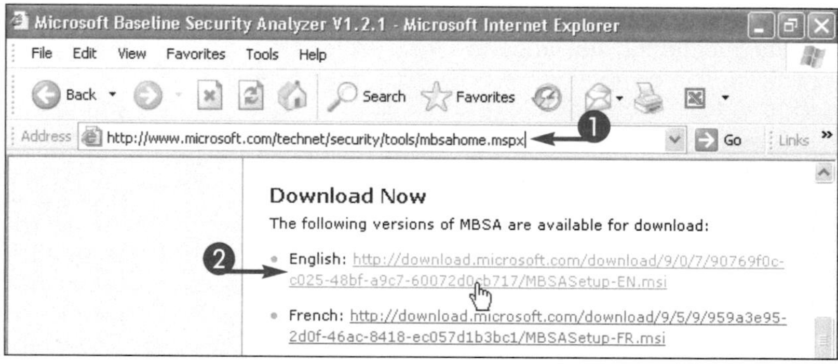

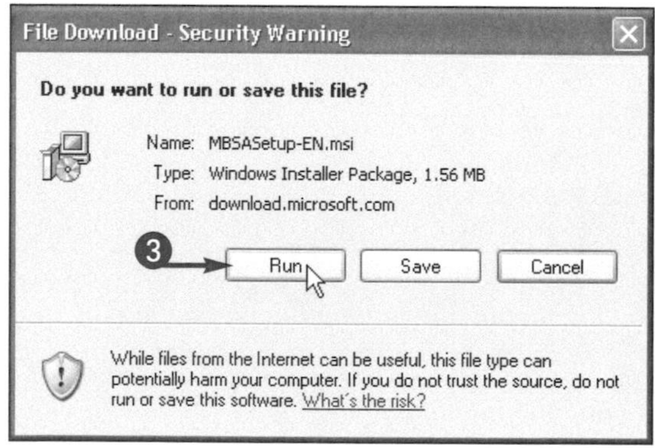

Analyze Your PC's Security

1. Double-click the Microsoft Baseline Security Analyzer icon on the Windows desktop.
2. Click Scan a computer.
3. Click here and select the PC you want to scan.
4. Click Start scan.

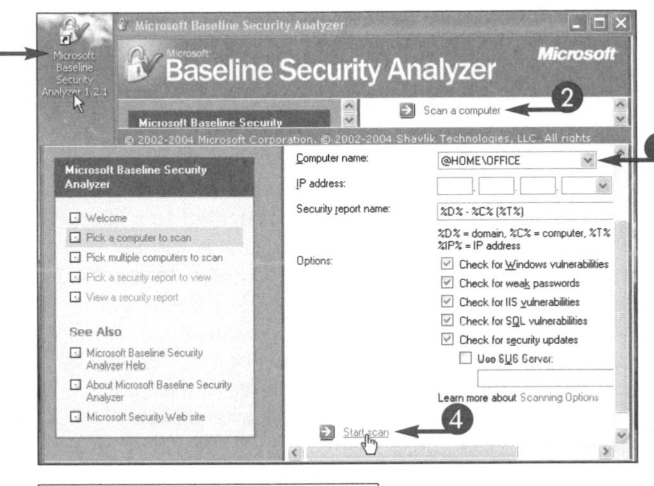

Microsoft Baseline Security Analyzer scans your PC and displays its security report.

- If MBSA identifies a problem, you can click the How to correct this link for instructions on how to repair the security hole.

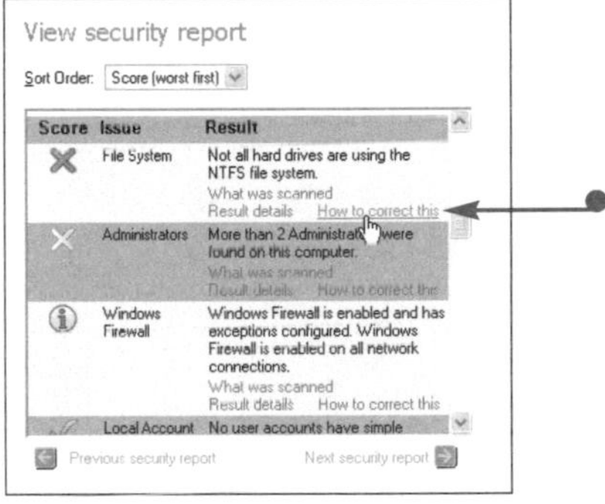

Can I find out more about what MBSA scanned and the problems that it found?

Yes. Below each item in the MBSA report are two links: What was scanned and Result details. Click the What was scanned link to find out the specific tests that MBSA peformed. Click the Result details link to determine which items were acceptable and which items did not pass the tests. After you correct problems that MBSA reports, analyze your PC again.

I have two or more PCs that share a network connection through a wireless router. Do I need to analyze all PCs on the network?

Yes. If one PC on the network is susceptible to unauthorized access, all PCs on the network run the risk of having their security breached. Run MBSA on every computer and fix all problems it identifies. You may be able to analyze multiple PCs from the PC on which you installed MBSA.

Does MBSA analyze my PC to ensure that an antivirus utility is installed and configured properly to protect my PC?

No. MBSA focuses on your Internet connection settings to ensure that no connections permit unauthorized access. However, MBSA does check the macro settings in your Office applications to ensure that macro security is configured to protect against macro viruses. It also checks Internet Explorer to ensure that security for the Internet zone is enabled.

Enable the Windows Firewall

When you connect your computer to the Internet, you place it on a network connected to millions of other computers. To help your computer navigate on this information superhighway, your Internet service provider assigns it a number that identifies it. With this number, anyone with a moderate amount of knowledge and desire can follow your every move on the Internet and even break into your computer to use your computer's resources, steal or destroy data, or perform other malicious activity without your knowledge.

To prevent your computer from becoming a fixed target for spies, thieves, and vandals, you can enable the Windows Firewall. The firewall stands between your computer and the Internet, hiding your computer's address from other users and preventing unauthorized access to your computer.

Whenever another computer attempts to send data or a program to your computer when you have not specifically requested that the computer do so, the Windows Firewall identifies the attempt as an *unsolicited request* and blocks the transaction. The firewall displays a dialog box asking if you want to permit an *exception*. You may want to permit an exception, for example, if a friend tries to send you a photograph or some other file via an instant messaging program.

Enable the Windows Firewall

1. Click Start.
2. Right-click My Network Places.
3. Click Properties.

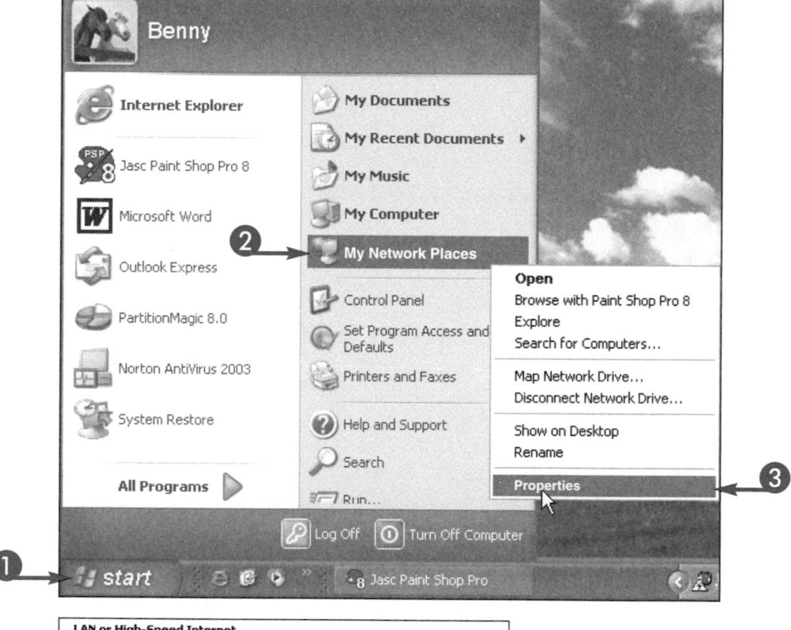

The Network Connections icons appear.

4. Double-click the icon for your Internet network connection.

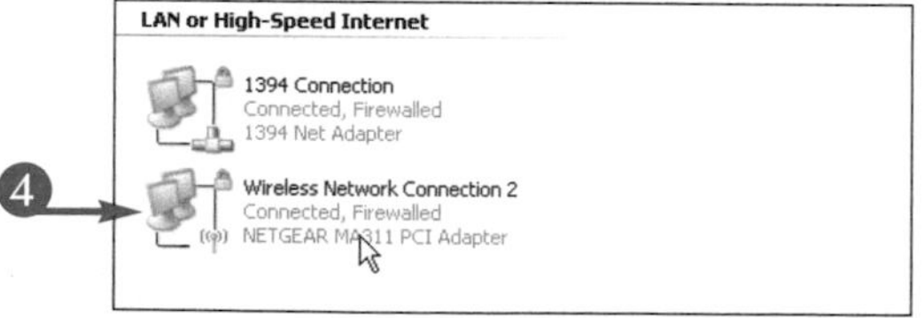

The Network Connection Status dialog box appears.

5 Click Properties.

The Network Connection Properties dialog box appears.

6 Click the Advanced tab.

7 Click Settings.

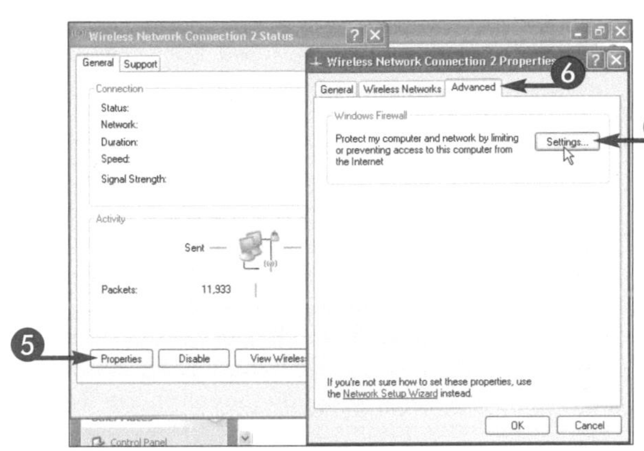

The Windows Firewall dialog box appears.

8 Click the On (recommended) option (○ changes to ◉).

9 Click OK.

Windows saves your settings and enables the firewall.

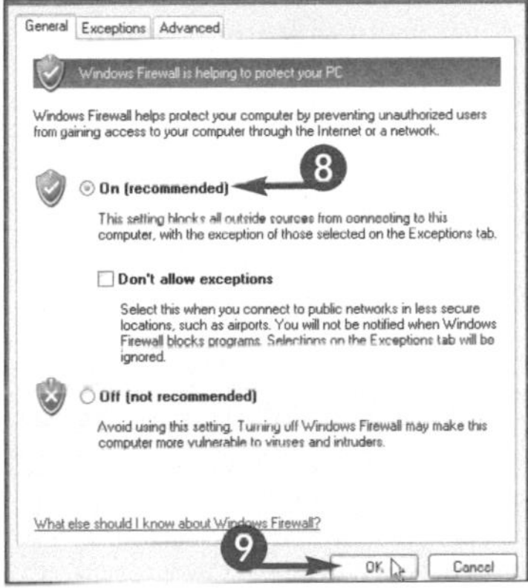

My PC has Windows XP installed, but the firewall settings differ from the settings shown in these steps. Why?

▼ The steps in this section show the firewall settings in Windows XP with Service Pack 2 installed. The firewall in this version is much more flexible than the firewall offered in earlier versions of Windows XP. It is recommended that you download and install the current service pack to provide your PC with additional security enhancements in addition to improved firewall software.

My PC is running an older version of Windows that does not have a firewall. What should I do?

▼ Several companies offer freeware or trialware versions of firewall software for different versions of Windows. Visit www.download.com or www.tucows.com to check out available firewalls. Sygate Personal Firewall, a freeware utility, has received consistently positive reviews. You can download it from smb.sygate.com. Zone Alarm, which you can download from www.zonealarm.com, also has a strong reputation, although early versions developed for Windows XP had compatibility problems with some systems.

Does the firewall prevent viruses and worms from reaching my PC?

▼ Yes. A firewall can help prevent viruses and worms from being placed on your PC by blocking unsolicited requests to access your PC. However, most firewalls, including the Windows Firewall, do not detect viruses, worms, or Trojan horses. This malicious software can find its way onto your PC from other sources, including e-mail attachments. Use antivirus software in addition to a firewall to protect your PC.

Allow Windows Firewall Exceptions

Your PC has a collection of ports that act as pipelines carrying data into and out of your PC. The Windows Firewall shuts down most of these ports to prevent unauthorized data flow. The more ports it shuts down, the more secure your PC is. However, some programs require that specific ports remain open. For example, a multiplayer game that you play over a network or over the Internet may require that one or more of the ports that the Windows Firewall normally blocks remain open. As long as the ports remain closed, you and the other player cannot play the game.

In most cases, when your PC attempts to communicate over a port that the Windows Firewall blocks, Windows Firewall displays a dialog box asking if you want to allow an exception. If you click Yes, Windows Firewall opens the port, so data can flow freely. In some cases, however, you may need to adjust Windows Firewall settings to allow an exception for a specific program.

Many programs select a port on startup or when they need to establish a connection, in which case you can allow an exception for the program. In some cases, however, the program requires the use of a specific port, so you must consult the program's documentation and then open the specified port.

Allow Windows Firewall Exceptions

1. Display the Windows Firewall dialog box.

Note: *Refer to the section "Enable the Windows Firewall" for details.*

2. Click the Exceptions tab.
3. Click Add Program.

The Add a Program dialog box appears, displaying a list of installed programs.

4. Click the program for which you want to allow an exception.
5. Click Change scope.

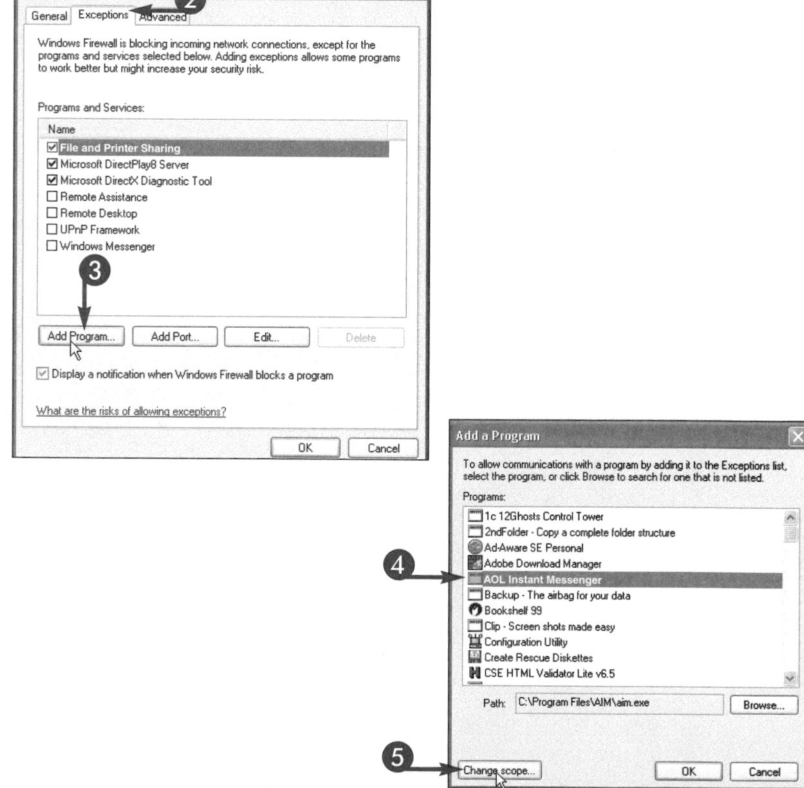

The Change Scope dialog box appears.

6 Click an option to specify the computers you want to allow access to the connection (○ changes to ◉).

You can choose to give access to all computers, only computers on the local network, or only the computers whose IP address you specify.

7 Click OK.

8 Click OK in the Add a Program dialog box.

The Windows Firewall dialog box reappears.

9 Click OK.

Windows saves your settings and allows the selected program unrestricted access.

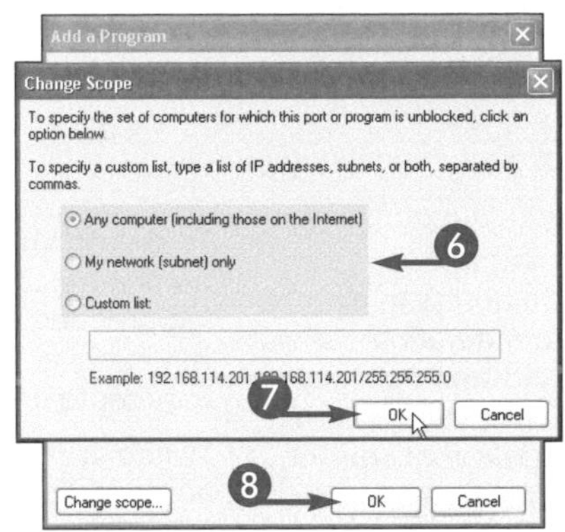

What should I do if I created an exception for a program, but it still cannot establish a connection?

▼ The program may require access to a specific port that Windows Firewall blocks. When you play multiplayer games over the Internet or run instant messaging programs with Webcams, you may have this problem. Instead of allowing an exception for the program, try opening the port. If your PC functions as an HTTP or FTP server, also try opening specific ports to enable access to the server. Check the program's documentation or online technical support to determine the correct port address. Then, display the Windows Firewall dialog box, click the Exceptions tab, and then Add Port. Type a name for the exception, type the specified port address, and click OK.

If someone is trying to access my PC remotely without my permission, can I find out who it is?

▼ Probably not with Windows Firewall, but you can examine a log of activity for your connection. To have Windows Firewall log Internet activity, display the Windows Firewall dialog box, click the Advanced tab, and under Security Logging, click Settings. Click the Log successful connections option (☐ changes to ☑), and then click OK. Click OK to close the Windows Firewall dialog box and save your settings. Windows Firewall records successful connections in the pfirewall.log file, which you can open in Windows Notepad or WordPad. Some third-party firewalls do a much better job of keeping you informed about successful and unsuccessful attempts to access your PC.

Using a Limited User Account

When you log on to Windows using an administrator account, you gain access to all accounts on your PC and all configuration settings. As administrator, you can install and uninstall software, change user account passwords, edit the Windows registry, and perform other administrative tasks that control the operation of your PC and enable network access to its files and other resources. If someone on the Internet gains remote access to your PC while you are logged on as administrator, the person has complete control of your PC and can perform those same administrative tasks. As you can imagine, this leaves your PC wide open to unauthorized users.

To protect your PC, Microsoft recommends that you limit the number of administrator accounts on your PC and that you log on using a limited user account whenever possible; that is, whenever you do not need to log on as an administrator in order to install software or configure your PC.

Windows requires that you have at least one administrator account. For optimum security, choose one account to use as an administrator account and then change the other accounts to limited accounts, as shown in the steps in this section.

Using a Limited User Account

1. Click Start.
2. Click Control Panel.
3. Click User Accounts.

The User Accounts window appears.

4. Click the account for which you want to change the account type.

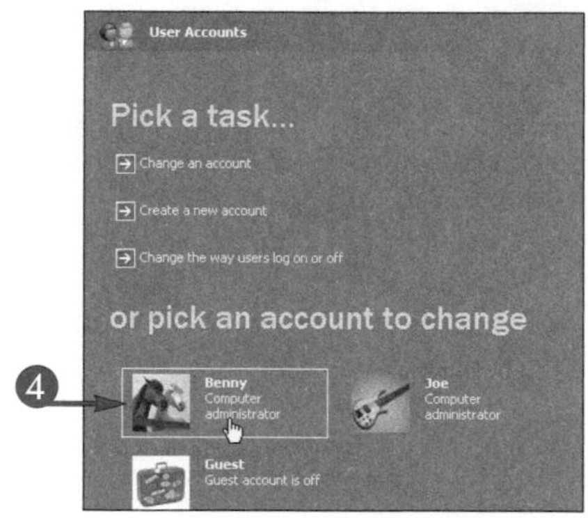

The options for the selected account appear.

5. Click the Change my account type link.

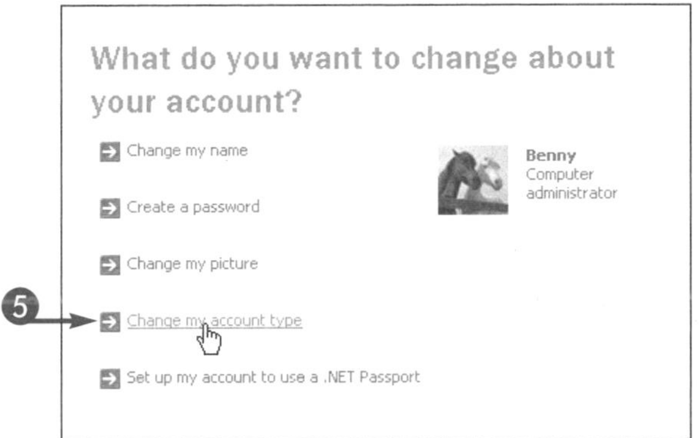

The Pick a new account type window appears.

6. Click the account type option you want to apply to this user (○ changes to ◉).

7. Click Change Account Type.

Windows changes the account type and closes the window.

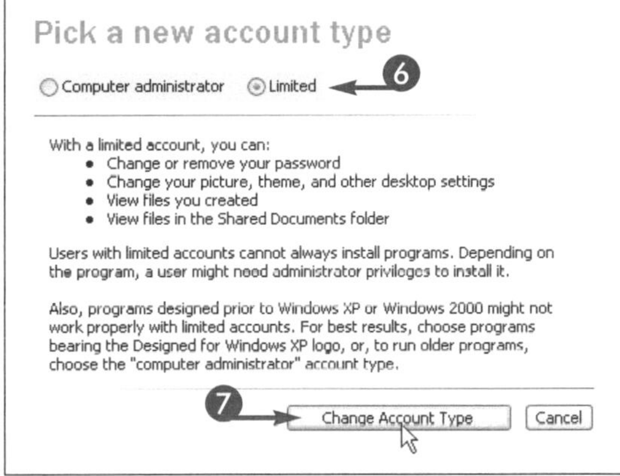

Should I assign passwords to all accounts?

▼ Account passwords provide an added level of protection against unauthorized access. You should always password protect your administrator account to prevent other users from taking control of your PC. Adding passwords to limited accounts is less important. When selecting a password, use a combination of letters and numbers to make the password difficult to guess.

Does logging on as an administrator place my PC at a greater risk?

▼ Yes. If you are logged on as an administrator when an unauthorized user gains access to your PC, the person has much more power to change configuration settings. If you are the administrator, create two accounts for yourself: an administrator account and a limited account. Log on with your limited account unless you need to install software or configure Windows.

Should I create a guest account?

▼ A guest account is useful if people, who are not regular users, need to use your PC temporarily; for example, if a friend occasionally logs on to check a Web-based e-mail account or to look something up on the Web. A guest account does not enable the user to install software or change account settings, but provides access to hardware, software, and shared documents. In Windows XP Professional, you can turn off the guest account for additional security.

Disable File and Printer Sharing

To connect to the Internet, you must enable various network settings, which open the lines of communication, but which can make your PC more vulnerable to unauthorized access. Network settings, for example, typically enable file and printer sharing, so that all computers on the network can exchange files and share hardware resources, including printers. When you enable file and printer sharing, however, you make your folders and files accessible to anyone who manages to log on to your computer.

File and printer sharing essentially transforms any PC on which it is enabled into a network server. To share a disk, folder, file, printer, or other resource, you can right-click the item's icon, click Sharing, and then enter your preferences. You can even assign the item a password to increase security. However, in the case of folders and files, the password provides little security.

You can disable file and printer sharing for any PCs on your network that do not need to share their resources. If you have only one PC, you can definitely do without file and printer sharing and significantly enhance your PC's security.

Disable File and Printer Sharing

1. Click Start.
2. Right-click My Network Places.
3. Click Properties.

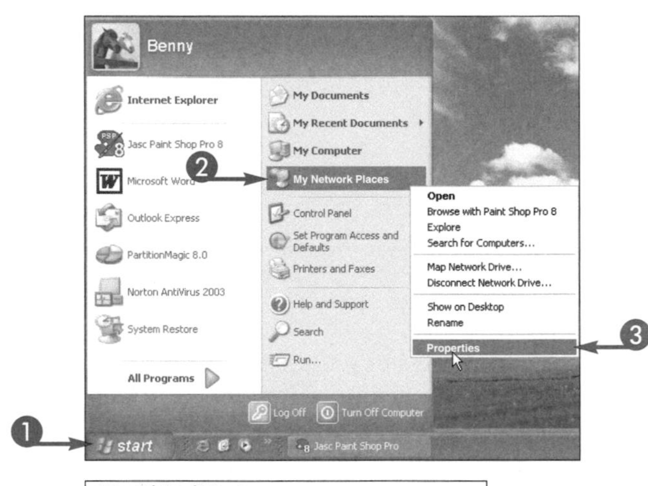

- The Network Connections dialog box appears, displaying icons for your network connections.

4. Right-click the icon for your network connection.
5. Click Properties.

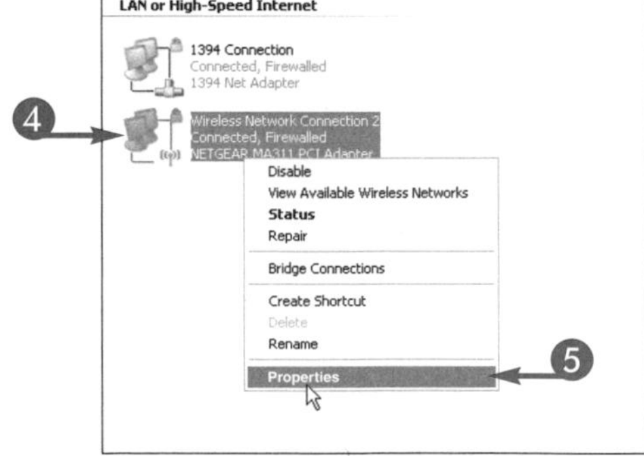

The network connection's Properties dialog box appears.

6 Click the "File and Printer Sharing for Microsoft Networks" option (☑ changes to ☐).

7 Click OK.

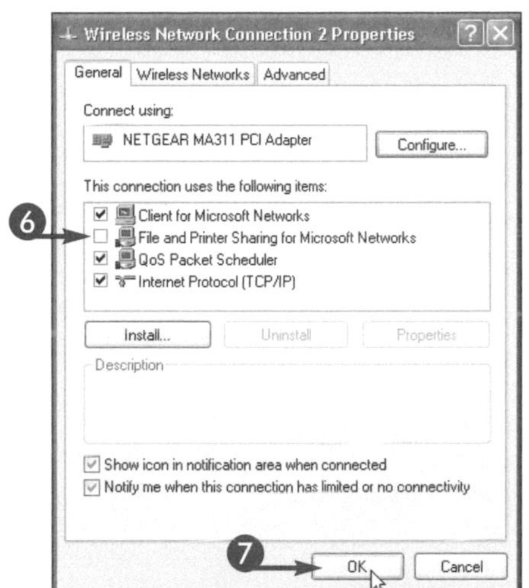

The network connection's Properties dialog box closes and returns you to the Network Connections window.

8 Click the Close button (☒).

The Network Connections window closes, and you can no longer mark items on this PC as shared resources.

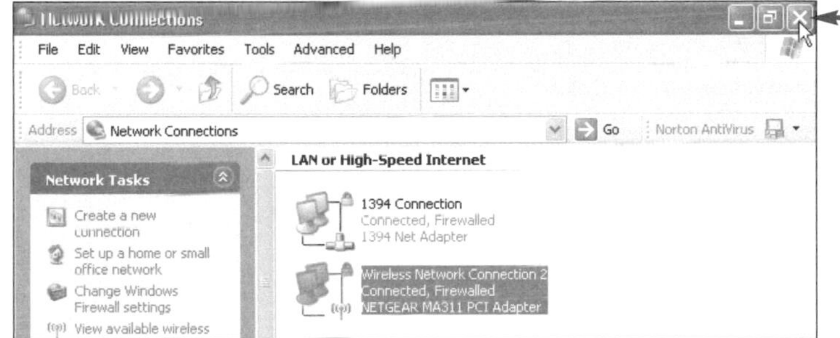

I just added my PC to a network. Can I enable File and Printer Sharing for Microsoft Networks?

▼ Yes. Perform the same steps shown in this section to enable the "File and Printer Sharing for Microsoft Networks" option (☐ changes to ☑). If your hard drive uses NTFS, you can further secure specific folders by setting access controls or encrypting them. See the section "Encrypt a Folder" for details.

Can I share every folder and file on my hard drive?

▼ Yes. By marking a drive as shared, you mark all folders and files on the drive as shared. However, Microsoft strongly recommends against marking an entire drive as shared, because this provides full access to the drive. Only mark as shared those folders and files that you need to share on the network.

Can I encrypt files and folders on a FAT32 drive?

▼ No. File encryption and compression are not available on FAT32 drives. Microsoft strongly recommends, for security purposes, that you convert drives to NTFS. To learn the benefits of the NTFS drive format and obtain instructions on how to convert a drive from FAT32 to NTFS, refer to Chapter 9.

Encrypt a Folder

If you store sensitive data on your PC, such as credit card statements, banking records, mortgage data, or your personal diary, you may want to encrypt the data so that if anyone does manage to gain access to your PC from a remote location, the intruder cannot view the contents of your files. In addition, if your computer is stolen and the thief is unable to log on to your user account, the encrypted files remain inaccessible. If someone tries to open the file or folder or decrypt it from another user account, the Access Denied message appears.

When you encrypt a file, Windows prompts you to specify whether you want to encrypt only the file or the folder that contains the file and all subfolders and files stored in it. When you encrypt a folder, Windows prompts you to choose whether you want to encrypt only the selected folder or the folder and all of its contents, including subfolders.

Encryption remains transparent to you, as a user. When you log on to your user account, all encrypted files and folders are accessible to you. When someone else logs on, however, encrypted files remain inaccessible.

Encrypt a Folder

1. Right-click a folder you want to encrypt.
2. Click Properties.

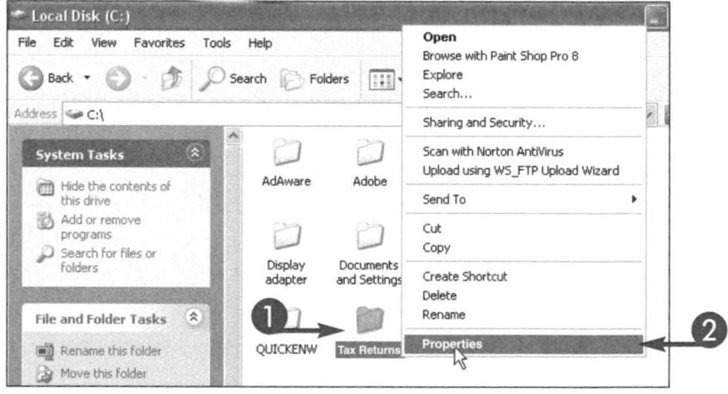

The folder's Properties dialog box appears.

3. Click Advanced.

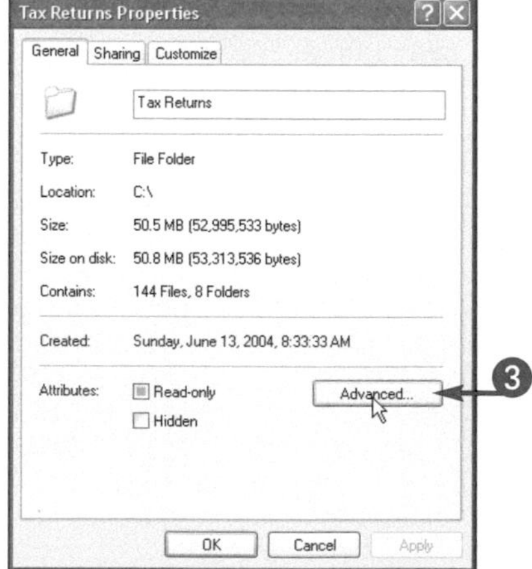

The Advanced Attributes dialog box appears.

4 Click the Encrypt contents to secure data option (☐ changes to ☑).

5 Click OK.

The Advanced Attributes dialog box closes.

6 Click OK in the folder's Properties dialog box.

The Confirm Attribute Changes dialog box appears.

7 Click either the "Apply changes to this folder only" or the "Apply changes to this folder, subfolders and files" option (○ changes to ◉).

8 Click OK.

Windows saves the settings for this folder and encrypts the folder and its contents, if specified.

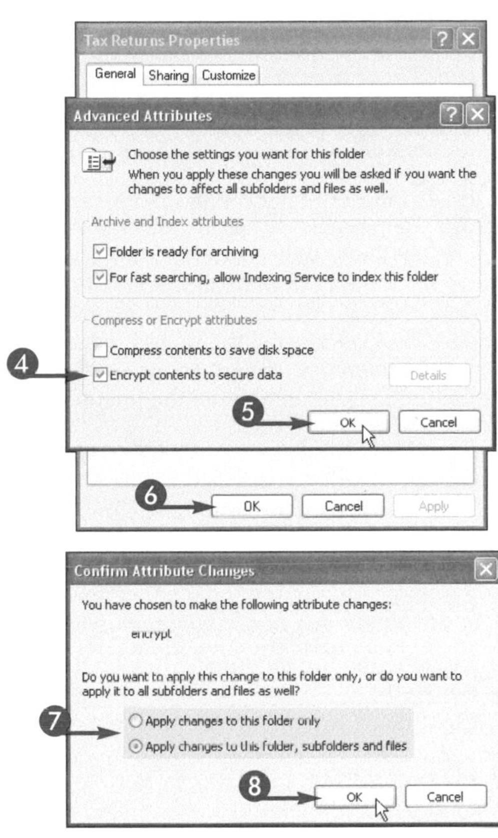

Can I decrypt a file or folder?

▼ Yes. You follow similar steps to decrypt a file or folder. Right-click the file or folder you want to decrypt and click Properties. Click Advanced, click the Encrypt contents to secure data option (☑ changes to ☐), and then click OK, and then OK in the item's Properties dialog box. Click either the option to decrypt only the selected item or to decrypt the selected item and related items, and then click OK.

I followed the steps in this section, but the Properties dialog box has no Advanced button. Why not?

▼ You have a version of Windows prior to XP or your PC's hard drive is formatted with the FAT or FAT32 file system rather than NTFS. You must have Windows XP and an NTFS-formatted drive in order to take advantage of file encryption. You can use a third-party file-encryption utility to encrypt files and folders.

Can I send encrypted files as e-mail attachments?

▼ Yes, but the files are no longer encrypted when you send them. Windows automatically decrypts a file when you send it as an e-mail attachment. In order to send encrypted e-mail messages and attachments, you must use a special utility designed for that purpose, such as PGP (Pretty Good Privacy). You can find several such utilities on the Web at www.tucows.com, www.download.com, or other shareware repositories.

Disable Universal Plug and Play

Windows Me and Windows XP feature support for a technology called Universal Plug and Play (UPnP), which extends the capability of Plug and Play technology to networks. With UPnP, computers on a network can automatically identify a new device installed on the network and install the drivers necessary to use the device. This is very convenient for network users, but it also makes a PC more vulnerable on the Internet.

In Windows Me, UPnP is not installed or enabled by default. In Windows XP, UPnP is installed and enabled by default. The threat to which UPnP opens your system is not very serious. Someone may be able to take advantage of the security flaw to degrade system performance and perhaps shut down the PC by sending repeated requests. Restarting Windows helps you recover. In addition, if you have a firewall installed and enabled, your PC is much more difficult to find on the Internet in order to exploit the security problem.

However, if you do not use UPnP to install network devices on the fly, you can uninstall UPnP to disable it and further enhance system security.

Disable Universal Plug and Play

1. Click Start.
2. Click Control Panel.

The Windows Control Panel appears.

3. Click Add or Remove Programs.

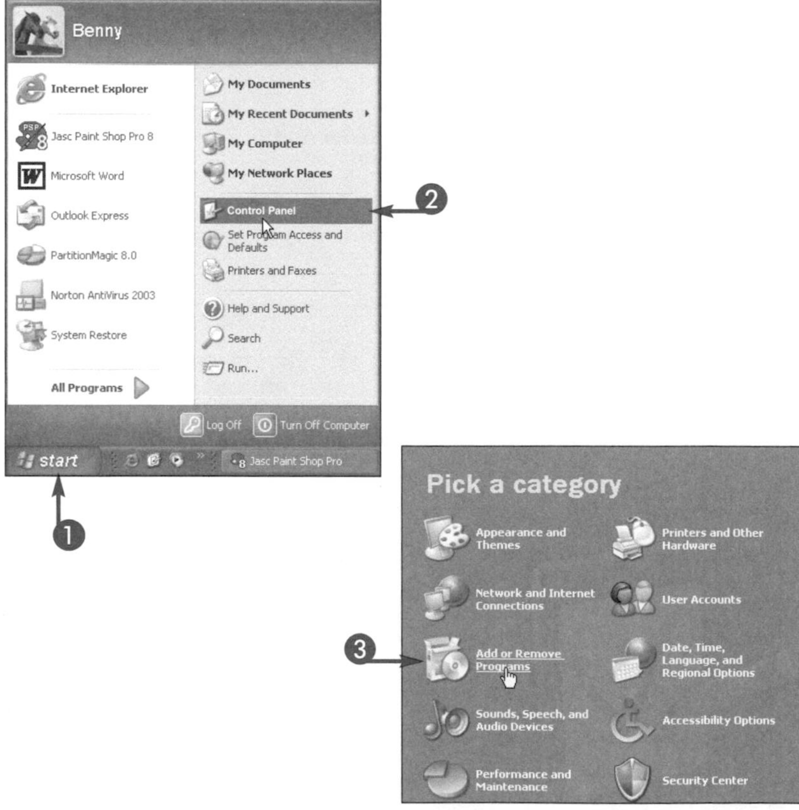

The Add or Remove Programs Window appears.

4 Click Add/Remove Windows Components.

The Windows Components Wizard appears.

5 Scroll down and click Networking Services.

6 Click Details.

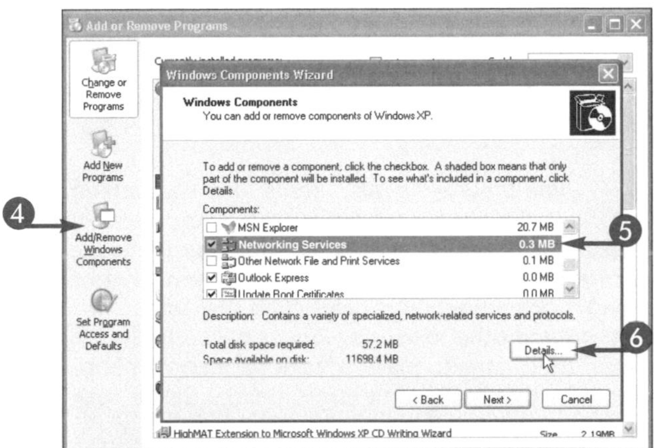

The Networking Services dialog box appears.

7 Click next to UPnP User Interface to deselect it (☑ changes to ☐).

8 Click OK.

9 Click Next.

Windows removes Universal Plug and Play from your PC.

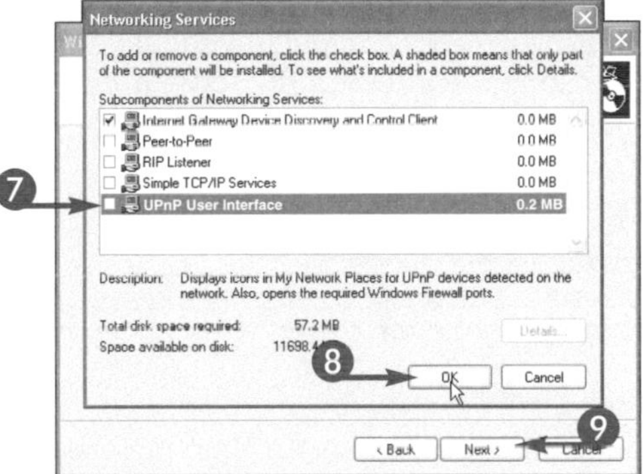

Does disabling Universal Plug and Play affect my ability to automatically install new hardware devices on my PC?

▼ No. Plug and Play and Universal Plug and Play are two separate features. When you connect a new device to your PC, the Plug and Play feature still detects the device, helps Windows identify it, and leads you through the process of installing the software required for Windows to use the device.

Can I disable Universal Plug and Play without removing it from my PC?

▼ Maybe. In Windows XP, click Start, right-click My Computer, click Manage, Services and Applications, double-click Services, click Universal Plug and Play Device Host, and click the Stop link. This shuts down the service without uninstalling it and protects your PC from attacks related to UPnP. In Windows Me, uninstall UPnP as shown in the steps in this section in order to disable it.

I installed and enabled UPnP, but it does not seem to be working. What could be wrong?

▼ Windows Firewall typically blocks the ports that UPnP requires to establish network connections. You may need to allow an exception for it. Refer to the section "Allow Windows Firewall Exceptions" for instructions. Also, in the Windows Firewall dialog box, click the Don't allow exceptions option (☑ changes to ☐). If this option is selected, Windows Firewall ignores the exceptions you set up.

Configure Security Zones

As you browse the Web, some Web sites attempt to install ActiveX controls or other components on your computer with or without your permission. In most cases, these small programs add functionality to the Web pages or browser, enhancing Web sites with animations and other dynamic, interactive content. However, they can also place adware on your computer, change your browser's home page, steal or delete data, and cause other problems.

To prevent ActiveX controls and other potentially harmful software from installing on your computer without your authorization, you can tighten the security settings in your Web browser. Most Web browsers, including Internet Explorer, provide settings for completely blocking ActiveX controls and Java applets, or for displaying a dialog box that requires your confirmation before installing them.

To protect your PC from malicious software and other Internet threats, Internet Explorer uses four security zones: Internet, Local Intranet, Trusted Sites, and Restricted Sites. The Internet zone controls security for all sites that are not on the Trusted or Restricted Sites lists and are not part of your local intranet, if you have a local intranet. You can relax or tighten security for each zone.

Configure Security Zones

Adjust Default Security Level

1. Launch Internet Explorer.
2. Click Tools.
3. Click Internet Options.

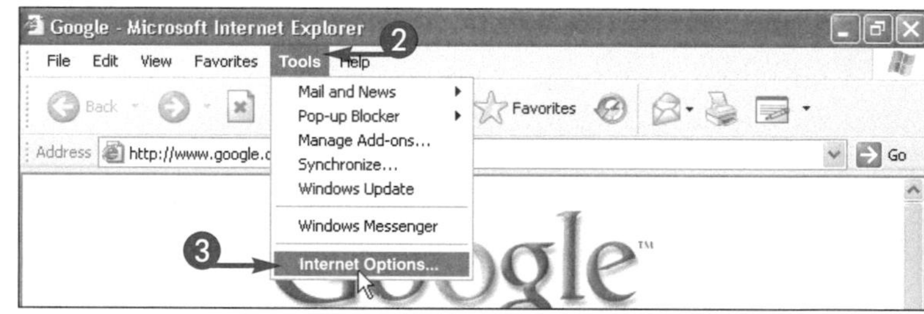

The Internet Options dialog box appears.

4. Click the Security tab.
5. Click the zone for which you want to change the security level.
6. Click and drag the slider up or down to the security level you want to use.
   - If the slider does not appear, click the Default Level button.

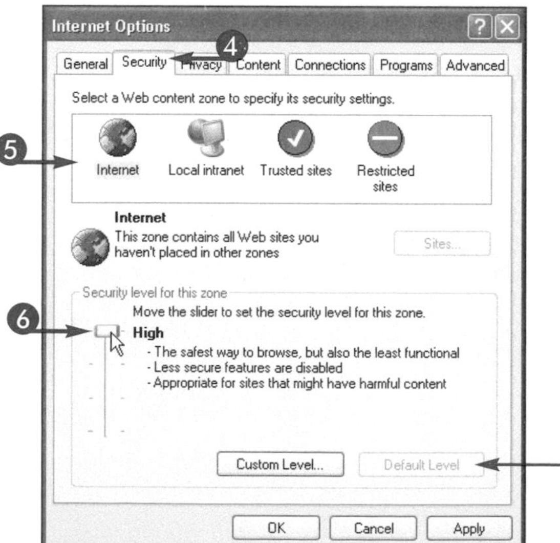

Enter Custom Security Settings

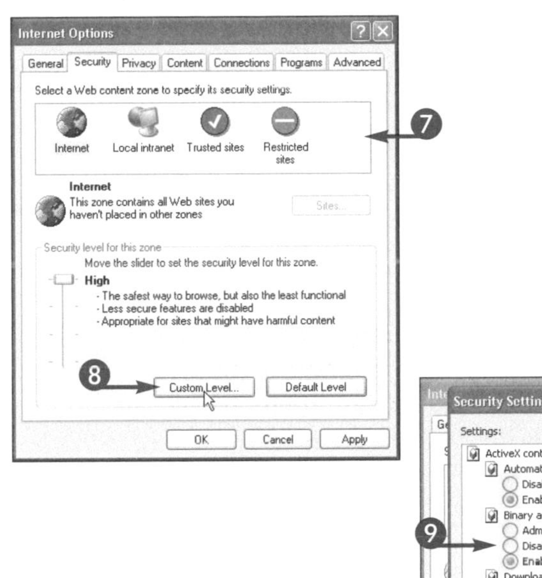

7. Click the zone for which you want to change the security level.
8. Click Custom Level.

The Security Settings dialog box appears.

9. Click the desired option or options for each security item (○ changes to ◉).
   - You can click here and click an option to learn more about it.
10. Click OK.
11. Click OK in the Internet Settings dialog box.

Your settings are saved.

Can I decide which content to view on a case-by-case basis?

▼ Usually. If you use the highest security setting, Internet Explorer may prevent the content from running at all. If you use a Medium or Medium-Low setting, Internet Explorer blocks some content and usually prompts you to choose whether to allow active content. The prompt may appear in a dialog box or in Internet Explorer's new Information Bar. See the section "Allow Blocked Content" for details.

I set the Internet zone security to High, and now I cannot access most of the features at my favorite site. What should I do?

▼ You can reset the security level to Medium or Medium low, or add the site to your list of trusted sites, as discussed in the section "Identify Trusted Sites." The security level for the Trusted Sites zone is Low, so you can access almost all features for sites in this zone.

Can I use a Web browser that is more secure than Internet Explorer?

▼ Some Web browsers, such as Opera and Mozilla, are more secure than Internet Explorer, but may not support features that Internet Explorer supports. When you deal with security, you always make trade-offs between functionality and security. For example, Internet Explorer's support for ActiveX controls enables your Web browser to play additional types of media files, but ActiveX controls can also function as spyware or adware or as a conduit for viruses.

Identify Trusted Sites

If you tighten security for the Internet zone, as discussed in the section "Configure Security Zones," some sites that make use of active content, Java applets, JavaScript, and other advanced Web page features may not function to your satisfaction. You can keep Web site security levels high while enabling functionality for specific Web sites by adding the sites to a list of trusted sites in Internet Explorer.

By default, the security setting for the Trusted Sites zone is Low, so any sites on the Trusted Sites list can freely run active content and make use of other advanced Web page features. When you add a site to the list of trusted sites, you provide it with a great deal of freedom on your PC, so be careful when adding Web sites to the list. Unless you specify otherwise, Internet Explorer enables you to add only *secure* Web sites to the list — that is, sites that have a URL starting with https:// rather than http://. You can change the setting to allow any Web site to be added to the list.

Identify Trusted Sites

1. Launch Internet Explorer.
2. Click Tools.
3. Click Internet Options.

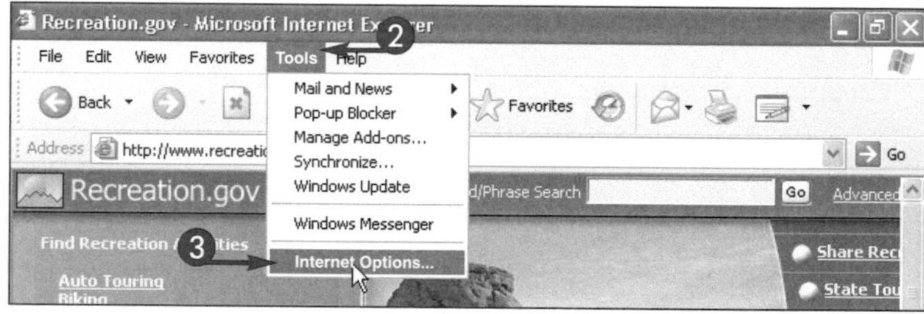

The Internet Options dialog box appears.

4. Click the Security tab.
5. Click Trusted sites.
6. Click Sites.

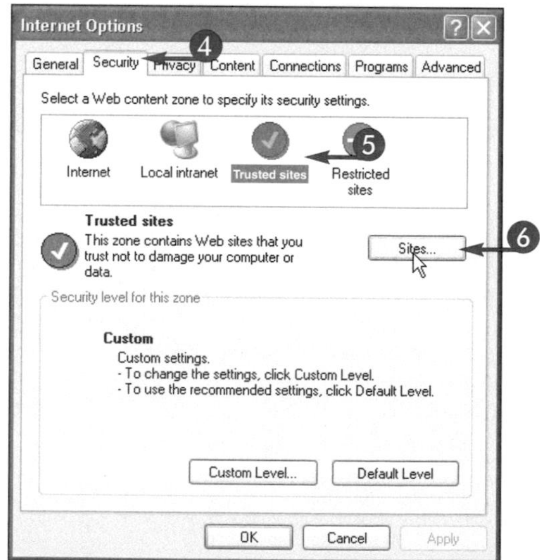

The Trusted sites dialog box appears.

7. Click the "Require server verification (https:) for all sites in this zone" option (☑ changes to ☐).

8. Click here and type the URL of the site you want to identify as a trusted site.

Note: *You must begin the URL with https:// or http://.*

9. Click Add.

10. Click OK.

The Trusted sites dialog box closes.

11. Click OK.

The Internet Options dialog box closes, and Internet Explorer relaxes security for the trusted site.

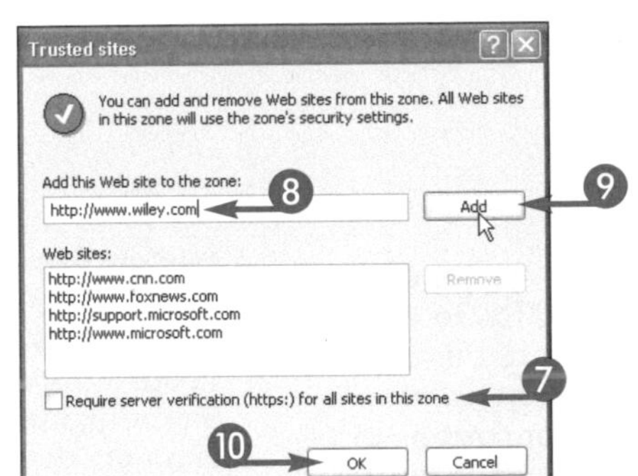

Can I increase security for specific sites?

▼ Yes. If you know of Web sites that you do not trust, you can add them to a list of restricted sites. On the Security tab in the Internet Options dialog box, click Restricted sites and then click Sites. Type the address of the site you want to restrict — the address must start with http:// or https:// — and click Add. Click OK to close the Restricted sites dialog box and save your changes.

I added a Web site to my list of trusted sites, but Internet Explorer is still blocking some content. What should I do?

▼ Sometimes a Web site redirects you to a related area of the same site that has a different URL. Unless this URL is on the trusted sites list, Internet Explorer uses the Internet zone security settings to determine which content to warn you about or block. Add the site's URL to the list of trusted sites.

I no longer trust one of the Web sites on the list of trusted sites. How do I remove it?

▼ Display the Internet Options dialog box and click the Security tab. Click Trusted sites, click Sites, click the URL of the site you want to remove from the list, and then Remove. Internet Explorer removes the site from the list of trusted sites. You can add the site to a list of Restricted sites if you want to tighten security for the site.

Allow Blocked Content

Most Web pages contain text, images, and video clips that do not pose a security risk to your PC. Internet Explorer enables access to this content, no questions asked. However, many Web pages contain *active content*, which can install and run programs or scripts on your PC to make sites more dynamic and interactive. Active content typically relies on ActiveX controls, JavaScript, and other scripted objects to display animations, interactive games and presentations, and components that run inside the Web browser window or in their own windows. This type of content significantly enhances the Web, but it can also be a source of spyware, adware, or other malicious software.

Internet Explorer uses its security zone settings, as discussed in the section "Configure Security Zones," to evaluate security risks posed by ActiveX controls and other active content. Unless you relax security, Internet Explorer displays a prompt asking for your permission to install or run active content. The prompt appears in a dialog box or in Internet Explorer's new Information Bar, as shown in the steps in this section. The Information Bar is a new feature that is part of the Windows XP Service Pack 2 update.

Allow Blocked Content

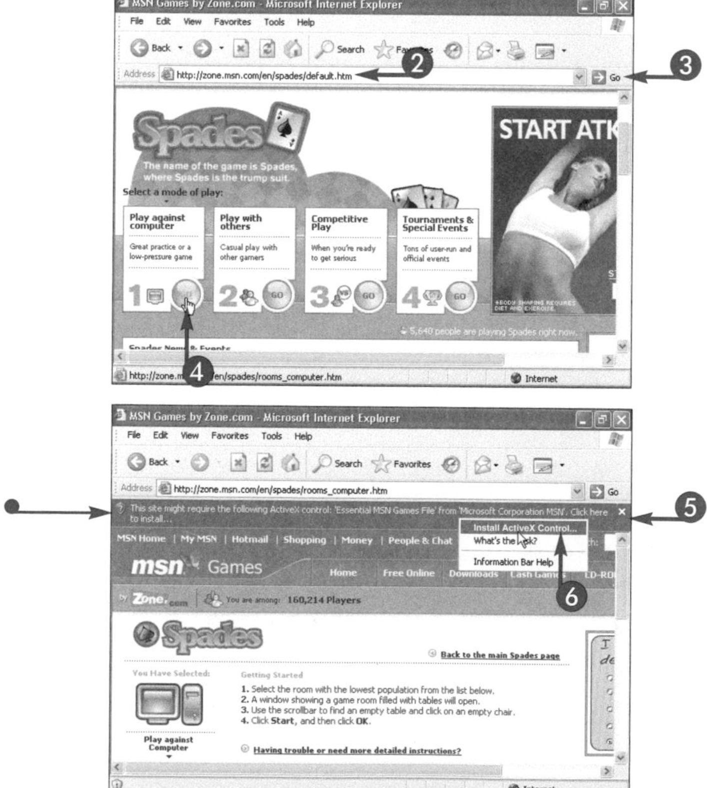

Allow Blocked Content Once

1. Launch Internet Explorer.
2. In the Address bar, type the address of a Web site that features active content.
3. Click Go.
4. Click a link for content that requires an ActiveX control or runs other active content.

- The Information Bar appears, indicating that Internet Explorer has blocked the content.

5. Click the Information Bar.
6. Click the link for installing the ActiveX control or allowing the blocked content.

   Internet Explorer allows the blocked content and installs the required ActiveX control, if it is not already installed.

Allow All Active Content

1. Launch Internet Explorer.
2. Click Tools.
3. Click Internet Options.

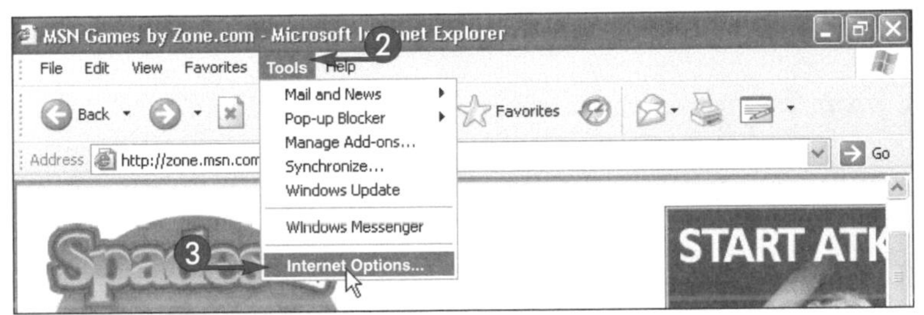

The Internet Options dialog box appears.

4. Click the Advanced tab.
5. Scroll down to the Security options.
6. Click the "Allow active content to run in files on My Computer" option (☐ changes to ☑).
7. Click OK.

Internet Explorer allows any Web site to run active content on your PC without prompting you for confirmation.

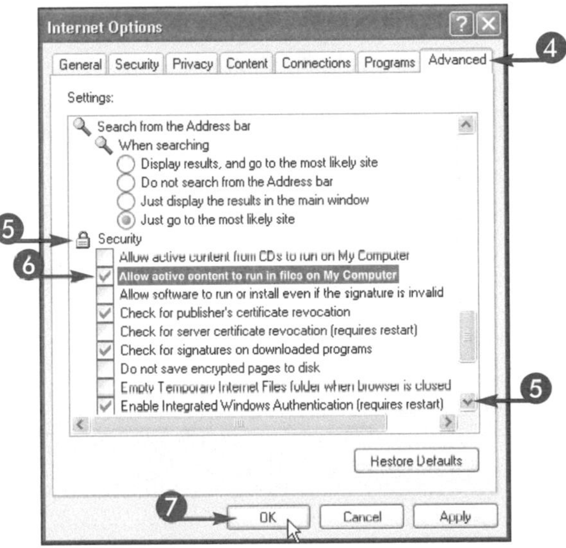

How do I know whether an ActiveX control that a site is trying to install on my PC is safe?

▼ Although Internet Explorer can determine whether an ActiveX control has a valid signature, you can never be completely sure that an ActiveX control is safe. Microsoft recommends that you ask yourself the following questions to determine how safe you think a control may be: *Were you trying to install the control? Do you trust the Web site providing the control? Do you know what the control is for and what it will do to your computer?* If you cannot answer *Yes* to all three questions, do not install the control.

What activities cause the Information Bar to appear?

▼ The Information Bar is available only in Windows XP with Service Pack 2 installed. By default, the Information Bar appears whenever a Web site attempts to display a pop-up window, install an ActiveX control or run it in a way that is unsafe, run active content on your PC, or download a file to your PC.

Can I prevent Internet Explorer from blocking pop-ups?

▼ Yes. Click Tools, click Pop-up Blocker, and then click Turn Off Pop-up Blocker. To disable other warnings that the Information Bar displays, you must disable the warnings for each type of message it displays. You can do this by changing the security zone settings. See the section "Configure Security Zones" for instructions.

Adjust Privacy Settings

When you visit an Internet site, it often sends a small file called a *cookie* to your computer that assigns your computer an identification number. The site can then check this cookie whenever you visit to determine who you are and what you have done at the site. If you select some products to purchase, for example, and then leave the site without paying, when you return to the site, it has a record of your selection, and you can complete the transaction.

In many cases, cookies enhance your Web browsing experience by helping Web sites deliver content that is tailored to your specific needs. However, cookies can enable a site to record your movements on the site without your knowledge. If you consider cookies to be an invasion of your privacy, you can prevent Internet Explorer from accepting them.

Internet Explorer features privacy settings that you can adjust to relax or tighten restrictions on cookies. You can control cookies in two ways — by relaxing or tightening restrictions for all sites, and by adding sites to a list of sites from which you want to allow or block cookies.

Adjust Privacy Settings

Adjust Cookie Restrictions

1. Launch Internet Explorer.
2. Click Tools.
3. Click Internet Options.

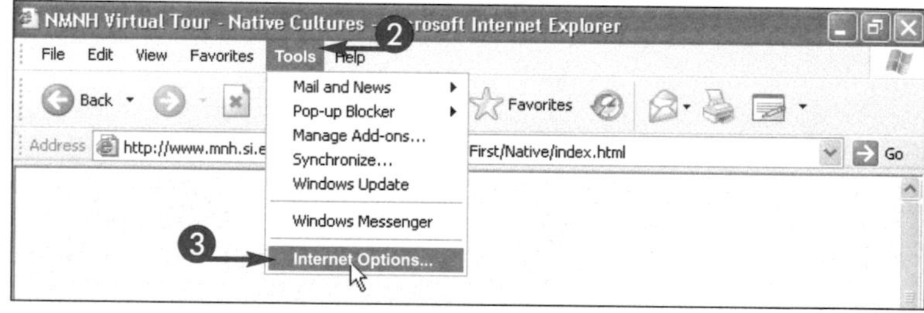

The Internet Options dialog box appears.

4. Click the Privacy tab.
5. Click and drag the slider to set the privacy level you want to use.

Internet Explorer sets itself up to restrict cookies based on the privacy level you set.

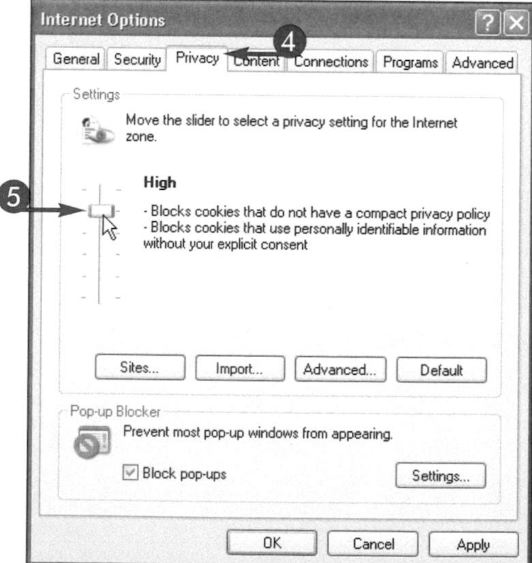

Block or Allow Cookies for Some Sites

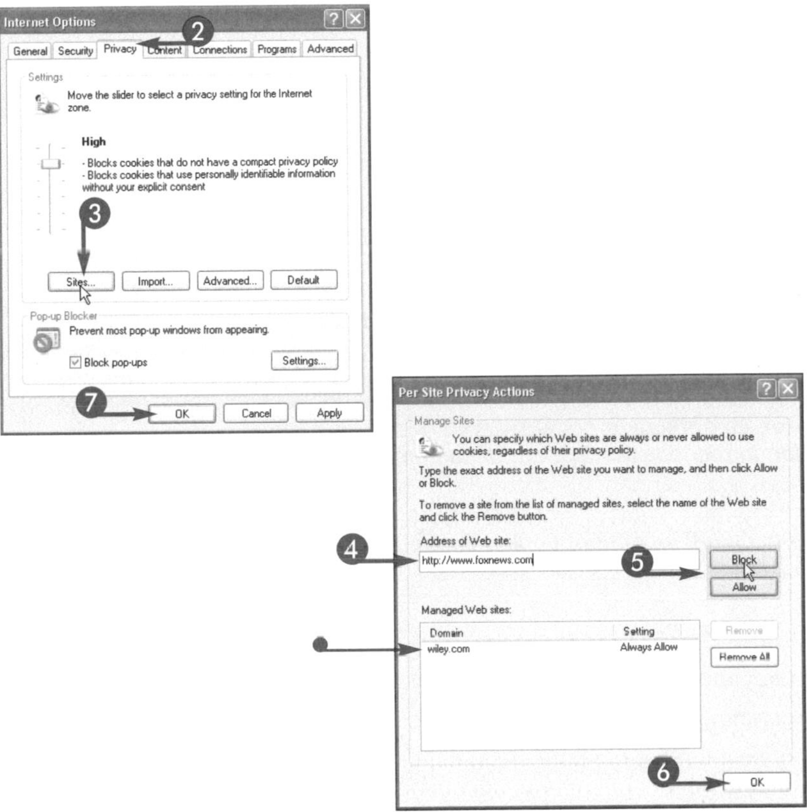

1. Display the Internet Options dialog box using steps 1 to 3 on the previous page.
2. Click the Privacy tab.
3. Click Sites.

The Per Site Privacy Actions dialog box appears.

4. Click here and type the address of a Web site for which you want to always allow or always block cookies.

Note: *You must begin the address with http:// or https://.*

5. Click either Allow or Block.

   - Internet Explorer adds the address to the list of sites.

6. Click OK.
7. Click OK in the Internet Options dialog box.

Internet Explorer saves your privacy settings.

MASTER IT

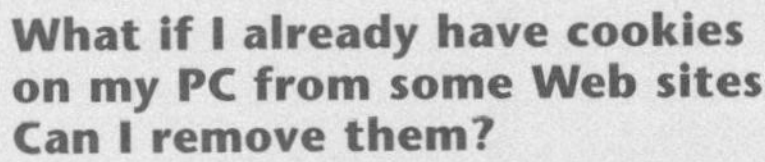

What if I already have cookies on my PC from some Web sites. Can I remove them?

▼ Yes. You can delete individual cookies or delete all cookies that are currently on your PC. Refer to the section "Delete Cookies" for instructions. When you delete a cookie, a Web site can no longer identify your PC, so you may lose access to usernames, passwords, order information, or other data at those sites.

If I already have cookies on my PC and I tighten restrictions on cookies, can Web sites read the existing cookies?

▼ That depends. If you drag the Privacy slider to the top to select Block All Cookies, Web sites cannot place cookies on your PC or read information from cookies that are already on your PC. If you drag the Privacy slider to a lower setting, Web sites can read information from the cookies stored on your PC.

Does Internet Explorer provide any additional control over how it handles cookies?

▼ Yes. By default, Internet Explorer uses the Privacy setting to automatically determine which cookies to accept and block. At the Low setting, for example, Internet Explorer accepts most first-party cookies and blocks most third-party cookies — cookies from sites other than the site you are currently viewing. You can click Advanced to enter settings that override Internet Explorer's automatic cookie handling.

Delete Cookies

Cookies typically enhance Web browsing, so keeping them on your computer rarely threatens your privacy. However, if you feel as though cookies are an invasion of privacy, you can tighten restrictions on cookies, as explained in the section "Adjust Privacy Settings." You can also view the cookies that are stored on your PC and delete one or all of the cookies.

The easiest way to remove cookies from your PC is to remove all of them at once. You can do this through an option in the Internet Options dialog box. You can also choose to delete individual cookies by displaying the contents of your Cookies folder and then deleting any of the cookie files that you want to remove. If you suspect that a cookie stores personal information it has collected about you, you can open the cookie to display its contents in Windows Notepad before you choose to delete it.

Cookie files are typically very small, so deleting them does not help you reclaim much hard drive storage space, but you can prevent sites from identifying your PC when you revisit the sites.

Delete Individual Cookies

1. Launch Internet Explorer.
2. Click Tools.
3. Click Internet Options.

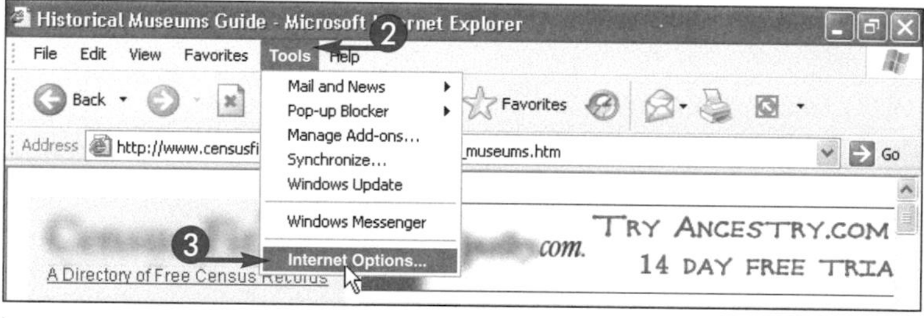

- The Internet Options dialog box appears.

4. Click Settings.

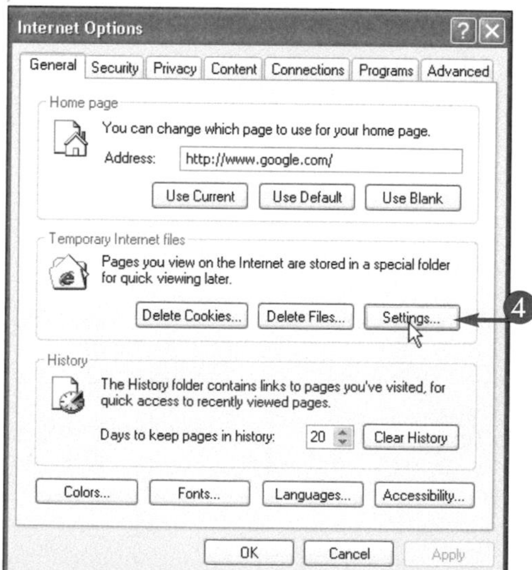

The Settings dialog box appears.

5 Click View Files.

My Computer displays the temporary Internet files.

6 Click the Up button ( ) twice.

7 Double-click the Cookies folder.

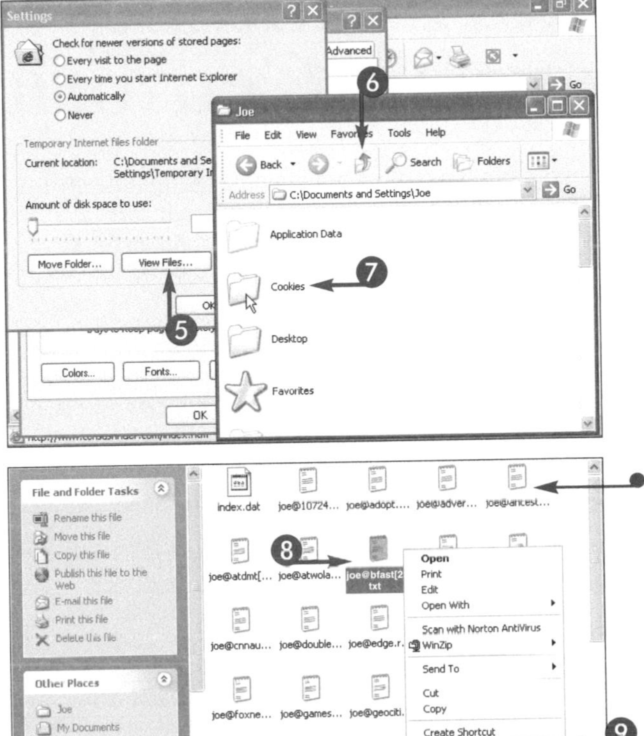

My Computer displays the contents of the Cookies folder.

- You can double-click a cookie to display its contents in Notepad.

8 Right-click a cookie you want to delete.

9 Click Delete.

My Computer deletes the cookie.

Can I delete all cookies at once?

Yes. In Internet Explorer, click Tools, then Internet Options to display the Internet Options dialog box. Click the General tab and click Delete Cookies. The Delete Cookies dialog box appears, prompting you to confirm. Click Yes. This removes all cookies from your PC.

Can I find out which site placed the cookie on my PC and when the site did it?

Yes. To find out when a site placed a cookie on your computer and when the site last modified the cookie, right-click the cookie and click Properties. The Properties dialog box appears, displaying the date and time the site created the cookie and most recently accessed it and modified it. You can block cookies at specific sites, as explained in the section "Adjust Privacy Settings."

Can Web sites other than the site that placed the cookie on my PC read that cookie?

Usually not. In most cases, the only Web site that can access the information stored in a cookie is the site that placed the cookie on your PC. Even if someone else can access the data stored in a cookie, the person can do little with that information; the information usually consists only of an ID number that a site uses to pull up other information.

Understanding Web Content Censoring

The Web is the largest information storage facility in the world, covering every subject from aardvarks to XXX videos. Most Web content is suitable for all ages and is not intended to be offensive. However, the Web has a dark side, where you can find pornography, violence, obscenity, bigotry, and other expressions of human indecency.

Because people of all ages, beliefs, and sensibilities access the Web, and because no central body governs its content, users must decide what they want to view, but avoiding potentially offensive content is not always simply a matter of choosing not to view it. Through spam, pop-up advertisements, and other intrusions, sites often display offensive content without asking permission. To prevent undesirable content from appearing on your screen, you must censor it.

You can use a variety of tools and techniques, alone or together, to censor Web sites and monitor Internet use. The following section lists your options, and then subsequent sections explain each option in greater detail.

Censoring Options

Effective censoring requires a combination of methods, some of which can be redundant. For example, you may use a system that blocks sites that are known to contain undesirable content and prevents the display of Web pages that contain unacceptable words. Several methods and tools are available to help users monitor Internet usage and prevent access to unacceptable content:

- Web browser content settings enable you to specify, in your Web browser, the types of content you want to display.
- Censoring software that you install on your PC can prevent your browser and e-mail program from downloading or displaying undesirable content. You may also install a router that includes its own censoring software for blocking sites based on a list of prohibited words.
- Monitoring software can record Web activity and keystrokes.
- Child-safe search directories can filter out links to sites that contain content unsuitable for children.
- Online services and Internet service providers may have their own tools for controlling content, such as America Online's Parental Controls. Consult your ISP or online service for details.
- Parents and guardians can supervise underage users to ensure that they are not abusing their computer privileges. Yahooligans! has an excellent parent guide at yahooligans.yahoo.com/parents/. The FBI also has some useful information about protecting children from online predators; you can access the information at www.fbi.gov/publications/pguide/pguidee.htm.

Web Browser Content Settings

Some Web browsers, including Internet Explorer, feature content filtering options that can prevent the Web browser from displaying pages that contain nudity, sexual content, violence, or obscenity. Internet Explorer's Content Advisor determines the suitability of Web sites based on their RSACi (Recreational Software Advisory Council information) rating. The RSAC has recently been folded into the ICRA (Internet Content Rating Association), which encourages companies to rate their own sites.

Content Advisor controls access to Web sites based on their RSACi rating. If the site has no rating, Internet Explorer blocks it, unless you choose to allow users to view sites that have no rating, which can allow too much questionable content. You can gain more control over Web content by configuring the Content Advisor's settings, as explained in the section "Enable Internet Explorer's Content Advisor."

Censoring Software

If you use a Web browser that does not filter content or you want a more robust censoring utility, you can purchase third-party censoring software that provides additional protections and filtering options. Several censoring programs are available, including CyberPatrol, CYBERsitter, Net Nanny, and Access Control. These programs typically filter e-mail, as well as Web content, and provide tools for limiting the number of hours and the times of day a person can use the PC. You learn how to download and install a trialware version of CYBERsitter in the section "Install CYBERsitter Censoring Software."

Another option is to subscribe to a censoring service, such as CrayonCrawler or SurfontheSafeside, which uses a combination of software on your computer and online filtering to more accurately and thoroughly control access to Web content and e-mail. These child-safe services cost a little extra but can provide an added level of security.

Monitoring Software

Because no system can block 100 percent of all potentially offensive content, you may consider using monitoring software instead of or in addition to censoring software. Monitoring software keeps track of the sites that your child visits, or tries to visit, and may even record keystrokes, so that you can keep track of what your child is communicating via e-mail and in instant messaging programs.

Some parents and guardians consider spying on their children unethical, because it invades the child's privacy, but others have found it to be a useful tool for supervising and protecting their children when they are unable to sit next to their children and supervise their activity personally.

Child-Safe Search Directories

The first thing that most people do after launching their Web browsers is go to one of their favorite Web sites or open a search page to look for something. If you have children, you can help prevent them from stumbling upon unsuitable Web pages by encouraging them to use a child-safe search directory:

- Yahooligans! at www.yahooligans.com is the kiddies version of Yahoo! The site includes information and tips for parents and guardians on how to protect youngsters on the Web.
- Ask Jeeves Kids at www.ajkids.com enables children to type their questions and find answers on pages that are suitable for children. A reference library and several online games accompany this site, making it a healthy hangout for kids of all ages.
- Education World at www.education-world.com provides a huge directory of resources that are suitable for children.
- Kids Click at sunsite.berkeley.edu/KidsClick! is a basic Web directory that enables kids to explore the Web by categories, including Weird & Mysterious, Home & Household, and Machines & Transportation.
- Lycos Zone at www.lycoszone.com is the child-friendly version of Lycos.

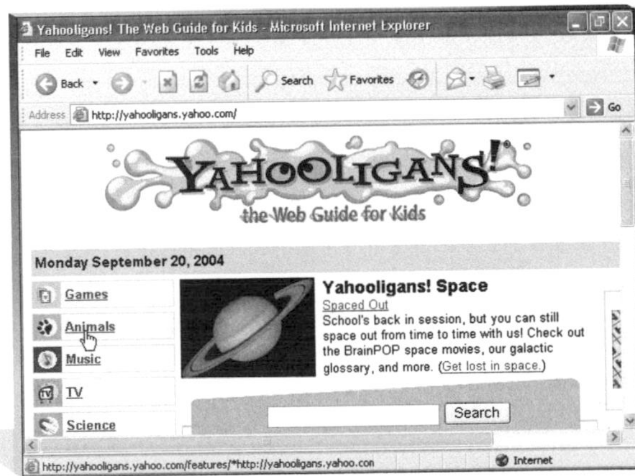

Enable Internet Explorer's Content Advisor

Internet Explorer features a Content Advisor, which is turned off by default. You can enable Content Advisor so that it can prevent access to Web sites based on their RSACi rating, which some companies use to rate the content at their Web sites. To enable Content Advisor, you must enter a password so that nobody can disable Content Advisor or configure it without entering the correct password. Write down the password and store it in a safe place.

When you enable Content Advisor, you may quickly notice that it blocks a wide variety of Web pages, including those that contain no potentially offensive content. Content Advisor blocks so many Web sites because it is initially configured to block unrated sites as well as those that have content ratings.

To prevent Content Advisor from filtering out content at acceptable sites, you can add approved Web sites to a list of acceptable sites. You can also indicate which Web sites are unacceptable. As a parent or guardian, you can work with a child to determine which sites to add to the list of acceptable sites. You can also broaden the list of sites that Content Advisor deems acceptable by installing additional rating systems, as explained in the section "Install a Rating System."

Enable Internet Explorer's Content Advisor

1. Launch Internet Explorer.
2. Click Tools.
3. Click Internet Options.

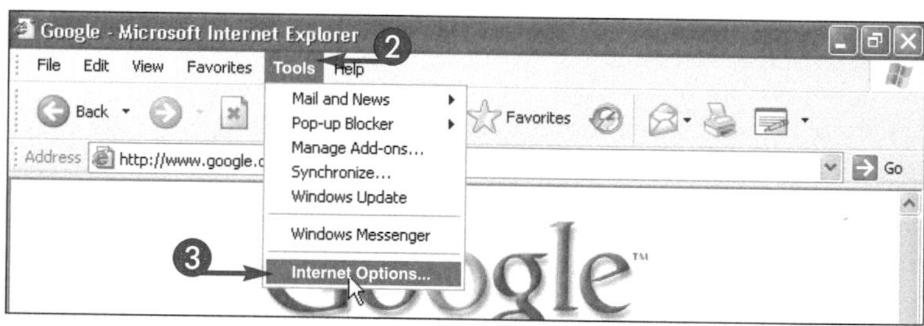

The Internet Options dialog box appears.

4. Click the Content tab.
5. Click Enable.

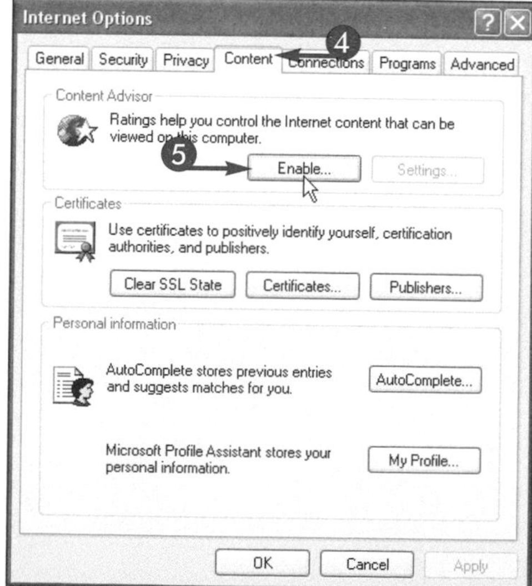

The Content Advisor dialog box appears.

6 Click a content category that you want to regulate.

7 Click and drag the slider to the type of content you want users to be able to access.

8 Repeat steps 6 and 7 for additional content categories.

9 Click OK.

The Create Supervisor Password dialog box appears.

10 Type a password.

11 Retype the password you typed in step 10.

12 Type a hint to help you remember your password.

13 Click OK.

14 Click OK in the Internet Options dialog box.

Content Advisor saves your settings and begins to filter content.

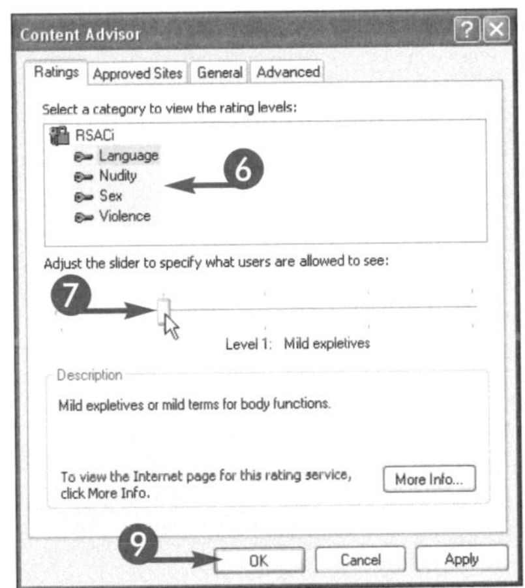

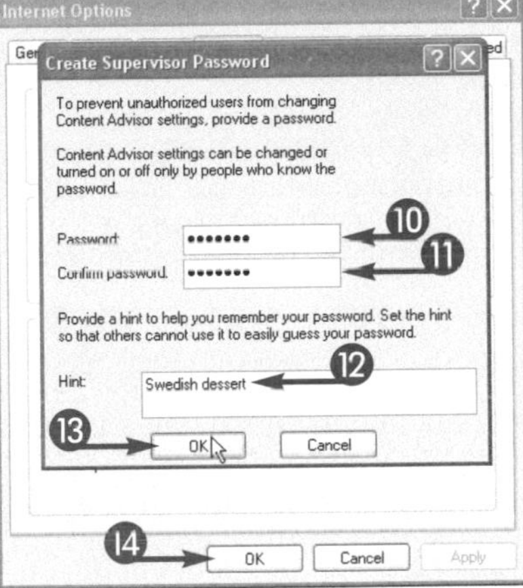

What happens when Content Advisor blocks a Web page?

▼ When Content Advisor blocks a Web page, it displays the Content Advisor dialog box, indicating that it is prohibiting you from viewing the content and often displaying a reason why. If you know the supervisor password, you can view the page by typing your password and clicking one of the following options: Always allow this Web site to be viewed (○ changes to ◉), Always allow this Web page to be viewed (○ changes to ◉), or Allow viewing only this time (○ changes to ◉). When you click OK, Internet Explorer loads the page and displays its content.

How can I add Web sites to the list of approved sites or block specific Web sites?

▼ The easiest way to add Web pages and Web sites to the list of approved sites is to enable Content Advisor and then, when Content Advisor blocks a page, select the option to always allow the Web site or Web page to be viewed, type your password, and click OK. You can also type addresses for acceptable and unacceptable Web sites in the Content Advisor dialog box. Click Tools, Internet Options, Content, Settings, type your password, then click OK and Approved Sites, type the address of an acceptable or unacceptable Web site, and then click Always or Never.

Install a Rating System

Content Advisor blocks all unrated Web pages and Web sites. You can select an option to enable users to view unrated Web sites, but then Content Advisor allows access to many sites that contain objectionable content. One way to expand the number of Web sites that Content Advisor allows without enabling access to too much objectionable material is to add acceptable Web sites to a list of approved Web sites, as explained in the section "Enable Internet Explorer's Content Advisor."

Another way you can broaden access to suitable sites is to install additional rating systems. Initially, Internet Explorer is set up to use the RSACi rating system, which is being phased out. Many Web sites use different rating systems, including SafeSurf and ICRA, which are more common. By installing additional rating systems, Content Advisor has fewer pages and Web sites to consider unrated, thus increasing the number of Web sites that it considers acceptable.

The steps in this section show you how to download and install the SafeSurf rating system. You can download the ICRA rating system from www.icra.org/_en/icra.rat and follow the same steps shown here to install it.

Install a Rating System

1. Launch Internet Explorer.
2. In the Address bar, type **www.safesurf.org**.
3. Click Go.
4. Click Update Your Browser.

   Update instructions appear.

5. Click SafeSurf.rat.

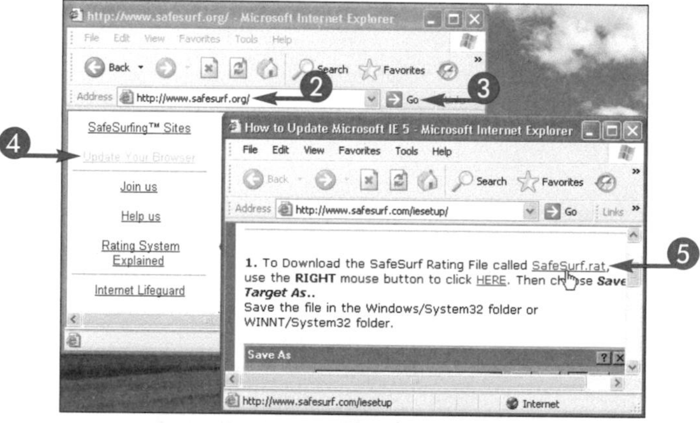

The File Download dialog box appears.

6. Click Save.
7. Navigate to the Windows\System32 folder.
8. Click Save.

   Windows saves the SafeSurf.rat file to the Windows\System32 folder.

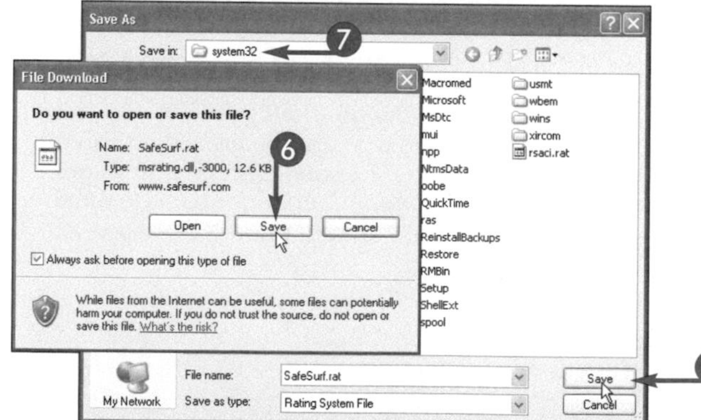

9 Display the Content Advisor dialog box.

Note: *Refer to the section "Enable Internet Explorer's Content Advisor" for more information.*

10 Click the General tab.

11 Click Rating Systems.

The Rating Systems dialog box appears.

12 Click Add.

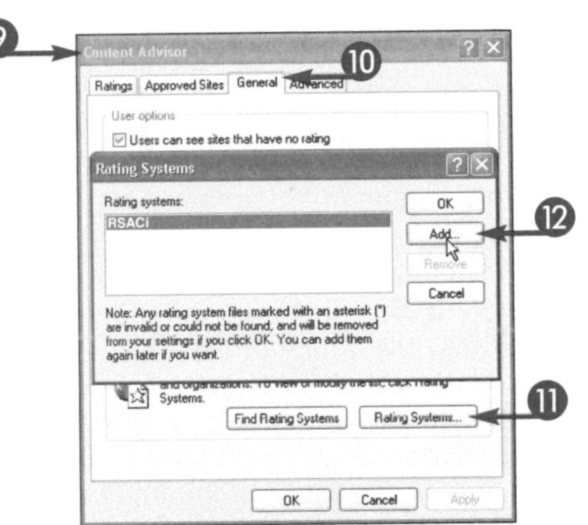

The Open ratings system file dialog box appears.

13 Click SafeSurf.rat.

14 Click Open.

15 Click OK.

Content Advisor incorporates the rating system.

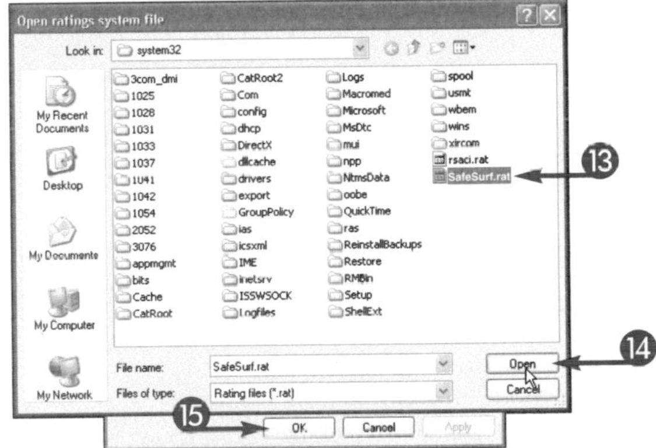

After I install the rating system, do I need to reconfigure Content Advisor?

Yes. By default, Content Advisor features four content categories: Language, Nudity, Sex, and Violence. When you install a rating system, it adds content categories. For example, SafeSurf adds Age Range, Drug Use, Gambling, and several other categories. By default, SafeSurf categories are set for strict content filtering. To view the categories and adjust their content filtering settings, click the Ratings tab.

How do I prevent Content Advisor from blocking unrated Web sites?

To prevent Content Advisor from blocking unrated Web sites, click Tools, Internet Options, and the Content tab, Settings, then type your password, and click OK, and then click the General tab, and the "Users can see sites that have no rating" option (☐ changes to ☑), then OK, and OK. With the "Users can see sites that have no rating" option enabled, many sites that contain violence, sexual content, nudity, and obscenity are accessible, because few of these sites bother to rate themselves.

Can I rely on these rating systems to prevent my children from viewing potentially offensive content?

No. Even with several rating systems installed, Content Advisor allows access to many Web sites that children should not view, especially if you enable Internet Explorer to display unrated Web sites. For additional protection, install third-party censoring software, as shown in the section "Install CYBERsitter Censoring Software." You should also personally supervise your children on the Internet.

Install CYBERsitter Censoring Software

Although Internet Explorer's Content Advisor provides a quick and easy way to block undesirable content, third-party content filters are much more effective and flexible. Many of these utilities include a database of Web sites that are known to provide content that is unsuitable for children. In addition, some contain a list of banned words that can help filter content from Web sites that are not on the list of prohibited sites. Some content filters also enable you to set restrictions on computer use — for example, you can limit computer use to one hour per day on weekdays and two hours on weekends and prevent one or more users from accessing the Internet after 11 p.m.

Many companies that develop content filters offer free trials of their software. You simply connect to the site, download and install the software, and use it for a limited time to evaluate its effectiveness. If you want to continue using the software, then you pay a registration fee to keep it or you can order a registered copy online. The steps in this section show you how to download and install CYBERsitter, one of the leading content-filtering utilities on the market.

Install CYBERsitter Censoring Software

1. Launch Internet Explorer.
2. In the Address bar, type **www.cybersitter.com**.
3. Click Go.
4. Click Free Trial.
5. Click the link to download CYBERsitter.

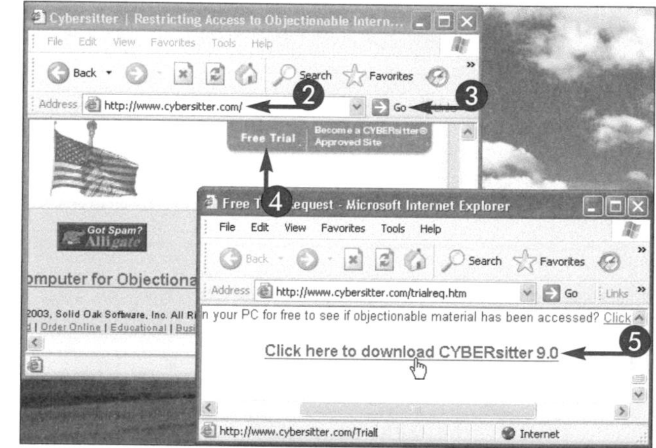

The Download Instructions page appears.

6. Read the download instructions.
7. Scroll down the page and click the link to start the download.

   The File Download dialog box appears.

8. Click Save.
9. Save the file to a folder on your PC.

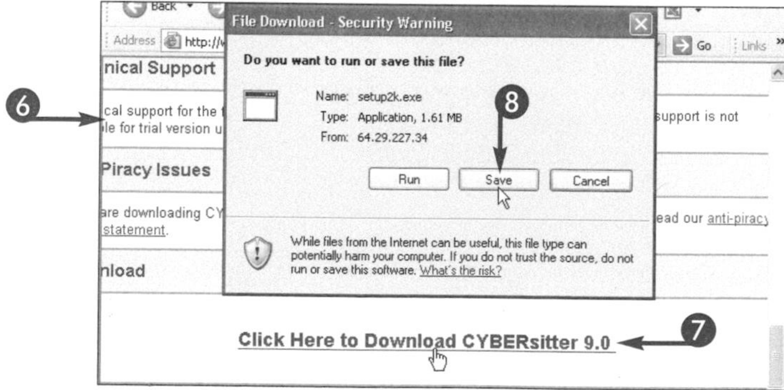

10 Open My Computer.

11 Navigate to the folder in which you saved the CYBERsitter installation file.

12 Double-click the CYBERsitter setup file.

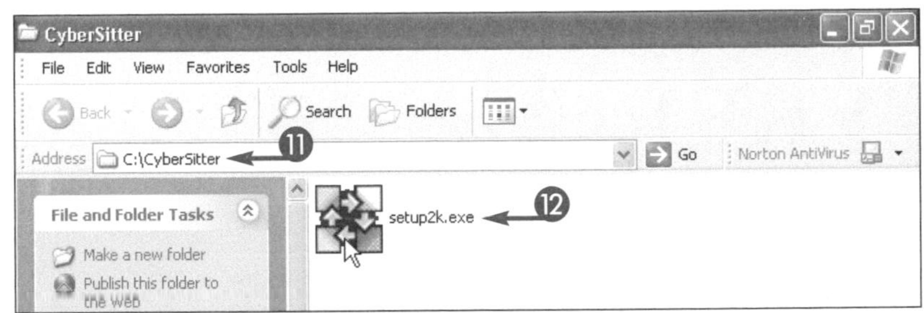

Windows initiates the CYBERsitter installation.

13 Follow the on-screen instructions to install and set up CYBERsitter.

CYBERsitter is installed and configured to start filtering Web content.

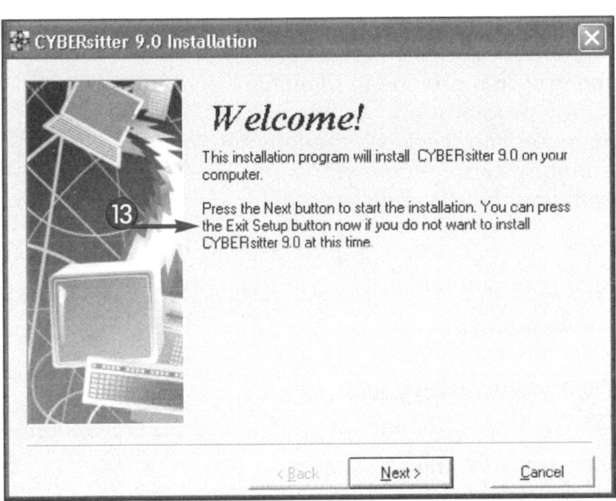

Where else can I obtain censoring software to try?

▼ Most shareware sites have a category for parental filtering or content filtering software. Go to www.download.com, www.tucows.com, or another shareware repository. You can also go directly to the developer's Web site: CyberPatrol at www.cyberpatrol.com, Enologic NetFilter at www.enologic.com, iProtectYouPro Web Filter at www.softforyou.com, and Net Nanny at www.netnanny.com. Trialware versions of all of these products are available. You can use most products for 10 to 30 days and then must register them. Before installing a new filter, uninstall the filtering software you were using so that it does not conflict with the new filter.

I thought CYBERsitter was trialware, but it requests a serial number. What should I do?

▼ CYBERsitter's trialware registration screen can be a little confusing. After you install CYBERsitter, a dialog box appears, prompting you to type your e-mail address. After you type your e-mail address and click Register, the dialog box requests your first and last name and the product's registration number. Type your first and last name, click Submit, and then close the Web page that prompts you to order the product. You can now use CYBERsitter for the duration of the free trial period. If, after that time, you want to continue using CYBERsitter, you must order it online to obtain a registration number.

Configure CYBERsitter

Nearly every censoring program features a set of options you can change to control the utility's operation. In most programs, you can specify the types of content you want blocked and how strict you want the censor to be. Most programs also enable you to create or edit a file that contains a list of banned sites or a list of prohibited words that the program can use to identify objectionable content. Some programs also enable you to limit the amount of time a user can spend on the Internet. By configuring the censoring software, you can make it perform more in tune with your beliefs and sensibilities.

The configuration options vary a great deal from one censoring program to another, depending on the available features and how those features operate. CYBERsitter provides a single dialog box that provides access to all of its configuration settings and is one of the easiest censoring programs to configure. The steps in this section show you how to enter some of the more common configuration settings in CYBERsitter. If you use a different censoring program, refer to its help system for specific instructions.

Configure CYBERsitter

1. Double-click the CYBERsitter icon on your desktop.

Note: *To install CYBERsitter, see the section "Install CYBERsitter Censoring Software."*

The CYBERsitter Control Panel appears.

- You can click options to disable filtering or to block all Internet access.

2. Click these options to disable specific Internet features or disable e-mail filtering (☐ changes to ☑).
3. Click one of these options to specify the startup mode (☐ changes to ☑).

- You can click Security to change your password.

4. Click Allowable Times.
5. Click and drag over time blocks to select the times when you want users to be able to access the Internet.

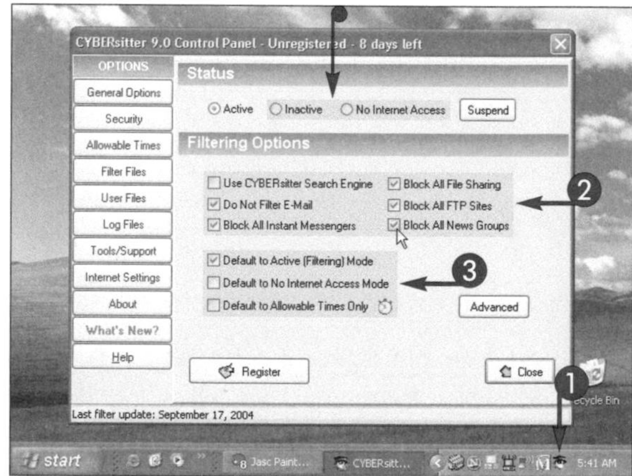

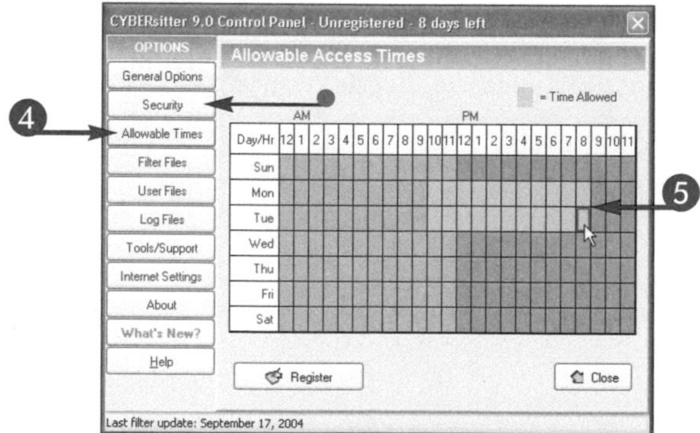

6 Click Filter Files.

7 Click to select each content area you want to filter (☐ changes to ☑).

- You can click Update Filters to download updated filter files.

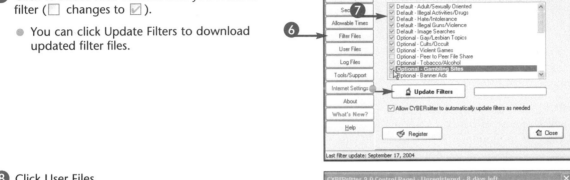

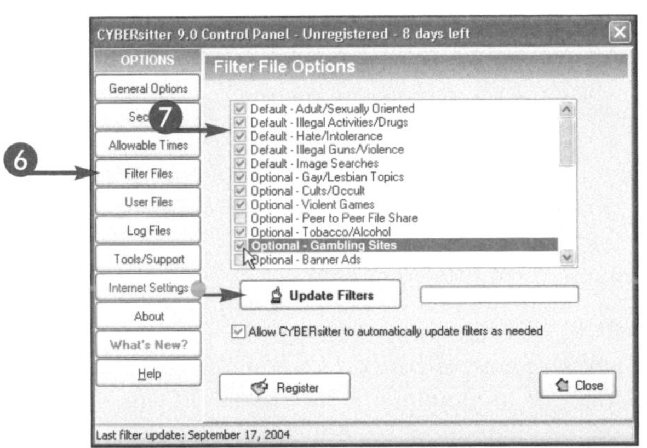

8 Click User Files.

9 Type Web site addresses and words that you want CYBERsitter to use to identify prohibited content.

- You can click the Always Allowable Sites tab to add addresses of sites that you never want CYBERsitter to block.

10 Click Save.

11 Click Close.

CYBERsitter saves your preferences and closes the Control Panel.

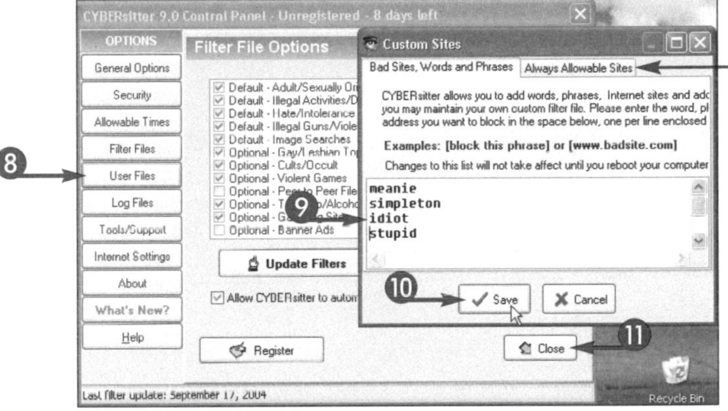

What are the Log File options for?

▼ You can click Log File for options that enable you to record user activity. CYBERsitter can record the user's name along with any blocked sites that the user attempts to view and all text typed during an instant messaging chat. You can click the Examine Violations button to display the contents of the report. Optionally, CYBERsitter can e-mail you the report, in case you forget to check it on your own.

Can I find out if my PC has any obscene or objectionable content stored on it?

▼ Yes. Click the Tools/Support button and then click the System Snooper button. CYBERsitter scans your PC's hard drive(s) for any Web pages that may contain prohibited content and displays a list of those pages. You can select the page and click the Delete button to remove it from your PC. You should delete these files soon after you install CYBERsitter, so you can start with a blank slate.

Can another user disable CYBERsitter?

▼ Yes. If a user is fairly sophisticated, the person can disable CYBERsitter. However, CYBERsitter has some built-in protections you can employ. In the CYBERsitter Control Panel, click Security and then Advanced. The Advanced Security Options dialog box appears, enabling you to hide the CYBERsitter icon on startup, disable registry editing, block access to the Windows Task Manager, and take other measures to prevent users from working around the filters.

31 Repair a Windows XP Installation

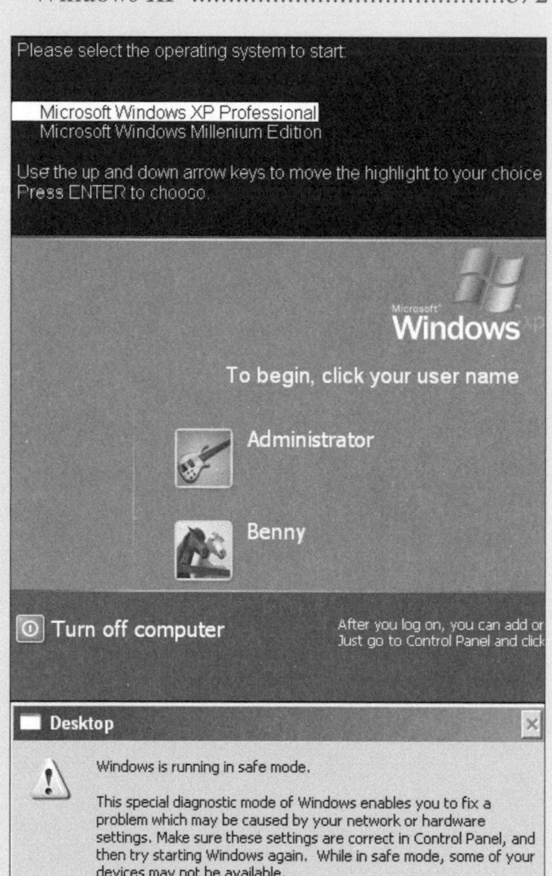

32 Re-Install Windows XP

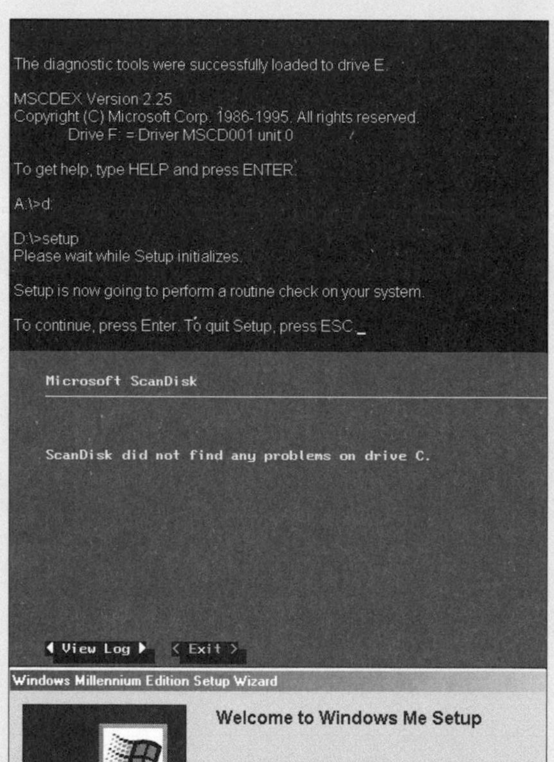

PART X
RETURNING YOUR PC TO PRISTINE CONDITION

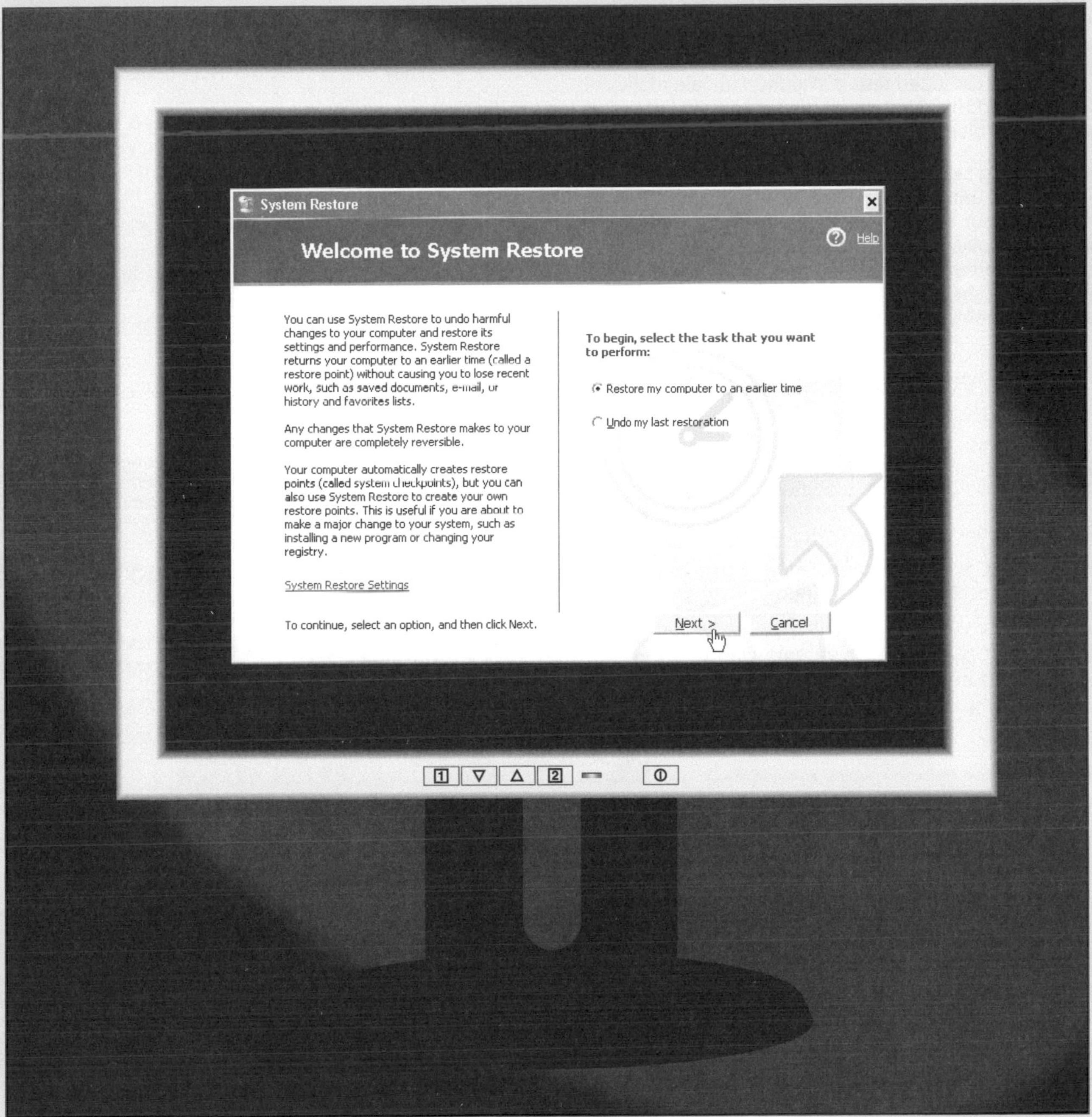

Run Windows in Safe Mode

If Windows does not start up when you turn on your PC, you can often restart Windows in Safe mode and then perform the steps necessary to troubleshoot and repair the problem.

The remaining sections in this chapter show you how to boot your PC using the Windows XP installation CD and then repair your Windows XP installation or use the Windows Recovery Console to restore damaged files. Before attempting to repair an installation or recover files, however, you should try to run Windows in Safe mode and correct the problem. Sometimes, starting your PC in Safe mode and then restarting it repairs the problem. In other cases, you may need to run the System Restore utility, as explained in Chapter 19, to restore your PC to a previous condition. If your PC cannot start Windows even in Safe mode, then you can boot from the Windows XP CD, as discussed in the section "Repair a Previous Installation of Windows XP."

When you start Windows in Safe mode, Windows displays the Advanced Options menu, which provides a list of alternative startup options, including Safe Mode and Safe Mode with Networking.

Run Windows in Safe Mode

1. If your PC is on, shut it down and turn it off.
2. Turn on your PC.
3. As your PC is starting, press F8 every two to three seconds until the Windows Advanced Options Menu appears.
4. Press the Up Arrow or Down Arrow key to highlight Safe Mode or Safe Mode with Networking.
5. Press Enter.

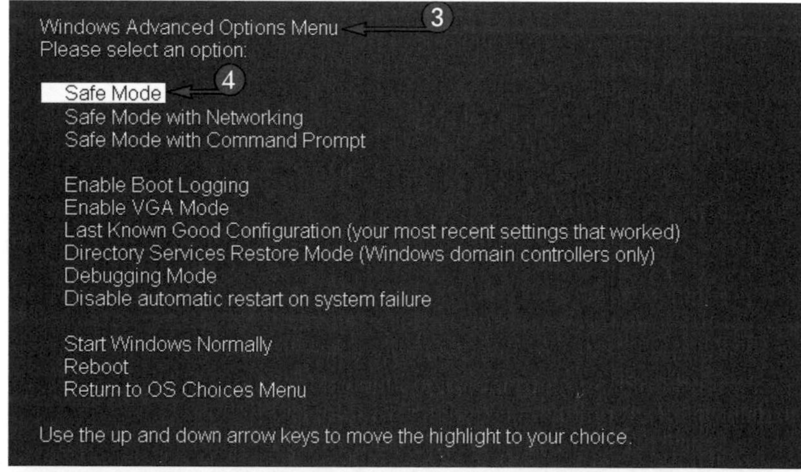

Windows prompts you to select the operating system you want your PC to run.

Note: *Most PCs have only one option.*

6. Use the Up or Down Arrow key to highlight the version of Windows you want to start in Safe mode.
7. Press Enter.

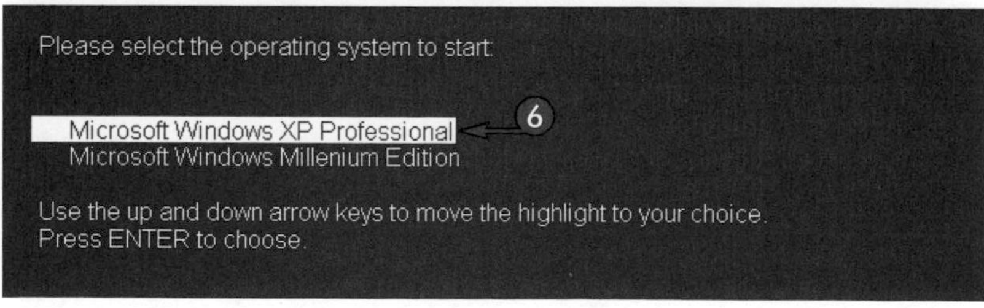

The Windows logon screen appears.

8 Click Administrator or click a user account that has administrator privileges and log on as you normally do.

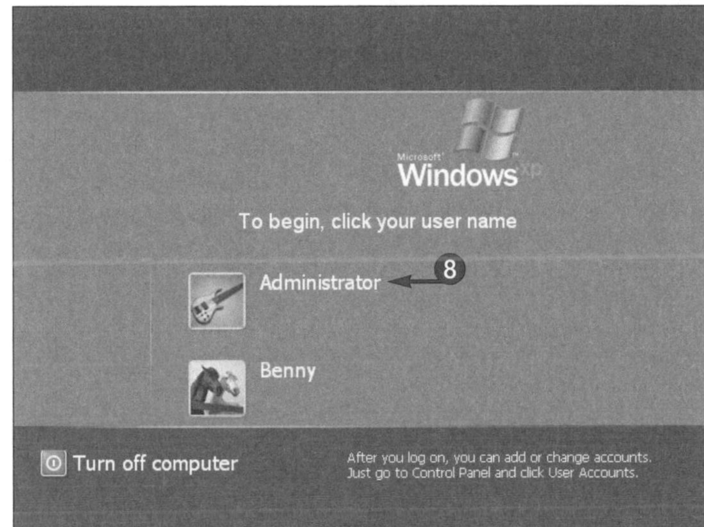

- The Desktop dialog box appears, indicating that Windows is running in Safe mode and asking if you want to continue running in Safe mode.

9 Click Yes.

A basic Windows desktop appears with a minimum of features, so you can troubleshoot and repair startup problems.

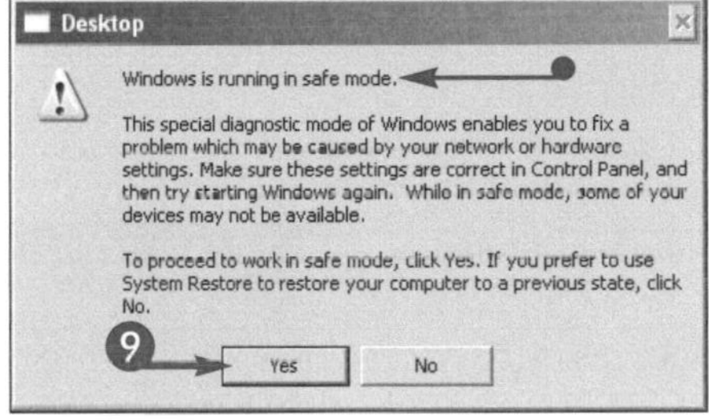

My PC runs a previous version of Windows. Can I start it in Safe mode?

▼ Yes. In Windows 98 and Windows Me, press Ctrl while turning on your PC and continue to hold down the key as your PC starts. Windows eventually displays the startup options, including the option to start in Safe mode. If you created a Windows Startup disk, you may have better success booting from the startup disk.

My PC started fine in Safe mode. Now what should I do to troubleshoot the problem?

▼ If you just installed a device or program that caused the problem, you can try uninstalling it and perhaps restoring your PC to its previous condition, as discussed in the section "Restore Windows on Startup." Chapter 13 provides instructions on how to perform a diagnostic startup. Windows also includes several troubleshooters that you can access via its help system; click Start, Help, and select the option for fixing a problem or troubleshooting.

When I start my PC normally, a message appears indicating that one of my system files is corrupt. What should I do?

▼ If you have the Windows XP installation CD, you can boot your PC from the CD, as explained in the section "Repair a Previous Installation of Windows XP," and then run the Recovery Console, which enables you to restore Windows system files from the CD to your PC's hard drive.

Start with the Last Known Good Configuration

Whenever you start your PC and Windows loads successfully, Windows saves the settings that are stored in the registry's HKLM\System\CurrentControlSet key. If you install a device that changes these settings and prevents Windows from starting normally, you can restart Windows with its last known good configuration. This does not guarantee that Windows will start normally, but it does provide another option you can try before attempting to repair your Windows installation.

Restoring your system in this way is a little riskier than starting in Safe mode and then troubleshooting a specific problem, because it resets a key in the registry, causing you to lose system configuration settings you entered since the last time you successfully started your PC. However, it is much safer and easier than trying to repair a Windows installation, as discussed in the section "Repair a Previous Installation of Windows XP."

The steps in this section show how to restore Windows XP to its most recent operable condition. If your PC is running Windows 98 or Me, or you want to perform a complete system restoration for Windows XP, refer to the section "Restore Windows on Startup."

Start with the Last Known Good Configuration

1. If your PC is on, shut it down and turn it off.
2. Turn on your PC.
3. As your PC is starting, press F8 every two to three seconds until the Windows Advanced Options Menu appears.
4. Press the Down Arrow key to highlight Last Known Good Configuration.
5. Press Enter.

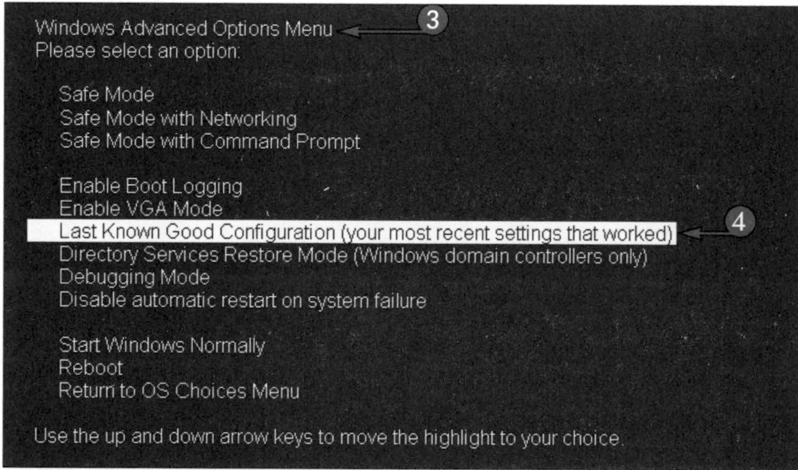

The name of each operating system installed on your PC appears.

6. Press the Up or Down Arrow key to highlight the version of Windows you want to restore.
7. Press Enter.

Please select the operating system to start:

Microsoft Windows XP Professional
Microsoft Windows Millenium Edition

Use the up and down arrow keys to move the highlight to your choice.
Press ENTER to choose.

6

The Windows logon screen appears.

8 Click your username and log on to Windows as you normally do.

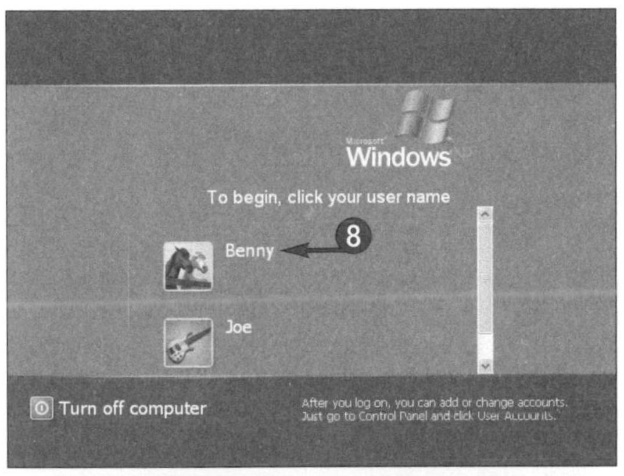

The Windows desktop appears.

Windows started with the last known good configuration, but it is not the configuration I want to use. What should I do?

▼ You can try restoring Windows using a different restore point, as explained in Chapter 19. The goal in this section is to get Windows up and running. Once it is running, you can use additional troubleshooting techniques to track down problems or reinstall the software or hardware that caused the problem.

My PC runs a previous version of Windows. Can I restore it to the last known good configuration?

▼ When Windows cannot start up properly, it typically defaults to the last known good configuration. If it does not, you can use the Windows Scanreg command to restore a previous copy of the Windows registry. See the section "Restore Windows on Startup" for details.

Does the Last Know Good Configuration option completely restore my system to its previously good operating condition?

▼ No. Starting Windows with the Last Known Good Configuration option only resets one key in the system registry that contains the most recent configuration changes. If Windows starts, you can run the System Restore utility, as explained in Chapter 19, and use it to perform a more complete restoration. If Windows does not run on startup, you can run the System Restore utility from the command prompt, as discussed in the section "Restore Windows on Startup." To recover from more serious problems, you can repair your Windows installation, as explained in the section "Repair a Previous Installation of Windows XP."

Restore Windows on Startup

Chapter 19 provides instructions on how to create system restore points and return your PC to a previous condition using a restore point. If your PC does not run Windows on startup, however, you cannot run the System Restore utility from Windows and use it to perform the restoration. You can run Windows with its last known good configuration, as explained in the previous section, but if that does not return Windows to an operable condition, you may need to perform a more thorough system restoration. You can do this by running the System Restore utility from the command prompt.

The command for restoring Windows from the command prompt differs depending on the version of Windows that your PC runs. In Windows 98 and Me, you can type **scanreg /restore** at the command prompt. In Windows XP, you can type the **rstrui.exe** command, as the steps in this section illustrate.

When your run Windows XP System Restore from the command prompt, it displays the System Restore window, which you can use to select a system restore point, as explained in Chapter 19. The scanreg /restore command in Windows 98 and Windows Me displays a list of registry backup files from which to choose.

Restore Windows on Startup

Restore Windows XP on Startup

1. Run Windows XP in Safe mode with the command prompt.

Note: *Refer to the section "Run Windows in Safe Mode" for details.*

2. Type **%systemroot%\system32\restore\rstrui.exe**.
3. Press Enter.

   The System Restore Wizard appears.

4. Click Next.
5. Follow the on-screen instructions.

   Windows is restored to a previous, working condition.

Note: *Refer to Chapter 19 for instructions on restoring Windows.*

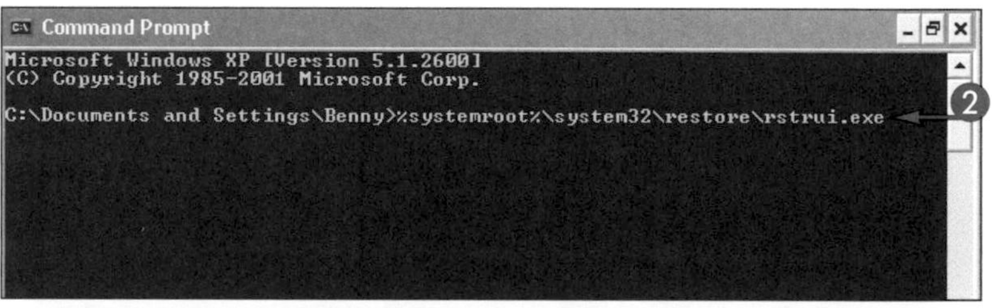

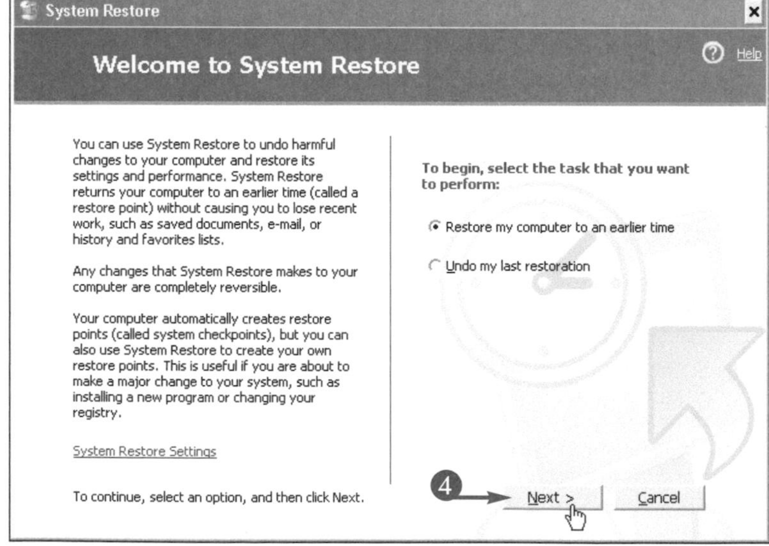

Restore Windows 98 or ME

1. Run Windows in Command Prompt Only mode.

Note: *Refer to the section "Run Windows in Safe Mode" for details.*

2. Type **scanreg /restore**.
3. Press Enter.
   - A list of backup registry files appears, and the word Started appears next to the name of each registry file that resulted in a successful startup.
4. Press the Down Arrow key to highlight the backup registry you want to use.
5. Press Enter to select Restore.

Windows restores the backup registry file.

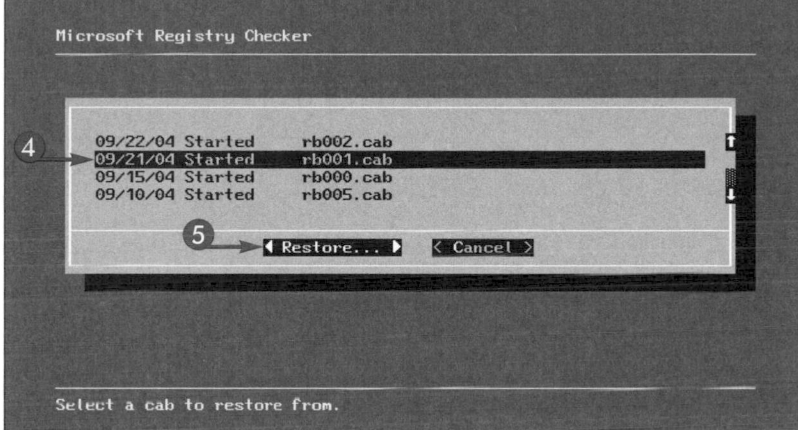

How do I choose which registry backup to restore?

▼ In most cases, you should choose the most recent registry backup or system restore point that resulted in a successful startup. This ensures that Windows loses the least possible number of configuration settings. For example, if you choose a registry backup or system restore point that is only one or two days old, you lose only the configuration settings you entered in the past day or two.

After I restore Windows, do I need to reinstall any of my applications?

▼ If you installed a registry backup or system restore point that predates the installation of an application, you may need to reinstall that application, assuming it is not the application that caused the problem. However, you do not need to reinstall applications that you installed prior to the date on which the registry backup or restore point was created. In addition, restoring Windows does not affect any of the data files you create.

Can I start Windows XP in Safe mode without the command prompt and then run System Restore?

▼ Yes. If Windows starts in Safe mode, you can run System Restore after starting Windows. In fact, when Windows XP starts in Safe mode, it displays a dialog box asking whether you want to continue working in Safe mode. Click No to start the System Restore utility and select a restore point.

Repair a Previous Installation of Windows XP

If you have Windows XP and your PC cannot load Windows on startup, you may be able to boot from the Windows installation CD and repair your Windows installation or use the Windows Recovery Console to restore damaged Windows system files to your PC's hard drive. However, if you purchased a PC on which Windows came pre-installed, and a Windows installation CD was not included, this option is unavailable.

Before you repair a previous installation of Windows XP, try starting Windows in Safe mode, as discussed in the section "Run Windows in Safe Mode." You can then attempt to restore your PC to a previous condition, as explained in Chapter 19, or troubleshoot other problems that may prevent Windows from starting properly. If you still cannot find the problem and correct it, you can try repairing the Windows installation, as shown in the steps in this section.

When you start a PC with a Windows XP installation CD loaded in the drive, Windows typically displays a message on startup instructing you to press a certain key to boot from the CD. If you press the specified key before Windows begins reading the operating system files from your PC's hard drive, Windows setup runs from the installation CD and provides you with options to repair a Windows installation or run the Recovery Console.

You must set up your PC to boot from the CD drive to perform these steps. Refer to Chapter 12 for more on changing the boot sequence.

Repair a Previous Installation of Windows XP

1. Insert the Windows XP CD into your PC's CD drive.
2. Restart your PC.
3. When the message appears instructing you to press any key to boot from the CD, press any key.

PC device listing ...

Bus No.	Device No.	Func No.	Vendor/Device		Class	Device Class	IRQ
0	7	1	1106	0571	0101	IDE Cntrlr.	14
0	7	2	1106	3038	0C03	Serial Bus Cntrlr	11
0	7	3	1106	3038	0C03	Serial Bus Cntrlr	11
0	7	4	1106	3058	0401	Multimedia Device	11
0	8	5	1260	3873	0280	Network Cntrlr	10
0	10	0	1002	4749	0300	Display Cntrlr	11
0	11	0	10CD	1200	0100	Mass Storage Cntrlr	11
0	12	0	12B9	1007	0780	Simple COMM. Cntrlr	11
2	12	0	1033	00CD	0C00	Serial Bus Cntrlr	11
2	13	0	11C1	5802	0C03	Serial Bus Cntrlr	11
						ACPI Controller	9

Verifying DMI Pool Data ....

Boot from CD :

Press any key to boot from CD.._ ③

The Windows Setup screen appears as Windows loads the necessary device drivers, and then the Windows XP Setup screen appears.

4. Press Enter to set up Windows XP.

Note: *You may be tempted to choose the repair option, but the option to set up Windows XP leads to an automated repair, which is much easier.*

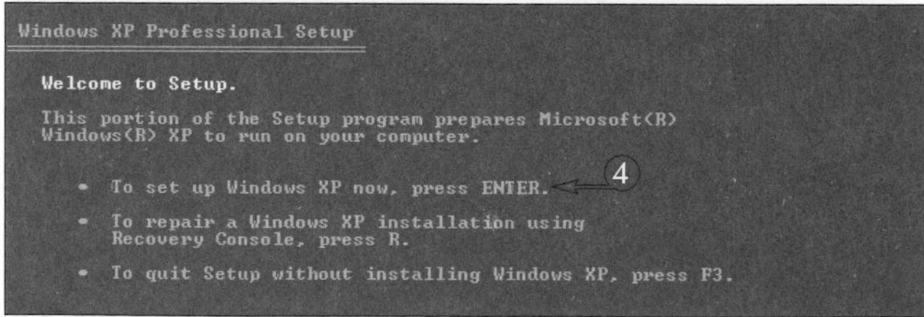

The End-User License Agreement appears.

5 Read the End-User License Agreement.

6 If you agree with the End-User License Agreement, press F8.

END-USER LICENSE AGREEMENT

IMPORTANT-READ CAREFULLY: This End-User License Agreement ("EULA") is a legal agreement between you (either an individual or a single entity) and Microsoft Corporation for the Microsoft software product identified above, which includes computer software and may include associated media, printed materials, "online" or electronic documentation, and Internet-based services ("Product"). An amendment or addendum to this EULA may accompany the Product. YOU AGREE TO BE BOUND BY THE TERMS OF THIS EULA BY INSTALLING, COPYING, OR OTHERWISE USING THE PRODUCT. IF YOU DO NOT AGREE, DO NOT INSTALL OR USE THE PRODUCT; YOU MAY RETURN IT TO YOUR PLACE OF PURCHASE FOR A FULL REFUND.

1. GRANT OF LICENSE. Microsoft grants you the following rights provided that you comply with all terms and conditions of this EULA:

* Installation and use. You may install, use, access, display and run one copy of the Product on a single computer, such as a workstation, terminal or other device ("Workstation Computer"). The Product may not be used by more than two (2) processors at any one time on any

F8=I agree ESC=I do not agree PAGE DOWN=Next Page

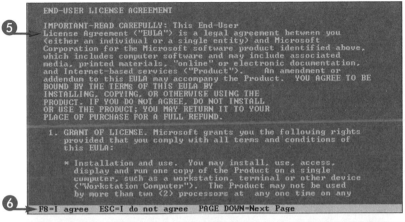

The Windows XP Setup screen displays options to repair a previous installation of Windows or proceed with a fresh installation.

7 Press R and follow the on-screen instructions to repair your Windows installation.

Windows setup replaces any damaged Windows files.

Note: *The repair installation installs the original version of Windows XP; reinstall Windows updates, as explained in Chapter 22.*

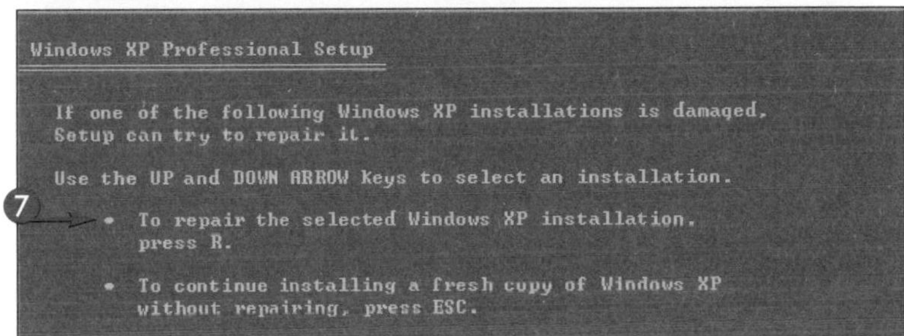

How do I use the Recovery Console?

Using the Recovery Console, you can type commands to copy or restore files from floppy disks or CDs to your PC's hard drive, which you may need to do if a Windows system file becomes damaged. To run the Recovery Console, perform steps 1 to 3 in this section. Instead of pressing Enter in step 4, press R. This runs the Recovery Console, which provides you with a command prompt that looks like C:\Windows>. You can type **help** at the prompt and press Enter to display a list of available commands. Type **help *commandname*** and press Enter to view information about a specific command.

My PC did not come with a Windows XP CD. What Should I do?

As of April 2000, Microsoft stopped allowing PC manufacturers to include the full retail version of Windows with their PCs. Manufacturers had three alternatives: include a version of Windows on CD designed only to be installed on a specific PC, copy the Windows installation files to a separate hard drive partition, or include no Windows backup at all. Unfortunately, some manufacturers choose the third option in order to trim costs. Check the operator's manual that came with your PC, check your PC's help system, or contact the PC manufacturer to determine if a Windows backup is available. You may need to purchase a copy of Windows.

Gather Essential Files and Information

No matter how much hard drive space you reclaim and how much you streamline Windows, your PC still retains a great deal of digital trash. If your PC's performance is satisfactory, you have little reason to do any more cleaning or optimizing. However, if your PC still runs slowly, you can take more drastic action and perform a clean installation of Windows on a newly formatted drive.

Before performing a clean installation, spend some time gathering irreplaceable files and configuration data:

- Back up all of your data files, as discussed in Chapter 4.
- Copy any programs that you downloaded and for which you do not have installation disks.
- Copy or print your e-mail address book and any e-mail messages you want to save.
- Locate your original Windows installation CD. To perform a clean installation, you need a full version Windows CD or an upgrade CD *and* the original CD of an older Windows version.

The steps in this section show you how to obtain some of the more important files and information that are stored on your PC.

Gather Essential Files and Information

1. Back up or copy any data files to CDs, DVDs, or a backup drive.
2. Back up or copy any program updates or installation files you downloaded to CDs, DVDs, or a backup drive.

Note: *Refer to Chapter 4 for instructions on backing up data files and programs.*

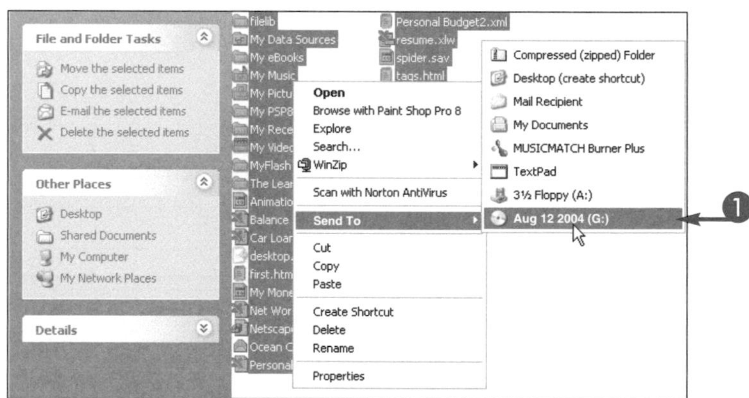

3. Export your e-mail address book and copy the file to a CD or another hard drive.
4. Export any e-mail messages you want to save and copy them to a CD or another hard drive.

Note: *Steps for exporting address books and e-mail messages vary depending on the e-mail program; refer to your e-mail program's help system.*

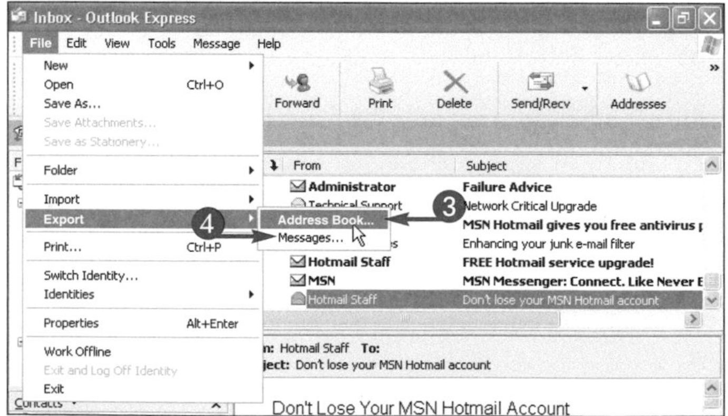

5 In your e-mail program, display your account settings.

6 Record the incoming mail server address.

7 Record the outgoing mail server address.

8 If you have a dial-up Internet connection, double-click its icon in the Network Connections window.

Note: *To open the Network Connections window, click Start, right-click My Network Places, and click Properties.*

9 Record your username.

10 Record the phone number required to connect.

11 Click Cancel.

You now have some of the important files and information you need for performing a clean installation of Windows.

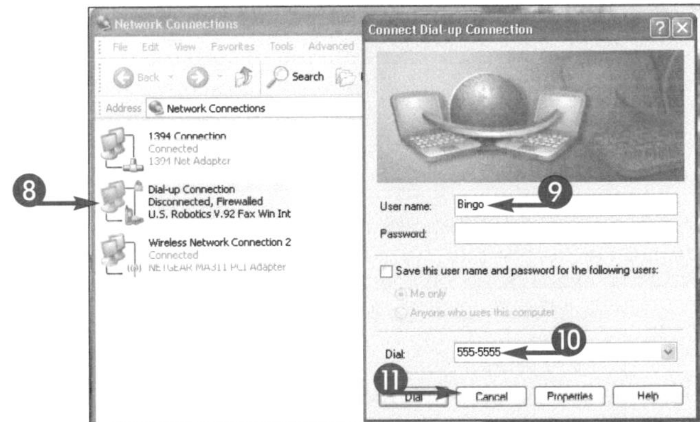

My PC is networked. Do I need to record any network settings?

▼ Yes. You should know your computer's name and the workgroup to which it belongs. Right-click My Computer and click Properties. Click the Computer Name tab and write down the full computer name and workgroup name. Right-click My Network Places, click Properties, right-click your network connection icon, and click Properties. Write down the items in the "My connection uses the following items" list. Double-click Internet Protocol (TCP/IP), and write down all IP and DNS settings; if you have broadband Internet service, such as a cable modem or DSL connection, you need these settings to establish a connection.

I share my PC with other users. Do I need to back up their data separately?

▼ Yes. Each user has his or her own My Documents folder with additional subfolders. You should back up the contents of every user's My Documents folder. In addition, each user typically has a separate e-mail address book and inbox. Consult with the other users to find out where they store their data files, and then back up those files. Export their address books and any e-mail messages they want to save and copy those files to CDs or to another drive. After installing Windows, you can recreate the user accounts and restore their files.

Re-Installing Windows XP

If you have a Windows XP installation CD, you can run the installation routine to clear everything from your PC's hard drive and perform a clean installation of Windows XP. Chapter 31 provides instructions on how to use the installation CD to repair an installation of Windows XP. The installation CD also provides the option to delete a hard drive partition, which essentially wipes everything off the hard drive. You can then select options to create a new, blank primary partition and then proceed to install Windows XP on the new partition. After installing Windows XP, you can then reinstall your application software, set up your Internet connection, and install any available software updates, including Windows updates.

The Windows XP CD uses a utility called FDISK to delete the existing hard drive partition on which Windows is installed and create a new partition. This permanently removes all files on the existing partition, including Windows files, application files, and the data files that you created. Make sure you have copies of all essential files and a record of any important configuration settings before you proceed, as explained in the section "Gather Essential Files and Information."

To perform the steps in this section, you must set up your PC to boot from the CD drive. Refer to Chapter 12 for instructions on how to change the boot sequence.

Re-Installing Windows XP

Note: *These steps permanently delete all files on your hard drive. Back up all files before proceeding.*

1. Insert the Windows XP CD into your PC's CD drive.
2. Restart your PC.
3. When the message appears instructing you to press any key to boot from the CD, press any key.

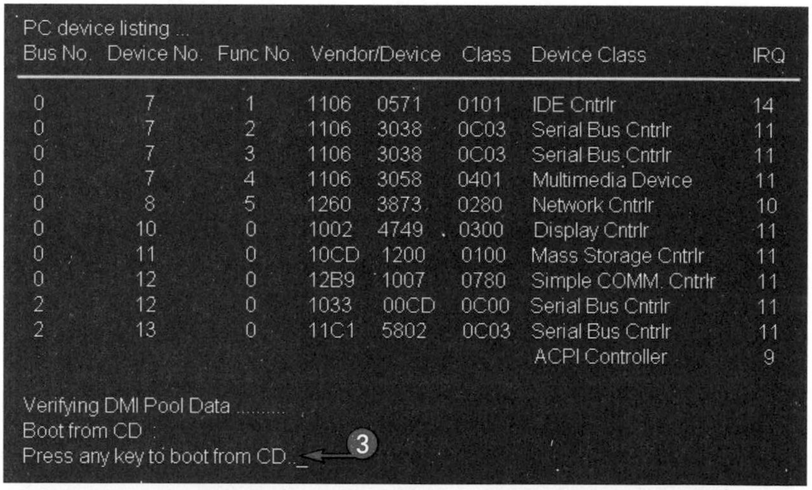

PC device listing ...

Bus No.	Device No.	Func No.	Vendor/Device		Class	Device Class	IRQ
0	7	1	1106	0571	0101	IDE Cntrlr	14
0	7	2	1106	3038	0C03	Serial Bus Cntrlr	11
0	7	3	1106	3038	0C03	Serial Bus Cntrlr	11
0	7	4	1106	3058	0401	Multimedia Device	11
0	8	5	1260	3873	0280	Network Cntrlr	10
0	10	0	1002	4749	0300	Display Cntrlr	11
0	11	0	10CD	1200	0100	Mass Storage Cntrlr	11
0	12	0	12B9	1007	0780	Simple COMM. Cntrlr	11
2	12	0	1033	00CD	0C00	Serial Bus Cntrlr	11
2	13	0	11C1	5802	0C03	Serial Bus Cntrlr	11
						ACPI Controller	9

Verifying DMI Pool Data ....

Boot from CD :

Press any key to boot from CD.._ 3

The Windows Setup screen appears as Windows loads the necessary device drivers, and then the Windows XP Setup screen appears.

4. Press Enter to set up Windows XP.

An End-User License Agreement appears.

5. Press F8 to accept the terms of the agreement.

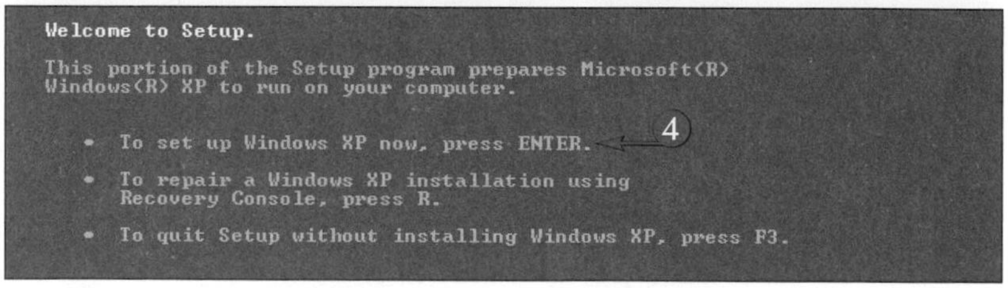

Welcome to Setup.

This portion of the Setup program prepares Microsoft(R) Windows(R) XP to run on your computer.

- To set up Windows XP now, press ENTER. 4
- To repair a Windows XP installation using Recovery Console, press R.
- To quit Setup without installing Windows XP, press F3.

- The installation routine displays the name of the currently installed version of Windows XP and offers to repair it.

6 Press Esc to continue installing a fresh version of Windows XP.

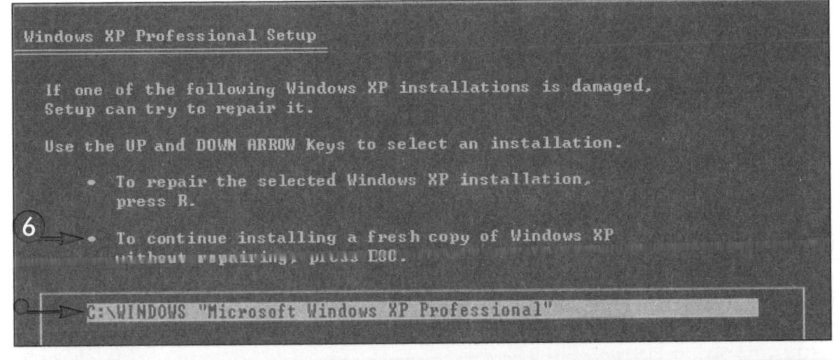

The installation routine displays the existing hard drive partitions.

7 Press the Up or Down Arrow key to highlight the partition on which Windows XP is installed.

Note: *Most PCs have a single hard drive partition, which is usually drive C.*

8 Press D to delete the partition.

9 Follow the on-screen instructions to create a new partition and install Windows XP on the new partition.

A fresh copy of Windows XP is installed on the new partition.

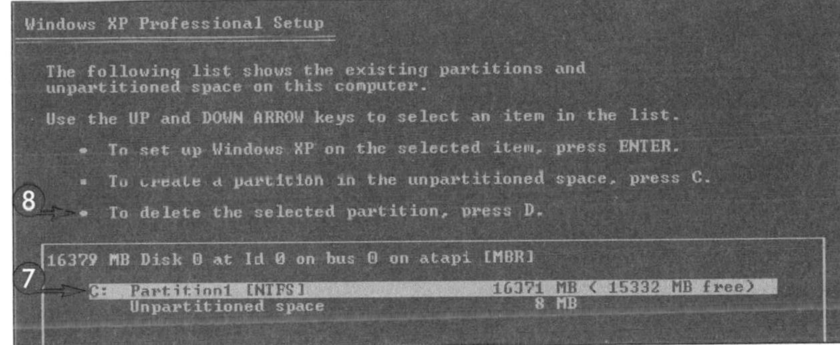

My PC runs Windows Me. Can I perform a clean installation of it on my PC?

▼ Yes. If you have the installation CD, you can use FDISK to delete the existing hard drive partition and create a new partition. You can then install Windows Me on the new partition. To use FDISK to delete an existing partition and create a new partition, refer to the sections "Delete a Hard Drive Partition" and "Create a Hard Drive Partition." To install Windows Me, see the section "Reinstall Windows 98 or Windows Me." If your PC included a Windows CD from the manufacturer, follow the manufacturer's instructions.

My PC runs Windows 98 or 95. Can I perform a clean installation of it on my PC?

▼ Maybe. You cannot boot your PC using the Windows 95 or Windows 98 installation CD, so you need to boot your PC with a bootable floppy disk that contains the files necessary to start your PC with CD-ROM support. If you created a Windows startup diskette, you can use it to boot your PC and then select the option to start with CD-ROM support. You can run FDISK from the startup disk to delete the existing partition and create a new partition, as explained in the following sections "Delete a Hard Drive Partition" and "Reinstall Windows 98 or Windows Me." After creating a new partition, you can run the Windows installation from the CD.

Delete a Hard Drive Partition

The Windows XP installation CD features all of the options necessary to perform a clean installation of Windows XP on a newly formatted hard drive. You can boot from the CD, delete a hard drive partition, create a new partition, and install Windows XP. Older versions of Windows, including Windows Me and Windows 98, do not provide this same convenience.

To perform a clean installation of Windows Me or Windows 98, you must first use the FDISK utility to delete the primary hard drive partition on which Windows is installed. Deleting a partition permanently removes all files from the drive, so copy all essential files and settings before deleting the partition, as explained in the section "Gather Essential Files and Information."

Some PC manufacturers include a bootable version of the Windows CD with their PCs. If you have a bootable Windows installation CD, you can boot from the CD and type the FDISK command to delete a hard drive partition and create a new one. Otherwise, you can boot your PC using a Windows startup disk and run the FDISK command from the startup disk. Refer to the Windows Help system to learn how to create a startup diskette.

Delete a Hard Drive Partition

Note: *These steps permanently delete all files on your hard drive. Back up all files before proceeding.*

1. Boot your PC from the Windows installation CD or startup disk.

Note: *If given the option of starting with or without CD-ROM support, start with CD-ROM support, so you can run Windows setup after clearing files from your drive.*

The DOS prompt appears.

2. Type **fdisk**.
3. Press Enter.

The FDISK Large Disk Support Screen appears, asking if you want to enable large disk support.

4. Type **y** to answer Yes.
5. Press Enter.

```
Your computer has a disk larger than 512 MB. This version of Windows
includes improved support for large disks, resulting in more efficient
use of disk space on large drives, and allowing disks over 2 GB to be
formatted as a single drive.

IMPORTANT: If you enable large disk support and create any new drives on this
disk, you will not be able to access the new drive(s) using other operating
systems, including some versions of Windows 95 and Windows NT, as well as
earlier versions of Windows and MS-DOS. In addition, disk utilities that
were not designed explicitly for the FAT32 file system will not be able
to work with this disk. If you need to access this disk with other operating
systems or older disk utilities, do not enable large drive support.

Do you wish to enable large disk support (Y/N)..........? [Y]
```
4

The FDISK Options menu appears.

6 Type **3** to select Delete partition or Logical DOS Drive.

7 Press Enter.

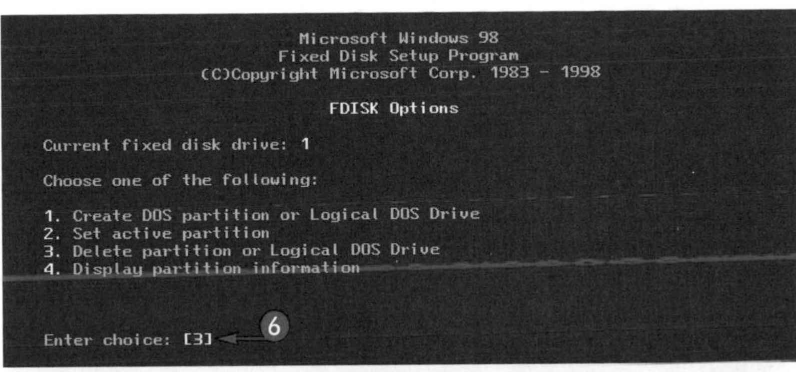

Microsoft Windows 98
Fixed Disk Setup Program
(C)Copyright Microsoft Corp. 1983 - 1998
FDISK Options
Current fixed disk drive: 1
Choose one of the following:
1. Create DOS partition or Logical DOS Drive
2. Set active partition
3. Delete partition or Logical DOS Drive
4. Display partition information
Enter choice: [3]
6

The Delete DOS Partition or Logical DOS Drive menu appears.

8 Type **1** to select Delete Primary DOS Partition.

9 Press Enter.

10 Follow the on-screen instructions to select the primary DOS partition on which Windows is installed and delete it.

FDISK deletes the partition on which Windows is installed, permanently removing all files from the partition.

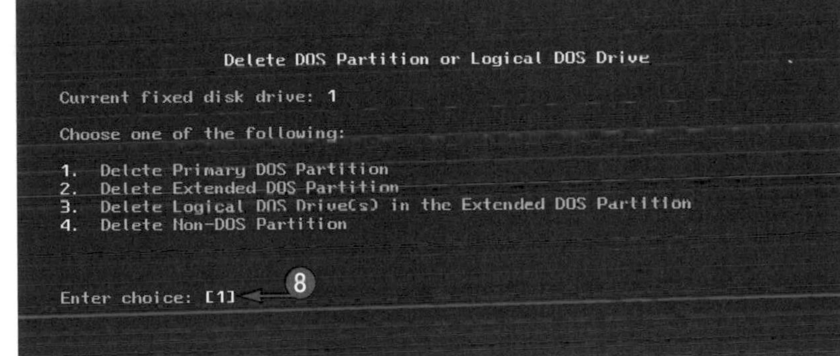

Delete DOS Partition or Logical DOS Drive
Current fixed disk drive: 1
Choose one of the following:
1. Delete Primary DOS Partition
2. Delete Extended DOS Partition
3. Delete Logical DOS Drive(s) in the Extended DOS Partition
4. Delete Non-DOS Partition
Enter choice: [1]
8

PART X

When asked for a Volume label, what should I enter?

▼ The Delete Primary DOS Partition menu displays the volume names of all partitions, so type the name of the partition you want to delete as it appears in the list. If the partition has no volume name, which is fairly common, simply press Enter when prompted to type a volume name. A partition has a volume name only if the person who created the partition gave it a name. See the section, "Create a Hard Drive Partition," for more information.

Are any utilities available that can help me delete, create, and manage partitions?

▼ Yes. Several utilities can help you manage your partitions. One of the more popular utilities, called PartitionMagic, is discussed in Chapter 9. PartitionMagic and similar utilities provide a more intuitive interface for creating and managing hard drive partitions. You can run PartitionMagic in Windows to adjust the size of partitions by dragging and dropping their borders. You can also run PartitionMagic from its installation CD.

My hard drive has both primary and logical DOS partitions. Do I need to delete all of them?

▼ Not necessarily. You can format the drive on which Windows is installed instead. For example, if Windows is installed on drive C, at the DOS prompt type **format c:** and press Enter. A message appears prompting you to confirm. Press Y to select Yes and press Enter. You can then type a volume name for the partition. To delete partitions, you must delete logical DOS drives first, then extended DOS partitions, then primary DOS partitions.

Create a Hard Drive Partition

You can reinstall Windows without deleting and re-creating the hard drive partition on which it is installed and retain your data files. This typically does not provide you with much of a performance boost, however, because it leaves many useless files and settings on the hard drive. You can restore your PC to its original operating system only by reinstalling Windows and your applications on a clean drive. To clear all files from the drive, you can delete the partition on which Windows is installed, as explained in the section, "Delete a Hard Drive Partition." You must then create a new primary DOS partition on which to install Windows.

When you run FDISK and choose the option to create a new partition, FDISK displays a menu with options for creating a primary DOS partition or an extended DOS partition. A primary DOS partition creates a bootable drive on which you can install Windows. FDISK also provides you with the option to use the maximum available space for the primary DOS partition. Most users choose to create a single partition that uses all available hard drive space, so they have a single hard drive to manage. However, you can divide your hard drive into multiple logical drives, as explained in Chapter 9.

Create a Hard Drive Partition

1. Boot your PC from the Windows installation CD or startup disk.

Note: *If given the option of starting with or without CD-ROM support, start with CD-ROM support, so you can run Windows setup after clearing files from your drive.*

The DOS prompt appears.

2. Type **fdisk**.
3. Press Enter.

The FDISK Large Disk Support Screen appears, asking if you want to enable large disk support.

4. Type **y** to answer Yes.
5. Press Enter.

```
Your computer has a disk larger than 512 MB. This version of Windows
includes improved support for large disks, resulting in more efficient
use of disk space on large drives, and allowing disks over 2 GB to be
formatted as a single drive.

IMPORTANT: If you enable large disk support and create any new drives on this
disk, you will not be able to access the new drive(s) using other operating
systems, including some versions of Windows 95 and Windows NT, as well as
earlier versions of Windows and MS-DOS. In addition, disk utilities that
were not designed explicitly for the FAT32 file system will not be able
to work with this disk. If you need to access this disk with other operating
systems or older disk utilities, do not enable large drive support.

Do you wish to enable large disk support (Y/N)..........? [Y]
```
4

The FDISK Options menu appears.

6 Type **1** to select Create DOS partition or Logical DOS Drive.

7 Press Enter.

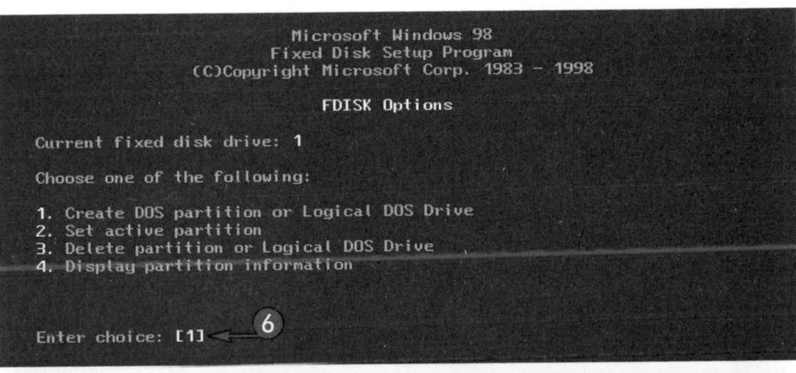

Microsoft Windows 98
Fixed Disk Setup Program
(C)Copyright Microsoft Corp. 1983 - 1998
FDISK Options
Current fixed disk drive: 1
Choose one of the following:
1. Create DOS partition or Logical DOS Drive
2. Set active partition
3. Delete partition or Logical DOS Drive
4. Display partition information
Enter choice: [1]
6

The Create DOS Partition or Logical DOS Drive menu appears.

8 Type **1** to select Create Primary DOS Partition.

9 Press Enter.

10 Follow the on-screen instructions to complete the process.

FDISK creates a new primary DOS partition on which you can install Windows.

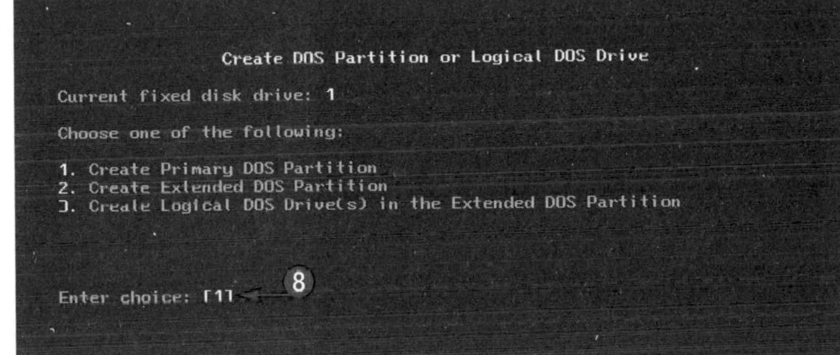

Create DOS Partition or Logical DOS Drive
Current fixed disk drive: 1
Choose one of the following:
1. Create Primary DOS Partition
2. Create Extended DOS Partition
3. Create Logical DOS Drive(s) in the Extended DOS Partition
Enter choice: [1]
8

Can I create more than one partition?

Yes. For example, you can create three partitions on one hard drive to create three logical drives — C, D, and E. When creating more than one partition, leave enough room on the primary partition for Windows, other applications, and free space to use as virtual memory. Because it is difficult to gauge the amount of space to reserve, most users set up a single partition. This provides you with more flexibility in the future. For more about disk partitions, refer to Chapter 9.

Do I need to reformat the drive before installing Windows 98 or Windows Me?

If you are installing Windows Me, you do not need to format the drive. The Windows Me installation formats the drive for you, if needed. To install Windows 98, you must format the drive. To format the drive, reboot your PC with the Windows startup disk and then choose to start without CD-ROM support. At the DOS prompt, type **format c:** and press Enter.

What is a primary DOS partition?

A primary DOS (Disk Operating System) partition is a division of a hard drive that is designed to be used as a bootable drive. FDISK also allows you to create and delete logical partitions, which are typically used to store data and applications rather than your PC's operating system. As discussed in Chapter 9, you can divide a single physical hard drive into multiple logical drives.

Re-Install Windows 98 or Windows Me

If your PC runs a version of Windows prior to Windows 2000/NT or Windows XP, such as Windows 98 or Windows Me, and you have the Windows installation CD for that version of Windows, you can reinstall Windows from the installation CD after using FDISK to create a blank hard drive partition. Most older PCs have a Windows installation CD or a backup Windows CD that you can use to reinstall Windows.

If you have a bootable Windows installation CD and your PC is set up to boot from the CD, as explained in Chapter 12, you can insert the CD, restart your PC, and then follow the on-screen instructions to install Windows. Otherwise, you must boot your PC with a Windows startup disk or another bootable floppy disk that enables you to start your PC with CD-ROM support. You can then type the **setup** command at the DOS prompt to initialize the installation.

Installing Windows 98 or Me is fairly easy. Once you start the installation routine, it leads you step by step through the process of installing the Windows files and configuring Windows to run on your PC.

Re-Install Windows 98 or Windows ME

1. Insert the Windows Me installation CD.
2. If the Windows installation CD is not bootable, insert a Windows startup disk in the floppy disk drive.
3. Restart your PC.
4. Select the option to start with CD-ROM support.

   The command prompt appears.
5. Type **d:** where *d* is the letter of your PC's CD drive.
6. Press Enter.
7. Type **setup**.
8. Press Enter.
   - A message appears, indicating that Windows Setup will check your system.
9. Press Enter.

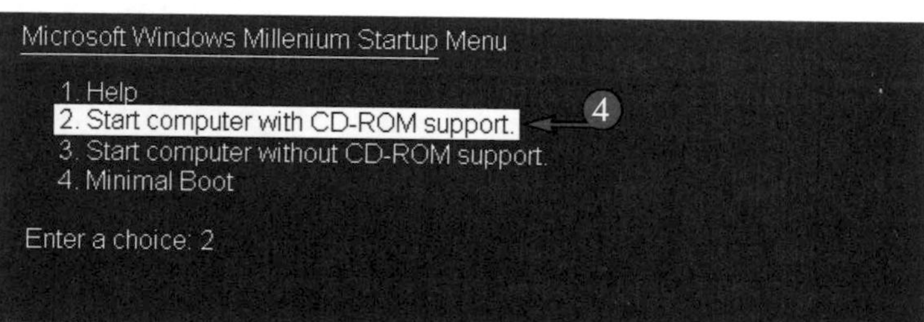

Microsoft Windows Millenium Startup Menu
1. Help
2. Start computer with CD-ROM support.
3. Start computer without CD-ROM support.
4. Minimal Boot
Enter a choice: 2
4

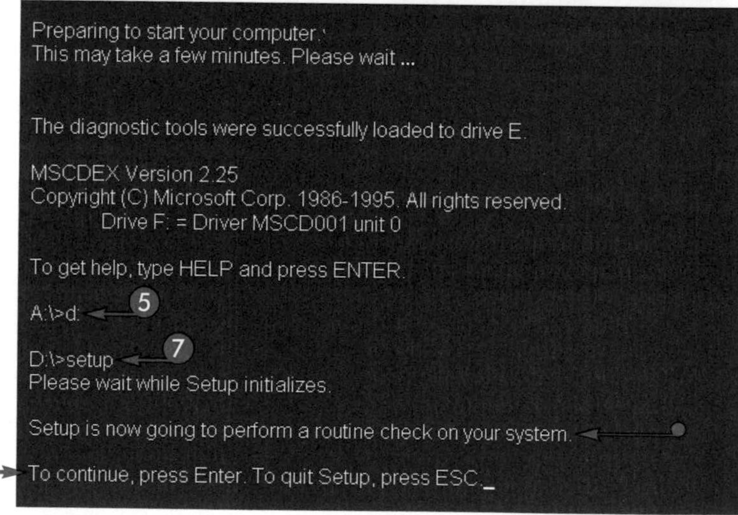

Preparing to start your computer.
This may take a few minutes. Please wait ...
The diagnostic tools were successfully loaded to drive E.
MSCDEX Version 2.25
Copyright (C) Microsoft Corp. 1986-1995. All rights reserved.
Drive F: = Driver MSCD001 unit 0
To get help, type HELP and press ENTER.
A:\>d:
5
D:\>setup
7
Please wait while Setup initializes.
Setup is now going to perform a routine check on your system.
9
To continue, press Enter. To quit Setup, press ESC.

Windows setup checks your PC's memory, hard drives, and processor to determine if it can install Windows on your PC and displays a screen similar to this one if your PC passes inspection.

10 Press the Right Arrow key to highlight Exit.

11 Press Enter.

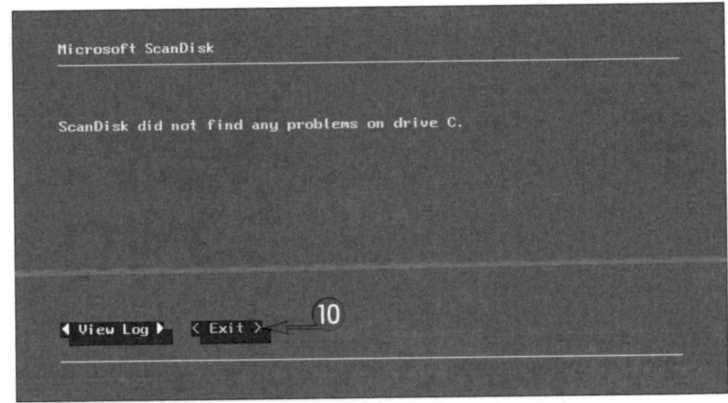

Windows Setup starts the installation process.

12 Click Next and then follow the on-screen instructions to install Windows on the new hard drive partition.

Windows Me is installed on the new hard drive partition.

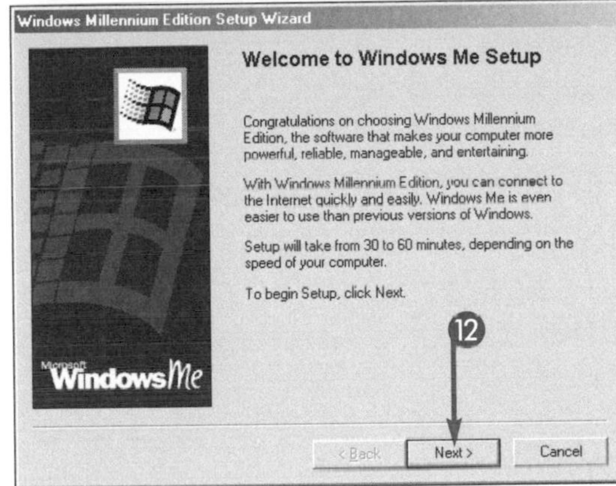

I do not have an original Windows installation CD. What should I do?

- You can purchase a new copy of the Windows version that was initially installed on your PC, or you can purchase a more recent version of Windows. Before purchasing a more recent version of Windows, check the system requirements for that version to make sure that your PC meets the minimum requirements for running it. Also, unless you have the installation CD for an older version of Windows, purchase a full version of Windows, not the upgrade version. The installation routine aborts the Windows installation if you cannot prove that you own a previous full version of Windows.

I am trying to install Windows 98, and a message appears indicating that the drive is not formatted. What should I do?

- Windows Me automatically formats a drive, if needed, during the installation process. Windows 98 requires that you format the drive before installing Windows. Exit the Windows installation and return to the DOS prompt. Type **a:** and press Enter to change to the drive that contains the Windows startup diskette. Type **format c:** and press Enter. A message appears indicating that all files on the specified drive will be deleted and asking if you want to proceed. Type **y** and press Enter. When prompted to type a volume label for the disk, type a label or press Enter to leave it blank.

Numbers

A

B

continued

D

continued

J

K

L

M

N

O

continued

R

INDEX

continued

T

INDEX

W

Y

Z

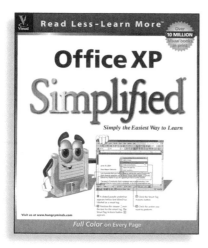

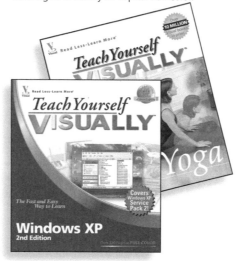

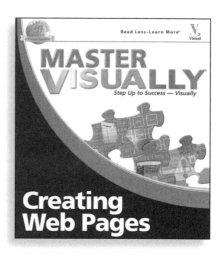